The European Union

The European Union has established itself as a leading text that provides readers from all disciplines with a sound understanding of the economics and policies of the EU. Its wealth of information, detail and analysis has ensured that previous editions have been read by a generation of students, researchers and policy-makers. It covers all major EU policy areas, as well as theories of economic integration, the theory of economic and monetary union (EMU), the measurement of the economic effects of European integration and the legal dimension of EU integration. It also includes an explanation and analysis of all recent developments affecting the EU, such as enlargement, the ratification of the Nice Treaty and the Convention for the Future of Europe. This edition has been thoroughly revised and updated and includes new resources to help students and teachers, including summaries, review questions, suggestions for essay titles and further reading lists.

Ali M. El-Agraa is Emeritus Professor of International Economic Integration at Fukuoka University, Japan. He has extensive teaching experience at universities in the UK and North America.

D1344830

NINTH EDITION

The European Union
Economics and Policies

Ali M. El-Agraa

With invited edited contributions

CAMBRIDGE
UNIVERSITY PRESS

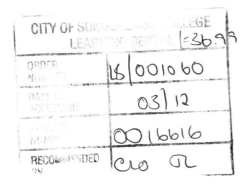
CAMBRIDGE UNIVERSITY PRESS
Cambridge, New York, Melbourne, Madrid, Cape Town,
Singapore, São Paulo, Delhi, Tokyo, Mexico City

Cambridge University Press
The Edinburgh Building, Cambridge CB2 8RU, UK

Published in the United States of America by
Cambridge University Press, New York

www.cambridge.org
Information on this title: www.cambridge.org/9781107400115

First published under the Philip Allan imprint in 1980
Second edition published 1983
Third edition published 1990
Fourth edition published under the Harvester Wheatsheaf imprint in 1994
Fifth edition published under the Prentice Hall Europe imprint in 1998
Sixth edition published under the Financial Times Prentice Hall imprint in 2001
Seventh edition published 2004
Eighth edition published by Cambridge University Press 2007

Ninth edition published 2011

Printed in the United Kingdom at the University Press, Cambridge

A catalogue record for this publication is available from the British Library

ISBN-13 978-1-107-00796-3 hardback
ISBN-13 978-1-107-40011-5 paperback

To Diana, Mark and Frances

and those who believe in and actively support
an ever closer unity for Europe

Contents

Figures

Tables

Boxes

Contributors

Brian Ardy is Reader in Economics and Head of the European Institute, the Business School at London South Bank University, UK.

Harvey W. Armstrong is Emeritus Professor of Economic Geography, Department of Geography, University of Sheffield, UK.

Ian Barnes is Professor Emeritus, Jean Monnet Professor of European Integration, Faculty of Business and Law, University of Lincoln, UK.

Kenneth Button is University Professor of Public Policy, School of Public Policy, George Mason University, USA, and is also director of both the University's Aerospace Research Center and the Center for Transportation, Policy, Operations and Logistics.

Ulrich Koester is Professor at the Institute of Agricultural Economics, University of Kiel, Germany.

Imelda Maher is Sutherland Professor in European Law, School of Law, University College, Dublin, Republic of Ireland.

Miriam Manchin is Lecturer in the Political Economy of European Union Integration, School of Slavonic and Eastern European Studies, University College London, UK.

Stephen Martin is Professor of Economics and Faculty Director of the Technology Transfer Initiative at the Krannert School of Management, Purdue University, USA, and is co-managing editor of the *International Journal of Industrial Organization*.

David G. Mayes is Professor of International Finance, the University of Canterbury, New Zealand, and Director of its National Centre for Research on Europe, and was Adviser to the Board of the Bank of Finland.

Wolf Sauter is with the Financial Markets Directorate, Ministry of Finance, the Netherlands, and was National Expert with the EU's Directorate General for Competition, Policy Adviser to the Independent Authority for Telecommunications and Posts (OPTA), The Hague, and Professor of Economic Law, Groningen University, the Netherlands.

Preface

The European Union (EU) is the most significant and influential of international economic integration (IEI) schemes. There are three reasons, the sum of which explains this significance:

1. Of the six EU founding states, (West) Germany, France and Italy were top ten world economies. Since then, two such economies have joined: the UK and Spain. Hence today the EU includes half of the world's top ten economies. The EU has also proved a magnet for new members: in addition to the founding member nations, known as the Original Six, there are now an additional twenty-one. The EU of twenty-seven continues to receive applications for membership; hence it is set to include practically the whole of Europe, and may go beyond the geographic area if Turkey succeeds in joining in 2015. No other scheme matches this economic size and diversity.

2. From a voluntary viewpoint, the EU is the oldest IEI scheme in operation; voluntary in the sense that countries are not coerced into joining, due to their being dominated by a foreign country or captured by war. This longevity is part of the EU's attraction.

3. Most vitally, the EU has the deepest scheme of IEI. It is almost a complete economic union: (a) it is practically a complete 'common market', where people, goods, services and capital move freely – the four freedoms; (b) sixteen of its twenty-seven member states have the same currency (euro), with the European Central Bank in charge of Eurozone monetary policy; (c) it has a system for monitoring and influencing fiscal policy – the Stability and Growth Pact; and (d) it has its own budget, financing a range of policies. Also, since the entry into force of the Treaty on European Union (TEU), popularly known as the Lisbon Treaty, on 1 December 2009, it has: (e) a single president of the European Council; and (f) a foreign policy chief who controls a vast diplomatic corps, now being established.

That is why the EU is fascinating to study, and this book attempts to guide those who care about an 'ever closer union' for the people of Europe. But it is not confined to 'Europeans', since the EU offers lessons for all countries that try to learn from it or even emulate it. This is not to suggest that the EU is heaven – far from it; it has always had its serious problems, some bringing it close to complete collapse: witness the financial and economic crises it has been experiencing since 2007, which prompted many to speculate on the imminent demise of the euro. But this is inevitable, given the diversity of EU peoples and economies.

This book is unique, and in more ways than one. First, when the first edition was published in 1980 there was no such text on the market; there were a few books for the layperson and the expert, which were naturally limited in scope. Second, this is the only text that covers every single major EU policy, but is inevitably slanted towards the economic, given the way the EU has developed. Third, although I am personally responsible for ten chapters of the book and co-author of another eight, the rest of the chapters are contributed by leading authorities in their particular area of EU expertise, but I have edited their contributions in such a way as to make the book read as a consistent whole. Naturally, in doing so, I have tried my best not to make them lose their unique style.

The book, together with its website, offers comprehensive coverage of all the major EU policy areas. It is written in such a way that the theoretical aspects are covered in separate chapters, so that those not comfortable with theory, either because they are averse to it or simply do not want to be diverted by it, can go straight to their chosen delight.

The book is in seven parts:

Part I EU history, institutions and legal dimension

Chapter 2 A history of European integration and the evolution of the EU

Chapter 3 EU institutions

Chapter 4 The legal dimension in EU integration

Chapter 5 The European economy: bare essentials

The aim of this part of the book is to provide a general background to the EU. Chapter 2 gives a short account of the history of European integration and the development of the EU. Chapter 3 provides a general description of EU institutions and their functioning. Chapter 4 explores the legal dimension in EU integration. Chapter 5 is a general survey of the bare essentials of the EU economy, using mainly charts, with the full statistical tables available on the website; it covers the major economic indicators for the present EU twenty-seven member states (MSs), as well as those involved in imminent enlargements and, to enable comparison, also for the rest of those in the group of eight (G8, now G20).

Part II EU market integration: theory and practice

Chapter 6 The theory of economic integration

Chapter 7 The economics of the single market

Chapter 8 Factor mobility

Chapter 9 Measuring the impact of economic integration

Part II of this book is devoted to a discussion of the theoretical and practical aspects of EU market integration. Chapter 6 covers the theory of economic integration, providing an overall picture of the analysis of the economic implications of the creation of a single market on both the partner nations and the rest of the world. It is followed by a consideration of these aspects in terms of the EU's Single European Market (SEM) in Chapter 7, with Chapter 8 dealing entirely with the question of the free movement of capital, labour and enterprise within the EU. Chapter 9 then deals with the nature and problems of the measurement of the impact of the formation of the EU on trade, production and factor mobility.

Part III EU monetary integration

Chapter 10 The theory of monetary integration

Chapter 11 The development of EU economic and monetary integration

Chapter 12 The operation of EMU

Part III covers all aspects of that far-reaching and most demanding element of integration, monetary unification, including the adoption of a single currency. The three chapters cover, respectively: the theoretical analysis of the gains and losses from economic and monetary union (EMU); the EU developments that have led to the present situation, where twelve of the fifteen pre-2004 EU member nations are using the euro as their only currency, and where all countries acceding after that are obliged to join them when deemed fit, with five of them already having done so; and the management of the euro by the European Central Bank (ECB) and how the euro is operated.

Part IV The single European market: policy integration

Chapter 13 Competition policy

Chapter 14 Industrial and competitiveness policy: the Lisbon Strategy

Chapter 15 Tax harmonization

Chapter 16 Transport policy

Chapter 17 Energy policy and energy markets

Chapter 18 Environmental policy

Part IV of the book covers areas that constitute the very foundations needed to facilitate a properly operating SEM. Hence it tackles in six chapters: competition rules; industrial and competitiveness policy; tax harmonization; transport policy; energy policy; and environmental policy. Industrial policy is included because variations in it would be tantamount to affording differing protection to national domestic industry. The absence of tax harmonization would have consequences equivalent to those of disparate industrial policies. Similar considerations apply to transport, energy and the environment. Of course, transport and energy are also dealt with as industries in their own right, as well as providers of social services, and the environment is treated in terms of tackling pollution and the consequent health benefits.

Part V EU budget and structural policies

Chapter 19 The general budget

Chapter 20 The Common Agricultural Policy

Chapter 21 The Common Fisheries Policy

Chapter 22 Regional policy

Chapter 23 Social policies: the employment dimension

Part V of this book covers all EU policies that address certain structural aspects of the EU economy and society. The EU affords special treatment to those in the agricultural sector, fishing industry and depressed regions, as well as dealing with EU-wide social problems, especially unemployment, hence employment. These areas are not only financed by the EU general budget, but also claim the bulk of its general budgetary resources. Thus this part of the book begins with the chapter on the budget and follows on with chapters on each of the mentioned areas.

Part VI EU external relations

Chapter 24 External trade policy

Chapter 25 The EU and the developing world

Part VI of the book deals with the external relations of the EU. Chapter 24 covers EU trade relations with its major partners within the context of the Common Commercial Policy (CCP) run by the European Commission on behalf of all EU member nations. Chapter 25 tackles EU relations with the developing world, in terms of trade, aid and preferential trading arrangements.

Part VII The future of the EU

Chapter 26 The future of the EU

Part VII of the book is naturally concerned with the future of the EU: where it is heading. It examines the views of all those who play influential roles in the drive behind European integration and sets them against the vision of the founding fathers.

Finally, I would like to thank all those who have contributed to this book over the years, especially those who are still with me since its inception, and to welcome Professors Ian Barnes and Imelda Maher and Dr Miriam Manchin to my team. Thanks are also due to Chris Harrison, Publishing Director for the Social Sciences at Cambridge University Press, for his encouragement and support, and to all his production teams for their excellent work.

Ali M. El-Agraa

Fukuoka University, Japan

October 2010

A reader's guide

The book is written in such a way that pure theory and measurement techniques are confined to separate chapters. This means that the policy chapters should be accessible to all readers. However, it also means that those who seek a rigorous, yet brief, background on international economic integration can find it handily in the same book. Moreover, as my contributors will no doubt attest, my editing style has been to ensure that the book reads as a whole, not as a collection of independent articles, each contributed for its own sake. This has been ensured through thorough editing and consultation with the contributors, cross-referencing, allowing repetition only where absolutely necessary, logical sequencing and a setting which begins with an introductory chapter and finishes with one on the future of the EU. In the process, I have tried my best not to distract from any contributor's own writing style. Therefore the reader has a unique product which offers a truly single entity, yet is authored by several acknowledged authorities in the various fields.

As to the reader's guide, for those truly interested in the EU as a whole, you will of course have to read the entire book, if you really want to understand it as a most successful scheme of international economic integration, with aspirations going beyond that. However, those who are simply interested in the EU itself without the global context can skip Chapters 6, 9 and 10, since these are devoted to theoretical and measurement considerations which pertain to all schemes. Those interested only in the EU policy areas can drop Chapters 2-6 and 9, although Chapter 2 is important for a proper understanding. Those interested only in the EU economic policies can drop Chapters 2-4 and 23 and, if not interested in the future of the EU, can also drop Chapter 26. Those interested only in EMU and the euro can confine themselves to Chapters 7, 8 and 10-12, but are advised to read Chapters 2 and 26 for a proper understanding; those interested in this area with an emphasis on the UK will find my book *The Euro and Britain: Implications of Moving into EMU* (2002) more appropriate. Also various combinations of chapters can be made, depending on what the user/reader has in mind – for example, those interested in a very basic understanding of the EU can use Chapters 2, 3, 5 and 26.

Finally, the entire book is written with those who want to pursue further study in mind. Thus, within every chapter the reader is referred to the most relevant research publications in the field and these are fully set out in the Bibliography at the end of the book. Nevertheless, there are also guides to further reading at the end of each chapter, but no guides to other texts, since it is not our task to supply them, especially when this book is a pioneer in its field and covers more than one field of study – it is not confined to economics.

Abbreviations

AAMS	Association of African and Malagasy States
AAU	Arab-African Union
ACC	Arab Cooperation Council
ACM	Arab Common Market
ACP	African, Caribbean and Pacific countries party to the Lomé Convention (now the Cotonou Agreement)
ADAPT	Community initiative concerning the adaptation of the workforce to industrial change
AEC	African Economic Community
AIM	advanced informatics in medicine
AL	Arab League
ALADI	Association for Latin American Integration
ALTENER	specific actions to promote greater penetration of renewable energy sources
AMU	Arab Maghreb Union
ANZCERTA	Australia and New Zealand Closer Economic Relations and Trade Agreement (also CER)
ARION	programme of study visits for decision-makers in education
ASEAN	Association of South East Asian Nations
ASEM	Asia-Europe meeting
AU	African Union
BAP	biotechnology action programme
BATNEEC	best available technology not entailing excessive cost
BC-NET	Business Cooperation Network
BCR	Community Bureau of References
BENELUX	Belgium, the Netherlands and Luxembourg Economic Union

BEP	biomolecular engineering programme
BEST	Business Environment Simplification Task Force
BLEU	Belgium–Luxembourg Economic Union
BRAIN	basic research in adaptive intelligence and neurocomputing
BRIDGE	Biotechnological Research for Innovation, Development and Growth in Europe
BRITE/EURAM	basic research in industrial technologies for Europe/raw materials and advanced materials
BSE	bovine spongiform encephalopathy
BU	Benin Union
CAA	Civil Aviation Authority
CACM	Central American Common Market
CADDIA	cooperation in automation of data and documentation for imports/exports and agriculture
CAEU	Council for Arab Economic Unity
CAP	Common Agricultural Policy
CARICOM	Caribbean Community
CARIFTA	Caribbean Free Trade Association
CCP	Common Commercial Policy
CCT	Common Customs Tariff
CEAO	Communauté Économique de l'Afrique de l'Ouest
CEC	Commission of the European Communities
CEDB	component event data bank
CEDEFOP	European Centre for Development of Vocational Training

CEEC	Countries of Central and Eastern Europe	CSF	Community support framework
CEEP	European Centre for Population Studies	CSTID	Committee for Scientific and Technical Information and Documentation
CEN	European Committee for Standardization	CTP	Common Transport Policy
CENELEC	European Committee for Electrotechnical Standardization	CTS	conformance testing services
		CU	customs union
CEP	common energy policy	DAC	Development Assistance Committee (OECD)
CEPGL	Economic Community of the Countries of the Great Lakes	DDR	German Democratic Republic (now part of Germany)
CER	closer economic relations	DELTA	developing European learning through technological advance
CERN	European Organization for Nuclear Research		
CET	common external tariff	DG IV	Directorate General Four
CFP	Common Fisheries Policy	DI	divergence indicator
CFSP	common foreign and security policy	DRIVE	dedicated road infrastructure for vehicle safety in Europe
CI	Community initiative	DV	dummy variable
CIS	Commonwealth of Independent States	EAC	East African Community
		EAGGF	European Agricultural Guidance and Guarantee Fund
CM	Common Market		
CMEA	Council for Mutual Economic Assistance	EBA	'Everything But Arms'
		EBRD	European Bank for Reconstruction and Development
CN	combined nomenclature		
CODEST	Committee for the European Development of Science and Technology	EC	European Community
		ECB	European Central Bank
		ECAA	European Common Aviation Area
COMECON	see CMEA	ECHO	European Community Humanitarian Office
COMETT	Community programme in education and training for technology		
		ECIP	European Community Investment Partners
CORDIS	Community research and development information service	ECJ	European Court of Justice
		ECLAIR	European collaborative linkage of agriculture and industry through research
COREPER	Committee of Permanent Representatives		
CORINE	coordination of information on the environment in Europe	ECMT	European Conference of Ministers of Transport
COSINE	cooperation for open systems interconnection networking in Europe	ECOFIN	European Council of Ministers for Financial Affairs
		ECOSOC	Economic and Social Committee (also ESC)
COST	European cooperation on scientific and technical research	ECOWAS	Economic Community of West African States
CREST	Scientific and Technical Research Committee	ECPE	European Centre of Public Enterprises
CRS	computerized reservation system		
CSCE	Conference on Security and Cooperation in Europe	ECSC	European Coal and Steel Community

ECU	European Currency Unit	EUROCONTROL	European organization for the safety of air navigation
EDC	European Defence Community		
EDF	European Development Fund	EURONET-DIANE	direct information access network for Europe
EDIFACT	electronic data interchange for administration, commerce and transport		
		EUROSTAT	statistical office of the EC/EU
EEA	European Economic Area	EVCA	European Venture Capital Association
EEC	European Economic Community	FADN	EEC farm accountancy data network
EEZ	Exclusive Economic Zone		
EFTA	European Free Trade Association	FAO	Food and Agriculture Organization of the United Nations
EGE	European Group on Ethics in Science and New Technologies		
		FAST	forecasting and assessment in the field of science and technology
EIB	European Investment Bank		
EIF	European Investment Fund	FCO	Foreign and Commonwealth Office
EMCF	European Monetary Cooperation Fund		
		FEER	Fundamental Equilibrium Exchange Rate
EMF	European Monetary Fund		
EMI	European Monetary Institute	FEOGA	European Agricultural Guidance and Guarantee Fund
EMS	European Monetary System		
EMU	European monetary union or economic and monetary union	FIFG	Financial Instrument for Fisheries Guidance
EP	European Parliament	FLAIR	food-linked agro-industrial research
EPC	European political cooperation		
EPOCH	European programme on climatology and natural hazards	FSAP	Financial Services Action Plan
		FSU	Former Soviet Union
EQS	environmental quality standard	FTA	free trade area
Erasmus	European Community action scheme for the mobility of university students	GATS	General Agreement on Trade in Services
		GATT	General Agreement on Tariffs and Trade (UN)
ERDF	European Regional Development Fund		
		GCC	Gulf Cooperation Council
ERM	Exchange Rate Mechanism	GDP	gross domestic product
ESA	European Space Agency	GFCM	General Fisheries Council for the Mediterranean
ESCB	European System of Central Banks		
ESF	European Social Fund	GNI	gross national income
ESI	electricity supply industry	GNP	gross national product
ESPRIT	European strategic programme for research and development in information technology	GSM	global system for mobile communication
		GSP	generalized system of preferences
ETUC	European Trade Union Confederation	HDTV	high-definition television
		HELIOS	action programme to promote social and economic integration and an independent way of life for disabled people
EU	European Union		
EUA	European Unit of Account		
Euratom	European Atomic Energy Commission		
		HS	Harmonized Commodity Description and Coding System
Eureka	European Research Coordinating Agency		
		IAEA	International Atomic Energy Agency (UN)
EURES	European Employment Services		

IATA	International Air Transport Association	JOP	joint venture programme PHARE-TACIS
IBRD	International Bank for Reconstruction and Development (World Bank) (UN)	JOULE	joint opportunities for unconventional or long-term energy supply
ICES	International Council for the Exploration of the Seas	JRC	Joint Research Centre
		KALEIDOSCOPE	programme to support artistic and cultural activities having a European dimension
ICONE	comparative index of national and European standards		
IDA	International Development Association (UN)	LAFTA	Latin American Free Trade Area
		LDC	less-developed country
IDB	Inter-American Development Bank	LEDA	local employment development action programme
IDO	integrated development operation	LIFE	Financial Instrument for the Environment
IEA	International Energy Agency (OECD)		
		M&A	mergers and acquisitions
IEM	internal energy market	MAGP	multi-annual guidance programme
IGC	intergovernmental conference		
IIT	intra-industry trade	MARIE	mass transit rail initiative for Europe
ILO	International Labour Organization		
IMF	International Monetary Fund (UN)	MAST	marine science and technology
		MB	marginal benefit
IMP	integrated Mediterranean programme	MC	marginal cost
		MCA	monetary compensatory amount
IMPACT	information market policy actions	MEDIA	measures to encourage the development of the audiovisual industry
INSIS	inter-institutional system of integrated services		
INTERREG	Community initiative concerning border areas	MEP	Member of the European Parliament
IPR	intellectual property rights	MERCOSOR	Southern Cone Common Market
IRCC	International Radio Consultative Committee	MERM	multilateral exchange rate model
IRIS	network of demonstration projects on vocational training for women	MFA	Multifibre Arrangement (arrangement regarding international trade in textiles)
IRTE	integrated road transport environment	MFN	most favoured nation
ISIS	integrated standards information system	MFP	multi-annual framework programme
ISPA	instrument for structural policies for pre-accession	MFT	multilateral free trade
		MISEP	mutual information system on employment policies
ITA	information technology agreement	MNE	multinational enterprise
ITER	international thermonuclear experimental reactor	MONITOR	research programme on strategic analysis, forecasting and assessment in research and technology
JESSI	Joint European Submicron Silicon Initiative		
JET	Joint European Torus	MP	marginal productivity
JHA	judicial and home affairs	MRU	Mano River Union

MS	member state	OSCE	Organization for Security and Cooperation in Europe
NAFTA	North Atlantic Free Trade Agreement; New Zealand Australia Free Trade Area	OSI	open systems interconnection
		PAFTAD	Pacific Trade and Development Conference
NAIRU	non-accelerating inflation rate of unemployment	PBEC	Pacific Basin Economic Council
NATO	North Atlantic Treaty Organization		
NCB	National Central Bank	PECC	Pacific Economic Cooperation Conference
NCI	new Community instrument		
NEAFC	North-East Atlantic Fisheries Commission	PEDIP	programme to modernize Portuguese industry
NET	Next European Torus	PETRA	action programme for the vocational training of young people and their preparation for adult and working life
NETT	network for environmental technology transfer		
NGO	non-governmental organization		
		PHARE	programme of community aid for Central and Eastern European countries
NIC	newly industrializing country		
NIE	newly industrializing economy		
NIEO	New International Economic Order	PO	producer organization
		POSEIDOM	programme of options specific to the remote and insular nature of the overseas departments
NIESR	National Institute of Economic and Social Research		
NiGEM	National Institute Global Econometric Model	PPP	polluter pays principle
		PPP	purchasing power parity
NIS	Newly Independent States (of the former USSR)	PTA	preferential trade area
		PTC	Pacific Telecommunications Conference
NMS	new member states		
NOHA	Network on Humanitarian Assistance	PTT	Posts, Telegraphs and Telecommunications
NPCI	national programme of Community interest	QMV	qualified majority voting
		RACE	research and development in advanced communication technologies for Europe
NPT	Treaty on Non-proliferation of Nuclear Weapons		
NTB	non-tariff barrier	RARE	réseaux associés pour la recherche européenne
NTM	non-tariff measure		
NUTS	Nomenclature of Territorial Units for Statistics	R&TD	research and technological development
OAPEC	Organization of Arab Petroleum Exporting Countries	RCD	Regional Cooperation for Development
OAU	Organization for African Unity	REGIS	Community initiative concerning the most remote regions
OCTs	overseas countries and territories		
ODA	overseas development aid	REIMEP	regular European interlaboratory measurements evaluation programme
OECD	Organization for Economic Cooperation and Development		
OEEC	Organization for European Economic Cooperation	RENAVAL	programme to assist the conversion of shipbuilding areas
OPEC	Organization of Petroleum Exporting Countries	REPAs	regional economic partnership agreements

RESIDER — programme to assist the conversion of steel areas

RIA — regional impact assessment

RoO — rules of origin

RTA — regional trade agreement

RTD — research and technological development

SACU — Southern African Customs Union

SAP — social action programme

SAST — strategic analysis in the field of science and technology

SAVE — Specific Actions for Vigorous Energy Efficiency

SCENT — system for a customs enforcement network

SCIENCE — plan to stimulate the international cooperation and interchange necessary for European researchers

SDR — special drawing rights

SEA — Single European Act

SEDOC — inter-state notification of job vacancies

SEM — Single European Market

SEM 2000 — sound and efficient management

SFOR — multinational stabilization force

SLIM — simpler legislation for the internal market

SMEs — small and medium-sized enterprises

SPD — single programme documents

SPEAR — support programme for a European assessment of research

SPES — stimulation plan for economic science

SPRINT — strategic programme for innovation and technology transfer

SPS — WTO's agreement on the application of sanitary and phytosanitary measures

STABEX — system for the stabilization of ACP and OCT export earnings

STAR — Community programme for the development of certain less-favoured regions of the Community by improving access to advanced telecommunications services

STEP — science and technology for environmental protection

SVER — structural vector autoregression

SYNERGY — multinational programme to promote international cooperation in the energy sector

SYSMIN — special financing facility for ACP and OCT mining products

TAC — total allowable catch

TACIS — Technical Aid to the Commonwealth of Independent States

TARIC — integrated Community tariff

TBT — WTO's agreement on technical barriers to trade

TEDIS — trade electronic data interchange systems

TELEMAN — research and training programme on remote handling in nuclear hazardous and disordered environments

TEMPUS — trans-European cooperation scheme for higher education

TENs — trans-European networks

TESS — modernization of the exchange of information between national social security institutions

TEU — Treaty on European Union

TFEU — Treaty of the Functioning of the European Union

TRIPs — trade-related aspects of intellectual property rights

TSEs — transmissible spongiform encephalopathies

t/t — terms of trade

TUC — Trades Union Congress

TVA — taxe à la valeur ajoutée

UDEAC — Union Douanière et Économique de l'Afrique Centrale

UEMOA — West African Economic and Monetary Union

UES — uniform emission standards

UN — United Nations

UNCLOS — United Nations Conference on the Law of the Sea

UNCTAD	United Nations Conference on Trade and Development	UTR	unilateral tariff reduction
UNECA	United Nations Economic Commission for Africa	VALOREN	Community programme for the development of certain less-favoured regions of the Community by exploiting endogenous energy potential
UNEP	United Nations Environment Programme		
UNESCO	United Nations Educational, Scientific and Cultural Organization	VALUE	programme for the dissemination and utilization of research results
		VAT	value added tax
UNHCR	United Nations High Commissioner for Refugees	VEIS	VAT information exchange system
		VER	voluntary export restraint
UNICE	Union of Industries of the European Community	VSTF	very short-term financing facility
		WEU	Western European Union
UNIDO	United Nations Industrial Development Organization	WFC	World Food Council (UN)
		WFP	World Food Programme (UN)
UNRWA	United Nations Relief and Works Agency for Palestine Refugees in the Near East	WIPO	World Intellectual Property Organization (UN)
		WTO	World Trade Organization
URAA	Uruguay Round Agreement on Agriculture	YES	'Youth for Europe' programme (youth exchange scheme)
URBAN	Community initiative for urban areas		

1 General introduction: the EU within the context of regional integration worldwide

ALI EL-AGRAA

1.1 Introduction

The European Union (EU) is the most prominent scheme of international economic integration (IEI). The first aim of this chapter is to provide a precise definition of IEI, since what it means to those specializing in trade theory is very different to what one would expect on purely linguistic grounds. IEI creates 'clubs' between some nations, which discriminate against non-members, in contrast to multilateralism, which extends agreed 'arrangements' to all nations. The World Trade Organization (WTO), which regulates trade, is based on the principle of non-discrimination, so the second aim of the chapter is to examine how IEI fits within the WTO framework. IEI can take several forms, and the third aim is to describe the various schemes that have actually been adopted worldwide and to set the EU within this broader context, substantiating the statement made in the opening sentence about the EU. The fourth aim is to show why most countries seek IEI – that is, to consider what economic or other benefits become possible as a consequence of IEI.

1.2 What is economic integration?

IEI is one aspect of 'international economics', which has been growing in importance since the middle of the twentieth century. The term itself has quite a short history; indeed, Machlup (1977) was unable to find a single instance of its use prior to 1942. Since then the term has been used at various times to refer to practically any area of international economic relations. By 1950, however, the term had been given a specific definition by international trade specialists to denote *a state of affairs or a process which involves the amalgamation of separate economies into larger free trading regions.* It is in this more limited sense that the term is used today. However, one should hasten to add that recently the term has been used to mean simply increasing economic interdependence between nations, now glamorized as *globalization.*

More specifically, IEI (also referred to as 'regional integration', 'regional trading agreements' (RTAs), 'preferential trading agreements' (PTAs) and 'trading blocs') is concerned with (a) the discriminatory removal of all trade impediments between at least two participating nations, and with (b) the establishment of certain elements of cooperation and coordination between them. The latter depends entirely on the actual form that IEI takes. Different forms of IEI can be envisaged and many have actually been implemented (see Table 1.1 for a schematic presentation):

1. In *free trade areas* (FTAs or PTAs), the member nations (MNs) remove tariffs among themselves, but retain their freedom to determine their own policies vis-à-vis the outside world (the non-participants). Recently, the trend has been to extend this treatment to investment.
2. *Customs unions* (CUs) are very similar to FTAs/PTAs, except that MNs must conduct and pursue common external commercial relations – for instance, they must adopt common external tariffs (CETs) on imports from the non-participants.
3. *Common markets* (CMs) are CUs that also allow for free factor mobility across MNs' frontiers – that is, capital, labour, technology and enterprises should move unhindered between MNs.
4. *Complete economic unions*, or economic unions (EcUs), are CMs plus the complete unification of monetary and fiscal policies – that is, MNs must introduce a central authority to exercise control over these matters, so that MNs effectively become regions of the same nation.

Table 1.1 Schematic presentation of economic integration schemes

Scheme	Free intra-scheme trade	Common commercial policy (CCP)	Free factor mobility	Common monetary and fiscal policy	One government
Free trade area (FTA)	Yes	No	No	No	No
Customs union (CU)	Yes	Yes	No	No	No
Common market (CM)	Yes	Yes	Yes	No	No
Economic union (EcU)	Yes	Yes	Yes	Yes	No
Political union (PU)	Yes	Yes	Yes	Yes	Yes

5. In *complete political unions* (PUs), MNs literally become one nation – that is, the central authority needed in EcUs should be paralleled by a common parliament and other institutions needed to guarantee the sovereignty of one state.

However, one should hasten to add that political integration need not be, and in the majority of cases will never be, part of this list. Nevertheless, it can of course be introduced as a form of unity and for no economic reason whatsoever, as was the case with the two Germanys in 1990, and as is the case with the pursuit of the unification of the Korean Peninsula, although we should naturally be interested in its economic consequences (see Section 1.5, page 14). More generally, we should stress that each of these forms of IEI can be introduced in its own right; hence they should not be confused with *stages* in a *process* which eventually leads to complete economic or political union.

It should also be noted that there may be *sectoral* integration, as distinct from general, across-the-board IEI, in particular areas of the economy, as was the case with the European Coal and Steel Community (ECSC; see Chapters 2 and 17), created in 1951, but sectoral integration is considered to be only a form of cooperation because it is inconsistent with the accepted definition of IEI, and also because it may contravene the rules of the General Agreement on Tariffs and Trade (GATT), which began to be run by the WTO in 1995 (see next page). Sectoral integration may also occur within any of the mentioned schemes, as is the case with the EU's Common Agricultural Policy (CAP; see Chapter 20), but then it is nothing more than a 'policy'.

It has been claimed that IEI can be *negative* or *positive*. The term 'negative IEI' was coined by Tinbergen

(1954) to refer to the simple act of the removal of impediments on trade between MNs. The term 'positive integration' relates to the modification of existing instruments and institutions, and, more importantly, to the creation of new ones so as to enable the market of the integrated area to function properly and effectively and also to promote other broader policy aims of the scheme. Hence, at the risk of oversimplification, according to this classification, it can be stated that sectoral integration and FTAs/PTAs are forms of IEI which require only negative integration, while the remaining types require positive integration, since as a minimum they need the positive act of adopting common external trade and investment relations. However, in reality this distinction is oversimplistic, not only because practically all existing types of IEI have found it essential to introduce some elements of positive integration, but also because theoretical considerations clearly indicate that no scheme of IEI is viable without certain elements of positive integration – for example, even the ECSC deemed it necessary to establish new institutions to tackle its specified tasks (see Chapter 2).

1.3 Economic integration and WTO rules

There are four basic WTO principles: (a) trade *liberalization* on a most favoured nation (MFN) basis (the lowest tariff applicable to one member must be extended to all members); (b) *non-discrimination*; (c) *transparency* of instruments used to restrict trade (now called *tariffication*); and (d) the promotion of *growth and stability* of the world economy. More generally, these principles are reduced to three: *non-discrimination*, *transparency* and *reciprocity*. GATT's Article XXIV (GATT 1986, p.

Box 1.1 GATT's Article XXIV.5

5. Accordingly, the provisions of this Agreement shall not prevent, as between the territories of contracting parties, the formation of a customs union or of a free-trade area or the adoption of an interim agreement necessary for the formation of a customs union or of a free-trade area; provided that:

   (a) with respect to a customs union, or an interim agreement leading to the formation of a customs union, the duties and other regulations of commerce imposed at the institution of any such union or interim agreement in respect of trade with contracting parties not parties to such union or agreement shall not on the whole be higher or more restrictive than the general incidence of the duties and regulations of commerce applicable in the constituent territories prior to the formation of such union or the adoption of such interim agreement, as the case may be;

   (b) with respect to a free-trade area, or an interim agreement leading to the formation of a free-trade area, the duties and other regulations of commerce maintained in each of the constituent territories and applicable at the formation of such free-trade area or the adoption of such interim agreement to the trade of contracting parties not included in such area or not parties to such agreement shall not be higher or more restrictive than the corresponding duties and other regulations of commerce existing in the same constituent territories prior to the formation of the free-trade area, or interim agreement, as the case may be; and

   (c) any interim agreement referred to in sub-paragraphs (a) and (b) shall include a plan and schedule for the formation of such a customs union or of such a free-trade area within a reasonable length of time.

Source: GATT 1986

42; see also WTO, which subsumed GATT in 1994, and hence can be used interchangeably) allows the formation of IEI schemes on the understanding that (a) they may not pursue policies which increase the level of protection beyond that which existed prior to their formation; (b) tariffs and other trade restrictions (with some exceptions) are removed on *substantially* (increasingly interpreted to mean at least 90 per cent of intra-MN trade) all the trade among MNs; and (c) they become established within a reasonable period of time. Box 1.1 provides the full text of item 5 of Article XXIV. The drafters of Article XXIV.5 recognized the benefits of closer IEI, even though this contradicted one of the basic WTO principles, that of *non-discrimination*.

There are more serious arguments suggesting that Article XXIV is in direct contradiction of the spirit of WTO (see Chapter 6 and, inter alios, Dam 1970). However, Wolf (1983, p. 156) argues that if nations decide to treat one another as if they were part of a single economy, nothing can be done to prevent them from doing so, and that IEI schemes, particularly the EU at the time of its formation in 1957, can have a strong impulse towards liberalization; in the EU case, the setting of CETs by 1969 (see Chapter 24) happened

to coincide with GATT's Kennedy Round of tariff reductions (by about 35 percent) in 1967. However, experience suggests that IEI can be associated with protectionism – for example, in the EU case, after the first oil crisis there was a proliferation of non-tariff barriers (NTBs), which is why the single European market (SEM) programme (Chapters 2 and 7) was introduced in 1992 – but the point about the WTO not being able to deter countries from pursuing IEI has general validity: the WTO is ultimately dependent on MSs respecting its rules.

Of course, these considerations are more complicated than is suggested here, particularly since there are those who would argue that nothing could be more discriminatory than for a group of nations to remove all tariffs and other trade impediments (import quotas and NTBs) on their mutual trade while *at the same time* maintaining the initial levels against outsiders. Indeed, it is difficult to find 'clubs' which extend equal privileges to non-subscribers, although the Asia Pacific Economic Cooperation (APEC) forum aspires to 'open regionalism', one interpretation of which is extending the removal of restrictions on trade and investment to all countries, not just MNs. This point lies behind the concern about whether IEI hinders or enhances the prospects for the free multilateral reductions in trade barriers that the WTO is supposed to promote (see El-Agraa 1999, for the arguments for and against). Moreover, as we shall see in Chapter 6, IEI schemes may lead to resource reallocation effects that are economically undesirable. However, to deny nations the right to form such associations, particularly when the main driving force may be political rather than economic, would have been a major setback for the world community. Hence, much as Article XXIV raises serious problems in terms of how it fits in with the general spirit of the WTO, and many proposals have been put forward for its reform, its adoption also reflects deep understanding of the future development of the world economy.

1.4 Economic integration worldwide

Although this book is concerned with the EU, it is important to view the EU within the context of the global experience of IEI. This section provides a brief summary of this experience. (See El-Agraa 1997 for full and detailed coverage, and Crawford and Fiorentino 2006 and the WTO website for the latest information.)

Since the end of the Second World War various forms of IEI have been proposed and numerous schemes have actually been implemented. Even though some of these were subsequently discontinued or completely reformulated, the number adopted during the decade following 1957 was so great as to prompt Haberler in 1964 to describe that period as the 'age of [IEI]'. Since 1964, however, there has been a further proliferation of IEI schemes, so Haberler's description may be more apt for the post-1964 era: by December 2008, 421 RTAs had been notified to the WTO,[1] and 230 of these are still in force.

1.4.1 Economic integration in Europe

The EU is the most significant and influential of IEI schemes. There are three reasons, which, when taken together, explain this significance:

1. Of the six EU founding states, Germany, France and Italy were top-ten world economies. Since then, two such economies have joined, the UK and Spain.

So the EU today includes five of the world's top ten economies. Also, the EU has proved a magnet for new members, so in addition to the founding MNs, known as the Original Six (hereafter, the Six), there are now an extra 21 MSs (see Table 1.2 for a tabulation of European states and their IEI arrangements). The EU of 27 continues to receive applications for membership, hence it is set to include practically the whole of Europe and may go beyond the geographical area if Turkey succeeds in joining in 2015 (see Chapter 2). No other scheme matches this economic size and diversity.

2. In terms of the voluntary nature of membership, the EU is the oldest IEI scheme in operation. This longevity is part of its attraction.

3. Most vitally, the EU has the deepest scheme of IEI. It is almost a complete economic union (EcU; see pages 1 and 2): (a) it is practically a complete CM; (b) 17 of its 27 MSs have the same currency (euro), with the European Central Bank in charge of eurozone monetary policy; (c) it has a system for monitoring and influencing fiscal policy, the *Stability and Growth Pact* (see Chapters 11 and 12); (d) it has its own budget, financing a range of policies; and since the Treaty of Lisbon came into force on 1 December 2009 it has (e) a single president of the European Council; and (f) a foreign policy chief who controls a vast diplomatic corps, now being established.

The influence of the EU is simply due to its relative global weight. Using 2008 data (see Table 1.3), the population of EU27 exceeds that of NAFTA (Canada, Mexico and the USA) by about 43 million (9.7 per cent) and is the third largest in the world, after China (1,325 million) and India (1,140 million). The combined economic weight of EU27, in terms of GNI, converted using the World Bank's Atlas method for exchange rates, exceeds that of NAFTA by about $249 billion (1.46 per cent), and, using purchasing power parity (PPP), falls short of it by about $2,384 billion (13.59 per cent).

The European Free Trade Association (EFTA) is the other major scheme of IEI in Europe. To understand its membership one has to know something about its history (detailed in Chapter 2). In the mid-1950s, when the European Economic Community (EEC) of the Six plus the UK was being contemplated, the UK was unprepared to commit itself to some of the economic and political aims envisaged for that Community

Table 1.2 Economic integration in Europe

Country	Scheme (year founded) and aim			
	EU (1957) CM/EcU	When to join EU? CM/EcU	EFTA (1960) FTA	EEA (1992) FTA
Austria	✓			✓
Belgium	✓			✓
Bulgaria	✓			✓
Cyprus	✓			✓
Czech Rep.	✓			✓
Denmark	✓			✓
Estonia	✓			✓
Finland	✓			✓
France	✓			✓
Germany	✓			✓
Greece	✓			✓
Hungary	✓			✓
Ireland	✓			✓
Italy	✓			✓
Latvia	✓			✓
Lithuania	✓			✓
Luxembourg	✓			✓
Malta	✓			✓
Netherlands	✓			✓
Poland	✓			✓
Portugal	✓			✓
Romania	✓			✓
Slovak Rep.	✓			✓
Slovenia	✓			✓
Spain	✓			✓
Sweden	✓			✓
UK	✓			✓
Albania		Applied in 2009		
Bosnia & Herzegovina		Hopes to apply soon		
Croatia		Negotiating since 2004		
Macedonia		Applied in 2004		
Montenegro		Applied in 2008		
Serbia		Applied in 2009		
Turkey		Negotiating since 2005 for 2015		
Iceland		Applied in 2009	✓	✓
Norway			✓	✓
Switzerland			✓	
(Liechtenstein)			✓	✓

Table 1.3 A Comparison of the EU and NAFTA, 2008

Scheme	Population (million)	GNI ($ billion)	GNI(PPP) ($ billion)
EU	496.7	17,338.3	15,155.3
NAFTA	443.8	17,089.1	17,539.6

– for example, the adoption of a Common Agricultural Policy and the eventual political unity of Western Europe were seen as aims that were in direct conflict with the UK's powerful position in the world and its interests in the Commonwealth, particularly with regard to 'Commonwealth preference', which granted special access to the markets of the Commonwealth. Hence the UK favoured the idea of a Western Europe which adopted free trade in industrial products only, thus securing for itself the advantages offered by the Commonwealth as well as opening up Western Europe as a free market for its industrial goods. In short, the UK sought to achieve the best of both worlds, but such an arrangement was not acceptable to those seriously contemplating the formation of the EEC, especially France, which stood to lose in an arrangement excluding a common policy for agriculture (see Chapter 20). As a result, the UK approached those Western European nations which had similar interests, with the purpose of forming an alternative scheme of IEI to counteract any possible damage due to the formation of the EEC. The outcome was EFTA, which was established in 1960 by the Stockholm Convention, with the object of creating a free market for industrial products only; there were some agreements on non-manufactures, but these were relatively unimportant.

The membership of EFTA consisted of Austria, Denmark, Norway, Portugal, Sweden, Switzerland (and Liechtenstein) and the UK. Finland became an associate member in 1961 and Iceland joined in 1970 as a full member. But Denmark, Ireland and the UK joined the European Community (EC; what the EEC became) in 1973; Portugal and Spain did so in 1986; and Austria, Finland and Sweden joined in 1995. All the remaining EFTA countries except Switzerland – that is, Iceland, Liechtenstein and Norway – now belong to the *European Economic Area* (EEA), a scheme introduced in 1992 which provides economic but not political membership of the EU – being part of the SEM without having a say in EU decisions.

Before the dramatic events of 1989–90, IEI schemes in Europe were not confined to the EU and EFTA. The socialist planned economies of Eastern Europe had their own arrangement: the Council for Mutual Economic Assistance (CMEA), or COMECON as it was generally known in the West. The CMEA was formed in 1949 by Bulgaria, Czechoslovakia, the German Democratic Republic, Hungary, Poland, Romania and the USSR; they were later joined by three non-European countries: Mongolia (1962), Cuba (1972) and Vietnam (1978). In its earlier days, before the death of Stalin, CMEA activities were confined to the collation of MNs' plans, the development of a uniform system of reporting statistical data and the recording of foreign trade statistics. However, during the 1970s the CMEA adopted a series of measures to implement a 'Comprehensive Programme of Socialist Integration', hence indicating that the organization was moving towards a form of integration based principally on plan coordination and joint planning activity, rather than on market levers (Smith 1977). The CMEA comprised a group of relatively small countries and one 'superpower', and the long-term aim of the association was to achieve a highly organized and integrated bloc, without any agreement ever having been made on how or when that was to be accomplished.

The CMEA's demise inevitably came about due to the dramatic changes that took place in Eastern Europe and the former USSR in the 1980s, together with the fact that the CMEA did not really achieve much in terms of economic integration – indeed some analysts have argued that the entire organization was simply an instrument for the USSR to dictate its wishes to the rest of the group (El-Agraa 1988b). However, soon after the USSR's demise, twelve of the fifteen former Soviet Republics formed the Commonwealth of Independent States (CIS) to bring them closer together in a relationship originally intended to match the EU's, but the relationship remains very limited.

Before leaving Europe, mention should be made of

the Central European Free Trade Agreement (CEFTA), the Council of the Baltic Sea States (CBSS) and the Nordic Community. CEFTA was originally formed by Czechoslovakia, Hungary and Poland in 1992, but with EU enlargement members have left when they joined the EU and new countries have joined, so it has moved southwards to include the republics of former Yugoslavia,[2] Albania and Moldova. The CBSS involves eleven states, nine EU states bordering the Baltic, Norway and Russia, and it involves cooperation but not economic integration. The Nordic Community involves five Nordic countries: Denmark, Finland, Iceland, Norway and Sweden.[3] In spite of claims to the contrary (Sundelius and Wiklund 1979), the Nordic scheme is one of cooperation rather than IEI, since its members belong to either the EU or the EEA, through which economic integration is organized.

1.4.2 Economic integration in Africa

Africa has numerous schemes of IEI (see Table 1.4), with practically all the African countries belonging to more than one scheme. If we include involuntary colonial integration, Africa could claim to have the oldest two schemes in the world: the Southern African Customs Union (SACU, 1910, which is dominated by South Africa, with all members except for Botswana part of a Rand-based common monetary area), and the East African Community (EAC, established by the British in 1919 for their own colonial administrative ease).

In West Africa, the Union Économique et Monétaire de l'ouest-Africaine (UEMOA) and Mano River Union (MRU) coexist with the Economic Community of West African States (ECOWAS), with considerable membership overlap. A similar situation exists in Central Africa, with the Economic Community of Central African States (ECCAS), the Communauté Économique et Monétaire des États de l'Afrique Centrale (CEMAC) and the Economic Community of the Countries of the Great Lakes (CEPGL). In eastern Africa there is the Common Market for Eastern and Southern Africa (COMESA), with the Intergovernmental Authority on Development (IGAD) and the East African Community (EAC) as smaller inner groups. In southern Africa there are the Southern African Development Community (SADC) and the Southern African Customs Union (SACU). Northern Africa used to be the only subregion with a single scheme, the Arab Maghreb Union (UMA),

but the recent creation of the Community of Sahel-Saharan States (CENSAD) has brought it in line with the rest of Africa.

UMA, created in 1989, aimed for a CU before the end of 1995 and a CM by 2000, but has yet to achieve a mere FTA. CENSAD, established in February 1998, has no clear objectives, not even with regard to a trade liberalization strategy, but since its MNs belong to other blocs, the aims of these are pertinent. ECOWAS was launched in 1975 with the aim of creating an economic and monetary union, but its revised treaty envisaged a mere CU by 2000, later delayed to 1 January 2003, and some MNs do not even apply an FTA. UEMOA, created in 1994 by the francophone MNs of ECOWAS, is now a CU, introducing its CETs in January 2000, but applying them to the rest of ECOWAS as well, and some MNs are still not even FTAs! MRU, established in 1973, is a CU with a certain degree of cooperation in the industrial sector. ECCAS has been dormant for almost a decade, but has recently been resuscitated. CEPGL was created in 1976, but is virtually inactive due to the conflicts within the bloc. Most activity in this part of Africa is confined to CEMAC, which has a common currency and has taken steps towards a CU. COMESA, established in 1993, launched an FTA in October 2000 comprising nine of its MNs. Note that of the MNs of the EAC (first *truly* established in 1967), Kenya and Uganda are also members of COMESA, while Tanzania also belongs to SADC, having earlier withdrawn from COMESA. The EAC and COMESA, in their May 1997 *Memorandum of Understanding*, agreed to become a CU. SADC aims to achieve an FTA within the next five years. Note that IGAD (formed in 1996 to replace the equivalent Association on Drought and Development of 1986) and the Indian Ocean Commission (IOC, set up in 1982, with vague aims and ambitions, except for concentration on some functional cooperation areas, such as fisheries and tourism) have agreed to adopt COMESA's aims.

Hence the unique characteristic of IEI in Africa is the multiplicity of overlapping schemes, made more complicated by the coexistence of intergovernmental cooperation organizations. For example, in West Africa alone, in 1984 there was a total of thirty-three schemes and intergovernmental cooperation organizations, and by the late 1980s, about 130 intergovernmental, multi-sectoral economic organizations existed simultaneously with all the above-mentioned IEI schemes (Adedeji 2002, p. 6). That is why the United Nations

Table 1.4 Economic integration in Africa

Country	Scheme															
	UMA	CENSAD	ECOWAS	UEMOA	CEMAC	ECCAS	CEPGL	MRU	COMESA	EAC	IGAD	IOC	SADC	SACU	AEC	AU
Algeria	✓														✓	✓
Angola						✓			✓				✓		✓	✓
Benin		✓	✓	✓											✓	✓
Botswana													✓	✓	✓	✓
Burkina Faso		✓	✓	✓											✓	✓
Burundi						✓	✓		✓	✓					✓	✓
Cameroon					✓	✓									✓	✓
Cape Verde			✓												✓	✓
Central African Rep.		✓			✓	✓									✓	✓
Chad		✓			✓	✓									✓	✓
Comoros									✓			✓			✓	✓
Congo					✓	✓									✓	✓
Congo Dem. Rep.						✓	✓		✓				✓		✓	✓
Côte d'Ivoire		✓	✓	✓											✓	✓
Djibouti		✓							✓		✓				✓	✓
Egypt		✓							✓						✓	✓
Equatorial Guinea					✓	✓									✓	✓
Eritrea		✓							✓		✓				✓	✓
Ethiopia									✓		✓				✓	✓
Gabon					✓	✓									✓	✓
Gambia		✓	✓												✓	✓
Ghana		✓	✓					–							✓	✓
Guinea-Bissau		✓	✓	✓											✓	✓
Guinea-Conakry		✓	✓					✓							✓	✓
Kenya		✓							✓	✓	✓				✓	✓
Lesotho, Kingdom of													✓	✓	✓	✓
Liberia		✓	✓					✓							✓	✓
Libya	✓	✓													✓	✓
Madagascar									✓			✓	✓		✓	✓
Malawi									✓				✓		✓	✓
Mali		✓	✓	✓											✓	✓
Mauritania	✓	✓													✓	✓
Mauritius									✓			✓	✓		✓	✓
Morocco	✓	✓													✓	
Mozambique													✓		✓	✓
Namibia													✓	✓	✓	✓
Niger		✓	✓	✓											✓	✓
Nigeria		✓	✓												✓	✓

PTA with an East Asian Community (see, inter alios, El-Agraa 2010a, b) in mind, was agreed with China, Japan and South Korea in 2003, but has yet to be finalized; the same is also true of an ASEAN+6, which includes Australia, India and New Zealand.

On 8 December 1985 the South Asian Association for Regional Cooperation (SAARC) was established by Bangladesh, Bhutan, India, Maldives, Nepal, Pakistan and Sri Lanka. Its aim is to accelerate the process of economic and social development of the members, but within the wider context of working together in a 'spirit of friendship, trust and understanding'. In November 2005, at the thirteenth summit, held in Dhaka, Bangladesh, SAARC agreed to admit Afghanistan as a member, to grant China and Japan observer status and to firmly commit to the realization of a South Asian Economic Union as well as an FTA (SAFTA).

In 1965 Australia and New Zealand entered into an FTA called the New Zealand Australia Free Trade Area. This was replaced in 1983 by the more important Australia New Zealand Closer Economic Relations and Trade Agreement (CER, for short): not only have major trade barriers been removed, but significant effects on the New Zealand economy have been experienced as a result.

A scheme for the Pacific Basin integration-cum-cooperation was being hotly discussed during the 1980s. In the late 1980s I argued (El-Agraa 1988a, b) that 'given the diversity of countries within the Pacific region, it would seem highly unlikely that a very involved scheme of integration would evolve over the next decade or so'.

Various fora involving governments, business and academics existed across the region,[4] but the Asia Pacific Economic Cooperation (APEC) forum was established in 1989 by ASEAN plus Australia, Canada, Japan, New Zealand, South Korea and the USA. These were joined by China, Hong Kong and Taiwan in 1991. In 1993 President Clinton galvanized it into its present form and its membership increased to eighteen nations by adding Chile, Mexico and Papua New Guinea. In Bogor, Indonesia, in 1994, APEC declared its intention to create a free trade and investment area embracing its advanced MNs by 2010, with the rest to follow ten years later. APEC tried to chart the route for realizing this vision in Osaka, Japan, in 1995, and came up with the interesting resolution that each MN should unilaterally declare its own measures for freeing trade and investment, but with agriculture completely left out of

the reckoning; China immediately obliged by declaring that it would do this for a vast number of products, an act conditional on WTO membership which China was negotiating at the time. In November 1998 Peru, Russia and Vietnam joined APEC, increasing its total membership to twenty-one nations. In its 2004 meeting in Bangkok, Thailand, APEC outlined its priorities to be the promotion of trade and investment liberalization, the enhancement of human security, and using the organization to help people and societies to benefit from globalization. And in the 2010 summit, with the financial crisis in mind, its leaders declared their support for the goals of the G-20 London 2009 Framework for Strong, Sustainable and Balanced Growth, by joining in their commitment to:

1. work together to ensure that macroeconomic, regulatory and structural policies are collectively consistent with more sustainable and balanced trajectories of growth;
2. promote current account sustainability and open trade and investment to advance global prosperity and growth sustainability;
3. undertake macro prudential and regulatory policies to help prevent credit and asset price cycles from becoming forces of destabilization; and
4. promote development and poverty reduction as part of the rebalancing of global growth.

Officially speaking, APEC aims to further enhance economic growth and prosperity as well as strengthening the Asia-Pacific region. It claims to be the only intergovernmental grouping in the world that operates on the basis of non-binding commitments, open dialogue and equal respect for the views of all participants. It has no treaty obligations and reaches decisions by consensus and commitments entered into voluntarily; hence it is consistent with the WTO.

1.4.5 Economic integration in the Middle East

There are several schemes in the Middle East, but some of them extend beyond the geographical area traditionally designated as such. This is natural since there are nations with Middle Eastern characteristics in parts of Africa. The Arab League (AL) clearly demonstrates this reality since it comprises twenty-two nations, extending from the Persian Gulf in the east to Mauritania and

Morocco in the west. Hence the geographical area covered by the scheme includes the whole of North Africa, a large part of the 'traditional' Middle East, plus Djibouti and Somalia. The purpose of the AL is to strengthen the close ties linking Arab states, to coordinate their policies and activities and to direct them to their common benefit, and to mediate in disputes between them. These are vague terms of reference, consistent with very limited achievements. For example, the Arab Economic Council, whose membership consists of all Arab Ministers of Economic Affairs, was entrusted with suggesting ways for economic development, cooperation, organization and coordination. The Council for Arab Economic Unity (CAEU), which was formed in 1957, had the aim of establishing an integrated economy of all AL states. Moreover, in 1964 the Arab Common Market was formed by Egypt, Iraq, Jordan and Syria, but in practice never got off the ground. The exception seems to be the Gulf Cooperation Council (GCC), established on 25 May 1981, which is keen to stress that long-lasting and deep religious and cultural ties link its members, and strong kin relationships prevail among its citizens. The GCC claims to have concrete objectives as an economic and political policy-coordinating forum, and has growing cooperation, inter alia, on customs duties, intellectual property protection, standard setting and intra-area investment, and has resolved most of the practical details for establishing a CU. This was set for 2003, but has yet to happen. The target date for introducing a single currency was 2010, but disputes regarding the location of the common central bank in Riyadh rather than the UAE have put this on hold. In short, the GCC wants to bring together the Gulf states and to prepare the ground for them to join forces in the economic, political and military spheres.

With regard to economic integration in the Middle East, UMA, which aims to create an organization similar to the EU, has already been mentioned in the context of Africa. But there is also the Arab Cooperation Council (ACC), founded on 16 February 1989 by Egypt, Iraq, Jordan and the Yemen Arab Republic, with the aim of boosting Arab solidarity and acting as 'yet another link in the chain of Arab efforts towards integration'.

1.4.6 An intricate web of relationships

All these schemes are connected by an increasing number of PTAs. This had resulted in an intricate web of interrelationships. Considering the EU alone, since it is the main protagonist of PTAs, and adding the seventy-eight African-Caribbean-Pacific (ACP) nations of the ACP–EU[5] arrangement (see Chapters 24 and 25) as well as those of the EEA, one can understand why the term 'spaghetti bowl' has been used to describe this web surrounding the EU.

1.4.7 Sectoral digressions

There are two schemes of sectoral IEI that are not based on geographical proximity. The first is the Organization for Petroleum Exporting Countries (OPEC), founded in 1960 with a truly international membership; its aim was to protect the main interest of its MNs, petroleum, by setting production quotas, and hence determining prices. The second is the Organization for Arab Petroleum Exporting Countries (OAPEC), established in January 1968 by Kuwait, Libya and Saudi Arabia, joined in May 1970 by Algeria and the four Arab Gulf Emirates (Abu Dhabi, Bahrain, Dubai and Qatar); in March 1972 Iraq and Syria became members, and Egypt followed them in 1973; Tunisia joined in 1982, but withdrew in 1986 (OAPEC was temporarily liquidated in June 1971). There are also the Organization for Economic Cooperation and Development (OECD) and the World Trade Organization (WTO). However, all these are organizations for intergovernmental cooperation rather than for economic integration. Therefore, except where appropriate, nothing more shall be said about them in this book.

1.5 The possible gains from economic integration

We shall see in Chapters 2 and 10 that the driving force behind the formation of the EU, the earliest and most influential of all existing IEI schemes (see page 4), was the political unity of Europe, with the aim of realizing eternal peace in the continent. Some analysts would also argue that the recent EU attempts for more intensive economic integration can be cast in the same vein, especially since they are accompanied by one currency, the euro, a full-time president and a 'foreign policy supremo' (see page 4 and Chapter 2). At the same time, during the late 1950s and early 1960s, IEI among developing nations was perceived as the only viable way to make some real economic progress; indeed that was the rationale behind the UN's encouragement and support of such efforts. More recently, the drive for IEI has been the belief that the opening up of markets would enhance the economic performance of the countries involved (see Chapter 6 for a list of possible gains). It is conceded that the gains would be even greater if pursued globally, but frustrations with the WTO's slowness in reaching agreement, due to the varied interests of its many participants, have led some to the conclusion that IEI would result in a quicker pace for negotiations since, by definition, it would reduce the number of parties involved. There are also practical considerations and countries may feel that IEI would provide security of markets among the participants. These possible gains will be addressed in Chapters 6 and 9.

1.6 Conclusion

Several conclusions are reached from this brief panorama of economic integration. First, although GATT's Article XXIV allows for the formation of IEI schemes, it sits uneasily within the general spirit of the organization. This is because the formation of clubs between some nations naturally discriminates between MNs and non-members, which is in direct contradiction of the principle of the WTO's non-discrimination. But because of the strength of the commitment to IEI of some European nations, a compromise was needed; hence the Article is in the nature of an accommodation of 'realities', which enabled a wide membership of GATT to be achieved at its inception. Second, practically every country in the world belongs to at least one scheme of IEI, with Africa going mad in terms of the number of schemes and overlapping membership. Third, the EU is the most significant and influential of all schemes. Fourth, the drive behind IEI is not confined to possible economic gains; indeed, political considerations are of the essence in some cases.

Summary

- IEI is defined as *a state of affairs or a process which involves the amalgamation of separate economies into larger free trading regions.*
- Conceptually, IEI can take several forms: free trade

areas or preferential trading agreements; customs unions; common markets; and complete economic unions. But actual schemes do not strictly conform to these terms.

- IEI promotes the creation of 'clubs' between some nations, and because clubs will always discriminate against non-members, this contradicts GATT's fundamental principle of 'non-discrimination'.
- GATT's Article XXIV allows the formation of IEI schemes *provided* that: (a) they do not increase their level of protection relative to what it was before their formation; (b) tariffs and other trade restrictions (with some exceptions) are removed on *substantially* all the trade among MNs; and (c) they become established within a reasonable period of time.
- Despite the provisos, many analysts are uncomfortable with GATT's Article XXIV since it still contradicts the WTO's principle of non-discrimination. They concede, however, that without it some European countries would not have joined GATT.
- There are over 400 schemes of IEI in the world, of which the EU is the most significant, influential and committed to the deepest type of economic integration.
- IEI has become popular for two reasons:
  1. One reason is that individual countries believe that their economies will benefit from free access to a larger market, lower costs through removal of barriers on trade, enhanced competition leading to better products and/or lower prices, greater innovation, and so forth.
  2. The other is that countries have become increasingly frustrated by the slow progress in achieving global agreements through the WTO because with 153 members it is difficult to reach a consensus: the Doha Round commenced in November 2001 and has yet to be finalized. It is also believed that the proliferation in IEI schemes may actually induce countries to galvanize the WTO into establishing the favoured multilateral regime.

Questions and essay topics

1. Discuss the claim that IEI as defined by trade theorists is far removed from what one would expect on purely linguistic grounds.

2. What form can IEI integration take?
3. What are 'positive' and 'negative' IEI?
4. What does 'WTO' stand for?
5. Under what conditions does GATT/WTO condone IEI? Assess the reasons for and the adequacy of these conditions.
6. What are the arguments for and against GATT's Article XXIV?
7. Multilateral trade negotiations under GATT/WTO have been reasonably successful. So why do countries pursue the formation of IEI schemes?
8. Is it true that a unique feature of IEI in Africa is its overlap and proliferation? If so, to what factors would you attribute such proliferation?
9. What makes the EU the most significant of all IEI schemes?
10. What makes the EU the most influential of all IEI schemes?
11. Discuss the proposition that IEI hinders efforts to achieve the multilateral freeing of trade.

FURTHER READING

El-Agraa, A. M. (1997) *Economic Integration Worldwide*, Macmillan and St Martin's, New York.

El-Agraa, A. M. (1999) *Regional Integration: Experience, Theory and Measurement*, Macmillan, London; Barnes and Noble, New York.

NOTES

1 305 of these agreements since 1995.
2 Except Slovenia.
3 Plus the autonomous territories of the Faroe Islands, Greenland and Åland.
4 There were and continue to be four such bodies: (1) Pacific Economic Cooperation Conference (PECC), which is a tripartite structured organization with representatives from governments, business and academic circles, with the secretariat work being handled between general meetings by the country next hosting a meeting; (2) Pacific Trade and Development Centre (PAFTAD), which is an academically oriented organization; (3) Pacific Basin Economic Council (PBEC), which is a private-sector business organization for regional cooperation; and (4) Pacific Telecommunications Conference (PTC), which is a specialized organization for regional cooperation in this particular field.
5 Cuba became the seventy-ninth member in 2000, but has not participated in the agreements.

Part I

EU history, institutions and legal dimension

2 A history of European integration and the evolution of the EU

3 EU institutions

4 The legal dimension in EU integration

5 The European economy: bare essentials

The aim of this part of the book is to provide a general background to the EU. Chapter 2 gives a short account of the history of European integration and the development of the EU. Chapter 3 provides a general description of EU institutions and their functioning. Chapter 4 explores the legal dimension in EU integration. Chapter 5 is a general survey of the bare essentials of the EU economy, mainly using charts, with the full statistical tables available on the website; it covers the major economic indicators for the present EU27 MSs, as well as those involved in imminent enlargements and, to enable comparison, for the rest of those in the group of eight (G8, now G20).

by the tradition of free trade and Adam Smith's argument, in *An Inquiry into the Nature and Causes of the Wealth of Nations* (1776), that 'the division of labour is limited by the extent of the market', which the German philosopher Friedrich Naumann utilized to propose in 1915 that European nation states were no longer large enough to compete on their own in world markets; therefore, they had to unite in order to guarantee their survival.

Despite the fact that there was no shortage of plans for creating a united Europe, it was not until 1945 that a combination of new forces and an intensification of old ones prompted action. First, Europe had been at the centre of yet another devastating war, caused by the ambitions of nation states. Those who sought and some of those who still seek a united Europe have always had at the forefront of their minds the desire to prevent any further outbreak of war in Europe. It was believed that if the nations of Europe could be brought closer together, such war would become unthinkable. Second, the Second World War left Europe economically exhausted, and this led to the view that if Europe were to recover, it would require a concerted effort on the part of the European states. Third, the Second World War also soon revealed that for a long time Western Europe would have to face not only a powerful and politically alien USSR, but also a group of European nations firmly fixed within the Eastern European bloc. It was felt that an exhausted and divided Europe (since the war embraced cobelligerents) presented both a power vacuum and a temptation to the USSR to fill it. Fourth, the ending of the war soon revealed that the wartime allies were in fact divided, with the two major powers, the USA and the USSR, confronting each other in a bid for world supremacy. Hence it should come as no surprise to learn that members of the European Movement, who wanted to get away from intergovernmental cooperation by creating institutions leading to a Federal Europe, felt the need for a third world force: 'the voice of Europe'. This force would represent the Western European viewpoint and could also act as a bridge between the eastern and western extremities.

2.2.1 Concrete unity efforts

The first concrete move for regional integration in Europe was made in 1947, with the establishment of the Economic Commission for Europe (ECE), which was set up in Geneva as a regional organization of the United Nations (UN). Its objective was to initiate and participate in concerted measures aimed at securing the economic restructuring of the *whole* of Europe. A year later, the Brussels Treaty Organization (BTO) was founded by the UK, France, Belgium, the Netherlands and Luxembourg. In recognition of the newer USSR threat, it was designed to create a system of mutual assistance in times of attack on Europe, but it simultaneously perpetuated the wartime alliance against Germany. The BTO took an Atlantic form in 1949, when the five nations, together with the USA and Canada, as well as Denmark, Iceland, Italy (significantly, since it had been an Axis power), Norway and Portugal, founded the North Atlantic Treaty Organization (NATO). The aim of NATO was, and continues to be, to provide military defence against attack on any of its members.[2]

Also, in 1948 the Organization for European Economic Cooperation (OEEC) was formed, followed a year later by the Council of Europe. These marked the beginning of the division of Western Europe into two camps, with, on the one hand, the UK and some of the countries that later formed the European Free Trade Association (EFTA), and, on the other, Belgium, France, West Germany, Italy, Luxembourg and the Netherlands, usually referred to as the Original Six (hereafter, the Six), who subsequently established the European Economic Community (EEC). The main reason for this division was that the UK was less committed to Europe as the main policy area than the Six. This was because, until the second half of the 1950s, the UK was still a world power which had been on the victorious side and a major participant in some of the fateful geopolitical decision-making at the time, and it still had the Empire to dispose of. Therefore, British policy was bound to incorporate this wider dimension: relations with Europe had to compete with Empire (later, Commonwealth) ties and with the 'special relationship' with the USA. In addition, the idea of a politically united Europe (as we have seen, in some quarters this meant a United States of Europe) was strongly held by the other countries, particularly by France and Benelux: Belgium, the Netherlands and Luxembourg agreed in 1944 to form a customs union (for a technical definition, see Section 1.2, page 1), which did not become effective until 1948. But despite the encouraging noises made by Winston Churchill, the British prime minister, both during the Second World War and afterwards, this was not a concept that thrilled British hearts (see Young 1998 for an excellent exposition of the British attitude towards European unification).

The different thinking between the UK and the Six about the political nature of European institutions was revealed in the discussions leading up to the establishment of the OEEC and the Council of Europe. The Second World War had left Europe devastated. The year 1947 was particularly bleak: bad harvests the previous summer led to rising food prices; the severe winter of 1946–7 led to a fuel crisis; the continental countries were producing very little, and what was produced tended to be retained rather than exported, while imports were booming, hence foreign exchange reserves were running out. It was at this juncture that the USA entered the scene to present the Marshall Plan. General George Marshall proposed that the USA should make aid available to help the European economy find its feet and that European governments 'should get together' to decide how much assistance was needed. In short, the USA did not feel it appropriate that it should unilaterally decide on the programme necessary to achieve this result. Although it seemed possible that this aid programme could be elaborated within the ECE framework, the USSR felt otherwise. Soviet reluctance was no doubt due to the fear that if its satellites participated, this would open the door to Western influence. Therefore, a conference was convened without the USSR, and the Committee for European Economic Cooperation (CEEC) was established.

The US attitude was that the CEEC should not just provide it with a list of needs; the USA perceived that the aid it was to give should be linked with progress towards European unification. This is an extremely important point, since it shows that from the very beginning the European Movement enjoyed the encouragement and support of the USA. Of course, the driving force behind the USA's insistence on European unity was its desire to establish a solid defence against any western advance by the USSR – that is, the USA did not insist on unity for unity's sake. Indeed, the USA also asked that its multinational companies should have free access to European markets. The CEEC, in turn, led to the creation of an aid agency: OEEC. Here, the conflict between the UK and the Six, especially France, came to a head over the issue of supranationalism. France in particular (and it was supported by USA)

wanted to introduce a supranational element into the new organization. But what is supranationalism? It can mean a situation in which international administrative institutions exercise power, for example, over the economies of the member states; or in which ministerial bodies, when taking decisions (to be implemented by international organizations), work on a majority voting system rather than insisting on unanimity.

The French view was not shared by the British, who favoured a body that would be under the control of a ministerial council in which decisions would be taken on a unanimous basis. The French, on the other hand, preferred an arrangement in which an international secretariat would be presided over by a secretary-general who would be empowered to take policy initiatives on major issues. Significantly, the organization that emerged was substantially in line with the British wish for unanimous rule. This was undoubtedly a reflection of the UK's relatively powerful position in the world at the time and her close alliance with the USA.

In the light of subsequent events, it is also interesting to note that the USA encouraged European nations to consider the creation of a customs union. Although this was of considerable interest to some continental countries, it did not appeal to the UK. In the end, the OEEC convention merely recorded the intention to continue the study of this proposal. For a variety of reasons, one of which was UK opposition, the matter was not pursued further.

The creation of the Council of Europe, with broad political and cultural objectives, including the notable contribution to protecting the individual through the Convention for the Protection of Human Rights and Fundamental Freedoms (its statute expresses a belief in a common political heritage based on accepted spiritual and moral values, political liberty, the rule of law and the maintenance of democratic forms of government), also highlighted the fundamental differences in approach between the countries which later founded the EEC, on the one hand, and the British and the Scandinavians, on the other. The establishment of the Council of Europe was preceded by the Congress of Europe at The Hague in May 1948. This was a grand rally of 'Europeans', attended by leading European statesmen, including Winston Churchill. The Congress adopted a resolution that called for the giving up of some national sovereignty before the accomplishment of economic and political union in Europe.

Subsequently, a proposal was put forward, with the support of the Belgian and French governments, calling for the creation of a European Parliamentary Assembly in which resolutions would be passed by majority vote. A Committee of Ministers was to prepare and implement these resolutions.

Needless to add, the UK was opposed to this form of supranationalism and in the end the British view largely prevailed. The Committee of Ministers, which was the executive organ of the Council of Europe, alone had power of decision and generally these were taken on the unanimity principle. The Consultative Assembly that came into existence was a forum (its critics called it a debating society), not a European legislative body. In short, the British and Scandinavian *functionalists* – those who believed that European unity, in so far as it was to be achieved, was to be attained by intergovernmental cooperation – triumphed over the *federalists* – those who sought unity by the radical method of creating European institutions to which national governments would surrender some of their sovereignty. The final disillusionment of the federalists was almost certainly marked by the resignation of Paul-Henri Spaak (see page 25), a devoted European federalist, from the presidency of the Consultative Assembly in 1951.

The next step in the economic and political unification of Western Europe was taken without the British and the Scandinavians. It was the creation in 1951 of the European Coal and Steel Community (ECSC) by the Six, and marked the parting of ways in post-war Western Europe. The immediate factor in these developments was the revival of the West German economy. The passage of time, the efforts of the German people and the aid made available by the USA through the Marshall Plan all contributed to this recovery. Indeed, the West German 'economic miracle' was about to unfold.

It was recognized that the German economy would have to be allowed to regain its position in the world, and that the Allied control of coal and steel under the International Ruhr Authority could not last indefinitely. The fundamental question was how the German economy in the sectors of iron, coal and steel, which were the basic materials of any war effort, could be allowed to regain its former powerful position without endangering the future peace of Europe. The answer was a French plan, elaborated by Jean Monnet, a French businessman turned adviser (see Box 2.1 for his true place in European unity), but put forward by Robert Schuman, the French minister of foreign affairs, in May 1950. The Schuman Plan was essentially political in character. It was brilliant since it sought to end the historic rivalry of France and Germany by making a war between the two nations not only unthinkable, but also materially impossible. This was to be achieved in a manner which ultimately would have the result of bringing about that European federation that is indispensable to peace. The answer was not to nationalize or indeed to internationalize the ownership of the means of production in coal, iron and steel, but to create, by the removal of customs duties, import quota restrictions and similar impediments on trade and factors of production – a 'common market' (for a technical definition, see Chapter 1, pages 1 and 2) in these products. Every participating nation in such a common market would have equal access to the products of these industries wherever they might be located; to reinforce this, discrimination on the grounds of nationality was to be forbidden.

The plan had a number of attractive features. First, it provided an excellent basis for solving the 'Saar problem': the handing back of the Saar region to West Germany was more likely to be acceptable to the French if Germany was firmly locked into such a coal and steel community. Second, the plan was extremely attractive to Germany, since membership of the community was a passport to international respectability; it was the best way of speeding up the end of occupation and avoiding the imposition of dampers on the expansion of the German economy. Third, the plan was also attractive to the federalists, who had found that the OEEC fell far short of their aspirations for the Council of Europe (its unanimity rule and the fact that no powers could be delegated to an independent commission or commissariat were extremely frustrating for them), and, in any case, the prospects for the OEEC were not very good, since by 1952 the four-year Marshall Plan period would be over, and the UK attitude was that thereafter the OEEC budget should be cut and some of its functions passed over to NATO.

As it turned out, the ECSC was much more to the federalists' taste, since its executive body, the High Authority, was given substantial direct powers that could be exercised without the prior approval of the Council of Ministers (the ECSC's second institution; it also had a Parliamentary Assembly, Court of Justice and Consultative Committee).

Box 2.1 Monnet, Father of Europe

Jean Monnet has a strong claim to be called the Father of Europe. Monnet deserves almost single-handed credit for creating in 1951 the first of Europe's epochal institutions for integration, the European Coal and Steel Community (ECSC) . . . As president from 1954 to 1975 of the Action Committee for the United States of Europe, a lobby for the integration cause, Monnet would be an inexhaustible front [for] unification and federation initiatives . . . the Frenchman's great achievements belong to the years immediately after World War II – when Europe was still recovering; the United States was supreme; power was held in relatively few hands; socialist, quasi-socialist, state corporatist, and organized capitalist systems were in vogue; and planning was *de rigueur* . . . [the ECSC] could not have . . . [developed] in any other setting.

Jean Monnet thought of himself as an institution builder and has often been so regarded by posterity, but his greatest gift . . . was in devising and circulating important ideas and putting words into action. He created, and to a considerable extent still shapes, the rhetoric of integration. To highlight this fact is not to denigrate Monnet's accomplishments but to underscore the inability of any other politician, technocrat, social scientist, or sloganeer to come up with comparable formulations: the big ideas that move the minds of men; concepts that can be organized, marshalled, and made to move in orderly fashion; terms that capture the realities that otherwise elude definition; and words that morph into policies, programs, and institutions when nurtured in bureaucratic hothouses. Monnet's idiomatic language has taken on a life of its own and captured the minds of many. Key analytical concepts – the big words used even today to describe the integration process in textbooks, in political discourse, and in public relations campaigns – are Monnet's words: terms that he and his associates coined or that other students of his work invented to give meaning to what he was doing. *Supranationalism*, *sectoral integration*, and *functionalism* are perhaps the most important examples of such interpretive concepts that still shape academic and professional research. Countless other terms have entered legal, administrative, and economic vocabularies, and out of them has oozed modern Eurospeak. The apparent inescapability of this linguistic legacy makes Monnet an avatar of integration, albeit less owing to his powers as a pure thinker than to his uncanny knack – in an age of science and technology, mass production, and instant communication – to harness the powerful and fertile minds of others to his goals and policies. One might well call him a modern prophet. Jean Monnet was pre-eminently a man of his times, one whose unsurpassed knack for getting things done derived from experience gathered over a long and extraordinary career. Monnet was driven by a stirring and powerful *idée fixe*: that the economic modernization and very political survival of both France as a nation and Europe as a civilization depended upon the creation of a federal union. Monnet was a go-getter and a deal maker *extraordinaire*, a man educated not so much formally or academically as on the job and in war management. As a remarkably young senior administrator responsible for France's overseas supply during the Great War, he soon understood the meaning of global interdependence and learned how to use the power of the state to strengthen the national economy. While serving in Washington in the unusual capacity of a French citizen on the British Lend-Lease mission during World War II, Monnet concluded from the miracle of American armaments production that the future would belong economically to the big battalions. Massive state intervention, huge markets, and central control were the order of the day.

Jean Monnet had plenty of additional experience. He had been deputy director of economic affairs for the League of Nations. He had made (and lost) a fortune between the wars as a financier and roving policy entrepreneur operating internationally in the realms of central banking, public finance, and project development. He had connections with powerful friends and policy makers on Wall Street, along the Potomac, and throughout Europe who would prove invaluable after 1945. Monnet's contacts, knowledge, indefatigability, and practicality opened doors to the movers and shakers of his age. But such political savvy would have counted for little without his intense commitment to European union. His determination to unite the continent deeply impressed the many brilliant and strong-willed individuals whose energies he channelled into the task of 'building Europe'. To them, quite simply, he was *l'Inspirateur* – The Inspiration.

Gillingham 2003, pp. 16–18

The plan received favourable responses from the Six. The UK was invited to join, but refused. Clement Attlee, British prime minister at the time, told the House of Commons: 'We on this side [of the House] are not prepared to accept that the most vital economic forces of this country should be handed over to an authority that is utterly undemocratic and is responsible to nobody.' However, the Six were not to be deterred, and in April 1951 the Treaty of Paris, valid for fifty years, was signed. The ECSC was born and it embarked on an experiment in limited economic integration on 1 January 1952.

The next stage in the development of European unity was also concerned with Germany. When the Korean War broke out in 1950, the USA, faced with the need to reduce its forces in Europe for deployment in Korea, put pressure on the Western European nations to do more to defend themselves against possible attack by the USSR. This raised the issue of a military contribution from West Germany, the implication being that Germany should be rearmed. However, this proposal was opposed by France, which was equally against Germany becoming a member of NATO. This was not a purely negative attitude. Indeed, René Pleven, French prime minister at the time, put forward a plan that envisaged that there would be no German army as such, but that there would be a European army to which each participating nation, including Germany, could contribute.

Britain was not against this idea, but did not wish to be involved. The Six were positively enthusiastic and discussion began in 1951 with a view to creating a European Defence Community (EDC). It was envisaged that there would be a Joint Defence Commission, a Council of Ministers, a Parliamentary Assembly and a Court of Justice. In other words, the EDC institutions were to parallel those created for the ECSC. The Six made rapid progress in the negotiations and the EDC Treaty was signed in May 1952.

Having gone so far, there were a number of reasons for further integrative efforts. First, the pooling of both defensive (NATO) and offensive capabilities (EDC) inevitably reduced the possibility of independent foreign policies. It was logical to follow integration in defence with measures that served to achieve political integration as well. Second, it was also desirable to establish a system whereby effective control could be exercised over the proposed European army. Third, there was also the Dutch desire that progress in the military field should be paralleled by more integration in the economic sphere. Therefore, the foreign ministers of the Six asked the ECSC Assembly, together with co-opted members from the Consultative Assembly of the Council of Europe, to study the possibilities of creating a European Political Authority.

A draft of a European Political Community (EPC) was produced in 1953 in which it was proposed that, after a period of transition, the ECSC political institutions and those proposed for the EDC be subsumed within a new framework. There would then be a European Executive responsible to a European Parliament (which would consist of a People's Chamber elected by direct universal suffrage, and a Senate elected by national parliaments), a Council of Ministers and a European Court to replace the parallel bodies created under the ECSC and EDC treaties.

This was a watershed in the history of the European movement. The Six had already successfully experimented in limited economic integration in the fields of iron, coal and steel; they had now signed a treaty to integrate defence; and they were about to proceed further by creating a community for the purposes of securing political unity. Moreover, the draft treaty proposed pushing economic integration still further by calling for the establishment of a general common market based on the free movement of commodities and factors of production.

However, on this occasion, the success that had attended the Six in the case of iron, coal and steel was not to be repeated. Five national parliaments approved the EDC treaty, but successive French governments felt unable to guarantee success in asking the French Assembly to ratify. Finally, the Mendès-France government attempted to water down the treaty, but failed to persuade the other five nations. The treaty as it stood was therefore submitted to the French Assembly, which refused to consider it, and in so doing obviously killed the EPC too.

There were a number of reasons for the refusal of the French Assembly to consider the treaty. First, there was opposition to the supranational elements that it contained. Second, the French 'left' refused to consider the possibility of the rearmament of Germany. Third, the French 'right' refused to have the French army placed under foreign control. Fourth, British aloofness was also a contributing factor: one of the arguments employed by those who were opposed to the treaty was that France, fearing German domination, could not participate in the formation of a European army with Germany if the UK was not a member.

It is perhaps worth noting that the failure of the EDC was followed by a British initiative also aimed at dealing with the problem of rearming Germany in a way that was acceptable to the French. A series of agreements was reached in 1954 between the USA, the UK, Canada and the Six, under which the BTO was modified and extended: Germany and Italy were brought in and a new intergovernmental organization was formed – the Western European Union (WEU). These agreements also related to the termination of the occupation of Germany and its admission into NATO. As a counterbalance to the German army, the UK agreed to maintain specified forces on the continent. In short, the gist of the agreements was to provide a European framework within which Germany could be rearmed and become a member of NATO, while also providing for British participation to relieve French fears that there would be no possible German predominance. It should be pointed out that the response of Eastern Europe to these agreements was a further hardening of the East/West division in the shape of the formation in 1955 of the Warsaw Pact (formally, The Treaty of Friendship, Cooperation and Mutual Assistance) by the USSR and its Eastern European satellites.

2.2.2 Unity via the back door

The year 1954 was a bad year for European unity, since those advocating the creation of supranational bodies had suffered a reverse, and the establishment of the WEU, an organization cast more in the traditional intergovernmental mould, had thereafter held centre stage. However, such was the strength of the European Movement that by 1955 new ideas were being put forward. The relaunching initiative came from Benelux. They produced a memorandum calling for the establishment of a general common market and for specific action in the fields of energy and transport.

The basic idea behind the Benelux approach was that political unity in Europe was likely to prove difficult to achieve. It was the ultimate objective, but it was one that could be realized in the longer run. In the short and medium term, the goal should be overall economic integration. Experience gained in working together would then pave the way for the achievement

of political unity – that is, political unity should be introduced through the back door. The memorandum called for the creation of institutions that would enable the establishment of a European Economic Community (EEC).

These ideas were considered at the meeting of foreign ministers of the Six at Messina, Italy, in June 1955. They met with a favourable response. The governments of the Six resolved that work should begin with a view to establishing a general common market and an atomic energy pool. Moreover, a committee should be formed that would not merely study the problems involved, but should also prepare the texts of the treaties necessary in order to carry out the agreed objectives. An intergovernmental committee was therefore created and, significantly enough, Paul-Henri Spaak (see page 22), by then foreign minister of Belgium, was made its president: what a triumph for members of the European Movement.

The Messina resolution recorded that since the UK was a member of the WEU and had been linked with the ECSC, through an Agreement of Association in 1954, it should be invited to participate in the work of the committee. The position of the other OEEC countries was not so clear. In fact, the question of whether they should be allowed to participate was left for a later decision by foreign ministers of the Six.

The Spaak Committee held its first meeting in July 1955. British representatives were present, and then and subsequently played an active role in the committee's deliberations. However, as the discussions continued, differences between the Six and the UK became evident. The UK was in favour of a free trade area (for a technical definition, see Section 1.2, page 1) arrangement, while the Six were agreed on the formation of a customs union: the Messina resolution had called explicitly for this type of arrangement. Moreover, the UK felt that only a little extra machinery was needed to put the new arrangement into effect; the OEEC, perhaps somewhat strengthened, would suffice. This view was bound to anger the federalists, who put emphasis on the creation of supranational institutions that should help achieve more than just economic integration. These differences culminated in the withdrawal of UK representatives from the discussions in November 1955 (for a detailed exposition, see Young 1998).

Meanwhile, the Spaak Committee forged ahead, although not without internal differences. For example, and research (see Chapter 14). Moreover, the summit envisaged a more active role for the EC in the area of regional policy (see Chapter 21) and decided that a European Regional Development Fund (ERDF) should be created to channel EC resources into the development of EC backward regions; the UK demanded such a fund during the accession negotiations, expecting to get most of it since it was the only country to have a 'regional policy', but events were to prove otherwise (see Chapters 19 and 21). Furthermore, later in the 1970s, the relationship between the EC and its ex-colonies was significantly reshaped in the form of the Lomé Convention, which became the EU-ACP agreements when the Caribbean and Pacific ex-colonies were later added (see Chapters 23 and 24), and is now managed as the EU Cotonou Agreement.

It was obvious from all these developments that the EC needed financial resources not only to pay for the day-to-day running of the EC, but also to feed the various funds that were established: the ESF, the ERDF and, most important of all, the European Guidance and Guarantee Fund (EAGGF; see Chapters 19–21) to finance CAP. In 1970 the EC took the important step of agreeing to introduce a system that would provide the EC and, specifically, the EC general budget, with its 'own resources' (see Chapter 19), thus relieving it of the uncertainty of annual decisions on national contributions for its finances as well as endorsing its political autonomy in this respect. Another important step was the decision that the European Parliament (EP; see Chapter 3) should be elected directly by the people, not by national parliaments. In addition, the EC decided to grant the EP certain powers over the EC general budget, which proved to be a very significant development (Chapter 19). Finally, but by no means least significant, was the development of the political cooperation mechanism. It is important not to forget that the dedicated members of the European movement had always hoped that the habit of cooperation in the economic field would spill over into the political arena, one aspect of which is foreign policy.

By the 1980s it was clear that the political and economic environment in which the EC operated was changing fast. Tumultuous events in the former USSR and the countries of the Warsaw Pact threw the institutional arrangements of Western Europe into disarray and brought the need to reassess defence requirements, NATO's role and the continuance of the US defence presence. The unresolved issue of whether the EC needed a foreign policy, or at least some half-way house towards one, was bound to be raised once more. Meanwhile, the economic base on which the EC had been able to develop became much more uncertain. Recession, industrial change, higher unemployment, slower growth and worries about European competitiveness undermined previous confidence (see Chapters 12, 13 and 22).

The twin issues of constitutional development and institutional reform continued to exercise EC circles, but little progress was possible and the EC seemed to be running out of steam. The deepening of the integrative process required action that governments found controversial; the new MSs – now including Greece (1981), Spain (1986) and Portugal (1986) – inevitably made for a less coherent group; while the recession hardened national attitudes towards the necessary compromise required for cooperative solutions. EC finances were constrained (the EC budget amounted to less than 1 per cent of EC GDP; see Chapter 19) such that new policies could not be developed, and this in turn led to bitter arguments about the resources devoted to the CAP (which exhausted more than 75 per cent of the EC budget) and its inequitable impact, especially on the UK. Internal divisions were compounded by fears of a lack of dynamism in the EC economy, threatening a relative decline in world terms. Such worries suggested that a significant leap forward was required to ensure a real common market, to encourage new growth and at the same time to modernize EC institutions.

2.3.2 The Single European Market

As the debate progressed, a major division emerged between those who were primarily interested in the ideal of political union and who wished to develop EC institutions accordingly, and those, more pragmatic in approach, who stressed the need for new policies. It was not until 1985 that the lines of agreement could be settled. These were brought together in the Single European Act (SEA), which came into effect on 1 July 1987.

The SEA contained policy development based on the intention of creating a true single market (usually referred to as the Single European Market, or SEM, and the 'internal market'; see Chapter 7) by the end of 1992 (hence the popular term 'EC92'), with free movement of goods, services, capital and labour (the so-called 'four freedoms'), rather than the patchy arrangements of the past (see page 26 and note 3 on page 36). The SEA also introduced, or strengthened, other policy fields. These included: responsibilities towards the environment; the encouragement of further action to promote health and safety at work; the promotion of technological research and development (R&D); work to strengthen economic and social cohesion so that weaker MSs could participate fully in the freer market; and cooperation in economic and monetary policy. In addition, the SEA brought foreign policy cooperation within its purview and provided it with more effective support than it had in the past, including its own secretariat, housed in Council buildings in Brussels. Institutionally, it was agreed that the Council would take decisions on a qualified majority vote (QMV; see Section 3.4, page 44) in relation to SEM, research, cohesion and improved working conditions, and that in such cases the EP should share in decision-making (see Chapter 3). These developments were followed later by agreement regarding the control of expenditure on the CAP (which, as we have seen, had been a source of heated argument for a number of years) and, most importantly, a fundamental change in the EC general budget.

The SEM provided a goal for the next few years and the EC became preoccupied with the necessary preparations (300 directives had to be passed and then incorporated into national law for this purpose; see Chapters 3 and 4), giving evidence of its ability to work together as one unit. However, it also brought new complications. It raised the question of how much power should be held by EC institutions, presented MSs with heavy internal programmes to complete the changes necessary for the SEM, and exposed the very different economic conditions in MSs that were bound to affect their fortunes in the SEM (see Chapter 7). Meanwhile, the unification of Germany in 1990 fundamentally changed its position within the EC, giving it more political and economic weight; but at the same time it was required to expend considerable effort eastwards.

A further challenge at the time came from new bids for membership (so far there has been one withdrawal: the position of Greenland was renegotiated in 1984, but it remains associated and has a special agreement to regulate mutual fishing interests). The SEM and the end of the cold war finally convinced the doubters in

Western Europe that they should try to join. This was both a triumph and an embarrassment for the EC, in that it was preoccupied with its own internal changes and a belief that it had not yet fully come to terms with the southern enlargement that had brought in Greece, Portugal and Spain. The reaction was mixed in that some MSs wished to press on with enlargement as a priority, while others wished to complete the SEM and tighten internal policies before opening the doors. A closer economic relationship was negotiated between EC and EFTA countries, except for Switzerland, to form the European Economic Area (EEA), on 2 May 1992, which was widely assumed to be a preliminary step towards membership, since it extended to these countries all EC privileges except in agriculture, but, understandably, without giving them voting rights. Austria, Finland, Sweden and Switzerland all formally applied between 1989 and 1992, and Norway followed them shortly afterwards; Switzerland's application remains on the table, which is odd, given its snub of the EEA.[4] Hungary, Poland and Czechoslovakia signed association agreements and hoped that they might join in a few years' time. Turkey and Morocco applied in 1987, although the former's application was laid aside and the latter's rejected. Cyprus and Malta applied in 1990. Later, most of the Central and Eastern European Countries (CEECs) expressed their desire to join and formal negotiations were opened in 1998, with those most likely to succeed being Cyprus, the Czech Republic, Estonia, Hungary, Poland and Slovenia. However, the instability in the Balkans and the war in Kosovo showed the need to hasten the process, and at Helsinki in December 1999 it was agreed to open accession talks with Bulgaria, Latvia, Lithuania, Malta, Romania and Slovakia. Moreover, after thirty-six years of temporizing, it was also agreed at the same summit that Turkey should be a recognized candidate, but negotiations were then not expected to start for a very long time, since the EU wanted to see big improvements in Turkey's political and human rights behaviour, including the rights of Kurds and other minorities, and the constitutional role of the army in political life, which might require changes in the Turkish constitution (these are known as the Copenhagen criteria, introduced in June 1993 at the Copenhagen summit; see page 30). Therefore, there was then an active list of thirteen candidates, which included Turkey, and a change in regime brought Croatia closer to joining

The Maastricht conference touched fears of the creation of a superstate. In an attempt to counter this, the subsidiarity principle was agreed during the Edinburgh summit in December 1992, and the Amsterdam Treaty tried to clarify it further. Article 5 (EC) explains that, where the EU does not have exclusive competence, it may proceed only if MSs cannot pursue the action themselves, or it is an objective better achieved by EU action. A protocol attached to the treaty has tried to clarify how this concept should be applied and, in particular, insists that the reasons for action must be stated, EU action must be simple and limited, and a report must be given to EU institutions on what has been done. These provisions are meant as a check on any insidious growth of EU power, allowing it to slip in a direction that has never been agreed. This brake is supported by the right of MSs to bring a case in the Court of Justice arguing that the EU is extending its powers unjustifiably.

One element in the debate about subsidiarity is doubt concerning the remoteness of decision-making in Brussels. There is a need to make the EU more responsive to the needs of the general public and more sensitive to the effects of the intrusiveness that EU legislation appears to bring. The 'democratic deficit' is an issue that has long been discussed and there are several ways of addressing it, of which greater powers to the EP is one (see Section 2.3.6, page 36 and Chapter 3). Individuals have long had the right to petition the EP and this has been supported by the appointment of an ombudsman, chosen by the EP but independent of it.

One particular issue is the undermining of national parliaments, especially those that have an important legislative function and have found it hard to devise ways for exercising control over the EU. In practice, this has been limited to scrutiny of proposals which, once they are at an advanced stage, are very difficult to change. Some efforts have also been made, through scrutiny committees, to discuss general issues, thus helping to suggest policy positions for the future, while Denmark, in particular, has tried to define the parameters within which ministers may negotiate. A protocol of the Amsterdam Treaty tries to increase the influence of national parliaments. Associated with this was the general acceptance of the need to keep the public better informed and to provide access to EU documentation. A declaration attached to the treaty stresses the importance of transparency, access to documents

and the fight against fraud, Article 255 (EC) giving citizens a right to access official documents. A further declaration accepts the importance of improving the quality of draft legislation. Over the years efforts have also been made to help individuals to question the EU. The right to petition the EP was buttressed by the establishment of the European Ombudsman. A further change, directly affecting individuals, was to confer EU citizenship on the nationals of MSs. Although such changes are intended to encourage greater openness in decision-making, their implementation will take time. Actual decision-making in the Council remains private.

Flexible policies and subsidiarity have been tackled together, although they deal with very different circumstances, because they both suggest that the EU is still uneasily balanced between the two opposing views on how to organize (Western) Europe, which have been so eloquently expressed since the end of the Second World War. To some observers the Amsterdam Treaty is one more step towards a federal Europe, but to others it is a means of keeping a check on this drive and retaining a degree of national governmental control. The final outcome remains uncertain.

2.3.5 The Nice Treaty

Hammered out over four bitter days and nights on the French Riviera, the Treaty of Nice of 11 December 2000 is both complex and insubstantial; one of its authors even called it 'lousy'. The treaty's main concern is with EU enlargement, especially with the institutional changes that would be needed to accommodate twelve to fifteen new members (see next page). Since its provisions will not make sense until we have discussed EU institutions, they will be dealt with in Chapter 3. Here it suffices to state that the treaty both amends QMV and extends it to new areas, including trade in services; asks the larger MSs to drop their second commissioner; limits the total number of commissioners to twenty after 2007; and proclaims the Charter of Rights, but without legal force.

One should add that the ratification of the treaty followed almost the same path as that of Maastricht. The Irish, whose constitution demands a referendum on such issues, were the first to kick off the process and shocked everyone by rejecting it on 7 June 2001 by 54 per cent to 46 per cent. Although technically that meant the death of the treaty, the other MSs stubbornly went ahead with ratification, leading to a dramatic situation in 2002 when all but Ireland had ratified. However, in a second referendum on 20 October 2002, Ireland recorded an emphatic 'yes' (by 62.9 per cent against 37.1 per cent). This then set the tone for the Copenhagen summit of 12–13 December 2002, when it was agreed that: (a united) Cyprus, the Czech Republic, Estonia, Hungary, Latvia, Lithuania, Malta, Poland, the Slovak Republic and Slovenia could join the EU on 1 May 2004; Bulgaria and Romania could join in 2007, provided they met the necessary criteria, which they have done; and Turkey could open accession negotiations immediately after the December 2004 summit, pending a favourable report by the Commission on its status with regard to the Copenhagen criteria. The first ten countries signed accession treaties with the EU on 16 April 2003 at the Athens summit, ratified their accession treaties (nine through popular referendums, with Cyprus not needing one) and became members on 1 January 2004 (but, alas, not a united Cyprus). And in the Brussels summit of 16–17 December 2004, in the light of a positive report from the Commission, Turkey was given the go-ahead to start negotiations on 3 October 2005; these negotiations are expected to take ten years. It should be added, however, that the decision to grant Turkey the right to negotiate EU membership has since proved controversial: France has decided that it will hold a referendum on Turkey's membership and many have attributed France's referendum rejection of the Constitutional treaty to this issue; the present German chancellor, Angela Merkel, is not keen on full membership, preferring a 'privileged partnership'; and there are many who are not happy with Turkey's claims to being 'European' in terms of both geography and character. Also, in June 2005, the 'Thessaloniki agenda' was reaffirmed, allowing the assessment of progress towards EU membership of the western Balkan countries: Albania, Bosnia and Herzegovina, Croatia, the former Yugoslav Republic of Macedonia, and Serbia and Montenegro, including Kosovo. Finally, on 26 September 2006, the Commission offered a positive report on the progress made by Bulgaria and Romania, which led to endorsement by MSs; they joined on 1 January 2007.

2.3.6 A Constitution for the EU?

At the Nice summit meetings it was decided to 'engage in a broader and more detailed analysis of the future of the EU, with a view to making it more democratic, more transparent and more efficient'. The ensuing debate culminated at the 2001 Laeken summit, when, on 12 December, it was decided to create a convention for this purpose. On 28 February 2002 the Convention for the Future of Europe was set up under the chairmanship of ex-French president Valéry Giscard d'Estaing, with ex-Italian prime minister Giuliano Amato and ex-Belgian prime minister Jean-Luc Dehaene as vice-chairpersons, to discuss the matter further and then report to an IGC in mid-2003. The convention had 105 delegates, representing EU governments, parliaments and institutions, and was set two tasks:

(a) to propose a set of arrangements to enable the EU to work with twenty-five to thirty MSs; and
(b) to express the purpose of the EU, so that the citizens whom it is meant to serve will understand its relevance to their lives and, with luck, feel some enthusiasm for its activities.

Surprisingly, the Convention issued a draft constitution for the EU on 6 February 2003, with the contents being mainly about the consolidation of the various EU treaties, but they included proposals for the reform of existing EU institutions and the future of the EU. A changed final draft was adopted on 20 June 2003 at the Thessaloniki summit, but although the December summit failed to endorse it, the Brussels June 2004 IGC did; hence it was set to become the EU Constitution if and when it was ratified by all MSs. However, during the early months of 2005, both France (on 29 May) and the Netherlands (on 1 June) rejected it in national referendums (by, respectively, 55/45 per cent and 62/38 per cent); therefore it was technically dead. However, as was the case with the Maastricht and Nice treaties, this was not a foregone conclusion. Indeed, eighteen MSs, including Bulgaria and Romania, representing two-thirds of the twenty-seven MSs and 56.12 per cent of the EU population, went ahead and ratified the Constitution. Moreover, on 26 January 2007 foreign ministers of twenty[5] so-called 'friends of the Constitution' declared in Madrid that far from slashing the original treaty to make it more palatable to voters, it should be more ambitious, giving the EU a bigger role in social policy, fighting climate change and immigration, which attracted the new headline, 'Use the pen not the scissors'. Later, almost all of the other MSs went ahead with ratification. This, in turn, led to a new draft, which removed some of the controversial terminology – that is, replacing 'constitution' with 'reform treaty' – and accommodated certain MSs' demands.

2.3.7 The Treaty of Lisbon

The eventual outcome was the Treaty of Lisbon, signed on 13 December 2007 and scheduled for full ratification by the end of December 2008. Ireland was the first to put it to the test and rejected it on 13 June 2008, by 53.4 per cent to 46.6 per cent, creating the by-now familiar havoc. This led to 'a time for reflection', since the other MSs repeated the game of proceeding with ratification. To shorten the familiar game, certain accommodations were finally agreed, which led to a second and overwhelmingly successful Irish referendum on 3 October 2009, by 67.1 per cent to 32.9 per cent. But the final ratification did not happen until the Eurosceptic Czech president, Vaclav Klaus, was accommodated. The treaty became final on 13 November 2009 and operative from 1 December 2009; it amends the two core treaties, the TEU and the treaty establishing the European Community, with the latter renamed the Treaty of the Functioning of the European Union (TFEU).

Here, is a skeleton of the Lisbon Treaty; skeleton since most of it simply incorporates what is in the previous treaties:

(a)   It sets out a single simplified EU treaty.

(b)   It creates the post of president of the EU Council (see Treaty on European Union, TEU, Article 9B.5), serving for thirty months, renewable once, instead of six-monthly rotations.

(c)   It creates the post of EU foreign policy chief, officially called the High Representative of the Union for Foreign Affairs and Security Policy (TEU, Article 9E), popularly referred to as 'foreign policy supremo' (FPS), who heads a yet to be created EU diplomatic service.

(d)   It gives greater scope for defence cooperation among MSs, including procurement.

(e)   It gives new powers to the EP over legislation and the EU budget.

(f)   It enables national parliaments to ensure that EU law does not encroach on MSs' rights.

(g)   It abolishes the national veto in some areas, including immigration and asylum policy.

(h)   It retains the national veto on tax, defence and foreign policy, and on financing the EU budget.

(i)   It introduces a new 'double majority' voting system for the Council, requiring at least 15 MSs, comprising 65 per cent of the EU population.

(j)   It introduces a mechanism for those MSs wishing to leave the EU.

(k)   It increases the power of the 'eurogroup' (the countries that have adopted the euro) to decide their own policies.

(l)   It incorporates an EU Charter of Fundamental Rights, including the right to strike, with legal provision limiting its application in national courts.

(m)   It reduces the size of the Commission, starting in 2014, with commissioners sent from only two-thirds of MSs on a rotation basis.

(n)   It raises the minimum number of seats in the EP for small MSs from four to six, and sets out a limit of ninety-six for the big MSs.

As mentioned, since a number of these points concern institutional changes, it makes more sense to discuss them in Chapter 3.

2.4 Conclusion

Adherents of the original ideal of European unity would stress that, from what has been stated in this chapter, one cannot escape the conclusion that although the EU has not yet reached the finishing line, it has gone a long way towards achieving the dream of its founding fathers: the creation of a United States of Europe. They would add that the long march is easily explicable in terms of the difficulties inherent in securing the necessary compromises needed, while accommodating new members, and the tackling of unforeseen economic and political problems, from both within and without. They would concede that it would, of course, require a big leap from the present 'union' to a full European state, but that much has been achieved and that this vision has been and will continue to be the guiding light for European integration (see Chapter 25). They would also add that it behoves all those who would like to reduce the EU to a mere trading bloc to think twice. The EU has already gone far beyond this, and as the problems of the Eurozone indicate, even to effectively maintain current economic integration may require further political developments. However, several member nations – most definitely the UK, and some would claim many EU citizens (they have never been asked the question directly and straight-forwardly) – do not share this view. They would insist that the EU has developed more than far enough, and would add that even though the creation of a powerful united European economy, with most of its members using the same currency, is a historic achievement, nothing further should ensue, and certainly not political unity.

I shall leave it there, since my own position, if it is not yet apparent, should not matter; it is what you believe in the light of the facts and your own deep reflection, as well as your personal vision, that really matters. I shall return to this issue, however, in the final chapter on the future of European integration (Chapter 25).

Summary

- The intellectual pursuit of voluntary European unity has a very long history, going back to the fourteenth century, but efforts to make it a practical reality did not start until the end of the Second World War.
- The driving force behind European unity is the achievement of eternal peace, putting an end to the continent's woeful history of conflict, bloodshed, suffering and destruction.
- The concrete effort for European unity began with:
  1. the Economic Commission for Europe in 1947, to initiate and participate in concerted measures aimed at securing the economic restructuring of the whole of Europe
  2. the Brussels Treaty Organization (BTO) in 1948, to create a system of mutual assistance in times of attack on Europe
  3. the North Atlantic Treaty Organization in 1949, adding the USA and Canada to the BTO
  4. the Organization for European Economic Cooperation in 1948, to facilitate the aid to Europe provided by the USA through the Marshall Plan
  5. the European Coal and Steel Community in 1951, a common market for iron, coal and steel
  6. the European Economic Community and European Atomic Energy Community in 1957.
- Since 1957 several integration-enhancing measures have been undertaken, bringing the EU to what it is today; most significant among these have been:
  1. the Single European Act of 1985, to ensure a true common market with freedom of movement for goods, services, people and enterprises
  2. the Treaty on European Union (TEU) in 1991, for further integration through a full EMU, institutional changes and developing political competences, with the EC forming only a pillar of a wider European Union, including common political, foreign and security concerns
  3. the Amsterdam Treaty of 1997, to tidy up the loose ends of the TEU and introducing the 'subsidiarity principle'
  4. the Nice Treaty of 2000, to facilitate enlargement to the east and south-east, adding over ten ex-Soviet bloc nations
  5. the Lisbon Treaty of 2007, to simplify the treaties and include a full-time president and foreign policy supremo.
- Although the EU is not a federal state, it exhibits many of its facets.

Questions and essay topics

1. Why did concrete European unity efforts not start until the end of the Second World War?
2. Why did the USA insist that the Europeans themselves should decide what reconstruction assistance should be provided by the USA through the Marshall Plan?
3. Why was the idea behind the creation of the ECSC brilliant?
4. Why was the ECSC's 'High Authority' a supranational institution?
5. Why does Jean Monnet deserve to be called the 'father of Europe'?
6. In what way did the end of the cold war affect European integration?
7. What is the rationale behind the Copenhagen criteria?
8. What is the subsidiarity principle?
9. What does *acquis communautaire* mean?
10. 'The United Kingdom is the black sheep of Europe.' Discuss.
11. 'The Lisbon Treaty is a disguised constitutional treaty.' Discuss.

FURTHER READING

Gillingham, J. (2003) *European Integration, 1950–2003: Superstate or New Market Economy?*, Cambridge University Press.

Lipgens, W. (1982) *A History of European Integration*, vol. I – *1945–47: The Formation of the European Unity Movement*, Clarendon Press, Oxford.

Marjolin, R. (1986) *Architect of European Unity: Memoirs 1911–1986*, trans. William Hall (1989), Weidenfeld and Nicolson, London.

Young, H. (1998) *This Blessed Plot: Britain and Europe from Churchill to Blair*, Macmillan, Basingstoke.

NOTES

1 His most noted books are Coudenhove-Kalergi (1926, 1938, 1943, 1953).

2 Greece and Turkey joined NATO in 1952, West Germany became a member in 1955 (see page 20), and Spain was added in 1982, after the disappearance of General Franco from the political scene. Following the collapse of communism in Eastern Europe, the Czech Republic, Hungary and Poland joined in 1999, Bulgaria, Estonia, Latvia, Lithuania, Romania, Slovakia and Slovenia in 2004, and Albania and Croatia in 2009, giving NATO twenty-eight members; and, vitally, NATO and Russia signed the Act on Mutual Relations, Cooperation and Security.

3 As mentioned, two of the major aims were the creation of the customs union (CU) and the common market (CM). The basic elements of the CU – that is, the removal of the internal tariffs, the elimination of import quota restrictions and the creation of the CETs – were established a year and a half ahead of schedule (Tables NT1.1 and NT1.2 provide their evolution).

As to the CM elements, initial steps were undertaken and measures proposed to tackle the many NTBs to the free movement of goods, services and factors of production. However, laying down the rules for mobility was no guarantee of it taking place, especially in the case of labour, since Europeans had a strong tendency to stay close to their birthplace and still largely do (see Chapter 7). Given this proviso, one can say that by 1969 a recognizable CM existed.

Recall that the aims also included the creation of common policies. Because of French demands, sometimes bordering on threats, the CAP was almost fully operational by 1969. However, the CTP was slow to evolve. But transport was not just an industry; it was and is largely a provider of services and publicly owned, thus not easy to tackle (witness the havoc created by privatization in some EU nations, especially the UK). Moreover, the ESF and the EIB were duly established and were fully operational at an early stage, with the EIB given a triple-A rating, the highest award. Furthermore, steps were taken to create a Common Commercial Policy, and the Six undertook appropriate trade and

Table NT1.1 EC intra-area tariff reductions (%)

Reduction date	Reduction based on the 1/1/1957 level	Cumulative reduction
1 January 1959	10	10
1 July 1960	10	20
1 January 1961	10	30
1 January 1962	10	40
1 July 1962	10	50
1 July 1963	10	60
1 January 1965	10	70
1 January 1966	10	80
1 July 1967	5	85
1 July 1968	15	100

Table NT1.2 The establishment of the CET (%)

Adjustment date	Industrial products		Agricultural products	
	Adjustment	Cumulative adjustment	Adjustment	Cumulative adjustment
1 January 1961	30	30		
1 January 1962			30	30
1 July 1963	30	60		
1 January 1966			30	60
1 July 1968	40	1,000	40	100

aid arrangements in respect of their colonial and ex-colonial dependencies. Also, a rudimentary system of macroeconomic policy coordination was devised. Thus there was complete success in the case of the CU, and variable and steady success with regard to the CM aspects, although, given their nature, that was hardly surprising.

There is no need to evaluate Euratom, since it then involved only France.

4 EEA membership smoothed negotiations and Austria, Finland and Sweden joined the EU in 1995.

5 The missing seven were the foreign ministers of the Czech Republic, Denmark, France, the Netherlands, Poland, Sweden and the UK.

3 EU institutions

ALI EL-AGRAA

3.1 Introduction

The EU has a unique institutional structure, which is not surprising, given that it is neither a federal state nor a purely intergovernmental cooperative venture – vital facts often forgotten, especially by EU sceptics comparing its institutions to their equivalents in single states. EU member states (MSs) pool sovereignty in specific areas and delegate them to independent institutions, entrusting them with defending the interests of the EU as a whole, as well as the interests of both its MSs and their citizens. The European Commission (hereafter, Commission) upholds the interests of the whole EU. The Council of the European Union (hereafter, Council) upholds the interests of the governments of MSs through their ministerial representatives, and the European Parliament (EP) upholds those of EU citizens, who directly elect its members.

The Commission, the Council and the EP, known as the 'institutional triangle', are flanked by the European Court of Justice (ECJ) and the Court of Auditors, as well as five other bodies: the European Central Bank (ECB), the European Investment Bank (EIB), the European Economic and Social Committee (EESC), the Committee of the Regions (CoR) and the European Ombudsman. There are also many agencies, created by specific legislation, taking care of specialized concerns, which are of a technical, scientific or managerial nature – for example, the European Data Protection Supervisor (EDPS).

This chapter provides basic coverage of these institutions, but does so more adequately for the institutional triangle. This is due not only to the fact that between them they initiate and finalize most new EU legislation, and thus constitute the core of the EU legislative process, but also because the others are dealt with in some detail in the chapters where they are most relevant – for example, ECB operations are fully covered in Chapter 12. Moreover, due to the obvious nature of the EDPS, established in 2001, no further consideration is needed.[1]

3.2 Important actors

Before explaining these institutions, we should recall from Chapter 2 that the EU also has the European Council and, since the adoption of the Treaty of Lisbon (Treaty on the Functioning of the European Union, TFEU) on 1 December 2009, a president (see Treaty on the European Union, TEU, Article 9B.5) and a High Representative of the Union for Foreign Affairs and Security Policy – the so-called foreign policy supremo (FPS; TEU, Article 9E). The European Council comprises EU political leaders (officially, heads of state or government of MSs), the EU president and Commission president, with the foreign policy supremo participating in its work. However, when necessary, the members may decide that each be accompanied by a minister, a member of the Commission in the case of the Commission president. It is convened twice every six months by the EU president, who can call to order special meetings when required. In the past, special meetings were held occasionally under the title of intergovernmental conferences (IGCs) for specific issues of major importance, such as the admittance of new member nations, or changes to existing treaties or the adoption of new ones. The European Council is meant to provide the EU with the 'necessary impetus for its development', and to 'define the general political directions and priorities thereof' – that is, it offers general guidelines and blueprints, but it has no legislative functions. Also, it generally decides by consensus unless otherwise required by the treaties, and elects the president by a qualified majority vote (QMV; see Section 3.4, page 43).

The EU president is expected to 'facilitate cohesion and consensus' within the European Council, present a report to the EP after each meeting and make sure that the EU is externally represented on common foreign and security policy (CFSP), naturally without prejudice to the powers of the FPS. The appointment is full-time for 30 months and can be renewed once.

The FPS assumes office for five years. The office-holder also acts as a vice-president of the Commission and controls a vast diplomatic corps, now in the process of being established.

3.3 The Commission

EU treaties assign the Commission a wide range of tasks, but these can be narrowed down to four major roles. The Commission initiates EU policy by proposing new legislation to the Council and the EP. It serves as the EU executive arm by administering and implementing EU policies. Jointly, with the ECJ, it acts as the guardian of EU treaties by enforcing EU law. And it acts as the EU spokesperson and negotiator of international agreements, especially in relation to trade and cooperation, such as the EU Cotonou Agreement, which links the EU with seventy-nine African, Caribbean and Pacific nations (EU–ACP; see Chapters 1 and 23).

As the initiator of EU policies, the Commission formulates proposals in several areas defined by the treaties. Due to the subsidiarity principle (see Chapter 2), such proposals should be confined to those where action at EU level would be more productive than at the national, regional or local level. However, once the Commission has lodged a proposal with the Council and the EP, the three institutions collaborate to try to achieve an agreement. Note that the Council generally reaches agreement by unanimity, only resorting to QMV for more controversial measures. Also, the Commission carefully scrutinizes amendments by the EP before offering, where deemed appropriate, an amended proposal.

As the EU executive arm, the Commission is involved in all the areas in which the EU is concerned. However, the role it plays assumes particular significance in certain fields. These include competition policy, where it monitors cartels and mergers and disposes of or monitors discriminatory state aid (see Chapter 13);

agriculture, where it drafts regulations (see Chapter 20); and technical R&D, where it promotes and coordinates through EU framework programmes (see Chapter 14). The Commission is also entrusted with the management of the EU general budget, and its discharge of this responsibility is assessed by the European Court of Auditors (see Chapter 19).

As the joint guardian of EU treaties, the Commission has to see to it that EU legislation is properly implemented in MSs. In doing so, it is hoped that it can maintain a climate of mutual confidence so that all concerned, be they MSs, economic operators or private citizens, can carry out their obligations to the full. If any MS is in breach of EU legislation – for example, by failing to apply an EU directive (see Chapter 4) – the Commission, as an impartial authority, should investigate, issue an objective ruling and notify the government concerned, subject to review by the ECJ, of the action needed to rectify the situation. If the matter cannot be dealt with through the infringement procedure, the Commission then has to refer it to the ECJ, whose decision is binding. Likewise, with the supervision of the ECJ, the Commission monitors companies for their respect of EU competition rules.

Until 2004, when the EU had 15 MSs, the Commission consisted of twenty members, one of whom was president and two vice-presidents. Two commissioners came from each of the then five large MSs and one from each of the remaining ten – that is, the number of commissioners was determined, roughly, by population size (see Table 5.1 on the website). However, the Nice Treaty required that the larger MSs should drop their second commissioner after 2005, so the number is now 27, including the president and the FPS since the entry into force of the Lisbon Treaty, which also dictates that as of 1 November 2014 the number should be limited to two-thirds of the total – that is, 18 for the EU of 27, unless the European Council unanimously decides otherwise.

All commissioners are appointed for five years (it was only four years until 1994) and have renewable terms. They are chosen for their competence and capacity to act independently in the interest of the EU itself, and not of their own nations. They have all been prominent politicians in their own countries, often having held ministerial positions: the incumbent Commission president, José Manuel Barroso, who was not the first choice for his first term (2004–9), was recruited while still prime minister of Portugal; his immediate predecessor, Romano Prodi, was prime minister of Italy (1996–8, and again during 2006–8); before him, Jacques Santer was prime minister of Luxembourg (1995–9); and the noted Jacques Delors was the French minister of economy and finance in 1981 and was expected to stand for the presidency. This political experience is necessary because commissioners need to be familiar with the political scene and be able to meet senior politicians on equal terms; without this stature and ability to understand political pressures they would lose the senses of touch and timing that are essential for the Commission to function effectively. Indeed, two of them have been so assertive that they have been accused of exceeding their duties: Hallstein (1958–62 and 1962–7) for trying to give more powers to the Commission to build it into a government for Europe; and Delors (1985–9, 1989–93 and 1993–5) for attempting to impose his French socialist approach on the rest of the MSs (Gillingham 2003). One has to recall, however, that Hallstein, the first ever Commission president, was following in the footsteps of Monnet and the Benelux drive for political unity of Europe through the back door, at a time when seeking the support of the European populace for a 'united states of Europe' was out of the question: who in his or her right mind would have attempted to seek the endorsement of the average person when the devastation of the Second World War was so fresh in people's minds? As for Delors, his record speaks for itself, but some claim that his misguided obsession with a 'socialist' Europe was shared by many EU organizations and citizens at the time. Of course, some would claim that all commissioners had become spent forces in their own countries before joining the Commission, but others would counter such an argument by stressing that 'experience' does not vanish overnight and many politicians return to office in their home countries after serving in the Commission.[2]

The commissioners' appointment process begins within six months of EP elections. This is to allow time for the necessary EP procedure to approve the Commission. This procedure commences with the appointment of the Commission president, who is nominated by MSs and has to be approved by the EP. Once confirmed, the Commission president, with the collaboration of MSs' governments, nominates the

---

> **Box 3.1** The need to reform the Commission
>
> Santer's Commission (1995–9) suffered the unique humiliation of having to resign nine months prematurely in March 1999. The resignation had been instigated by the EP, following a report by a committee of independent experts which condemned the Commission and the Commission president for not assuming responsibility for financial irregularities and other acts of misconduct within their services. Serious allegations were also made against Commissioner Édith Cresson of France, regarding the appointment of her former dentist to a research job within the Commission. Cresson's stubborn refusal to resign and the belief of several commissioners that her resignation was necessary, if only to clear their names, left Santer with no alternative but to announce the resignation of the entire Commission, even though the EP had not censured it, but Santer's Commission stayed in a caretaker capacity.

remaining commissioners. The EP then gives its opinion on the entire college of twenty-seven through an approval process – the EP has the power to dismiss the entire Commission, but not individual commissioners (see page 45). Once the college is approved by the EP, the new Commission assumes its official responsibilities in the following January; six of the commissioners are now vice-presidents.

It is pertinent to add here that, following the exposure of ineptness and laxity in some parts of the Commission (see Box 3.1), the EP has taken the question of approval even more seriously and has subjected nominees to detailed scrutiny, including their suitability for their intended posts (see Box 3.2), the allocation of which is the prerogative of the Commission president. Indeed, the EP succeeded in doing precisely that when, for his first term, Barroso nominated Rocco Buttiglione of Italy for the justice portfolio (see Box 3.2).

It has also been made clear that the commissioners must work under the political guidance of the Commission president (EC, Article 219), while the commissioners have had to agree to resign if asked to do so by the Commission president. The procedures have enhanced the EP's powers considerably, since the EP

After two days of arguing with EP members (MEPs) over his nomination of Rocco Buttiglione – a Catholic Italian conservative who believes that homosexuality is a sin and that women should stay at home to raise children – as justice commissioner, a post which includes antidiscrimination policy, Barroso had to back down. One hour before the EP was to vote, he told MEPs that if the vote were to go ahead on 27 October 2004, the outcome would 'not be positive'. Then, to loud cheers and clapping, he added that under 'these circumstances I have decided not to submit a new commission for your approval today'. He went on to say, 'I need more time to look at this issue and to consult with the [European] Council and consult further with you, so we can have strong support for the new Commission. It is better to have more time to get it right.' Then, displaying some of the diplomatic skills for which he was chosen to lead the new Commission, he uttered: 'Ladies and gentlemen, these last days have demonstrated that the European Union is an intensely political construction and that this Parliament, elected by popular vote across all of our member states, has indeed a vital role to play in the governance of Europe.' The crisis came to an end when the Italian prime minister, Silvio Berlusconi, replaced Buttiglione with Franco Frattini.

can satisfy itself about the Commission's programme and intended initiatives before giving its approval.

While these moves are intended to ensure a more efficient Commission, the episode has brought a latent contradiction to the surface. The Commission was designed as the powerhouse of EU political momentum. Although, as we have seen, this function is to some extent now shared with the European Council and the EP, it has been less effective in administrative and managerial functions, where its weaknesses have been exposed. This has led some critics to argue that reform should include a shift of responsibility, away from policy and towards execution, so that the Commission becomes more like a national civil service (Vaubel 2009).

Each commissioner is responsible for a portfolio, which in many cases is a mixture of policy areas and administrative responsibilities, for a long time referred to as Directorates General (DGs), but now called Departments and Services. However, since there are forty-six Departments and Services (see Table 3.1), some commissioners have more than one portfolio. That does not mean that they are busier, however, as the workload for each Department depends on its relative weight within the EU. The Departments used to be numbered in roman style (e.g. DG I, DG II), but the numbers have now been dropped, so Table 3.1 gives the latest designations.

A director general is in charge of a DG; under him or her is a director, followed by a head of division. Each commissioner has a private office or cabinet, the staff of which is selected by the commissioner and has traditionally come from the same member nation for ease of communication (but see next paragraph). When the commissioner is away, the head of his or her private office, the *chef de cabinet*, will act on his or her behalf at the weekly meetings, held on Wednesdays in Brussels, but in Strasbourg during EP plenary sessions.

One should add that, over time, some DGs have acquired greater prestige than others. Not surprisingly, those that deal with core EU policies are most prominent, and as the EU has developed, so the possibility for conflict between DGs over policy matters has arisen. Agricultural, competition and regional and external trade policies, especially imports from the LDCs, are obvious examples. A new development brought in with the 1999 Commission was to have a senior commissioner responsible for an oversight of external affairs, whether of an economic or political nature, but this is now the job of the FPS (see page 38). The personal cabinets of the commissioners are being opened to wider recruitment, so that they are less obviously national enclaves attached to a particular commissioner. Reform of financial controls and stronger management systems are being put into place and merit is to account for more, and nationality less, in promotion to senior posts. Personnel are to receive more training and be subject to tighter controls.

Once the Commission has reached a decision on a matter presented by the commissioner concerned, the decision becomes an integral part of its policy and will have the unconditional backing of the entire college, even if simple majority voting led to its adoption. In

Table 3.1 EU Departments (Directorates General) and Services

Policies	External relations
Agriculture and rural development	Development
	Enlargement
Climate action	EuropeAid – Cooperation Office
Competition	External Relations
	Humanitarian Aid
Economic and financial affairs	Trade
Education and culture	
Employment, social affairs and equal opportunities	**General services**
Energy	Communication
Enterprise and industry	European Anti-Fraud Office
Environment	Eurostat
Executive agencies	Historical archives
	Joint Research Centre
Health and consumers	Publications Office
Home affairs	Secretariat-General
Information society and media	**Internal services**
Internal market and services	Budget
	Bureau of European Policy Advisers
Justice	European Commission Data Protection Officer
	Human Resources and Security
Maritime affairs and fisheries	Informatics
Mobility and transport	Infrastructures and Logistics – Brussels
	Infrastructures and Logistics – Luxembourg
Regional policy	Internal Audit Service
Research	Interpretation
	Legal Service
Taxation and customs union	Office for administration and payment of individual entitlements
	Translation

a sense, the Commission follows the British practice of collective responsibility – that is, it acts as a collegiate body, accepting responsibility as a group, but in practice policy rests mainly with the responsible commissioner, perhaps in association with two or more colleagues.

In carrying out its responsibilities, the Commission seeks the opinions of national parliaments, administrations, and professional and trade union organizations. For the technical details of its legislative provisions or proposals, it consults the experts meeting in the committees and working groups that it organizes. In carrying out implementing measures, the Commission is assisted by committees of representatives of MSs. Also, it works closely with the EESC and the CoR, since it has to consult them on many proposed legislative acts. The Commission also attends all EP sessions, where it must clarify and justify its policies, and regularly replies to both written and oral questions posed by MEPs.

One should point out that, in some ways, both for interest groups and for the layperson who wishes to make the effort, the Commission is more accessible than national administrations. This is due, in part, to the fact that the consultation processes, although clumsy, do bring a wide range of people in touch with

EU affairs. The danger of this web of machinery and consultation is indecision and slowness of action. At the same time, it puts a premium on the views of those who are effectively organized. Additionally, there is a well-established Commission policy of informing and educating the public in order to mobilize public opinion behind the integration process. Unfortunately, this has not been very effective, so that considerable unease remains, and its success in establishing relations with bankers, industrialists and other interest groups has contributed to a widespread belief that the EU is an elitist institution, far removed from the ordinary citizen. Hence better information and public access to the Commission have been a priority since the Maastricht Treaty.

Finally, one should add that it is possible that the term 'Commission' itself may be confusing. This is because it is used to refer to both the college of twenty-seven commissioners and to the entire institution, with approximately 32,000 staff.[3] However, one should encounter no major difficulties, since it is easy to judge from the context which meaning is being used on any given occasion.

3.4 The Council of the European Union

As mentioned in Chapter 2, the three Councils of Ministers, one for each of the ECSC, the EEC and Euratom, were merged in 1965. With the adoption of the Treaty on the European Union (TEU; the Maastricht Treaty), the name was changed in 1993 to the Council of the European Union (hereafter, Council; see page 30) to reflect the three EU pillars.

The Council consists of representatives of MSs' governments, who are accountable to their national parliaments and citizens; hence it is the embodiment of national interests, but representatives of the Commission always attend its meetings. Note that although the Commission has no voting rights, it plays an active role in helping to reach a decision, and that it is here that it can perform an important mediating function between national viewpoints and its own, which, as we have seen, is intended to represent the general EU interest. Who constitutes the Council depends on the matter under consideration: for financial matters, it would be the ministers of finance; for agriculture, it would be the ministers of agriculture,

and so on. Thus, unlike the Commission, the Council is not made up of a fixed body of people. The Council is located in Brussels and most of its meetings are held there, except during April, June and October, when they take place in Luxembourg.

Since Council membership varies according to the subject matter under review, this has led to problems for MSs. Because EU issues are handled by various ministers, briefed by their own civil servants, it becomes harder for any government to see its EU policy as a coherent whole. In turn, coordination within the government machine becomes problematic. For the EU, too, the greater specialization of business creates difficulties, since it has become far harder to negotiate a package deal whereby a set of decisions can be agreed, and each MS has gains to offset against its losses, although in the long run governments need to show the benefits they have achieved.

Council presidency rotates, with each MS holding it in turn for a period of six months, and the chairmanship of the many committees alters correspondingly. The Council president plays an active role as the organizer of the Council's work and as the chairperson of its meetings; as the promoter of legislative and political decisions; and as an arbiter between MSs in brokering compromises between them. It has become the practice for each MS to try to establish a particular style of working and to single out certain matters to which it wishes to give priority. Since any chairperson can influence business significantly, the president may occupy an important, albeit temporary, role. The Council president also fulfils some representational functions towards other EC institutions, notably the EP.

The Council has six major responsibilities. It is the main EU legislative body, but in many areas it exercises this prerogative jointly with the EP through the co-decision procedure (see page 46). The Council coordinates the broad economic policies of MSs. It also concludes EU international agreements. Together with the EP, it has authority over the EU general budget. On the basis of general guidelines from the European Council, it used to take the necessary decisions for framing and implementing the CFSP, but this task has now gone to the FPS. It coordinates MSs' activities as well as adopting measures in the area of judicial and home affairs (JHA).

It may prove helpful to elaborate on three of these

roles. With regard to its decision-making powers, generally speaking the Council only acts on a proposal from the Commission (see page 39), and in most cases acts jointly with the EP in the context of a co-decision, consultation or assent procedure (see page 46). Under the co-decision procedure, the Council and the EP share legislative authority in general areas, including the completion of the internal market, environment and consumer protection, non-discrimination, free movement and residence, and combating social exclusion. However, the Council plays a dominant role when it comes to JHA when it relates to essential components of national policy, since both the EP and the Commission have more limited roles in this area. Also, although the Commission is entrusted with the enforcement of EU legislation, the Council may reserve the right for it to perform executive functions.

The Maastricht Treaty introduced economic policy coordination to achieve this task; each year the Council adopts draft guidelines for MSs' economic policies, which are then incorporated into the conclusions of the European Council. They are then converted into a Council recommendation and accompanied by a multilateral surveillance mechanism. This coordination is performed in the context of EMU, where the Economic and Financial Affairs (ECOFIN) Council plays a leading role (see Chapters 10–12).

Finally, with regard to the joint responsibility of the Council and the EP for the EU general budget, the Commission submits a preliminary draft budget to the Council for approval each year. Two successive readings allow the EP to negotiate with the Council on the modification of certain items of expenditure and to ensure that budgetary revenues are allocated appropriately. In the case of disagreement with the EP, the Council is entrusted with making the final decision on the so-called 'compulsory expenditures' (see Chapter 19), relating mainly to agriculture and financial commitments emanating from EU agreements with non-MSs. However, with regard to 'non-compulsory expenditures' and the final adoption of the whole budget, the EP has the final say.

Council decisions are taken by unanimous, simple or QMV (see page 38), with QMV being the most common. When QMV is used, each MS is endowed with a number of votes. The votes are weighted so that at least some of the smaller member nations must assent. For the EU27 the distribution of the votes is: twenty-nine for each of France, Germany, Italy and the UK; twenty-seven for Poland and Spain; fourteen for Romania; thirteen for the Netherlands; twelve each for Belgium, the Czech Republic, Greece, Hungary and Portugal; ten each for Austria, Bulgaria and Sweden; seven each for Denmark, Finland, Ireland, Lithuania and Slovakia; four each for Cyprus, Estonia, Latvia, Luxembourg and Slovenia; and three for Malta. A decision requires a majority of MSs and a minimum of 255 votes (73.9 per cent of the total of 345), and the blocking minority is ninety-one votes. The proviso is added that a Council member can request verification on whether the MSs constituting the 255 votes represented at least 62 per cent of the total EU population; if not, the decision cannot be adopted. Thus a decision requires a triple majority. This general picture is reinforced in the Lisbon Treaty, which defines QMV from 1 November 2014 to be at least 55 per cent of Council members, comprising at least fifteen of them and representing MSs comprising at least 65 per cent of the EU population. That being the case, one is left wondering why the arithmetic is needed, unless one is interested in the trivial pursuit of playing exercises with them.

As a final word on QMV, one should add that its proponents often claim that it is a device meant to ensure that the large MSs cannot impose their wishes on the smaller MSs. However, it can equally be claimed that it is a system that prevents majority opinion from being stymied by a few smaller nations, which is what could happen in the case of a decision requiring a simple majority of EU nations – that is, fourteen out of the twenty-seven, or of course unanimity.

The Council is served by its own secretariat and is supported by an important body called the Committee of Permanent Representatives (COREPER). The membership of COREPER comprises senior representatives from MSs holding ambassadorial rank. This body prepares Council work, except for agricultural matters, since these are entrusted to the Special Committee on Agriculture. The Council is also assisted by working groups, which consist of officials from MSs' national administrations.

In 1966 it was agreed that it would be desirable for the Commission to contact MSs' governments via COREPER before deciding on the form of an intended proposal. As a result of its links with both the Council and the Commission, COREPER is involved in all major stages of EU policy-making. Many matters of policy are in fact agreed by COREPER and reach the Council only in a formal sense. While this is one way of keeping business down to manageable proportions, it has meant that the Council itself has become concerned only with the most important matters, or those which may not be of great substance but which are nevertheless politically sensitive. This has encouraged domestic media to present Council meetings as national battles in which there has to be victory or defeat, and politicians have become extremely adept at using publicity to rally support for their point of view. As a result, the effect has been the opposite of what was originally intended – that is, that the experience of working together would make it progressively easier to find an answer expressive of the general good, and for which majority voting would be a suitable tool. Instead, conflict of national interests is often a better description. The Council also encounters practical problems. The great press of business, the fact that ministers can only attend to Council business part-time, the highly sensitive nature of their activities and the larger number of members all contribute to a grave time lag in reaching policy decisions, and the move towards QMV was one measure designed to overcome this difficulty.

The General Affairs, ECOFIN and Agriculture Councils meet once a month, while the others meet between two and four times a year, the frequency depending on the number and urgency of the issues under consideration. Because the ministers of finance and foreign affairs also meet in other capacities, due to the nature of EU activities, their (ECOFIN) meetings have attracted the term 'Senior Council'.

3.4.1 Types of EU decision

It will become clear later that all EU institutions have a part to play in the decision-making process, depending on a modus vivendi existing between them to allow the process to operate. It is, however, at Council that outcomes are declared; hence this is the appropriate place to specify their nature. Formally, an EU 'action' results in: a *regulation*, a *directive*, a *decision*, a *common action/position*, a *recommendation* or an *opinion* (TFEU, Article 249; see also Chapter 4). Other measures, such as *conclusions*, *declarations* and

resolutions, can be adopted. A regulation is directly applicable and binding in its entirety in all MSs, without the need for any national implementing legislation; hence it is automatic EU law. A directive binds MSs to the objectives to be achieved within a certain period of time, while leaving the national authorities the choice of form and means to be used; thus directives have to be implemented by national legislation in accordance with the procedures of the individual MSs, and in this respect the UK has been the fastest and Italy the slowest. A decision, which is a more specific act and often administrative in nature, is binding in all its facets only for the party it is addressed to, whether it be all MSs, an individual MS, an enterprise, an individual or individuals. Recommendations and opinions have no binding force, but they express detailed EU preferences on an issue. Formal acts, notably regulations and directives, are constantly adding to EU law (see Chapter 4). The majority of legislation is now directives: in 2009 there were 1,521 directives and 976 regulations relating to the Single European Market (SEM; CEU 2010a).

3.5 The European Parliament

Originally, the EP was a consultative rather than a legislative body, since the Council had to seek its opinion, albeit without obligation, before deciding on a Commission proposal. It did have the power to dismiss the entire Commission, but because it did not possess the right to appoint commissioners, many analysts did not attach much significance to this. However, as mentioned in Chapter 2 and above (see page 40), the EP acquired budgetary powers in 1970, financial provisions powers in 1975 and the right to elect the president of the Commission in 1992. Also, the SEA gave it more powers in 1986, and the Maastricht (1992), Amsterdam (1997) and Lisbon (2009) treaties have turned the EP into a true legislative body, as well as strengthening its role as the democratic overseer of the EU. Some elaboration of this is warranted.

The EP acts together with the Council in formulating and adopting certain legislation emanating from the Commission. Here, the most common path is through the *co-decision procedure*, renamed the *ordinary legislative procedure* in the Lisbon Treaty (TFEU, Article 294), which gives equal weight to both and results in the

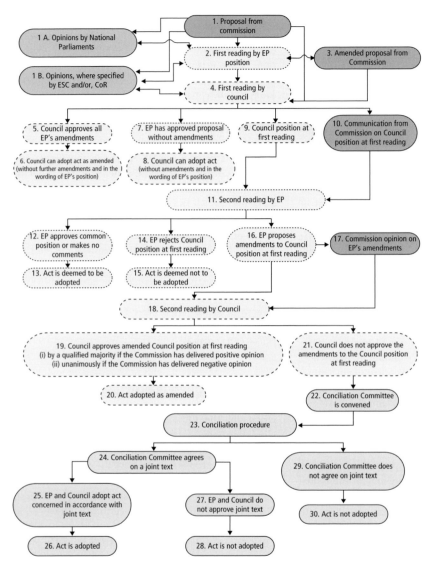

Figure 3.1 The co-decision procedure

adoption of joint acts (see Figure 3.1). In the case of disagreements between the two, conciliation committees are convened to find common ground. The co-decision procedure applies particularly in the case of the single market, freedom of movement of workers, technological research and development, the environment, consumer protection, education, culture and public health.

Also, the EP's approval is needed in certain areas. These include accession by new member nations; association agreements with non-members; decisions

affecting the right of residence for EU citizens; its own electoral procedures; and the task and powers of the ECB.

Moreover, although the Commission remains the main instigator of new legislation, the EP also provides significant political momentum, especially through its examination of the annual programme for the Commission and asking it to submit appropriate proposals.

With regard to the EU general budget (see Chapter 19), the EP and the Council are the key players. Each year, the Commission has to prepare a preliminary draft budget, which has to be approved by the Council. Then two readings ensue, providing the EP with the occasion to negotiate with the Council to amend certain items of expenditure (although such amendments are generally subject to the financial constraints of the budget), and to ensure that the budgetary resources are appropriately allocated. Finally, it is the EP that has the right to adopt the final budget, which needs the signature of the EP president before it can come into force. Also, the EP's committee on budgetary control is entrusted with monitoring the implementation of the budget, and each year the EP grants a discharge to the Commission for the implementation of the budget for the previous year.

Thus the EP of today performs three important functions together with the Council: it legislates, it shares authority on the EU general budget, and it elects the president of the Commission and approves the nominations of EU president and commissioners. Independently, it has the right to censure the Commission, forcing its resignation, and exercises political supervision over all the institutions.

The EP operates in three different places. It meets in Strasbourg, where it is seated, for its plenary sessions, which all members must attend. Its twenty parliamentary committees (covering everything from women's rights to health and consumer protection), which prepare work for the plenary sessions, hold their meetings in Brussels, and additional plenary sessions are held there too. Its secretariat is located in Luxembourg. This set-up has attracted harsh criticism, not only for its inconvenience and wasting of money and time, due to the travel and accommodation expenses involved, but more importantly for making it difficult for the EP to become a more coherent and effective organization. It is often claimed that the reasons for these locations are mainly historical, going back to the creation of the ECSC, the EEC and Euratom, but the history was no accident, given the prestige the EP extends to the countries where it is located and the economic value of having EU institutions operating in one's country.

The EP is still in an evolutionary stage and cannot be expected to follow the path of national parliaments, which, in any case, differ among themselves. Some have suggested (e.g. Gillingham 2003) that it should become merely an advisory body, just falling short of the powers of the British House of Lords, on the assumption that the EU is not a single state. Others argue for the creation of a second chamber consisting of representatives of national parliaments, determined by lot and with its only power to be the blocking of centralizing legislation (Vaubel 2009). But such propositions would not be consistent with the very nature of the EU as a dynamic association still in the making (see Chapter 2). The EP operates in a different environment and its power struggles, so far, have been with the Council and the Commission rather than with national parliaments.

The EP had its first elections by direct universal suffrage in 1979. Elections are based on a system of proportional representation and are held either on a regional basis (as in, for example, Belgium, Italy and the UK) or nationally. The EP elected in June 2009 has 736 members (MEPs); the Lisbon Treaty dictates that the number should not exceed 750 plus the EP's president (elected for 30 months). As Table 3.2 clearly shows (see page 48), the national distribution of MEPs is very roughly proportional to the member countries' populations.

MEPs are elected for a term of five years and each has a parliamentary assistant. Once elected, they are organized in EU-wide political rather than national groups (presently seven; see Table 3.2), although in some cases national identity remains very strong. Twenty-five MEPs from at least one quarter of the EU member nations are needed for a group and no member can belong to more than one group. Each group appoints its own chairperson, bureau and secretariat. Belonging to a group is important because the groups attract funding and receive guaranteed seats on committees.

Since the ideologies of the different factions in a group are not identical, one might wonder how such motley collections ever get anything useful done. The response would be that in reality they do agree on many issues, but of course the pace at which they do so is dictated by the time needed to reach consensus. Moreover, for the EP to be effective, it has proved necessary to have such large coalitions (Tsoukalis 2005).

3.6 The courts

3.6.1 The European Court of Justice

There are three reasons why the ECJ is needed. First, a body of legal experts is indispensable for ensuring

Table 3.2 Members of the European Parliament elected in June 2009

Country	EPP	S&D	ALDE	G/EFA	ECR	GUE/NGL	EFD	NA	Total
Austria	6	4		2				5	17
Belgium	5	5	5	4	1			2	22
Bulgaria	6	4	5					2	17
Cyprus	2	2				2			6
Czech Republic	2	7			9	4			22
Denmark	1	4	3	2		1	2		13
Estonia	1	1	3	1					6
Finland	4	2	4	2			1		13
France	29	14	6	14		5	1	3	72
Germany	42	23	12	14		8			99
Greece	8	8		1		3	2		22
Hungary	14	4			1			3	22
Ireland	4	3	4			1			12
Italy	35	21	7				9		72
Latvia	3	1	1	1	1	1			8
Lithuania	4	3	2		1		2		12
Luxembourg	3	1	1	1					6
Malta	2	3							5
Netherlands	5	3	6	3	1	2	1	4	25
Poland	28	7			15				50
Portugal	10	7				5			22
Romania	14	11	5					3	33
Slovakia	6	5	1				1		13
Slovenia	3	2	2						7
Spain	23	21	2	2		1		1	50
Sweden	5	5	4	3		1			18
United Kingdom		13	11	5	25	1	13	4	72
Total	**265**	**184**	**84**	**55**	**54**	**35**	**32**	**27**	**736**

Note:

EPP: a group of the European People's Party (Christian Democrats)

S&D: a group of the Progressive Alliance of Socialists and Democrats

ALDE: a group of the Alliance of Liberals and Democrats for Europe

Greens/EFA: a group of the Greens and European Free Alliance

ECR: a group of the European Conservatives and Reformists

GUE/NGL: a group of the European United Left and Nordic Green Left

EFD: the group of the Europe of Freedom and Democracy

NA: the non-attached

that the EU institutions act in a constitutional manner, fulfilling the obligations laid out for them by the treaties. Second, a court is essential for seeing that the MSs, firms and individual citizens observe the (increasing number of) EU rules. And a court at the EU level is vital for guiding national courts in their interpretation of EU law, and hence for ensuring that EU legislation is uniformly applied (see Chapter 4).

The Court system consists of three courts: the ECJ, the General Court and the Civil Service Tribunal, all seated in Luxembourg (see Chapter 4 for details). The ECJ has a president, elected by and from twenty-seven judges, one from each EU MS, for a three-year term. There are eight Advocates General who are responsible for (a) the preliminary investigation of a matter, and (b) presenting publicly and impartially reasoned opinions on the cases brought before the ECJ to help the judges in reaching their decisions. Each judge has a cabinet to take care of administrative responsibilities and its members are recruited directly by the judge. A cabinet comprises three law clerks to the ECJ and two to the General Court. Clerks help the judges draw up their reports and draft their rulings. The EJC administrative service is led by the registrar, who is also responsible for following the cases procedurally.

In carrying out its responsibilities, the ECJ has a wide jurisdiction that it exercises in the context of various categories, the most common of which are: preliminary rulings, failure to fulfil obligations, annulment, failure to act and appeals. A few words on how business is handled by the ECJ might be in order. After cases are lodged with the registry, they are distributed among the judges. A specific judge and Advocate General assume responsibility for each case. A judge, appointed as *juge rapporteur*, has to write a report for the hearing, providing a summary of the legal background to the case and the observations of the parties to the case submitted in the first written phase of the procedure. In the light of the reasoned opinion of the responsible Advocate General, the *juge rapporteur* writes a draft ruling, which is then submitted to the other EJC members for examination. Thus the procedure has both a written and an oral phase. The Advocate General then submits his or her conclusion – that is, reasoned opinion – before the judges deliberate and deliver their judgment on the case.

The ECJ sits as a full court, a grand chamber of thirteen judges or a chamber of three or five judges, depending on the nature, complexity or importance of the case. Chambers of five have three-year presidents; those of three have one-year presidents. The full court considers cases prescribed by its statutes, such as the dismissal of a member of the Commission; a grand chamber deals with a request by a MS or institution and exceptionally important cases; and the other chambers deal with the rest. An ECJ judgment is reached by majority decision and is pronounced at public hearings. There is no expression of 'dissenting opinions' and all the judges partaking in the deliberations must sign the judgment.

3.6.2 The General Court

Because the ECJ had been too busy to reach quick decisions, essential for the smooth operation of the integration process, the SEA introduced a Court of First Instance in 1989, renamed the General Court in 2009. The court deals with: (a) the enforcement of competition rules, (b) disputes between EU institutions and (c) actions brought by individuals against EU institutions and agencies, except in cases concerning trade protection. The court's rulings are subject to appeal to the ECJ on points of law only. In 2004 the Council decided to establish the European Union Civil Service Tribunal, comprising seven judges, to deal with disputes involving the civil service, with its decisions subject to appeal to the General Court only for points of law, which in turn may be reviewed by the ECJ in exceptional cases.

The court has the same number of judges as the ECJ – that is, twenty-seven, and they are subject to precisely the same conditions. It elects its own president as well as the presidents of its chambers of three or five judges, all on three-year renewable terms, and can meet as a grand chamber in especially important cases. Although it has no Advocates General, a judge may be nominated for the task in a limited number of cases. It appoints its own six-year term registrar, but depends on the ECJ for its administrative needs.

3.6.3 The Court of Auditors

The Court of Auditors was established in 1975 by the Treaty of Brussels and became operative in 1977 when EC budgetary arrangements were revised. It is located in Luxembourg.

The main function of the court is to ensure that the EU budget is properly implemented – that is, it is entrusted with the external monitoring of EU revenues and expenditures. In exercising this function, it also tries to secure sound financial management and to enhance the effectiveness and transparency of the whole system. It has no legal enforcement powers, so it informs the European Anti-Fraud Office when it detects any irregularities.

To carry out these responsibilities, the court needs to be independent, as indeed it is. However, the court does communicate and collaborate with other institutions. It assists the EP and the Council, the joint budgetary authority, by presenting them each year with observations on the execution of the budget for the previous year. These observations are taken seriously by the EP and influence its decision on the granting or otherwise of the implementation of the budget. It also submits to them statements of assurance regarding the proper use of EU revenues. Moreover, it gives its opinion on the adoption of financial regulations; it can submit observations on specific issues and responds with opinions to any request from any EU institution. Furthermore, in the reports issued by the court, based on its investigation of documents and, where necessary, of organizations managing revenues and expenditures on behalf of the EU, it draws the attention of both the Commission and MSs to any outstanding problems.

The court consists of twenty-seven members, one from each MS, appointed by the Council, but consulting the EP, and it must decide by unanimous agreement. The appointees are chosen from those who have worked for auditing institutions in their MSs or are specifically qualified for the job, and must meet the requirements of independence and full-time work. They have six-year renewable terms, they elect one of them to be president for three years and they have the option of operating in chambers. The court has a staff of about 500, 200 of whom are qualified auditors (CEU 2010b), divided into 'audit groups' according to the nature of their work, and they prepare reports for the court in order to help the court to reach its decisions.

3.7 The Ombudsman

Following the TEU call for the establishment of a European Ombudsman to deal with complaints raised by EU citizens, the post was created in 1995. The appointment, which is for a renewable term of five years, is the prerogative of each new EP; hence it coincides with each EP's life. The office is located in Strasbourg, where there is a secretariat whose principal administrator is appointed by the Ombudsman.

Being authorized to act independently as a full-time intermediary between EU citizens, including foreigners residing or having registered offices in the EU, and the authorities (only the ECJ and the General Court, in their judicial roles, do not come under the Ombudsman's jurisdiction), the Ombudsman uncovers malpractices in EU institutions and bodies and

makes recommendations for their elimination. The Ombudsman can also investigate on his or her own initiative. The Ombudsman's findings are referred to the EP to act on. The Ombudsman also presents an annual report to the EP on his or her activities.

Complaints to the Ombudsman must be submitted within two years of their being brought to the attention of the offending party, provided that the administrative procedures have already been undertaken and no legal proceedings have been initiated. When the Ombudsman has lodged comments on an issue with the institution or body concerned, it has the opportunity to respond to them and it is also obliged to provide the Ombudsman with any solicited information or access to relevant files, except where there are justifiable confidentiality grounds. If a case of malpractice has been established, the Ombudsman notifies the institution or body involved and the latter must respond within three months with a detailed opinion. The Ombudsman then lodges a report with both the EP and the institution or body involved, and notifies the complainant of the outcome of the investigations.

3.8 The European Economic and Social Committee

The Economic and Social Committee (ESC), now referred to as the European Economic and Social Committee (EESC), was first established as a result of the ECSC Treaty. The EESC is a forum for organized EU civil society. It comprises the various categories of economic and social activity, such as employers, unions and the self-employed, together with representatives from community and social organizations (in particular, producers, farmers, carriers, workers, dealers, craftsmen, professional occupations, consumers and general interest groups). These are considered as three groups: (1) employers' representatives from both the private and public sectors; (2) mainly members of national trade union organizations; and (3) a miscellaneous group, including members of farmers' organizations, small and medium-sized enterprises (SMEs) and various NGOs.

The EESC plays an important role of a general consultative and informative nature. Its opinions are sought by the Commission, the Council and the EP (since the Amsterdam Treaty) on all matters under its jurisdiction, some of which are mandatory. Since 1972 the EESC itself can also formulate its own opinions on issues it deems to be important. It also offers 'exploratory opinions' when approached by the Commission or the EP to discuss and make suggestions on an issue that could lead to a Commission proposal.

The TEU endowed the EESC with a status akin to that of the other EU institutions, especially in terms of its procedural rules, budget, the reinforcement of its right of initiative and the management of its staff with a secretariat-general. In 1997 the EESC saw a broadening in its field of action, notably in social matters, in accordance with the Amsterdam Treaty.

The EESC has 344 members, appointed by the Council by lists forwarded by the governments of MSs. Each member is appointed (and can be reappointed) for four years and acts independently, in a personal capacity, in the interests of the whole EU. The national distribution of the 344 members is such that France, Germany, Italy and the UK have twenty-four members each; Poland and Spain have twenty-one each; Romania has fifteen; Austria, Belgium, Bulgaria, the Czech Republic, Greece, Hungary, the Netherlands, Portugal and Sweden have twelve each; Denmark, Finland, Ireland, Lithuania and Slovakia have nine each; Estonia, Latvia and Slovenia have seven each; Cyprus and Luxembourg have six each; and Malta has five.

The EESC is housed in Brussels, but although most of its meetings and plenary sessions are held there, meetings are also scheduled in other locations. It has a plenary assembly, a bureau, the three groups just mentioned, six sections (dealing with the main EU activities) and a secretariat-general, with a staff of 135. It elects its own bureau of thirty-seven members, a president and two vice-presidents from the three groups in rotation, who hold office for two-year terms. The president acts as its external representative.

In reaching its decision, the EESC follows a certain procedure. When the president receives a request for an opinion from the Council, the Commission or the EP, the bureau lodges it with the appropriate section. The section then sets up a study group, consisting of about twelve people, and appoints a rapporteur, assisted by about four experts in the field. Based on the group's recommendations, the section adopts its opinion on the basis of simple majority and this is then considered in the plenary session, which decides in the same way before addressing it to the requesting

institution. Usually about ten plenary sessions are held every year.

3.9 The Committee of the Regions

The Committee of the Regions (CoR) was set up in 1994, as dictated in the TEU, in response to demands by several MSs that regional and local authorities should be directly involved in deliberations at EU level. In many countries these authorities enjoy wide-ranging powers, either because of the federal structure of the country concerned or by virtue of legislative or constitutional measures adopted over the past few decades; hence they are in direct touch with the average EU citizen, whose involvement in EU affairs, as we saw in Chapter 2, has been a major issue. The TEU specifies that members of the CoR must hold a regional or local authority electoral mandate or be politically accountable to an elected assembly, but must act independently.

The CoR is an advisory body to the Council, the Commission and the EP, and its main work entails advancing its own opinions on Commission proposals. Also, as is expected, it ensures that the subsidiarity principle is safeguarded. Moreover, the Council and the Commission must consult the CoR on any issue of direct relevance to local and regional authorities, and it can initiate its own opinions on matters of particular concern to itself and lodge them with either the Council, the Commission or the EP. Hence the CoR's work is guided by three principles: subsidiarity, proximity to citizens and partnership between those involved at all levels.

The structure and procedures of the CoR resemble those of the EESC in most respects. The exceptions are fourfold. First, for every one of the 344 members there is an alternate. Second, as just mentioned, the members are mainly politicians, either elected or exerting influence on local or regional authorities. Third, the members are assigned to six specialist commissions (set up by each plenary assembly, hence their designation varies with each term), whose job is to prepare for the five annual plenary sessions (it also holds two extraordinary meetings, each in the member nation acting as president at the time), which decide its 'opinion'. Fourth, its bureau consists of its president, the first vice-president, twenty-seven other vice-presidents (one from each MS), twenty-seven other members and the leaders of its political groups. The bureau has three seats for each of France, Germany, Italy, Poland, Spain and the UK, and one for each of the remaining twenty-one.

3.10 The European Central Bank

The ECB was established on 1 June 1998 and is located in Frankfurt, but its foundations were laid down through the European Monetary Institute (EMI), introduced on 1 January 1994, during the second stage of EMU (see Chapter 11). It is given total independence to carry out its mandate (see Chapter 12).

The ECB and the seventeen central banks of the euro nations are known as the Eurosystem, which distinguishes them from the European System of Central Banks (ESCB), since the latter includes the central banks of all twenty-seven EU nations. The ECB lies at the very heart of the Eurosystem (see Chapter 12), whose primary task is to ensure price stability in the Eurozone. Price stability has been defined as an annual increase in the consumer price index of less than 2 per cent. How this is achieved is explained in Chapter 12.

In executing its task, the ECB defines and implements the monetary policy of the Eurozone; holds and manages the foreign exchange reserves of the Eurozone and conducts foreign exchange operations; issues euro notes and coins; and promotes the smooth operation of the payment systems.

The executive board of the ECB is responsible for the daily running of the bank, the implementation of its monetary policy and transmitting the necessary instructions to the national central banks. It comprises the president, vice-president and four other members, all six being appointed on the agreement of the heads of state or government of the nations in the Eurozone. All six hold non-renewable eight-year terms.

The ECB's top decision-making body is the governing council, which comprises the six members of the executive board and the seventeen governors of the Eurozone central banks. The ECB president acts as its chairperson. The governing council meets twice a month, and during the first meeting it normally examines the economic conditions and the position of monetary policy, and determines the key interest rate; in the second meeting it concentrates on its other tasks (see Chapters 11 and 12).

There is also the general council, consisting of the ECB president and vice-president, as well as the governors of the national central banks of all EU27 MSs. Its task is to contribute to ECB advisory and coordinating work and to assist with the future enlargement of the Eurozone.

3.11 The European Investment Bank

The European Investment Bank (EIB) was set up in 1958 in Luxembourg, to fund both private and public investment projects that enhance economic integration, and to update and promote the balanced development and economic and social cohesion of EU MSs (see Chapters 2, 21 and 22). In global terms, the EIB meets the financial obligations of EU agreements on development aid and cooperation policies (see Chapter 24). EIB capital is provided by MSs, each contributing according to its relative GNP standing within the league of EU MSs. The EIB is empowered to make its own decisions on which projects to finance.

The EIB has a board of governors, a board of directors, a management committee and an audit committee. The board of governors, consisting of ministers appointed by MSs (usually the finance ministers), defines the general guidelines for lending, approves the balance sheet and annual report, decides on the funding of projects outside the EU and further capital generation, and appoints the members of the other three boards. The board of directors, which comprises twenty-eight members on five-year terms (one nominated by each MS and one by the Commission) and is headed by the EIB's president, has sole responsibility for decisions on loans, guarantees and borrowings, and ensures that the EIB is run properly and in accordance with EU treaties. The board also has sixteen alternates, necessitating sharing between MSs, and can co-opt up to six non-voting experts (three members and three alternates) for their advice. Since 1 May 2004, it has been deciding by a majority of those eligible to vote, but who must constitute a minimum of 50 per cent of the subscribed capital. The management committee is the full-time executive and consists of the EIB president and eight vice-presidents, appointed for six-year renewable terms. The audit committee, comprising three members and three observers on three-year terms, not only oversees the proper management of

EIB operations and financial resources, but also cooperates with the Court of Auditors for the EIB's external auditing.

The EIB is usually invited by the EP to participate in the committees concerned with EIB operations. It also has input in preparing the work of the Council (hence the EIB president may be asked to attend some meetings of the Council), and cooperates with other institutions concerned with its activities.

The EIB finances its activities by borrowing on the financial markets; thus it does not receive any EU budgetary contribution, and is run as a non-profit-making entity. It is different from traditional banks, however, since it does not offer current and savings accounts. It follows three criteria in deciding which investment projects it should fund: first, the investment must be instrumental in enticing other sources of funding; second, it must be in specified fields; third, it must be in the most disadvantaged regions. It has steadily grown in stature and is now ranked AAA, the highest credit rating on the capital markets, which enables it to raise funds on the most competitive of terms. It is also a majority shareholder in the European Investment Fund (EIF), created in 1994 and located in Luxembourg, to assist with the financing of investments in SMEs. The EIB deals directly with those promoting large-scale projects, worth at least 25 million euros, but cooperates with about 180 banks and specialist European financial intermediaries in the case of SMEs and local authorities.

EIB activities promote EU integration in a wider sense, with about 10 per cent of its funding going to projects in applicant countries, Mediterranean nations and ACP countries, as well as to some Asian and Latin American nations for ventures of common interest.

3.12 Conclusion

The main conclusion is that because the EU is neither one nation nor a very loose assortment of completely independent nations, the nature of its institutions should not be examined within the narrow context of a 'united states of Europe'. Hence those who argue that the Commission should be no more than an 'executive' are oblivious to the fact that somehow there must be an institution responsible for initiating integrative efforts, unless they are simply interested in the demise of the

EU itself. Likewise, those who compare the powers of the EP with those of national parliaments are misguided, since it is not a parliament for one nation, and so on and so forth.

The second conclusion is that the worries stated in the last edition have not all been removed by the adoption of the Treaty of Lisbon. Take, for example, the appointment of the full-time president of Council to champion the EU's internal agenda and represent it to the outside world. Those who supported this change insisted that it made sense only if the Commission itself were strengthened at the same time, with its president elected directly by the EP. Those who opposed it, however, including then Commission president, Romano Prodi, believed that this solution had a number of drawbacks. It needed to ensure that rivalry between the presidents of the Commission and the Council did not become a divisive factor; to avoid any risk of creating a second administration; to ensure that reforms actually improved the quality of work in the Council and the various Council configurations; and to settle satisfactorily the issue of the accountability of the presidents of the Council and the General Affairs Council (speech delivered by Romano Prodi to the French National Assembly in Paris on 12 March 2003). Prodi pushed for a clarification of how competences should be shared by the two presidents and how long their terms of office should be; who the president of the Council should be accountable to; how to avoid duplicating the administration; and how the work of the Council, and in particular the presidency of the General Affairs Council, should be organized. Although some of these concerns have now been met, the gist of the reservations remains valid.

Summary

- The EU has a unique institutional structure, which is not surprising, given that it is neither a federal state nor a purely intergovernmental cooperative venture.
- EU MSs delegate sovereignty in specific areas to independent institutions, entrusting them with defending the interests of the EU as a whole, as well as of both its MSs and its citizens: the Commission upholds the interests of the whole EU; the Council upholds the interests of MSs' governments through

their ministerial representatives; the European Parliament (EP) upholds those of EU citizens, who directly elect EP members.

- The Commission, the Council and the EP are known as the institutional triangle. They are the most significant institutions, so this summary is confined to them.
- EU treaties assign the Commission a wide range of tasks, but these can be narrowed down to four major roles:
  1. The Commission initiates EU policy by proposing new legislation to the Council and the EP.
  2. The Commission serves as an EU executive arm by administering and implementing EU policies.
  3. Jointly, with the ECJ, the Commission acts as the guardian of EU treaties by enforcing EU law.
  4. The Commission acts as EU spokesperson and negotiator of its international agreements, especially in relation to trade and cooperation.
- The Council consists of representatives of the governments of MSs, who are accountable to their national parliaments and citizens; hence it is the embodiment of national interests. It has six major responsibilities:
  1. The Council is the main EU legislative body, but in many areas it exercises this prerogative jointly with the EP through the co-decision procedure.
  2. The Council coordinates the broad economic policies of MSs.
  3. The Council concludes EU international agreements.
  4. Together with the EP, the Council has authority over the EU general budget.
  5. On the basis of general guidelines from the European Council, the Council used to take the necessary decisions for framing and implementing the common foreign and security policy (CFSP), but this task has now gone to the foreign policy supremo (FPS).
  6. The Council coordinates MSs activities, as well as adopting measures in the area of judicial and home affairs.
- Originally, the EP was a consultative rather than a legislative body, but it is now part of the legislative process:
  1. The EP acts with the Council to formulate and adopt certain legislation emanating from the Commission, and here the most common path is through the co-decision procedure, which gives equal weight to both and results in the adoption of joint acts.
  2. The EP has budgetary powers by having the right to make certain alterations and to adopt the final budget.
  3. The EP's consent is needed for the appointment of EU and Commission presidents, and to approve all commissioners, as well as to dismiss the entire Commission.

Questions and essay topics

1. What functions does the EU president perform?
2. What functions does the EU foreign policy supremo perform?
3. What functions does the Commission president perform?
4. The Commission has four major roles to play. What are these?
5. Do you agree that the Council is the ultimate EU legislative authority?
6. What is qualified majority voting?
7. What is the co-decision procedure?
8. Is the EP a purely consultative EU chamber?
9. 'EU institutions share a vested interest in ever-closer union because this enhances their power and prestige.' Discuss.
10. 'The fact that the Commission has executive, legislative and quasi-judicial powers is incompatible with the classical separation of powers.' Discuss.
11. '[The EP] lacks many characteristics of a normal parliament. A second chamber ought to be added which includes representatives of national parliaments determined by lot and which shall have no other power than to block centralizing legislation' (Vaubel 2009). Explain and discuss.

FURTHER READING

Rittberger, B. (2005) *Building Europe's Parliament: Democratic Representation beyond the Nation-State*, Oxford University Press.

Vaubel, R. (2009), *The European Institutions as an Interest Group*, Institute of International Affairs, London.

NOTES

1 The call for this goes back to Article 286 of the EEC Treaty, but it was Council/EP regulation 45/2001 (of 18 December 2000) that enacted the protection of individuals with regard to the processing of personal data by EU institutions and bodies, and the free circulation of such data; and the appointment of the first five-year-term supervisor, who has a deputy, was made in 2004, following a public call for candidates.

2 Although not usually in the large MSs.

3 Most of the 23,000 staff are in Brussels, but nearly 4,000 are in Luxembourg; there are representatives in every EU MS, and Commission agencies are spread across the EU, as well as in delegations in almost all other countries. Although the number of people working for the Commission may seem excessive, it is actually less than that employed by a medium-sized EU city council (CEU 2010b).

4 The legal dimension in EU integration

IMELDA MAHER

4.1 Introduction

This chapter sets out to describe the normative and functional nature of European Union (EU) law, with particular focus on the role of the European Court of Justice (ECJ). In doing so, it aims to shed light on how and to what extent law is an essential part of the European project, and to show how the ECJ, through its constitutionalizing role, has defined the EU as a new legal order.

Section 4.2 provides a general background, setting the scene. Section 4.3 discusses how the rule of law lies at the heart of the EU legal order. Section 4.4 describes the ECJ institutionally and in terms of its jurisdiction. The following sections then examine the framing function of EU law (Section 4.5); rule-making (Section 4.6); the implementation and enforcement of EU law (Section 4.7); and interpretation and dispute resolution (Section 4.8). The final section (4.9) is a conclusion on the nature of EU law.

4.2 Background

EU law, to state a truism, is a form of law that in many ways adheres to conventional understandings of law. Thus it has normative and functional dimensions. From a normative perspective, the EU legal order is predicated on the rule of law. Compliance with the rule of law means that:

- nobody is above the law;
- the law embodies certain fundamental principles; and
- it is consistent with certain procedural norms designed to ensure fairness and the appropriate exercise of discretion.

Thanks are due to Suzanne Kingston for her helpful comments.

From a functional perspective, EU law has four main functions:

1. Framing
2. Rule-making
3. Implementation and enforcement
4. Interpretation and dispute resolution.

Thus the treaties – themselves instruments of international law – describe the institutional framework and also frame competences, responsibilities, prohibitions and rights within the EU. The mandate within the treaties to articulate and give effect to agreed policies is executed through rule-making, which can take many different forms, ranging from statute-like regulations (Treaty on the Functioning of the European Union, TFEU, Article 228) to soft law, the latter being norms that have practical and even legal effects, but are not formally constituted as law (Snyder 1995, p. 64; Stefan 2008). The EU differs fundamentally from other legal orders in that it does not have any police or border officials and very few inspectors. Instead, it has a dependent relationship, with national enforcement agencies putting EU law into effect. The obligation on member states (MSs) to do so is achieved in four main ways:

1. Through the general duty of loyalty in the Treaty on the European Union (TEU, Article 4(3)), which requires states to meet their obligations in EU law.
2. Through the risk of an enforcement action being brought against an MS for non-compliance before the ECJ.
3. Through the use of directives which set out the objective to be achieved and usually give MSs two years to implement the directive in a manner that they think fits best with their own legal and political structures (TFEU, Article 288; Prechal 2005).

4. Specifically in relation to the Single European Market (SEM; see Chapter 7) legislation, MSs have to report how they have implemented EU legislation, with scoreboards being drawn up by the Commission.

Failure to notify the Commission of national implementing legislation will negate that legislation (CEU 2009a; Treutlein 2009).

Once transposed, the directive is enforced indirectly through national law by the national enforcement agencies and courts (Daintith 1995; Maher 1996a). Thus the EU is parasitic on national legal orders for the enforcement of EU law. Even in the field of competition law (see Chapter 13), where the Commission has extensive enforcement powers, in 2003 national competition agencies were also given the power to enforce the European competition rules on private market behaviour (TFEU, Articles 101 and 102), with the Commission investigating and enforcing issues that affect three or more MSs (Council 2003b; CEU 2004l, paragraph 14).

The EU is unusual in the international legal order in that from the outset the MSs had willingly delegated the interpretation of the law to the ECJ. This autonomy was to prove critical to the development of the legal order, especially when combined with the preliminary reference procedure whereby national courts refer questions of interpretation and validity of EU law to the ECJ (TFEU, Article 267). It is through its interpretation of the treaties in particular that the ECJ shaped the EU legal order, developing the doctrines of direct effect and the supremacy of EU law so that the EU legal order is seen as constitutionalizing – a process commenced in the early 1960s and which continues, despite the collapse of the EU Constitution following the negative referenda in the Netherlands and France (see Chapters 2 and 25; Grimm 1995; Craig 2001a; Curtin 2006). The opinion of the ECJ can often prove decisive regarding the outcome of a case; thus its interpretive and dispute resolution roles are combined. The ECJ plays a crucial role in dispute resolution, in particular in cases involving EU institutions, MSs and private parties (although there were severe limitations on private individuals challenging the validity of legislation, recently relaxed in the Treaty of Lisbon (TFEU, Article 263(4); Arnull 2006, pp. 76–94)).[1] It is an outstanding achievement of the ECJ that it has fashioned a unique legal order, neither international nor national, but one that

is nonetheless clearly predicated and committed to the rule of law and fundamental rights.

4.3 The rule of law and the EU

According to TEU Article 2, the EU is founded on the rule of law. The rule of law constrains the exercise of all public power, but it also legitimates it. By stating at the very start of the Treaty that it is founded on the rule of law, the EU is making law pre-eminent over the exercise of power. This means that no one is above the law and that all public power must be exercised in a manner consistent with the law. Provided it is exercised in this way, it is legitimate. Thus it has both a political and a legal dimension, and the challenge for a legal order committed to the rule of law is to ensure an appropriate balance between law as a constraint on the exercise of power on the one hand, and, on the other hand, law as a means of ensuring individual freedom (Tamanaha 2004, pp. 33–6; Maher 2009, p. 422). One tool with which to achieve this balance is adherence to rules of procedure that aim to ensure that all are treated fairly and no one is privileged before the law. This narrow conception of the rule of law is perhaps best seen in Fuller's articulation of the eight characteristics of law: generality, promulgation, no retroactivity, clarity, no contradictory rules, no impossible prescriptions, stability and consistent application (Fuller 1964, Chapter 2). These characteristics are aimed for, if not always achieved, by the rulings of the ECJ, and act as a constraint on the way in which law is made and exercised in the EU. For example, it is a fundamental principle of the EU legal order that a measure adopted by public authorities is not applicable to those concerned before they have the opportunity to acquaint themselves with it. Thus the measure must be promulgated and should not apply retroactively – although the ECJ has been willing to allow retroactive measures in exceptional circumstances, but only where the purpose requires it and where the legitimate expectations of individuals are fully respected.[2]

The narrow and procedural conception of the rule of law is problematic, however, as it is so thin that a highly legalistic society can formally comply with these rules and yet fail to realize the values of justice, fairness and equality that are also inherent in the rule of law. Thus this narrow conception can be seen as a necessary but not sufficient condition for a liberal democracy (and a polity like the EU) (Rose 2004, p. 260). Instead, a 'thick' understanding of the rule of law is also needed, but the difficulty is that it is not possible to provide an agreed definition of justice, for example, that can be measured within any particular legal order. This may explain why TEU, Article 2, not only mentions the rule of law but also expressly refers to human dignity, freedom, democracy, equality and human rights. This suggests that the Treaty itself recognizes that the rule of law needs to be expressly grounded in a wider set of values, so that even if a narrow conception of it is taken, procedures within EU law will also have to pay due regard to these more difficult to define but nonetheless vital values of freedom, democracy, equality and human rights:

The Union is founded on the values of respect for human dignity, freedom, democracy, equality, the rule of law and respect for human rights, including the rights of persons belonging to minorities. These values are common to the Member States in a society in which pluralism, non-discrimination, tolerance, justice, solidarity and equality between women and men prevail (TEU, Article 2)

The commitment to the rule of law is further complemented by explicit commitments to fundamental rights. Thus the EU Charter of Fundamental Rights (see Chapter 2) has the same legal value as the treaties (TEU, Article 6.1) and the EU is now required to accede to the European Convention on Human Rights (TEU, Article 6.2), a 1950 Treaty adopted under the aegis of the Council of Europe (see Chapter 2), with its own court, the European Court of Human Rights, which sits in Strasbourg. This is a separate international treaty and legal regime from that of the EU, although all EU MSs have ratified the Convention. Finally, the constitutional traditions common to the MSs also provide a basis for the recognition of fundamental rights in the EU. This reflects the early case law of the ECJ, where the principle of supremacy was established. There was no reference to fundamental rights in the then treaties, and the advisability of what, in the 1960s, was essentially a partial economic union based on law having priority over the rights-rich constitutions of MSs was challenged. The ECJ responded by identifying fundamental human rights as inherent in the general principles of EU law and inspired by the constitutional traditions common to MSs.[3] The requirement that the

constitutional tradition be common to MSs is rarely referred to by the ECJ. Even if MSs agree on a particular right, there can be differences as to the scope and nature of it. For example, the right to life is commonly recognized, but in Ireland this extends to the unborn under the constitution, so grounds for abortion are extremely restrictive, unlike in most other MSs.

Thus there is a long and complex history behind the status, scope and nature of fundamental rights in the EU legal order. This explains why there are three bases to EU rights, recognized in Article 6:

1. the EU Charter;
2. the European Convention; and
3. the common constitutional traditions of the MSs.

ECJ case law is also significant. The complexity of sources in part reflects the absence of any reference to fundamental rights in the treaties until the TEU (Article F) in 2003, when it was expressly stated that the EU was founded, inter alia, on respect for human rights and, more recently, the political sensitivity around the legal status of the Charter, which is now a protocol of the Treaty. This is because there is some anxiety as to the extent to which EU rights can bind national governments and 'trump' national constitutional rights; thus Irish sensitivities around family values (including the constitutional right to life) were seen as one reason for the rejection of the Lisbon Treaty the first time round (Quinlan 2009) and there are considerable British concerns around the social rights relating to workers' collective rights (Goldsmith 2001, p. 1214).

ECJ case law is also significant in supporting the commitment of the EU to the rule of law – both in relation to process and in terms of a substantive commitment to justice:

[I]t is to be borne in mind that the [EU] is based on the rule of law, inasmuch as neither its Member States nor its institutions can avoid review of the conformity of their acts with the basic constitutional charter, the [EU] Treaty, which established a complete system of legal remedies and procedures designed to enable the Court of Justice to review the legality of acts of the institutions (Case C-402/05P and C-415/05P *Kadi and Al Barakaat International Foundation* v. *Council* [2008] ECR I-6351, paragraph 281)

First, through its review of decision-making and law-making by the EU institutions (TFEU, Article 263) and of the MSs' compliance with their EU law obligations

(TFEU, Articles 258–60), the ECJ has ensured that procedural rights are protected. Second, it has developed through its case law general principles which inform how it interprets the rules (Tridimas 2006; Craig 2006, Chapters 15–19). Some of the principles are now articulated in the Treaty – for example, the principles of proportionality (TFEU, Article 5.3) and equality (TFEU, Articles 2 and 9). Others, such as the principle of legitimate expectation (closely linked to legal certainty), also enrich the development of procedural requirements in the EU and provide a basis on which to challenge the validity of specific rules (Craig 2006, Chapter 10; Tridimas 2006, Chapter 6). They also provide a means by which soft-law measures, such as guidelines, can be considered by the ECJ in its deliberations, thus bringing new governance tools within the purview of judicial review (Stefan 2008). Under Article 6, the fundamental rights recognized by the EU are general principles of the EU, following the practice developed by the ECJ. Finally, as the sole authoritative interpreter of EU law (TFEU, Article 19), the ECJ has wielded considerable power in relation to how the bare bones of the treaties have developed into the complex and extensive *acquis communautaire* (the entire corpus of EU law) and, in particular, into a supranational legal order where EU law is supreme over national law (see Chapter 2) and confers rights on individuals that can be invoked before national courts. It is these two characteristics of supremacy and direct effect – both judge-made law – that distinguish the EU from other international legal regimes (Hartley 1999, p. 128). This is because the EU recognizes persons (natural people, as well as legal persons such as firms and charities) as subjects of its law, while only states and international organizations are subjects of international law. The supremacy of EU law means that MSs are bound by EU law, and where there are conflicting national and EU laws, the EU law prevails and the national courts must disapply the national law (see Section 4.7, page 64).

Thus the rule of law is the cornerstone of the EU legal order. The difficulty is that apart from a narrow conception, based on legal procedures, there is little agreement as to what exactly is the rule of law. Nonetheless, commitment to the rule of law ensures the legitimacy of the EU, of its institutions and of the decisions taken and the rules made under the powers conferred by the treaties. Thus while there is much debate as to the existence and extent of the democratic deficit in the EU (see Chapters 2, 3 and 25; inter alios, Crombez 2003; Majone 2008; Moravcsik 2006; Snell 2008), the commitment to the legal dimension of the rule of law as protecting individual freedom and acting as a constraint on power exercised remains unchallenged. The functional aspects of an EU based on the rule of law are the focus of the rest of this chapter. Given the importance of the ECJ, we will describe the court and its jurisdiction first.

4.4 The European Court of Justice

The Court system consists of three courts: the ECJ, the General Court and the Civil Service Tribunal. All are based in Luxembourg. Originally, there was only one court (so the ECJ and Court were used interchangeably), but as the volume of cases grew, the Court of First Instance (as the General Court was known) was set up in 1988, following the Single European Act (Council 1988, Chapter 2). The Treaty of Nice introduced further reform, allowing for the creation of specialist tribunals (now TFEU, Article 257). So far, the only one set up is the Civil Service Tribunal, which hears labour disputes between the EU institutions and their individual employees (Council 2004b). Since the Lisbon Treaty specialist tribunals no longer require unanimity in the Council to be set up; it is sufficient to have a qualified majority voting (QMV; see Chapter 3 on QMV and Chapter 2 on most of the items mentioned in this section). This makes the creation of further specialist tribunals (such as a Patents Court) more likely.

The working language of the ECJ is French and the French judicial model informed its structure. The proceedings are conducted mainly on the basis of paper submissions, with oral hearings used mainly to clarify certain points. The ECJ will hear cases in any of the official EU languages. The ECJ consists of no more than one judge from each MS and hence has 27 judges (TEU, Article 19; TFEU, Article 253). No matter how many judges hear a case, only one judgment is ever delivered and the deliberations of the judges are confidential. This has been important in preventing the ECJ from becoming politicized along the lines of the nationality of its judges, as it is not possible to point to the view of any single judge. This aspect has also been criticized as a constraint on legal reasoning, and as inhibiting the ECJ from bringing into the open the legal debate about the conflicting methods and values that inform its judgments (Perju 2009). What the ECJ does have is Advocates General (AGs), of whom there are eight (TEU, Article 19.2; TFEU, Article 253). The AG to a case provides a learned opinion to the ECJ after all submissions, setting out what the law is and how he or she thinks the case should be decided (Burrows and Greaves 2007). In effect, the AGs represent the public interest. The opinion is not binding on the ECJ, but is followed in about 80 per cent of cases. An AG now only sits on about half the cases before the ECJ (European Court of Justice 2009a, p. 11).

The ECJ sits in chambers of three or five judges and, occasionally, as a grand chamber of thirteen judges, with the important cases being assigned to larger chambers (TFEU, Article 251; TFEU, Article 16, Statute of the ECJ Protocol 3). It can sit as a full court, but does so very rarely (Arnull 2006, p. 8). Thus the ECJ is a composite court. The risk for a composite court is that predictability, consistency and certainty – all important requirements for adherence to the rule of law – could be weakened where there are multiple chambers. Thus it is important for the office of the president of the ECJ (elected for three years from the ranks of the judges; TFEU, Article 253) to ensure that information about decisions in different chambers is circulated to all ECJ members. On the other hand, the chambers system allows judges to specialize, developing their expertise, and hence ensuring better-quality judgments. The chamber system is designed to address the huge workload of the ECJ, which delivered 588 judgments in 2009 (European Court of Justice 2009a, p. 81). This system reflects the relatively open nature of the ECJ – it does not generally 'vet' the substance of cases in advance to see if it is worth hearing them. In other words, the Court does not exercise a docket system of only hearing the cases that it deems important, as in the US Supreme Court (Chalmers *et al.* 2010, p. 179). Nonetheless, the parties do have to meet the strict standing requirements set down in the treaty. This relatively 'open-door' ECJ policy, particularly in the early years in relation to references from national courts, helps to ensure its position at the centre of the European court system, and also ensures that national courts also become European courts in so far as they send questions to the ECJ and give effect to European law. The downside of the policy is that there is currently a waiting period of fifteen to seventeen months for a case before the ECJ gives judgment (European Court

of Justice 2009a, p. 94; Chalmers *et al.* 2010, p. 178). There has been a gradual reduction in this time lag since 2005.

The junior partner of the ECJ is the General Court, which is required to have at least one judge from each MS, and hence could have more. At the moment it has 27 judges. It also works on a chamber system, but, unlike the ECJ, it does not have any AGs, with one of the judges fulfilling that role in a case if it is deemed necessary. It is also a very busy court, with 555 cases decided in 2009 (European Court of Justice 2009a, p. 165). Duration of proceedings ranges from sixteen months for appeals, to twenty months for intellectual property cases, thirty-three months for other actions and fifty-two months for staff case appeals (European Court of Justice 2009a, p. 173).

The ECJ is the more senior court in that decisions from the General Court can be appealed to it on a point of law (not fact), giving it the final word on the interpretation and validity of the law. It also hears preliminary rulings from national courts and so remains the sole authoritative interpreter of EU law for all courts across the 27 MSs. It hears all disputes between MSs and the institutions, as well as between the institutions, and offers opinions on the legality of international agreements negotiated by the EU. The General Court has more limited jurisdiction, focused mainly on individuals (TFEU, Article 256). Thus it can carry out judicial review cases from individuals claiming illegality of acts of the institutions (TFEU, Article 263.4), failure to act by the institutions (TFEU, Article 265(3)) or claims for damages for non-contractual liability (TFEU, Articles 268 and 340.2). It also hears appeals in staff cases and from the Office for Harmonization in the Internal Market (OHIM) in relation to granting an EU trademark.

The ECJ has no jurisdiction over the EU's common foreign and security policy (TFEU, Articles 24.1 and 275; see Chapter 3). It has limited powers to review a decision to expel an MS from the EU (TFEU, Article 269), and in the field of judicial cooperation in criminal matters and police cooperation, it has no jurisdiction over the validity and proportionality of actions of national police, or over MSs' actions to maintain law and order and safeguard internal security (TFEU, Article 276). Table 4.1 provides a summary of the main heads of jurisdiction for both courts.

Table 4.1 Jurisdiction of the courts

TFEU	Jurisdiction	ECJ	General Court
A267	Preliminary reference	Questions on EU law referred from national courts	
A263	Judicial review	Actions brought by the institutions Actions brought against Parliament or Council by an MS	Actions brought by private parties Actions brought by an MS against the Commission, ECB or European Council
A265	Failure to act	Actions brought by an MS and institutions	Actions brought by private parties
A263(4) A265(3) A268 A340(2)	Liability		Non-contractual liability of the EU
A258, 259 and 260	Enforcement	Actions brought by the Commission or an MS against an MS for failing to fulfil a treaty obligation, including action to impose a fine	
A272	Contract		Arbitration clause conferring jurisdiction on the ECJ
A256	Appeals	From General Court on points of law	From Civil Service Tribunal and OHIM
A218(11)	Opinions	Compliance of international treaties concluded by the EU	

4.5 The framing function of EU law

The EU is founded on the treaties, which are the primary reference for the values inherent in the Union (TEU, Article 2), its aims and objectives (TEU, Article 3), and the powers conferred on it and each of its institutions to realize those objectives (TEU, Articles 4 and 5; TFEU, Article 1.1). Failure to exercise powers according to the treaties renders those actions void and illegal. In other words, while the competences of the EU have expanded with each treaty revision, it remains a polity limited and framed by law, as it cannot lawfully exercise any powers other than those conferred on it (either expressly or under the implied powers doctrine developed by the ECJ). This is known as the principle of conferred powers (Craig 2004), which means that all laws made must give reasons for their enactment and specify the treaty provision on which they are based. These technical requirements have two effects:

1. They ensure accountability, as the institutions have to explain why particular legislation is enacted; if that explanation is not consistent with the rules that follow, its validity can be challenged before the ECJ.
2. There are many different forms of law-making in the treaty, and how a law is enacted will be determined by the provision relied on – for example, whether it is by QMV or unanimity, by ordinary or special procedures.[4]

With the expansion of co-decision (see Chapter 3) by the Lisbon Treaty (now called the ordinary legislative procedure under TFEU, Article 289) this is less of an issue than it was in the past (Klamert 2010).

With the historically limited democratic credentials of the EU, power came not from the people but from the law. Thus compliance with the law and the constraints imposed by it were all the more important in the EU legal order. The paradox, perhaps, is that despite the constraints of limited competence, and foundational documents in the form of treaties rather than a constitution adopted by the citizens of the EU, the competences of the Union have grown exponentially since 1958. Legal integration is explained mainly by the strong integrationist stance adopted by the ECJ when interpreting the treaties and by the extraordinary success it has had in creating a unique supranational legal order (Alter 2001; Burley and Mattli 1993). The ECJ adopts a teleological approach in its judgments – that is, the law is interpreted in order to achieve the aims and objectives of the treaties, which were framed mainly in terms of market integration until the Lisbon Treaty (Scott 1992). The ECJ also changed its original position from seeing the EU as having limited competence to recognizing its ever expanding competence:

The European Economic Community [now the EU] constitutes a new legal order of international law for the benefit of which the states have limited their sovereign rights albeit within limited fields.[5]

The ECJ had become more expansive a few years later, in Opinion 1/91:

In contrast, the EEC Treaty [now the TEU], albeit concluded in the form of an international agreement, none the less constitutes the constitutional charter of a Community [now Union] based on the rule of law, as the Court of Justice has consistently held, the Community Treaties established a new legal order for the benefit of which the States have limited their sovereign rights, in ever wider fields and the subjects of which comprise not only Member States but also their nationals.[6]

This issue of creeping competence was initially addressed through the introduction of the subsidiarity principle in the TEU (Article 5; see Chapter 2). The requirement that actions only be taken at EU level if they cannot be sufficiently achieved at national level has proved largely unsuccessful, leading to the new arrangement in the treaty for national parliaments to review draft EU legislation (TEU, Article 12; TEU, Protocols 1 and 2; Estella 2002). Thus the Lisbon Treaty now expressly states that powers not conferred on the EU remain with the MSs (TEU, Articles 4.1 and 5). This suggests that it is for the ECJ to decide whether or not the EU has competence where there is a dispute. However, the question of who or what court decides on the competence of the EU is a vexed one, with national courts looking to their constitutions to see the scope of

what has been conferred, and the ECJ looking only to the treaties (see Section 4.9, page 67).

4.6 Rule-making

As well as the overarching framework provided by the TEU and TFEU, there are three main types of laws that are legally binding: regulations, directives and decisions (see Chapter 3). Regulations are binding in their entirety and are generally and directly applicable; they apply without the need for any 'converting' national law, and in fact MSs are prohibited from taking any steps to so convert them.[7] They provide uniform rules for all the Union and can be seen as the statutes of the EU. Directives are binding as to outcome, but leave to the MSs the means according to which that outcome is achieved through national law. Directives thus depend on national law for implementation. Finally, decisions are laws issued to specifically named individuals or groups (TFEU, Article 288; see Section 3.4.1, page 45). For example, the Commission has power to issue decisions fining firms in breach of EU competition rules (Regulation 1/2003, Article 7; see Chapter 13).

There was no express provision for secondary legislation in the treaty. This has now been remedied in the Lisbon Treaty (TFEU, Article 290), although the power to make legislation has long been delegated to the Commission in order for the EU to function. Such delegated legislation does not go through the full democratic procedures for enactment, instead being overseen by a committee procedure where national interests are represented. This process, known as comitology, has raised concerns in relation to the importance of the powers being delegated, the amount of delegation that takes place and the dilution of accountability (Franchino 2004). The increased role of the European Parliament (EP) in the TFEU (Article 290) is designed to address these accountability concerns (Hoffmann 2009).

Finally, a recent phenomenon in the EU has been the emergence of soft law as a form of governance (Senden 2004). This has arisen especially following the Lisbon Strategy, where the open method of coordination (OMC) was identified as a key governance tool (Hodson and Maher 2001). Under OMC and its many variants, networks play an important role, with an emphasis on information gathering and sharing, and evaluation according to agreed benchmarks, with or without escalation to sanctions and hard law where states fail to meet those benchmarks (Trubek and Trubek 2007; Armstrong and Kilpatrick 2007). In addition to the Lisbon Strategy, soft law can be found in other policy areas. For example, the Commission has long issued guidelines to supplement and support legislation in the competition field and to set out Commission thinking (see Chapter 13). The legal status of such guidelines is murky. They are not legally binding and often expressly say so, but are capable of having practical effects in that they can shape behaviour. Soft law may also have legal effects – for example, in some cases the Commission may be bound by its own soft law measures, such as norms it sets down in its Annual Competition Reports, notices and guidelines (Snyder 1995; Stefan 2008).[8] Nonetheless, there can be accountability concerns, as the EP is not involved in the development of soft law; and while recommendations and opinions are expressly mentioned in the treaty as having no binding force (Article 288.5), other forms of soft law, such as guidelines and notices, are not. Thus soft law bypasses to some degree the framing role of the treaties. At the same time, as a tool of policy learning and coordination, such coordination being required, as in economic policy (see Chapter 14), it has taken on an increasingly important role within the toolkit of norm creation in the EU.

Legislation is now adopted mainly under the ordinary procedure, which was formerly known as co-decision, and involves the adoption of legislation jointly by the EP and the Council. The treaty now refers to all other procedures as special procedures, making it clear that co-decision, with its better democratic credentials given the involvement of the EP, is the most common (TFEU, Article 289; see Chapter 3).

4.7 Implementation and enforcement

The relationship between the EU and its MSs is such that the states carry primary (though not sole) responsibility for compliance with and enforcement of EU law. They must comply with regulations that are directly applicable within their jurisdictions, and implement directives within the timeframe set out and in a manner faithful to the measure. Failure to do so can lead to an enforcement action brought against an MS by the Commission before the ECJ (TFEU, Article 258), or, exceptionally, by another MS (TFEU, Article 259). Failure to comply with that judgment can lead to another action, this time for a fine to be imposed on the MS (Wenneras 2006).[9] Under the Lisbon Treaty, where an MS has failed to fulfil its obligation to notify the Commission of its measures transposing a directive, the Commission can recommend a fine at the initial hearing, removing the need to go through a two-stage process (TFEU, Article 260).

Why would states fail to comply with legislation they have negotiated and adopted at the EU level? They may not have voted in favour of the measure on its adoption. There may be systemic problems where, for example, the new EU regime does not fit well with the existing national regime, or the fault lies with regional or local government and central government is unable to secure compliance. There is also the possibility that non-compliance or compliance only when coerced to do so may be seen as politically desirable if the policy in the EU measure is not popular domestically (Falkner and Treib 2008; Maher 1996a).

The ECJ has adopted a number of strategies that have strengthened its enforcement role:

1. The concept of 'state' is very broadly interpreted, and no differentiation is made between different organs of the state and different levels of government. Once the body is an emanation of the state, it is subject to the responsibilities of the state, even if it is constitutionally independent of the government.[10] While this has cast the net wide, it is also a fiction to some extent, especially when the failure to implement a directive gives rise to liability – for example, for a regional health body that cannot be deemed responsible for the transposition of directives.[11]

2. Provisions, practices or circumstances in their existing legal system cannot justify failure to implement.[12]

3. The doctrines of supremacy and direct effect have had a profound impact on the constitutionalization of the EU (de Witte 1999) that extends far beyond questions of enforcement, but they both have had an important impact on enforcement and the efficacy of EU law.

Thus the ECJ has repeatedly held that EU law is supreme over national law, including constitutional law:

Recourse to the legal rule or concepts of national law in order to judge the validity of measure adopted by the institutions of the Community [now EU] would have an adverse effect on the uniformity and efficacy of Community law. The validity of such measures can only be judged in the light of Community law. In fact, the law stemming from the Treaty, an independent source of law, cannot because of its very nature be overridden by rules of national law, however framed, without being deprived of its character as Community law and without the legal basis of the Community itself being called into question. Therefore the validity of a Community measure or its effect within a Member State cannot be affected by allegations that it runs counter to either fundamental rights as formulated by the constitution of that State or the principles of a national constitutional structure (Case 11/70 *Internationale Handelsgesellschaft mbH* v. *Einfuhr-und Vorratsstelle für Getreide und Futtermittel*[13])

This means that MSs cannot avoid their obligations under EU law by passing subsequent national law that negates EU law.[14] Where national law contradicts and conflicts with EU law and both laws are before a national court, the national court is required by this doctrine to disapply the conflicting national law. EU law cannot and does not declare national law void. The supremacy doctrine simply prevents national law from being applied where it would conflict with EU law.

While the doctrine of direct effect has important constitutional implications, it also has a more mundane but nonetheless important impact on the enforcement of EU law and the obligations of the MSs. Thus while we know from the treaty that regulations are directly applicable in the states without the need for any implementing legislation at the national level, under the doctrine of direct effect developed by the ECJ measures that are clear and precise, unconditional and require no implementing legislation can be relied on by private persons before their national courts, even if they are not contained in a regulation (Pescatore 1983).[15] The ECJ has gone on to interpret each of these requirements in a fairly broad manner, leaving it with some discretion as to the scope of the doctrine (Craig and de Búrca 2008, p. 275). Individuals affected by the failure of an MS government to give effect to an EU law can rely on it before their own courts, and the national courts will have to give effect to it (as it is supreme over national law) and disapply any conflicting national law (Craig 1992). The implications of this are considerable, and even more so because directives that are not

implemented within the time limit set down in them can become directly effective and be enforced subject to one very significant limitation: directives only can be relied on or used against the state (vertical direct effect) (Prechal 2005). They do not have horizontal direct effect – that is, a private party cannot rely on a directive against another private party, even after the time limit for implementation has passed.[16] This is because it is not the duty of a private party to implement an EU directive. This limitation has been severely criticized, but the ECJ has retained it as a means of preserving the distinction between regulations and directives (Curtin 1990a; Coppel 1994; Tridimas 1994).

Nonetheless, the potential scope for enforcement of EU laws in national courts where states have failed to carry out their obligations has been expanded in a number of ways:

1. As noted above, directives can have direct effect against any organ of the state (Curtin 1990b).[17]
2. National courts are obliged to interpret all national law, irrespective of when enacted, as far as possible in a manner consistent with EU law.[18] Known as the doctrine of indirect direct effect, this is a far-reaching obligation as it applies to all national law and goes a long way in overcoming the limitations on horizontal direct effect for directives (Betlem 2002; Drake 2005). There are some limitations on this – for example, the time limit for transposition of a directive must have expired before the national court is required to interpret in light of it,[19] and the application of the doctrine must not breach the requirements of the rule of law, such as legal certainty.[20]
3. Incidental direct effect can also arise in relation to litigation between private parties where a party is allowed to rely on a directive as a shield to a claim based on national law or even as the basis for an action. There is no clearly articulated rule to be applied for this small number of cases mainly concerned with the failure of an MS to notify new technical standards as required by a directive designed to prevent non-tariff barriers on trade (NTBs; see Chapter 1) being hidden at national level (now Directive 98/34). As a result of failure to notify a measure, parties have been able to invoke the directive without imposing an obligation on a private party. How far this case law may extend is not clear. What is significant, however, is that there is scope

for directives to be invoked in private litigation (Weatherill 2001).

4. Also significantly, the ECJ has held that where MSs have failed to meet their obligations under EU law they can be liable for damages against the affected private parties:

Community [now EU] law confers a right to reparation where three conditions are met: the rule of law infringed must be intended to confer rights on individuals; the breach must be sufficiently serious; and there must be a direct causal link between the breach of the obligation resting on the State and the damage sustained by the injured parties (C-46/93, C-48/93 *Brasserie du Pêcheur SA* v. *Germany* and *R.* v. *Secretary of State for Transport, ex parte Factortame Ltd. and Others*, paragraph 51[21])

What is important to note is that liability for damages is not a first but a last resort and is aimed at the seriously recalcitrant state. This is what the ECJ means by a sufficiently serious breach of EU law. There must be little discretion open to the MS (Chalmers *et al.* 2010, p. 307). The state, as we saw earlier, is not disaggregated by the ECJ; therefore, controversially, the exposure to liability for damages extends to actions of national courts.[22] The same test is applied, but with one additional requirement. Because of the need for cases to be finalized (the principle of res judicata) and the importance of judicial independence and authority, liability is only triggered in the exceptional case where a national court has manifestly infringed EU law, including ECJ case law (Beutler 2009). Liability is limited to courts adjudicating at last instance – that is, there is no prospect of an appeal for their decision.

The TEU also requires MSs to provide remedies sufficient to ensure effective legal protection in the fields covered by EU law (TEU, Article 19.1). Thus MSs must not only ensure that they comply with EU law, but where there are transgressions and matters are brought before national courts, they must ensure that there are appropriate remedies provided for breach of EU law. This is supported by two well-established ECJ principles:

1. Any remedies for breach of EU law must be equivalent to what would be offered for breach of national law (the principle of equivalence).
2. The right to a remedy for breach of EU law must not be impossible to achieve in practice (the principle of practical possibility).[23]

The principle underlying this treaty provision and ECJ case law is efficacy: the ECJ is intent on ensuring that EU law is rendered effective and that the national courts have an important role to play in realizing that principle.

This TEU provision may be significant where a private party has suffered damage as a result of another private party's failure to comply with EU law. This has arisen in the context of competition law, where the ECJ has held that it should be possible to sue for damages for losses caused by contract or conduct liable to restrict or distort competition (contrary to the TFEU, Articles 101 and 102). The competition provisions of the TEU are the only ones that are expressly addressed to private conduct and hence are something of an anomaly. Thus while there is a strong efficacy argument for requiring damages actions between private parties for breach of the competition rules, it is not clear how much further this right can extend (Craig and de Búrca 2008, p. 334; cf. Drake 2006), though arguably the new Article 19 in the TEU may be relied on by private parties in national courts when seeking a remedy, and even to bring an action against the state itself for damages for failing to provide a remedy.

4.8 Interpretation and dispute resolution

The ECJ has been part of the institutional framework of the EU from the outset. Treaties are incomplete contracts between states: as legal documents, it is not possible to record every eventuality and some text is ambiguous to reflect the need to establish consensus; as foundational documents, the treaties are by definition not designed to be exhaustive. Thus an authoritative interpreter of the treaties is required, hence the establishment of the ECJ (Alter 1998a). In the early days the ECJ had little work (Arnull 2006, p. 5); Arnull refers to the apocryphal story of champagne being opened when the first preliminary reference arrived (p. 26). This has all changed with a busy court – some would argue too busy (Chalmers, *et al.* 2010, p. 178; Tridimas and Gari 2010). The ECJ resolves disputes between the MSs and the institutions. Enforcement actions are brought against the MSs (TFEU, Articles 258–60). On the other hand, judicial review actions are brought by the MSs and the institutions, challenging the legality of legislative acts and acts of bodies, offices and agencies of the EU that have legal effects (TFEU, Article 263). Individuals can also bring actions, but historically their standing was severely limited. This issue has been relaxed in the Lisbon Treaty, making actions by individuals more likely. The extension of the basis on which private individuals can challenge the validity of EU acts is long overdue – in a seminal opinion, A. G. Jacobs stated that the standing rules should be changed, but his view was rejected by the ECJ in the same case[24] (Granger 2003). As citizens can invoke directly effective EU legislation before national courts, it was important for them to have access to the EU courts also. This reflects a maturing of the relationship between the citizen, the EU and its courts.

Partly as a result of the very restricted access to the EU courts for individuals, the national courts became the principal route for individuals looking to assert their rights under EU law or to challenge the validity of EU law and actions, assisted by the doctrines of supremacy and direct effect. Just under half of the cases heard by the ECJ (and only the ECJ can hear them) are preliminary references (TFEU, Article 267; European Court of Justice 2009a, p. 82). This is the procedure whereby national courts can (or if they are courts of last resort, generally must) refer questions on the validity and interpretation of EU law to the ECJ. The procedure is a two-hander between the national court and the ECJ. A case starts in the national court and, when it becomes clear that there is an EU law dimension, the court may make a reference if a decision on the validity or interpretation of EU law is necessary for the outcome of the case. If it is a court of last resort – that is, there is no further appeal – it must make a reference, subject to the qualifications described below. The court sends the case to the ECJ with its questions. The ECJ then answers the questions (having first established whether they have already been addressed in previous case law, in which case it simply sends the earlier answer), and the matter is referred back to the national court for completion of the proceedings. The ECJ will redraft the questions if necessary, answer only some of them, or answer them in the order it deems best, in order to provide the answer it deems most appropriate to the case. Thus there is an element of uncertainty in making the reference, which can take on average seventeen months (European Court of Justice 2009a, p. 94). The ECJ never rules on national law. Instead it will hold that a rule of the type referred to by the national court is inconsistent with EU law – leaving it to the national court to disapply the law.[25] Sometimes ECJ judgments are rather Delphic, making it difficult, if not impossible, for national courts to decide how to proceed. On other occasions, ECJ rulings can be so precise as to leave little or no discretion to the national court in deciding the case. For example, in the notorious Sunday trading cases, the ECJ held that Sunday trading laws did have an effect on inter-state trade, but the effect would be lawful if its objective were to ensure that working and non-working hours were so arranged as to accord with the national or regional sociocultural characteristics and the law was proportionate.[26] No criteria were given to help national courts to apply the test, leading to chaos in the lower English courts and culminating in another reference, where a clear-cut answer was provided by the ECJ that the laws complied with EU law, leaving little discretion at the national level (Rawlings 1993; Maher 1996b).[27]

This procedure has proved to be the lynchpin of the EU judicial system (Alter 1998a; Stone Sweet and Brunell 1997). The national courts have embraced the procedure sufficiently to provide a vital line of communication between them and the ECJ, such that the ECJ undoubtedly has the authoritative voice on the validity and interpretation of EU law and the national courts can be regarded as EU courts (Maher 1994). In fact, the procedure has been so popular that the ECJ has had to constrain the obligation to refer in a number of ways (Craig and de Búrca 2008, p. 448). Thus it does not hear cases where the parties are not in genuine dispute.[28] EU law must be necessary for the resolution of the case, and the case referred must be sufficiently well set out that the ECJ can divine what the questions are and what the facts are.[29] The ECJ has also held that a national court does not have to refer if the matter has already been dealt with in an earlier case. And even if there is no precedent, there is no obligation to refer if the matter is so clear as to leave no scope for any reasonable doubt as to how the question is to be resolved.[30] This doctrine can only apply to interpretive questions: it is not for national courts to declare EU law invalid. The initial ECJ open-door approach has thus been modified, with steps taken to assist national courts, while also managing cases that do not raise significant legal issues and can safely be left to national courts. To facilitate national courts in preparing a case for reference, the ECJ has published a notice that summarizes its case law (European Court of Justice 2009a).

The partnership between the ECJ and national courts is now demarcated by the ECJ, which, on the one hand, restricts the scope for references from national courts, while on the other, trusts them to give effect to EU law. This procedure is the key to the constitutionalization of EU law. As a result of hearing such references, the ECJ developed the doctrines of supremacy and direct effect and its fundamental rights jurisprudence. The procedure is the basis for a form of dialogue between the ECJ and the higher national courts in particular. It is through this procedure that the key constitutional questions of the relationship between the EU legal order, national law and (what are now) EU citizens have arisen. Through this seemingly technical and innocuous procedure, the ECJ revolutionized EU law, creating a new legal order and giving national courts new powers to review national laws in the light of EU law and to disapply them. In doing so, the ECJ challenged the constitutional frameworks of MSs while simultaneously making national courts European courts and key participants in the development of the EU legal order.

4.9 Conclusion: the nature of EU law

The ECJ has been central to the development of EU law. It deals with many technical debates and discussions, hearing appeals on matters such as competition law, employment rights, social security entitlements and taxation. In addition to the bread-and-butter matters of a court, at the heart of a market integration project dealing with trade rules relating to goods and services, it also brought the EU on a constitutionalizing journey. The development of the twin doctrines of supremacy and direct effect at the very early stages of the Union (both in the early 1960s) has embedded them in the legal order at a time when the market integration project was struggling, such that as the competences of the Union grew, the penetration of the Union into the national legal orders increased to a greater degree than perhaps was ever envisaged by the original framers.

At the same time, the dual nature of the legal order places quite profound limits on this constitutionalizing process. The basis on which the doctrine of supremacy has been accepted by national constitutional courts differs from that of the ECJ. The ECJ predicated the

supremacy of EU law on its vision of the EU as a new legal order, where MSs had voluntarily given up their sovereign powers to the Union (or Community as it then was), and supported it with a strong pragmatic argument: that for the efficacy of EU law it had to apply consistently across all MSs and thus could not become a patchwork depending on variations introduced in national law. ECJ vision was strong, but it is fair to say that its jurisprudential reasoning was weak: there was little in the then treaties to support this view. Nonetheless the doctrine is now well established. However, its acceptance at national level was based not on EU law, but on national constitutional traditions (de Witte 1999). National constitutional courts derive their power and authority from their constitutions. This vantage point provides a stronger and democratically more secure basis for recognizing the supremacy of EU law. There is a confluence between the EU and national constitutional traditions in the doctrine of supremacy, but from different, yet equally valid, legal perspectives (MacCormick 1999). Furthermore, the national constitutional courts, and most notably the German constitutional court, have consistently noted that while they accept the supremacy doctrine, this is not without reservation: that the supremacy doctrine can only apply as long as fundamental rights are adequately protected in the EU.[31] Thus through its widely discussed judgments, the German court in particular, and other constitutional courts also,[32] have put down a benchmark that the EU as a creature of the MSs has its legal boundaries ultimately determined by those national constitutions (Hoffmann 2009; Halberstam and Möllers 2009). These considerations of the boundaries of the constitutionalizing process of the EU are first-order questions that arise infrequently in ECJ case law. They do, however, affect the grand moments of Union development, shaping how we understand the EU. What direction this constitutionalizing process will take after the Treaty of Lisbon is not clear, but undoubtedly the ECJ will remain a powerful integrating force in the Union.

Summary

- EU law is based on the rule of law, which means:
  - No one is above the law.
  - EU law aims to meet procedural norms to ensure fairness and consistency.

- EU law is based on principles of justice and fundamental rights. EU fundamental rights are based on the EU Charter of Fundamental Rights, the European Convention on Human Rights, the constitutional traditions common to the MSs and ECJ case law.
- The ECJ is central to how EU law develops, as its sole authoritative interpreter. Its doctrines of supremacy (EU law takes primacy over conflicting national laws) and direct effect (private parties may rely on EU law before national courts in certain circumstances) made the EU a new legal order.
- EU law has four main functions:
  - Framing – the treaties set out EU competence and what the institutions can do.
  - Rule-making – the treaties specify how law is made. New governance methods have become significant in the last decade.
  - Implementation and enforcement – MSs have primary responsibility for implementing EU law. To ensure EU law efficacy, the ECJ developed the doctrines of supremacy and direct effect. MSs may also be liable for damages if they breach their obligations. The new treaty requires the states to provide adequate remedies for breach of EU law – subject to the long-standing principles of equivalence (the remedy must be equivalent to one offered for the breach of a national law) and practical possibility (it must be possible to avail of the remedy).
  - Interpretation and dispute resolution – the new treaty loosens the previously very strict rules on standing for private individuals before the ECJ. Because individuals had such limited access to the court, national courts became the main means through which they could assert their EU rights. Thus the preliminary reference procedure, whereby national courts can refer questions of validity and interpretation of EU law to the ECJ, became a key mechanism in EU constitutionalization. Over half of the workload of the ECJ is preliminary references. It developed its human rights jurisprudence, the doctrines of direct effect and supremacy through preliminary reference cases. National courts embraced their role under EU law, working in partnership with the ECJ.

- While national courts generally accept the doctrines of direct effect and supremacy, they do so mainly by reference to their own constitutions. National constitutional courts, in particular the German court, also place limits on the EU legal order, suggesting that national constitutions determine its boundaries. The ECJ, on the other hand, seeks to determine those boundaries. This matter remains unresolved.

Questions and essay topics

1. What does it mean to say that the EU is based on the rule of law?
2. What are the main functions of EU law?
3. How does EU law seek to ensure that MSs meet their obligations under EU law?
4. On what bases are fundamental rights recognized in EU law?
5. What constraints are there on EU competences?
6. What are the main kinds of law that the EU can enact and how do they differ?
7. How has the ECJ strengthened its enforcement role?
8. 'The doctrines of supremacy and direct effect are fundamental to understanding the nature of EU law.' Discuss.
9. 'National courts are EU courts.' Discuss.

FURTHER READING

Alter, K. (2001) *Establishing the Supremacy of European Law: The Making of an International Rule of Law in Europe*, Oxford University Press.

Chalmers D., Davies G. and Monti, G. (2010) *European Union Law*, 2nd edn, Cambridge University Press.

Craig, P. and de Búrca, G. (eds.) (2011) *The Evolution of EU Law*, 2nd edn, Oxford University Press.

NOTES

1 C-50/00 P *Unión de Pequeños Agricultores* v. *Council* [2002] ECR I-6677, Opinion of Advocate General Jacobs.

2 Case 98/78 *Firma A. Racke* v. *Hauptzollamt Mainz* [1979] ECR 69.

3 Case 11/70 *Internationale Handelsgesellschaft* v. *Einfuhr- und vorratstelle für Getreide und Futtermittel* [1970] ECR 1125.

4 See e.g. C-94/03 *Commission* v. *Council* [2006] ECR I-1.

5 Case 26/62 *Van Gend en Loos* v. *Nederlandse Administratie der Belastingen* [1963] ECR 1, paragraph 3.

6 [1991] ECR I-6079, paragraph 21.

7 Case 39/72 *Commission* v. *Italy* [1973] ECR 101, paragraph 17.

8 For example see C-51/92 *Hercules Chemicals* v. *Commission* [1999] ECR I-4235, compare with C-189/02P, C-202/02P, C-208/02P. C-213/02P *Dansk Rørindustri A/S and others* v. *Commission* [2005] ECR I-5425.

9 See e.g. the first case where a fine was imposed, case C-387/97 Commission v. Greece [2000] ECR I-5047.

10 Case 77/69 *Commission* v. *Belgium* [1970] ECR 237.

11 Case 152/84 *Marshall* v. *Southampton and SW Hampshire Area Health Authority* [1986] ECR 723.

12 E.g. case C-298/97 *Commission* v. *Spain* [1998] ECR I-3301, paragraph 14.

13 [1970] ECR 1125, paragraph 3.

14 Case 106/77 *Amministrazione delle Finanze dello Stato* v. *Simmenthal SpA* [1978] ECR 629.

15 See note 5.

16 Case C-91/92 *Dori* v. *Recreb Srl* [1994] ECR I-3325.

17 Case C-188/89 *Foster* v. *British Gas* [1990] ECR I-3313.

18 Case 14/83 *Von Colson and Kamann* v. *Land Nordrhein-Westfalen* [1984] ECR 1891; case 106/89 *Marleasing* v. *La Comercial* [1990] ECR I-4135.

19 Case C-212/04 *Adeneler et al.* v. *Ellinikos Organismos Galaktos* (ELOG) [2006] ECR I-6057.

20 Case 14/83 *Von Colson and Kamann* v. *Land Nordrhein-Westfalen* [1984] ECR 1891, paragraph 26.

21 [1996] ECR I-1029.

22 Case C-224/01 *Köbler* v. *Austria* [2003] ECR I-10239; C-173/03 *Traghetti del Mesiterraneo SpA* v. *Italy* [2006] ECR I-5177.

23 Case 33/76 *Rewe-Zentralfinanz eG and Rewe-Zentral AG* v. *Landwirtschaftskammer für das Saarland* [1976] ECR 1989; case 45/76 Comet [1976] ECR 2043.

24 Case C-50/00 P *Unión de Pequeños Agricultores* v. *Council* [2002] ECR I-6677.

25 Case 6/64 *Costa* v. *ENEL* [1964] ECR 585.

26 Case 145/88 *Torfaen BC* v. *B&Q plc* [1989] ECR 3851.

27 Case C-169/91 *Council of the City of Stoke on Trent and Norwich City Council* v. *B&Q plc* [1992] ECR I-6635.

28 Case 104/79 *Foglia* v. *Novello* [1980] ECR 745.

29 See e.g. cases C-343/90 *Dias* v. *Director da Alfandega do Porto* [1992] ECR I-4673; C-318/00 *Bacardi-Martini SAS and Cellier des Dauphins* v. *Newcastle United Football Club* [2003] ECR I-905; C-320-322/90 *Telemarsicabruzzo spa* v. *Circostel, Ministero delle Poste e telecommunicazioni and Ministerio della Difesa* [1993] ECR I-393.

30 Case 283/81 *Srl CILFIT and Lanificio di Gavardo SpA* v. *Ministry of Health* [1982] ECR 3415.

31 Re Wünsche Handelsgesellschaft (Solange II) [1987] 3 CMLR 225; *Brunner* v. *The European Union Treaty* [1994] 1 CMLR 57; Lisbon Case BVerfG, 2 be/08 from 30 June 2009.

32 E.g. Polish membership of the EU (Accession Treaty) Polish Constitutional Court judgment K18/04, 11 May 2005.

5 The EU economy: bare essentials

ALI EL-AGRAA

The tables referred to in this chapter can be found online at www.cambridge.org/el-agraa

5.1 Introduction

This chapter describes the bare realities of the EU economy. The presentation is basically graphic, with the statistical tables on the accompanying website due to space limitations and for ease of regular updating. The graphs and statistics also consider EU immediate candidates, including the member nations of the European Free Trade Association (EFTA), because, apart from Switzerland, they all belong to the European Economic Area (EEA). Recall that the EEA is considered a stepping-stone to full EU membership (see Chapters 1 and 2, where it is also stated that Switzerland has a pending EU membership application). In order to preserve a general sense of perspective, similar information is given where appropriate for Canada, Mexico and the USA (the member nations of the North American Free Trade Agreement, or NAFTA), as well as for Japan and the Russian Federation (Russia), since, together with the four largest EU nations, they comprise the group of eight (G8). Data are also provided for China, due to its rapid ascent in the league of GDI, and for India, which is trying to emulate China and Brazil, because these three together with Russia, form what is referred to as the BRICs, which are becoming increasingly influential in international negotiations, especially in the World Trade Organization (WTO; see Chapters 1 and 24) and the group of twenty (G20).

The main purpose of this chapter is to provide the latest information, since the analysis of longer-term trends and the economic forces that influence them is one of the main tasks of the rest of this book. For example, the analysis of the composition and pattern of trade prior to EU inception and subsequent to its formation is the aim of Part II of the book (EU market integration: theory and practice), especially Chapters 8 and 9. Moreover, all the policy chapters are concerned

with the analysis of particular areas of interest, such as social policies, emphasizing the employment/unemployment problem, the Common Agricultural Policy (CAP), the role of the EU budget, competition and industrial policies, EU regional policy, and so on, and these specialist chapters contain detailed pertinent information.

5.2 Area and population concerns

Table 5.1a gives information on area, population and life expectancy at birth. Table 5.1b provides longer-term data on life expectancy for a selected number of countries. Table 5.2 offers supporting data on various aspects of health. Table 5.3 has data on the labour force and its distribution in terms of the broad categories of agriculture, industry and services, as well as on employment and unemployment. Table 5.4 completes the picture by providing information by economic activity during 2004–8. Hence the information in these tables is mainly about 'people'. The data are self-explanatory, but a few points warrant particular attention.

The EU of twenty-seven (EU27) has a larger population (about 500 million) than any country in the advanced Western world. This population exceeds that of the USA (just over 300 million) by about two-thirds, is over three and a half times that of Russia (just over 140 million) and about four times that of Japan. It exceeds the combined population of the USA, Canada and Mexico by 53 million, and that of the USA and Japan, the world's two largest economies, by 65 million (although China may have assumed Japan's position by the time this book is published).

The average annual rate of population growth during 1990–2008 was between –0.9 and 1.3 for the EU27, the highest being recorded for Ireland and the lowest for

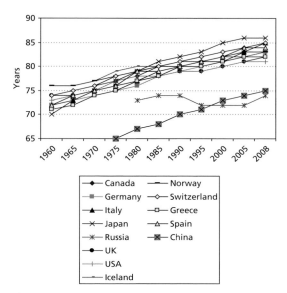

Figure 5.1 Female life expectancy at birth, 1960–2008

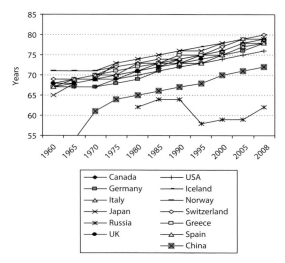

Figure 5.2 Male life expectancy at birth, 1960–2008

Estonia and Latvia. It is 1 for Canada and 1.1 for the USA, both with high immigration rates. Thus Turkey and Mexico, with 1.5, are the truly exceptional cases within the sample.

Average life expectancy at birth in 2008 was 72–82 years for the EU27 (79–82 for the EU15 – that is, without the twelve members joining in 2004 and 2007) and 78–83 years for Canada, Japan and the USA. It is 72, 73 and 75 years for Brazil, China and Mexico respectively, so they are not that far behind, but for Russia with 68 years and India with 64 years it is rather different. For the EU27 it is 77–85 (81–85 for the EU15) years for females and 66–79 (75–78 for the EU15) years for males, and 81–86 years for females and 76–78 years for males for Canada, Japan and the USA. For Brazil, China and Mexico it is 76, 65, 78 years and 69, 71, 73 years for females and males respectively; thus only Brazil is much different, but it still fares better than India, with 65 and 62 years for females and males. On the assumption that a difference of, say, four years for women and two years for men is of no major significance (there is hardly any need for a calculation of standard deviations here), one can assert that the advanced nations of the world have similar life expectancies for females and males. Indeed, this has been the case since 1960, as Figures 5.1 and 5.2, drawn from data in Table 5.1b, clearly reveal for females, males and the average; Russia is not an advanced nation. What is of

special interest is that China does not seem to be doing badly relative to the advanced world. One can therefore throw out of the window all the claims for food affording the Japanese longer lives, for three reasons. First, they lagged behind the rest in the earlier years – that is, they have not always been at the top. Second, in 2008 it is only Japanese women who are at the top, but by merely one year over their French, Italian and Swiss counterparts. Third, and vitally, Japanese life expectancy is highest in Okinawa, where the main diet is pork! It should be added that I make an exception using long-term data here, simply because the issue is not discussed in this way elsewhere in the book. What is even more interesting is that the USA has the lowest average among the advanced world, yet it spends much more on health (15.7 per cent) than any of them (8–11 per cent), as Table 5.2 clearly shows.

One should note that the EU unemployment rate (in 2008) as a whole is high (7 per cent) relative to the 4, 4.2 and 5.8 per cent rates in Japan, China and the USA respectively. The highest is recorded for Spain (11.3 per cent), with Slovakia (9.5 per cent) not far behind. There are, however, four countries with rates below 4 per cent, with the Netherlands achieving the lowest overall rate (2.8 per cent), and Slovenia at 4.4 per cent. Six countries fall in the 5.1–5.8 per cent range, four in the 6–6.7 per cent range and ten in the 7–7.7 per cent range. There is therefore a wide variation around the overall average. What may seem strange is the 7.5 per cent average rate for the Eurozone being higher than

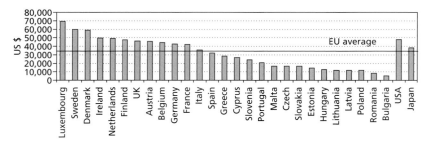

Figure 5.3 Per capita GNI, 2008

for the EU as a whole, but having one currency run by a single (European) central bank (ECB) does not guarantee otherwise, especially when unemployment is not an ECB remit. The variation within the Eurozone is much wider since it includes Spain, the country with the highest rate: three countries are below 4 per cent, one has 4.4 per cent, another four below 7 per cent. It is interesting that Denmark (3.3 per cent) and the UK (5.6 per cent) are on the low side, but to attribute this to their staying out of the euro glosses over the Netherlands' 2.8 per cent, the lowest for the entire EU. Unemployment has become such an important EU issue that it has developed into a policy area of its own: Chapter 22 on social policy is devoted almost entirely to it and it is also considered in other chapters, especially Chapters 11 and 12, since EMU impinges on it. All the tables and graphs in Chapter 22 are pertinent, so one can turn to them immediately without loss of continuity.

One should also note the dominance of the services sector in total employment. Services are mainly part of the tertiary sector, comprising such divergent items as banking, distribution, insurance, transport, catering and hotels, laundries and hairdressers, professional services of a more varied kind, publicly and privately provided, and so on. For the EU27 it is 35–71 per cent for men, but for eight of the twelve new members (NMSs) joining in 2004 and 2007 it is 52 per cent and lower. The rate is 46–90 per cent for women and 81–90 per cent if one excludes ten NMSs, the exceptions being Cyprus and Malta. This is significant, particularly since it has frequently been alleged that the size of this sector was the cause of the slow rate of growth in the UK economy a few decades ago; the USA, with its high growth rate, is on a par with the UK in this respect and the other advanced nations are not much different either (see next section). Also, the increasing size of this sector

over time led to the doctrine of deindustrialization: as this sector grows in percentage terms, it automatically follows that the other sectors, especially industry, must decline in relative terms.

5.3 GNI, per capita GNI and growth of GDP

Table 5.5 gives per capita GNI in 2008, using both the Atlas method (applied by the World Bank to smooth fluctuations in prices and exchange rates by utilizing a conversion factor that averages the exchange rate for a given year and the two preceding years, adjusted for differences in inflation rates) and purchasing power parity (PPP). The table also provides the ranking of nations in terms of both measures, as well as the basic industry distribution of GDP. Table 5.6 provides the average annual rate of GDP growth for 1990–2000 and 2000–2008.

As noted in Chapter 1, five EU member states (MSs) are ranked as the 4th to 8th largest GNI economies of the world, and the combined economic weight of the EU27, in terms of GNI, converted using the Atlas method (see above), exceeds that of NAFTA by about $249 billion (1.46 per cent), but falls short of it by about $2,384 billion (13.59 per cent), using PPP. However, one of the salient features is the disparity between EU MSs in terms of per capita GNI: the rank ranges from 3 (Luxembourg, with $69,390) to 96 (Bulgaria, with $5,490), and from 5 (again, Luxembourg, with $52,770) to 91 (again, Bulgaria, with $11,370) for the respective measures (see Figure 5.3 for how EU MSs fare relative to EU average per capita GNI). Indeed, the dispersion of income levels among EU MSs is much wider that between US states (see Figure 19.1, page

192). However, for the EU15, the respective ranges are 3–50 and 5–56; 3–32 and 5–39 if Greece, Portugal and Spain are excluded. For the twelve NMSs joining in 2004 and 2007, the ranges are 46–96 and 45–91. Hence, there is a very wide gap between the two groups, especially when Greece, Portugal and Spain are left out of the first group. Of EFTA countries, Norway and Liechtenstein outperform Luxembourg on the Atlas measure; Norway does so on the PPP method too, but most likely so does Liechtenstein (data are not available for the PPP method). Note that one should not read too much into Luxembourg's number 1 ranking among the EU27, given the dominance of high-ranking and well-paid EU officials there.

Of particular concern is the growth of GDP. As can be seen from Table 5.6, of the EU15, only Ireland has performed consistently well over the two periods: 7.4 per cent during 1990–2000 and 5 per cent during 2000–2008. For the other fourteen, except for Luxembourg, the rates were 1.5–3.2 per cent during 1990–2000; and except for Finland, Greece and Spain, they were –0.9 and 2.8 per cent respectively for the two periods. The twelve NMSs have done well over the second period (3.6–8.2 per cent), suggesting hope for the EU's future. The hope is enhanced by the good performance of the potential members: except for EFTA nations minus Iceland, the rates were 3.2–8.1 per cent during the second period. Note that Canada, Japan, Mexico and the USA have not fared any better than the EU15: 1.1–3.5 and 1.6–2.7 during the two respective periods. China and India are in a league of their own.

Another major concern is the distribution of income between the rich and the poor. Table 5.7 gives information on the distribution of income and consumption, but note that the survey years vary greatly: 1993 for Japan and 2008 for Mexico and Serbia; and within the EU27, 1995 for France and 2007 for Latvia. The table shows that for all the countries under consideration the highest 10 per cent received between 21.1 per cent in Germany and 43 per cent in Mexico; for the EU27 the respective percentages are obviously Germany's and the 29.8 per cent in Portugal. The Gini index ranges from 24.7 for Denmark to 55 in Brazil; for the EU27 obviously Denmark and the 38.5 for Portugal. Recalling that a Gini index of 0 represents perfect equality, it is interesting to note that the disparity is widest for Brazil (55), Mexico (51.6), the Russian Federation (43.7), Macedonia (42.8), China (41.5), Turkey (41.2), and the USA (40.8).

5.4 Demand

The structure of demand in 2008 is given in Table 5.8. It shows the percentage distribution of GDP between household final consumption expenditure (private consumption), general government final consumption expenditure (public consumption), gross capital formation (investment expenditure), gross domestic savings and the export/import of goods and services. Tables 5.9 and 5.10 then provide detailed information on the government, export and import sectors, gross international reserves, official development assistance (ODA) and gross foreign direct investment (FDI) as percentages of GDP. Note that data on any of these items are not available for Liechtenstein.

With regard to private consumption as a percentage of GDP in the EU in 2008, except for Greece with 71, it is 46–68 for the rest, but data are not available for Cyprus, Luxembourg and Malta. In Denmark, Ireland, the Netherlands and Sweden it is 46–49, while in Bulgaria, Hungary, Lithuania, Poland, Portugal, Romania and the UK it is 60–68. Of EU candidates, Norway has a low 39, followed by Switzerland (58) and Croatia (59), with the rest having 70–97. As to the comparators, except for the USA matching Greece (71), and China (34, the lowest of all) and Russia (48), the picture is similar to the EU.

The 9–27 for EU public consumption is a much narrower range compared to that of consumption. Hungary is the only one below 10, twelve are 16–19 and eleven are 20–27; again data are not available for Cyprus, Luxembourg and Malta. EU candidates and comparators fit well in this picture, with Albania and India matching Hungary's 9.

As to gross capital formation, of all the countries considered, the lowest percentage belongs to the UK (17 per cent), which is closely followed by the USA (18), and Canada and Germany (19 each). China has a high 44. Of the remaining 25 EU MSs, nineteen are 20–29 and six 30–38.

Ignoring Slovakia's –16, the percentage of gross domestic savings for EU MSs ranges from 5 (Cyprus) to 28 (Sweden). Of all the nations considered, China stands out with 54, followed by Bosnia and Herzegovina and Norway with 42, and Russia with 32. Note that in all the twelve NMSs joining the EU since 2004, gross savings fall short of gross capital formation, with a significant difference in Bulgaria, Estonia, Latvia, Lithuania and Slovakia.

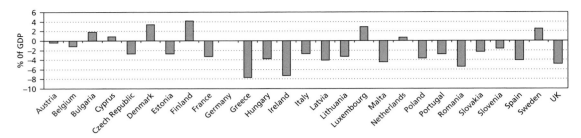

Figure 5.4 Budget deficits, 2009

Exports of goods and services loom large in the case of Luxembourg (179 per cent). It is followed by Belgium (92), Malta (88), Slovakia (83) and Hungary (81). Of the remaining EU MSs, five are 23–29, two are 30–33, five are 42–47, four are 54–59, one is 60 and five are 70–79. Of the other nations considered, India is 81 and is followed by Switzerland (56) and Macedonia (53), with all the others below 50.

Imports of goods and services behave in a roughly similar fashion, the exceptions being Bulgaria, with exports at 60 per cent and imports at 83 per cent, Cyprus (47 and 59), Lithuania (59 and 71) and the Netherlands, where it is the other way round (77 and 69). Of EU candidates, except for Norway (48 and 29) and Switzerland (56 and 47), all have imports exceeding exports. Of the comparators, only China (37 and 28), Russia (31 and 22) and the USA (12 and 17) are different.

Considering all these items together, the USA is almost in a league of its own in terms of high private consumption coupled with low gross domestic savings, exports and imports. Japan has high gross domestic savings and capital formation and low export/import rates.

Table 5.9 shows the dissimilarity between EU MSs with respect to both their total government expenditure and current revenue as percentages of 2008 GDP (see Chapter 19 for details and analysis). In terms of total expenditure, the range is between 26.3 per cent for Spain and 48.3 per cent for Malta. This is in stark contrast to China (11.4 per cent), Mexico (15 per cent), Japan (15.3 per cent), India (16.2 per cent), Canada (17.8 per cent), Switzerland (17.6 per cent) and even the USA (22.7 per cent).

Of particular interest for the EU are the sizes of budget deficit and public borrowing, since they are two of the five Maastricht criteria for EMU membership and a requirement of the Growth and Stability Pact

(GSP; see Chapters 11 and 12). These are specified as a maximum of 3 per cent of GDP for the former and 60 per cent of GDP for the latter. These are presented in Figures 5.4 and 5.5. Of the Eurozone seventeen, in 2008 Ireland (–7.3 per cent), Greece (–7.7), Spain (–4.1), France (–3.3) and Malta (–4.5) failed on the budget deficit count, with Italy and Estonia not far behind (–2.7). Of the remaining EU MSs, Hungary, Latvia, Lithuania, Poland, Romania and the 'opt-out' UK also failed, with the Czech Republic close behind. And of EU candidates, Iceland failed too, and terribly so, at –13.5. Note that the USA would also fail. With regard to public borrowing, the picture is not very different: of the Eurozone seventeen, Italy (106.1 per cent), Greece (99.2), Belgium (89.9), Hungary (72.9), France (67.5), Portugal (66.3), Germany (66), Malta (63.7) and Austria (62.5) fail, with the Netherlands not far behind (58.2). All the rest are fine except for Japan, which stands in a league of its own with 164.

A frequently cited figure is the percentage of GDP spent on ODA extended to developing countries and multilateral agents, given in Table 5.10, due to the developing countries' plea (through UNCTAD) that it should be 0.5 per cent (originally 1 per cent) of the major donor countries' GDP. As the table shows, of EU MSs, Luxembourg (1.22 per cent), Sweden (1.01 per cent), Denmark (0.87 per cent), the Netherlands (0.86 per cent), Ireland (0.6 per cent) and Belgium (0.53) meet the target. But, given that the low percentages for Greece and Portugal are understandable and that the NMSs have been having special EU assistance through Agenda 2000 (see Chapters 2, 21 and 24) and its successor, except for Italy (0.23 per cent), the EU as a whole seems to be doing very well. Yet even Italy leaves Japan (0.2 per cent) and the USA (0.18) as the black sheep of the family.

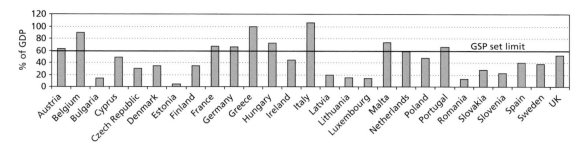

Figure 5.5 Net public borrowing, 2008

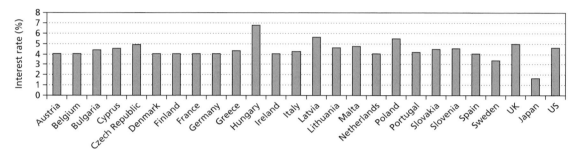

Figure 5.6 Long-term interest rates, 2007

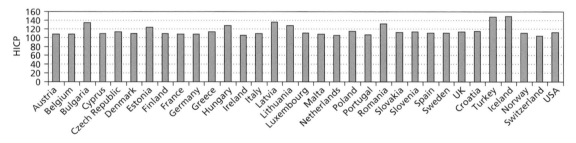

Figure 5.7 Harmonized index of consumer prices (HICP), 2009 (2005 = 100)

5.5 Price indices and real interest and exchange rates

Table 5.11 provides information on consumer and wholesale price indices, and on real interest and exchange rates. The first two items are under the control of the ECB, which has a set inflation target (see Chapter 12) and hence dictates the nominal interest rate for the Eurozone nations. Of particular interest is the variation in the price indices – and hence in the real interest rates, which are noted for their absence – for the seventeen, given a one-interest-rate policy for them all. Figure 5.6 shows the long-term interest rates for the

EU27 in 2007; the nominal rates after the financial crisis since 2007 do not make much sense, due to their being pushed unusually low to deal with the situation. Figure 5.7 depicts the inflation rates in terms of the EU harmonized index of consumer prices (HICP).[1]

5.6 Direction of trade

Table 5.12 gives the percentage share in total exports by a country going to the EU, and Table 5.13 does the same for imports, while Figure 5.8 provides a graph for both. Hence the two tables together are for EU member

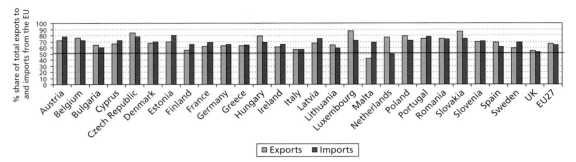

Figure 5.8 Exports to and imports from the EU, 2009

nations about the extent of intra-EU trade. As the notes to the tables clearly indicate, these percentages are not strictly comparable, due to the changing number of EU nations; note, for example, the differences in the two columns for 2000, where the first relates to the EU15 and the second to the EU25. For an analysis of the proper trends, the reader should consult Chapter 9, and for a full analysis El-Agraa (1989a, 1999).

Table 5.12 and Figure 5.8 show that in 2009 all EU MSs bar Malta sent more than 50 per cent of their total exports to each other, but although Malta sent only 42.4, the year 2009 is not typical, since it sent 49.4 and 49.3 in 2004 and 2007 respectively. Finland, Italy, Sweden and the UK sent 55–58.5 per cent of their exports to other EU MSs, twelve sent 61.5–69.3, seven sent 71.8–79.3, and the Czech Republic, Luxembourg and Slovakia sent more than 80 per cent. Thus most export trade is intra-EU, with the average being 66.6 per cent. This picture is matched by all those EU candidates for whom we have data, with Albania and Norway on more than 80 per cent and Iceland on 75.9 per cent. Of the comparator countries, Mexico sends a high 90.4 per cent, India 65 per cent, Russia 59.9 per cent and Brazil 49.8 per cent, so they too act likewise. The USA (21.2 per cent) and China (20.5 per cent) export about a fifth to the EU; not so Japan (14.1 per cent) and Canada (7.5).

Table 5.13 and Figure 5.8 provide a similar picture for imports. It shows that in 2009 all EU MSs bought more than 50 per cent of their total imports from each other, but at 49.2 per cent the Netherlands is not too much of an odd one out. Hence most import trade is intra-EU. Italy, Lithuania and the UK are on 52.7–58.8, eleven are on 60.3–69.9 and twelve are on 70.8–79.7. The table also shows that EFTA countries, Brazil, India,

Mexico and Russia conduct most of their trade with the EU.

Taking exports and imports together, it follows that most EU trade is intra-EU – that is, EU MSs conduct most of their trade between themselves, not with the 'outside world'.

5.7 Tariff barriers

One of the major concerns of the world economy is the level of protectionism practised by all nations, especially by the advanced. Table 5.14 provides the level of tariff barriers for our group of countries; there is one figure for each item for the EU, simply because it has a common commercial policy – that is, all member nations have the same policy, conducted by the European Commission (see Chapters 1 and 23).

The table clearly shows that for all products the simple mean EU tariff rate is lower than that in Japan and the USA, being almost half of the latter's. But the weighted mean EU tariff rate is higher (1.7 per cent), albeit marginally so (1.3 and 1.5 per cent for Japan and the USA respectively). However, on both the primary and manufactured product categories, both the means in the EU are lower, much lower on the simple bound rates (2.3 as against 4.9, and 2.5 and 1.5 versus 2.3 and 3.1) and on the weighted primary products (0.4 versus 2.3 and 1.0). In comparison, Canada is almost on a par, but Switzerland, with zero rates all round, is the most open and Norway is next, but closer to the EU.

It is well known, however, that tariffs have been coming down ever since the General Agreement on Tariffs and Trade (GATT, run by the World Trade Organization, WTO, since 1995) was established in

1947, so the real question is the extent of non-tariff barriers (NTBs), but these are difficult to quantify in terms of what is on this table (see Chapters 1, 7 and 23).

NOTES

1 HICPs are economic indicators constructed to measure the changes over time in the prices of consumer goods and services acquired by households. HICPs give comparable measures of inflation in the Eurozone, the EU, the European Economic Area and for other countries, including accession and candidate countries. They are calculated according to a harmonized approach and a single set of definitions. They provide the official measure of consumer price inflation in the Eurozone for the purposes of monetary policy in the Eurozone and assessing inflation convergence, as required under the Maastricht criteria.

Part II   EU market integration: theory and practice

6 **The theory of economic integration**
7 **The economics of the single market**
8 **Factor mobility**
9 **Measuring the economic impact of European integration**

Part II of this book is devoted to a discussion of the theoretical and practical aspects of EU market integration. Chapter 6 covers the theory of economic integration, providing an overall picture of the analysis of the economic implications of the creation of a single market on both the partner nations and the rest of the world. It is followed by a consideration of these aspects in terms of the EU's Single European Market (SEM) in Chapter 7, with Chapter 8 dealing entirely with the question of the free movement of capital, labour and enterprise within the EU. Chapter 9 then deals with the nature and problems of the measurement of the impact of the formation of the EU on trade, production and factor mobility.

The theoretical aspect of this part of the book is basically concerned with three concepts: trade creation, trade diversion and unilateral tariff reduction. These can be illustrated quite simply as follows. In Table II.1 the cost of beef per kg is given in pence for the UK, France and New Zealand (NZ). With a 50 per cent non-discriminatory tariff rate, the cheapest source of supply of beef for the UK consumer is the home producer. When the UK and France form a customs union, the cheapest source of supply becomes France. Hence the UK saves 10p per kg of beef, making a total saving of £1 million for 10 million kg (obviously an arbitrarily chosen quantity). This is trade creation: *the replacement of expensive domestic production by cheaper imports from the partner.*

In Table II.2 the situation is different for butter as a result of a lower initial non-discriminatory tariff rate (25 per cent) by the UK. Before the customs union, New Zealand is the cheapest source of supply for the UK consumer. After the customs union, France becomes the cheapest source. There is a total loss to the UK of £1 million, since the tariff revenue is claimed by the government. This is trade diversion: *the replacement of cheaper initial imports from the outside world by expensive imports from the partner.*

Table II.1 Beef illustrating trade creation

	UK	France	NZ
The cost per unit (p)	90	80	70
UK domestic price with a 50% tariff rate (p)	90	120	105
UK domestic price when the UK and France form a customs union (p)	90	80	105

Table II.2 Butter illustrating trade diversion

	UK	France	NZ
The cost per unit (p)	90	80	70
UK domestic price with a 25% tariff rate (p)	90	100	87.5
UK domestic price when the UK and France form a customs union (p)	90	80	87.5

Table II.3 Beef illustrating unilateral tariff reduction

	UK	France	NZ
The cost per unit (p)	90	80	70
UK domestic price with a 50% tariff rate (p)	90	100	105
UK domestic price with a non-discriminatory tariff reduction of 80% (i.e. tariff rate becomes 10%) (p)	90	80	77

Table II.4 Butter illustrating unilateral tariff reduction

	UK	France	NZ
The cost per unit (p)	90	80	70
UK domestic price with a 25% tariff rate (p)	90	100	87.5
UK domestic price with a non-discriminatory tariff reduction of 80% (i.e. tariff rate becomes 5%) (p)	90	80	73.5

In Tables II.3 and II.4 there are two commodities: beef and butter. The cost of beef per kg is the same as in the previous example, as is the cost of butter per kg. Note that Table II.3 starts from the same position as Table II.1, and Table II.4 from the same position as Table II.2. Here the UK does not form a customs union with France; rather, it reduces its tariff rate by 80 per cent on a non-discriminatory basis – that is, it adopts a policy of unilateral tariff reduction.

Total cost before the customs union = 90p × 10 million kg = £9 million

Total cost after the customs union = 80p × 10 million kg = £8 million

Total savings for the UK consumer = £1 million

Total cost to the UK government before the customs union = 70p × 10 million kg = £7 million

Total cost to the UK after the customs union = 80p × 10 million kg = £8 million

Total loss to the UK government = £1 million

Total cost to the UK before the tariff reduction = 90p × 10 million kg = £9 million

Total cost to the UK after tariff reduction = 70p × 10 million kg = £7 million

Total savings for the UK = £2 million

Now consider Tables II.3 and II.4 in comparison with Tables II.1 and II.2.

Total cost for Tables II.1 and II.2 before the customs union = £9 million + £7 million = £16 million

Total cost to the UK before the tariff reduction = 70p × 10 million kg = £7 million

Total cost to the UK after the tariff reduction = 70p × 10 million kg = £7 million

Total savings for the UK = nil

The combined total cost for Tables II.1 and II.2 after the customs union = £8 million + £8 million = £16 million

The combined total cost for Tables II.3 and II.4 after the unilateral tariff reduction = £7 million + £7 million = £14 million

This gives a saving of £2 million in comparison with the customs union situation. Hence a non-discriminatory tariff reduction is more economical for the UK than the formation of a customs union with France. Therefore, *unilateral tariff reduction is superior to customs union formation.*

This dangerously simple analysis (since a number of simplistic assumptions are implicit in the analysis and all the data are chosen to prove the point) has been the inspiration for a massive literature on customs union theory. Admittedly, some of the contributions are misguided in that they concentrate on a non-problem due to definitional misspecification, as explained in the following chapter.

Chapter 6 tackles the basic concepts of trade creation, trade diversion and unilateral tariff reduction, considers the implications of domestic distortions and scale economies for the basic analysis, and discusses the terms of trade effects. Chapter 7 discusses the measurement of the theoretical concepts discussed in Chapter 6.

6 The theory of economic integration

ALI EL-AGRAA

6.1 Introduction

In reality, some existing schemes of economic integration, especially the EU, were either proposed or formed for political reasons, even though the arguments popularly put forward in their favour were expressed in terms of possible economic gains. However, no matter what the motives for economic integration are, it is still necessary to analyse the economic implications of such geographically discriminatory groupings; that is why I included political unions as schemes of economic integration in Chapter 1 (see Section 1.2, page 1).

The chapter begins with a static analysis of the effects of economic integration on trade and production, first in partial- and then in general-equilibrium terms; static in the sense of immediate effects that do not allow for changes in consumption and production patterns. It goes on to examine these effects in dynamic terms, allowing time for changes to occur in the consumption and production patterns. Domestic distortions in the markets are then included, followed by the incorporation of changes in international prices on the analysis. Then elements of factor mobility are ushered in before various other considerations are briefly dealt with and conclusions stated. It should be stressed, however, that this chapter requires an understanding of trade theory, but the basic concepts involved have already been introduced in the introduction to this part of the book.

To understand these effects, one needs to appreciate the *possible* sources of economic gain from economic integration. At the customs union (CU) and free trade area (FTA) level they can be attributed to:

1. enhanced efficiency in production made possible by increased specialization in accordance with the law of comparative advantage;

2. increased production level due to better exploitation of economies of scale made possible by the increased size of the market;

3. an improved international bargaining position, made possible by the larger size, leading to better terms of trade (t/t);

4. enforced changes in economic efficiency brought about by enhanced competition;

5. changes affecting both the amount and quality of the factors of production arising from technological advances.

If the level of economic integration is to proceed beyond the CU level to the economic union level, then further sources of gain become *possible* as a result of:

6. factor mobility across the borders of member nations;

7. the coordination of monetary and fiscal policies;

8. the goals of near full employment, higher rates of economic growth and better income distribution becoming unified targets.

I shall now discuss these considerations in some detail.

6.2 The customs union aspects

6.2.1 The basic concepts

Before the theory of second best was introduced, it used to be the accepted tradition that CU formation should be encouraged. The rationale for this was that since free trade maximized world welfare, and since CU formation was a move towards free trade, CUs increased welfare, even though they did not maximize it. This rationale certainly lies behind the guidelines of the GATT-WTO Article XXIV (see Section 1.3, page 2), which permits the formation of CUs and FTAs as the special exceptions to the rules against international discrimination.

Viner (1950), and arguably Byé (1950), challenged this proposition by stressing that CU formation is by no means equivalent to a move to free trade, since it amounts to free trade between the members and protection vis-à-vis the outside world. This combination of free trade and protectionism could result in trade creation and/or trade diversion. Trade creation (TC) is *the replacement of expensive domestic production by cheaper imports from a partner*, and trade diversion (TD) is *the replacement of cheaper initial imports from the outside world by more expensive imports from a partner*. Viner stressed that TC is beneficial since it does not affect the rest of the world, while TD is harmful; it is the relative strength of these two effects that determines whether or not CU formation should be advocated. It is therefore important to understand the implications of these concepts.

Assuming perfect competition in both the commodity and factor markets, automatic full employment of all resources, costless adjustment procedures, perfect factor mobility nationally, but perfect immobility across national boundaries, prices determined by cost, three countries, H (the home country), P (the potential CU partner) and W (the outside world), plus all the traditional assumptions employed in tariff theory, we can use a simple diagram to illustrate these two concepts.

In Figure 6.1, I use partial equilibrium diagrams, but will employ general equilibrium ones in most of the rest of this chapter, even though it has been demonstrated that partial and general equilibrium analyses are, under certain circumstances, equivalent (see El-Agraa and Jones 1981). S_W is W's perfectly elastic tariff-free supply curve, for this commodity; S_H is H's supply curve, while S_{H+P} is the joint H and P tariff-free supply curve. With a non-discriminatory tariff (t) imposition by H of AD ($= t_H$), the effective supply curve facing H is $BREFQT$ – that is, its own supply curve up to E, then that of W inclusive of the tariff [$SW(1 + t_H)$]; obviously $S_H(1 + t_H)$ will lie above S_H and hence would be out of the picture. The domestic price is therefore OD, which gives domestic production of Oq_2, domestic consumption of Oq_3 and imports of q_2q_3. H pays q_2LMq_3 ($= a$) for the imports, while the domestic consumer pays q_2EFq_3 ($a + b + c$), with the difference ($LEFM = b + c$) being the tariff revenue which accrues to the H government. This government revenue can be viewed as a transfer from

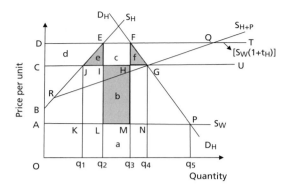

Figure 6.1 Trade creation and trade diversion

the consumers to the government, with the implication that, when the government spends it, the marginal valuation of that expenditure should be exactly equal to its valuation by the private consumers, so that no distortions should occur.

If H and W form a CU, the free trade position will be restored, so that Oq_5 will be consumed in H and this amount will be imported from W. Hence free trade is obviously the ideal situation. But if H and P form a CU, the tariff imposition will still apply to W while it is removed from P. The effective supply curve in this case is $BRGQT$. The union price falls to OC, resulting in a fall in domestic production to Oq_1, an increase in consumption to Oq_4 and an increase in imports to q_1q_4. These imports now come from P.

The welfare implications of these changes can be examined by employing the concepts of consumers' and producers' surpluses. As a result of increased consumption, consumers' surplus rises by $CDFG$ ($= d + e + c + f$). Part of this (d) is a fall in producers' surplus due to the decline in domestic production, and another part (c) is a portion of the tariff revenue now transferred back to the consumer subject to the same condition of equal marginal valuation. This leaves e and f as gains from CU formation. However, before we conclude whether or not these triangles represent net gains, we need to consider the overall effects more carefully.

The fall in domestic production from Oq_2 to Oq_1 leads to increased imports of q_1q_2. These cost q_1JIq_2 to import from P, while they originally cost q_1JEq_2 to produce domestically. (Recall the assumption that these resources are to be employed elsewhere in the economy without any adjustment costs or redundancies.) There is therefore a saving of e. The increase in consumption from Oq_3 to Oq_4 leads to new imports of q_3q_4, which cost q_3HGq_4 to import from P. These give a welfare satisfaction to the consumer equal to q_3FGq_4. There is therefore an increase in satisfaction of f. However, the *initial* imports of q_2q_3 cost the country a, but these imports now come from P, costing $a + b$. Therefore these imports lead to a loss in government revenue of b (c being a retransfer). It follows that the triangle gains ($e + f$) have to be compared with the loss of tariff revenue (b) before a definite conclusion can be made regarding whether or not the net effect of CU formation has been one of gain or loss.

It should be apparent that q_2q_3 represents, in terms of our definition, TD, and $q_1q_2 + q_3q_4$ represents TC, or, alternatively, that areas $e + f$ are TC (benefits), while area b is TD (loss). (The reader should note that I am using Johnson's (1974) definition so as to avoid the unnecessary literature relating to a trade-diverting welfare-improving CU promoted by Gehrels (1956–7), Lipsey (1960) and Bhagwati (1971).) It is obvious, then, that TC is economically desirable, while TD is undesirable: hence Viner's conclusion that it is the relative strength of these two effects that should determine whether or not CU formation is beneficial or harmful.

The reader should note that if the initial price is that given by the intersection of D_H and S_H (due to a higher tariff rate), the CU would result in pure TC, since the tariff rate is prohibitive. If the price is initially OC (due to a lower tariff rate), then CU formation would result in pure TD. It should also be apparent that the size of the gains and losses depends on the price elasticities of S_H, S_{H+P} and D_H, and on the divergence between S_W and S_{H+P} – that is, international cost differences.

6.2.2 The Cooper–Massell criticism

Viner's conclusion was challenged by Cooper and Massell (1965a). They suggested that the reduction in price from OD to OC should be considered in two stages: first, by reducing the tariff level indiscriminately – that is, for both W and P – to AC, which gives the same union price and production, consumption and import changes; second, by introducing the CU starting from the new price OC. The effect of these two steps is that the gains from the TC ($e + f$) still accrue, while the losses from TD (b) no longer apply, since the new effective supply curve facing H is $BJGU$, which ensures that imports continue to come from W at the

cost of a. In addition, the new imports due to TC ($q_1q_2 + q_3q_4$) now cost less, leading to a further gain of $KJIL$ plus $MHGN$. Cooper and Massell then conclude that *a policy of unilateral tariff reduction (UTR) is superior to customs union formation*. This criticism was challenged by Wonnacott and Wonnacott (1981), but their position was questioned by El-Agraa and Jones (2000a, b), although El-Agraa (2002a) demonstrates that it can be validated when WTO's Article XXIV rules are incorporated into the analysis; I shall return to these considerations in Section 6.2.7, since a different theoretical model is needed for these analyses.

6.2.3 Further contributions

Immediately following the Cooper–Massell criticism came two independent but somewhat similar contributions to the theory of CUs. The first development was by Cooper and Massell (1965b) themselves, the essence of which is that two countries acting together can do better than if each acts in isolation. The second was by Johnson (1965b), and was a private plus social costs and benefits analysis expressed in political economy terms. Both contributions utilize a 'public good' argument, with Cooper and Massell's expressed in practical terms and Johnson's in theoretical terms. However, because the Johnson approach is expressed in familiar terms, this section is devoted to it, since space limitations do not permit a consideration of both. There is, however, another reason for doing so: most of the new developments mentioned later can be tackled within this framework.

Johnson's method is based on four major assumptions:

1. Governments use tariffs to achieve certain non-economic (political, etc.) objectives.
2. Actions taken by governments are aimed at offsetting differences between private and social costs. They are, therefore, rational efforts.
3. Government policy is a rational response to the demands of the electorate.
4. Countries have a preference for industrial production.

In addition to these assumptions, Johnson makes a distinction between private and public consumption goods, real income (utility enjoyed from both private and public consumption, where consumption is the sum of planned consumption expenditure and planned investment expenditure) and real product (defined as total production of privately appropriable goods and services).

These assumptions have important implications. First, competition among political parties will make the government adopt policies that will tend to maximize consumer satisfaction from both 'private' and 'collective' consumption goods. Satisfaction is obviously maximized when the *rate of satisfaction per unit of resources is the same in both types of consumption goods*. Second, collective preference for industrial production implies that consumers are willing to expand industrial production (and industrial employment) beyond what it would be under free international trade.

Tariffs are the main source of financing this policy, simply because GATT-WTO regulations rule out the use of export subsidies, and domestic political considerations make tariffs, rather than the more efficient production subsidies, the usual instruments of protection.

Protection will be carried to the point where the *value of the marginal utility derived from collective consumption of domestic and industrial activity is just equal to the marginal excess private cost of protected industrial production.*

The marginal excess cost of protected industrial production consists of two parts: the marginal production cost and the marginal private consumption cost. The marginal production cost is equal to the proportion by which domestic cost exceeds world market costs. In a very simple model this is equal to the tariff rate. The marginal private consumption cost is equal to the loss of consumer surplus due to the fall in consumption brought about by the tariff rate that is necessary to induce the marginal unit of domestic production. This depends on the tariff rate and the price elasticities of supply and demand.

In equilibrium, the proportional marginal excess private cost of protected production measures the marginal 'degree of preference' for industrial production. This is illustrated in Figure 6.2, where S_W is the world supply curve at world market prices; D_H is the constant-utility demand curve (at free trade private utility level); S_H is the domestic supply curve; S_{H+u} is the marginal private cost curve of protected industrial production, including the excess private consumption cost (*FE* is the first component of marginal excess cost

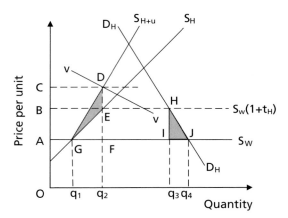

Figure 6.2 Marginal 'degree of preference' for industrial production

– determined by the excess marginal cost of domestic production in relation to the free trade situation due to the tariff imposition (*AB*) – and the area *GED* (= *IHJ*) is the second component, which is the dead loss in consumer surplus due to the tariff imposition); the height of *vv* above S_W represents the marginal value of industrial production in collective consumption; and *vv* represents the preference for industrial production that is assumed to yield a diminishing marginal rate of satisfaction.

The maximization of *real* income is achieved at the intersection of *vv* with S_{H+u}, requiring the use of tariff rate *AB*/*OA* to increase industrial production from Oq_1 to Oq_2 and involving the marginal degree of preference for industrial production *v*. Note that the higher the value of *v*, the higher the tariff rate, and that the degree of protection will tend to vary inversely with the ability to compete with foreign industrial producers. It is also important to note that, in equilibrium, the government is maximizing real income, not real product: maximization of real income makes it necessary to sacrifice real product in order to gratify the preference for collective consumption of industrial production. It is also important to note that this analysis is not confined to net importing countries. It is equally applicable to net exporters, but lack of space prevents such elaboration (see El-Agraa 1984b for a detailed explanation).

The above model helps to explain the significance of Johnson's assumptions. It does not, however, throw any light on the CU issue. To make the model useful for this purpose it is necessary to alter some of the assumptions. Let us assume that industrial production is not one aggregate, but a variety of products in which countries have varying degrees of comparative advantage, that countries differ in their overall comparative advantage in industry as compared with non-industrial production, that no country has monopoly–monopsony power (conditions for optimum tariffs do not exist) and that no export subsidies are allowed (GATT-WTO).

The variety of industrial production allows countries to be both importers and exporters of industrial products. This, in combination with the preference for industrial production, will motivate each country to practise some degree of protection.

Given the third assumption, a country can gratify its preference for industrial production only by protecting the domestic producers of the commodities it imports (import-competing industries). Hence the condition for equilibrium remains the same: $vv = S_{H+u}$. The condition must now be reckoned differently, however: S_{H+u} is slightly different because, first, the protection of import-competing industries will reduce exports of both industrial and non-industrial products (for balance of payments purposes). Hence, in order to increase total industrial production by one unit, it will be necessary to increase protected industrial production by more than one unit so as to compensate for the induced loss of industrial exports. Second, the protection of import-competing industries reduces industrial exports by raising their production costs (because of perfect factor mobility). The stronger this effect, *ceteris paribus*, the higher the marginal excess cost of industrial production. This will be greater the larger the industrial sector compared with the non-industrial sector and the larger the protected industrial sector relative to the exporting industrial sector.

If the world consists of two countries, one must be a net exporter and the other necessarily a net importer of industrial products, and the balance of payments is settled in terms of the non-industrial sector. Therefore for each country the prospective gain from reciprocal tariff reduction must lie in the expansion of exports of industrial products. The reduction of a country's own tariff rate is therefore a source of loss, which can be compensated for only by a reduction of the other country's tariff rate (for an alternative, orthodox, explanation, see El-Agraa 1979b, c).

What if there are more than two countries? If reciprocal tariff reductions are arrived at on a most-favoured

nation basis, then the reduction of a country's tariff rate will increase imports from *all* the other countries. If the tariff rate reduction is discriminatory (starting from a position of non-discrimination), however, then there are two advantages: first, a country can offer its partner an increase in exports of industrial products without any loss of its own industrial production by diverting imports from third countries (TD); second, when TD is exhausted, any increase in partner industrial exports to this country is exactly equal to the reduction in industrial production in the same country (TC), thus eliminating the gain to third countries.

Therefore, discriminatory reciprocal tariff reduction costs each partner country less, in terms of the reduction in domestic industrial production (if any) incurred per unit increase in partner industrial production, than does non-discriminatory reciprocal tariff reduction. On the other hand, preferential tariff reduction imposes an additional cost on the tariff-reducing country: the excess of the costs of imports from the partner country over their cost in the world market.

The implications of this analysis are as follows:

1. Both TC and TD yield a gain to the CU partners.
2. TD is preferable to TC for the preference-granting country, since a sacrifice of domestic industrial production is not required.
3. Both TC and TD may lead to increased efficiency due to economies of scale.

Johnson's contribution has not been popular because of the nature of his assumptions. His economic rationale for CUs, resting on public goods grounds, can only be established if for political or similar reasons governments are denied the use of direct production subsidies. While this may be the case in certain countries at certain periods in their economic evolution, there would appear to be no acceptable reason why this should generally be true. Johnson's analysis demonstrates that CUs and other acts of commercial policy 'may make economic sense under certain restricted conditions, but in no way does it establish or seek to establish a general argument for these acts' (Krauss 1972).

6.2.4 General equilibrium analysis

The conclusions of the partial equilibrium analysis can easily be illustrated in general equilibrium terms. To simplify the analysis we shall assume that H is a 'small'

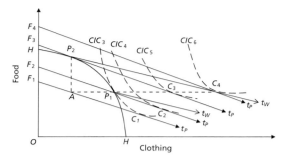

Figure 6.3 General equilibrium of the Cooper–Massell argument

country, while P and W are 'large' countries – that is, H faces constant t/t (t_p and t_w) throughout the analysis. Also, in order to avoid repetition, the analysis proceeds immediately to the Cooper–Massell proposition.

In Figure 6.3, HH is the production possibility frontier for H. Initially, H is imposing a prohibitive non-discriminatory tariff which results in P_1 as both the production and consumption point, given that t_w is the most favourable t/t – that is, W is the most efficient country in the production of clothing. The formation of the CU leads to free trade with the partner, P; hence production moves to P_2 where t_p is at a tangent to HH, and consumption to C_3 where CIC_5 is at a tangent to t_p. A unilateral tariff reduction (UTR), which results in P_2 as the production point, results in consumption at C_4 on CIC_6 (if the tariff revenue is returned to the consumers as a lump sum) or at C_3 (if the tariff is retained by the government). Note that at C_4 trade is with W only.

Given standard analysis, it should be apparent that the situation of UTR and trade with W results in exports of AP_2, which are exchanged for imports of AC_4, of which C_3C_4 is the tariff revenue. In terms of Johnson's distinction between consumption and production gains and his method of calculating them (see El-Agraa 1983b, Chapters 4 and 10), these effects can be expressed in relation to food only. Given a Hicksian income compensation variation, it should be clear that: (i) F_1F_2 is the positive consumption effect; (ii) F_2F_3 is the production effect (positive due to curtailing production of the protected commodity); and (iii) F_3F_4 is the tariff revenue effect. Hence the difference between CU formation and a UTR (with the tariff revenue returned to the consumer) is the loss of tariff revenue F_3F_4 (C_4 compared with C_3). In other words, the consumption gain F_1F_2 is positive and applies in both cases, but

in the Cooper–Massell analysis the production effect comprises two parts: (i) a *pure* TC effect equal to F_2F_4; and (ii) a *pure* TD effect equal to F_3F_4. Hence F_2F_3 is the difference between these two effects and is, therefore, rightly termed the *net* TC effect.

Of course, the above analysis falls short of a general equilibrium one, since the model does not endogenously determine the t/t (El-Agraa 1983b, Chapter 5). However, as suggested above, such analysis would require the use of offer curves for all three countries, both with and without tariffs. Unfortunately such an analysis is still awaited – the attempt by Vanek (1965) to derive an 'excess offer curve' for the potential union partners leads to no more than a specification of various possibilities; and the contention of Wonnacott and Wonnacott (1981) to have provided an analysis incorporating a tariff by W is unsatisfactory, since they assume that W's offer curve is perfectly elastic (see El-Agraa 1999, Chapter 4; see also Section 6.2.7).

6.2.5 Dynamic effects

The so-called dynamic effects (Balassa 1961) relate to the numerous means by which economic integration may influence the rate of growth of GNP of the participating nations. These include the following:

1. scale economies made possible by the increased size of the market for both firms and industries operating below optimum capacity prior to integration;
2. economies external to the firm and industry which may have a downward influence on both specific and general cost structures;
3. the polarization effect, by which is meant the cumulative decline either in relative or absolute terms of the economic situation of a particular participating nation, or of a specific region within it, due either to the benefits of TC becoming concentrated in one region or to the fact that an area may develop a tendency to attract factors of production;
4. the influence on the location and volume of real investment;
5. the effect on economic efficiency and the smoothness with which trade transactions are carried out due to enhanced competition and changes in uncertainty.

Hence these dynamic effects include various and completely different phenomena. Apart from economies of

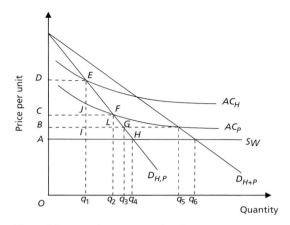

Figure 6.4 Internal economies of scale

scale, the possible gains are extremely long-term and cannot be tackled in orthodox economic terms – for example, intensified competition leading to the adoption of best business practices and to an American type of attitude, and so on (Scitovsky 1958), seems to be a naive socio-psychological abstraction that has no solid foundation with regard to either the aspirations of those countries contemplating economic integration or to its actually materializing.

Economies of scale can, however, be analysed in orthodox economic terms. In a highly simplistic model, like that depicted in Figure 6.4, where scale economies are internal to the industry, their effects can be demonstrated easily – a mathematical discussion can be found in, inter alios, Choi and Yu (1984), but the reader must be warned that the assumptions made about the nature of the economies concerned are extremely limited – for example, H and P are 'similar'. $D_{H,P}$ is the identical demand curve for this commodity in both H and P, and D_{H+P} is their joint demand curve; S_W is the world supply curve; AC_P and AC_H are the average cost curves for this commodity in P and H respectively. Note that the diagram is drawn in such a manner that W has constant average costs and is the most efficient supplier of this commodity. Hence free trade is the best policy resulting in price OA with consumption that is satisfied entirely by imports of Oq_4 in each of H and P, giving a total of Oq_6.

If H and P impose tariffs, the only justification for this is that uncorrected distortions exist between the privately and socially valued costs in these countries (see Jones 1979 and El-Agraa and Jones 1981). The best

tariff rates to impose are Corden's (1972a) 'made-to-measure' tariffs, which can be defined as *those that encourage domestic production to a level that just satisfies domestic consumption without giving rise to monopoly profits*. These tariffs are equal to AD and AC for H and P respectively, resulting in Oq_1 and Oq_2 production in H and P respectively.

When H and P enter into a CU, P, being the cheaper producer, will produce the entire union output – Oq_5 – at a price OB. This gives rise to consumption in each of H and P of Oq_3, with gains of $BDEG$ and $BCFG$ for H and P respectively. Parts of these gains, $BDEI$ for H and $BCFL$ for P, are cost-reduction effects. There is also a production gain for P and a production loss in H due to abandoning production altogether.

Whether or not CU formation can be justified in terms of the existence of economies of scale will depend on whether or not the net effect is a gain or a loss, since in this example P gains and H loses, as the loss from abandoning production in H must outweigh the consumption gain in order for the tariff to have been imposed in the first place. If the overall result is net gain, then the distribution of these gains becomes an important consideration. Alternatively, if economies of scale accrue to an integrated industry, then the locational distribution of the production units becomes an essential issue.

6.2.6 Domestic distortions

A substantial literature has tried to tackle the important question of whether or not the formation of a CU may be economically desirable when there are domestic distortions. Such distortions could be attributed to the presence of trade unions that negotiate wage rates in excess of the equilibrium rates, or to governments introducing minimum wage legislation – both of which are widespread activities in most countries. It is usually assumed that the domestic distortion results in a *social* average cost curve which lies below the private one. Hence, in Figure 6.5, which is adapted from Figure 6.4, I have incorporated AC^s_H and AC^s_P as the *social* curves in the context of economies of scale and a separate representation of countries H and P.

Note that AC^s_H is drawn to be consistently above AP_W, while AC^s_P is below it for higher levels of output. Before the formation of a CU, H may have been adopting a made-to-measure tariff to protect its industry,

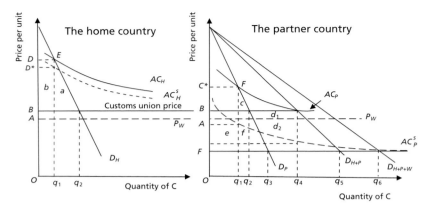

Figure 6.5 Social costs and economies of scale

but the first best policy would have been one of free trade, as argued in the previous section. The formation of the CU will therefore lead to the same effects as in the previous section, with the exception that the cost-reduction effect (Figure 6.5(a)) will be less by DD^* times Oq_1. For P, the effects will be as follows:

1. as before, a consumption gain of area c;
2. a cost-reduction effect of area e, due to calculations relating to social rather than private costs;
3. gains from sales to H of areas d_1 and d_2, with d_1 being an income transfer from H to P, and d_2 the difference between domestic social costs in P and P_W – the world price;
4. the social benefits accruing from extra production made possible by the CU – area f – which is measured by the extra consumption multiplied by the difference between P_W and the domestic social costs.

However, this analysis does not lead to an economic rationale for the formation of CUs, since P could have used first best policy instruments to eliminate the divergence between private and social cost. This would have made AC^s_P the operative cost curve, and, assuming that D_{H+P+W} is the world demand curve, this would have led to a world price of OF and exports of q_3q_5 and q_5q_6 to H and W respectively, with obviously greater benefits than those offered by the CU. Hence the economic rationale for the CU will have to depend on factors that can explain why first best instruments could not have been employed in the first instance (Jones 1980). In short, this is not an absolute argument for CU formation.

6.2.7 Terms of trade effects

So far the analysis has been conducted on the assumption that CU formation has no effect on the terms of trade (t/t). This implies that the countries concerned are too insignificant to have any appreciable influence on the international economy. Particularly in the context of the EU and groupings of a similar size, this is a very unrealistic assumption.

The analysis of the effects of CU formation on the t/t is not only extremely complicated but is also unsatisfactory, since a convincing model incorporating tariffs by all three areas of the world is still awaited (see Mundell 1964; Arndt 1968, 1969; and Wonnacott and Wonnacott 1981). To demonstrate this, let us consider Arndt's analysis, which is directly concerned with this issue, and the Wonnacotts' analysis, whose main concern is the Cooper–Massell criticism, but which has some bearing on this matter.

In Figure 6.6 O_H, O_P and O_W are the respective offer curves of H, P and W. In section (a) of the figure, H is assumed to be the most efficient producer of commodity Y, while in section (b) H and P are assumed to be equally efficient. Assuming that the free trade t/t are given by OT_O, H will export q_6h_1 of Y to W in exchange for Oq_6 imports of commodity X, while P will export q_1p_1 of Y in exchange for Oq_1 of commodity X, with the sum of H and P's exports being exactly equal to OX_3.

When H imposes an *ad valorem* tariff (percentage tariff), its tariff revenue-distributed curve is assumed to be displaced to O^*_H, altering the t/t to OT_1. This leads to a contraction of H's trade with W and, at the same

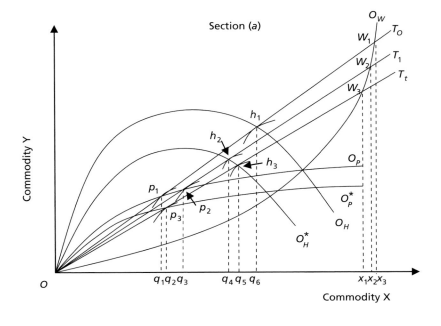

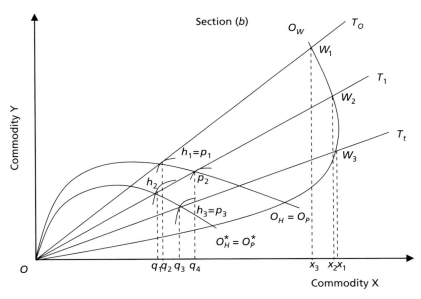

Figure 6.6 Customs unions and the terms of trade

time, increases P's trade with W. In section (a) of the figure it is assumed that the net effect of H and P's trade changes (contraction in H's exports and expansion in P's) will result in a contraction in world trade. It should be apparent that, from H's point of view, the competition of P in its exports market has reduced the

appropriateness of the Cooper–Massell alternative of a (non-discriminatory) UTR.

Note, however, that H's welfare may still be increased in these unfavourable circumstances, provided that the move from h_1 to h_2 is accompanied by two conditions. It should be apparent that the larger the size of P relative to H, and the more elastic the two countries' offer curves over the relevant ranges, the more likely it is that H will lose as a result of the tariff imposition. Moreover, given the various offer curves and H's tariff, H is more likely to sustain a loss in welfare the lower its own marginal propensity to spend on its export commodity, X. If, in terms of consumption, commodity Y is a 'Giffen' good in country H, h_2 will be inferior to h_1.

In this illustration country H experiences a loss of welfare in case (a), but an increase in case (b), while country P experiences a welfare improvement in both cases. Hence it is to H's advantage to persuade P to adopt restrictive trade practices. For example, let P impose an *ad valorem* tariff and, in order to simplify the analysis, assume that in section (b) H and P are identical in all respects such that their revenue-redistributed offer curves completely coincide. In both sections of the figure, the t/t will shift to $OT_{p'}$ with h_3, p_3 and W_2 being the equilibrium trading points. In both cases, P's tariff improves H's welfare, but P gains only in case (b), and is better off with unrestricted trade in case (a) in the presence of tariff imposition by H.

The situation depicted in Figure 6.6 illustrates the fundamental problem that the interests, and hence the policies, of H and P may be incompatible. H stands to gain from restrictive trade practices in P, but the latter is better off without restrictions, provided H maintains its tariff. The dilemma in which H finds itself in trying to improve its t/t is brought about by its inadequate control of the market for its export commodity. Its optimum trade policies and their effects are functions not only of the demand elasticity in W, but also of supply conditions in P and of the latter's reaction to a given policy in H. H will attempt to influence policy-making in P. Given the fact that the latter may have considerable inducement to pursue independent policies, H may encounter formidable difficulties in this respect. It could attempt to handle this problem in a relatively loose arrangement, such as international commodity agreements, or in a tightly controlled and more restrictive set-up involving an international cartel. 'The difficulty is that neither alternative may provide effective control over the maverick who stands to gain from independent policies. In that case a [CU] with common tariff and sufficient incentives may work where other arrangements do not' (Arndt 1968, p. 978).

Of course, the above analysis relates to potential partners who have similar economies and who trade with

W, with no trading relationships between them. Hence it could be argued that such countries are ruled out, by definition, from forming a CU. Such an argument would be misleading, since this analysis is not concerned with the static concepts of TC and TD; the concern is entirely with t/t effects, and a joint trade policy aimed at achieving an advantage in this regard is perfectly within the realm of international economic integration.

One could ask about the nature of this conclusion in a model that depicts the potential CU partners in a different light. Here, Wonnacott and Wonnacott's (1981) analysis may be useful, even though the aim of their paper was to question the general validity of the Cooper–Massell criticism (see below), when the t/t remain unaltered as a result of CU formation. However, this is precisely why it is useful to explain the Wonnacotts' analysis at this juncture: it has some bearing on the t/t effects and it questions the Cooper–Massell criticism.

The main point of the Wonnacotts' paper was to contest the proposition that UTR is superior to the formation of a CU; hence the t/t argument was a side issue. They argued that this proposition does not hold generally if the following assumptions are rejected:

1. that the tariff imposed by a partner (P) can be ignored;
2. that W has no tariffs;
3. that transport is costless between members of the CU (P and H) and W.

Their approach was not based on t/t effects or economies of scale, and, except for their rejection of these three assumptions, their argument is set entirely in the context of the standard two-commodity, three-country framework of CU theory.

The basic framework of their analysis is set out in Figure 6.7. O_H and O_P are the free trade offer curves of the potential partners, while O_H^t and O_P^t are their initial tariff-inclusive offer curves. O_W^1 and O_W^2 are W's offer curves, depending on whether the prospective partners wish to import commodity X (O_W^1) or to export it (O_W^2). The inclusion of both O_H^t and O_P^t meets the Wonnacotts' desire to reject assumption (1), while the gap between O_W^1 and O_W^2 may be interpreted as the rejection of (2) and/or (3) (see Wonnacott and Wonnacott 1981, pp. 708–9).

In addition to these offer curves, I have inserted in Figure 6.7 various trade indifference curves for

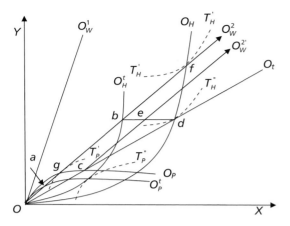

Figure 6.7 UTR versus customs unions

countries H and P (T_H . . . and T_P . . . respectively) and the pre-CU domestic t/t in H (O_t). O_W^1 is drawn parallel to O_W^2 from the point c where O_p intersects O_t (see next paragraph).

The diagram is drawn to illustrate the case where a CU is formed between H and P, with the common external tariff (CET) set at the same rate as H's initial tariff on imports of X, and where the domestic t/t in H remain unaltered so that trade with W continues after the formation of the CU. With its initial non-discriminatory tariff, H will trade along O_W^2 with both P (Oa) and W (ab). The formation of the CU means that H and P's trade is determined by where O_p intersects O_t – that is, at c – and that H will trade with W along (drawn parallel to). The final outcome for H will depend on the choice of assumptions about what happens to the tariff revenue generated by the remaining external trade. If there is no redistribution of tariff revenue in H, then traders in that country will remain at point d. The tariff revenue generated by the external trade of the CU with W is then shown to be equal to ed (measured in units of commodity X), which represents a reduction of be compared with the pre-CU tariff revenue in H. Further, if procedures similar to those of the EU were adopted, the revenue ed would be used as an 'own resource' (see Chapter 18) to be spent or distributed for the benefit of both members of the CU, whereas the pre-union tariff (bd) would be kept by country H.

It can be seen that country P will benefit from the formation of the CU, even if it receives none of this revenue, but that H will undoubtedly lose, even if it keeps all the post-union tariff revenue. This is the case

of pure TD, and, in the absence of additional income transfers from P, H clearly cannot be expected to join the CU, even if it considers that this is the only alternative to its initial tariff policy. There is no rationale, however, for so restricting the choice of policy alternatives. UTR is unambiguously superior to the initial tariff policy for both H and P, and, compared with the non-discriminatory free trade policies available to both countries (which take country H to T_H' at f and country P to T_P' at g), there is no possible system of income transfers from P to H that can make the formation of a CU Pareto-superior to free trade for both countries. It remains true, of course, that country P would gain more from membership of a CU with H than it could achieve by UTR, but provided that H pursues its optimal strategy, which is UTR, country P itself can do no better than follow suit, so that the optimal outcome for both countries is multilateral free trade (MFT).

Of course, there is no a priori reason why the CU, if created, should set its CET at the level of country H's initial tariff (see WTO rules in Section 1.3, page 2, and the final part of this section). Indeed, it is instructive to consider the consequences of forming a CU with a lower CET. The implications of this can be seen by considering the effect of rotating O_t anticlockwise towards O_W^2. In this context, the moving O_t line will show the post-union t/t in countries H and P. Clearly, the lowering of the CET will improve the domestic t/t for H compared with the original form of the CU, and it will have a trade-creating effect, as the external trade of the CU will increase more rapidly than the decline in intra-union trade. Compared with the original CU, H would gain and P would lose. Indeed, the lower the level of the CET, the more likely H is to gain from the formation of the CU *compared with the initial non-discriminatory tariff*. As long as the CET remains positive, however, H would be unambiguously worse off from membership of the CU than from UTR, and, although P would gain from such a CU compared with any initial tariff policy it might adopt, it remains true that there is no conceivable set of income transfers associated with the formation of the CU that would make both H and P simultaneously better off than they would be if, after H's UTR, P also pursued the optimal unilateral action available – the move to free trade.

It is of course true that if the CET is set to zero, so that the rotated O_t coincides with O_W^2, then the outcome is identical to that for the unilateral adoption of free trade for both countries. This, however, merely illustrates how misleading it would be to describe such a policy as 'the formation of a CU'; a CU with a zero CET is indistinguishable from a free-trade policy by both countries and should surely be described solely in the latter terms.

One can extend and generalize this approach beyond what has been done here (see El-Agraa 1989b and Berglas 1983). The important point, however, is what the analysis clearly demonstrates: the assumption that the t/t should remain constant for members of a CU, even if both countries are 'small', leaves a lot to be desired. But it should also be stressed that the Wonnacotts' analysis does not take into consideration the tariffs of H and P on trade with W; nor does it deal with a genuine three-country model, since W is assumed to be very large: W has constant t/t.

Back to the Cooper–Massell criticism

Before finishing this section, it is important to address the question regarding what would happen to the Cooper–Massell criticism when the WTO's Article XXIV is catered for within the context of the orthodox offer curve analysis. Such an analysis is fully set out in El-Agraa (2002a), so here is a brief taste of it.

The clearest way to demonstrate how the incorporation of the requirements of Article XXIV into the analysis would impact on the Cooper–Massell criticism is by adapting the very case that the Wonnacotts use to illustrate its validity. Here, W is 'very large' and has no tariffs or transportation costs, and the potential CU partners H and P are 'very small'. Hence, in Figure 6.8, W's offer curve (O_W) is a straight line: H and P, being very small, can trade with W without influencing in any way the prices of commodities X and Y. Before the formation of the CU, O_H^t and O_P^t are the respective H and P tariff-inclusive offer curves. H trades at A, exporting X in exchange for imports of Y, while P trades at C, exporting Y in exchange for imports of X, the relevant distances along O_W determining the volume of trade. When H and P form a CU with a prohibitive CET – the Wonnacotts' assumption (1981, p. 707) – the respective offer curves for H and P become their tariff-ridden ones – that is, their free trade offer curves O_H and O_P – and the equilibrium trading point becomes E, since W is excluded from trade by assumption.

The Wonnacotts stress that the move from A to E represents an improvement for H (they afford it better

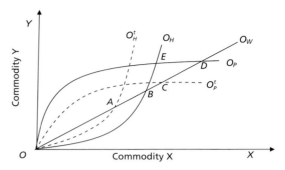

Figure 6.8 Vindicating the Cooper–Massell when dominant W has no tariffs/transport costs

t/t), and that E is also superior for H in comparison with the position it can achieve by UTR (point B). However, not only is E inferior to C for P, but also P can reach a superior position (point D) by simply adopting UTR policy. Hence the formation of the CU will depend on whether H can persuade P to join: H will have to compensate P for the loss of welfare, measured by the difference between E and D. This compensation cannot be met by H since, given standard assumptions, P's loss at E (vis-à-vis D) exceeds H's gain at E (vis-à-vis B). Hence UTR dominates CU and both H and P are better off adopting UTR. The Cooper–Massell criticism is therefore vindicated.

We have just seen that it is essential for the Wonnacotts to resort to their assumption of the CU needing a prohibitive CET in order to justify the only case they have that negates the Cooper–Massell criticism. Yet such an assumption is not only puzzling but is also in direct contradiction to the WTO's Article XXIV, which clearly specifies that the CET must not exceed the (weighted) average of the pre-CU tariffs (see Section 1.3, page 2). If WTO rules were to be adhered to, at least one of the CU partners would continue to trade with W (and at an expanded rate), since the CET must be lower for that country than its pre-CU tariff rate.

To put it differently, the analysis illustrated in Figure 6.8 can be true only if the *non-discriminatory* tariffs imposed by H and P prohibit trade *between* them. This can be so only if W is both 'large' and the most efficient producer of the three countries, while H and P are small; otherwise the Wonnacotts' reference to a country being 'dominant' has no theoretical meaning. However, such an interpretation does not dispose of the problem altogether, since the formation of the CU need

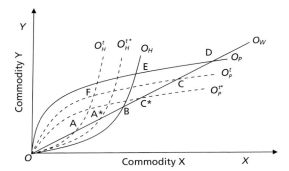

Figure 6.9 Dominant *W* has no tariffs/transport costs – non-discriminatory tariffs by *H* and *P* and a CET consistent with WTO rules: case I

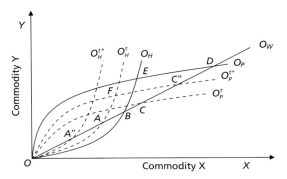

Figure 6.10 Dominant *W* has no tariffs/transport costs – non-discriminatory tariffs by *H* and *P* and a CET consistent with WTO rules: case II

not result in a CET that is prohibitive of trade between *H* and *P* and *W*: as long as the CET is a (weighted) average of the initial tariffs, either *H* or *P* must end up with a lower tariff after the formation of the CU (unless their tariffs were initially equal, but as will be shown below the inferences are similar), and this *may* open up trade between the relevant CU partner and *W*.

Hence Figure 6.8 needs to be adapted to cater for Article XXIV requirements. Assuming that *H*'s initial tariff is higher than *P*'s, the CET will ensure a reduction in *H*'s tariff; hence *H* must continue to trade with *W* after the formation of the CU. Moreover, the elimination of *H* and *P*'s mutual tariffs may open up trade between them. Hence, in Figure 6.9, *H* and *P* initially have the same (tariff-inclusive) offer curves for trade with all countries, but after the formation of the CU have in effect two offer curves each: one tariff-free for mutual trade, and another CET-inclusive for trade with *W*, with O_H and O_P defined as before. and are *H* and *P*'s respective offer curves when a CET consistent with WTO rules is adopted. Since after the formation of the CU *W* faces a lower *H* tariff, *H* and *W* will trade at A^*, and since *H* and *P* have no mutual tariffs, *H* will want to trade with *P* at *E*: the vector *OE* (not drawn) indicates better t/t for *H* in comparison with vector OO_W. Note that both the movement from *A* to A^* and from A^* to *E* indicate welfare improvement for *H*.

Taking these considerations into account, it should be apparent that the Wonnacotts' analysis of this 'most general' case does not necessarily vindicate the Cooper–Massell criticism of UTR dominating a CU. One needs to evaluate not only *E* and *D* and *E* and *B* (an evaluation that leads to the conclusion that UTR

dominates a CU since *H* cannot bribe *P* into joining the CU and still be better off – see the analysis illustrated by Figure 6.8), but also AA^* (which is a gain for *H*) and CC^* (which is a loss for *P*). Since AA^* may be equal to, longer or shorter than CC*, it follows that if AA^* is either equal to or shorter than CC^*, UTR must dominate a CU. However, if AA^* is longer than CC^*, the difference may enable *H* to bribe *P* into joining the CU and still become better off. Therefore, UTR need not dominate a CU.

This is a significant conclusion, given that this case is conceded by the Wonnacotts as vindicating the Cooper–Massell criticism. Surprisingly, it turns out that a WTO rule-consistent (as opposed to a prohibitive) specification of the CET provides a clearer and more general case supporting a negation of the criticism. However, theoretical completeness necessitates that one should consider the alternative situation, where the initial *H* tariff is lower than *P*'s before dwelling on this conclusion. Hence, in Figure 6.10, after the formation of the CU, *H* would be interested in trading with *P* only (at *E*), since trade with *W* (at *A''*) would not be desirable: *A''* indicates a lower level of welfare relative to *A*, while *E* indicates better t/t and a higher level of welfare. However, *P* will want to trade at *C''*, since it gives a higher level of welfare relative to *C*, but will have no interest in trading with *H*, since *OE* are worse t/t relative to OO_W. Therefore, it should be evident that since UTR takes *P* to *D* (giving a higher level of welfare relative to *C''*), P would have no interest in the CU. Whether *H* can bribe *P* to join the CU would depend on the relative lengths of *A''A* and *CC''*: more precisely, on *A''A* being shorter than *CC''* by a distance sufficient to make *BE* exceed *CD*. Hence, again, UTR need not dominate a CU, and therefore the conclusion reached here reinforces that arrived at in the previous case.

Note that in both cases, initially H would have been interested in trading with P rather than W, since trade with P offers better t/t (OF relative to OO_W in both Figures 6.9 and 6.10). However, H's desires are frustrated simply because P chooses to trade with W at better t/t for itself; once P chooses to trade with W, H has no alternative but to follow suit.

Analytical completeness requires a discussion of the two alternatives, where the offer curves for H intersect O_W to the north-east of all the points where P's offer curves intersect it. However, it should be obvious that under such circumstances the same conclusions would be reached. Hence, UTR need not dominate CU formation.

A final question remains: would the assumption of equal initial H and P tariff rates nullify this generalization? The answer is in the negative and can be explained in the following way. If they were equal, the CET would also be equal to them. Hence, O_H^t and O_P^t will continue to be the respective H and P offer curves for trade with W. Therefore, in Figure 6.8, trade with W would continue at the initial level: OA trade between H and W and OC trade between P and W. It follows that the evaluation of the CU formation versus UTR must lead to the same conclusion as that reached in the case illustrated by Figure 5.8. However, there would be one significant difference: in the Wonnacotts' analysis, the conclusion reached from Figure 6.8 rests entirely on the CET being prohibitive of trade between the CU partners and W, while in this (generalized) case, trade between the CU partners and W would continue on the same basis and to the same extent as before the CU formation. The implication of this result is that the outright vindication of the Cooper–Massell criticism would depend on assuming that the H and P tariffs were equal rather than on the CET being prohibitive. This implication is consistent not only with some of the literature on the subject, but also with practical notions: in the real world the formation of CUs has never completely eliminated trade with the non-members, W (see, inter alios, El-Agraa 1999).

6.3 Customs unions versus free trade areas

The analysis so far has been conducted on the premise that differences between CUs and FTAs can be ignored.

However, the ability of the member nations of FTAs to decide their own commercial policies vis-à-vis the outside world raises certain issues. Balassa (1961) pointed out that FTAs may result in deflection of trade, production and investment. Deflection of trade occurs when imports from W (the cheapest source of supply) come to the higher tariff partner via the member country with the lower tariff rate, assuming that transport and administrative costs do not outweigh the tariff differential. Deflection of production and investment occurs in commodities whose production requires a substantial quantity of raw materials imported from W – the tariff differential regarding these materials might distort the true comparative advantage in domestic materials, therefore resulting in resource allocations according to overall comparative disadvantage.

If deflection of trade does occur, then the FTA effectively becomes a CU with a CET equal to the lowest tariff rate, which is obviously beneficial for the world (see page 84 and Curzon Price 1974). However, most FTAs have been adopting 'rules of origin' so that only those commodities that originate in a member state are exempt from tariff imposition (see Shibata 1967 for a different analysis). If deflection of production and investment does take place, we have the case of the so-called tariff factories; but the necessary conditions for this to occur are extremely limited (see El-Agraa in El-Agraa and Jones 1981, Chapter 3 and El-Agraa 1984b, 1989a).

6.4 Economic unions

The analysis of CUs needs drastic extension when applied to economic unions. First, the introduction of free factor mobility may enhance efficiency through a more rational reallocation of resources, but it may also result in depressed areas, therefore creating or aggravating regional problems and imbalances (see Mayes 1983 and Robson 1985). Second, fiscal harmonization may also improve efficiency by eliminating non-tariff barriers (NTBs) and distortions and by equalizing their effective protective rates (see Chapter 15). Third, the coordination of monetary and fiscal policies that is implied by monetary integration may ease unnecessarily severe imbalances, hence resulting in the promotion of the right atmosphere for stability in the economies of the member nations.

These economic union elements must be tackled

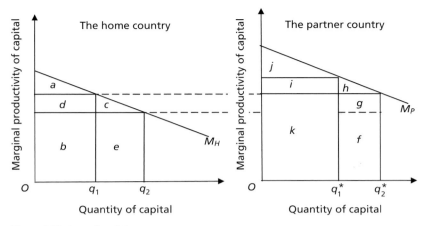

Figure 6.11 Capital mobility

simultaneously with TC and TD, as well as economies of scale and market distortions. However, such interactions are too complicated to consider here; the interested reader should consult El-Agraa 1983a, b, 1984a, 1989a. This section will be devoted to a brief discussion of factor mobility. Since monetary integration is probably the most crucial of commitments for a regional bloc and is a main pillar of EU integration for practically all member nations, Chapters 10–12 are devoted to it.

With regard to factor mobility, it should be apparent that the removal (or harmonization) of all barriers to labour (L) and capital (K) will encourage both L and K to move. L will move to those areas where it can obtain the highest possible reward – that is, net advantage. This encouragement need not necessarily lead to an increase in actual mobility, since there are socio-political factors that normally result in people remaining near their birthplace – social proximity is a dominant consideration, which is why the average person does not move (Chapter 8). If the reward to K is not equalized – that is, differences in marginal productivities (MPs) exist before the formation of an economic union – K will move until the MPs are equalized. This will result in benefits that can be clearly described in terms of Figure 6.11, which depicts the production characteristics in H and P. M_H and M_P are the schedules that relate the K stocks to their MPs in H and P respectively, given the quantity of L in each country (assuming two factors of production only).

Prior to the formation of an economic union, the K stock (which is assumed to remain constant throughout the analysis) is Oq_2 in H and in P. Assuming that K is immobile internationally, all K stocks must be nationally owned and, ignoring taxation, profit per unit of K will be equal to its MP, given conditions of perfect competition. Hence the total profit in H is equal to $b + e$ and $i + k$ in P. Total output is, of course, the whole area below the M_p curve but within Oq_2 in H and in P – that is, areas $a + b + c + d + e$ in H and $j + i + k$ in P. Therefore, L's share is $a + c + d$ in H and j in P.

Since the MP in P exceeds that in H, the removal of barriers to K mobility or the harmonization of such barriers will induce K to move away from H and into P. This is because nothing has happened to affect K in W. Such movement will continue until the MP of K is the same in both H and P. This results in $q_1 q_2$ $(= q_1^* q_2^*)$ of K moving from H to P. Hence the output of H falls to $a + b + d$, while its *national* product, including the return of the profit earned on K in P $(= g + f)$, increases by $(g - c)$. In P, *domestic* product rises by $(f + g + h)$, while *national* product (excluding the remittance of profits to H) increases by area h only. Both H and P experience a change in the relative share of L and K in national product, with K owners being favourably disposed in H and unfavourably disposed in P.

Of course, the analysis is too simplistic; apart from the fact that K and L are never perfectly immobile at the international level and multinational corporations have their own ways of transferring K (see McManus 1972; Buckley and Casson 1976; Dunning 1977), the analysis does not take into account the fact that K may actually move to areas with low wages after the formation of an economic union. Moreover, if K moves predominantly in only one direction, one country may become a depressed area; hence the 'social' costs and benefits of such an occurrence need to be taken into consideration, particularly if the economic union deems it important that the economies of both H and P should be balanced. Therefore, the above gains have to be discounted or supplemented by such costs and benefits.

6.5 Macroeconomics of integration

We have seen that TC and TD are the two concepts most widely used in international economic integration. We have also seen that their economic implications for resource reallocation are usually tackled in terms of particular commodities under conditions of global full employment. However, the economic consequences for the outside world and their repercussions on the integrated area are usually left to intuition. Moreover, their implications for employment are usually ruled out by assumption.

In an effort to cater for these aspects, I have used a macroeconomic model (see El-Agraa and Jones 1981, Chapters 6–8, and El-Agraa 1989a); the model has been refined by Jones (1983) and presented in the light of the Lisbon Treaty provision for withdrawal in El-Agraa and Jones (2007). However, even the crude model indicates that the advantages of using a macro model are that it clearly demonstrates the once-and-for-all nature of TC and TD. It also shows the insignificance of their overall impact given realistic values of the relevant coefficients: marginal propensities to import, marginal propensities to consume, tariff rates, and so on. The model also demonstrates that TC is beneficial for the partner gaining the new output and exports, but is detrimental to the other partner and the outside world, and that TD is beneficial for the partner now exporting the commodity, but is detrimental for the other partner and the outside world.

6.6 Economic integration in developing countries

It has been claimed that the body of economic integration theory as so far developed has no relevance for least-developed countries. This is because the theory suggests that there would be more scope for TC if the countries concerned were initially very competitive in production, but potentially very complementary, and that a CU would be more likely to be trade-creating if the partners conducted most of their foreign trade among themselves (see Lipsey 1960 and Meade 1980). These conditions are unlikely to be satisfied in the majority of the developing nations. Moreover, most of the effects of integration are initially bound to be trade-diverting, particularly since most of the least-developed countries seek to industrialize.

On the other hand, it was also realized that an important obstacle to the development of industry in these countries is the inadequate size of their individual markets (see Brown 1961; Hazlewood 1967, 1975; and Robson 1980, 1983, 1997). It is therefore necessary to increase the market size so as to encourage optimum plant installations: hence the need for economic integration. This, however, would result in industries clustering together in the relatively more advanced of these nations – those that have already commenced the process of industrialization.

I have demonstrated elsewhere (El-Agraa 1979a) that there is essentially *no theoretical difference* between economic integration in the advanced world and in the least-developed countries, but that there is a major difference in terms of the *type* of economic integration that suits the particular *circumstances* of developing countries and that is politically feasible: the need for an equitable distribution of the gains from industrialization and the location of industries is an important issue (see page 89). This suggests that any type of economic integration that is being contemplated must incorporate as an essential element a common fiscal authority and some coordination of economic policies. But then one could argue equally that *some degree* of these elements is necessary in *any* type of integration (see the Raisman Committee (1961) recommendations for the EAC).

This raises the interesting question of what happens when economic integration takes place between advanced and poor nations, such as Mexico in NAFTA (on this see Section 6.8).

6.7 Economic integration among communist countries

The only example of economic integration among communist countries was the CMEA. However, there the economic system perpetuated a fundamental lack of interest by domestic producers in becoming integrated with both consumers and producers in other member countries. As Marer and Montias (1988) emphasize, the integration policies of member nations must focus on the mechanism of state-to-state relations rather than on domestic economic policies, which would make CMEA integration more attractive to producers and consumers alike – that is, integration must be planned by the state at the highest possible level and imposed on ministries, trusts and enterprises. It should also be stated that the CMEA operated different pricing mechanisms for intra- and extra-area trade. Moreover, the attitude of the former USSR was extremely important, since the policies of the East European members of the CMEA were somewhat constrained by the policies adopted by the organization's most powerful member, for economic as well as political reasons. CMEA integration, therefore, had to be approached within an entirely different framework, but this is not the appropriate place to discuss it, especially since the CMEA met its demise soon after the collapse of socialism in the former USSR and Eastern Europe.

6.8 New theoretical developments

There are many new developments in the analysis of economic integration, but they are mostly concerned with minute aspects, and hence do not amount to a body coherent enough to be briefly explained and discussed within the general introductory nature of this chapter. I shall mention only three. First, Schiff and Winters (1998) examine regional integration as diplomacy. They do this by modelling a scheme motivated by security concerns. Assuming that trade can help reduce frictions among antagonistic neighbouring nations by raising trust between them, they show that: a regional bloc is optimum or first-best under traditional static welfare terms; optimum CETs fall over time; the CETs fall in the aftermath of deep integration, which includes such NTBs as harmonization and mutual recognition of standards, investment codes and the like (see Chapter 1); and enlargement enhances the welfare of the members of the bloc, with optimum CETs likely to rise. Their general conclusion is that the optimum intervention under these circumstances is a subsidy on imports from the neighbour, and the

equivalent solution is for the neighbouring countries to tax imports from the rest of the world – that is, to form a trading bloc – as well as to have domestic taxes.

The second is by Venables (2003), who examines the distribution between the participants of the benefits from integration. He finds that the outcome would depend on their comparative advantage, relative to both each other and the rest of the world: countries with a comparative advantage between that of their partners and the rest of the world fare better than those with an extreme comparative advantage. This means that economic integration between poor (rich) countries would lead to a divergence (convergence) in their incomes. Venables concludes that the results suggest that developing countries are likely to be better served by north–south than by south–south agreements.

The third is concerned with the enlargement of existing schemes and is based on Buchanan's classic work on the economic theory of clubs (Buchanan 1965). It is elaborated by, inter alios, Alesina and Spolaore (2003) and Gros and Stenherr (2004). Making simplifying assumptions – for example, that members have a well-defined common interest and are identical – it can be shown that the optimum number of members or scheme size would depend on the costs and benefits of belonging.

6.9 Conclusion

The conclusion reached here is consistent with that of El-Agraa (1979a, b, 1989a), and Jones (in El-Agraa and Jones 1981). It has four points.

First, the rationale for regional economic integration rests on the existence of constraints on the use of first-best policy instruments. Economic analysis has had little to say about the nature of these constraints, and presumably the evaluation of any regional scheme of economic integration should incorporate a consideration of the validity of the view that such constraints do exist to justify the pursuit of second- rather than first-best solutions.

Second, even when the existence of constraints on superior policy instruments is acknowledged, it is misleading to identify the results of regional economic integration by comparing an arbitrarily chosen common policy with an arbitrarily chosen national policy. Of course, ignorance and inertia provide sufficient reasons why existing policies may be non-optimal; but it is clearly wrong to attribute gains that would have been achieved by appropriate unilateral action to a policy of regional integration. Equally, although it is appropriate to use the optimal common policy as a point of reference, it must be recognized that this may overstate the gains to be achieved if, as seems highly likely, constraints and inefficiencies in the political processes by which policies are agreed prove to be greater among a group of countries than within any individual country.

Although the first two conclusions raise doubts about the case for regional economic integration, in principle at least, a strong general case for economic integration does exist. In unions where economies of scale may be in part external to national industries, the rationale for unions rests essentially on the recognition of the externalities and market imperfections that extend beyond the boundaries of national states. In such circumstances, unilateral national action will not be optimal while integrated action offers the scope for potential gain.

As with the solution to most problems of externalities and market imperfections, however, customs union theory frequently illustrates the proposition that a major stumbling block to obtaining the gains from joint optimal action lies in agreeing an acceptable distribution of such gains. Thus the fourth conclusion is that the achievement of the potential gains from economic integration will be limited to countries able and willing to cooperate to distribute the gains from integration so that all partners may benefit compared with the results achieved by independent action. It is easy to argue from this that regional economic integration may be more readily achieved than global solutions, but, as the debate about monetary integration in the EU illustrates (see Chapters 10 and 11), the chances of obtaining potential mutual gain may well founder in the presence of disparate views about the distribution of such gains and weak arrangements for redistribution.

Summary

- Before serious analysis of economic integration was undertaken, economists believed that economic integration was beneficial. This was due to the prevailing wisdom at the time: free trade maximized

world welfare, restricted trade impacted negatively on world welfare and economic integration reduced the restrictions, and hence brought the world closer to free trade.
- Viner challenged this belief by pointing out that economic integration can bring economic benefits to the member countries, but it can also harm them.
  1. The source of the benefits is trade creation: *the replacement of expensive domestic production by cheaper imports from the partner.*
  2. The losses arise from trade diversion: *the replacement of cheaper initial imports from the outside world by expensive imports from the partner.*
  3. Hence the economic viability of a scheme of economic integration would depend on whether or not trade creation exceeds trade diversion.
- Cooper and Massell, in turn, challenged Viner by arguing that a country can secure the benefits of trade creation without incurring the losses from trade diversion by simply *unilaterally reducing its tariffs for all countries without discrimination.*
- Yet all these effects are the result of static analysis based on 'orthodox' methodology; using 'unorthodox' methodology greatly improves the chances for gain. Here we considered Johnson's 'preference for industrial production' model to demonstrate this, but new developments can do likewise.
- Also, ushering in dynamic analysis improves the chances for economic gains.
- New theoretical developments do not add up to a coherent body, since they deal with economic integration in an ad hoc fashion, catering for its impact on diplomacy and the like.

Questions and essay topics

1. According to trade theorists, what is the definition of international economic integration (IEI)?
2. Why did pre-1950 trade theorists believe that IEI is economically beneficial, and hence should be encouraged?
3. What IEI schemes are technically feasible and how do real-world ones compare with them?
4. What do GATT-WTO rules say about IEI?
5. What is trade creation (TC)?
6. What is trade diversion (TD)?
7. Use simple data to explain TC and TD.

8. What is a policy of unilateral tariff reduction (UTR) and how does it compare with TC/TD?

9. Use partial-equilibrium analysis to explain TC, TD and UTR.

10. What is preference for industrial production?

11. What are domestic distortions and how do they impact on the analysis of the economic effects of IEI?

12. How does the introduction of transportation costs and tariffs by non-members impact on the analysis of economic integration?

13. Show how economic integration may impact on the terms of trade.

14. Does the incorporation of GATT's article XXIV alter the Viner and Cooper–Massell conclusions?

15. Show how economic integration may impact on the terms of trade.

16. 'The rationale for IEI should not be based on strict economic criteria.' Discuss.

17. 'Without IEI, developing countries stand no chance of improving their economies, let alone catching up with the advanced world.' Discuss.

FURTHER READING

El-Agraa, A. M. (ed.) (1997) *Economic Integration Worldwide*, Macmillan and St Martin's, New York.

(1999) *Regional Integration: Experience, Theory and Measurement*, Macmillan, London; Barnes and Noble, New York.

Frankel, J. A. (1997) *Regional Trading Blocs in the World Trading System*, Institute for International Economics, Washington D.C.

Schiff, M. and Winters, L. A. (2003) *Regional Integration and Development*, Oxford University Press.

7 The economics of the single market

BRIAN ARDY AND ALI EL-AGRAA

Unlike many areas of EU policy-making, the single market, more precisely the Single European Market (SEM),[1] has been seen in a positive light, perhaps because it has been central to EU development, although today, amid widespread disillusion with the EU, even the SEM is seen as 'less popular than ever, more needed than ever' (Monti 2010, p. 20). The SEM is an important stepping-stone on the route from the customs union to a fully-fledged economic union (see Chapter 1), and many regard monetary union (EMU; see Chapters 10–12) as the last stage and thus the final piece in the jigsaw of 'negative' integration. The SEM is defined as 'an area without internal frontiers in which the free movement of goods persons, services and capital is ensured' (Single European Act (SEA), Article 12; CEU 1987c). This means that borders should disappear within the EU: goods, services, capital and people should be able to move between member states (MSs) as they move between regions within a country. This requires the removal of customs and passport controls at borders; the elimination of any national barriers to the sale of other EU countries' goods and services; and the ending of any national controls on the movement of capital. This is a very extensive agenda that has such wide implications that the subject of virtually every chapter of the book has been affected by its developments. This chapter, therefore, considers the development of the SEM, emphasizing its key characteristics and the continuing debates about its effects.

7.2 Why 'the single market'?

There were provisions for a single market in the 1957 EEC Treaty: Article 3 required not only the removal of all internal tariffs and quotas, but also 'of all other measures having equivalent effect', and 'of obstacles to freedom of movement of persons, services and capital'. The procedure to eliminate these non-tariff barriers (NTBs) was harmonization or the approximation of laws (EEC Treaty, Article 100). After the successful early completion of the customs union (see Chapter 2), internal factors and external events conspired against the completion of the single market. The EEC economy was under strain in the 1970s because of: the world recession associated with the oil price shocks of 1973 and 1979; rapid changes in technology; the changing structure of the world economy; and the emergence of significant new competitors, first Japan and then the newly industrializing countries of South East Asia. With growth slow or negative and unemployment rising rapidly, national governments tried to protect their economies, but with tariffs fixed by GATT (see Chapter 1) and EEC Treaty commitments, only NTBs could be used – the 'New Protectionism'. Barriers went up within as well as without the EU, and these economic strains made countries much less willing to agree to integration initiatives in general and harmonization in particular.

The progress of harmonization was extremely slow for other reasons. It proved difficult to reach agreement on what were often complex technical issues, which were politically sensitive and often the subject of long-standing national legislation – for example, it was difficult to agree a definition for chocolate because in the UK significant amounts of non-cocoa fat could be added, but in the rest of Europe this was not the case. So an agreed definition was seen as either undermining continental European standards or requiring UK manufacturers to change their products. The UK was able to hold up the process in this instance because harmonization required unanimous agreement in the Council. Harmonization was also seen in some countries as over-regulation. The treaty also allowed national measures 'on grounds of public morality, public policy or public security; the protection of health and life of humans, animals or plants; the protection of national treasures possessing artistic, historic or archaeological value; or the protection of industrial and commercial property' (Article 36). This was exploited by some MSs to restrict trade. As a result, between 1969 and 1985, the EC managed to adopt only 270 directives (Schreiber 1991, p. 98). This was too slow to bring about any reduction in technical barriers, since new regulations were being introduced by MS governments at a faster rate.

Gradually, attitudes towards the single market began to change. There was concern over the performance of EC economies, slow growth and the falling share of world exports of hi-tech goods. Big business began to see the segmentation of the EC market into national markets as hampering their international competitiveness. They were unable to get the long production runs to keep costs down and to spread the costs of research and development (R&D). The Round Table of European Industrialists was particularly influential, lobbying national governments and the Commission. The limitations of nationalistic economic policies were being revealed by generally poor performance and failures, such as President Mitterand's abortive attempt to expand the French economy from 1981 to 1983. The European Monetary System (see Chapter 11) was seen as a successful example of what could be achieved by European cooperation. There was also support for further integration, demonstrated by the European Parliament (EP) majority in favour of the Draft Treaty of European Union[2] in 1984. The awkward partner in the EC, the UK, was also prepared to cooperate on further integration for three reasons. First, in 1984 a more permanent solution to the UK's budgetary problems was agreed (see Chapters 2 and 19). Second, SEM was in tune with the free market orthodoxy of the time, particularly with the Thatcher government's philosophy. Third, the British prime minister, Margaret Thatcher, believed that there were large potential gains for the UK from freer trade in services, especially for financial services in the City of London.

The new Commission in 1984, presided over by Jacques Delors, was pushing at an open door when it chose the SEM as the priority for its period in office. Lord Cockfield, the vice-president of the Delors Commission responsible for the SEM, drew up the Internal Market White Paper (CEU 1985a) – at the time

a novel approach for the EC – setting out an ambitious but feasible strategy, including a legislative programme designed to sweep away cross-border restrictions and to restore the momentum of economic integration. The necessary institutional changes were contained in the SEA. The features of the strategy and legislation that characterize the SEM programme are as follows:

1. Minimum harmonization: New Approach Directives restrict harmonization to essential requirements: health, safety, environmental and consumer protection. The general harmonization method, originating in too rigid an interpretation of the treaty, was to be abandoned; in most cases, an 'approximation' of the parameters was sufficient to reduce differences in rates or technical specifications to an acceptable level.
2. The deadline of 31 December 1992, combined with regular monitoring, was designed to speed progress.
3. Qualified majority voting (QMV; see Chapter 3) is to apply to most SEM measures, but not to fiscal (tax) provisions, the free movement of persons, or the rights of employed persons.
4. Control of the emergence of new NTBs.
5. Mutual recognition, facilitated by the landmark judgment by the European Court of Justice (ECJ) in the Cassis de Dijon case (see Chapter 2): goods which are 'lawfully' made and sold in one EU MS should in principle be able to move freely and go on sale *anywhere* within the EU, and the same was true of tradable services such as banking or insurance.
6. European standards are to be developed, but (except where they coincide with legal requirements) their absence should not be allowed to restrict trade. The detailed technical definition of these requirements should, where possible, be entrusted to European standards institutions.

To make the SEM for the EU like a national market required the removal of three types of barriers: physical, fiscal and technical.

Physical barriers were checks at borders for the following reasons: (1) the control of the movement of persons for immigration purposes; (2) customs borders were required due to differences in indirect taxes; (3) animal and plant health was protected by inspections at borders; and (4) checks on lorries and drivers were ostensibly for safety reasons and to enforce national restrictions on foreign hauliers. Considerable expense was incurred in preparing the documentation needed and there were delays at borders, further increasing the cost of inter-EU transport. Fiscal barriers were needed to check the goods crossing borders because differences in indirect taxes, VAT, and excise duties on alcohol, tobacco, and so on, were dealt with by remitting these taxes on exports and imposing them on imports (see Chapter 15).

Technical barriers cover an enormous range of measures that affect trade. The most pervasive of these are technical regulations and standards. *Regulations* are legal requirements that products must satisfy before they can be sold in a particular country; these cover health, safety and environmental requirements. Regulations are also important in relation to services (see Section 7.4.1, page 107). *Standards* are not legally binding in themselves; they are technical requirements set by private standardization bodies, such as DIN in Germany, BSI in the UK and AFNOR in France. Although they are only voluntary, they often assume a quasi-legal status because they are used in technical regulations and in calls for tenders in contracts. They are also important in marketing the product. The existence of different regulations and standards imposed additional costs on EU producers, who had to make alterations to their products before they could sell them in other MSs.

Another technical barrier related to *public procurement*: private sector purchases by governments. Governments frequently discriminated against bids from firms in other MSs for a variety of reasons: strategic (e.g. weapons); support of employment; and encouragement of emerging high-tech industries, to maintain employment. However, such policies imposed costs on both the public authorities (who ended up paying more than they needed to) and on firms (because the market available for selling their goods was too limited). One consequence was too many producers, making it difficult to achieve an optimum scale in industries such as defence, electricity generation and telecommunications equipment.

Technical barriers were the main impediment to trade in services. For a range of services, from plumbing to legal services, the problems related to the recognition of qualifications[3] and the rights to establish businesses. For financial services, trade was limited by government regulatory measures. In banking there were particular problems with establishing capital adequacy. Insurance could not be sold in most MSs unless the insurer had a local permanent establishment. Capital movements were controlled by several MSs, which interfered with free trade in financial services.

What was remarkable about the SEM programme was its broad aims and ambitions, and the development of a clear approach to achieving them. It embraced measures as diverse as animal health controls and licensing of banks; public procurement and standards for catalytic converters for car exhausts. It covered not just traditionally tradable services, such as banking, insurance and transport, but also the new areas of information, marketing and audiovisual services. With regard to transport, the agenda included the 'phasing out of all quantitative restrictions (quotas) on road haulage', and further liberalization of road, sea and air passenger services through the fostering of increased competition (see Chapter 16). The aim for audiovisual services was to create a single, EC-wide broadcasting area.

7.3 The economics of non-tariff barriers

NTBs are any non-tariff government policy measure, which intentionally or unintentionally alters the amount or direction of trade. These are government, not private measures. They are artificial, not natural conditions: transport costs, language and cultural factors influence trade flows, but are not NTBs. Natural conditions can, however, be exploited as NTBs – for example, by requiring extensive documentation in the home language. Whether intentional or unintentional, it is the effect on trade that is important, not the declared purpose of the measure. It is notoriously difficult to establish intentions. A trade barrier implies a reduction of trade, but the volume of trade or its direction could be altered by subsidies, which could lead to an excessive amount of trade.

The effects of NTBs are analogous to those of tariffs (see Chapter 6). Figure 7.1, adapted from Figure 6.1 (see page 84), is the basis for a partial equilibrium comparison of tariffs and NTBs. The world supply of this product to the EU, S_W, is assumed to be infinitely elastic at a price D, and this would be the price in the absence of restrictions on trade. At this price, EU demand (D_{EU})

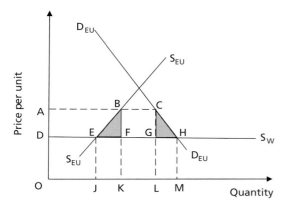

Figure 7.1 The effects of tariffs and non-tariff barriers

would be OM, EU supply (S_{EU}) OJ and imports JM. If a tariff of AD were levied on imports, the EU price would rise to A, EU demand would contract by LM to OL, EU supply would increase by JK to OK, and imports would fall to KL. Thus the effects of the tariffs are as follows:

1. Consumption is reduced and consumers are worse off. The consumers' loss is equal to the area ACHD,[4] made up of the higher price on their current consumption, an amount equal to the area ACGD, and the loss of the opportunity to buy LM at the lower price OD, the area CHG.
2. Government tariff revenue is BCGF, so part of the consumer loss is transferred to the government.
3. Domestic producers' revenue increases from DEJO to ABKO; of this, EBKJ is the additional cost of production, so producers' surplus[5] increases by ABED.
4. The deadweight (net) loss associated with the tariff is relatively small, equal to the two dark triangles EBF and CGH; most of the additional cost to the consumer is extra tariff revenue for the government or producer surplus.[6]

If instead of a tariff there was an NTB of the same size, the effects on EU consumption, production, imports and producer surplus would be the same. There are, however, two important differences:

1. NTBs are cost-increasing rather than revenue-generating. NTBs protect the market by imposing additional costs on importers – for example, by requiring products to be modified to comply with different national regulations; this increases costs both directly and indirectly by reducing

production runs. Complying with customs requirements involves administrative and other costs for importers, in addition to costs for the government of policing the measures. Thus the area BCGF is not government tariff revenue; it is an additional deadweight loss associated with NTBs.

2. Levels of NTB protection can be very high. Tariffs are relatively transparent: tariff rates are published and are subject to international negotiation. It is difficult to measure NTBs and thus levels of protection can be very high. Table 7.1 shows that NTBs in the EC were much higher than tariffs, and their variation across industries considerably greater.

This means that the benefits from the elimination of NTBs are likely to be large for three reasons. First, the cost savings are large. Second, they apply to a larger proportion of output than with tariff reduction. And, third, they may impact more directly on economies of scale because production can be standardized. Thus there are potentially substantial benefits from the elimination of NTBs (OECD 2005b).

7.4 An evolving programme

The White Paper (CEU 1985a) contained 300 proposals for legislation. By the 1992 deadline, 95 per cent of the measures were in place. However, this was not the end of the process, since additional legislation was needed: to close the remaining gaps in the SEM – for example, finance, energy and services; to update and improve the existing legislative framework to ensure it achieves its objectives; and to minimize the administrative burdens on business. Existing legislation needs to be transposed, and directives (see Chapters 3 and 4) need to be incorporated into national legislation, and this can take a considerable time. Continuing vigilance is needed to ensure the implementation of existing legislation; enforcement is the responsibility of national governments and sometimes this is problematic. In addition to legislation, there is the enormous task of developing European standards, which is still far from complete.

By October 2009 there were 1,521 directives and 976 regulations (see Chapters 3 and 4) related to the SEM (CEU 2010f, p. 7), which gives some idea of the increased coverage of the programme.[7] Despite this, the Commission continues to identify areas where

Table 7.1 Measures of protection by country and industry

	Tariff rate		Non-tariff barrier rate	
	Rate[1]	Standard deviation	Rate[1]	Standard deviation
Protection by country				
Belgium	7.0	7.6	19.6	28.2
Denmark	7.1	4.1	18.2	27.0
Germany, West	7.4	6.0	22.3	27.4
Greece	7.0	8.6	25.5	25.8
Spain	6.8	4.8	13.9	22.1
France	7.4	14.3	18.4	26.1
Ireland	7.5	7.5	20.8	27.0
Italy	7.6	14.4	20.9	27.1
Netherlands	7.1	7.6	20.6	28.1
Portugal	7.1	3.4	19.1	20.2
Protection by industry				
Food products	9.8	33.6	45.9	30.0
Textiles	11.7	24.5	69.8	38.2
Apparel	12.3	30.4	71.7	35.7
Footwear	13.3	44.5	33.8	41.9
Furniture	6.4	46.2	0.9	46.5
Industrial chemicals	10.2	23.5	9.1	30.1
Iron & steel	9.8	38.0	47.7	34.6
Machinery electric	8.6	28.3	14.3	33.3
Transport equipment	7.9	30.7	25.5	38.8
Professional & Scientific equipment	6.5	23.6	2.7	30.3

Note:
[1] Import weighted measure.
Source: Lee and Swagel 1997

further progress is needed (Monti 2010; CEU 2007a). These can broadly be divided into three: the traditional SEM; extension beyond its traditional boundaries or into new areas; and improving the context within which SEM operates. The free movement services, standards, consumer rights, network industries; reducing tax obstacles; public procurement; improving conditions for small and medium-sized enterprises, including simplifying the regulatory environment; cross-border debt recovery; a statute for a European Private Company; and EU patent are all traditional SEM issues. Extensions include the digital single market and green industry. The context is both economic and political. The 1985 White Paper recognized that the

measures to reduce barriers should be accompanied by an expanding market and a flexible market (CEU 1985a). So the SEM can be seen as both complementary to and dependent on the Lisbon process (see Chapter 14). Politically, if SEM is to operate effectively, there should be a consensus on its importance and its continued development.

Another important issue, which relates to political support, is SEM integrity, the extent to which the existing measures apply and are enforced. Most SEM legislation takes the form of directives, which means that national legislation is necessary to introduce the measure. As a result, two problems occur: first, failure of transposition by national governments to pass the necessary legislation by the deadline contained in the directive; and, second, incorrect transposition – that is, national legislation does not comply with directive. These two problems mean that 1.5 per cent of directives do not apply correctly across the whole EU; this percentage is improving, but it still remains an issue for the operation of the SEM. The effectiveness of the SEM is also compromised by the problem of enforcement. Measured by infringement proceedings, in cases where MSs are brought before the ECJ for failing to correctly apply the legislation, only limited progress is being made. So SEM rules for the most part apply and are enforced, but further improvements can and should be made.

7.4.1 The services market

A major SEM disappointment has been the limited extent to which services markets have been integrated (Gros 2006; OECD 2005b); in 2009 services accounted for 74 per cent of output and 70 per cent of employment in the EU27 (see Tables 5.4 and 5.5).[8] The limited impact of the SEM in this area is illustrated by the low proportion of Gross Value Added (GVA) that is traded[9] (see Figure 7.2) and the low level of foreign direct investment (FDI) in services industries, which seems to be related to regulatory problems (Kox *et al.* 2004a, b).

The EU has sought to open up the services market with two particular measures: a general services directive and the Financial Services Action Plan (see page 108). The barriers to cross-border trade in non-financial services remain high; national regulatory regimes are very different and complex, with a high level of discretion by MSs, and there is little confidence that they would not be used to protect domestic companies. In sectors such as accountancy, retailing, wholesale trade and IT services, barriers remain high and the gains from their elimination significant. Trade in commercial services could rise by 30–60 per cent and the stock of FDI by 20–35 per cent (Kox *et al.* 2004a, p. 66); this could raise EU consumption by 0.6 per cent and employment by 600,000 (Copenhagen Economics 2005, p. 13).

The original proposal for a services market directive (CEU 2004k) sought to extend the principle of mutual recognition to services: a company able to operate a service in one MS should, in principle, be able to operate that service in any other MS. The directive proposed various measures to achieve these ends: freedom of

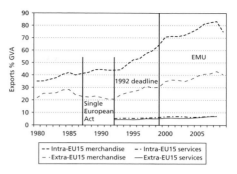

Figure 7.2 Intra- and extra-exports' share of GVA
Source: **IMF 2010b; Eurostat 2010e; CEU 2010c**

establishment (easing of administrative requirements); freedom of movement (country of origin principle and rights of recipients to use services in other MSs); and measures to establish consumer confidence in services provision. Coming as they did at a time of growing economic nationalism, these proposals proved so controversial as to be labelled the Frankenstein directive, in a pun on the name of Frits Bolkstein, the internal market commissioner at the time. There were concerns over social dumping: social standards (minimum wages and health and safety) would be undermined because foreign services companies could use cheap foreign workers employed on lower standards. Particular concerns were raised over the regulation of private security and social care, where the vetting of workers' suitability – for example, for criminal convictions – could be undermined.

Although there were some problems with the directive, these criticisms were exaggerated. The Posted Workers Directive (Council 1997c) requires employers to pay the minimum wages and satisfy the employment conditions, including health and safety, of the host country, although it would still have been possible to employ foreign workers at below normal wages for the service. Are standards that much lower in other countries? Wages are lower, but whether standards are lower is questionable. A lot of the criticisms are special pleading by interest groups.

These objections have resulted in a significantly modified services directive (CEU 2006a). The modification includes a considerable number of exemptions from the directive: to the original exemptions on financial,[10] electronic communication networks and transport services,[11] are added healthcare and pharmaceutical services, audiovisual services, whatever their means of transmission, gambling services, social services in the area of housing, childcare and support to families and persons in need.[12] The other significant modification is that the principle of regulation by country of origin has gone, to be replaced by the freedom to provide services. The original proposal for mutual recognition was important, since it would potentially have made cross-border services provision much more straightforward, because it meant that cross-border services providers would only have to satisfy one set of regulations. But under the agreed directive, two sets of regulations are going to have to be satisfied. Provided requirements of non-discrimination, necessity[13] and proportionality are met, national authorities may regulate foreign services providers. There are some useful requirements on the authorization regime, such as a single point of contact, charges and processing time. The impact of the directive will only become apparent later, but these modifications are likely to reduce its impact significantly by increasing the difficulty of establishing new services provision in another MS. These difficulties are such that some suggest that from a legal viewpoint little has changed: 'the legal framework of the revised Services Directive remains predominantly the same as under the current legal status quo' (Badinger and Maydell 2009, p. 711). This implies that the benefits of the measure will be limited (de Bruijn *et al.* 2006; Badinger *et al.* 2008).

7.4.2 Financial services

The integration of financial markets is an essential SEM component which not only yields direct benefits, but is essential for the SEM as a whole. The Cecchini Report (CEU 1988a) attributed as much as a quarter of the potential gains for EC GDP from the SEM to the liberalization of financial services. The SEM review in the mid-1990s (Monti 1996) was markedly less optimistic, largely because remaining regulatory and other barriers had inhibited the emergence of genuine pan-EU provision of services. This was especially the case for retail financial services (Schüler and Heinemann 2002), but some barriers also remained in other areas and there was limited cross-border consolidation of the financial services industry. This led in 1999 to the Financial Services Action Plan (FSAP) (CEU 1999j), to restore the impetus towards financial integration, because the

potential gains from greater capital market efficiency were being lost. There is still plenty of potential for further integration of financial markets and this will substantially enhance economic growth (Kyla *et al.* 2009).

The key mechanisms through which financial integration translates into improved economic performance can be summarized as follows:

- Improvements in the 'x-efficiency' of financial intermediaries as competitive pressures oblige them to adopt new technologies, to pare operating costs and to restructure to more optimal sizes.
- Lower cost or more innovative provision, such as electronic trading, may lead to increases in retail demand for financial services especially.
- Pooling of liquidity that deepens the supply of finance, an effect estimated to be capable of lowering the cost of capital.
- The potential benefits from integration of financial markets are considerable.

FSAP (CEU 1999j) was designed to raise the efficiency of financial intermediation in the EU and especially to lower the costs of cross-border financing. It had four broad aims:

1. Completing a single wholesale market.
2. Developing open and secure markets for retail financial services.
3. Ensuring the continued stability of EU financial markets.
4. Eliminating tax obstacles to financial market integration.

The first legislative phase of FSAP is now complete: all the original measures have been adopted and transposed (CEU 2010l). The Lamfalussy Directives on securities markets are all adopted, but five MSs still need to complete transposition of three directives (CEU 2010m). But the process continues, with a further thirteen directives adopted, only two of which have been transposed in all MSs.

With the legislative programme still recent, it is early to judge the impact of FSAP. The one study that has been published (Kyla *et al.* 2009) found evidence that FSAP was having an impact in the three areas examined (banking, securities and insurance), but it was difficult to evaluate because of the financial crisis and the short time the measures had been in operation.

The financial crisis has fundamentally changed the

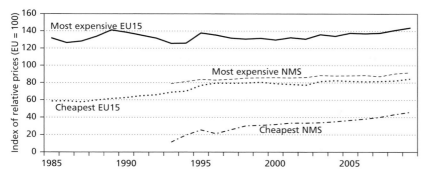

Figure 7.3 Price dispersion in the EU *Source:* CEU 2010c

environment within which financial market integration is occurring. The EU has responded by changing financial legislation in the areas of deposit guarantees, capital requirements and credit rating agencies, and further measures are in the pipeline (CEU 2010n). One fundamental change has been the development of a new EU supervisory financial framework, consisting of a European Systemic Risk Assessment Board and three new supervisory authorities dealing with banks, insurance/pensions and securities markets (European Parliament 2010). Regulation will still be by national authorities, but more closely monitored at EU level. How effective this framework will prove to be is questionable, but it does mark a significant step towards EU regulation of financial markets.

7.5 Assessment of the single market

The assessment of the SEM has two aspects: (a) the evaluation of the extent to which it has been achieved; and (b) the measurement of its effects on economic performance. These are the subject of the next two subsections.

7.5.1 The extent of integration in the single market

There is a very wide range of potential measures of the extent of integration in the SEM, but two stand out for their generality: price convergence and the extent of trade. A further indicator that needs examination is FDI, because, particularly in services, FDI could be a substitute for trade (see Chapter 8).

The SEM makes trade easier between MSs, which should make it harder to maintain price differences between national markets.[14] Arbitrage[15] and consumer cross-border trade should be much easier in the SEM. There was price convergence in the EU15 associated with the SEM from 1989 to 2000, but since 2000 there has been some divergence (see Figure 7.3). The new member states (NMS) show signs of price convergence both within their group and with the EU15.

The problem, of course, is one of causation: is the SEM the cause of price convergence? Price convergence of tradable goods is the result of arbitrage, but price convergence of non-tradable goods may be the result of the Balassa–Samuelson effect. In poorer countries the price of goods, such as housing, and services, such as restaurant meals, haircuts, and so on, is cheaper. This is partly the result of lower demand relative to supply (causing lower land prices and rents), but also because lower wages mean lower costs of production. The development of these economies leads to increases in productivity, especially in the tradable sector, so wages here can rise without affecting competitiveness. Wages in non-tradable sectors also rise, but without the accompanying increase in productivity, thus prices rise.[16] Therefore, the process of convergence in income levels will cause a reduction in price dispersion within the EU; so is price convergence the result of the SEM or income convergence? Indeed, is some of the income convergence the result of the SEM? In addition, the price convergence process may be very long-term (Mathä 2006).

The SEM should cause price convergence by increasing the proportion of output that is traded. Figure 7.2 shows intra- and extra-EU15 exports as a percentage of

GVA. Intra-EU15 exports increased their share of GVA rapidly after the introduction of SEM measures and this growth has continued. Extra-EU15 exports increased their share of GVA from 1992, but at a slower rate than for intra-EU15 trade. The greater rate of increase of intra-EU share of GVA is a clear indication of the effect of the SEM, because extra-EU15 exports should have been boosted by the faster growth of non-EU GDP. Both intra- and extra-EU15 imports fell in 2009 as a result of the crisis, but the fall in extra-EU15 exports is less, as EU15 GDP fell more than world GDP. The high level of intra-EU15 merchandise trade is a strong indication of the success of the SEM in integrating the EU's economy.[17]

The situation with trade in services is very different: both intra- and extra-EU imports have low shares of GVA in services and, while there is some growth, trade remains at a very low level. Given that a significant proportion of services is non-tradable, a lower share of GVA traded is to be expected. But the low overall growth and the fact that intra-EU15 trade in services is growing no faster than extra-EU15 trade is an indication that the integration of services markets has not been achieved. Trade is of course not the only indicator; the effects of integration could occur in the absence of trade if foreign services providers set up in other economies, but this does not seem to be happening (see Section 7.4.1, page 107). This is also indicated by the significant difference in services trade between countries (Roca Zamora 2009).

These conclusions relate to the EU15; the NMSs have higher overall levels of trade and growth of trade for both goods and services (Roca Zamora 2009). Here it is difficult to disentangle the impact of the SEM from the impact of enlargement, but they do seem to be more willing and able to exploit the potential of the SEM.

The SEM should increase the amount of FDI as companies locate and concentrate production at least-cost locations in the EU; companies invest in new local production for markets that have to be served locally (e.g. retailing); market competition is reconfigured by mergers that were previously off-limits. An acceleration of intra- and extra-EU15 FDI can be noted in 1998 (see Figure 7.4), a time of booming FDI across the world; but from 1999 onwards intra-EU15 FDI began to exceed outward FDI significantly and a clear gap between the two has been maintained. The timing of this development indicates that the single currency has had a

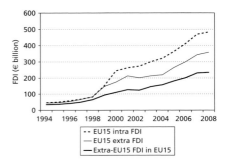

Figure 7.4 EU15 foreign direct investment
Source: Eurostat (2010e)

significant role in encouraging intra-EU FDI. While there is some tendency for FDI to decline with distance, other factors affecting FDI would tend to encourage extra- rather than intra-EU FDI – for example, differences in labour costs and market access. Extra-EU15 FDI has risen continuously, indicating that the SEM is attractive to non-EU multinational companies.

7.5.2 The single market and economic performance

The rationale for the SEM is that it reinforces the market opening principle of the common market by focusing not just on existing trade flows, but also on subjecting hitherto protected sectors to greater cross-border competition. In so doing it establishes a number of channels for improved resource allocation and efficiency gains that, in turn, offer the promise of improved economic performance. The economic gains are both micro- and macroeconomic. Achieving these benefits will require some dislocations: unemployment can result from the changes needed to achieve overall benefits. The benefits and costs of the SEM are analogous to the benefits of the formation of customs unions discussed in Chapter 6.

7.5.3 Empirical research on the single market: Commission studies

There are three major problems in estimating the effects of the SEM. First, the very wide nature of the programme means that its effects are spread across the whole EU economy. Second, both the implementation of the SEM and businesses' response take considerable periods of time. One estimate suggests that by 2007 less than half of the long-term income gains had been achieved (Straathof *et al.* 2008). For example, the elimination of barriers will encourage the relocation of production to least-cost sites within the EU, but this is a slow process. Third, these two problems compound the general difficulty of identifying the counterfactual: what would have happened in the absence of the SEM (see Chapter 9). SEM is not exogenous since some economic integration would have occurred in its absence, but how much? These general benefits of the SEM are calculated as part of the measurement of the effects of EU integration analysed in Chapter 9. So only a short summary of the potential size of the effects is included here.

The Cecchini Report (CEU 1988a) is based on Commission economic research (Emerson *et al.* 1988) highlighting the benefits of the SEM in the run-up to the 1992 deadline. The study predicted the total potential gain for the EC12 to be 4–7 per cent of EC GDP and 2–5 million jobs. It is important to emphasize the speculative nature of this exercise, and the fact that it was undertaken by a Commission keen to underscore the benefits of the flagship policy. Compared with this very optimistic picture, the findings of the second major exercise conducted by the Commission in the mid-1990s have to be regarded as a disappointment. Enormous effort was put into this research, which comprised some thirty-eight studies, plus a business survey (CEU 1996f). The headline figure this time was that the SEM had raised EU GDP by just over 1 per cent by 1994 and had increased employment by about half a million.

Why was there such a difference in the assessed impact? The Commission (CEU 1996f) identified three main problems. First, it was too soon to observe the medium-term effects of the SEM. Some SEM measures were not implemented until 1994–5, but also economic agents had not yet had time to adjust. Second, the data that could be used were, at best, only up to 1994, and thus only allowed a very short assessment period. Third, separating out the relatively small and incremental impact of market integration is difficult. While the impact of the SEM on economic performance was disappointing, surveys of opinion of company representatives reported a strong and significant impact on output and employment. In particular, the protection the SEM programme provides 'against the introduction of new barriers and the refragmentation of the market' was seen as important, thus indicating a role of the SEM in protecting existing gains rather than providing new ones.

On the tenth anniversary of 1992, the Commission was keen to celebrate the achievements of the SEM. It produced new estimates indicating that the SEM had raised EU GDP in 2002 by 1.8 per cent and increased employment by 1.46 per cent, which means that around 2.5 million extra jobs have been created (CEU 2002q). The latest estimates are provided by Ilkovitz *et al.* (2007), who suggest gains during 1992–2006 of 2.2 per cent of GDP and 1.4 per cent of employment. This indicates a significant, but far from earth–shattering, impact of the SEM, undermining the Commission's explanations for the low estimates in 1996. The idea that the SEM would transform EU economic performance has proved to be wide of the mark: there is no indication in the growth of output or productivity over this period that would support this contention (see Chapter 14).

It is only with the availability of a longer run of post-1992 data and the gradual refining of techniques that more reliable estimation of the overall effects of the SEM has become possible. A good recent example is Straathof *et al.* (2008), who suggest that internal market integration, including the customs union, have raised EU GDP by 2–3 per cent, but that the effect differed significantly between countries, amounting to 4–6 per cent for the Netherlands, for example.

7.6 Conclusion

In political terms the SEM must be regarded as a success. Despite some foot-dragging in the implementation of key measures, the strategic aim of opening up goods markets has been consistently advanced and has retained wide political support. Although, in a sense, the SEM will never be fully completed, because there will always be barriers that give some advantage to indigenous producers, there can be little doubt that the EU has moved a long way. The scope of the SEM has also expanded significantly to encompass most production. Economic nationalism and protection remain potent forces, and the development of the SEM continues to be a battle with these forces. The pace of regulation has slowed and the emphasis has gradually shifted to quality of regulation, implementation and enforcement.

Although much of the rhetoric surrounding the SEM has been about liberalization and deregulation, with the implication that it is principally concerned with *negative* integration (see Chapter 1), the reality is more complex. In a number of areas the outcome has been more a recasting of the regulatory framework than its dismantling, and the resulting regulatory style is one that reflects European values.

In economic terms, the outcome of the SEM is much less clear-cut: ultimately its objective was to raise the performance of the EU's economy, by raising productivity growth. To paraphrase Robert Solow, you can see the SEM programme everywhere but in the productivity statistics.[18] The interesting issue is why this should be so. Various responses are possible: the limited progress in services, the long-term nature of the project and the difficulties of implementation. An alternative view is that the impact of the SEM may have been a transitory shock, with little long-term impact on productivity growth. A balanced view might be that expectations were overblown and limited, but that worthwhile benefits have been achieved. It is also important to note that the SEM is merely part of an increasingly globalized world market, generally subject to liberalization and deregulation; ultimately these developments may have more profound impacts on economic performance. Indeed, European companies' search for competitiveness in this market was at the heart of the SEM, and in this sense it has been successful, enabling large companies to emerge and be competitive in the globalized economy. The SEM remains central to the EU and, despite its apparently limited economic impact, it is a powerful attraction for potential members and a model for its many imitators.

Summary

- The SEM is central to the development of the EU because it is the basis of economic integration and has such wide implications for other policies.
- Provision for the SEM was made in the EEC Treaty, but although the customs union was completed early, NTBs were not removed. This was a particular problem because the costs associated with NTBs are potentially larger than those associated with tariffs.
- After 1973, with the oil crisis and its associated recession, NTBs increased so that the SEM was regressing.
- Attitudes began to change in the early 1980s, with the failure of nationalistic economic policies,

the resolution of the UK's budget problem and a dynamic new Commission led by Jacques Delors.
- The Internal Market Programme was supported by all MSs, and in 1987, the SEA, the first major revision of the EEC Treaty, came into force.
- The SEA defined the internal market as an area without barriers, in which the freedom of movement of goods, services, capital and person is ensured.
- The SEA set a deadline of 1992 for the measures and reformed decision-making to make it easier to agree new laws.
- This was a very ambitious programme to remove internal borders, to harmonize taxes and laws relating to product safety, the environmental impact of products, and so on.
- The original legislative programme was completed more or less on time, but there have been problems getting the legislation transposed and enforced.
- Over time the programme has expanded to additional areas, such as network industries (telecommunications, electricity); the scope of existing measures has expanded and updating has taken place, so it is a continuous process.
- The SEM is largely complete, but there are problem areas such as services, where it has been difficult to implement.
- The SEM's economic purpose was to raise the EU's efficiency/productivity by enhancing competition, providing a larger market in which economies of scale could be achieved, and encouraging R&D.
- There is clear evidence that the SEM has integrated markets, as shown by price convergence and increasing trade and FDI.
- The assessed impact on economic performance is significant, but has not lived up to early expectations. This may be because there are problems with the operation of the SEM in relation to services, for example, or that the benefits take a long time so they are not yet complete.
- The SEM is an enormous achievement that has proved to be a magnet for new members and an example for the rest of the world.

Questions and essay topics

1. Why has the SEM been so central to EU development?

2. Why did the EC fail to eliminate NTBs using the powers contained in EEC Treaty?

3. Why are NTBs potentially more costly than tariff barriers?

4. What factors led to the development of the SEM programme in the early 1980s?

5. What were the major provisions of the SEA which facilitated the development of the SEM?

6. What are the problems of transposition and enforcement and why are they important?

7. What does the evidence on price convergence suggest about the SEM's effect on economic integration?

8. How is the SEM expected to raise economic performance of MSs?

9. How has the SEM affected trade in goods?

10. How has the SEM affected trade in services?

11. Why has the SEM had a greater effect on trade in goods than trade in services?

12. What has been the impact of the SEM on FDI?

13. Why is it difficult to estimate the SEM's effect on MSs' economic performance?

14. How would you explain the fact that the impact of the SEM on MSs' economic performance has been relatively limited?

FURTHER READING

Badinger, H. and Maydell, N. (2009) 'Legal and economic issues in completing the EU internal market for services: an interdisciplinary perspective', *Journal of Common Market Studies*, vol. 47, no. 4.

Monti, M. (2010) 'A new strategy for the single market: at the service of Europe's economy and society', Report to the President of the Commission, J. M. Barroso (http://ec.europa.eu/bepa/pdf/monti_report_final_10_05_2010_en.pdf).

OECD (2009) 'Deepening the single market', *OECD Economic Surveys: European Union 2009*, OECD, Paris, Chapter 3.

NOTES

1 The official expression is 'internal market', but 'single market' is the commonly used term. We shall use 'SEM' throughout to refer to this programme so as not to confuse it with the general expression of 'single market'.

2 An EP initiative which got no further, not to be confused with the Treaty *on* European Union (TEU), the Maastricht Treaty.

3 This was also a particular problem for labour mobility.

4 This is the reduction in consumer surplus: the difference between the maximum amount consumers are prepared to pay and the amount they actually have to pay (see Chapter 6).

5 Producers' surplus is the excess of revenue over cost (see Chapter 6).

6 Over time, losses could be larger as a result of inefficiency of protected producers.

7 Although it also relates to limitations in the original strategy, with additional legislation being required.

8 Excluding public services and administration, commercial services account for about half of GDP.

9 Even allowing for the fact that services are less tradable than merchandise goods and services.

10 Subject to separate legislation (see page 108).

11 The exclusion of urban transport, taxis and ambulances, as well as port services, is made explicit.

12 This means that the directive only applies to about one-third of GDP.

13 For example, justified for reasons of public policy, public security, public health or the protection of the environment.

14 This effect should be further reinforced by the single currency.

15 The movement of products from low-price to high-price markets for profit.

16 Competitiveness is not affected because these goods/services are not traded.

17 See also Roca Zamora 2009.

18 The original was Robert Solow's 1987 remark: 'You can see the computer age everywhere but in the productivity statistics.'

8 Factor mobility

DAVID MAYES

8.1 Introduction

Although the freedom of mobility of labour and capital were objectives enshrined in the Treaty of Rome itself, only fairly limited progress had been made by the early 1980s in turning this into reality. Most countries had capital controls of one form or another, and labour faced considerable constraints on movement through lack of recognition of qualifications and other problems over establishment and transfer of benefits. The slow progress stemmed from two sources. In the case of capital, member states (MSs) were worried that having free movement would lead to destabilizing flows that would disturb the running of the domestic economy. The main fear was a capital outflow that would depreciate the currency, drive up the rate of inflation and require monetary and fiscal contraction to offset it. Labour controls, on the other hand, were more concerned with inflows. Employees in the domestic economy feared that an inflow from other countries would lose them their jobs – countries would export their unemployment. Much of this was dressed up as a need to have certain skills, standards and local knowledge for the protection of consumers. Much of the fear stemmed from ignorance of what others' qualifications meant, and overcoming this required a long and tedious process of determination and negotiation.

This chapter begins by exploring the role of the movement of capital and labour in the EU and the history of its development, before moving on: first, to study capital mobility, and direct investment in particular; and then labour mobility.

8.2 The mobility of capital and labour in the EU

The 1985 White Paper on completing the Single European Market (SEM; see Chapter 7) and the 1986 Single European Act (SEA) signalled the determination to break through this complex of restrictions and move to a much more open market. In the case of capital, this was to be achieved by 1 July 1990. This target was largely not met for the EC of nine, and Portugal and Spain managed to participate in 1992, only for the Exchange Rate Mechanism (ERM) crisis of September 1992 (see Chapter 11) to require some controls to be reintroduced by MSs in the hope of stabilizing their exchange rates. The setback proved to be short-lived. The Treaty on European Union (TEU, or Maastricht Treaty), which came into force in 1993, had advanced progress further, and capital markets have become even more open with the introduction of the euro at the beginning of 1999.

The SEM legislative programme was intended to be complete by the end of 1992. While this was largely achieved, some of the labour mobility measures are yet to have their full effect (see Chapter 7). However, it has since become evident that these measures were by no means ambitious enough to achieve anything like a single capital market and this problem is still being tackled.

At the end of the millennium, attention turned to the various problems in the capital markets, including rigidities in capital movements across EU borders. Consequently, the Commission undertook an important political initiative aimed at enhancing the development of the risk capital markets and, more generally, dealing with related problems in the financial markets, the rationale being that Europe had lost opportunities

The previous version of this chapter was co-authored by Juha Kilponen; no doubt some of his work remains in this version. I am grateful to Jeremy Clegg for comments.

to create jobs and increase investment because its risk capital markets were underdeveloped, mainly due to the fragmentation of the regulation of the securities market (CEU 1998d). Following the Lamfalussy Report (2001), a new Financial Services Action Plan was implemented, which was given special fast-track procedures. This may have brought cross-border capital movement noticeably closer in the Eurozone to that within individual nations, but many aspects, such as the Single European Payments Area, remain elusive and may require direct action by the authorities if they are to materialize – for example, provision of services by the European Central Bank (ECB; see Chapters 3 and 11–12).

There are also some contradictions in these approaches. The logic behind the EU itself and the four freedoms is largely built on the neoclassical paradigm of perfect competition and its advantages. Yet the new development in the field, with its associated knowledge-based economies, is founded on notions based on new growth theory, increasing returns to scale and monopolistic competition. This means that earlier models of international factor mobility, basically static in character, are no longer useful for analysing international factor mobility, since they consider the optimal allocation of given factors of production. In the new 'endogenous growth' literature, a country or region's factor endowments are allowed to change over time under conditions of balanced growth. Growth is endogenous in the sense that it depends on the amount of resources allocated to accumulating production factors, such as human capital. Consequently, factor mobility can have an important influence on growth and convergence of growth rates between the countries. In the earlier literature, per capita output grows in accordance with the exogenous growth rate of technology, with policies that affect savings only altering the level of per capita income. Hence countries that have the same long-run growth rate in technology should have the same long-run growth rate in their per capita incomes, irrespective of their prevailing technology, size or level.

For new growth theories, the accumulation of knowledge, the generation of ideas, the development of human capital and the capacity to absorb new technologies are of the essence in explaining the forces underlying economic growth and determining the competitive position of individual countries. Thus the long-term growth prospects of EU MSs importantly depend on the flexibility and efficiency of the EU's own internal factor markets. Ongoing reallocation of production factors should transfer resources to those industries and sectors with comparative advantage and ability to achieve increasing returns to scale in the generation and application of new technology.

Moreover, according to the recent economic geography models, foreign direct investment (FDI) is not simply determined by relative costs of production or national tax structures. Firms may be drawn to particular regions due to the possibility of obtaining 'agglomeration economies'. The idea is that growth can be faster if competitors, suppliers, customers and related services are all close together in dynamic interaction. Agglomeration effects can be compounded by the wider impact of inward investment. While this has certainly been beneficial for large multinational companies, the problem for economic development is that it leads to greater spatial polarization. Not surprisingly, regions do not want to be without such poles (see Chapter 22).

Globalization has turned physical capital into a much more mobile factor of production. Due to FDI, firms may own the export sector of another nation, and these foreign owners may repatriate most of their profits (Gill and Law 1988). In such a case, the eventual problem from the point of view of economic development is the hierarchical and possibly exploitative character of transnational firms in a global economy: growth may be achieved, but only at the cost of international inequalities, combined with dependence on financial headquarters elsewhere. This may also apply to the EU's eastern enlargement, if increasing flows of profit repatriation eventually outweigh the inward FDI flows to the new member states (NMSs). It is thus not surprising to see that at the same time that the existing MSs have been pulling down the barriers to the free movement of capital and labour, they have been cautious in both fields, increasing the protection of labour through the social chapter in the TEU, insisting on a transition period for NMSs and seeking to limit the powers of company takeover.

However, Grossman and Rossi-Hansberg (2006) argue that many complex industrial goods nowadays are a result of a multitude of tasks that are performed in separate locations. Because of dramatic developments in communication and information technologies, improved possibilities for relocating the tasks offshore generate almost the same effects as technological progress in a standard neoclassical model of production and trade. If this productivity effect dominates the relative price, and labour supply affects offshoring, wages for low-skilled jobs will actually *rise* in the country where offshoring takes place. Moreover, along with improved possibilities for offshoring, high-skilled tasks can also boost the wages of domestic white-collar workers.

There is a basic distinction between direct investment, which involves the setting up or acquisition of a 'subsidiary' in a foreign country, and portfolio investment, involving the purchase of shares and bonds or the making of other forms of loan to a company in a foreign country. In the case of labour movement, individuals physically move from one country to another and then provide their labour services in the second country. Capital, on the other hand, involves the transfer of claims through a financial transaction and not the transfer of capital goods themselves in the form of plant, machinery and vehicles. If existing physical capital is exported, then the financial transfer is lowered. If new physical capital is purchased from the home country there is an additional export, but the net inflow of physical capital is smaller. The net flow is largest when the new physical capital is all produced in the country where the new plant is set up.

8.3 Capital movements

Exchange controls were eliminated in the UK in October 1979, for reasons that had little to do with EU membership (see Chapter 11). At that stage, the remaining MSs all had restrictions on capital flows, although these varied in their degree of tightness. After the start of the SEM programme, these restrictions were steadily removed and there has been effective freedom of capital movements since the start of Economic and Monetary Union's (EMU) stage 2. With the exception of NMSs, freedom throughout the Community was in place by July 1990, the start of EMU's stage 1. In most cases there was a distinction between controls applied to residents and those applied to non-residents, with the restrictions being lighter in the latter case. However, such restrictions as did apply to non-residents usually applied equally to all such non-residents, regardless of whether they were residents of another EC country or of a third country. There is thus no counterpart to the

preference system applied to trade through differential tariffs as far as capital movements are concerned; nor, it seems, was there any intention of taking the opportunity of introducing discrimination against third countries by making this freedom of movement only in respect of fellow MSs.[1]

In general, the movement of financial capital among financial centres now entails only minimal intrinsic costs, due to the liberalization and development of information technology. FDI and the (re-)establishment of productive capacity are neither costless nor prohibitively costly in terms of time and financial effort. The GATT and WTO rounds aimed at liberalization in world trade have also enhanced direct investments (see Chapter 24).

However, the restrictions that matter are not in the capital movements themselves, but in how those funds can be used to purchase physical assets. Constraints, or indeed incentives, apply to inward investment, to mergers and acquisitions (M&A) and to the operation of multinational enterprises (MNEs). Thus freedom of capital movements is to some extent a myth if there are further constraints on how the funds can be used. Nevertheless, it is clear that restrictions are being progressively eliminated. Although it has been somewhat difficult to detect any direct growth benefits for financial integration as such, there is evidence that the strengthening of financial sectors has contributed to strong growth in the emerging Europe.

According to the OECD (2000) and Nicoletti *et al.* (2000), barriers to intra-MS trade are now fairly low in all EU countries – in some cases even lower than in the USA. There are, however, still quite large differences across countries; in particular, indicators are the highest in Greece, Portugal and France.

As in the case of trade flows, we would expect to observe a more rapid increase in direct investment abroad than in GDP itself. This duly occurred in the second half of the 1980s, but was not confined to the EU. Increased trade flows are likely to involve changes in capital flows – to set up distribution networks and to establish local production as market penetration increases – although the direction of the change is still problematic, as we cannot tell a priori the extent to which trade and direct investment might be substitutes rather than complements.

Nevertheless, recent trends in capital movements in Europe give a clear message about the importance of capital flows in open economies. Gross flows of capital are of immense magnitude, many of the flows representing offsetting movements through which financial and other institutions achieve portfolio diversification and protection against exchange rate and other financial risks. FDI flows are naturally smaller, but since the second half of the 1990s they have continued to surge and have become substantially more important in the process of capital formation as well (see Table 8.1, page 118). This in part reflects the globalization process, which has entailed the rapid expansion of the number and coverage of MNEs in Europe. The overall scale of FDI began to increase strikingly during recent decades as countries began to locate portions of their manufacturing, sales and service enterprises in many other countries. For example, the sum of outward and inward FDI as a share of total 1997 investment exceeded 20 per cent for ten of the EC15. The corresponding figure was less than 10 per cent for all but the UK and the Netherlands in 1975.

Traditionally, the main net outward investors include Germany, Japan and the UK. The Netherlands, Sweden and Switzerland also rank high as net outward investors. One of the main reasons is that several MNEs reside in these countries, which invest extensively abroad. On the other hand, other countries receive more FDI than they invest abroad. These include countries such as Hungary and Poland, as well as Australia and Spain. Recently, however, the picture has changed. Ranking EU MSs according to the size of their respective cumulative inflows over 1992–2000, it appears that Germany has changed its position, since in 2000 it became a net recipient of EU FDI, while the Netherlands switched to a position of net recipient (see Table 8.1, page 118), but the figures for 2005 restore the German and Dutch positions.

8.4 On the determinants of direct investment

Investment flows between countries cannot really be treated in the same manner as investment within the economy because, although total investment can be explained through well-known relationships, the split between home and foreign expenditure, on an economy-wide basis, is not so clear. We are concerned in this case not just with what resources firms are prepared to put into capital for future production, but where they are going to site them. Most consideration, therefore, has been devoted to the problem at the level of the firm itself, rather than through modelling the components of the capital account of the balance of payments. Even within the confines of aggregate explanation there has been a tendency to avoid modelling FDI flows directly, and modelling them indirectly through the determination of the exchange rate as a sort of reduced-form approach (see Cuthbertson *et al.* 1980 for a discussion of this work).

Such an approach may be appropriate for the explanation of portfolio investment, in particular, since much short-term portfolio investment is described as speculative in nature. It is much less useful for direct investment, because of the degree of permanence embodied in the existence of physical capital held abroad and changes in the logic with which MNEs organize their production.[2]

Nowadays a large proportion of trade is accounted for by large MNEs, and a significant proportion of global trade (estimates are between 30 and 40 per cent) runs through the international production and distribution networks of MNEs as *intra-company trade*. The increase in intra-company trade reflects the motives of MNEs for diversifying risk and deepening economies of scope in the world market. The increasing information content in nearly all products requires experts in various fields to participate in the design and development of almost every commodity. Consequently, many global companies seek to establish both production and research and development activities in different locations all over the world, providing them with either cost-effective production or an abundance of educated people and information infrastructure.

Another factor that may have affected the upsurge of FDI is related to changes in MNEs' production model. In the typical 'Fordist' production model, MNEs seek growth by expanding into new sectors and connected horizontal integration with diversification. Vertical integration, which was the characteristic of the Fordist production model, was a means of internalizing possible market risks in different phases of the value chain. Globalization, however, has drastically changed the Fordist production model. In recent years, an increasing number of companies have chosen to narrow their segment of products and services and of the value

Table 8.1 Direct investment flows of EU countries, 1987–2009 (ECU/euro million)

	1987			1993			1998			2005			2009 (provisional figures)		
	Intra[1]	Extra[2]	Total	Intra[1]	Extra[2]	Total	Intra[1]	Extra[2]	Total	Intra[1]	Extra[2]	Total	Intra[1]	Extra[2]	Total
Outward															
BLEU[3]	1,655	545	2,200	2,675	1,333	4,008	16,778	6,035	22,813	69,488	52,726	122,214	163	124,796	124,959
Denmark	278	219	497	297	779	1,076	3,734	240	4,054	9,800	2,115	11,915	6,969	4,410	11,379
Germany	1,610	5,266	6,876	18,821	9,610	28,431	47,744	108,558	156,302	21,696	14,999	36,695	36,867	8,271	45,138
Greece	1	9	10	na	na	na	na	na	na	na	na	na	1,141	183	1,324
Spain	270	227	497	1,584	937	2,521	5,241	11,680	16,921	14,420	16,757	31,177	4,121	7,638	11,759
France	3,639	3,483	7,122	6,012	4,381	10,393	26,101	17,343	43,444	66,871	26,137	93,008	91,149	26,370	117,519
Ireland	65	86	151	na	na	na	1,126	2,363	3,489	10,250	659	10,909	10,422	4,515	14,937
Italy	998	495	1,493	4,732	1,442	6,174	5,183	5,605	10,788	27,225	6,352	33,577	29,979	1,480	31,459
Netherlands	1,998	3,607	5,605	4,832	5,228	10,060	18,724	15,985	34,718	93,145	21,784	114,929	-7,512	20,311	12,799
Portugal	8	6	2	84	7	91	1,491	2,129	3,620	1,620	-698	922	1,613	-682	931
UK	1,730	16,728	18,458	7,866	11,700	19,566	16,940	91,777	108,716	23,314	59,370	82,684	-17,681	30,576	12,895
Austria				na			1,329	1,036	2,452	2,816	5,244	8,060	478	2,679	3,157
Finland				1,190	13	1,203	15,411	1,245	16,656	4,817	-1,322	3,495	1,919	165	2,084
Sweden				1,192	127	1,319	9,519	5,509	15,028	12,833	5,968	18,801	18,941	5,263	24,204
EU12/15	12,344	30,670	43,014	40,711	24,377	65,088	149,443	218,754	368,197	399,477	208,704	608,181	217,887	263,335	481,222
Inward															
BLEU[3]	1,265	693	1,958	6,302	2,899	9,201	12,229	6,331	18,560	81,729	34,165	115,894	54,512	51,137	105,649
Denmark	2,127	151	24	843	582	1,425	1,053	4,640	5,747	5,657	4,888	10,545	4,284	1,416	5,700
Germany	250	215	465	1,048	-439	609	38,615	4,661	43,276	19,967	6,297	26,264	18,568	7,062	25,630
Greece	102	87	189	na	na	na	na	na	10	na	na	na	2,091	324	2,415
Spain	1,976	1,338	3,314	6,963	1,087	8,050	9,493	1,049	10,542	15,553	2,932	18,485	5,561	5,258	10,819
France	1,654	2,056	3,710	7,803	2,647	10,450	22,458	5,227	27,685	36,552	14,572	51,124	33,812	10,431	44,243
Ireland	160	327	487	na	na	na	4,647	3,271	7,919	-19,956	-5,078	-25,034	17,026	949	17,975
Italy	1,310	1,745	3,055	2,528	673	3,201	2,117	208	2,325	14,101	1,926	16,027	17,902	2,963	20,865
Netherlands	1,315	664	1,979	5,869	680	6,549	13,222	20,662	33,884	27,804	5,533	33,337	16,720	2,679	19,399
Portugal	230	97	327	1,062	232	1,294	1,112	1,588	2,700	2,952	-448	2,504	1,354	713	2,067
UK	4,085	5,619	9,704	2,037	10,609	12,646	16,863	46,146	63,010	103,166	25,124	128,290	-1,514	33,997	32,483
Austria				na	na	na	4,342	-184	4,050	6,131	1,141	7,272	2,143	3,162	5,305
Finland				512	227	739	10,332	516	10,848	3,437	-278	3,159	2,211	-375	1,836
Sweden				1,264	1,002	2,266	12,950	1,522	14,472	9,686	782	10,468	11,052	-2,000	9,052
EU12/15	12,344	12,991	25,335	37,231	20,775	58,006	135,847	96,432	232,279	366,052	77,214	443,266	154,909	221,734	376,643

Notes:

[1] 'Intra' = flows to or from other EU countries.

[2] 'Extra' = flows to or from the rest of the world.

[3] 'BLEU' = Belgium–Luxembourg Economic Union.

Source: Adapted from Eurostat database for 1993–2005; *European Union Direct Investment Yearbooks* (1984–93) for 1987.

chain, to concentrate on accumulating and developing core competencies.

Moreover, due to more open international competition and the complexity of the products, companies find it harder to achieve and maintain competitive advantage in several sectors or product and service segments at once. This has affected the factor flows across territorial boundaries, in particular FDI, and reinforced the development of a more concentrated economy.

This multinational structure of production and pressures to expand it also have consequences for trade. In the case of vertical FDI, where companies allocate different parts of their production chain to those countries where production costs are lower, FDI typically boosts international trade. In the case of horizontal FDI, a company places its production close to foreign markets. In this case, FDI acts as a substitute to trade, and provides strategic market access for the investor.

8.5 Capital movements in Europe

It is noticeable that most modelling of inward FDI relates to flows into the EU from outside, not to flows within the EU itself. Yet it is these internal flows that should be of prime interest in the case of the SEM and the development of a knowledge-based society. The studies of external FDI flows suggest that there are three basic mechanisms at work. First, investment tends to increase with sales to the EU – that is, supporting trade rather than substituting for it (Scaperlanda and Balough 1983). Barrell and Pain (1993) suggest, following Vernon (1966), that there is an initial level of exports that is required before it becomes worthwhile setting up dealer networks and other downstream services. Second, investment takes place to overcome trade barriers (Culem 1988; Heitger and Stehn 1990) or anti-dumping duties (Barrell and Pain 1993). However, overseas investors with a choice of locations and flows are also affected by relative costs and relative barriers. Thus, when anti-dumping actions were at their height in the USA in the mid-1980s, this acted as a spur to Japanese investment there. Finally, investment flows are crucially affected by the availability of funds in the investing country.

The UK has been the largest investor overseas in the EU and is the second largest in the world after the USA.[3] Only the Netherlands among other EU MSs has been a net FDI exporter since 2000, although West

Germany had substantial net exports during 1975–90. More recently there have been striking year-to-year variations, with strong outward FDI by France and strong inward FDI in Germany. Towards the end of the millennium large parts of EU outward FDI flows were accounted for by the UK, France, the Netherlands and Germany. In 2000 they made up 60 per cent of outward FDI flows outside the EU (excluding the USA) and 73 per cent of flows to the USA. At the same time, these four countries accounted for 55 per cent of intra-EU FDI flows. Figures for 2009 are particularly distorted by the financial crisis.

More generally, in 2000 the EU participated in the strong worldwide FDI activity that was closely related to the reorganization of the telecommunications sector, and thus may not be indicative of the longer run. At the other end of the scale is the very low level of FDI in Greece and Italy. Thus, despite any attractiveness that may have existed from surplus and cheaper labour in those countries, this factor advantage has been met by labour outflow rather than capital inflow

Outward FDI has been rising considerably faster than in the USA, while inward FDI has risen more slowly. Much EU FDI is outside the EU rather than to other EU MSs. FDI abroad, like domestic investment, has traditionally been affected by trade cycles. It is also not realistic to treat the EU as a largely homogeneous unit from the point of view of FDI. For example, FDI flows between the UK and the Netherlands were far larger than relative economic size would suggest, both before and after accession to the EU. This presumably reflects, among other things, the number of Anglo-Dutch MNEs.

As noted earlier, between one-half and three-quarters of net FDI abroad by the UK is composed of profits from overseas subsidiaries and associated companies that are not remitted to the UK. Net acquisition of overseas companies' share and loan capital is, partly by consequence, around one-sixth to one-third of the total.[4]

The Commission put together a database called AMDATA that provided a rather detailed list of M&A activity involving EU enterprises (sadly now discontinued). There has been a marked increase in M&A activity in the EU since the early 1990s. On the one hand, there has been a strong upward trend in MNEs since 1992. On the other hand, cross-border M&A inside the EC started to increase steadily only after 1996 (see Table

Table 8.2 Mergers and acquisitions involving EU firms

Year	Total (no.)	National (%)	EC (%)	International (%)
1987	2,775	71.6	9.6	18.8
1991	10,657	54.3	11.9	14.5
1995	9,854	57.4	12.9	22.8
1999	14,335	55.7	14.2	26.4
2003	8,700	59.0	14.0	21.0
2004	9,000	57.0	14.0	24.0

Note:

Figures do not necessarily add up to 100 per cent since in some cases the bidder is unknown. Figures for 1991–2001 are based on the recent revisions of the AMDATA, while those for 1987–90 are based on 1999 revisions. Figures from 2002 onwards are based on the EU25, while earlier figures are based on the EU15.

Source: European Economy (CEU 2001j, 2005k)

8.2). In 2004 there were 9,000 instances where EU companies were the target. While these recent numbers refer to the EU25 and thus the enlarged EU, M&A still predominantly takes place in the EU15.

Intra-EU FDI flows have been expanding during the second half of the 1990s, confirming the importance of the deepening integration of the product and factor markets in the EU. During 1999 and 2000 in particular, intra-EU FDI showed a significant increase in volume relative to GDP and trade. One of the reasons behind this upsurge was associated with the reorientation of UK FDI flows in favour of EU MSs. This, in turn, was largely due to a few huge cross-border mergers, in particular the acquisition of Mannesmann by Vodafone Air Touch, and successive ownership changes in two of the most important telecoms businesses (CEU 2001j). Total FDI flows into EU MSs increased substantially in 2005 over the previous year. There has also been a clear upsurge in intra-EU FDI flows. Much of this upsurge is explained by an increase in investments to the UK. This increase has largely been due to the merger of Shell Transport and Trading Company plc and the Royal Dutch Petroleum Company into Royal Dutch Shell. Country-by-country breakdown of FDI flows shows that the situation varies considerably across countries and time.

8.6 Labour movements

Labour mobility is often assumed to be a substitute for capital mobility. However, this is rather misleading,

given that labour migration is in many ways a much more complex process than international capital flows. Simply put, because the migration of labour necessarily requires the movement of a person or persons, such a move involves more than just the labour market and income considerations. Capital may be allocated internationally without requiring the movement of the capital owner. Moreover, there are many situations where the movements of capital and labour do not substitute but rather complement each other (Fischer 1999). Such differences in behaviour are enormous from a practical and policy point of view.

On the one hand, total FDI statistics are sometimes affected by the behaviour of a single or very few large MNEs in a particular country; a single company can dominate the total effect of flows between any particular pair of countries. Labour flows, on the other hand, are the result of the decisions of a large number of independent households (although actions by companies and communities can have a strong influence on these decisions). With some limited exceptions involving transient staff and actions in border areas, movement of labour simply involves a person shifting his or her residence from one country to another to take up a job in the second country. There is not the same range of possible variations as in the case of capital movements. There is also the considerable simplification that there is not the equivalent problem of the relation between the financial flows (or retained earnings) and the physical capital stock. The number of foreign nationals employed will be the sum of the net inflows, without any revaluation problems and only a relatively limited difficulty for 'retirements' (through age, naturalization, and so on).

On the other hand, early theories of migration argued that a major incentive to move is an income differential in real terms. However, it is not merely that the same job will be better paid in the second country; it may be that the person moving will be able to get a 'better' job in the second country (in the sense of a different job with higher pay). There are severe empirical problems in establishing what relative real incomes are, not just in the simple sense of purchasing power parities, but in trying to assess how much one can change one's tastes to adapt to the new country's customs and price patterns, and what extra costs would be involved if, for example, the household had to be divided, and so on. This is difficult to measure, not just in precise terms for the outside observer, but even in rough terms for the individual involved.

This sort of uncertainty for the individual is typical of the large range of barriers that impede the movement of labour, in addition to the wide range of official barriers that inhibit movement. Ignorance of job opportunities abroad, living conditions, costs, ease of overcoming language difficulties, how to deal with regulations, and so on, is reduced as more people move from one country to another and are able to exchange experiences. Firms can reduce the level of misinformation by recruiting directly in foreign countries.

Even if it were possible to sort out what the official barriers are and to establish the relative real costs, there would still be a multitude of factors that could not be quantified but could perhaps be given implicit values. These other factors involve differences in language, customs, problems of transferring assets (both physical and financial), disruptions to family life, changes in schooling, loss of friends, and so on.

These considerations have led to the development of so-called microeconomic behavioural models of labour mobility or immobility. These theories argue, quite convincingly, that migration decisions are made in a complex environment, where the decisions are influenced by family or group considerations as well as by time and life-course events. In some of these approaches, location-specific information and the ability to make use of insider advantage play an important role in the decision to move (Fischer 1999). Gaining knowledge about location-specific economic,

social and cultural opportunities, building up a social network or getting involved in the activities of various interest groups all require a certain time of immobility. Thus immobility has a value, and in moving investment, gaining such insider advantage represents a sunk cost that needs to be covered by expected utility gains in the receiving region.

Of course, some of these factors could work in a favourable direction: it might be easier to find accommodation abroad, and setting up a new household and finding new friends might be an attractive prospect. Moreover, the development of information technologies and the consequential reduction in communication and organizational costs across territorial borders help in solving at least some of the problems associated with insider advantage. Nevertheless, all this suggests that margins in labour rewards between countries may be considerable in practice, even if free movement of labour is theoretically permitted. It should thus be no surprise to find that many differences in labour rewards exist between EC MSs. However, it would also be a mistake to think that there are no barriers in practice to employment in other EU MSs, as is clear from the next section.

8.7 Labour flows in the EU

While freedom of movement of labour was part of the framework of the 1957 Treaty of Rome itself, the original six EU MSs had to start from a position of considerable restrictions of labour movement, and it was not until 1968 that work permits were abolished and preferences for home country workers no longer permitted. The SEM involved a range of measures to try to eliminate those fiscal barriers, not just for the worker but for the accompanying family as well. Merely permitting geographic labour mobility does not in itself either facilitate or encourage it. It is quite possible to make mobility difficult through measures relating to taxes and benefits, which make a period of previous residence or contribution necessary for benefit.

EU labour markets are in general characterized by relatively low levels of geographic mobility; EU citizens have about half the mobility rate of US citizens. According to Eurobarometer, 38 per cent of EU citizens changed residence over the course of a decade, the majority of whom moved within the same town or village (68 per cent), and 36 per cent moved to another town in the same region. However, only 4.4 per cent moved across national borders into another MS. Furthermore, it has been estimated that annual migration between MSs amounts to around 0.75 per cent of the resident population and perhaps only 0.4 per cent of resident EU nationals. In the USA these figures appear about six times larger. Moreover, occupational or professional reasons account for only a small proportion of the house moves; when people move it is mainly for family and housing reasons. Movements increased with respect to NMSs after 2004.

Of course, these relatively low labour mobility figures reflect cultural and institutional heterogeneity in the EU, but may also be due to a more systematic failure in the functioning of factor markets. In particular, it has been argued that real wage unresponsiveness to regional labour demand fluctuations and wage compression policies have hindered the functioning of internal labour markets.

The principal concern raised in the EU recently is that various barriers still exist and continue to keep labour mobility within the EU at a low level. Given the political commitment to enhance EU competitiveness and growth in the global economy by establishing a knowledge-based economy the EU has taken a look at the impediments on mobility of skills and labour.

The potential barriers to labour mobility in the EU can be roughly divided into man-made and natural barriers. Man-made barriers include inconsistent labour market institutions; problems in the portability of pensions and social security rights; and the lack of full mutual recognition of qualifications and experience. Natural barriers include a range of social, cultural and language barriers and also the ageing of the labour force. Given that the young tend to be more mobile than the old, demographic change will imply that there will be considerably fewer potential movers among the working-age population. Many empirical studies have found that, in both the EU and the USA, moving declines sharply after the age of thirty to thirty-five.

The actual path of labour migration is, of course, heavily affected by the cyclical fluctuation of the economy. If an economy is growing and able to maintain full employment, it is likely to attract more labour from abroad for two reasons: first, because there are more job opportunities, and second, because there is less domestic opposition to immigration. In the period after

the first oil crisis, when unemployment rose sharply and EU economies moved into recession, there was much more resistance to the flow of labour between MSs and encouragement for reversing the flow.

The clearest feature of the development of the permitted mobility of labour among EU MSs was that restrictions were lifted on workers from other MSs rather than non-members. Nevertheless, only Belgium and Luxembourg have had a higher proportion of their foreign workers coming from within the EU than from outside it. The position has changed relatively little in recent years, with the exception of Germany, where there has been a small rise, and Luxembourg, where there has been a small fall in the number of non-nationals in the workforce. Looking at it from the point of view of country of origin, in all cases except Ireland, only a very small percentage of the labour force from the old MSs has moved to other MSs. It appears that size and percentage of working population abroad are inversely related. It is EU MSs with the lowest incomes that had the highest outward mobility. Greece, Portugal and Spain alter the picture fairly considerably. They all had above-average numbers of people working elsewhere in the EU even before they joined, particularly Portugal. NMSs have emphasized the picture. The real income gaps with the rest of the EU have been larger and the incentives to move that much greater. Although there was an opportunity for a phased reduction in barriers against immigration from NMSs, this has not proved to be a problem by and large. It is immigration from outside the EU, particularly where it is illegal, that has put pressure on the system.

The picture is a little more complex for inward flows. Luxembourg stands out, with around one-third of the working population coming from foreign countries. Belgium, France and Germany form a second group, with a little less than 10 per cent of their workforce coming from abroad; and the remaining countries have smaller proportions, down to negligible numbers in the case of Italy.

Some special relationships are apparent which relate to previous history rather than the EC as a determinant of the pattern of flows: former colonies in the case of France and the UK and, to a lesser extent, in the case of Belgium and the Netherlands; and the relationship between the UK and Ireland. The West German policy of encouraging foreign workers is clear, with large numbers coming from Turkey and (the former)

Yugoslavia. What is perhaps surprising is that despite the recruitment ban on countries outside the EU in 1973, the shares of MSs and non-member countries in the number of foreign nationals employed in West Germany remained at approximately the same levels after 1974, the share of non-members falling only as some of the countries joined the EC. Subsequently there was a fall in foreign labour in most countries by 1990 and stabilization thereafter. However, the switch is much larger for those from non-member countries than for those from the other MSs.

At first glance it appears that labour, in proportionate terms, is rather less mobile than capital. The balance of labour and capital flows tends to be in opposite directions according to the development of the various economies. However, there are many specific factors overriding this general relation. The wealthier countries have attracted labour and invested overseas at the same time, thus helping to equilibrate the system from both directions. Yet there is little evidence inside the EU that there are large labour movements purely as a result of the EU's existence. Some movement between contiguous countries is to be expected, especially where they are small, and also movements from those countries with considerable differences in income, primarily Greece, Ireland, Italy, Portugal and, to a lesser extent, Spain. However, the major movements have been the inflow of workers from outside the EU, primarily into France, Germany and the UK. Thus, despite discrimination in favour of MSs' nationals, the relative benefits to employers (the ability to offer worse conditions, readier dismissal, lower benefits, and so on) and to employees (the size of the income gain and the improvement in living standards for their families) make flows from the lower-income countries more attractive to both parties.

Worries about the competitive exploitation of employees through reducing social protection (known colloquially as 'social dumping') have led the EU to develop the SEM's social dimension, expressed through the Charter of Fundamental Rights for Workers and the action programme for its implementation (see Chapters 2 and 23). The measures are specifically designed to ensure an EU 'single market' for labour. This does not necessarily mean that labour will be more mobile or labour markets more flexible as a consequence. In practice, the social dimension has led to relatively limited changes in labour market legislation. Even the Working Time Directive, which caused a major debate, was ultimately watered down to the point where it did not much change existing behaviour (see Chapter 23).

It should be no surprise that international mobility is limited when one sees the extent of reluctance to respond to economic stimuli for movement within countries. The existence of sharply different regional unemployment levels and regional wage differentials reveals this reluctance. In the UK, the system of public sector housing is thought to aid labour rigidity. Possession of a council house in one district does not give any entitlement to one elsewhere. However, even for private sector house owners, negative equity and the very considerable transaction costs of sale and purchase act as a substantial restriction on mobility.

Yet regional and industrial data in EU MSs reveals only moderate differences in wages across sectors for homogeneous labour. These moderate wage differentials more likely reflect the institutional rigidity of wages per se, rather than the efficient functioning of the factor markets. This is evident from the fact that regional unemployment rates are widely dispersed. Unemployment differentials across sectors are also fairly persistent in many EU MSs. EU MSs exhibit bigger variations across regional migration flows than between the corresponding US states.

Decressin and Fatás (1995) note that in the EU region-specific shocks in the demand for labour are reflected in changes in regional participation rates, while unemployment rates react to a small extent during the first three years. Migration, in turn, plays a substantial role in the adjustment process only after three years. A large part of the changes in labour demand is met by people moving in and out of the labour force, instead of migrating or experiencing short unemployment spells. However, more recent evidence suggests that EU nationals may be significantly more mobile than was previously thought. Based on a panel of 166 regions for the period 1988–97, Tani (2002) shows that labour demand shocks trigger fairly similar responses in local labour markets across the EU and the USA. According to his study, the absorber of a labour demand shock is net migration, accounting for around 50 per cent of the response in the first year and about 80 per cent during the next. In the USA the corresponding numbers are about 40 per cent and 50 per cent.

8.8 Agglomeration considerations

In recent years Krugman and Venables (1996), inter alios, have argued that the pattern of location of industry will be rather different from that initially expected, as there are several factors that lead to increasing economies of scale and agglomeration, at least over a range above the position applying in the early 1990s. Proximity to the main markets, networks of suppliers, skilled labour, and so on, may actually attract firms to the main centres of existing industry even though costs may be higher, thus encouraging labour and capital to move in the same direction and exacerbate rather than ease existing disparities.

This idea of the clustering of activity both in terms of location and in range of industrial activity has a long history, although it has more recently been popularized by Porter (1990). Porter offers not so much an explanation of why activity concentrates, as an encouragement to governments to reorient their policies to encourage the process so that they can reap a competitive advantage. The key to this comes from the exploitation of the immobile and less mobile factors of production, such as land, physical and business infrastructure and services and, particularly in the EU's case, highly skilled labour. The increasing returns occur because the process feeds on itself – endogenous growth.

EU structural policy has followed this line of argument (see Chapters 22 and 23), using this policy as a means of helping disadvantaged regions compete through improving public and private infrastructure and human skills. Thus there have been counterforces to those of increasing concentration in existing centres that market forces alone might have fostered.

This process of concentration has clearly been followed in practice in the EU, but it is by no means the only force for development, as the Irish economy demonstrates. Here high-technology and IT-based industries have been able to flourish where their location was not very important, aided by favourable macroeconomic, wage bargaining and other direct incentives. High-value, low-weight items, with a worldwide market, are not so dependent on location, but do require skilled labour. Similarly, call centres, internet services and computer software can be located in any lower-cost region and their results transmitted electronically immediately.

The experience with migration from Central and Eastern Europe after 1989 increased caution over opening up the labour market more widely, and it was no surprise that most countries imposed a phase-in agreement for allowing unlimited migration from NMSs when they joined in 2004. This has been eased since, in part because those MSs that did permit migration, particularly the UK, seem to have benefited from an influx of skilled workers, and in part because the scale of flows has been fairly modest. It reinforces the suspicion that labour movement has been widely regarded as a key EU ingredient largely because it has not occurred on a substantial scale. Labour markets and capital markets once again complement and, importantly, interact with each other and factor endowments can no longer be taken as given. Regions that are open to factor flows have additional means of adjusting to external shocks and the changing economic and political environment. Factor flows, however, are not instantaneous, but proceed at a rate that reflects economic incentives, intrinsic costs of adjustment, economic policy and institutional settings, as well as the reorganization of industrial production structures. In this sense, factor flows reflect a continuous process of adjustment towards equilibrium. What is crucial to the rate of integration in the internal market is whether differences in factor rewards persist across territorial boundaries of Europe.

8.9 Conclusion

Recent trends indicate that labour and capital are neither perfectly mobile nor perfectly immobile, but rather adjust gradually to market conditions and economic policies. EU MSs do experience inter-regional movements of labour and capital that are of significant magnitude. Yet these movements are far from instantaneous. Labour and capital are clearly linked across regions, but there are still some obstacles to rapid adjustments of labour and capital stocks. At the same time, liberalized immigration policies, EU enlargements and other steps that promote integration of the factor markets of Western Europe with those of surrounding regions present a challenge to policy-makers to maintain social cohesion and stable development across different EU regions.

Summary

- The freedom of movement of capital and labour, while being two of the four fundamental freedoms laid down by the Treaty of Rome, have been slow to become a reality. While direct barriers to the free movement of capital were removed in the early 1990s in the first stage to EMU, it is still far from a single market for capital as in the USA.

- Freedom of movement of labour also experiences many practical difficulties, but labour is relatively reluctant to move in the EU, even when there are considerable incentives. Thus the free movement of both labour and capital are far more limited than in the USA.

- Modern developments in endogenous growth theory and the new economic geography suggest that in a modern, knowledge-based economy there are increasing returns from the agglomeration of production and skills in particular industry groups in certain locations.

- As a result, many of the fears about the loss of jobs from inward migration and the loss of control from foreign ownership have proved to be outweighed by positive effects.

- As a result, the pattern of production and ownership in the EU has changed markedly since the beginning of the 1980s.

- However, MNEs operate on a global scale and investment by EU MSs outside and by outsiders in the EU has formed a critical part of the process of development.

- FDI tends to go in cycles and hence developments have been bunched. Some MSs have been more active than others, with France, Germany, the Netherlands and the UK being more active in FDI and also in receiving labour migration. The rest of the EU is also uneven, with Belgium and Luxembourg attracting the greatest proportionate labour flows.

- A new round of development is in progress with the latest EU enlargements, and the pattern is unlikely to stabilize for some years yet, given the extent of the differences in relative prices.

Questions and essay topics

1. What are the main forces leading to FDI?
2. Why is labour so reluctant to move in the EU compared to the USA?
3. How has the new economic geography changed views on the importance of factor mobility?
4. What is the role of MNEs in transforming the structure of trade and investment in the EU?
5. What impact are NMSs likely to have on migration and the siting of production in the EU?
6. What is social dumping? Why has it been a concern?
7. Why is it so difficult to attain a single market for capital in the EU?
8. How does endogenous growth theory impart a positive role to inward migration in EU MSs?
9. In what ways is investment a complement rather than a substitute for trade?
10. How do capital flows and labour flows interact? To what extent are they substitutes?

FURTHER READING

Fassmann, H. J., Haller, M. and Lane, D. (2009) *Migration and Mobility in Europe: Trends, Patterns and Control*, Edward Elgar, Cheltenham.

Liebscher, K., Christl, J., Mooslechner, P. and Ritzberger-Grunwald, D. (2007) *Foreign Direct Investment in Europe: A Changing Landscape*, Edward Elgar, Cheltenham.

NOTES

1 There are, of course, differential restraints on the activities of financial institutions depending on whether or not they are registered within the EU.

2 It is interesting to note that the pressure for the SEM came just as strongly from European MNEs as it did from political sources. Wisse Dekker, then head of Philips and the European Round Table of major companies, put forward a plan in January 1985 to achieve a single market in five years – that is, by 1990, thus anticipating the White Paper.

3 On an annual basis, the UK was overtaken by Japan, but the UK's outstanding stock of FDI was still larger.

4 Unremitted profits by UK MNEs as a percentage of total net outward FDI in the EU alone and in all countries (in brackets) were 74 per cent (40 per cent) in 1975, 112 per cent (71 per cent) in 1979, 40 per cent (80 per cent) in 1982 and 122 per cent (55 per cent) in 1985 (Business Monitor).

9 Measuring the economic impact of European integration

ALI EL-AGRAA

9.1 Introduction

This may not seem to be the appropriate place in the book to discuss the impact of European integration on the economy of the EU and member states (MSs), since economic and monetary union (EMU; Chapters 10–12), as well as all EU policy areas, are yet to come. However, the overall economic aims of the EU have already been stated (Chapter 2), the theoretical considerations identifying what needs measurement delineated (Chapter 6), and the changes expected from the single European market (SEM) pinpointed (Chapter 7). Also, each policy area is unique, requiring its own analytical approach, hence its specific measurement technique, so all cannot be lumped together to be tackled in unison. Of course, there are close theoretical associations between EMU, tax harmonization (Chapter 15) and the EU budget (Chapter 19), but even these have their own peculiarities, so they need separate treatment.

The issues raised in the mentioned chapters inform us of what needs measuring as a consequence of EU formation: the short-term resource reallocation effects – that is, trade creation (TC) and trade diversion (TD); changes in the terms of trade (t/t); changes in rates of economic growth and welfare; and the longer-term dynamic effects. This chapter briefly deals with each of these, but several aspects are covered in other chapters so will only be touched on. The chapter finishes with conclusions.

It should be pointed out here that most of the measurements obviously require methodologies to inform about how they should be carried out. The methodologies that were pioneered in the early EEC years remain popular, with most of the recent work being devoted to refining the techniques and of course to using the latest data. This means that it is vital to explain the earlier methodologies more carefully and to treat the latest as the icing on the cake. Fortunately, the methodologies are fully covered elsewhere (El-Agraa 1989a, updated in 1999 edn), so, due to space limitations, we can be brief here; those keen on the details are advised to turn to that book.

It should also be mentioned here that a proper understanding of this chapter requires familiarity with economic statistics and econometrics. The results are easy to see, but they should not be taken at face value since they depend crucially on the nature of the methodologies employed in calculating them.

9.2 It is a tough real world

Economic theory is meant to help us see the forest from the trees, not always successfully, as witnessed by the doubts raised regarding the belief in the efficiency of markets since the 2007 economic and financial crises. When it comes to the real world, it is often the case in economics to find that it bears little resemblance, if at all, to what is in the textbooks. In the case of the measurement of the impact of economic integration, it immediately became apparent that TC, *the replacement of expensive domestic production in the home country (H) by cheaper imports from the partner (P)*, and TD, *the replacement of cheaper initial imports from the outside world (W) by expensive imports from P* (see Chapter 6) are far from being straightforward and are not the only effects to be observed. Williamson and Bottrill (1971) recognized other effects too:

Sections 9.1–9.6 are updates of my chapter in the 6th edition and the rest is a brief adaptation from the second part of Nigel Grimwade's chapter in the 8th, for which thanks are due, but without implicating him for my errors and omissions. I am also grateful to Susan Senior for helpful comments and suggestions.

- supply-side diversion, which is the replacement of exports to non-partners (W) with exports to P
- external TC (ETC), which is the replacement of expensive domestic production with cheaper imports from W due to a reduction in common external tariffs (CETs), as has happened after the Kennedy and further rounds of WTO/GATT tariff reductions
- balance of payments induced adjustments due to the effects of TC, TD and ETC.

Others have added trade suppression (TS), which occurs when production in one P is moved altogether to another P (due to costs there becoming cheaper with integration), which used to import the product from W. In short, when one delves into the real world, confidence in theoretical predictions is shattered and may even turn out to be completely misguided.

9.3 How/what to measure?

The measuring of the impact of economic integration relates to the empirical calculation of all the above changes. Thus any sensible approach to estimating them should have the following characteristics:

1. It should be capable of being carried out at the appropriate level of disaggregation in terms of both countries and products.
2. It should be able to distinguish between TC, TD and ETC.
3. It should be capable of discerning the effects of economic growth on trade that would have taken place in the absence of economic integration.
4. It should be analytic – that is, it should be capable of providing an economic explanation of the actual post-integration situation.
5. It should be a general-equilibrium approach, capable of allowing for the effects of economic integration on an interdependent world.

These relate to the measurement of changes in only the trade flows, but, as we saw in Chapter 1, economic integration is not confined to customs unions (CUs) and free trade areas (FTAs). In the case of common markets (CMs), the impact of factor mobility needs to be taken into account, and in complete economic unions (EcUs; see Chapter 1), so too must the effects of common economic and fiscal policies, which are especially pertinent in the EU's case (see Chapters 1 and 8). However, as mentioned in the introduction, these are tackled in the specialist chapters, but a brief statement on factor mobility may be in order.

Factor mobility complicates the estimation of the impact of economic integration on goods and services since they can be both complements to and substitutes for them. A new foreign direct investment (FDI) may require an inflow of skilled labour and imports of some of its inputs, and may export part of its output; China does precisely this by asking all FDI ventures to sell their products outside China (see El-Agraa and Liu 2006a, b; El-Agraa 2007). Alternatively, a firm may decide to invest in a new plant using local labour to supply the local market, both substituting for goods and services it previously supplied from its home market. These interactions are very difficult to separate, especially since the theoretical literature on factor movements is relatively undeveloped and factors may not respond to any changes that are meant to enhance their movement (see Chapter 8).

9.4 The effects on trade

The general trend of the empirical work on economic integration has been to examine various specific aspects of integration (mainly the effects on trading Ps) and to analyse them separately. The most important practical distinction made is between 'price' and 'income' effects. This is largely because the main initial instruments in economic integration are tariffs, import quotas and non-tariff trade barriers (NTBs; see Chapter 6), which act mainly on relative prices in the first instance. However, all sources of possible economic gain (see Chapter 6) incorporate income as well as price effects.

The removal of quotas and NTBs is usually subsumed within the tariff changes for estimation purposes. These tariff changes are thought to result in a series of relative price changes: the price of imports from P falls, for commodities where the tariff is removed, relative to the price of the same commodity produced in H. In W, which is excluded from the union, relative prices may change for more than one reason. They will change differently if the tariff with respect to W is shifted from its pre-integration level, or they may change if producers in W have different pricing reactions to the change in price competition. Some W producers may decide to absorb rather more of the potential change by reducing profits rather than by increasing prices relative to domestic producers. Relative prices are also likely to change with respect to different commodities, and hence there is a complex set of interrelated income and substitution effects to be explained.

The immediate difficulty is thus the translation of tariff changes and other agreed measures in the economic integration treaty into changes in prices and other variables that are known to have an impact on economic behaviour. The evidence that exists suggests that there are wide discrepancies among the reactions of importers benefiting from tariff cuts and also among competitors adversely affected by them (EFTA Secretariat 1969), and that reactions of trade to tariff changes are different from those to price changes (Kreinin 1961). Two routes would appear to be open: one is to estimate the effect of tariff changes on prices and then to estimate the effects of these derived price changes on trade patterns; the other is to operate directly with observed relative price movements. This latter course exemplifies a problem which runs right through the estimation of the effects of economic integration and makes the obtaining of generally satisfactory results almost impossible. It is that to measure the effect of integration one must decide what would have happened if integration had not occurred. Hence the major obstacle in carrying out research on these effects is devising a convincing *anti-monde* (an alternative world in which all events except one are identical). Thus, if in the present instance any observed change in relative price was assumed to be the result of the adjustment to tariff changes, all other sources of variation in prices would be ignored, which is clearly an exaggeration and could be subject to important biases if other factors were affecting trade at the same time.

9.5 The dynamic effects

While in the discussion of the exploitation of comparative advantage, the gains from a favourable movement in t/t and often those from economies of scale are expressed in terms of comparative statics, it is difficult to disentangle them from feedback on to incomes and activity. The essence of the gains from increased efficiency and technological change is that the economy should reap dynamic gains. In other words, integration should enhance the rate of growth of GDP rather than just giving a step-up in welfare. Again, it is necessary to explain how this might come about explicitly.

There are two generalized ways in which this can take place: first, through increased productivity growth at a given investment ratio, and second, through increased investment itself. This is true whether the increased sales are generated internally (in H and P) or through the pressures of demand for exports from W through integration. Growth gains can, of course, occur temporarily in so far as there are slack resources in the economy. Again, it is possible to observe whether the rate of growth has changed, but it is much more difficult to decide whether that is attributable to economic integration.

Krause (1968) attempted to apply a version of Denison's (1967) method of identifying the causes of economic growth, but suggested that all changes in the rate of business investment were due to EC formation (or EFTA in the case of those countries). Mayes (1978) showed that if the same contrast between business investment before and after the formation of the EC/EFTA were applied to Japan, a bigger effect would be observed than in any of the integrating countries. Clearly, changes in the rate of business investment can occur for reasons other than integration.

9.6 The pioneering studies

9.6.1 Methodologies

As stated in the introduction to this chapter, a comprehensive survey of the studies covering the period up to the late 1980s is available in El-Agraa (1999). There is therefore no need to go through these studies in detail; a few general comments and a short summary should suffice.

Most of the measurements can be broadly classified as *ex ante* or *ex post*. The *ex ante* estimates are based on a priori knowledge of the pre-integration period (termed structural models), while the *ex post* studies are based on assumptions about the actual experience of economic integration (residual-imputation models). Either type can be analytic or otherwise.

There are two types of *ex ante* studies: those undertaken before the EC/EFTA came to be and those conducted afterwards;[1] it is inevitable that the EC and EFTA are dealt with together, given that they were created at more or less the same time and were of equal economic size. The most influential studies to use this approach are those of Krause (1968), who predicted the TD that would be brought about by the EC/EFTA on the basis of assumptions about demand elasticities, and Han and Leisner (1971), who predicted the effect on the UK by identifying those industries that had a comparative cost advantage/disadvantage vis-à-vis the EC and finding out how they were likely to be affected by membership (on the assumption that the pattern of trade prior to UK membership provided an indication of the underlying cost conditions and that this would be one of the determinants of the pattern of trade and domestic production after membership). This approach is of very limited value, however, for the simple reason that 'it does not provide a method of enabling one to improve previous estimates on the basis of new historical experience' (Williamson and Bottrill 1971, p. 326).

The most significant studies to use the *ex post* approach are as follows. Lamfalussy (1963) and Verdoorn and Meyer zu Schlochtern (1964) employ a relative shares method. Balassa (1967, 1975) uses an income elasticity of import demand method.[2] The EFTA Secretariat (1969, 1972) adopts a share of imports in apparent consumption method.[3] Williamson and Bottrill (1971) utilize a more sophisticated share analysis.[4] Prewo (1974a, b) pioneers an input–output method.[5] And Barten *et al.* (1976) use a medium-term macroeconomic method.[6] The advantage of the *ex post* method is that it can be constructed in such a way as to benefit from historical experience and hence to provide a basis for continuous research. However, the major obstacle in this approach concerns the difficulty regarding the construction of an adequate hypothetical post-integration picture of the economies concerned.

9.6.2 Findings

This section now provides an integrated summary of the studies of the impact of economic integration up to the early 1970s. But, as mentioned above, later contributions are refinements, so will be briefly considered later, and the most significant contributions are fully covered in El-Agraa (1999). To appreciate the

summary, it is vital to bear in mind the distinction between short-term static effects, whereby changes in the impediments to trade lead to once-and-for-all changes in the composition and pattern of trade, and longer-run dynamic effects, whereby economic integration over time leads to permanent changes in the rate of change of economic parameters. With this distinction in mind, one can classify the studies into static and dynamic along the lines suggested above.

The static studies can be put together into two major groups, under the headings of residual and analytic models.

Residual models

Residual models depend largely on their ability to quantify the situation in the absence of economic integration – that is, on the construction of the *anti-monde*. It should be clear from the contributions discussed that the construction of a satisfactory *anti-monde* will depend on a thorough accounting for the omissions mentioned above. These models are set out here in order of increasing complexity.

(a) Import models

The general tendency in import models is to emphasize variables drawn from only the importing country. This has the advantage of easy data collection, but one must ask whether or not this adequately compensates for the inaccuracy of the estimates. To answer this question meaningfully, it may prove helpful to follow Mayes' (1978) classification of this category of studies, which distinguishes between the following:

(i)   The demand for imports
    Studies of the demand for imports are based on the assumption that in the absence of economic integration imports would have grown over time as they did in the past. These studies have the obvious limitation that the extrapolation of trends has cryptic drawbacks for a cyclical activity such as international trade. Hence many of the contributors assumed that imports would continue to be subject to the same linear relation to total expenditure, GDP and GNP respectively in the *anti-monde* as they had been prior to the integration era (see, for example, Wemelsfelder 1960; Walter 1967; Clavaux 1969).
    These contributions were built on the untenable premise that the marginal propensity to import remained constant throughout; evidence

Table 9.1 Predictions of trade creation (TC) and trade diversion (TD) in the EEC

	TC					TD		
Year	Estimate	Value ($ billion)	Year	Estimate	Value ($ billion)	Year	Estimate	Value ($ billion)
1959	A	0.9	1965	H	1.7	1962	T	0.5
	B	1.1	1966	A	8.6		U	0.5
1960	A	1.6		B	9.8	1965	D	−1.6
	B	2.5		H	2.2		E	−0.3
1961	A	2.3	1967	A	9.2	1965	F	0.1
	B	3.3		B	11.1		H	0.6
1962	A	3.2		H	2.3	1966	H	0.7
	B	4.1		J	1.8	1967	H	0.9
	C	1.0		K	9.2		J	3.0
1963	A	4.7		L	2.5		K	−1.0
	B	5.2		M	10.1		L	0.5
1964	A	5.7	1968	I	10.8		N	1.1
	B	6.4	1969	N	9.6	1968	I	−2.9
	D	4.5	1969/70	O	20.8	1969	N	0.0
	E	2.6		P	7.2	1960/70	O	−4.0
1965	A	6.9		Q	16.0		P	2.4
	B	8.2	1970	R	11.4		Q	−2.8
	F	1.9		S	18.0	1970	R	0.1
	G	5.0					S	−3.1

Notes:
A = Atkin (1973, projection); B = Atkin (1973, dummy variable); C = Waelbroeck (1964, method 1); D = Truman (1969, disaggregated; 1958, base); E as D (1960, base); F = Balassa (1967); G = Clavaux (1969); H = EFTA (1972); I = Major and Hayes (1970; 1958 base); J = Resnick and Truman (1974); K = Truman (1975); L as K (adjusted); M = Verdoorn and Schwartz (1972); N = Williamson and Bottrill (1971); O = Kreinin; (1972, not normalized); P as O (US normalized and adjusted); Q as O (UK normalized); R = Balassa (1974); S = Prewo (1974b); T = Lamfalussy (1963); U as C (method 2)
Source: Adapted from Mayes 1978, p. 6

suggests that this parameter rises as income grows. Moreover, the estimation of the actual marginal propensity to import over the pre-integration periods would always be obscured by other changes in the international trading arrangements that had occurred then, and would not represent an *anti-monde* where no change had taken place. Table 9.1 provides a summary of TC/TD found by the major studies during this period, and a glance will reveal that the use of more observations tends to improve the results.

(ii) Shares in apparent consumption

Estimation can also be carried out by examining the relative share performance in total consumption, as against the absolute value of imports, of different suppliers. Truman (1969) adopted the simplest solution by assuming that the relative share of each supplier would remain constant over time, but, as already indicated, it would be desirable to allow changes in these ratios over time on the basis of historical experience. The studies by the EFTA Secretariat (1969, 1972) tackle this by assuming that the linear trend in relative shares during the period from 1954 to 1959 would have been maintained by the participating nations in the absence of economic integration. There are two objections

Table 9.2 Changes in *ex post* income elasticities of import demand in the EEC

Product group	*Ex post* income elasticity of import demand		Difference 1959–70/1953–9
	1953–9	1959–70	
Total imports			
Non-tropical food, beverages, tobacco	1.7	1.5	−0.2
Raw materials	1.1	1.1	0
Fuels	1.6	2.0	+0.4
Chemicals	3.0	3.2	+0.2
Machinery	1.5	2.6	+1.1
Transport equipment	2.6	3.2	+0.6
Other manufactured goods	2.6	2.5	−0.1
Total of above	1.8	2.0	+0.2
Intra-area imports			
Non-tropical food, beverages, tobacco	2.5	2.5	0
Raw materials	1.9	1.8	−0.1
Fuels	1.1	1.6	+0.5
Chemicals	3.0	3.7	+0.7
Machinery	2.1	2.8	+0.7
Transport equipment	2.9	3.5	+0.6
Other manufactured goods	2.8	2.7	−0.1
Total of above	2.4	2.7	+0.3
Extra-area imports			
Non-tropical food, beverages, tobacco	1.4	1.0	−0.4
Raw materials	1.0	1.0	0
Fuels	1.8	2.1	+0.3
Chemicals	3.0	2.6	−0.4
Machinery	0.9	2.4	+1.5
Transport equipment	2.2	2.5	+0.3
Other manufactured goods	2.5	2.1	−0.4
Total of above	1.6	1.6	0

Source: Balassa 1974

to this premise: first, 1954 and 1959 may not lie on the actual trend, and second, the form of the trend itself is too simple. Estimation by regression analysis, for example, to improve on the results is not really worthwhile, given the naivety of the original assumption.

(iii) Changes in the income elasticity of demand for imports

This method tries to tackle the problem of changes in the relative shares from the opposite direction, by discerning what the actual changes imply for the elasticity of demand for different types of imports with respect to income. Balassa (1967) estimates

the income elasticities of demand for imports from *P*s separately from those from *W*. He advanced the proposition that an increase in the elasticity of demand for imports from all sources indicated TC, and that a decline in the elasticity of demand for imports from *W*, given an increase in the elasticity for imports from *P*s, indicated TD. The results are given in Table 9.2. Note that the *anti-monde* here was that these elasticities would not have changed in the absence of economic integration. To reiterate the criticism advanced in El-Agraa (1989a), since the estimated elasticities are not unitary and not equal for imports from *P*s and *W*s, this means that changes in the shares of total imports in apparent consumption and imports from W (and hence Ps) in total imports can and do take place in the *anti-monde*. Although Balassa made allowances for changes in prices, his estimates were similar to those of the general trend (Mayes 1978), but both positive and negative results were observed.

Both Balassa (1967) and the EFTA Secretariat's (1969) methods leave unanswered the question why the substantial liberalization in world trade prior to economic integration left unaffected the estimation of trade relationships during that period. Indeed, Clavaux (1969) showed that if this factor were taken into consideration – that is, if trade liberalization were excluded from the *anti-monde* – Balassa's calculations for TC by 1966 would have more than doubled. However, as Mayes (1978, p. 9) clearly argues, the most important aspect of this criticism is that price elasticities imply a level of sophistication not reflected in the methods employed: without equations depicting supply conditions, there would arise identification problems which would bias estimates of price elasticities towards zero; the negative of supply conditions implied that the price elasticities of supply would be infinite. Note that Balassa's (1974) calculation of *ex post* income elasticities incorporated supply constraints, but for the pre-integration situation as well. Moreover, Sellekaerts (1973) demonstrated that income elasticities varied widely over both the pre- and post-integration eras. Hence, the selection of appropriate periods for comparison purposes is of the utmost importance.

(b) Inclusion of supply parameters

The explicit incorporation of supply conditions would improve the specification of models since trade between any two countries is determined by parameters within both of them. The simplest method of dealing with this was built on the premise that, under normal circumstances, trade between any two countries would be purely a function of the total trade of each of the two countries. Most particularly, the trade between any two countries would vary proportionately with the total exports of the exporting country and the total imports of the importing country in the *anti-monde*. The RAS advanced by Stone and Brown (1963) was the earliest input–output model to be adapted by Kouevi (1964) and Wealbroeck (1964) for this purpose.

The major deficiency of this model is that total imports and exports were constrained to their actual values; hence it was not possible to estimate TC.

An advance on this simple approach was the gravity method pioneered by Tinbergen and developed by Pulliainen (1963), Polyhonen (1963a, b) and Linnemann (1966). The model presumed that the trade flow between any two countries would be a function of their respective national incomes and populations and the distance between them.[7] The model was estimated by cross-section data, and the economic impact of any integration scheme was calculated by the unexplained residual in the regression, or by the inclusion of dummy variables (DVs) for trade between participating nations, as was the case in the estimates by Aitken (1973). These two methods gave very different results because of the substantial variability over time in the parameters. The estimates by Aitken (1973) gave a figure of $1,264 million for TC by EFTA in 1967, employing 1958 values, while the use of 1967 values themselves together with DVs made the results increase by 92 per cent. Note that Aitken's results were the only ones to be estimated over a sequence of years. Even though these estimates are fairly consistent with the others, they tend to form an upper bound in some instances – for example, in 1965 they were three to four times as large as the lower bound. But one should hasten to add that the absolute magnitude of all the estimates was small. The main reason for these differences was the variability in the estimated parameters from year to year, indicating that to project with fixed parameters one needs to take great care; this was confirmed in a disaggregated study by Bluet and Systermanns (1968). Mayes (1978, pp. 11–12) argued that much of the variability in the estimators occurs because a cross-section cannot represent a relationship which responds to cycles in economic activity and the very process of trade liberalization in general. Pooling data helps to some extent, but the model's main disadvantage is the omission of relative prices.

Verdoorn and Schwartz (1972) tried to tackle this drawback in their second model, where they combined the advantages of the gravity method with the effects of prices, both on the overall demand for imports and the substitution between imports from different sources. While the results were mainly calculated on a residual basis, two DVs were used to explain some of the residual, but the explanation was statistical, not economic. The results are given in Table 9.3; they

Table 9.3 Comparing the 1974 Resnick and Truman (R&T) estimates of trade creation and trade diversion in the EEC and EFTA with the 1972 Verdoorn and Schwartz estimates (V&S) ($ million)

	Trade creation		Trade diversion	
	R&T	V&S	R&T	V&S
	1968	1969	1968	1969
EEC				
BLEU	152	913	281	183
Netherlands	93	868	190	216
W. Germany	−659	3,874	1,732	267
Italy	1,022	1,336	62	154
France	582	3,073	737	248
Total	1,190	10,064	3,002	1,068
EFTA				
UK	81	204	394	249
Other EFTA	131	161	231	547
Total	212	365	625	796
EEC+ EFTA	1,402	10,429	3,627	1,864

Source: Mayes 1978, p. 12

Table 9.4 A comparison of the effects of different *anti-mondes* on the imports of the EEC and EFTA in 1969 ($ million)

Anti-monde	Exporter	Importer	
		EEC	EFTA
[1]		5,091.00	−1042.00
[2]	EEC	1,081.00	−3610.00
[1]/[2]		5.00	0.29
[1]		−2258.00	2542.00
[2]	EFTA	−1594.00	2644.00
[1]/[2]		1.42	0.96
[1]	*W*	2,833.00	−1500.00
[2]		576.00	966.00

Note: W is the rest of the world.
Source: Mayes 1978, p. 13

generally conform with the broad results, thus indicating that more sophisticated models do not leave us much the wiser.

(c) Incorporating information from third countries

Estimation using the share approach, without incorporating supply factors, could include third country behaviour. Lamfalussy (1963) showed that if one took into consideration the change in the shares of trade of *W* and EC MSs in other markets, where neither was affected by economic integration, as the basis of one's expectations of how shares in *P*s' markets would have changed in the absence of integration, one would get a different set of answers relative to those from trend extrapolation in MSs' markets alone. This is shown in Table 9.4, where the differences depict a fairly clear pattern: the share of EC exports in both EC and EFTA imports is much greater under the first hypothesis, and the share of *W* in both markets falls under the first hypothesis but rises under the second. EFTA shares in both markets are greater under the second hypothesis, but only very marginally so for intra-EFTA trade. As we

observed earlier, it is also apparent that Lamfalussy's pessimistic conclusions were largely due to a limited period of observation: the first three years in the EC's life. This was demonstrated by Williamson and Bottrill (1971), by using more observations and sophisticated extrapolation methods of the *anti-monde* shares; their approach, however, does not allow one to estimate TC/TD without introducing further assumptions concerning their relative sizes.

Third countries can be used as a 'control' group or a 'normalizer' for estimating what the *anti-monde* would have been by incorporating them explicitly in the model. Kreinin (1972) does so by adapting the technique of projecting the *anti-monde* on the basis of predicted import/consumption ratios. The advantage of this method is that it allows one to observe more clearly how the normalization procedure works, and, therefore, should enable one to evaluate the tenability or otherwise of the assumptions on which it is built. However, it is an illusion to believe that a control group can be found, particularly for such schemes of integration as EC and EFTA, since the control variables themselves are affected by the very experiment one is seeking to isolate.

(d) Estimation of the *anti-monde*

We have observed that the number and range of estimates of the impact of economic integration of the unaccounted-for residual are large, and it should be apparent that, the more relevant parameters that are incorporated into the estimation of the *anti-monde*, the more acceptable the results. Also, the incorporation of such refinements as disaggregation and intermediate products should lead to even more satisfactory results. However, the results of the study by Prewo (1974), shown in Table 9.1, gave a very different pattern of estimates relative to other models, but this may be attributable to the simplicity of some of his other assumptions. Yet the problem of establishing a hypothetical *anti-monde* is in itself not an attractive proposition: while 'it is possible to point out the existence of biases it is not possible to know whether an unbiased estimate has been achieved, one can merely judge on the grounds of plausibility' (Mayes 1978, p. 15). Plausibility is determined by the incorporated parameters, not just in the importing and exporting countries, but also in the way they influence the trade cycle and changes in world prices. Hence it is necessary to develop analytic models that are capable of explaining actual trade flows and their changes, as opposed to the estimation of *anti-monde*s and the imputation of residual differences to determine the impact of economic integration.

Analytic models

By analytic models one means methods that provide an economic rationale for the actual situation after economic integration has taken place. Such approaches are vital for all *ex ante* methods, since the future values of trade flows are not known. Owing to the inherent complexity of prediction, such models are usually very simple and rely mainly on economic behaviour in the importing country. As we have seen, they assume that imports are determined by a measure of income or economic activity and the level of prices of imported and domestic products. Therefore, on the premise of a relationship between tariffs and prices, TC can be predicted from the change in the level of tariffs. Also, if one has knowledge about the elasticity of substitution with regard to changes in prices between Ps and W, one can estimate TD.

This simple method will not provide acceptable estimates, even if more sophisticated import demand functions are incorporated, unless the effect of price changes on the level of prices can be explained. The EFTA Secretariat (1969) expected prices to fall by the amount of tariff changes, but it turned out that only part of the tariff changes seemed to be passed on. There

is also a fair amount of evidence, at the microeconomic level, to suggest that the pricing of imports of many commodities depends mainly on the prices of existing competing domestic products. It is even suggested that the situation is far worse since importers tend to anticipate tariff changes, indicating that the growth of trade will anticipate the 'determining' tariff changes; see Walter (1967). Moreover, the attempts by Krause (1962) and Kreinin (1972) to calculate the tariff elasticities directly have not been successful. Mayes (1974) demonstrates that the estimates from this method do not correspond closely to those from the residual models.

Since different goods and/or nations are unlikely to behave in an identical fashion, one should expect that the greater the extent of disaggregation, the more reasonable the estimates will be. Mayes (1971) uses a ninety-seven-commodity breakdown of manufactures and allows for a complete system of demand equations, with the volume and price of imports from each country being distinguished to give a whole matrix of direct substitution elasticities (with those of Barten 1970) to reach estimates for a projected Atlantic Free Trade Area comprising Canada, EFTA, Japan and the USA. These results are given in Table 9.4. They display an expected pattern of signs for overall TC and TD, and are also robust to quite significant changes in the variables. Other estimates utilize more global values, based on either simple assumptions or crude extrapolation from calculations for the USA; the different sets of assumptions employed by Balassa (1967), Kreinin (1967) and Krause (1968) lead to estimates given respectively in columns (3) and (4) of the table, as recalculated by Mayes (1978). The results are somewhat similar, but this is attributable to offsetting changes: greater TC being matched by greater TD. However, the striking feature of these results is that they are small relative to those given by residual models – for example, Kreinin (1969) found the effect of EC formation for the period 1962–5 to be less than $100 million.

More elaborate models (Armington 1970; Resnick and Truman 1975) allow for the determination of imports by a series of allocation decisions, while the studies by Balassa (1967) and Kreinin (1967) use simple assumptions for supply constraints, but, as can be seen from Tables 9.1 and 9.2 (pages 130 and 131), the estimates of these models do not fit happily with those from the residual models – for example, the estimates of TD from the Resnick and Truman model are only one-eighth of those from Verdoorn and Schwartz's (1972). Also, because the establishment of CETs meant that West Germany had to raise its tariff level, TC is negative in the analytic case, but is the largest positive estimate in the residual model. This indicates that factors other than tariff changes had a very substantial and positive effect on West Germany's post-EC trade. There is, therefore, much more to be explained that is not covered by the analytic models and cannot be covered by the residual ones.

However, the main attraction of the analytic models is that they can be tested after the event and can be used for forecasting as well as for *ex post* estimation. In this respect, the models used by Grinols (1984) and Winters (1984), which cannot be discussed here owing to space limitations, are a sort of improvement (see El-Agraa 1999).

Dynamic studies

The static models are predominantly concerned with the impact of price changes alone on the level, composition and pattern of trade. However, it could be argued that the static models leave out the most dominant effects of economic integration. This is due to the fact that the feedback into incomes and the rate of economic growth, or the necessity for the use of expenditure-switching policies for balance-of-payments equilibrating purposes, may be considerable and either positive or negative. For example, Kaldor (1971) argues not only that EC membership will inflict costs on the UK, but that the costs will be reinforced by adverse dynamic effects. However, there are very few estimates of the dynamic effects, with Krause (1968) being the exception. Krause tries to explain changes in the rate of real economic growth in the EC and EFTA by increasing business investment and efficiency. The expectation is that an increase in the ratio of investment to GDP will increase capital accumulation, and if the marginal capital/output ratios are constant, both output and the rate of growth must increase. But the fixity of the capital/output ratios automatically excludes economies of scale which lie at the very heart of the dynamic effects. The increase in efficiency is due to a decrease in input costs from imports; hence the increase in the ratio of imports to output is estimated and multiplied by the average tariff rate to calculate the income effect of the cost reduction, and this can be expressed as an annual rate.

Clearly, this method suffers from the same limitations as the static models: equating tariff changes and consequent price changes, and attributing all changes to economic integration.

A critique of previous studies

There is no need to offer a criticism of the pioneering studies. This is because each new study justifies its undertaking by pointing out the limitations of previous studies. So this section is limited to a few general criticisms. Before doing so, however, one should have noticed the absence of any estimates on the effects of economic integration on t/t, and this is because it has been almost non-existent; there will be some mention where appropriate, but a whole section cannot be justified.

First, practically all the studies assume that the formation of the EC or EFTA has been the sole factor to influence the pattern of trade. Since the EC and EFTA were established more or less simultaneously and were of equal economic size, this must cast great doubt on the findings.

Second, most of the later studies ignore the fact that the UK used to be a member of EFTA before joining the EC. Since the UK is a substantial force as a member of either scheme, it seems misleading to attempt estimates that do not take into consideration this UK switch.

Third, in the period prior to EC/EFTA formation, certain significant changes were happening on the international scene. The most important of these was that discrimination against the USA was greatly reduced. It seems far-fetched to assume, as many of the studies have, that such developments had no effect whatsoever on EC/EFTA trade patterns.

Fourth, all the studies, except for Truman's (1975) and, to some extent, Winters' (1984), dealt with trade data in spite of the fact that a proper evaluation of the effects of economic integration requires analysis of both trade and production data. TC indicates a reduction in domestic production combined with new imports of the same quantity from the partner, while TD indicates new imports from the partner combined with fewer imports from the rest of the world (W) and a reduction in production in W.

Fifth, tariffs are universally recognized as only one of the many trade impediments, yet practically all the studies, except Krause's (1968) and Prewo's (1974), are based on the assumption that the only effect of integration in Western Europe was on discriminatory tariff removal. NTBs are everywhere; witness France's diversion of Japanese video recorders to Poitiers (poorly manned for customs inspection) to slow down their penetration of the French market (see El-Agraa 1988a).

Finally, the Dillon and Kennedy Rounds of tariff negotiations resulted in global tariff reductions which coincided with the first stage of the removal of tariffs by the EC. Does this not mean that any evidence of external TC should be devalued, and any evidence of TD undervalued?

9.7 A taste of the latest estimates

As mentioned at the beginning of this chapter, the latest estimation techniques are more or less refinements of the old, so in this section only a sample of these are considered.

9.7.1 Gravity's pull

Gravity has become the standard technique for the measurement of the effects of economic integration. Bayoumi and Eichengreen (1995), Frankel (1997), Wang and Winters (1991), Baldwin (1994), Rose (1999) and the CEPR/EU Commission (1997) have all used it in major exercises. However, only the first two have come up with unique changes to the gravity equation, with the rest making a fairly straightforward application of it. Therefore, the first two must be tackled, but so too must the last, simply because it is about SEM, and hence of direct relevance to Chapter 7, where technicalities are avoided.

Nevertheless, here is a brief statement on what the others have done. Wang and Winters (1991) analyse the effects of increased integration between Western and Eastern Europe, following the collapse of communism and the demise of the CMEA, by estimating bilateral trade flows between seventy-six countries over the period 1984–6, excluding the Central and East European countries (CEECs) and former Soviet Republic (FSR) countries. Their results predicted a big increase in trade between Western and Eastern Europe, but a reduction in trade between the CEECs.

Baldwin (1994) estimates the effects of increased integration between the EC and EFTA using trade flows between their member countries and between the member countries and the USA, Japan, Canada and Turkey for the period 1979–88. He finds a significant medium-term potential for export growth from Western to Eastern Europe, with Germany being the largest potential beneficiary. CEECs and FSR countries also enjoy potential for enhanced exports to the EU and EFTA countries, but exports to other CEECS and FSR countries are expected to fall. He also allows for an increase in per capita incomes of CEECs and FSRs as they approach the levels of poorer West European countries, and finds that the West European countries' exports to Eastern Europe rise by 10–15 per cent annually over several decades.

Rose (1999) assesses the effects of EMU on trade by estimating for 186 countries for five different years, beginning with 1970 and at five-year intervals thereafter, to finish in 1990. He is able to explain 63 per cent of trade flows, with all the expected results. Also, vitally, he finds that exchange rate volatility (measured by the standard deviation of bilateral nominal exchanges in the preceding five years) has a strong negative effect on trade, and the single currency has an even larger positive impact.

Bayoumi and Eichengreen (1995) utilize a gravity equation estimated in differences rather than levels so that variables that do not change over time could be ignored – for example, distance. Also, being concerned about the omission of third-country influences in previous studies, they included a variable for each country's real exchange rate vis-à-vis the US dollar to serve as a proxy for competitiveness. The model is estimated for twenty-one industrial countries over three separate periods during 1953–92, when EEC MSs expanded from six (first period) to nine (second) to twelve (third). They find that EEC/EFTA formation significantly impacted on their trade. For the first period, intra-EEC trade increased annually by about 3.2 per cent, due to both TC and TD, and for EFTA by 2.3 per cent, all TC. The accession of Denmark, Ireland and the UK in the second period increased their intra-trade significantly faster than the model's predictions, again due to both TC and TD. In the third period, when Greece (1981) and Portugal/Spain (1986) joined, intra-nine trade with the three new MSs also increased faster than predicted by the model, entirely due to TC in the Portugal/Spain case.

Frankel (1997) employs a gravity model to estimate

the explanatory power of all the conventional variables determining a comprehensive cross-section of data covering the period 1965–94. He adopts ordinary least squares to estimate an equation that includes total bilateral exports and imports as the dependent variable, and GNP, per capita GNP, distance, adjacency, language and membership of a regional trading scheme as the independent variables. Five separate trading blocs were included in the equation. Bilateral trade flows from the UN's trade matrix covering some sixty-three countries were included. An estimated 75 per cent of all bilateral trade flows were explained by the model. With regard to Europe, integration had a positive effect on trade flows between MSs, although much depended on whether the EU15 or EC12 is considered to be the relevant trading bloc. For the EU, there was no statistically significant effect until after 1985. By 1990, trade between EU MSs was found to be 35 per cent more than trade between two similar countries. The EC bloc effect was stronger, but not statistically significant until 1980. The results indicate that by 1992 bilateral trade between any two EC MSs was 65 per cent higher than it would have been in their absence. Both the 1973 and 1985 enlargements are found to have contributed about half of the increase.

The CEPR/EU Commission (1997) used three demand equations for fifteen three-digit sensitive goods sectors for France, Germany, Italy and the UK to estimate the effects of the creation of the single European market (SEM; see Chapter 7). The equations estimate the share of nominal, sectoral expenditure accounted for by domestically produced goods, intra-EU imports and extra-EU imports. A separate DV is included to capture the effect of SEM creation, which was expected to affect trade flows not only through the *direct* effects of reductions in trade costs on demand, but also through the *indirect* effects of enhanced competition and reductions in price-cost margins. Separate price equations for each of the sectors covered are utilized to estimate these indirect, supply-side effects. The estimated impact of SEM on price-cost margins is then used to simulate the impact of price reductions on trade flows, applying the estimated demand equations. They find that the overall SEM impact is a reduction of 4.2 per cent in the domestic producers' share in the fifteen sectors covered, and a rise of 2.1 per cent in the share of EU producers and of 2 per cent in that of *W*. The results are summarized in Table 9.5. A similar

exercise was carried out for the manufacturing sectors and found that for manufacturing as a whole, the fall in the domestic producers' share is 2.3 per cent, with EU producers increasing their share by 0.5 per cent and *W* by 1.8 per cent. In other words, the impact of SEM was overwhelmingly one of both internal and external TC.

9.7.2 Computable general equilibrium models

The use of computable general equilibrium (CGE) models in this field is somewhat recent. The CEPR/EU Commission (1997) employs one to simulate SEM effects for twelve countries and 118 manufacturing industries. It comprises two sectors, one perfectly competitive for non-agriculture, the other imperfectly competitive for manufactures. Both products are presumed to be differentiated and subject to economies of scale.

CGE models operate in two stages. In the first, the model is calibrated for a base year, for which the model's equations are estimated for a particular year using a data set containing values for all the variables involved. But not all parameters are estimated, they are simply borrowed from available studies – an act once labelled 'junkyard econometrics'. In the second, the model goes through a number of external shocks to simulate what is being estimated. The outcome is contrasted with the *anti-monde*: what would have happened without SEM in this case.

The CEPR/EU Commission uses *ex ante* as well as *ex post* simulations. The *ex ante* exercise simulates the SEM's possible impact on intra-EU trade costs by borrowing sectoral estimates from Buigues *et al.* (1990). These are then incorporated into the model for 1990 and the impacts on the equilibrium are recalculated. It is found that the share of domestic producers in home consumption falls by just over 2 per cent in most MSs, while EU producers' share is enhanced by about 3 per cent and *W*'s declines by less than 1 per cent. This suggests that roughly two-thirds of SEM's effect on intra-EU trade is TC, with TD accounting for the remaining third.

The *ex post* simulation required a reverse operation. The necessary changes in trade costs for reproducing the equilibrium in import penetration that actually materialized between 1988 and 1994 are calculated on the presumption that producers only had time to make minor adjustments to the changes occurring during

Table 9.5 Estimated impact of SEM on market shares (%)

	Direct demand			Price competition			Overall impact		
	Home	EU	W	Home	EU	W	Home	EU	W
Glassware	−1.3	−0.1	+1.4	+0.7	−0.1	−0.5	−0.7	−0.2	+0.9
Ceramics	−4.2	+1.8	+2.4	−0.2	+0.3	−0.1	−4.4	+2.0	+2.4
Basic industrial chemicals	−4.3	+2.5	+1.8	+1.1	−0.7	−0.3	−3.3	+1.8	+1.5
Pharmaceuticals	−1.9	+0.4	+1.5	−0.1	+0.2	−0.1	−2.0	+0.5	+1.4
Boiler making, etc.	−5.3	+4.4	+0.9	+0.9	−0.9	+0.0	−4.4	+3.5	+0.9
Machine tools for metals	−2.0	−2.2	+4.2	−0.6	+0.2	+0.4	−2.6	−2.0	+4.6
Machine tools for foodstuffs	−7.4	+3.0	+4.4	+0.5	−0.4	−0.1	−6.9	+2.6	+4.3
Plant for mines	−1.7	+1.0	+0.7	+1.1	−0.6	−0.5	−0.6	+0.4	+0.2
Office machines	−7.8	+2.8	+5.0	+1.1	+0.1	−1.2	−6.7	+3.0	+3.8
Tele-communications equipment	−2.7	+1.7	+1.0	+1.0	−1.5	−0.5	−1.7	+0.2	+1.5
Electronic equipment	−15.7	+4.6	+11.1	+4.0	−2.2	−1.8	−11.7	+2.2	+9.5
Motor vehicles	−4.9	+3.7	+1.2	+0.3	−0.7	+0.3	−4.6	+3.0	+1.5
Aerospace equipment	−15.3	+14.6	+0.8	+7.0	−2.5	−4.4	−8.3	+12.0	−3.8
Brewing and malting	−6.3	+5.9	+0.4	+1.5	−1.4	−0.1	−4.8	+4.5	+0.3
Clothing	−2.9	−2.5	+5.4	+0.7	−0.5	−0.2	−2.1	−3.1	+5.2
Weighted average for 15 sensitive areas	−5.4	+3.0	+2.5	+1.2	−0.8	−0.4	−4.2	+2.1	+2.0
Rest of manufacturing	−0.4	−0.9	+1.3	+0.8	+0.4	+0.4	−1.2	−0.4	+1.7
Aggregate manufacturing	*−2.2*	*+0.5*	*+1.7*	*−0.1*	*+0.0*	*+0.1*	*−2.3*	*+0.5*	*+1.8*

Note: W = rest of world

Source: CEPR/EU Commission 1997

the period. Of course, they are assumed to be fully adjusted in the long term. Two simulations then ensue: the first based on price-cost margins being fixed (due to absence of competitive behaviour); and the second based on the full SEM impact being realized. Again, the outcome is contrasted with the *anti-monde* – what would have happened without SEM. It is found that in the case of manufacturing as a whole, the share of domestic producers fell by about 1.5 per cent, whereas that of EU producers increased by 2 per cent. Also, that

of W fell by roughly 0.5 per cent. However, no consideration is allowed for a decline in extra-EU trade costs that SEM may have generated. In a second simulation, the results of a fall in extra-EU trade costs are calculated; Table 9.6 provides their summary.

9.7.3 Intra-industry trade

Soon after the estimation exercises got under way, it became clear that countries traded varieties of the

Table 9.6 Changes in trade patterns in manufactures resulting from SEM: an ex post simulation

	Changes in shares: base (%)			Change in EU share (%)	Changes in shares: competition effect (%)			Change in EU share (%)
	Home	EU	RoW		Home	EU	RoW	
France	−3.22	2.12	1.11	1.13	0.08	−0.04	−0.02	1.13
Germany	−2.78	1.63	1.14	1.12	0.04	−0.02	−0.03	1.12
Italy	−2.7	1.82	0.88	1.14	0.1	−0.07	−0.03	1.14
UK	−2.79	1.7	1.08	1.12	0.08	−0.05	−0.04	1.12
Netherlands	−2.8	1.78	1.02	1.07	0.19	−0.12	−0.06	1.07
Belgium-Luxembourg	−2.76	1.98	0.77	1.06	0.22	−0.16	−0.07	1.07
Denmark	−2.36	1.4	0.96	1.06	0.55	−0.34	−0.21	1.08
Ireland	−2.58	1.74	0.84	1.09	0.48	−0.34	−0.15	1.1
Greece	−1.46	0.92	0.54	1.05	0.61	−0.4	−0.21	1.07
Spain	−2.41	1.74	0.67	1.11	0.21	−0.16	−0.05	1.12
Portugal	−1.31	1.03	0.28	1.05	0.3	−0.24	−0.06	1.06

Note: RoW = rest of the world
Source: CEPR/ EU Commission 1997

same products (cars, computers, etc.), rather than exchanging those of different industries as predicted by the traditional Heckscher-Ohlin-Samuelson (HOS) model. This is called intra-industry trade (IIT), as against the inter-industry trade of the HOS model (see El-Agraa 1989b, Chapter 16). Balassa (1974) was the first to apply this to the estimation of economic integration effects on trade. He was followed by Grubel and Lloyd (1975), Greenaway and Hine (1991), the CEPII/EU Commission (1997) and others. Here, space is devoted to the last simply because it is of relevance to SEM and is relatively recent.

CEPII/EU Commission (1997) measures IIT for what is termed 'vertical' (differentiated goods being of different quality) and 'horizontal' (products are identical in their use of the same technology and cost equality, but differ in minor respects which are nonetheless of particular significance for the consumer – for example, whether the same car model is red or yellow). Bilateral trade flows in about 10,000 differentiated products during 1980–94 are examined. It is found that that IIT has increased during the period, mainly in the vertical rather than horizontal IIT. Table 9.7 summarizes the results. Note that France, Belgium-Luxembourg and Germany have, in that order, levels of horizontal IIT in excess of 20 per cent, while the UK, Germany, France, Belgium-Luxembourg and the Netherlands

have vertical IIT of more than 4 per cent. Denmark, Greece, Portugal and Spain have high levels of inter-industry trade. Ignoring Denmark, this suggests a positive relationship between IIT and the level of economic development. Also note the increase in IIT in all but Ireland and Denmark.

9.8 Estimating the income effects

In reviewing the studies above we have concentrated on measuring the impact of economic integration on trade. What about the effects on real incomes? Balassa (1974) estimates the welfare gains from TC in manufacturing in 1970 to be $0.7 billion. He achieves his estimates by multiplying the increase in trade in this sector, $11.4 billion, by half (see Chapter 6) a 12 per cent average tariff. With minuscule TD, this amounts to 0.15 per cent of GNP. In the case of agricultural products, of $1.3 billion, and a 47 per cent average external rate of protection, the loss is estimated at $0.3 billion.

Many explanations can be advanced for such trivial changes. Among these are that trade forms a small percentage of GDP; tariffs are greatly reduced through GATT rounds; and gains from enhanced variety due to increased IIT are not amenable to measurement.

Table 9.7 Share of inter-industry and intra-industry trade in intra-EC trade (% change), 1987–1994

Country	Shares in 1994 (%)			Variation 1987–94 (%)		
	Inter-industry trade	Horizontal intra-industry trade	Vertical intra-industry trade	Inter-industry trade	Horizontal intra-industry trade	Vertical intra-industry trade
France	31.6	24.1	44.3	−6.4	2.8	3.6
Germany	32.6	20.5	46.9	−5.4	1.9	3.4
Belgium-Luxembourg	34.8	23.2	42.0	−3.8	1.6	2.2
United Kingdom	35.6	16.5	47.9	−7.0	−1.9	8.9
Netherlands	39.3	18.9	41.9	−4.8	−0.3	5.1
Spain	45.9	18.9	36.9	−12.0	8.7	3.3
Italy	46.9	16.2	36.9	−2.8	5.8	−3.1
Ireland	57.7	7.9	34.4	2.2	−0.9	−1.3
Denmark	60.0	8.1	60.0	1.1	−1.1	0.0
Portugal	68.6	7.5	23.9	−8.6	3.9	4.8
Greece	86.0	3.7	10.3	−0.2	0.8	−0.6
EC12	38.5	19.2	42.3	−5.1	2.0	3.1
EC without Spain and Portugal	37.4	19.5	43.1	−5.0	1.7	3.3

Source: CEPII/EU Commission 1997

Also, time is of the essence if gains from intra-industry specialization are to be realized, and, as Keynes vehemently uttered, in the long run we are all dead. Economies of scale are due to increased plant specialization and longer production runs, rather than plant size. Expanding the number of varieties available, IIT also enhances competition among producers, which may lead to the elimination of X-inefficiency (managerial slack). If producers respond to this process by cutting their prices, consumers stand to gain a further boost in their real incomes.

Thus Owen (1983) tries to capture the gains from economies of scale and enhanced competition. Calculating the efficiency gains in three manufacturing industries, he finds gains of 54 per cent for washing machines, 135 per cent for refrigerators, 53 per cent for cars and 4 per cent for trucks. Also, he finds savings in costs due to the elimination of high-cost marginal producers in importing countries. The total benefit from the two effects for the EEC six MSs is found to be 3–6 per cent of their combined GNP. In contrast, the pure static

welfare gains are only 0.67 per cent. Note that Owen is strongly criticized for extrapolating from a limited selection of industries.

Finally, there are the benefits attributed to SEM, calculated on behalf of the Commission by Paolo Cecchini (then governor of Italy's central bank, although Emerson (1988) is known to have been the driving force) and fully set out in the voluminous Cecchini Report (CEU 1988a). Here the method is to calculate the cost of non-Europe by estimating the welfare gain from removing a wide range of NTBs. On the assumption of passive macroeconomic policies, the gains are estimated at ECU (=$) 70–190 billion, or 2.5–6.5 per cent of EC12 GDP, spanning a five-year period or more, and an increase in employment of about two million jobs. With macroeconomic policy support, they rise to 7 per cent for EC12 GDP and about five million jobs.

However, this is essentially an *ex ante* estimate; but, as pointed out in Chapter 7, both the Commission itself and other researchers have conducted *ex post* studies (those interested are advised to turn to that chapter).

Table 9.8 The effects of economic integration on the growth rate of member states, 1961–72 and 1974–81

	1961–72		1974–81	
	Actual growth rate (%)	Growth rate due to EC	Actual growth rate (%)	Growth rate due to EC
Germany	4.39	–0.02	2.65	0.91
France	5.40	–2.71	2.66	1.57
Italy	4.97	1.04	2.74	0.42
Netherlands	5.17	2.94	1.99	0.53
Belgium-Luxembourg	4.56	2.45	2.03	0.71
UK	–	–	1.24	0.37
Ireland	–	–	3.84	0.31
Denmark	–	–	1.98	–0.64

Source: Summarized from Marques-Mendes 1986

9.9 Economic growth effects

The pioneering studies make little attempt to measure the effect of economic integration on the rate of economic growth. Balassa (1974) finds that EC formation adds another 1 per cent to GNP, due to increased savings and investment. This enhances the growth rate by 0.05 per cent. And if economies of scale are exploited, leading to further new investment (fixed investment in EEC6 GNP did rise from 21 per cent in 1958 to 25 per cent in 1970), another 0.2 per cent will be added.

Marques-Mendes (1986) utilizes a simple balance of payments constrained growth model, based on that of Thirlwall (1979, 1982), for the same purpose. The model makes use of the foreign trade multiplier, whereby an increase in export volume causes an increase in output, not only in the exporting country, but also in trading partners, through an increase in imports. Some of the increase in output in trading partners returns to the country that experiences the initial export expansion through increased imports by trading partners. The size of the foreign trade multiplier depends on the income elasticity of demand for imports in both countries. However, the extent to which output can grow is constrained by the need to achieve balance of payments equilibrium. Marques-Mendes' findings for the two integration periods, 1961–72 and 1974–81, are summarized in Table 9.8.

For the first period, although France and, to some

extent, Germany are negatively affected, there is a sizeable positive impact on economic growth. As to the second period, all countries, except Denmark, experienced faster growth. The total effect is that EC GDP is 2.2 per cent higher than it would have been had integration not taken place, and, by 1981, 5.9 per cent higher.

Baldwin (1989) is unhappy with the Cecchini Report (CEU 1988a) and Emerson *et al.* (1988) SEM estimates of potential economic gains due to their once-and-for-all nature. He distinguishes between two effects on economic growth: *medium-term* acceleration due to higher incomes boosting savings and investment; and *long-term* additions because the increased investment rates induce further increases in other parts of the economy. Starting with the Cecchini estimates (above) and applying a Romer (1986) endogenous growth model, he finds that SEM enhances the EC's rate of long-term growth by 0.28–0.92 percentage points. Although this might appear trivial on first sight, it actually amounts to a boost in EC GDP of 11–35 per cent. Whatever went wrong?

Finally, Henrekson *et al.* (1996) adopt an econometric analysis to inform us further. They use a base regression, in which the average growth rate of real per capita GDP is a function of the initial real per capita GDP, schooling years, the investment/GDP ratio, a DV variable for EC/EFTA membership, and the real exchange rate to separate the effects of regional integration from those of trade policy in general. For the period from

1976 to 1985 they find that EC/EFTA membership has a positive and significant effect of one percentage point to the growth rate. An interesting aspect of their work is the evidence they produced to show that technology transfer was the main mechanism through which growth was affected.

9.10 Conclusion

The conclusion is straightforward and simple. Applied economists and econometricians will never be able to devise *anti-monde*s that can be taken at face value. Therefore, interesting as all these studies have been and continue to be, they are more a delight to the experts engaged in carrying them out than providers of solid information that we can comfortably throw around. Here is a quotation from a long time ago:

All estimates of [TC] and [TD] by [the EC] which have been presented in the empirical literature are so much affected by ceteris paribus assumptions, by the choice of the length of the pre- and post-integration periods, by the choice of benchmark year (or years), by the methods to compute income elasticities, changes in trade matrices and in relative shares and by structural changes not attributable to [the EC] but which occurred during the pre- and post-integration periods (such as the trade liberalisation amongst industrial countries and autonomous changes in relative price) that the magnitude of no . . . estimate should be taken too seriously (Sellekaerts 1973, p. 548)

Moreover, given the validity of those criticisms, one should not take seriously such statements as the following:

There are a number of studies that have reported attempts to construct . . . estimates. Individually the various methods must be judged unreliable. . . But collectively the available evidence is capable of indicating conclusions of about the same degree of reliability as is customary in applied economics. That is to say, there is a wide margin of uncertainty about the correct figure, but the order of magnitude can be established with reasonable confidence (Williamson and Bottrill 1971, p. 323)

No single study can be justified in its own right, and the degree of reliability in applied economics and econometrics leaves a lot to be desired, so it is difficult to see the collective virtue in individual misgivings.

Summary

- It is not straightforward to estimate TC and TD because in the real world economic integration has other effects. These include, supply-side diversion, external trade creation (ETC) and trade suppression.
- Any sensible approach to estimating TC/TD should meet certain conditions. It should be:
  1. capable of being carried out at the appropriate level of disaggregation in terms of both countries and products
  2. able to distinguish between TC, TD and ETC
  3. capable of discerning the effects of economic growth on trade that would have taken place in the absence of economic integration.
  4. analytic – that is, it should be capable of providing an economic explanation of the actual post-integration situation
  5. of general-equilibrium nature, capable of allowing for the effects of economic integration on an interdependent world.
- In order to measure the effect of integration one must decide what would have happened if integration had not occurred. Hence the major obstacle in carrying out research on these effects is devising a convincing *anti-monde* (an alternative world in which all events except one are identical).
- The most popular method for estimating the economic impact of integration is the gravity equation. In its simplest form, it presumes that the trade flow between any two countries would be a function of their respective national incomes, populations and the distance between them.
- Practically none of the studies reviewed has found an overwhelming positive impact on the EU or its MSs as a consequence of economic integration. Even the SEM has not established itself in this particular respect.

Questions and essay topics

1. What is supply-side diversion?
2. What is external trade creation (ETC)?
3. What are the five requirements for a sensible approach to estimating the impact of economic integration?

4. How can one distinguish between *ex ante* and *ex post* studies in this field?

5. What are residual models?

6. What are analytical models?

7. What are dynamic studies in this field?

8. What is the gravity equation?

9. What is intra-industry trade?

10. Of all the studies reviewed in this chapter, which one would you single out, and why?

11. Evaluate the proposition that no study of the economic effects of regional integration should be taken seriously.

12. Prognosticate on how you would go about trying to estimate the impact of economic integration.

FURTHER READING

El-Agraa, A. M. (1999) *Regional Integration: Experience, Theory and Measurement*, Macmillan, London; Barnes and Noble, New York.

Frankel, J. A. (1997) *Regional Trading Blocs in the World Trading System*, Institute for International Economics, Washington D.C.

NOTES

1 See, for instance, Verdoorn (1954), Janssen (1961), Krause and Salant (1973a) and the EC study discussed in Chapter 7 (page 111).

2 *Ex post* income elasticities of import demand were defined as the ratio of the average annual rate of change of imports to that of GNP, both expressed in constant prices. Under the assumption that income elasticities of import demand would have remained unchanged in the absence of integration, a rise in the income elasticity of demand for intra-area imports would indicate gross TC (increases in intra-area trade), irrespective of whether this resulted from substitution for domestic or for foreign sources of supply. In turn, a rise in the income elasticity of demand for imports from all sources taken together would give expression to TC proper – that is, a shift from domestic to partner-country sources. Finally, TD, a shift from foreign to partner-country producers, would be indicated by a decline in the income elasticity of demand for extra-area imports (see Balassa 1975, p. 80).

3 The EFTA Secretariat's study is based on the assumption that had EFTA not been established, the import share in the apparent consumption of a particular commodity in any EFTA country would have developed in the post-integration period in precisely the same fashion as it had during the pre-integration period 1954–9 (see EFTA Secretariat 1969, 1972).

4 We believe that the most promising hypothesis is that originally introduced by Lamfalussy. According to this, the share performance of the *j*th supplier in markets where he neither gains nor loses preferential advantages gives a good indication of his hypothetical performance in markets which were in fact being affected by integration. *W* provides a control which indicates what share performance would have been in EEC and EFTA markets if these two organizations had not been formed (Williamson and Bottrill 1971, p. 333).

The methods selected are:

1. Using an a priori formula which ensures that the predicted gain in market shares will be small if the previous market share was either very small or very large.

2. Extrapolating from a regression of data on relative export shares.

3. Assuming that market shares would have remained constant in the absence of economic integration.

5 Prewo (1974a, b) uses a gravity model (see note 7 below), which links EC countries' national input–output tables by a system of trade equations. In this model, trade between EC MSs is assumed to be proportional to demand in the importing, and supply in the exporting, country and inversely proportional to trade impediments, whereas extra-area imports are assumed to be related to demand in EC countries. In this model, changes in final demand have a direct effect on imports of final goods, as well as an indirect effect through their impact on the imports of inputs for domestic production.

The basis of the analysis is that the 'difference between the actual trade flows of the customs union and the hypothetical trade flows of the customs union's [anti-monde] is taken to be indicative of the integration effects' (Prewo 1974, p. 380).

6 It basically consists of eight similarly specified country models, which are linked by bilateral trade equations and equations specifying the formation on import and export prices (Barten *et al.* 1976, p. 63).

7 A gravity model attempts to explain bilateral trade flows between pairs of countries by variables drawn from both importing and exporting countries. The standard variables in a gravity equation are the two countries' GNP/GDP, population and geographical distance separating them. The equation incorporates both supply- and demand-side trade determinants. The importer

country's GNP/GDP has a positive influence on trade flows, and so does the exporting country's. The importer country's population can also be expected to increase the demand for its imports, but that of the exporting country exhibits a negative relationship with its exports. This is due to population being a proxy for size, which leads to greater self-sufficiency. Naturally, distance has a negative effect on trade flows. Additional DVs can be added (see page 132) for countries next to each other and/or with a common language or cultural affinity.

Using logarithms, the regression equation looks like this:

$$\log X_{ij} = \log A + \beta \log Y_i + \beta \log Y_j + \mu \log H_i \\ + \mu \log H_j + \gamma \log N_i + \gamma \log N_j + \alpha \log D_{ij} \\ + \log \varepsilon_{ij}$$

where i and j stand for countries, Y is GDP, H is geographical size, N is population, D is distance between the two countries and e is the error term. Such an equation is then estimated using ordinary least squares.

Part III

EU monetary integration

Part III covers all aspects of that far-reaching and most demanding element of integration, monetary unification, including the adoption of a single currency. The three chapters cover, respectively: the theoretical analysis of the gains and losses from economic and monetary union (EMU); the EU developments that have led to the present situation, where twelve of the fifteen pre-2004 EU member nations are using the euro as their only currency, and where all countries acceding after that are obliged to join them when deemed fit, with five of them already having done so by 1 January 2007; and the management of the euro by the European Central Bank (ECB) and how the euro is operated.

10 The theory of monetary integration
ALI EL-AGRAA

10.1 Introduction

Chapter 6 was devoted mainly to a theoretical analysis of the economic consequences of tariff removal, the establishment of the common external tariff (CET) and factor mobility – that is, the common market (CM) aspects of regional integration (see Chapter 1). However, economic and monetary union (EMU) is by far the most challenging commitment for any scheme of economic integration. Therefore this and the two subsequent chapters deal in turn with: the theoretical analysis of EMU (this chapter); the current and planned development of the EU's European monetary union (Chapter 11); and an appraisal of the operation of the EU's EMU (Chapter 12). Between them, these chapters explain the reasons for the challenge, as well as tracing EU endeavours in this respect.

This chapter begins by explaining the differences between the 'monetary' and 'economic' parts of EMU. Concentrating on the economic, it then provides the proper definition of EMU, permanent fixity of member nations' (hereafter, 'member' stands for 'member nation') exchange rates and the complete mobility of capital between them, and what requirements are needed to satisfy it. Then the economic aspect of monetary union is discussed, and the role of fiscal policy analysed. Two sections follow dealing respectively with the expected benefits and costs of EMU. A clarification of elements identified in the costs follows. The chapter finishes with conclusions. It should be stressed, however, that a *proper* understanding of what is in this chapter requires prior knowledge of international monetary economics, hence of monetary economics, as well as of public economics.

10.2 Disentangling the concepts

The acronym EMU is often misinterpreted as European monetary union. This is understandable because the largest element of EMU (economic and monetary union) has been the setting up of the EU's monetary union, with the establishment of a single currency, the euro, and the new central banking system to run it. The provisions of the treaty setting up EU EMU are heavily dominated by the monetary aspect and it is this which forms the heart of the present chapter.

However, in a unitary country, or even a fairly weakly federal one, economic *and* monetary integration would involve having a countrywide fiscal policy as well as a single monetary policy. Arrangements vary as to how much of fiscal policy is handled at the country/federal level and how much at lower state/regional levels. But the norm is that the largest proportion of government expenditure and revenue is at the federal level, which also imposes some limitations on what the states/regions can do, even in very loose federations. The EU, however, has not attempted this level of integration. The centralized budget amounts to only around 1 per cent of EU GDP (see Chapter 19) and at this level cannot constitute a real macroeconomic policy instrument. It is a structural budget whose form is largely set for periods of around five years. It is thus both too small and too inflexible to be used in any sense to manage the path of the EU economy in either real or nominal terms.

The EU adopts a different approach, which is to constrain the ability of the members to run independent fiscal policies. There are three types of constraints. The first are laid down in the treaty, as part of the conditions for EMU membership – the so-called Maastricht criteria. These are considered in detail in the next chapter, but in the present context they can be regarded as constraints designed to impose prudence on fiscal policy so that no one country's debt can start to raise the interest rates/lower the credit ratings of the other EMU countries. The constraints relate to the ratio of debt to GDP as a measure of long-run sustainability, and to the ratio of the government deficit to GDP in the short term.

The second set of constraints operationalizes the membership requirements for the continuing behaviour of the members inside EMU. These constraints are known as the Stability and Growth Pact (SGP) and are also dealt with in Chapters 11 and 12. The coordination among the members takes place through the framework of ECOFIN (European Council of Ministers for Financial Affairs), assisted by the Commission (see Chapter 2), and includes the ability to impose financial penalties on members that do not adhere to the prudent limits.

However, even though the SGP has the effect of coordinating fiscal policy to some extent through its constraints, the third aspect of policy among the members is a more positive form of cooperation. This occurs through the annual setting of Broad Economic Policy Guidelines (BEPGs). Here, there is not only discussion among the members to try to set a framework for policy consistent with EU longer-term objectives, but also an informal dialogue between the fiscal and monetary authorities.

The ability to levy taxation is normally one of the key elements of economic independence, and EU countries have only agreed fairly limited constraints on their individual behaviour. These relate to the nature of indirect taxation (VAT and specific duties; see Chapter 15), which is largely a facet of the treatment of trade and the internal market discussed in Chapter 7. It is proving very difficult to get agreements on the nature of the taxation of income from capital and of company profits. Discussion of agreements on the levels of taxation of personal incomes is even further from practical realization, as the range between the highest and lowest is very large (Chapter 15). It has, however, been possible to get agreement that reductions in the level of non-wage taxes on labour would assist the overall EU economic strategy.

Taken together, these measures represent rather soft and limited coordination, which affects the nature of the theoretical discussion on monetary integration. Fiscal policy in the EU is neither a single coordinated policy nor a set of uncoordinated national policies run for the individual benefit of each member. Indeed the

degree of automatic or discretionary coordination is difficult to estimate before the event. This makes the assessment of the impact of monetary integration a somewhat uncertain exercise.

10.3 What is monetary integration?

Monetary integration has two essential components: an exchange rate union and capital (K) market integration. An exchange rate union is established when members have what is in effect one currency. The actual existence of one currency is not necessary, however, because if members have *permanently* and *irrevocably* fixed exchange rates among themselves, with currencies *costlessly* exchangeable at par, the result is effectively the same. But having a single currency makes the permanence and irrevocability more plausible, as there would be severe repercussions from exit, not least the need to produce new coins and notes. Giving the impression of permanence is a crucial ingredient for a monetary union. Hence, quasi monetary unions like currency boards, which permit the continuation of the domestic currency, but backed by another currency, tend to be less stable. This is because a currency board offers the abandonment of the backing currency as a way out of a crisis. In the same way, exchange rate unions between more equal partners have tended to back the two currencies by a common medium, such as silver or gold. Again, this offers a more rather than less unifying way forward.

Exchange rate integration requires convertibility: the *permanent* absence of all exchange controls for both current and K transactions, including interest and dividend payments (and the harmonization of relevant taxes and measures affecting the K market) within the union. It is, of course, absolutely necessary to have complete convertibility for trade transactions, otherwise an important requirement of customs union (CU) formation is threatened, namely the promotion of free trade among members, which is an integral part of an economic union (see Chapter 1). That is why this aspect of monetary integration does not need any discussion; it applies even in the case of a free trade area (FTA). Convertibility for K transactions is related to free factor mobility (see Chapters 7 and 8) and is therefore an important aspect of K market integration, which is necessary in CMs, but not in simple CUs or FTAs.

Nevertheless, the pattern of both trade and production will be affected if there are controls on K transactions.

In practice, monetary integration should specifically include three elements if it is to qualify under this definition:

1. a common monetary policy
2. a common pool of foreign exchange reserves and a common exchange rate policy
3. a single central bank or monetary authority (MA) to operate these policies.

There are important reasons for including these elements. A country entering a fixed exchange rate system gives up monetary policy autonomy because monetary policy must be used to maintain the exchange rate. In a fixed peg system, the MA is usually a single country, the USA in the Bretton Woods system and Germany in the European Monetary System (EMS; see Chapter 11). This country has monetary autonomy, but the other countries have to adjust their monetary policy to maintain the fixed exchange rate. This monetary policy may not suit the economic circumstances of the other countries in the system. Thus one of the reasons that countries such as France supported EMU was that a common monetary policy would be more suitable for their economy than a German monetary policy. Monetary policy conventionally targets inflation and controls interest rates to adjust economic activity to achieve the inflation target. To control interest rates the MA must also control the money supply, which also implies control of foreign exchange reserves, because of the interaction between foreign exchange operations and the money supply. The exchange rate is not specifically targeted, but it becomes the MA's responsibility. So in a monetary union the single MA must take responsibility for four elements of monetary policy: interest rates, money supply, foreign exchange reserves and exchange rate.

In short, monetary integration, as defined, requires the unification and joint management of monetary policy as well as of the union's external exchange rate policy. This has two further consequences. First, the rate of increase of the money supply must be decided jointly. Beyond an agreed amount of credit expansion, allocated to the central bank of each member, a member would have to finance any budget deficit in the union's K market at the ruling interest rate. A unified monetary policy would eliminate one of the main reasons for disparate price level movements in the members, and a major factor for the prevalence of intra-union payment imbalances prior to monetary union. Second, the balance of payments of the entire union with the outside world must be regulated at the union level. For this purpose, MA must dispose of a common pool of exchange reserves, and the union exchange rates with other currencies must be regulated at the union level.

Monetary integration which explicitly included these three requirements would therefore enable the partners to do away with all these problems right from the start. Incidentally, this also suggests the advantages of having a single currency: with a single currency the members can all have a say in the setting of policy. With a reference currency, the tendency will always be for the country whose currency it is to dominate the decision-making, as the others will have to follow or leave the arrangement. A tighter arrangement is likely to give them explicit rights in decision-making, perhaps even including a veto.

10.4 The gains and losses

10.4.1 Gains from EMU

The gains from EMU membership could be purely economic, non-economic (e.g. political) or both. Some of the non-economic benefits are obvious – for example, it is difficult to imagine that a complete political union could become a reality without the establishment of a monetary union. However, because political, security and other issues lie beyond the scope of this chapter, the discussion will be confined to the economic benefits, which can be briefly summarized as follows:

1. A common pool of foreign exchange reserves economizes their use, since it is unlikely that members will go into deficit *simultaneously*, so one country's surplus can offset another's deficit. Intra-union trade transactions will no longer be financed by foreign exchange, so the need for foreign exchange is reduced for any given trade pattern. Frankel and Rose (2002) argue that having EMU will in itself lead to an increase in intra-trade at the expense of trade with non-members. In the EU context, this will reduce the role of the US dollar or reduce EU dependence on the dollar.

2. In the case of the EU, the adoption of the common currency (the euro) has transformed the currency into a major world medium which competes with the US dollar and the Japanese yen. The advantages of such a currency from seignorage[1] are well established, but not huge. How long it would take the euro, if it were even possible, to supplant much of the role of the US dollar as an international vehicle currency is of course a moot point (see Chapter 11). One facet of having a second major currency to compete with the US dollar is that international market conditions can become more or less stable, depending on whether the two authorities decide to cooperate or permit major swings. Since, for a large currency bloc, foreign trade forms a small proportion of total transactions, wide swings in exchange rates can be accommodated with limited impact on the overall economy. These swings can have more striking effects on smaller countries, so large currency areas normally feel an obligation to consider the wider implications. Indeed, the group of seven (G7; which became G8, and now we have G20) was created in 1986 to establish a system of international coordination between the most advanced nations in the world for precisely such a reason.

3. Transaction costs incurred when one currency is exchanged for another are avoided within a monetary union, leading to a saving in the use of resources. The high costs that individuals incur when making foreign exchange transactions would seem to suggest these costs are large. These gains, however, are thought to be small (the Commission estimated them in 1990 at 0.2–0.5 per cent of EU GDP).

4. Competition in the SEM will be enhanced by a single currency because of the greater transparency and certainty it provides. Prices can be more easily compared across national borders, so competition will intensify. Since exchange rate movements have been eliminated, differences in prices and costs between locations become more apparent, so production can be shifted to where costs are lowest.

5. There is normally a clear interest rate gain for the smaller and previously high-inflation countries, if the area as a whole has credible institutions and policies. These countries will be able to borrow at lower interest rates because inflation expectations are reduced and because of the greater efficiency of larger and deeper capital markets in monetary unions.

6. There are also the classical advantages of having permanently fixed exchange rates (or one currency) among EMU members for free trade and factor movements. Stability of exchange rates enhances trade, through reduced price uncertainty, encourages K to move to where it is most productively rewarded, and encourages labour (L) to move to where the highest rewards prevail. Of course, hedging can tackle the problem of exchange rate fluctuations, but at a cost. Here again, however, the evidence suggests that hedging costs and penalties from uncertainty are relatively minor, except for smaller companies that tend not to hedge. The much greater advantage is that it seems to cement integration, encouraging greater trade and foreign direct investment (FDI) than would be expected; this is shown very clearly in the gravity model literature (see Mélitz 2001).

7. The integration of the K market has a further advantage. If an EMU member is in deficit, it can borrow directly on the union market using the K inflow to finance the deficit, while adjustment takes place. However, as mentioned above, the integration of economic policies within the monetary union may ensure that this help will occur automatically under the auspices of the common central bank.

8. When a monetary union establishes a central fiscal authority with its own budget, then, as already mentioned, the larger the size of this budget, the higher the scope for fiscal harmonization (CEU 1977a; Chapters 15 and 19). This has some advantages: regional deviations from internal balance can be financed from the centre, and the centralization of social security payments, financed by contributions or taxes on a progressive basis, would have some stabilizing and compensating effects, modifying the harmful effects of EMU (see Chapter 19).

Specific to the EU, there are also negative advantages in that EMU is helpful for maintaining the EU as it exists. For example, realizing SEM – that is, making prices transparent (see page 000) – would become more difficult to achieve, and the common agricultural prices enshrined in the Common Agricultural Policy (CAP; see Chapter 20) would become more complicated when members' exchange rates were flexible. These

EMU benefits are clear and there are few economists who would question them; the only disagreement is about their extent (see point 6 opposite and Chapter 7), and most of those who minimize them tend to give little weight to the psychological benefits of dealing with a single currency. However, there is no consensus with regard to the costs.

10.4.2 Losses from EMU

The losses from EMU have been elaborated in terms of the theory of optimum currency areas (OCAs), pioneered by Mundell (1961), with immediate contributions coming from McKinnon (1963) and Kenen (1969), and followed by, inter alia, Mundell (1973a, b) himself and, within the context of the UK and the euro, Buiter (2000) and Barrell (2002). Given the broad nature of this issue, this section is confined to a presentation of its main message; those interested in a more comprehensive coverage should consult de Grauwe (2009).

Before presenting the bare OCA essentials, it may prove helpful to begin with later contributions by Fleming (1971) and Corden (1972a). Assume that the world consists of three countries: the home country (H), the potential partner country (P) and the rest of the world (W). Also assume that, in order to maintain both internal and external equilibrium (as defined in standard open-economy macroeconomics), H needs to devalue its currency relative to W, while P needs to revalue vis-à-vis W. Moreover, assume that H and P use fiscal and monetary policies for achieving internal equilibrium. If H and P were partners in EMU, they would devalue together (which is consistent with H's policy requirements in isolation) or revalue together (which is consistent with P's requirements in isolation), but they would not be able to alter the rate of exchange in a way that was consistent with both. Under such circumstances, the alteration in the exchange rate could leave H with an external deficit, forcing it to deflate its economy, increasing or creating unemployment, or it could leave it with a surplus, forcing it into accumulating foreign reserves or allowing its prices and wages to rise. If countries deprive themselves of rates of exchange (or trade impediments) as policy instruments, they impose on themselves losses that are essentially the losses emanating from *enforced departure from internal balance* (Corden 1972a).

In short, the rationale for retaining exchange rate flexibility rests on the assumption that governments aim to achieve both internal and external balance, and, as Tinbergen (1952) has shown, to achieve these *simultaneously* at least an equal number of targets and instruments is needed. This can be explained in the following manner. Internal equilibrium is tackled via financial instruments, which have their greatest impact on the level of aggregate demand, and the exchange rate is used to achieve external equilibrium. Of course, financial instruments can be activated via both monetary and fiscal policies, and may have a varied impact on both internal and external equilibrium. Given this understanding, the case for maintaining flexibility in exchange rates depends entirely on the presumption that the loss of one of the two policy instruments will conflict with the achievement of both internal and external equilibrium.

With this in mind, it is vital to follow the Corden–Fleming explanation of the enforced departure from internal equilibrium. Suppose a country is initially in internal equilibrium but has a deficit in its external account. If the country were free to vary its rate of exchange, the appropriate policy for achieving overall balance would be a combination of devaluation and expenditure reduction. When the rate of exchange is not available as a policy instrument, it is necessary to reduce expenditure by more than is required in the optimal situation, which results in extra unemployment. This *excess* unemployment, which can be valued in terms of output or some more direct measure of welfare, is the cost to that country of depriving itself of the exchange rate as a policy instrument. The extent of this loss is determined by the potential size of balance of payments deficits, and the effectiveness as an instrument of adjustment of the exchange rate and of the alternatives still available in a monetary union.

This analysis is based on the assumption that there exists a trade-off between rates of change in costs/inflation and in levels of unemployment – the Phillips curve. Assuming that there is a Phillips (1958) curve relationship (a negative response of rates of change in money wages – W^* – and the level of unemployment – U), the Fleming–Corden analysis can be explained by using a simple diagram, adapting one devised by de Grauwe (1975). Hence, in Figure 10.1, the top half depicts the position of H, while the lower half that of P. The upper and lower right-hand corners represent the two countries' Phillips curves, while the remaining quadrants

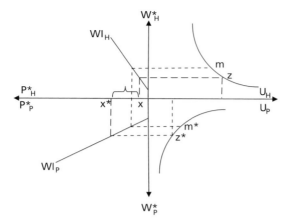

Figure 10.1 The Fleming–Corden analysis of monetary integration

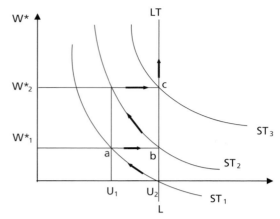

Figure 10.2 The expectations-augmented Phillips curve

show their inflation rates corresponding to the rates of change in wages – P^*. WI (which stands for *wage rate change* and corresponding *inflation*) is determined by the share of L in total GNP, the rate of change in the productivity of L, and the degree of competition in both the factor and the commodity markets, with perfect competition resulting in WIs being straight lines. Note that the intersection of WIs with the vertical axes will be determined by rates of change of L's share in GNP and its rate of productivity change. The diagram has been drawn on the presumption that the L productivity changes are positive.

The diagram is drawn in such a way that countries H and P differ in all respects: the positions of their Phillips curves, their preferred trade-offs between W^* and P^*, and their rates of productivity growth. H has a lower rate of inflation (x), than P (x^*), equilibrium change in wages and unemployment level being at z and z^*. Hence, without EMU, P's currency should depreciate relative to H's.[2] Altering the exchange rates would then enable each country to maintain its preferred internal equilibrium: z and z^* for countries H and P, respectively.

When H and P enter EMU, their inflation rates cannot differ from each other, given a model without non-traded goods. Each country will therefore have to settle for a combination of U and P^*, which is different from what it would have liked (m and m^*). The Fleming–Corden conclusion is thus vindicated.

However, this analysis rests entirely on the acceptance of the Phillips curve, but the consensus today is

that there is no long-term trade-off between unemployment and inflation. If there is any relationship, it must be a short-term one, such that the rate of unemployment is in the long term independent of the rate of inflation: there is a natural rate of unemployment (NRU), generally defined as the non-accelerating inflation rate of unemployment (NAIRU) – that is, the rate of unemployment consistent with an unchanging inflation rate (see Stiglitz 1997), which is determined by rigidities in the L market. Thus the simple version of the Phillips curve has been replaced by an expectations-augmented one along the lines suggested by Phelps (1968) and Friedman (1975) – that is, the Phillips curves become vertical in the long run. This is shown in Figure 10.2, which depicts three Phillips curves for one of the two countries. Assume that unemployment is initially at point U_2 – that is, the rate of inflation is equal to zero – given the short-term Phillips curve indicated by ST_1. The expectations-augmented Phillips curve suggests that, if the government tries to lower unemployment by the use of monetary policy, the short-term effect will be to move to point a, with positive inflation and lower unemployment. However, in the long term, people will adjust their expectations, causing an upward shift of the Phillips curve to ST_2, which leads to equilibrium at point b. The initial level of unemployment is thus restored, but with a higher rate of inflation. A repetition of this process gives the vertical long-term curve labelled LT.

If both H and P have vertical LT curves, Figure 10.1 will have to be adjusted to give Figure 10.3. The implications of this are:

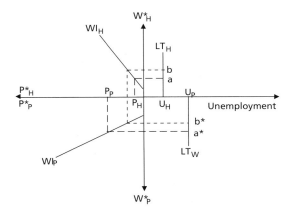

Figure 10.3 Monetary integration with expectations-augmented Phillips curves

1. EMU will have no long-term effects on either partner's rate of unemployment, since this will be fixed at the appropriate NAIRU for each country – U_H, U_P.
2. If EMU is adopted to bring about balanced growth and NRU, this can be achieved only if, inter alia, other policy instruments are introduced to bring about uniformity in the two L markets. This is, however, only a necessary condition; other aspects of similarity in tastes and production structures would be necessary to make it a sufficient condition.

Therefore, this alternative interpretation of the Phillips curve invalidates the Fleming–Corden conclusion.

It should be noted that Allen and Kenen (1980) and Allen (1983) have demonstrated, using a sophisticated and elaborate model with financial assets, that, although monetary policy has severe drawbacks as an instrument for adjusting cyclical imbalances within EMU, it may be able to influence the demand for the goods produced by members in a differential manner within the short term, provided members' markets are not too closely integrated. Their model indicates that EMU, in this sense, can come about as a consequence of the substitutability between nations' commodities, especially their financial assets, and of country biases in the purchase of commodities and financial assets. The moral is that the EMU central bank can operate monetary policies in such a manner as to have differing impacts on the various partner countries, and thus achieve real effects without compromising their internal and external equilibria. Moreover, once non-traded goods are incorporated into the model and/or K and

L mobility is allowed for, it follows that the losses due to deviating from internal equilibrium vanish, a point which Corden (1972a, 1977) readily acknowledged. Finally, this model does not allow for the fact that EMU involves at least three countries – that is, W has to be explicitly included in the model. Allen and Kenen (1980) tried to develop a model along these lines, but their model is not a straightforward extension of that depicted in Figure 10.1.

To recap, it may be helpful to clarify some misconceptions and highlight others:

1. The fixity of exchange rate parities within EMU does not mean that the different member currencies cannot vary in unison relative to extra-union currencies; the adoption of one currency by the union would clearly show that.
2. In a 'proper' EMU – that is, one which satisfies all the elements specified in the definition given above (see Section 1.3, page 148) – an extra deficit for one region (country) can come about only as a result of a revaluation of the union currency: the union as a whole has an external surplus vis-à-vis the outside world. Such an act would increase the foreign exchange earnings of the surplus region, and therefore of the union as a whole, provided that the conditions for a successful revaluation existed. The integration of monetary policies through the common central bank will ensure that the extra burden on the first region is alleviated: the overall extra earnings will be used to help the region with the extra deficit. Such a situation may lead to surplus regions financing those in deficit indefinitely, but that is not likely.
3. One can perhaps think of the reservations in terms of Tinbergen's (1952) criterion of an equal number of policy instruments and objectives (see page 151). Although a country may lose an instrument individually, it is gaining other instruments from other aspects of EMU. The union as a whole does not lose the exchange rate route of adjustment (point (1) above). A voluntary EMU of depth is likely to offer a sufficient degree of 'political' union for unacceptably adverse effects on a particular country or part of it to be recognized and acted on (witness the agreed deal in 2010 between the EU and the IMF for the rescue of Greece; see Chapters 11 and 12). When countries are in a voluntary union they will be prepared, within limits, to act in favour of

other members, even when it is not in their immediate economic interest. Next time it may be they who would benefit from the voluntary assistance of others. Taking either a legalistic view of what actions union agreements lay down or a relatively short-run perspective of economic gains can be misleading. Ultimately, the alternative would be that the member would leave the union, which could also harm the other members and threaten the credibility of the union thereafter. Relevance to reality therefore requires taking a somewhat broader view of the policy problem.

4. Devaluation can work effectively only when there is 'money illusion'; but are today's trade unionists so deluded?

5. In practice there would never be a separation between the exchange rate union and K market integration. Once convertibility for K transactions is allowed for, K will always come to the rescue. Of course, this raises the spectre of a permanently depressed member, but, again, how likely is that?

6. More fundamentally, but arguably, a very crucial element is missing. The analysis relates to a country in internal equilibrium and external deficit. If such a country were outside EMU, it could devalue its currency. Assuming that the necessary conditions for effective devaluation prevailed, then devaluation would increase the national income of the country, increase its price level or result in some combination of the two. Hence a deflationary policy would be required to restore the internal balance. However, if the country were to lose its freedom to alter its exchange rate, it would have to deflate in order to depress its imports and restore external balance. According to the above analysis, this alternative would entail unemployment in excess of that prevailing in the initial situation. The missing element in this argument can be found by specifying how devaluation actually works. Devaluation of a country's currency results in changes in relative price levels and is price inflationary for both exportables and importables, at least. These relative price changes, given the necessary stability conditions, will depress imports and (perhaps) increase exports. The deflationary policy that is required (to accompany devaluation) in order to restore internal balance should therefore eliminate the *newly injected* inflation as well as the *extra* national income. Only if the inflationary implications of devaluation are completely disregarded can one reach the a priori conclusion that membership of EMU would necessitate extra sacrifice of employment in order to achieve the same target.

7. Even within a purely economic context, there will be a limit to how far the argument will go for the costs for a country from forgoing the ability to have its own exchange rate and monetary policy. The whole net benefit of the increased integration has to be taken into account. Hence, even if the rates of inflation and unemployment differed from those that would be preferred without EMU, they may dwindle to nothing when combined with other benefits to real incomes and wealth. Similar agreements with parts of W may not be politically superior, even if they might be economically so. Similarly, monetary integration may reinforce the barriers to reversion to less desired examples of economic dominance (a point emphasized by some of the countries involved in the 2004 EU accession).

Against the above, one should add that monetary independence offers an element of contingency planning. Sweden explicitly and Denmark implicitly have argued that even though they may wish to shadow EMU very closely, maintaining a separate currency gives them the opportunity to respond rather better to a very large adverse shock. Thus, with care, they can manage to secure most of the gains from EMU and yet retain an element of flexibility.

10.4.3 Back to OCAs

OCA is generally presented in terms of national incomes and prices, relegating wages to the background. This is useful, since it provides a complementary picture to the above analysis, ensuring a better understanding, but, of course, inevitably leading to overlaps. Mundell (1961) attributed the loss to a shift in demand, due, say, to a change in consumer preferences, away from P, in favour of H. This is depicted (not by Mundell) in Figure 10.4, where the vertical axis measures prices (P_H, P_P), the horizontal the level of national economic activity (Y_H, Y_P), and S and D, respectively, are the aggregate national supply and demand curves. The two countries are initially in the equilibrium situations depicted by the solid S and D

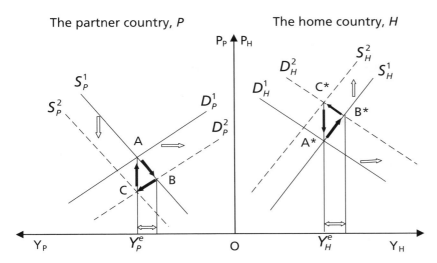

Figure 10.4 Shifts in EMU partners' aggregate supply and demand

curves (D_H^1, S_H^1 for H and D_P^1, S_P^1 for P), with H at A* (i.e. income Y_H^e) and P at A (income Y_P^e). The indicated shifts in demand (the dotted lines D_H^2 and D_P^2; follow the blank arrows) mean that H moves to the right while P moves to the left. Thus the equilibrium points move to B* and B respectively – that is, H experiences an increase in Y, hence in employment – while P experiences the opposite – that is, an increase in unemployment. As mentioned above, it is the extent of these deviations from equilibrium Y_H^e and Y_P^e that constitutes the costs of EMU for the two partners.

Given that the original income levels (Y_H^e; Y_P^e), hence of employment/unemployment, were the nations' desired ones, the question is then how to restore them. As above, there are two ways to do so. The first is that if *wages are flexible* in both countries, then the increased level of economic activity in H will push up H's wages, while the increased unemployment in P will depress P's wages. The result will be an upward shift in S in H to S_H^2 (since S reflects costs, which have risen with increased wages), and a downward shift in P to S_P^2. The figure has been drawn in such a way that the new equilibrium positions (C* and C) precisely restore the original Y levels (A* and A), but of course increase H's price level and reduce P's. These price changes will stimulate demand in P and depress it in H, and their change relative to each other in favour of P will result in reinforcing shifts in demand that take both countries back to their original curves (D_H^1, D_P^1) – that is, to points A* and A.

The second is that if labour (L) can move freely between the two countries, then those losing jobs in P will migrate to H. The reduction (or increase) in L in P (or H) will enable both countries to maintain their initial wages; thus they can stay at B* and B. Of course, this means different income levels from the initial ones, but there is no disequilibrium due to the changes in L endowments.

What happens if wages are inflexible and L is immobile? Obviously, equilibrium in P will remain at C. In H, however, the increase in D will lead to increases in wages and shift the S curve upwards, resulting in higher prices there. Hence, H has to bear the full brunt of the adjustment, through higher prices – that is, higher inflation. These increased prices, again, will make P products more competitive, leading to shifts in demand in their favour. The upshot is that, by being a member of EMU, H will have to accept higher inflation than it desired.

But how would the two countries fare outside EMU? If they followed a freely flexible exchange rate system, H would raise its interest rate, depressing demand, while P would do the opposite, enhancing demand. These policy changes lead to an appreciation of H's currency and a depreciation of P's, enhancing the competitiveness of P products in the H markets. The interest and exchange rate changes will thus enhance demand in P and depress it in H. The net effect of these policy changes is to shift the demand curves back to their original levels and restore equilibrium – that is, go back to A* and A.

This is the same conclusion reached above: as a member of EMU, a country will have to either persevere with more unemployment than it desired or put up with more inflation than it deemed acceptable – that is, such a country cannot adjust to asymmetric shocks. Hence the major contribution of OCA theory is to point out that for nations to form OCAs they have to have symmetric shocks, or, they must have flexible wages and free labour mobility. Recall, however, that this conclusion is null and void in the long run in the previous case, and is valid here only if the change in demand is permanent (if it is short-lived, then what is the fuss about?) (see de Grauwe 2005); for the EU, Gros (1996) and others find that shocks are sectoral, hence cannot be tackled in terms of exchange rate changes.

10.4.4 OCA in a nutshell

The previous section considered explicitly only two prerequisites of OCA, but the others have been dealt with in the section on the definition and some will be catered for in the next section. So here is a brief enumeration of all the factors.

OCA's message is very simple: two countries would gain from having a single currency when the benefits of the elimination of exchange rate risks and enhanced price transparency outweigh the costs of adjusting to country-specific (asymmetric) shocks due to loss of control over their own interest and exchange rates. *OCA is not about the overall costs and benefits of EMU; it is a cost-benefit analysis of the costs of EMU.* The theory sets out the conditions that would ensure against costs, or at least limit their extent:

1. Price/wage flexibility, which would enable markets to clear fully, thus eliminating the need for the lost policy instruments (page 155).
2. Labour/capital mobility, which would fully compensate for the adjustments that the lost policy instruments would achieve (page 155).
3. Financial market integration, which would cater for inter-area payments imbalances and enhance long-term adjustment through wealth effects (see previous section).
4. Open economies, meaning members have high exports/income ratios and trade mainly with each

other, and thus would benefit from fixed exchange rates between them (see previous section and next page).
5. Production spread across a variety of goods and services, which would insulate against fluctuations in the demand for individual commodities, dispensing with the necessity for frequent changes in the terms of trade by way of exchange rate changes (see previous section and next page).
6. Similarity of production structures, which ensures similar shocks, eliminating the need for individually tailored policies (see previous section and next page).
7. Similarity of inflation rates, which would minimize payment imbalances (page 152).
8. Greater degree of fiscal integration, which would make it easier to eliminate divergent shocks through fiscal transfers (see Section 10.6 page 159 and Chapters 11 and 12).

Note that these need not apply inclusively, since an acceptable performance in one criterion may compensate for a poorer performance on another – for example, a high degree of labour mobility would reduce the need for a high degree of wage flexibility. Also note, importantly, that these criteria say nothing about the gains from integration (see left column), but the next section does so.

Before we proceed, however, it should be mentioned that a later Mundell (1973a) is less sceptical of EMUs. This is due to his adding a new dimension to his analysis: EMU provides an insurance mechanism, enabling members to manage asymmetric shocks better, relative to having their own exchange rate uncertainty outside. Suppose members experience a temporary asymmetric shock. Inside EMU, consumers in the adversely affected country can borrow automatically from a member to mitigate their circumstances. In the absence of EMU, the existence of separate monies and uncertain exchange rates would deter the lenders; hence temporary shocks cannot be alleviated. Also, under uncertainty, movements in the exchanges themselves may be the cause of asymmetric shocks, rather than enabling members to cope with them.

10.5 A 'popular' cost approach

As mentioned, OCA theory is concerned with only the loss of the exchange rate as a policy instrument when what is needed is an examination of the overall costs and benefits of EMU. Before dealing with this, here is a simple version of the losses, made popular in the context of the discussions concerning the euro as the single currency for the EU. It is known as the impossible trilogy, or inconsistent trinity, principle.

The principle states that only two out of the following three are mutually compatible:

1. Completely free capital mobility
2. An independent monetary policy
3. A fixed exchange rate.

This is because, with full capital mobility, a nation's own interest rate is tied to the world interest rate, at least for a country too small to influence global financial markets. More precisely, any difference between the domestic and world interest rates must be matched by an expected rate of depreciation of the exchange rate – for example, if the interest rate is 6 per cent in the domestic market, but 4 per cent in the world market, the global market must expect the currency to depreciate by 2 per cent this year. This is known as the interest parity condition, which implies that integrated financial markets equalize expected asset returns; hence assets denominated in a currency expected to depreciate must offer an exactly compensating higher yield for the expected depreciation.

Under such circumstances, a country that wants to conduct an independent monetary policy, raising or lowering its interest rate to control its level of employment/unemployment, must allow its exchange rate to fluctuate in the market. Conversely, a country confronted with full capital mobility, which wants to fix its exchange rate, must set its domestic interest rate to be exactly equal to the rate in the country to which it pegs its currency. Since monetary policy is then determined abroad, the country has effectively lost its monetary independence.

The loss caused by EMU membership is as already indicated, but here its extent is determined by the combined Mundell–McKinnon–Kenen (respectively, 1961, 1963 and 1969) criteria, which render price adjustments through exchange rate changes less effective or less compelling:

(a) Openness to mutual trade
(b) Diverse economies
(c) Mobility of factors of production, especially of labour.

Greater openness to mutual trade implies that most prices would be determined at the union level, which means that relative prices would be less susceptible to being influenced by changes in the exchange rate. An economy more diverse in terms of production would be less likely to suffer from country-specific shocks, reducing the need for the exchange rate as a policy tool. Greater factor mobility enables the economy to tackle *asymmetric shocks* via migration, hence reducing the need for adjustment through the exchange rate.

EU nations score well on the first criterion, since the ratio of their exports to their GDP is 20–70 per cent (combining both exports and imports for 2001 gives the EU 12.3 per cent, with Belgium 91.7 per cent and France, Germany, Italy and the UK around 30 per cent), while that for the USA and Japan is, respectively, 11 per cent (13.5) and 7 per cent (10.8). Note that the USA is the preferred reference nation, but there is no evidence that it is an OCA (de Grauwe 2005, and references cited there), which invokes the criticism that the only area that meets OCA conditions is one that already has a currency – a circular argument. EU nations also score well in terms of the second criterion, even though they are not all as well endowed with oil or gas resources as the Netherlands and the UK. As to the third criterion, they score badly in comparison with the USA, since EU labour mobility is lower (see Chapters 7 and 8) due to, inter alia, the Europeans' tendency to stick to their place of birth, not only nationally, but also regionally. There is also a tendency for migration to be temporary and only involve part of a larger family (see Chapter 8).

Although there is no definitive estimate of the costs, due to the relative lack of labour mobility, it is generally thought to be considerable. However, it would have to be very large to offset the gains from EMU. In any case, much of the problem from lack of mobility is as relevant within the members as between them, and this applies to the USA too. It therefore requires addressing through structural policy in each member, regardless of EMU, or regardless of membership of the EU itself for that matter. Tackling the problem has become more important since the late 1960s and will remain so in the face of faster rates of technical change in products and production methods; in part, it is a consequence of globalization, so it is a change that will have to be made in any case.

Nonetheless, even on purely economic grounds, the longer-term perspective will not lend support to some

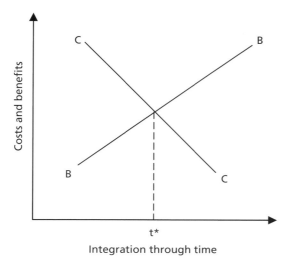

Figure 10.5 Krugman's (1990) cost–benefits of EMU

of the more pessimistic assessments. Consider, for example, Krugman's (1990) model, which utilizes such a perspective when examining the costs and benefits of EMU. In Figure 10.5 the costs are represented by line CC and the benefits by line BB, and both are expressed in relation to GDP. The benefits from the single currency are shown to rise with integration, since, for example, intra-EU trade, which has been rising with integration over time (see Figure 5.8 in Chapter 5, page 76), Tables 5.11–5.13 on the website and El-Agraa 1999), will be conducted at lesser costs (Frankel and Rose 2002), while the losses from ceding the exchange rate as a policy variable decline with time. In the economic jargon used above, changes in the exchange rate are needed to absorb asymmetric shocks, but these will decline with time, becoming less asymmetric as integration proceeds and becomes more intensive. In short, as the member economies become more integrated, the use of the exchange rate instrument for variations against members' currencies would become undesirable. Thus, for countries seriously and permanently involved in EMU, sooner or later a time would arrive when the benefits will exceed the costs. All this is tantamount to stating that OCA is non-operational, if not altogether irrelevant; indeed, a very long time ago, Corden (1972b) castigated it as one of 'feasibility', rather than 'optimality', and although Bayoumi and Eichengreen (1996) developed methods for identifying the suitability of various EU nations for EMU, their method only succeeds in ranking suitability rather than calculating actual costs/benefits, which would indicate where the line separating included from excluded countries should be (see Capie and Wood in El-Agraa 2002b). Moreover, Issing (2008, p. 50) points out that OCA criteria are neither definitive nor complete, and conditions such as the necessary market flexibility can also be created *after* the event, and hence are endogenous – that is, dependent on the process itself.

In many respects the key policy choice issue relates to uncertainty about the future. If a prospective EMU member could be certain that the economies would grow more closely together, in the sense of becoming more economically similar, and that the chance of having a serious external shock that affects only one of them or both in opposite directions, then worries about a single monetary policy being inappropriate would be reduced – that is, symmetry would be enhanced.

However, a priori, such developments can only be assessed; they cannot be known. Moreover, OCA analysis tends to ignore the fact that behaviour is likely to change after the event and assesses net EMU benefits on the basis of *ex ante* behaviour (Issing 2008). Mayes and Suvanto (2002) take this even further and argue that in the case of Finland, for example, one of the factors swaying the authorities in favour of EMU membership is that it would force generally favourable changes in labour market behaviour. In other words, knowing that the exchange rate mechanism is not available to accommodate asymmetric shocks may actually cause people to change their behaviour, so that the impact of the shocks is reduced to acceptable levels.

Furthermore, there is a tendency to ignore positive asymmetric shocks. In such cases the impact of the favourable shock will be magnified by EMU membership. Out of the union, such a shock would increase the demand for the currency as investors from other countries sought to join in the benefits. The surge in demand would probably push the domestic central bank into raising interest rates to head off any inflationary pressure, thereby also raising the exchange rate and reducing the expected rate of growth. Inside EMU, the capital inflow will have a much more limited impact on the exchange rate, as it relates only to a part of the union. Similarly, the response of monetary policy will be negligible. Knowing that there will be no offsetting policy changes, in turn, will help keep down inflationary pressures. Such an experience seems to have occurred with the favourable technology shock, or Nokia phenomenon, in Finland. The growth/inflation combination that occurred in the early EMU years was considerably more favourable than that which prevailed in earlier decades. Other factors, such as the continuing impact of the collapse of the former Soviet Union and the banking crisis in the early 1990s, may also have been influential, but the evidence is, at the very least, suggestive.

10.6 Fiscal policy in monetary unions

Although this chapter is concerned with EMU theory, EMU is essentially an EU phenomenon in the sense that sovereign nations voluntarily decide to adopt it. The USA is, of course, an EMU, and, as we have seen, it is used by all analysts as the benchmark against which to judge EMUs, but it is a single nation. It may therefore prove helpful, before drawing overall conclusions, to digress somewhat by examining the role of fiscal policy in monetary unions, including the USA. Aspects of this are dealt with in Chapter 12, but a bit of overlap is warranted.

Durable EMUs are characterized by large central budgets that facilitate fiscal policy and transfers between regions. Fiscal policy is the manipulation of the balance between government expenditure and revenue so as to influence aggregate demand in the economy. This has three elements in EMU: the overall fiscal situation, interactions and transfers between members. Macroeconomic policy is more effective if monetary and fiscal policies are coordinated. This was apparent in the recent recession, starting in 2007, where a loose monetary policy needed to be augmented by a fiscal stimulus. However, with individual members' fiscal policies responding to their individual macroeconomic situation, the overall fiscal stance is likely to be suitable.

Interactions between members can occur in two ways: first, the potential effect of national fiscal policy on EMU's monetary policy, and second, absorption. If national fiscal policy of some EMU members is too loose, this could lead the MA (see Chapters 12 and 19) to raise interest rates at the expense of the responsible members. This is possible, but for it to be significant the members involved would have to be large and the looseness great. So this seems to be a marginal problem.

Absorption relates to the national income accounting identity that a country's balance of payments current account balance (CA) is equal to national income/output minus absorption: the national use of goods and services in consumption, government expenditure and investment. Or that CA is equal to net private saving plus the government fiscal balance (government revenue minus government expenditure). So the national fiscal stance will affect other countries in EMU via their balance of payments. For example, in EMU, Germany's high level of private saving more than offset the modest fiscal deficits and the country has a large surplus on CA. With most EMU trade being internal, the counterpart of this large surplus is deficits in other Eurozone members. So there is an important interaction between national fiscal positions, CA and national macroeconomic situations. In EMU with a large central budget, the effects of these regional imbalances would be at least partially offset by fiscal transfers between regions, the issue to which the discussion now turns.

With automatic transfers from the central/federal budget, fiscal policy will act as a means of inter-regional risk sharing by transferring resources between regions (see Chapters 11 and 12). These transfers perform three types of function (Fatás 1998): inter-temporal stabilization, inter-regional insurance and inter-regional redistribution. The first two stabilize regional income and the third reduces inequalities in income levels between regions. Inter-temporal stabilization smoothes fluctuations in regional income levels due to the stabilization of the national economy by movements in the national public sector deficits: the Keynesian stabilization function. Inter-regional insurance transfers tax revenue from fast-growing regions to slow-growing ones when economic cycles are imperfectly correlated between regions. Inter-regional redistribution involves the transfer of resources from more to less prosperous regions, so it is related to levels of rather than changes in income. Such redistribution might be justified in terms of the solidarity of the nation state, to achieve a fairer individual distribution of income, or to enhance overall economic efficiency. The delineation of these transfers in theory and their separation in reality are another matter; in national monetary unions transfers between regions fulfil all three functions.

These three functions relate to three problems that regions face in EMU: asymmetric shocks, competitiveness and differences in regional income. Differences in regional income levels relate to long-term economic growth, not stabilization, so are not a concern for EMU except in terms of its long-term political cohesion. Asymmetric shocks and competitiveness relate to stabilization, so are an EMU issue. Regions within EMU that face an adverse asymmetric shock have this partially offset by higher receipts from and lower payments to the federal budget, but how important is this stabilization? Initial research (Sala-i-Martin and Sachs 1992), indicated that inter-regional flows of public finance were important in reducing fluctuations in regional income. Gradually, more refined research techniques have whittled away at the estimated effects, and more recent research suggests that federal taxes and transfers only reduce regional income fluctuations by 10 per cent (Fatás 1998; Asdrubali *et al.* 2002). These estimates of stabilization are for the USA, a monetary union comparable in size to EMU. Whether it is a good basis for comparison with EMU could be questioned because of the difference between US states and EU countries. The national economies[3] of EMU remain diversified, so their vulnerability to asymmetric shocks and, consequently, the need for inter-regional stabilization is less. The greater separation of EU nations may also enhance the potential for differences in rates of wage and price inflation: an effective alternative adjustment mechanism (see page 157). By comparison with the USA, European national economies lack adjustment mechanisms such as labour mobility and cross-border capital holdings and flows, but are perhaps less vulnerable to asymmetric shocks than US states. Although, as the recent recession indicates, the vulnerability of national economies, even to symmetric shock, can vary substantially.

By contrast, competitiveness issues loom much larger for a monetary union such as EMU; the separation of national economies makes wider divergences in wage/price inflation possible. The ability to reduce these divergences may also be more difficult if they are related to structural features of the economy. It may have been thought that a common monetary policy and some coordination of fiscal policies would be sufficient to ensure similarity of national inflation rates in EMU, but this has not proved to be the case. In the absence of exchange rate adjustment, the adjustment of competitiveness is a long and painful process, with lower growth and higher unemployment being

needed to bear down on inflation. If these are insufficient to adjust competitiveness, then EMU could find itself with nations with persistently high unemployment and lower income levels, in the same way that nation states have such regions – for example, the Mezzogiorno in Italy. This indicates that EMU may require fiscal transfers from prosperous to problem nations.

Fiscal policy and government deficits lead to government debt, which is an issue for EMUs. National governments can adopt a relatively relaxed attitude to their debt, because the debt in developed countries is predominantly held by national citizens and institutions, and, in the worst case, the debt could be repaid by expanding the domestic money supply.[4] Membership of EMU changes the nature of government debt, and foreign financing of debt within the EMU may increase because it is denominated in the same currency. With the money supply controlled by the ECB, national governments can no longer service their debts by creating money. So EMU encourages looser fiscal policy, but makes its debt consequences more serious. A nation with high government debt in EMU would have to increase taxes and reduce government expenditure, which would reduce national income, making servicing the debt more difficult. The hope would be that this deflation would restore price competitiveness and expand demand in the private sector, but this is a slow and uncertain process. This is, of course, a description of the current dilemma of Greece. It follows that it is important that countries enter EMUs with manageable government debt, and that there are mechanisms to prevent the excessive accumulation of debt.[5]

This analysis indicates that EMU either requires a significant central budget or very tight controls on national governments' budgets and limits on debt. When reading Chapters 11 and 12, you should consider whether the EU's EMU meets this requirement.

10.7 Conclusion

This chapter has gone to some lengths to emphasize three EMU facets, the wider process of economic and monetary integration that has been dominating the integration process in Europe since before the turn of the century. These are:

1. The development of EMU has to be seen in the light of both the longer-term and the wider political context. Narrow short-run economic assessments can make the decisions that have been taken look illogical.
2. EMU is expected to change the behaviour and structure of the European economy. Assessment of the likely impact therefore has to include these structural changes. Many traditional models that have been used to assess the impact of integration either do not take this into account adequately or have sometimes been used in ways that ignore these essential structural components of the process of change.
3. While the focus on the monetary aspect of EMU is understandable, it is the economic 'E' in EMU that is both the more complex issue and the key to the ultimate success of the enterprise.

Hence the next two chapters appraise both the development of EMU over the last forty years, and the way in which it is currently operating and will develop as the accession countries join, in the light of these three observations.

Summary

- EMU requires the complete and irrevocable fixing of members' exchange rates, as well as the complete mobility of capital between them.
- For EMU to work in practice, three elements need to be added:
  1. a single monetary policy
  2. a common pool of foreign exchange reserves and their management
  3. a single central bank or monetary authority.
- EMU economic benefits come from various sources, including:
  1. savings in foreign exchange reserves
  2. reductions in the costs of financial management
  3. certainty and stability of prices.
- EMU economic costs are due to the loss of the exchange rate as a policy instrument.
- The losses from EMU stem from the optimum currency area (OCA) analysis, which shows that to minimize them would require, inter alia, labour and capital mobility and/or flexibility in wages and prices, and/or common central fiscal arrangements.
- OCA analysis is not operational and its conditions may be met after EMU creation, so it is not the be-all and end-all.

Questions and essay topics

1. What is EMU?
2. What are the economic benefits of EMU?
3. What are the economic costs of EMU?
4. What is an optimum currency area?
5. What conditions have to be met in order to reduce the costs of EMU?
6. What is the impossible trilogy or inconsistent trinity?
7. What is the interest parity condition?
8. How does Mundell reconcile his later OCA optimism with his earlier scepticism?
9. 'OCA is a cost-analysis of EMU, not a cost-benefit analysis of it.' Explain and discuss.
10. 'OCA conditions can be met after the event, so what is all the fuss?' Explain and discuss.

FURTHER READING

de Grauwe, P. (2009) *Economics of Monetary Union*, Oxford University Press.

NOTES

1 Seignorage is the benefit to a country if its currency is accumulated as reserves by other governments, companies or individuals in other countries. This reserve accumulation means that the currency issue country can acquire foreign goods, services or assets in exchange.
2 There is only a minute chance that the two countries' inflation rates would coincide.
3 It is national economies that are important here, because the persistence of large national budgets means that inter-regional transfers can continue within nation states, albeit constrained by the requirement of the Stability and Growth Pact.
4 There are potential problems, such as crowding out, government borrowing reducing private borrowing and investment. Expanding the money supply to finance the government debt servicing can be inflationary or

hyperinflationary. This places constraints on governments' use of such financing.

5 Debt markets should have constrained Eurozone government borrowing by requiring much higher rates of interest from governments with high levels of debt. This did not happen until the credit crunch made obvious the problems of these countries – yet another example of the failure of financial markets.

11 The development of EU economic and monetary integration

DAVID MAYES AND ALI EL-AGRAA

11.1 Introduction

The aim of achieving economic and monetary union (EMU), although enshrined in the Treaty on European Union (TEU, or the Maastricht Treaty), and hence in the Treaty of Lisbon, is not a new phenomenon for the EU (see Chapter 2). This chapter provides a historical perspective by travelling the route taken by the EU in this direction. The actual route followed has been the combination of the objectives for increasing economic integration, paving the way for what some hoped to be the political unity of Europe (see Section 2.2.2, page 25), and the more immediate economic needs and shocks along that path. Nevertheless, the initial ideas, sketched out as early as 1970, bear striking similarities to what has eventually been accomplished.

The chapter begins by considering the first attempt at EMU, based on the 1971 Werner Report, which committed then European Community (EC) member states (MSs) to achieving it in three stages, beginning in 1971 and finishing in 1980. After examining the reasons for its failure, it goes on to tackle the 1979 European Monetary System (EMS), a limited arrangement aimed at dealing with the monetary upheavals of the time by creating a zone of monetary stability. It then turns to the revival of EMU in the two Delors reports, which culminated in its formal adoption in the 1992 Maastricht Treaty, again to be achieved in three stages, beginning in 1990 and finishing in 1997, or 1999 at the very latest. We then look into how it has progressed and why some MSs remain outside, before offering our conclusions.

11.2 The Werner Report

From 1967, the prevailing world order for exchange rates, established as part of the Bretton Woods agreement in 1944, began to fall apart. Until that point

the system of having exchange rates that were 'fixed', but adjustable occasionally when the existing rate was shown to be unsustainable, had worked rather well. Fixity permitted fluctuations within 1 per cent of a peg with the US dollar, which in turn was convertible to gold at $35 per ounce. Despite some initial repositioning after the war, the number of occasions on which pegs had been changed meant that the system had seemed credible. The contrast with problems after the First World War, with hyperinflation in Germany and then the deflationary impact of trying to return to the gold standard, was striking. However, while the early problems lay with other countries trying to stabilize themselves with respect to the USA, the problem in the 1960s was that the USA, hindered by the cost of the Vietnam war, was no longer able to act as the anchor for the international system.

Other countries therefore had to look elsewhere for stability. While the main initial thrust was towards a reform of the Bretton Woods system, the EC looked at the possibility of trying to create a locally stable system with the same sort of architecture for itself. In 1969, during The Hague summit (see Chapter 2), the original six MSs (the Six) decided that the EC should progressively transform itself into an EMU, and set up a committee, led by Pierre Werner, then prime minister of Luxembourg, to consider the issues involved. The Werner Committee presented an interim report in June 1970 and a final report in October of the same year. The latter became generally known as the Werner Report, and was endorsed by the Council in February 1971.

According to Council resolution, the EC would (*OJ C* 1971):

1. Constitute a zone where persons, goods, services and capital would move freely – but without distorting competition, or creating structural and regional imbalances.

2. Form a single monetary entity within the international monetary system, characterised by the total and irreversible convertibility of currencies; the elimination of fluctuation margins of exchange rates between [members]; the irrevocable fixing of their parity relationships. These steps would be essential for the creation of a single currency, and they would involve a Community-level organisation of central banks.

3. Hold the powers and responsibilities in the economic and monetary field that would enable its institutions to ensure the administration of the economic union. To this end, the necessary economic policy decisions would be taken at EC level and the necessary powers would be attributed to community institutions.

EC organization of central banks would assist, in the framework of its own responsibilities, in achieving the objectives of stability and growth in the EC.

As progress was made in moving closer to the final objectives, EC instruments would be created whenever they seemed necessary to replace or complement the action of national instruments. All actions would be interdependent; in particular, the development of monetary unification would be backed by parallel progress in the convergence, and then the unification, of economic policies.

The Council decided that EMU could be attained during that decade, if the plan had the permanent political support of MSs' governments. Implementation was envisaged in three stages, with the first beginning in 1971 and the third completed by 1980. The Council made quite clear how it envisaged the process leading to full EMU (emphasis added):

(a) The first phase should begin on January 1, 1971, and could technically be completed within three years. This phase would be used to make [EC] instruments more operational and to mark the beginnings of [the EC's] individuality within the international monetary system;

(b) The first phase should not be considered as an objective in itself; it should be associated with the complete process of economic and monetary integration. *It should therefore be launched with the determination to arrive at the final goal*;

(c) In the first phase consultation procedures should be strengthened; the budgetary policies of [MSs] should accord with [EC] objectives; some taxes should be harmonised; monetary and credit policies should be coordinated; and integration of financial markets should be intensified.

The EMU launched by the EC in 1971 was thus consistent with the requirements for a full EMU discussed in Chapter 10. While the problems of integrating product markets may not have been clear then, the intention to have the free flow of capital and labour rather than just free trade and ordered payments is set out, foreshadowing later developments.

Although the 1971 venture did fail, after an earlier than expected successful negotiation of the first phase and making some progress during the second, the failure was not due to lack of commitment, determination or both. The Nixon shock, the first oil shock and the enlargement shock (the admission of three new members, each bringing with it its own unique problems) were the real culprits. The first step in coordinated monetary management had been that EC MSs would keep all their bilateral exchange rates within 2.25 per cent of each other. Their joint rates would therefore move quite closely together in a 'snake' round the dollar, which was still treated as the numeraire of the system, and since the dollar rate itself fluctuated, this led to the term 'snake in the tunnel'. (The Smithsonian Agreement that was in force at the time would have limited each currency's fluctuation with respect to the dollar to 2.25 per cent. Thus without the 'snake', EC currencies could have moved up to 4.5 per cent from each other. This would clearly have been more than is acceptable without renegotiating prices, and hence would have violated the degree of stability required within the EC.) Not only were the lira, sterling and the French franc unable to hold their parity within the first year or so, but the Smithsonian Agreement itself had collapsed into generalized floating by 1973.

11.3 The European Monetary System

In some quarters, the European Monetary System (EMS) has been considered as the next EC attempt at EMU, but some would argue that it was little more than a mechanism devised to check the monetary upheavals of the 1970s by creating a zone of monetary stability. The route to the EMS was a fairly short one. The idea was floated not by the EC Commission but by the German chancellor, Helmut Schmidt, and the French president, Valéry Giscard d'Estaing, and was discussed in Council in Copenhagen in April 1978. Roy Jenkins, Commission president, had called for such a corrective

Box 11.1 Provisions of the EMS (OJ C 1971)

1. In terms of exchange rate management . . . EMS . . . will be at least as strict as the 'snake'. In the initial stages of its operation and for a limited period of time, member countries currently not participating in the 'snake' may opt for somewhat wider margins around central rates. In principle, intervention will be in the currencies of participating countries. Changes in central rates will be subject to mutual consent. Non-member countries with particularly strong economic and financial ties with [the EC] may become associate members of the system. The European Currency Unit (ECU) will be at the centre of the system; in particular, it will be used as a means of settlement between EEC monetary authorities.

2. An initial supply of ECUs (for use among [EC] central banks) will be created against deposit of US dollars and gold on the one hand (e.g. 20% of the stock currently held by member central banks) and member currencies on the other hand in an amount of a comparable order of magnitude.

   The use of ECUs created against member currencies will be subject to conditions varying with the amount and the maturity; due account will be given to the need for substantial short-term facilities (up to 1 year).

3. Participating countries will coordinate their exchange rates policies *vis-à-vis* third countries. To this end, they will intensify the consultations in the appropriate bodies and between central banks participating in the scheme. Ways to coordinate dollar interventions should be sought which avoid simultaneous reserve interventions. Central banks buying dollars will deposit a fraction (say 20%) and receive ECUs in return; likewise, central banks selling dollars will receive a fraction (say 20%) against ECUs.

4. Not later than two years after the start of the scheme, the existing arrangements and institutions will be consolidated in a European Monetary Fund.

5. A system of closer monetary cooperation will only be successful if participating countries pursue policies conducive to greater stability at home and abroad; this applies to deficit and surplus countries alike.

initiative in a speech in Florence the previous October. By 5 December the Council had adopted the idea, in the form of a resolution 'on the establishment of [EMS] and related matters', after a period of intensive discussion (Ludlow 1982 gives a full account of the negotiations involved).

The EMS, which started operating in March 1979, was introduced with the immediate support of six of EC MSs at the time. Ireland, Italy and the UK adopted a wait-and-see attitude; 'time for reflection' was needed by Ireland and Italy, which required a broader band of permitted fluctuation of ±6 per cent when they did enter, and a definite reservation was expressed by the UK. Later, Ireland and Italy joined the system, while the UK expressed a 'spirit of sympathetic cooperation'.

The main EMS features are given in the annex to the conclusions of the EC presidency (*Bulletin of the European Communities*, no. 6, 1978, pp. 20–1) set out in Box 11.1.

In essence, the EMS is concerned with the creation of an EC currency zone within which there is discipline for managing exchange rates. This discipline is known as the Exchange Rate Mechanism (ERM), which asks a member nation to intervene to reverse a trend when 75 per cent of the allowed exchange rate variation of ±2.25 per cent is reached; this is similar to what happened within the preceding 'snake' arrangements. The crucial differences, however, were twofold. First was the creation of the European Currency Unit (ECU) as the centre of the system against which divergence of the exchange rate was to be measured; the ECU followed on directly from the European Unit of Account as a basket of *all* EC currencies, not just those participating in the ERM. Weights in the basket, based on economic importance in the system, were revised every five years.[1] It was the means of settlement between the EC central banks. Second, the EMS was to be supported by a European Monetary Fund (EMF), which, supposedly within two years, was to absorb the short-term financing arrangements operating within the snake, the short-term monetary support agreement that was managed by the European Monetary Cooperation Fund (EMCF), and the medium-term loan facilities for balance of payments assistance (*Bulletin of the European*

Communities, no. 12, 1978). The EMF was to be backed by approximately 20 per cent of national gold and US$ reserves and by a similar percentage in national currencies. The EMF was to issue ECUs to be used as new reserve assets, and an exchange stabilization fund able to issue about US $50 billion was to be created.

It is clear from the above that the EMS asks neither for permanently and irrevocably fixed exchange rates between member nations nor for complete capital convertibility. Moreover, it does not mention the creation of a common central bank to be put in charge of the member nations' foreign exchange reserves and to be vested with the appropriate powers. Hence the EMS was not EMU, although it could be seen as paving the way for it.

11.3.1 The success of the EMS

The EMS's survival belied the early scepticism, and there is little dispute that it was something of a success. There was, however, a period from 1992 onwards when it looked as if the EMS might collapse altogether, just at the time when the final push to EMU was being agreed (see page 174). This success can be seen as embodied in three principal achievements.

First, despite occasional realignments and fluctuations of currencies within their preset bands, it seems that the EMS succeeded in its proximate objective of stabilizing exchange rates – not in the absolute sense, but in bringing about more stability than would have been enjoyed without it. Moreover, up to 1992 this was done without provoking periodic speculative crises of the Bretton Woods system. This stability had two elements. Not only did the number of realignments in the central rates fall (with one minor exception there were none in the five years following 1987), but the variation of exchange rates between ERM countries fell much faster than that of those outside, even in the early period up to 1985 (Ungerer *et al.* 1986). Just having scope for realignments meant that, unlike the 'snake', a parity change did not entail a confidence-shaking exit from the system.

Second, the claim is made for the EMS that it provided a framework within which member countries were able to pursue counter-inflationary policies at a lesser cost in terms of unemployment and lost output than would have been possible otherwise. The basis of the claim is that the structure of the EMS began

to attach a measure of 'reputation' to countries that managed to avoid inflation and hence depreciation of their exchange rate. This element of loss of reputation through 'failure' may have reduced the expectation of inflation and hence made counter-inflatory policy less 'costly'. However, estimates of the change in the sacrifice ratio (ratio of the rise in unemployment to the fall in inflation in a period) do not indicate any improvements compared to countries outside the ERM (which were also successful in lowering inflation), although, as generally expected, sacrifice ratios observed did rise as inflation fell.

Third, while it is claimed that nominal exchange rate stability was secured, it is also argued that the operation of the EMS prevented drastic changes in *real* exchange rates (or competitiveness). This is contrasted with the damaging experience in this respect of both the UK and the USA over the same period. However, in one sense it may merely have encouraged countries to put off necessary realignments, leading ultimately to the drastic changes and crisis in 1992–3 (see page 174 and Section 11.5, page 170).

Finally, while it was not an immediate objective of the EMS as such, the ECU became established as a significant currency of denomination of bond issues, which is testimony to the credibility of the EMS and the successful projection of its identity. In part, the use of the ECU in international bond issues may have reflected its role as a hedge by being a currency 'cocktail'. It also provided a means of getting round some of the currency restrictions in force, particularly in France and Italy. The high point for new ECU issues was 1991, and external issues never recovered after the 1992–3 crisis (see page 174).

These achievements have not been without some qualifications. For example, the divergence indicator mechanism, for triggering intervention before the limits of the band were reached, did not withstand the test of time.

The enforced changes to parities in and after September 1992 considerably reduced the credibility of the EMS and called into question the validity of the idea of approaching monetary union through increasingly fixed exchange rates while having no control over capital flows. Although the widening of the bands to ±15 per cent in August 1993 appeared to remove much of the effective distinction between the ERM and freely floating exchange rates, the practice was a very considerable convergence and a system which took only limited advantage of the flexibility available.

11.4 The Delors Report and the Maastricht Treaty

As already mentioned, by 1987 the EMS, and the ERM within it, appeared to have achieved considerable success in stabilizing exchange rates. This coincided with legislative progress towards EMU on other fronts. The EC summit held in Hanover on 27 and 28 June 1988 decided that, in adopting the Single European Act (SEA; see Chapter 2), thus paving the way for the creation of the Single European Market (SEM), EC MSs had confirmed the objective of 'progressive realization of economic and monetary union'. The heads of state agreed to discuss the means of achieving this in their meeting in Madrid in June of the following year, and to help them in their deliberations they entrusted to a committee chaired by Jacques Delors, then Commission president, and composed of the central bank governors and two other experts, the 'task of studying and proposing concrete stages leading towards this union'. The committee reported just before the Madrid summit and its report is referred to as the Delors Report on EMU.

The committee was of the opinion that the creation of EMU must be seen as a single process, but that this process should be in stages, which progressively led to the ultimate goal. Thus the decision to enter into the first stage should commit an MS to the entire process. Emphasizing that the creation of EMU would necessitate a common monetary policy and require a high degree of compatibility of economic policies and consistency in a number of other policy areas, particularly in the fiscal field, the report pointed out that the realization of EMU would require new arrangements which could be established only on the basis of a change in the Treaty of Rome and consequent changes in national legislation.

According to the report, the first stage should be concerned with the initiation of the process of creating EMU. During this stage there would be a greater convergence of economic performance through the strengthening of economic and monetary policy coordination within the existing institutional framework. The economic measures would be concerned with SEM

completion and the reduction of existing disparities through programmes of budgetary consolidation in the MSs involved and more effective structural and regional policies. In the monetary field the emphasis would be on the removal of all obstacles to financial integration and on the intensification of cooperation and coordination of monetary policies. Realignment of exchange rates was seen to be possible, but efforts would be made by every MS to make the functioning of other adjustment mechanisms more effective. The committee was of the opinion that it would be important to include all EC currencies in the EMS's ERM during this stage. The 1974 Council decision defining the mandate of central bank governors would be replaced by a new decision indicating that the committee itself should formulate opinions on the overall orientation of monetary and exchange rate policy.

In the second stage, which would commence only when the Treaty had been amended, the basic EMU organs and structure would be set up. The committee stressed that this stage should be seen as a transition period leading to the final stage; thus it should constitute a 'training process leading to collective decision-making', but the ultimate responsibility for policy decisions would remain with national authorities during this stage. The procedure established during the first stage would be further strengthened and extended on the basis of the amended Treaty, and policy guidelines would be adopted on a majority basis. Given this understanding, the EC would achieve the following:

1. [establish] a medium-term framework for key economic objectives aimed at achieving stable growth, with a follow-up procedure for monitoring performances and intervening when significant deviations occurred;
2. set precise, although not yet binding, rules relating to the size of annual budget deficits and their financing;
3. assume a more active role as a single entity in the discussions of questions arising in the economic and exchange rate field.

In the monetary field, the most significant feature of this stage would be the establishment of the European System of Central Banks (ESCB) to absorb the previous institutional monetary arrangements. The ESCB would start the transition with a first stage in which the coordination of independent monetary policies would be carried out by the Committee of Central Bank

Governors. It was envisaged that the formulation and implementation of a common monetary policy would take place in the final stage; during this stage, exchange rate realignments would not be allowed, barring exceptional circumstances.

The report stresses that the second stage would require a number of actions – for example:

1. National monetary policy would be executed in accordance with the general monetary orientations set up for the EC as a whole.
2. A certain amount of foreign exchange reserves would be pooled and used to conduct interventions in accordance with the guidelines established by the ESCB.
3. The ESCB would have to regulate the monetary and banking system to achieve a minimum harmonization of provisions (such as reserve requirements or payment arrangements) necessary for the future conduct of a common monetary policy.

The final stage would begin with the irrevocable fixing of MSs' exchange rates and the attribution to EC institutions of the full monetary and economic consequences. It is envisaged that during this stage the national currencies will eventually be replaced by a single EC currency. In the economic field, the transition to this stage is seen to be marked by three developments:

1. EC structural and regional policies might have to be further strengthened.
2. EC macroeconomic and budgetary rules and procedures would have to become binding.
3. The EC role in the process of international policy cooperation would have to become fuller and more positive.

In the monetary field, the irrevocable fixing of exchange rates would come into effect and the transition to a single monetary policy and a single currency would be made. The ESCB would assume full responsibilities, especially in four specific areas:

1. The formulation and implementation of monetary policy.
2. Exchange market intervention in third currencies.
3. The pooling and management of all foreign exchange reserves.
4. Technical and regulatory preparations necessary for the transition to a single EC currency.

As agreed, the report was the main item for discussion at the EC summit which opened in Madrid on 24 June 1989. In that meeting MSs decided to call a conference that would determine the route to be taken to EMU. This agreement was facilitated by a surprisingly conciliatory Margaret Thatcher, British prime minister, on the opening day of the summit. Instead of insisting (as was expected) that the UK would join the ERM 'when the time is ripe', she set out five conditions for joining:

1. a lower UK inflation rate and in the EC as a whole;
2. abolition of all exchange controls (at the time, and for two years after, Italy, France and Spain had them);
3. progress towards an SEM;
4. liberalization of financial services;
5. agreement on competition policy.

Since these were minor conditions relative to the demands for creating EMU, all MSs endorsed the report and agreed on 1 July 1990 as the deadline for the commencement of the first stage.

The three-stage timetable for EMU did start on 1 July 1990, with the launch of the first phase of intensified economic cooperation during which all MSs were to submit their currencies to the ERM. The main target of this activity was the UK, whose currency was not subject to the ERM discipline; the UK joined in 1991 (the decision was announced at the Madrid Summit of June 1989 while Margaret Thatcher was still in office), but withdrew from it in 1992, as did Italy.

The second stage is clarified in the TEU. It was to start in 1994. During this stage the EU was to create the European Monetary Institute (EMI) to prepare the way for a European Central Bank (ECB), which would start operating on 1 January 1997. Although this was upset by the 1992 turmoil in the EMS, the compromises reached at the Edinburgh summit of December 1992 (deemed necessary for creating the conditions which resulted in a successful second referendum on the TEU in Denmark and hence in UK ratification; see Chapter 2) did not water down the TEU too much. Be that as it may, the TEU already allowed Denmark and the UK to opt out of the final stage when EU currency rates would be permanently and irrevocably fixed and a single currency floated. However, in a separate protocol, all the then twelve EC MSs declared that the drive to a single currency in the 1990s was 'irreversible'. Denmark, which supported the decision, was an exception, because its constitution demands the holding of a referendum on this issue. The rationale for the UK was its very specific problems (see El-Agraa 2002b).

A single currency (the euro), to be managed by an independent ECB, was to be introduced as early as 1997 if seven of the then twelve EC MSs passed the strict economic criteria required for its successful operation, and in 1999 at the very latest. These conditions were as follows:

1. *Price stability* – Membership required 'a price performance that is sustainable and an average rate of inflation, observed over a period of one year before the examination, that does not exceed by more than [1.5] percentage points that of, at most, the three best performing' EC [MSs]. Inflation 'shall be measured by means of the consumer price index on a comparable basis, taking into account differences in national definitions'.
2. *Interest rates* – Membership required that, 'observed over a period of one year before the examination, a [MS] has had an average nominal long-term interest rate that does not exceed by more than two percentage points that of, at most, the three best performing [MSs] in terms of price stability. Interest rates shall be measured on the basis of long-term government bonds or comparable securities, taking into account differences in national definitions.'
3. *Budget deficits* – Membership required that an MS 'has achieved a government budgetary position without a deficit that is excessive' (Article 109j). However, what is to be considered excessive is determined in Article 104c.6, which simply states that the Council shall decide after an overall assessment 'whether an excessive deficit exists'. The protocol sets the criterion for an excessive deficit as being 3 per cent of GDP. However, there are provisos if 'either the ratio has declined substantially and continuously and reached a level that comes close to the reference value; or . . . the excess over the reference value is only exceptional and temporary and the ratio remained close to the reference value'.
4. *Public debt* – Here the requirement in the protocol is that the ratio of government debt should not exceed 60 per cent of GDP. But again there is an important proviso: 'unless the ratio is sufficiently diminishing and approaching the reference value at a satisfactory pace'. Whether such an excessive

deficit exists is open to interpretation and is decided by the Council under qualified majority voting (see Chapter 3). In helping the Council decide, the Commission is to look at the medium term and quite explicitly can have the opinion that there is an excessive deficit if there is risk, 'notwithstanding the fulfilment of the requirements under the criteria'.
5. *Currency stability* – 'Membership required that a[n] MS has respected the normal fluctuation margin provided for by the exchange rate mechanism . . . without severe tensions for at least two years before the examination. In particular, [it] shall not have devalued its currency's bilateral central rate against any other [MS's] currency on its own initiative for the same period.

One is, of course, perfectly justified in asking about the theoretical rationale for these convergence criteria. The answer is simply that there is none – for example, the inflation criterion is not even based on NAIRUs (that is, inflation could be convergent simply because the economy is out of internal equilibrium over the examination period; see Chapter 10) – and there is no way to evaluate whether or not a 60 per cent of GDP public debt is better or worse than, say, a 65 per cent of GDP rate. Normally the criterion used for assessing the debt position of a country in rating its debt is 'sustainability', which is subject to a wide range of considerations. One easy rationalization that could be applied is that 3 per cent of GDP happened to be the average level of public investment at that time, and MSs deemed this percentage acceptable. Given this, it is often also accepted that investment – provided it has an equivalent financial rate of return – can be sustainably financed by a budget deficit. Calculating this at the steady state of equilibrium and a compound rate of interest of 5 per cent per annum results in a public borrowing of 60 per cent of GDP (see Buiter *et al.* 1993), which also happened to be the average at the time; alternatively, one could start the calculation with 5 per cent.

The important requirements for a stable system are that no MS should be able to run its economy in a way that increases the cost for the others. Provided that the minimum standard set is high enough, the Eurozone as a whole will get the finest credit ratings/lowest interest costs. Unless there is some means of differentiation, the single exchange and interest rate for EMU will reflect the aggregate behaviour. In a more developed federal system it becomes possible to have two sorts of public debt, such as in the USA, for example. Then states have the ability to raise their own debt, but subject to limits and very explicitly without a guarantee from the federal authorities. The USA therefore shows noticeable spreads for local and state debt, and some have indeed got into difficulty.

It is interesting to note that the timing of these convergence tests has been crucial. If they had occurred in 1992, only France and Luxembourg would have scored full marks – that is, five points. The others would have scored as follows: Denmark and the UK four points each; Belgium, Germany and Ireland three points each; Netherlands two points; Italy and Spain one point; Greece and Portugal no points. Hence EMU could not have been introduced, since seven countries would have needed to score full marks for this purpose. The position at the end of 1996 was even worse, since only Luxembourg qualified. Thus the third stage of EMU did not begin by the earlier date of 1997. What is extraordinary is the turnaround by the final qualifying date of 1998. Then only one country, Greece, was deemed not to qualify, and even Greece was able to qualify at the first reassessment in 2000 (although it has subsequently been revealed that some of the statistics involved were knowingly inaccurate, and this was confirmed during the recent financial crisis). However, one should hasten to add the proviso, regarding this test, that the text permitted the exercise of considerable discretion, reinforced by Article 6 of the protocol, which states that the Council shall, acting unanimously on a proposal from the Commission and after consulting the European Parliament, EMI or ECB, as the case may be, and the Committee referred to in Article 109c, adopt appropriate provisions to lay down the details of the convergence criteria referred to in Article 109j of the TEU, which shall then replace this Protocol.

The data on which the decision on 2 May 1998 was based (see Table 11.1, page 172) were deemed, in the opinion of the Commission, to indicate that eleven nations had passed the test. Of the remaining four, three (Denmark, the UK and Sweden) had already decided not to join in the first wave, and Greece was not in the running. The Commission's interpretation of MSs' performance was clearly flexible (the EMI, which was also charged with issuing a convergence report, was of exactly the same opinion as the Commission (EMI 1998)).

Fourteen MSs had government deficits of 3 per cent of GDP or less in 1997: Austria, Belgium, Denmark, Finland, France, Germany, Ireland, Italy, Luxembourg, the Netherlands, Portugal, Spain, Sweden and the UK. MSs had achieved significant reductions in the level of government borrowing, in particular in 1997. This remarkable outcome was the result of MSs governments' determined efforts to tackle excessive deficits, combined with the effects of lower interest rates and stronger growth in the European economy.

In 1997 government debt was below the TEU reference value of 60 per cent of GDP in four MSs – Finland, France, Luxembourg and the UK. According to the TEU, countries may exceed this value as long as the debt ratio is 'sufficiently diminishing and approaching the reference value at a satisfactory pace' (see page 169). This was deemed to be the case in almost all MSs with debt ratios above 60 per cent in 1997. Only in Germany, where the ratio was just above 60 per cent of GDP and the exceptional costs of unification continued to bear heavily, was there a small rise in 1997. All countries above the 60 per cent ratio were expected to see reductions in their debt levels. The Commission concluded that 'the conditions were in place for the continuation of a sustained decline in debt ratio in future years' (CEU 1998e, p. 33).

Thus it should be clear that the EMU envisaged in the Delors Report and detailed and endorsed in the TEU is consistent with and satisfies all the requirements of a full economic and monetary union in the sense described in Chapter 10.

11.5 The transition to EMU

As the EU progressed towards EMU it was opening itself up to the possibility of severe strains through the EMS, as exchange controls were removed as part of stage 1. The removal posed two problems for the EMS. First, a protection against speculation was lost. Second, because interest parity was no longer prevented, interest rates everywhere were tightly linked, as the amount of expected depreciation was confined by the bands of permissible fluctuations of the currencies against one another. Because Germany was by far the largest EMS economy, this meant that interest rates, and hence monetary policy, everywhere in the system were dominated by Germany. Unless Germany, in turn, tempered its monetary policy by concern for the economic situation in other countries, this could turn out to be an unacceptable state of affairs, as indeed proved to be the case in 1992–3.

These problems were realized and various solutions proposed. First, as regards the problem of speculation, EMS mechanisms were improved by measures to accommodate automatic lending by a strong currency country to a weak currency country in the event of need; whereas previously this automaticity applied only when intervention was taking place at the edge of the band, since the deliberations of EMS finance ministers in Nyborg in September 1987, it applied also to so-called intra-marginal intervention – that is, foreign exchange operations taking place to support a currency before it has reached its limit. These new provisions were tested by a speculative run on the French franc in the autumn of 1987 and proved successful; the Bundesbank lent heavily to the Banque de France, but the lending was rapidly repaid once the speculation subsided and confidence returned. The second problem, concerning excessive German dominance, was only resolved by moving on to full EMU. The Nyborg provisions called for much closer monetary cooperation, implying more continuous exchange of information, and interest rate movements within the EMS after that time displayed a high degree of synchronization. However, the cooperation called for also seemed to imply a degree of common decision-making, going beyond simply following a German lead, in a prompt and well-prepared way. Progress on this front is less evident. The anxiety of France on this score, however, led to important initiatives. First, France called on Germany to discuss economic policy on a regular basis and an economic council was set up for this purpose. Second, it was on French initiatives that the EC was led to call for an investigation into the requirements of full EMU, an investigation subsequently carried out by the Delors Committee, the recommendations of whose report were endorsed by all twelve EC MSs in June 1989, leading to the TEU (see page 167).

The path that EMS participants agreed to follow thus called for increasing intervention resources and other devices to combat the threat of speculation, and for increased economic and monetary cooperation between MSs, eventually leading to the creation of the European Central Bank (ECB). But we should note that

there were alternative short-run solutions. One way in which countries can recover a greater measure of independence from the dominant power is to enlarge the bands of exchange rate fluctuation, which is what they did in 1993; another would have been to compromise on SEM by retaining a measure of exchange control. Either device has obvious counter-speculative advantages too. If maintained over the long term, these alternative solutions would have been, in effect, a defeat for the higher aspirations of EMU. The second mechanism was not used, but it is not difficult to think of circumstances in which it might have been, given the increasing popularity in the late 1990s of the idea of putting 'sand in the wheels' of international financial transactions in order to limit their volatility.

The forecast threat to the system duly occurred in September 1992. Uncertainty about the outcome of the French referendum on the TEU contributed to speculation against the weakest currencies in the ERM, sterling and the lira. Neither was able to resist the pressure, despite substantial increases in interest rates. By the summer of 1993 not even the French franc could survive the pressure, and the bands had to be widened to ±15 per cent to allow it to devalue without realigning within the system.

Other currencies also came under pressure and were forced to devalue. There was considerable pressure on the French franc in September 1992, but it survived, aided by substantial intervention by the Bundesbank on its behalf. It is arguable that all the currencies that were devalued were in some sense overvalued in terms of their long-term sustainable values. One interpretation of this is the Fundamental Equilibrium Exchange Rate (FEER), the rate at which the balance of payments is sustainable in the long run. However, the problem was not merely one of great domestic inflation by the devaluing countries, but of the special problems of the dominant German economy leading to a divergence from the domestic objectives of the other MSs.[2] German interest rates were driven up by the need to finance unification over and above the willingness to raise taxes. With the tight linkage of EMS interest rates, other states also had to have rates that were high in real terms.

In the UK case it was clearly a relief that ERM constraints could be broken. Interest rates had already been progressively cut to the point that sterling was close to its lower bound. A domestic recession was being

Table 11.1 EU member states' performance with regard to the convergence criteria

	Inflation	Government budgetary position		Debt (% of GDP)	Change from previous year			Exchange rates	Long-term interest rates[d]
	HICP[a]	Existence of an excessive deficit[b]	Deficit (% of GDP)[c]					ERM participation	
	1998		1997	1997	1997	1996	1995	March 1998	January 1998
Reference value	**2.7**[e]		**3**	**60**					**7.8**[f]
Austria	1.1	yes[g]	2.5	66.1	-3.4	0.3	3.8	yes	5.6
Belgium	1.4	yes[g]	2.1	122.2	-4.7	-4.3	-2.2	yes	5.7
Denmark	1.9	no	-0.7	65.1	-5.5	-2.7	-4.9	yes	6.2
Finland	1.3	no	0.9	55.8	-1.8	-0.4	-1.5	yes[h]	5.9
France	1.2	yes[g]	3.0	58.0	2.4	2.9	4.2	yes	5.5
Germany	1.4	yes[g]	2.7	61.3	0.8	2.4	7.8	yes	5.6
Greece	5.2	yes	4.0	108.7	-2.9	1.5	0.7	yes[i]	9.8[j]
Ireland	1.2	no	-0.9	66.3	-6.4	-9.6	-6.8	yes	6.2
Italy	1.8	yes[g]	2.7	121.6	-2.4	-0.2	-0.7	yes	6.7
Luxembourg	1.4	no	-1.7	6.7	0.1	0.7	0.2	yes[k]	5.6
Netherlands	1.8	no	1.4	72.1	-5.0	-1.9	1.2	yes[g]	5.5
Portugal	1.8	yes[g]	2.5	62.0	-3.0	-0.9	2.1	yes[g]	6.2
Spain	1.8	yes[g]	2.6	68.8	-1.3	4.6	2.9	yes[g]	6.3
Sweden	1.9	yes[g]	0.8	76.6	-0.1	-0.9	-1.4	no	6.5
UK	1.8	yes[g]	1.9	53.4	-1.3	0.8	3.5	no	7.0
EU(15)	1.6		2.4	72.1	-0.9	2.0	3.0		6.1

Notes:

[a] Percentage change in arithmetic average of the latest twelve-monthly harmonized indices of consumer prices (HICPs) relative to the arithmetic average of the twelve HICPs of the previous period.

[b] Council decisions of 26 September 1994, 10 July 1995, 27 June 1996 and 30 June 1997.

[c] A negative sign for the government deficit indicates a surplus.

[d] Average maturity ten years; average of the last twelve months.

[e] Definition adopted in this report: simple arithmetic average of the inflation rates of the three best-performing member states in terms of price stability plus 1.5 percentage points.

[f] Definition adopted in this report: simple arithmetic average of the twelve-month average of interest rates of the three best-performing member states in terms of price stability plus two percentage points.

[g] Commission-recommended abrogation.

[h] Since March 1998.

[i] Average of the available data during the past twelve months.

[j] Since November 1996.

[k] Since October 1996.

Source: CEU 1998e, Table 1.1, p. 34

exacerbated by the inability to use monetary policy to alleviate it. On exit, interest rates were lowered by four percentage points in virtually as many months. There was no immediate prospect of sterling re-entering the ERM, and indeed its fall of over 15 per cent is no larger than that suggested by the FEER, and its subsequent rise as the economy recovered was predictable.

The EMS suffered considerably through being unable to organize an orderly realignment of exchange rates. The mechanisms existed, but political pressures meant that MSs could not agree among themselves. Blame has been placed in a number of quarters – on the Bundesbank for not taking greater account of the impact of its policy on other MSs, and on the UK for not being sincere in trying to maintain parity within the bounds – but the basic weakness of the system remained: that trying to have narrow bands without exchange controls is really not sustainable when there are substantial shocks to the system. This was admitted in practice by widening the bands.

The EMS took a back seat after the devaluations of September 1992 and the widening of the band to ±15 per cent in August 1993. However, the EMS remained intact and slowly regained credibility. Despite three devaluations of the peseta and the escudo between November 1992 and March 1995, the participating currencies moved back into closer alignment. At the end of 1996 all bar the Irish punt were within the ±2.25 per cent band. Although sterling and the drachma remained outside the ERM and the Swedish krona did not join, Italy rejoined in November 1996 and Finland (October 1996) and Austria (January 1995) also became participants.

As we have noted, the EMS survived through to its replacement by the Eurosystem at the start of 1999 primarily because of the determination of EU governments to qualify for EMU under TEU criteria. The restraints on fiscal policy from needing to keep deficits below 3 per cent of GDP and debt below 60 per cent (or make credible progress towards 60 per cent) simultaneously helped inflation to converge and MSs to get their business cycles in line. The steady development of the SEM has integrated them further.

In part, the reason why stage 3 of EMU did not begin in 1997 was simply that the convergence period after the shocks of 1992–3 was just too short, particularly for countries like Sweden and Finland, where the shocks were greatest, but the evolution of the general economic cycles was not favourable. From then onwards, however, convergence was easier. Just as the adverse circumstances in the mid-1990s were bad luck, so the EU was extremely lucky that 1996–8 was a period of very considerable stability. Even the Asian crisis did not have a marked effect, and decreased the chance of importing inflation from the rest of the world.

Once financial markets felt that fiscal convergence and EMU were likely, this expectation brought the required convergence in real interest rates. Had it not been possible for some MSs that had experienced the greatest difficulty in converging to join then, it is likely that they would have experienced considerable pressures in the period immediately after the decision. The loss of credibility involved would then have made joining at a subsequent date much more expensive than it was for those who were successful earlier on.

Eurosystem creation has established three groups of countries within the EU: those who are in the Eurozone, those who are outside but intend to join at some date in the reasonably near future, and those who are outside but have no immediate plans to join. In one sense, all MSs that are outside the Eurozone, except Denmark and the UK, fall into the second group, as they are supposed to join as soon as they have met the convergence criteria – which are still the same as those applied originally under the TEU. Thus, rather than the more logical idea of converging to the performance of the existing Eurozone MSs, convergence is still required to that of the three best-performing members of the EU as a whole, which on some occasions have all been non-Eurozone MSs in the case of inflation. Denmark and the UK have a derogation from this requirement to join, and are free to pursue their own independent monetary policies, just as they could outside the ERM of the previous EMS. However, it appears that Sweden is at present a de facto member of the third group as well, since Eurozone membership was decisively rejected (by 14 percentage points) in a referendum on 14 September 2003 (see Mayes 2004, and the other contributors to the same symposium in *Cooperation and Conflict* for a deeper discussion). The ten new MSs (NMSs) that joined the EU in May 2004 and the two that joined in 2007 varied in their enthusiasm for how fast they wished to join the Eurozone, with Estonia, Lithuania and Slovenia indicating that they wished to join at the first opportunity. Latvia and then Cyprus, Malta and Slovakia have also opted for rapid entry, but others have set more cautious timetables.

The Eurosystem has created an extension of the ERM labelled ERM II, which MSs that wish to adopt the euro should join during the convergence period. Thus the countries mentioned above – Cyprus, Estonia, Latvia, Lithuania, Malta and Slovenia – joined, along with Slovakia, which entered in November 2005. Denmark is also participating in ERM II voluntarily, but operating in a tighter band. The rules are similar to those that faced the new members Austria, Finland and Sweden under the original ERM. Their currencies did not form part of the ECU basket, and hence if their exchange rate moved with respect to the other members it did not affect the value of the ECU itself. Membership is notional for Estonia and Lithuania as they have currency boards based on the euro and their exchange rates with it are completely fixed.

A central value is agreed between the ECB and an MS for the exchange rate with the euro. The intention then appears to be for the rate to remain within the same 2.25 per cent range that prevailed within the ERM. Realignments are possible and indeed have already happened for Greece (upwards). However, the terms are not precise. In its 2006 Convergence Report, the ECB explains its application of TEU provisions as 'whether the country has participated in ERM II for a period of at least two years prior to the convergence examination without severe tensions, in particular without devaluing against . . . [the] euro.' However, actual membership is not compelled for the full period: 'absence of "severe tensions" is generally assessed by (i) examining the degree of deviation of exchange rates from ERM II central rates against [the] euro; (ii) using indicators such as exchange rate volatility vis-à-vis eurozone and their development; and (iii) considering the role played by foreign exchange interventions' (ECB 2006, p. 17).

ERM II is thus a rather one-sided affair, very much reminiscent of the early days of the original ERM. It is for the applicants to adjust to the behaviour of the Eurozone: euro monetary policy is run without regard to their problems; it is the ECB that determines the parities. The ECB (and the Commission) will offer an opinion on whether convergence has occurred. In the case of Greece, the government was keen to go ahead with Eurozone membership as soon as possible. It was accepted for membership in June 2000 and joined the Eurosystem at the beginning of 2001. Even if all twelve NMSs were to join ERM II, the system would be highly unbalanced in favour of the Eurosystem in terms of relative economic size. In

some ways dependency will actually afford strength to the system, as it makes stable alternatives substantially more costly for the applicants. Thus not only will they have a strong incentive to try to remain in the system and not follow policies that are likely to lead to downward realignments, but the existence of these incentives will be obvious to everybody else as well, thereby increasing the credibility of the commitment.

However, NMSs have found ERM II a difficult proposition, as they are still undergoing a major process of structural change and have not in some cases achieved sustainably low inflation. It is therefore likely that, as with the original ERM, the weaker NMSs will experience real exchange rate increases that will ultimately force them into realignments. Adopting a currency board based on the euro may offer greater credibility. Ironically, one element of convergence to the behaviour of the Eurosystem may be easier than for some of the existing ESCB MSs, as the applicants are in the main heavily integrated with the Eurozone economy already, even though geography might have led one to expect closer links with third countries. Particularly in the case of the former Soviet bloc countries, the economic ties further east have been thoroughly broken. It is thus the problems of transition that are likely to present the greatest strains, rather than worries about asymmetric shocks that have affected countries like the UK with substantial economic linkages outside the Eurozone.

Transition is likely to be slow in some cases, particularly for those countries that have not yet been accepted for EU membership, so ERM II is also likely to be a relatively long-lived arrangement. However, in many cases NMSs will feel that they would rather complete the process of adjustment within EMU than outside. The credibility and hence much lower real interest rates offered by membership may very well be thought to outweigh the gains from exchange rate flexibility. Massive changes in their labour markets are known to be inevitable, so there may be a willingness to accept the pressures on non-monetary and non-fiscal routes to adjustment, a process that has presented considerable difficulties for many of the current EU MSs.

The combination of the SEM and the absence of exchange controls clearly added to the risk from speculative pressures for EMS. It is not surprising, therefore, that there was very strong pressure to move to stage 3 of EMU, despite the costs of transition. This still applies, and Lithuania and Slovenia asked to be evaluated in 2006. Slovenia succeeded and became the thirteenth Eurosystem member at the beginning of 2007, but Lithuania failed by the narrowest possible margin – its inflation rate was 0.1 per cent too high: 2.7 per cent compared to the average of the lowest three inflation MSs of 1.1 per cent (and the area average of 2.3 per cent); it met all the other conditions. Attention was also drawn to its substantial current account balance of payments deficit (5.6 per cent of GDP). Since the three lowest inflation MSs were Finland, Sweden and Poland, two of which were not in the Eurozone, there are strong grounds for contesting the economic sense of the process. (Estonia did not bother to apply, because although it met all the other criteria easily, it knew its inflation at the time would be clearly too high.) Since then Cyprus and Malta, then Slovakia and finally Estonia have joined, the last on 1 January 2011.

11.6 The decision over membership of EMU

We address two questions in this section – the sensible strategy for NMSs in the face of EMU membership criteria, and the decision of Denmark, Sweden and the UK to stay out of the Eurozone – as they both reflect clearly on the economic logic of membership of EMU for potential and existing members.

It might appear odd, prima facie, in purely economic terms, that the UK, Sweden and Denmark have chosen to stay out of stage 3 of EMU, while other countries that seem less convergent on standard optimum currency area (OCA) criteria (see Chapter 10), such as Finland, Greece and the Irish Republic, have chosen to join. Setting aside the political issues, there are three simple economic reasons that help explain the decisions, but the case of the UK stands out for a further reason. The UK is larger in economic terms than the other five countries mentioned above taken together. It is the only EU MS with a world-scale financial market, although Frankfurt has been improving its relative position. We therefore spend rather more time on the UK in the rest of this section.

The simple economic reasons are:

1. Life on the outside has been successful. It is very difficult in the case of Denmark, for example, to point to the extra costs from staying outside, but shadowing the euro very closely, except in terms of forgoing a seat at the table (both in the ECB and the Eurozone). With little right of veto, the impact of a single small country is rarely going to be decisive.

2. Some of the joining countries, particularly Finland (see Mayes and Suvanto 2002), have put a much higher weight on the expectation that Eurozone membership would change behaviour for the better. Furthermore, in the case of both Finland and the Irish Republic, the expectation has been that membership would support their propensity for faster than average growth by offering lower real interest rates and dampening inflationary pressures through the threat of competition.

3. It is better to adjust first, making use of the extra flexibility available, and join second. This has been very much the view in Sweden, set out at length in the report of the Calmfors Commission that was appointed by the Swedish government to assess the costs and benefits of full EMU participation (Calmfors *et al.* 1997). This caution, particularly about being able to cushion the impact of shocks on employment and unemployment, remains in the more recent Commission on Stabilization Policy for Full Employment in the Event of Sweden Joining the Monetary Union (Johansson *et al.* 2002). The commission concludes: 'Our view is that changes in the degree of nominal wage flexibility are likely to compensate only to a minor extent for the loss of national monetary policy as an instrument of stabilization policy' (p. 3). Indeed they see that wages in Sweden might themselves be a source of shocks. This reaction reflects a general expectation that flexibility will not work. The same argument is applied to fluctuations in working hours. Because so much of the area of working hours is statutorily controlled, the commission (pp. 5–6) did not see this as being able to act as a shock absorber. If rules were changed they would apply to all sectors. The rigidities imposed on the labour market mean that it is necessary to look elsewhere for offsetting fluctuations in the system. This implies that much of the successful readjustment of the Swedish economy to the crisis at the beginning of the 1990s can be attributed to the operation of monetary policy and to the movement in the exchange rate.

One might wish to add two further reasons. The first is a much more pessimistic view of the secondary benefits that could accrue under a more complete EMU than in the partial or 'pseudo' union envisaged in the Corden–Fleming model (see Chapter 10). This would be particularly true for countries that expect to be net payers rather than net recipients. The second is that, if a country feels that it is already more flexible than its potential partners, membership and a tendency towards common behaviour might actually be retrogressive and result in a structure that generates slower growth. Some of this flavour emerges from UK discussion.

NMSs face a rather different balance of interests. In general, their economic position and policies are less credible than those of Eurozone MSs and hence they will get clear benefits from lower interest rates. Similarly, the constraints that qualifying imposes on fiscal policy will provide helpful external pressures that domestic political conditions might otherwise find difficult. Most of the countries, Poland excepted, are also small, which limits their ability to build up an effective anchor for inflation on their own. They tend to meet many OCA criteria, with the exception of real convergence, and their trade pattern is strongly integrated with the EU. It is really only one main factor that inhibits their rushing to join stage 3 of EMU before something goes wrong. With the exception of Cyprus and Malta, they have low price levels, wages and output per head, and expect to grow faster than existing Eurozone MSs over at least the next twenty to thirty years – that is, they expect an extended period of real convergence. This in turn will mean that their rate of inflation is likely to exceed that of current members. While this gives them a straightforward problem of meeting the convergence criteria – they would have to go through a period of unusually low inflation that looks sustainable – it also poses problems of whether it is better to adjust partly through the nominal exchange rate. The Czech Republic in particular regards it as beneficial to keep domestic inflation low by inflation targeting, which means that it will have comparable inflation to the Eurozone, but some exchange rate appreciation. Countries that join early can only make such adjustments through the real exchange rate. If the process were smooth this might not matter, but if it overshoots then adjustment through an independent exchange rate may well prove easier than having to rely entirely on fiscal policy to disinflate.

As noted earlier, it is largely an empirical question whether a country can achieve structural change rapidly without inflating. As noted above, Bulgaria, Cyprus, Estonia, Latvia, Lithuania and Malta have all successfully (thus far) already pegged their exchange rate and hence know how easy/difficult it is to adjust when they get asymmetric shocks that do not affect their partners.[3] The Baltic states have already had one such shock, with the Russian crisis of 1998, and weathered it without the system collapsing. Other countries, including Poland and particularly Hungary, have experienced more difficulty, both in fiscal restraint and, in Hungary's case, in maintaining a smooth exchange rate regime. The Czech Republic also encountered difficulties in the aftermath of the Asian crises, as there was a general move of investors away from higher-risk countries.

The most common exposition of the problem, however, is to refer to the Balassa–Samuelson effect (Björksten 1999), which points out that prices of highly traded goods will tend to be at international levels around the world. Typically they will also show productivity growth relative to domestic services. Hence achieving balanced growth across the industrial spectrum will tend to involve non-traded goods and services rising in relative price. It may prove difficult for market forces to manage this without excess inflation in the price level as a whole. There have been a variety of estimates of the size of this effect, but something of the order of 1 per cent a year, or a little more, seems to be widely accepted.

Taken together, this will tend to mean that MSs that are currently pegging to the euro will want to join early and will hope that at some stage they will meet the convergence criteria, as they have nothing to gain from being outside except leaving the peg, which would be a serious blow to credibility and have a cost for several years to come. Inflation-targeting countries, on the other hand, along with countries that are managing the real exchange rate, as has been the case with Slovenia, are likely to want to wait longer until they are closer to real convergence. At that point, nominal exchange rate movements are likely to be compatible with the convergence criteria.

In 2010–11, we have seen the consequences of asymmetric shocks for Eurozone countries. First Greece, then Ireland and finally Portugal got into such difficulty that their governments' debts rose to the point that a joint bail-out by other MSs and the IMF was agreed.

11.6.1 The UK

The UK declined to participate in the operation of the EMS to begin with, out of a belief that it would be operated in a rigid way that would threaten the UK, with its high propensity to inflate and a decline in its competitiveness, especially vis-à-vis Germany. Opposition on different grounds was propounded by the incoming Conservative government headed by Margaret Thatcher, which wished to run an experiment in monetary policy in order to bring down inflation, and reasoned, correctly, that if the instruments of monetary policy (principally interest rates) were to be directed at reducing the rate of growth of the money supply, they could not simultaneously be used to target the exchange rate. Technically, this dilemma could be avoided by maintaining a suitably strong set of exchange controls; such controls would allow a government some freedom to maintain two different targets for monetary policy, but Thatcher's government was keen to remove these controls in any case and did so not long after taking office.

Events were to turn out somewhat paradoxically. The first phase of the Thatcher government's monetary experiment was associated with a very marked *appreciation* of the exchange rate – so competitiveness would have been *better* preserved inside EMS – and the deep recession that soon set in was attributed by many observers to this cause. In particular, the exchange rate would be steadier and competitiveness more assured, while inflation would be dragged towards the modest German level. This view gained momentum as official British policy towards the exchange rate as a target changed, and as it became clear that monetary policy was no longer aimed in single-minded fashion at controlling the supply of money.

In September 1986, at IMF meetings, the Chancellor of the Exchequer advertised the non-speculative EMS realignment process and, not long afterwards, followed this up with a policy of 'shadowing EMS', keeping the sterling exchange rate closely in line with the Deutschmark. This policy initiative lasted for just over a year; by the end of February 1988, following a well-publicized exchange of views between the chancellor and the prime minister, sterling was uncapped. Higher interest rates, invoked as a means of dampening monetary growth and in response to forecasts of inflation, caused the exchange rate to appreciate through

its previous working ceiling. The incident underlined the inconsistency between an independent monetary policy and an exchange rate policy. Even when sterling ultimately went into the ERM in October 1990, it appeared to be with considerable reluctance.

ERM membership only lasted until September 1992, when markets pushed sterling out of the system (see page 174). It did not rejoin, even when a government with a more favourable attitude was elected in May 1997. The issue had been overtaken by whether the UK should join EMU. While a close shadowing of the euro, as has been followed by Denmark, could make sense in its own right to help acquire greater stability, the main reason for such a policy would be as part of the preconditions for Eurozone membership. UK monetary policy was immediately focused on an explicit inflation target of 2.5 per cent per year in May 1997. Pursuit of this target, with only narrow bands of 1 per cent either side, almost inevitably means that UK monetary policy will vary from the ECB's, with its medium-term target of inflation being less than but close to 2 per cent (see Chapter 12).

That UK government turned to a serious consideration of Eurozone membership. It decided that it would recommend euro adoption in a referendum to the British people, provided that five tests, set by Chancellor Gordon Brown in October 1997, were met. UK performance against these tests was evaluated during the summer of 2003 and gave a negative result, but the government said it would try again.

What are the five Brown economic tests? The first is about business cycles and economic structures being compatible, 'so that we and others could live comfortably with euro interest rates on a permanent basis'. The second relates to whether there would be 'sufficient flexibility to deal with' any problems if they emerge. The third concerns whether euro adoption would 'create better conditions for firms making long-term decisions to invest in Britain'. The fourth is about what the impact of euro adoption would be 'on the competitive position of . . . [the] UK's financial services industry, particularly the City's wholesale markets'. The final sums up the other four, since it is about whether euro adoption would 'promote higher growth, stability and a lasting increase in jobs'.

However, when announcing these tests in October 1997, Brown added that the Treasury must decide that there is a 'clear and unambiguous' economic case for recommending British euro adoption. Since that would be unlikely in any circumstances, it would seem that this addition has been made to ensure that any decision on the matter would be based on purely political grounds.

It was generally agreed that it is also vital to include an economic test, omitted by Brown, that would determine the UK's economic performance for years to come: namely, the value at which sterling would enter the euro. Contrary to popular perception, this need not be the prevailing market exchange rate. This raises the question of how much lower sterling should be relative to the euro at the appropriate time.

Since the decision on euro entry rested on the Treasury's own assessment of the performance of the British economy against its own tests, we did not advance our own. However, several such assessments had been published (see, inter alios, Barrell 2002; and the various papers in the 2,000 pages that accompanied Treasury assessment (UK Treasury 2003)). While all agreed that the British economy had been converging with the Eurozone, the overall assessment was firmly negative, although leaving open the opportunity for reassessment. The problem was straightforward. There was (is) no general public support for euro membership, so it would be pointless to incur the embarrassment of a defeat, or follow Sweden into an extended period of non-membership following a referendum. The relative success of the UK economy would inevitably influence the economic judgement over the appropriate timing of entry. A clear and unambiguous case can never be made, as the result depends on a comparison of two hypothetical futures that are unknowable by definition and cannot even be validated after the event. Moreover, even if the economic case can be established, it will ebb and flow as the performances of the EU and UK economies move relative to each other. The final decision, therefore, is bound to be a political rather than an economic one, and will continue to be so since the present Conservative-Liberal Democratic coalition government that assumed power in 2010 does not see eye to eye on this issue, or even on membership of the EU itself.

11.7 Conclusion

Only a few years before it occurred, conclusions on the prospects for EMU in the EU were cautious. In 1996, at the time for assessing whether stage 3 could start at the beginning of 1997, it was not even worth looking, as only one country, the smallest, qualified under the Maastricht criteria. Only two years later the ECB was up and running, and eleven MSs had both qualified and decided on membership. By 2002 the notes and coin of the euro currency were in circulation and the national currencies of MSs, by then increased to twelve, had been withdrawn. There was a large element of luck in the specific timing, but nevertheless one must conclude that the process to EMU has been a remarkable success. It is difficult to tell whether those framing the Maastricht Treaty a decade earlier really believed their efforts would turn out so well. Previous attempts had run into difficulty.

It will be some time before it is possible to estimate EMU's degree of success in economic terms. In any case, any such assessment will always be highly contested, as it rests on comparison with a hypothetical alternative that did not occur. The years 1999 and 2000 were good years, not just in the Eurozone but also more generally, although 2001 and 2002 saw a serious setback, which has continued in many Eurozone MSs, with the overall economy only taking a clear turn upwards in 2006. Public support for EMU has risen and fallen with the general economic climate, irrespective of whether EMU was actually causal. It is, however, difficult to gainsay the beneficial impact on those countries that previously faced problems of credibility in their macroeconomic policy. The enthusiasm of some of the NMSs for moving on to membership of stage 3 of EMU as soon as possible after joining the EU, and the caution of some of the others, continue to illustrate the debate. The difficulties of Greece, Ireland and Portugal in facing rapidly rising government debts since 2010 have also emphasized the downsides of membership.

In this chapter we have deliberately concentrated on the 'M' in EMU, leaving the 'E' for the discussion in Chapter 12 – not because it is less important, but because the main developments have occurred more recently as the Eurozone became a reality. This emphasis on the monetary side is strongly reflected in the literature and may help to explain some of the emphasis on the potential difficulties stemming from adverse asymmetric shocks within an EMU. The monetary side of EMU in Europe involves new institutions and a strong legal basis for a single monetary policy. The economic side, on the other hand, relies on relatively soft coordination among MSs through a series of processes regulated by the Stability and Growth Pact (SGP; see Chapter 12). As soon as SGP constraints have started to bind, those affected have tended to complain and seek ways round the restrictions. This has led to both popular scepticism and academic criticism, because the terms of the pact are rather simplistic and pragmatic and not founded on clear economic principles.

The reality, however, has been a major turnaround in the macroeconomic behaviour of many EU economies, particularly those that were facing the greater inflationary and budgetary problems. This change has been perpetuated after the initial convergence conditions for membership of stage 3 were met and has resulted in a much more prudent fiscal basis for the EU. Conditions are not as good as they were in the period when the countries were seeking membership, but much better than in the previous period since the 1960s. As noted elsewhere (Chapters 12 and 22), this process is by no means complete, given the challenges from ageing and the continuing problems of adjustment caused by increasing competition and the more rapid change in products and technology. It has, however, achieved a degree of success well beyond what many expected, despite the problems of Greece, Ireland and Portugal in 2011–11.

A key feature of this success is that assessments of the potential benefits of EMU based on pre-existing structures of behaviour have proved mistaken. The economies have become more symmetric. Thus, not only has the chance of adverse asymmetric shocks fallen, but also the automatic response of other countries (through the automatic stabilizers) has helped to offset some of the anticipated loss of flexibility from having a single monetary and exchange rate policy. Furthermore, there is evidence that bargaining and other structures have themselves responded, irrespective of regulatory reform, to offer more flexibility and hence reduce the real impact of shocks.

Lastly, countries such as Finland and the Irish Republic have demonstrated that in EMU favourable asymmetric shocks are also amplified, resulting in faster growth and more inflation than would otherwise have been possible – a combination which ultimately proved disastrous for Ireland, but successful for Finland, where fiscal policy has been highly prudent and, as a result, inflation has remained below the Eurozone average.

In the next chapter we will look at the operation of EMU in more detail.

Summary

- From 1967, the prevailing world order for exchange rates, established as part of the Bretton Woods agreement in 1944, began to fall apart. The main problem was that the USA, hindered by the cost of the Vietnam war, was no longer able to act as the anchor for the international system.

- Other countries therefore had to look elsewhere for stability. The EC tried to create a locally stable system with the same sort of architecture for itself. In 1969 the Six decided that the EC should progressively transform itself into an EMU, and set up a committee, led by Pierre Werner, to consider the issues involved. The Committee's October 1970 final report, the Werner Report, was endorsed by the Council in February 1971. EMU implementation was envisaged in three stages, with the first beginning in 1971 and the third completed by 1980.

- Although the 1971 EMU failed, after an earlier than expected successful negotiation of the first phase and some progress during the second, the failure was not due to lack of commitment, determination or both. The Nixon shock, the first oil shock and the enlargement shock (the admission of three new members, each bringing with it its own unique problems) were the real culprits.

- In some quarters, the European Monetary System (EMS), which began operating in 1979, has been considered as the next EC attempt at EMU, but it was really little more than a mechanism devised to check the monetary upheavals of the 1970s by creating a zone of monetary stability. In essence, EMS is concerned with the creation of an EC currency zone within which there is discipline for managing exchange rates. This discipline is known as the Exchange Rate Mechanism (ERM), which asks a member nation to intervene to reverse a trend when 75 per cent of the allowed exchange rate variation of ±2.25 per cent is reached; this is similar to what happened within the preceding 'snake' arrangements. By 1987, the EMS, and the ERM within it, appeared to have achieved considerable success in stabilizing exchange rates, but the system was put under considerable strain in 1992, leading to widening of the band to ±15 per cent.

- Before then, the EC Hanover summit, held on 27 and 28 June 1988, decided that, in adopting the Single European Act, thus paving the way for the creation of the Single European Market (SEM), EC MSs had confirmed the objective of progressive realization of EMU. The heads of state agreed to discuss the means of achieving this in their meeting in Madrid in June of the following year, and to help them in their deliberations they entrusted to a committee, chaired by Jacques Delors, then Commission president, and composed of the central bank governors and two other experts, the 'task of studying and proposing concrete stages leading towards this union'. The committee reported just before the Madrid summit, the Delors Report on EMU. It too called for a three-stage EMU, to start in 1990 and finish with a single currency in 1997, or 1999 at the very latest.

- Five strict criteria on inflation and interest rates, budget deficits, public debt and currency stability were set for Eurozone membership, and by 1996 only Luxembourg qualified, so the earlier date for the final stage had to be abandoned. However, by 1998, although most qualified, eleven were admitted. By 2002 EMU was fully operational and in 2011 the Eurozone comprises seventeen members.

Questions and essay topics

1. What did the Werner Report state as the necessary conditions for EMU?
2. How did the Werner Report envisage the achievement of EMU?
3. Why did the EMU of the Werner Report meet its demise?
4. What were the 'snake' and 'snake in the tunnel'?
5. What is EMS?
6. What is ERM?
7. How did the Delors Report envisage the achievement of EMU?
8. What is the Eurozone and who belongs to it today?
9. Which countries have no intention of entering into the Eurozone, and why?
10. Has the process beginning with the EMU of the Werner Report, moving to the EMS and finishing with today's EMU been well planned since the inception of the EC, and executed accordingly?
11. Discuss the proposition that the EU never needed to have EMU.
12. Discuss the proposition that the UK will never seriously consider Eurozone membership.

FURTHER READING

Alesina, A. and Giavazzi, F. (eds.) (2009) *Europe and the Euro*, University of Chicago Press, Chicago and London.

Issing, O. (2008) *The Birth of the Euro*, Cambridge University Press.

Young, H. (1998) *This Blessed Plot: Britain and Europe from Churchill to Blair*, Macmillan, Basingstoke.

NOTES

1 These revisions ended in 1989 when Portugal and Spain were added, and the same weight continued until the ECU was replaced by the euro. Thus, when Austria, Finland and Sweden joined the EU in 1995, their currencies did not become components of the ECU, even though the first two later joined the ERM.

2 Cobham (1996) provides a helpful exposition of the different possible explanations of the crisis.

3 Other countries that are currently outside the EU but are hoping to join, such as Croatia and Albania, also experience constraints through substantial euroization. Bosnia-Herzegovina has a currency board backed by the euro, and Montenegro and Kosovo use the euro and do not have their own currencies. Thus several of those wanting to adopt the euro at an early stage may also be those that are a long way off real convergence.

12 The operation of EMU

DAVID MAYES

12.1 Introduction

The EU's European monetary union (EMU) has four broad ingredients: the euro and the single European monetary policy (SMP); the coordination of European macroeconomic policies through the Stability and Growth Pact (SGP), the Broad Economic Policy Guidelines (BEPG) and related processes; the completion of the Single European Market (SEM); and the operation of the structural funds and other cohesion measures. This chapter will consider only the first two, as the others are dealt with in Chapters 7, 11, 12 and 19.

Although the euro did not come into existence until 1 January 1999, and then only in financial markets, most of the characteristics of stage 3 of EMU (Chapter 11) were operating once the European Central Bank (ECB) opened in June 1998. The ECB, in the form of the European Monetary Institute (EMI), had been preparing for the day with all EU national central banks (NCBs) since 1994. The form of the coming SMP was already known by 1998, in both framework and instruments. In the same way, much of the framework for the operation of the economic coordination among the member states (MSs) had been developed with the SGP of July 1997 and BEPG commencement in 1998. The generalized framework was incorporated in the Treaty of Amsterdam (October 1997). There was thus no great break in behaviour at the beginning of 1999, especially since the main qualification period under the Treaty on European Union (TEU) convergence criteria had related to 1997. However, the SGP effectively broke down in 2003 and had to be revised in 2005 after a period of debate.

In what follows we begin by looking at the provisions for the SMP, then consider those for policy coordination, before we explore how they have worked. EMU weathered the global financial crisis quite well until 2010, when problems for the most exposed states, particularly Greece, followed by Ireland and then Portugal, imposed strains on the whole system and prompted extraordinary measures.

12.2 The Eurosystem and the euro

The institutional system behind the SMP is quite complex because it has to deal with the fact that some EU MSs are not (yet) participants in stage 3 of EMU. The TEU sets up the European System of Central Banks (ESCB), which is composed of all the national central banks and the ECB, which is sited in Frankfurt. The ECB and the participating NCBs form the Eurosystem, which is what is running the monetary side of the Eurozone. The term 'Eurosystem' has, however, only been coined by its members in order to make the set-up clearer; it is not in the TEU. The body responsible for the ECB and its decisions is the Governing Council, which is composed of the governors of the NCBs and the six members of the Executive Board, who provide the executive management of the ECB. The Executive Board is composed of the president and vice-president and four other members, responsible for the various parts of the ECB, which are labelled Directorates General in the same manner as the Commission. If that were not enough, the ECB also has a General Council, which is composed of the president, vice-president and the governors of *all* EU NCBs, whether participating in the Eurozone or not. Thus the General Council has twenty-nine members, including Bulgaria and Romania (twenty-seven governors + two), but the Governing Council has twenty-three members (seventeen governors + six) since Slovenia joined at the beginning of 2007, Cyprus and Malta in 2008, Slovakia in 2009 and Estonia in 2011, and it will increase in size as more MSs join the Eurozone.[1] A representative from the Commission and the presidency may also attend,

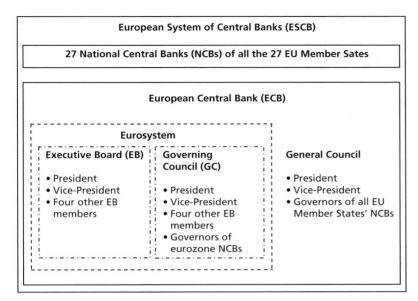

Figure 12.1 Structure of the European System of Central Banks *Source*: adapted from the ECB's website

but may not vote. Figure 12.1 may help to clarify the structure.

The Eurosystem is relatively decentralized compared to the USA's Federal Reserve System, although the names for the various institutions imply the opposite relative structures. The central institution in the USA, the Board of Governors of the Federal Reserve System, which is the controlling body, having powers over the budgets of the twelve Federal Reserve Banks, does not have another label for its staff and administrative operations. The seven governors of the Federal Reserve Board hold a voting majority on the monetary policy-making body, the Federal Open Market Committee (FOMC), where only the president of the New York Fed and four of the presidents of the other Fed Banks, by rotation, are voting members (although all are present at each meeting and can speak).[2]

The Eurosystem, on the other hand, operates through a network of committees, where each NCB and the ECB has a member.[3] The ECB normally provides the chairman and the secretariat. It is the Governing Council that takes the decisions, but the Executive Board coordinates the work of the committees and prepares the agenda for the Governing Council. Many of these committees meet in two compositions, one for the Eurosystem and one for the whole ESCB, depending on the subject.

To complete the confusion over labels, the Eurosystem has a Monetary Policy Committee, but, unlike the UK and many other central banks around the world, this is not the decision-making body on monetary policy. It organizes and discusses the main evidence and discussion papers to be put before the Governing Council on monetary matters.

There are, however, some key characteristics of this structure and other elements of the institutional set-up of the Eurosystem that have important implications for policy. As the Delors Committee (see Chapter 11), which designed the set-up for the Eurosystem, was composed almost entirely of central bank governors, it is not surprising that it is very well adjusted to the current views about the needs of monetary policy. First of all, although the TEU sets down the objective of monetary policy (maintaining price stability) – in general terms – the Eurosystem has a high degree of independence from political influence in exercising responsibility. Not only is the taking or seeking of advice explicitly prohibited, but Governing Council members are protected in a number of ways in order to shield them from interest group pressures. First, they have long terms of office – eight years in the case of the Executive Board – but these are not renewable, so they are less likely to have any regard for the prospects for their next job while setting monetary policy.

Second, the proceedings are secret, so that people cannot find out how they voted. Each member is supposed to act purely in a personal capacity and solely with the aims of price stability at the Eurozone level in mind, without regard to national interests. No system can ensure this, but a well-designed one substantially increases the chance of this happening. More importantly, it can reduce any belief that the members will act with national or other interests in mind. Third, the Eurosystem is explicitly prohibited from 'monetizing' government deficits.[4]

The point of trying to achieve this independence is simply credibility – to try to maximize the belief that the Eurosystem will actually do just what it has been asked to do – namely, maintain price stability. The stronger that belief can be, the less costly monetary policy will be. If people do not believe that the ECB will be successful, they will base their behaviour on that belief. Hence price- and wage-setters who believe that there will be increases in inflation substantially beyond what the ECB says it will deliver will set their prices with that higher outcome in mind. That means that the ECB then has to struggle against that belief, thereby entailing high interest rates. Thus, even though the ECB may intend exactly the same outcomes in both cases, it does not have to run such high interest rates to achieve them if it is credible.

This credibility comes from other sources as well as independence. The structure of the Governing Council is strongly reminiscent of that of the Bundesbank. The Bundesbank was highly successful in maintaining low inflation. By having a similar structure (probably assisted by the Frankfurt location just a few kilometres down the road), the Eurosystem has been able to 'borrow' much of the Bundesbank's credibility.

12.2.1 The monetary policy of the Eurosystem

The Eurosystem is further assisted in the inherent credibility of its policy by having a single, simple objective of price stability laid down by the TEU. If a central bank has multiple objectives, it will have difficulty explaining the balance between them, especially when they conflict. There was, for example, a short period of confusion at the outset over exchange rate policy, as the Eurosystem is not responsible for the regime, only the execution. However, it rapidly

became clear that since exchange rate policy and the objective of monetary policy are inextricably linked, one of the two must have primacy, and ministers made it clear that it was price stability that was the driving force. The other common objectives for a central bank of maximizing employment and the rate of economic growth – in this case expressed as 'without prejudice to the objective of price stability . . . [the] ESCB shall support the general economic [EU] policies' – are clearly subservient.

However, for monetary policy to be credible it is necessary that the objective should be clear enough for people to act on and that the central bank's behaviour in trying to achieve that objective should be both observable and understandable as a feasible approach to success. Here the ECB had to define the objective, since the TEU's concept of price stability is far too vague to be workable. They opted for inflation over the medium term of less than 2 per cent. They also defined the inflation they were talking about as that in the harmonized index of consumer prices (HICP). After a swift clarification that this meant that zero inflation was the lower bound, the specification was widely criticized for being too inexact (compared with other central banks). Not only is the length of the medium term not spelt out, but it is not clear how much and for how long prices can deviate from the target. Nor is there any indication of how fast inflation should be brought back to the target after a shock hits. In 2003 the target was reappraised and 'clarified' as being 'less than but close to 2 per cent'.

This means that a range of policy settings would be consistent with such a target. Policy is thus inherently not very predictable – something the Governing Council has sought to offset by trying to give clear signals about interest rate changes. Despite the inevitably diffused structure of decision-making with eighteen (now twenty-three) independent decision-makers, the Eurosystem has come to offer a single explanation of how it regards the working of the economy and the appropriate response to it. One facet of Eurosystem strategy that came in for criticism was what is known as the 'two pillars' approach. Rather than adhering to any specific model or suite of models, the Eurosystem announced that it would base its decisions on a wide range of indicators under two pillars. The first of these assigned a prominent role to money and has included a 'reference value' for the growth of broad money (M3).

The second was a broadly based assessment of the outlook for price developments. In the 2003 reappraisal it was made clear that the monetary pillar was assigned a medium-term role and acted as a cross-check on the broad-based assessment that underpins policy decisions. While some controversy remains, this brings Eurosystem policy more into line with thinking in other central banks. If anything, the problems of the global financial crisis have stimulated new interest in the monetary pillar.

Assigning money such an important role by at least some of the members of the Governing Council was inevitable, given that this was the Bundesbank's policy, as well as that of some other successful predecessor NCBs. The particular reference value of 4.5 per cent growth (based on the sum of the expected medium-term inflation of around 1.5 per cent, the expected rate of growth of around 2 per cent and the drift in the velocity of circulation of around 1 per cent) has proved a problem, as it has been exceeded almost all of the time and a lot of effort has had to be spent explaining the discrepancies. Similarly, the price assessment began as a narrative rather than a firmly based discussion of options and their possible outcomes. However, the process has developed steadily. The Eurosystem publishes its forecasts (broad macro-economic projections) twice a year, with updating by ECB staff in the intervening quarters. Although these are 'staff' forecasts and do not necessarily represent the views of the Governing Council, they are increasingly being used as a basis for explaining policy. The decentralized structure of the Eurosystem would make any closer 'ownership' of the forecasts by decision-makers impossible.

The Eurosystem is, of course, in good company. The USA's Federal Reserve has multiple objectives and offers no quantification at all for its target for the price level/inflation. It only publishes the staff forecasts by the Board of Governors with a lag.

Thus far policy has been generally successful, but between mid-2000 and 2011 inflation was stubbornly above 2 per cent. It is possible to blame the rapid rise in oil prices and some other shocks, but the deviation reached the stage where it had an effect on expectations (as calculated from French index-linked bonds). At that point, the Governing Council reacted by raising interest rates ahead of a clearly revealed recovery in the economy. This helped to enhance the Eurosystem's reputation as an inflation fighter, but has been controversial in some political circles.

One concern, which does not seem to have proved relevant, was the fear that NCB governors and Executive Board members would, either explicitly or unconsciously, as a result of their backgrounds, tend to promote monetary policy decisions that supported the particular economic conditions in their country of origin rather than in the Eurozone as a whole. As a result, complex models of coalitions have been developed and there have been worries about whether those voting in favour are sufficiently representative of the Eurozone as a whole. The first reason why this is not relevant is that the Governing Council has not been voting on these issues. It has operated by consensus, in the sense that decisions are taken when the majority in favour is such that the minority withdraws its objection and does not feel the need to register dissent in some public manner.

The possible objection to that form of behaviour is not some form of country bias, but that it might engender conservatism in policy-making. Since the records of the debates are not published, there is no way of finding out whether the particular structure has inhibited or delayed action. The simplest way of judging the issue is to look at the voting records in the FOMC, where the results are published with a lag. Here it is immediately clear that deep divisions over what to do are relatively unusual. Most of the time there is not only no division at all, but also no proposal to change policy. When there are divisions, the number of dissenters, even before the vote in the debate, tends to be quite small. The problem is thus predicated on a much more random and indeed contentious approach to policy-making than is actually the case.

There has been strong pressure on the Governing Council to be more open and to publish minutes of its discussions, as this would inhibit the members from following obviously national interests. However, it is not at all clear what the impact would be. Publishing minutes or resolutions leads to more formal proceedings or taking positions for the sake of having them recorded if US and Japanese experiences are anything to go by (Pollard 2003). If the real discussion is pushed outside the meeting into informal sub-groups and consultations, the result may be counterproductive and it will be even more difficult to sort out which opinions were responsible for which decisions.

12.3 The coordination of fiscal and other macroeconomic policies

Operating an SMP for a diverse area has proved quite tricky. Policy that is well suited to some economies has been ill suited to others. It is important to be clear about the extent of the differences. Mayes and Virén (2000, 2002c) have shown that in some MSs the exchange rate is at least twice as important as a determinant of inflation (as compared with interest rates). Similarly, the length of time it takes for the impact of policy on inflation to take its full effect also varies by a factor of two. Thus if the main problem lies in a region where policy has both a relatively small and a relatively slow effect, a policy based on the average experience of the Eurozone would not be very efficient.

The problem is further complicated because the main economic relationships involved, such as the Phillips curve (see Chapter 10), are non-linear and asymmetric. To spell this out a little: whereas a low unemployment/positive output gap has quite a strong upward pressure on inflation, high unemployment and a negative output gap have a considerably smaller downward impact for the same-sized difference. This means that simply adding up inflation rates and growth across the Eurozone and exploring aggregate relationships will be misleading. The analysis needs to be at the disaggregated level and then summed using the appropriate estimates of the effect in each region/MS.

However, once we look at fiscal and structural policy these differences become even more important, because they have to offset the differential impact of monetary policy. The coordination of fiscal and other policies therefore needs not merely to permit different policy settings by each MS, subject to the constraints of prudence, but to expect them.

12.3.1 The coordination processes for macroeconomic policies

The structure of the 'economic' side of macroeconomic policy-making thus involves constraints from following policies that could harm the system as a whole – the excessive deficit procedure (EDP) with the SGP, and the system of enhanced policy learning or soft coordination under the BEPG. The annual BEPG forms the framework that brings together three main elements:

- the orientation of general fiscal policy (EDP, SGP and multilateral surveillance);
- the European Employment Strategy (the Luxembourg process; see Chapter 23); and
- the actions on structural reforms (the Cardiff process).

There is actually a fourth process – the Cologne process – which involves an informal exchange of views twice a year between, inter alios, the current, past and future presidents of ECOFIN, the Employment and Social Affairs Councils, the ECB, the Commission and the social partners. These processes are named after the location of the meeting places at which they were agreed.[5] The coordination is somewhat broader than this, as the annual SEM reviews are also taken into account by the Economic Policy Committee (EPC): the committee of officials responsible for overseeing the Cardiff process. This is not to be confused with the Economic and Financial Committee (EFC), also composed of officials, which undertakes the preparation and offers advice for the decision-making Council of Economics and Finance Ministers (ECOFIN).

The general approach, spelt out in some detail in the Conclusions of the Lisbon Council in 2000 (see European Council 2000c and Chapters 7 and 14), was to set 'a *new strategic goal* for the next decade: to become the most competitive and dynamic knowledge-based economy in the world, capable of sustainable economic growth with more and better jobs and greater social cohesion'. This involves aiming to change the structure of EU development so that it could achieve a rate of growth of 3 per cent a year (without inflationary pressure), which should have been enough to bring down unemployment/increase employment to acceptable levels over the course of a decade. The key ingredients in this were continuing structural reform (overseen by the Cardiff process), a labour market strategy (Luxembourg) and the development of the appropriate fiscal incentives through a sound budgetary system within MSs. (It was amended at the end of 2002, at the Laeken Council, by the addition of a social policy strategy, which follows the same form of process as for the labour market.) Despite a thorough appraisal and rethink at the halfway stage (Sapir *et al.* 2003a, b, c), the strategy showed only limited success and was finally swept aside by the global financial crisis that rendered its targets irrelevant. However, a new strategy with similar structure and ambitions, labeled Europe 2020, has been implemented to replace it.

These processes do not compel, but by agreeing objectives, setting out how each MS intends to achieve the objectives, and evaluating progress, particularly through annual reports by the Commission, they act as considerable moral suasion. The meetings and the annual round of plans and evaluations enable MSs to learn from each other and encourage a search for best practice. These plans can be quite detailed. The annual National Action Plans under the Employment Strategy (see Chapter 22), for example, have covered over twenty guidelines grouped under four pillars: employability, entrepreneurship, adaptability and equal opportunities. Although the Commission produces assessments, much of the point of the arrangement is that it involves multilateral surveillance, so that each country is looking at the successes and failures of the others.

While there are obvious opportunities for window-dressing, this process, labelled the Open Method of Coordination, appears to have worked remarkably well. The key feature of the method is that it does not compel specific actions, but allows each MS, and indeed the regions within them, to respond to the challenges in the manner that best meets their local conditions, institutions and structures. Given that the whole structure of social welfare varies across the EU (Mayes *et al.* (2001) distinguish four different sorts of regime, for example), any given measure will have different outcomes in different MSs. In a sense, this is an example of the operation of the subsidiarity principle (see Section 2.3.4, page 30).

12.3.2 The Stability and Growth Pact and the excessive deficit procedure

As was argued above, the SGP and EDP have two features: a general orientation to ensure a policy that is sustainable over the longer term, and a constraint on short-term actions – the excessive deficits – to ensure that the process is not derailed on the way. This general orientation is to achieve budgets that are 'in surplus or near balance'. This orientation will actually result in a continuing reduction in debt ratios. While this is necessary anyway for MSs exceeding the 60 per cent limit, it has been thought generally more desirable because of the expected strains on the system that are likely to occur with the ageing of the population. In any case,

it makes sense to have sufficient headroom to meet shocks, as vividly illustrated by the global financial crisis. This headroom is required in two respects. First, given the structure of automatic stabilizers, each MS needs to be far enough away from the 3 per cent deficit ratio limit for the normal sorts of adverse economic shock not to drive them over that limit. If that threatens to happen, the MS would need to take contractionary fiscal action when the economy is performing weakly.

This was precisely the problem that faced German authorities in 2003. The combination of being too close to the limit and lower than expected growth forced them a little over the limit. Needing to raise taxes and restrain expenditure proved politically difficult. At the same time, French authorities also breached SGP terms, although it is more arguable that this was deliberate rather than a result of incorrect forecasting. As a result, ECOFIN agreed to suspend the SGP rather than declare the two countries in breach of it, as recommended by the Commission. The Commission appealed this decision to the European Court of Justice (ECJ), which ruled that ECOFIN could decide to take no action but that it could not suspend the process. This provoked an intensive debate on how to improve the SGP in the light of the difficulties, and a new agreement was reached in March 2005.

The extent to which an MS needs to be inside the 3 per cent boundary to avoid an undue risk of a breach and to maintain a stance that is sustainable in the long run depends on the extent of the automatic stabilizers and the distribution of expected shocks. Thus a country like Finland, which has fairly large stabilizers and seems prone to above-average shocks, would need to run a small surplus if it is to avoid hitting the 3 per cent boundary.

There is a danger (von Hagen and Mundschenk 2002) that having the 3 per cent deficit boundary will have a deflationary longer-term bias on the EU if MSs compete too strongly to have very strong stabilizers. Sweden might be regarded as a case in point, as its reaction to the pressures from membership has been to advocate the establishment of a substantial buffer fund (Johansson *et al.* 2002). These funds, if implemented, would be far larger than Finnish buffer funds, which were put in place when Finland joined the Eurozone. However, Ricardian equivalence would suggest that simply repaying debt should have no influence on longer-term growth; it is only having a higher tax burden today at the benefit of a lower burden in the future.

The SGP can be viewed as having two parts: a preventative part that tries to discourage MSs from running imprudent and unsustainable fiscal policies, and a corrective part that requires them to return to prudence as soon as possible if a mistake has been made. The 2005 agreement eased both sides of this, allowing more latitude for problems before declaring a breach (an excessive deficit) and hence permitting a less onerous return to compliance. This was not the full extent of the changes, as MSs also took the opportunity to improve the governance process of surveillance, tightening up the quality of statistics and accounting practices.

The general principles of the SGP remain unchanged. Attempts to correct underlying problems with the SGP, such as the failure to take proper account of the economic cycle and to focus on the underlying problem of sustainable debt, were discussed extensively in the debate on revision, but ultimately not adopted, despite pressure from the Commission. While the changes did not address the fundamental economic problems, they do represent a set of arrangements that are more likely to be adhered to. In practice, the idea that a country could ever be harshly penalized was ambitious. The penalties were intended as a deterrent. If naming and shaming did not work, the SGP was always likely to change if a significant number of countries were affected. With the global financial crisis, the SGP is effectively suspended, as economic performance is generally too weak to generate the EDP. This is proving a major headache, as in just three years a decade or so of fiscal consolidation has been unwound in many MSs, and the financial position of the most exposed – Greece, Ireland, Italy, Portugal and Spain – has become a cause for concern.

Various proposals were put forward for reforming the SGP, and indeed the Commission itself advanced proposals (Buti *et al.* 2002; CEU 2002a), which were then taken into account in considering SGP reform. These can be classified under three main headings, but they all relate to means of easing the constraints somewhat without altering the overall principles. The first set of proposals relates to *symmetry*. MS behaviour is constrained when deficits are in danger of becoming too large. There is no such restraint on surpluses, but a switch from a 2 per cent surplus to balance can have just as much impact on aggregate demand as a switch from balance to a 2 per cent deficit. Hence countries which notch up major surpluses could destabilize the system somewhat, simply by switching rapidly to a

modest deficit well within the permissible limit. The Commission in particular suggested enhancing the ability to affect fiscal policy in 'good times' and this is reflected, albeit weakly, in the revised provisions shown in Box 12.1.

The second set of proposals sought to differentiate between MSs according to whether they are well inside, near or above the 60 per cent limit for the debt ratio. Here the argument was simply that countries with no sustainability problem should be allowed more licence in the short run over deficits. This line of argument, of course, runs against that in the first group, as such licence could easily result in much bigger swings in fiscal policy that will affect the overall level of inflationary pressure in the Eurozone if we are talking about larger countries.

The third group of suggestions related to measurement issues. In the traditional literature the concern is with cyclically adjusted deficits. While measurement has indeed been improved, the idea of cyclical adjustment has not been followed. In the main, this is because what is trend and what is cycle can only be established after the event, which is incompatible with the preemptive rather than corrective SGP orientation.

There was a fourth set of suggestions that looked for more of a market solution to the question of fiscal discipline. One of the big advantages of EMU has been that interest rates on sovereign debt in the previously more inflation-prone and more indebted parts of the Eurozone converged on the lowest. Credit ratings similarly increased. Although there was explicitly no agreement to bail out MSs across the Eurozone, the market is behaving as if there were. Or at least behaving as if the EDP would restrain MSs from running policies that will ever get them near default. This means that there is not so much pressure on marginal borrowing by those states that have debt or deficit ratio problems.

This has all been completely changed by the financial crisis. Interest rate spreads widened extensively and reflected lenders' concerns that some MSs might default. The extent of the market pressure was such that the EU and the IMF drew up a joint fund, with strong conditionality, that Greece could draw on if it proved impossible for it to raise new debt or roll over existing debt satisfactorily in the market. This fund, the European Financial Stability Facility, had to be enlarged and extended to the Eurozone as a whole

Box 12.1 Revisions to the Stability and Growth Pact agreed in March 2005

The revisions agreed by the Council on the recommendation of ECOFIN are quite detailed, but can be summarized as follows:

(i)   The basic precepts are unchanged both in terms of the 60 per cent debt ratio and the 3 per cent deficit ratio, and in terms of the sanctions to be applied if an MS is determined to have an excessive deficit and has undertaken insufficient measures to end it.

(ii)   The adjustment processes required have been eased slightly, extending the time allowed by four months (to sixteen).

(iii) The criteria under which there can be exceptions to the 3 per cent rule for an excessive deficit have been softened. A decline in GDP or an extended period of low growth below potential are now admissible, and 'all relevant factors' can be taken into account – although these are not specified in any detail.

(iv)   The medium-term adjustment to a sustainable fiscal position has been eased slightly, and MSs' structural balance should be 'close to balance or in surplus' (CTBOIS) and now allows a lower limit of a 1 per cent deficit.

(v)   While MSs are still required to reduce their structural deficits to reach CTBOIS by 0.5 per cent of GDP per year, it is now admitted that they should do so faster in 'good times' and may do so more slowly in 'bad times' in the economic cycle.

(vi)   Temporary divergences can be allowed for the costs of structural reforms aimed at improving the longer-term position.

(vii) If there are unforeseen events, ECOFIN can issue changed deadlines and requirements.

(viii) Implicit liabilities, such as those for the pension system from the ageing of the population, should be taken into account.

In addition, there is a set of requirements that should improve the governance and operation of the generalized system of preferences, which includes: stronger peer pressure, better national fiscal rules and institutions – such as greater scrutiny by parliaments – improved forecasting, and better statistics and standards.

* Structural balance is defined as the cyclically adjusted deficit after removing the effect of temporary and one-off measures (as determined by the Commission).

when the problem threatened to spread to Ireland, Italy, Portugal and Spain. By 2011, Greece, Ireland and Portugal were all subject to fund arrangements, with associated strong conditionality requiring determined efforts to bring the rising government debt under control. This facility, in conjunction with the IMF, only lasts for three years, and its extension into a more permanent arrangement has been subject to considerable debate in the fiscally prudent countries that will be the lenders.

The Eurozone has thus got itself to a position that it previously resisted. MSs did not want to bail each other out, and SGP and TEU criteria were designed to make such a threat implausible. By admitting states with debt problems, albeit assisted in the Greek case by incorrect national accounts statistics, and by not having a stronger SGP, it has reached the point where

the weaker states can threaten the system. Much of the reason for the compromise, however, was that financial institutions in the other MSs had bought Greek government debt and hence stood to make major losses in the event of a default.

12.3.3 Policy coordination

The type of policy coordination described thus far differs from that normally discussed in the literature, where much of the point is the coordination of monetary and fiscal policy. The argument is that there are some choices that can be made over how much to use fiscal policy rather than monetary policy to smooth fluctuations in the real economy or to maintain price stability. The set-up within EMU rests on a fairly simple economic model. The first side of it is that monetary policy cannot be used effectively to achieve longer-term real objectives, except in two senses:

- first, that having higher rates of inflation beyond levels near zero will tend to result in reductions in the overall rate of economic growth, and indeed having falls in the price level may also be damaging; and
- second, that inept policy that does not generate credibility will also impose a cost on society.

In general, taking these together, the argument is, in effect, that the long-run Phillips curve is vertical and monetary policy per se will not have adverse effects on the longer-term level of unemployment (see Chapter 10). Monetary policy can therefore be targeted appropriately at the stabilization of the price level rather than on objectives for the real economy. The scope for using monetary policy for smoothing real behaviour beyond that point is limited. As Thornton (2002) puts it, in general, the impact of monetary policy on inflation variation and output gap variation should be regarded as one of complements rather than trade-offs. A credible monetary policy aimed at restricting inflation to a fairly narrow range in a smooth manner should, *ipso facto*, also restrain the fluctuations in output round the sustainable path.

Similarly, in this simple paradigm, fiscal policy can affect the rate of growth in terms of how funds are raised and spent – for example, one can view this in terms of incentives. Moreover, as discussed above, for fiscal policy to be consistent with price stability over the medium term it has to be sustainable (and believed to be so by markets). But discretionary fiscal policy, beyond the automatic stabilizers, is unlikely to be of much value, except to help exit the deflationary spiral, as Keynes identified in the 1930s; Feldstein (2002) offers a clear exposition of this view. One of the main reasons for avoiding discretionary fiscal policy to address fluctuations in the economy is that policy operates with a lag, and there is a danger that by the time the problem is identified, the necessary measures are agreed by the legislature and implemented, and the impact occurs, it may destabilize what is then going on.

In the event of a major adverse shock, such as the global financial crisis, the model is still not disturbed. The shock is so great that emergency action is warranted. Each country acting in its own interests nevertheless acts to stimulate joint demand and reduce the short-run impact (albeit at the expense of higher taxation in the future to pay for the surge in debt).

Under these circumstances there is no need for much policy coordination between the monetary and fiscal authorities beyond transparency. The monetary authorities need to be able to make a reasonable assessment of the inflationary pressure likely to stem from fiscal policy, and the fiscal authorities need to know what to expect from monetary policy when setting their fiscal objectives. The potential conflict comes from the fact that, unlike fiscal policy, monetary policy can be changed quickly and substantially, and indeed with fairly limited transaction costs. In the EU's framework the coordination works because the monetary authorities are predictable. If they do react quickly it is to specific crisis signals, like the shock of 11 September 2001. Given the time lag for fiscal changes, the fiscal authorities need to be confident that their monetary counterparts will not do anything in the intervening period that will render their policy stance inappropriate.

Pinning the ECB down to a single objective helps to achieve this predictability, in the same way that SGP rules and macroeconomic coordination ensure that the ECB has plenty of warning about the way in which fiscal policy is likely to develop and hence is less likely to set inappropriate levels for interest rates. EMU coordination will not work if the Eurosystem believes that the fiscal authorities will always be too inflationary and/or if ECOFIN always believes that the Eurosystem will set interest rates that are too high. In these circumstances the problem will be self-fulfilling, and monetary policy and fiscal policy will tend to push against each other. The resulting bias will be a cost. Fiscal policy needs to be credible to the monetary authority and vice versa. There is a danger of paying too much attention to the rhetoric in this regard.

The final part of the simple model which underlies the coordination mechanism is the belief that it is structural policies that will change the underlying rate of economic growth. Hence these form a key part of the continuing annual policy discussion. Once fiscal policy is largely automatic with respect to shocks, the surveillance mechanisms can focus on sustainability and on whether the size of budgetary swings that the automatic processes deliver are appropriate. If there were little concern for fine-tuning, then having more than the current six-monthly informal dialogue laid down by the Cologne process would seem unnecessary.

12.3.4 Asymmetry

Traditionally, the focus on the suitability and sustainability of EMU has been on asymmetry in the sense of the differences between MSs, as discussed at the beginning of Section 12.2 (page 182). However, a different asymmetry is also present in MSs' behaviour, namely asymmetry over the cycle (Mayes and Virén 2002a).[5]

The total deficit is much more responsive in the downward than the upward phase. While responsiveness over the cycle as a whole is of the order of 0.2–0.3 (a 1 per cent increase in real GDP lowers the deficit ratio by 0.2–0.3 per cent) in the first year, it is five times as large in the downturn as the upturn. This bundles together all the influences – automatic stabilizers, discretionary policy changes, interest rate changes and any special factors. On unbundling, we can see that the automatic or cyclical part of the deficit behaves in a fairly symmetric manner. It is what governments choose to do with the structural part of the deficit that causes the asymmetry. What has happened is that governments increased the structural deficit in both downturns and upturns. Thus in good times governments tend to allow the system to ratchet up. The effect is split between revenues and expenditures, but the asymmetry is more prominent on the revenue side. Tax rates are cut in upturns so that revenue to GDP ratios do not rise.

The SGP, EDP and other components of macroeconomic coordination in EMU would have to lean against this tendency for asymmetric behaviour to reduce the pressures it generates. In practice, the pressure is placed somewhat more on the downside: the area where governments have themselves responded more effectively in the past. Tackling this asymmetry and 'procyclicality in good times' was incorporated in general terms in the revised SGP (see Box 12.1). Whether this will have much effect is debatable, especially after the experience of the financial crisis.

12.4 Completing EMU

It has to be said that the earlier discussion of coordination leaves a lot to the credibility of the process.

Institutional credibility would be much greater if the degree of control over fiscal actions at EU level were larger and there were some parallel institution to the ECB on the fiscal side. While this is not on the political agenda, its relevance would be much greater if one further plank, which characterizes most economic and monetary unions, were in place, namely a significant revenue-raising and spending capability at EU level. This does not have to take the form of a larger budget per se (see Chapters 10 and 19), as transfers from one region or MS to another in a form of fiscal federalism would also suffice (see Chapter 10). Currently stabilization takes place automatically within MSs. It only takes place between them to the extent that their agreed and automatic actions spill over from one to another because of their economic interdependence. The actual size of such a budget – around 2.5 to 7 per cent of EU GDP – would be highly effective (MacDougall Report/CEU 1977a; Mayes *et al.* 1992; Chapter 19), but is quite small compared to many existing federal states. It is, however, large compared to the structural funds and the current budgetary limit.

EU enlargement has increased the need for fiscal federalism, although the current small economic size of new member states (NMSs) keeps down the scale of any transfers needed in the short term. We are concerned here with cross-border fiscal flows to help balance out the effect of asymmetric shocks; dealing with income inequality is a problem of a very different order. Nevertheless, given the persistence of shocks, particularly with respect to their impact on the labour market, if fiscal flows do not ease the pressure then other changes will result to compensate. The most obvious would be an increase in migration. That is also not politically attractive at present (see Chapter 8). It remains to be seen whether some greater integration on the macroeconomic side of EMU may not be preferred to increasing flexibility through cross-border migration. The relative attraction of stabilizing flows is that, according to their definition, they should be temporary. However, the shape of economic cycles does vary across the EU. Nevertheless, as economic and financial integration increases across the EU, so self-insurance increases with diversification of income and wealth generation across the EU as a whole, helping to smooth the asymmetric shocks hitting any particular region without recourse to fiscal transfers (Mundell 1973b; Chapter 10).

12.5 Conclusion: enlargement

Before EMU moves further towards 'completion', it is likely to continue to expand through the inclusion of new members. Thus far the five NMSs that have joined – Cyprus, Estonia, Malta, Slovakia and Slovenia – are all small. Even if many of the NMSs were to join, the economic effect would be limited. Only Poland and, to a lesser extent, Romania are of any size. Their effect on the dynamics of decision-making would be much more dramatic, and indeed the Eurosystem may well invoke its ability to alter the voting arrangements on monetary policy to move the balance back in favour of the large, original members. Adding Denmark and Sweden would make little difference to the structure of the Eurozone or the issues that have been raised in this chapter. If the UK were to join, the position would be different, as the country is large enough to alter the balance of the SMP. Also, since the UK is somewhat different, both in its flexibility of response and its symmetry with the other MSs, the consequences could be measurable. Adding more NMSs is likely to take place with a level of income per head well below the average of the existing members, as convergence in these real terms is not one of the criteria. This could alter the character of the Eurozone.

We have already noted that in the run-up to membership there was greater convergence of MSs than there has been in the period since. This was because they had to run their monetary and fiscal policies individually to converge to quite a narrow band. Once inside, the SGP, EDP and the rest of the coordination under the BEPG apply, but the SMP is no longer related to the inflation concerns of each country, just the total, so more inflation, and indeed growth variation, is possible and feasible. This experience is likely to be reflected even more strongly by the new members, as they are generally expected to 'catch up' quite rapidly with the existing members in real terms. This means that they will have faster rates of growth than the existing members, driven primarily by productivity. It has also been pointed out that this may have implications for inflation and monetary policy. While the price of tradable goods and services may be reasonably similar across the EU, the same is not the case for non-tradables. Large portions of non-tradables are public and private services, where their principal input is labour. As productivity grows in the tradable industries, so wages are likely to rise with it. In turn, in a competitive economy, this is likely to result in wage increases in the non-tradable sector. There it will not be so easy to find productivity growth to offset it and prices will tend to rise. In so far as there are no offsets elsewhere, this will result in a rise in the general price level that is faster than in the rest of the euro area (see Chapter 11).

This process, known as the Balassa–Samuelson effect, will probably not be substantial by the time NMSs join the Eurozone – perhaps of the order of 1 per cent a year (Björksten 1999). Given that NMSs, taken together, will only contribute a fraction of Eurozone GDP, this implies that the total effect on inflation would be of the order of 0.2 per cent a year. That may seem very small, but with a medium-term target of inflation below 2 per cent, it could represent an increase in the rate of interest. The actual impact is speculative and could vary from the disastrous to the trivial. It would be disastrous if some countries cannot cope with the increase in the real exchange rate that this relative inflation might imply. The problems of asymmetry that have worried some of the old EU MSs could be much larger for NMSs, yet the drive for locking in credibility and buying lower interest rates by Eurozone membership may be sufficient to play down the worries about sustainability at the time of joining. Too rapid an expansion of EMU could actually harm the prospects of the enterprise as a whole. It is therefore not surprising that the ECB has already blown relatively cold on some of the ideas implying early membership and has sought to toughen the interpretation of the convergence criteria.

Nevertheless, the harsh experience of the Baltic States in the global financial crisis has shown that, by and large, they can cope with the largest adverse shocks that are likely to hit them and, in the case of Estonia, bounce back sufficiently to meet the convergence criteria for joining the Eurozone. With a currency board, Estonia has effectively been a member of the Eurozone since the outset, but without a vote.

Summary

- The structure of EU monetary institutions set up in 1998 for euro introduction on 1 January 1999 have a lot in common with the USA's, but the nomenclature is confusingly different and the arrangements complex. The Governing Council, chaired by the ECB president, composed of the six members of the Executive Board and governors of the participating central banks, currently seventeen, decides on monetary policy (MP).

- Eurozone MP is focused on price stability, defined as inflation below but close to 2 per cent over the medium term. The system's structure emphasizes the Eurosystem's independence.

- Although there is no single fiscal policy (FP) to match the single MP, EU MSs have an elaborate annual cycle of policy coordination under Broad Economic Policy Guidelines (BEPG).

- The most important element in FP management is the Stability and Growth Pact (SGP), which on the one hand tries to keep MSs' fiscal position on a path of consolidation towards a low and sustainable public debt, and, on the other, has an excessive deficit procedure (EDP) to try to prevent fiscal deficits in excess of 3 per cent of GDP in any year. The system was revised in 2005 and the EDP is not operating in the financial crisis because of the severity of the downward pressure on GDP.

- Coordination between MP and FP occurs through open discussion and having a rule-based system for MP that makes it predictable for FP-making.

- The SGP is inherently asymmetric and does not have matching rules for surpluses; nevertheless, the focus on deficits counters the previous asymmetric trend towards a worsening fiscal position in most MSs.

- There is little enthusiasm for a clear, EU-level fiscal capability, but countries remain keen to join the Eurozone, with Cyprus, Estonia, Malta, Slovakia and Slovenia having joined since the notes and coin were introduced in 2002. It is the inflation criterion that makes enlargement so difficult, as a country must be within 1.5 per cent of the inflation rate of the lowest three inflating countries in the entire EU of 27, not just the Eurozone.

Questions and essay topics

1. Compare the structure of the monetary institutions and decision-making in the EU and the USA.

2. What is the objective of MP in the EU? How is it achieved?

3. Is the Eurosystem really independent?

4. How is coordination of FP among MSs achieved in the Eurozone?

5. What is the excessive deficit procedure? Does it work?

6. How does the SGP hope to achieve a prudent FP in the EU?

7. Are MP and FP coordinated in the EU?

8. What is the Balassa–Samuelson effect? Will it inhibit the expansion of the Eurozone?

9. What problems does the lack of an EU-level fiscal capability create for macroeconomic policy in MSs?

FURTHER READING

CEU (2008h) *EMU@10: Successes and Challenges after 10 Years of Economic and Monetary Union*, DG ECOFIN, Brussels.

de Grauwe, P. (2009) *The Economics of Monetary Union*, Oxford University Press.

ECB (2004) *The Monetary Policy of the ECB*, ECB, Frankfurt.

NOTES

1 ECB (2001) is one of the most comprehensive and straightforward of the many available descriptions of the institutional arrangements; see also Chapter 3.

2 The Eurosystem is also planning to move to a system where only some of the governors have a vote (by rotation) when the number of MSs exceeds fifteen. However, it will still be the case that the number of voting governors will substantially exceed the number of Executive Board members. Despite the number being seventeen for the start of 2011, this system is yet to be implemented.

3 Sometimes more than one.

4 The special measures taken during the global financial crisis show that this is not really true in practice, at least in the short run, as the ECB has bought extensive amounts of governmental debt from commercial banks, particularly from the troubled MSs, in order to maintain liquidity and effectively ease monetary policy once interest rates approached zero.

5 See Hodson and Maher (2004) for a clear exposition of the processes and their role in policy-making. These various processes are brought together under the 'Helsinki process'.

6 The study uses annual data for the period 1960–99 for the 2002 EU MSs, excluding Luxembourg, and treats them as a panel. The structural deficits are as defined by the Commission.

Part IV The single European market: policy integration

Part IV of the book covers areas that constitute the very foundations needed to facilitate a properly operating Single European Market (SEM). Hence it tackles in six chapters: competition rules; industrial and competitiveness policy; tax harmonization; transport policy; energy policy; and environmental policy. Industrial policy is included because variations in it would be tantamount to affording differing protection to national domestic industry. The absence of tax harmonization would have consequences equivalent to those of disparate industrial policies. Similar considerations apply to transport, energy and the environment. Of course, transport and energy are also dealt with as industries in their own right, as well as providers of social services, and the environment is treated in terms of tackling pollution and the consequent health benefits.

13 Competition policy
WOLF SAUTER

13.1 Introduction

The main purpose of competition policy is generally seen as protecting the market mechanism from breaking down. It does so by promoting competitive market structures and policing anti-competitive behaviour, thereby enhancing both the efficiency of the economy as a whole and consumer welfare in particular. In the EU this objective is pursued by means of enforcing prohibitions against (1) anti-competitive agreements between different companies, as well as against (2) anti-competitive behaviour by companies that are large enough – either individually or jointly – to harm competition by means of independent behaviour, and (3) by vetting mergers between previously independent companies to verify whether these are likely to result in non-competitive market structures.

EU competition policy has three important characteristics that are not commonly found elsewhere. First, it not only aims to protect the competitive process as such, but also to promote and protect market integration between EU member states (MSs). Second, apart from addressing private distortions of competition, it also curbs distortions of the market process by its MSs, notably as a result of state aid. Both result from the third distinguishing feature of EU competition policy: it is implemented in a multi-level political system, that of the EU and its MSs. In this context, it is worth noting that although until recently the application of EU competition rules was highly centralized in the hands of the European Commission (Commission), due to its exemption monopoly for agreements infringing the cartel prohibition, this changed fundamentally in May 2004. A decentralized system based on enforcement by (and coordination between) the twenty-seven national competition authorities (NCAs) was moved into place. All these aspects are examined further below.

This chapter first discusses in greater detail the rationale for competition policy generally, and for EU competition policy in particular. Next, it sets out the basic instruments of EU competition policy, its rules and procedures, and the manner in which they are implemented. Finally, three important developments in EU competition policy are addressed: the focus on public intervention, its shift to a more economic approach and, most recently, a move towards decentralization.

13.2 The rationale for EU competition policy

The reasons for introducing competition rules have varied, both between different jurisdictions and over time. The first set of modern competition rules is contained in the USA's Sherman Act (1890). They were adopted as the result of political concern over the railroad, oil and financial 'trusts' emerging in the USA at the end of the nineteenth century, generating an economic concentration of power that threatened to upset the popular consensus underpinning the economic as well as the political system of that country. In various European states from the early twentieth century onwards, national competition rules typically sought to provide protection against the socially and therefore politically undesirable results of 'unfair' competition (Gerber 2001). In some cases, the legislation concerned even enabled public authorities to impose the terms of existing private cartel agreements on entire economic sectors, as an alternative to state-designed market regulation – for example, in order to control prices.

American ideas about competition policy that were more critical of restraints were exported to both Germany and Japan after the Second World War, when the Allied occupation forces imposed new anti-monopoly legislation to curb the influence of the financial–industrial combines that were widely seen as having powered the war effort of these two countries. For similar reasons, coal and steel being the essential components of the war industry of the time, anti-trust provisions were introduced into the 1951 Paris Treaty creating the European Coal and Steel Community (ECSC; see Chapter 2), which, unlike the EEC Treaty, included the control of concentrations from the outset. This check on concentrations of economic power was therefore in line with the objective of the ECSC of eliminating the threat of future wars between its participant MSs.

For the EC beyond coal and steel, competition rules were likewise introduced in the 1957 EEC Treaty, albeit for a different reason. In this case, the competition rules served primarily to ensure that restrictions on trade between MSs – tariff and non-tariff barriers – that the MSs' governments agreed to remove under this treaty would not be replaced by cartels between undertakings following national lines (Goyder and Albors-Llorens 2009). This is why competition rules addressed to undertakings were introduced into what at the outset was still regarded as an international treaty between independent states.

Initially, therefore, EU competition rules essentially served to complement an inter-state trade policy of reducing trade barriers and promoting market integration. From this starting point, promoting market integration has developed into an overriding rationale of EU competition policy, alongside that of maintaining 'effective competition' (Bishop and Walker 2002) and, more recently, promoting the consumer interest. The integration rationale has had a profound impact on the orientation of EU competition policy that has at times led it into conflict with the emerging economic consensus favouring efficiency considerations.

For example, the integration rationale has long tended to lead to a negative view of vertical agreements with territorial effects. This conflict is clearly seen in the groundbreaking ruling by the European Court of Justice (ECJ) *Consten & Grundig* of 1966.[1] Consten was the exclusive distributor in France for Grundig, a German producer of consumer electronics. Consten agreed not to market products competing with those of Grundig in exchange for an exclusive licence to use Grundig's trademark in France. Thereby, in practice, Consten enjoyed absolute territorial protection. In economic terms, such territorial protection may have been required, for example, to recover Consten's investments in setting up a sales network and an aftersales

service in France. However, the ECJ ruled that this contract infringed the cartel prohibition of the Treaty as it had a market partitioning effect. Agreements that reinforce national divisions in trade frustrate the EC objective to abolish the barriers between MSs and therefore could not be allowed. Although economic theory shows that restrictions of intra-brand competition (between different suppliers of Grundig products) are unlikely to have harmful effects on competition, so long as there is sufficient competition between brands (that is, between suppliers of Grundig products and suppliers of comparable products), the ECJ considered the protection of both forms of competition equally important here. This view has evolved over time: the current competition rules on vertical restrictions recognize that vertical agreements generally produce efficiencies and should be treated more leniently. However, absolute territorial protection is still prohibited.

13.3 The role of economics

While it is difficult to find an example where pure economic reasoning motivated the introduction of competition rules, the rationale of EU competition policy is increasingly defined in economic terms. Evidently, the relevant economic theory has evolved over time as well (Motta 2004).

The economic reasoning concerning the goals and limits of competition policy has been developed in particular in the USA, where an early willingness of courts to entertain economic arguments was subsequently stimulated by the appointment of law and economics scholars to the bench and to influential regulatory positions. Over the past century, the resulting debate has had a profound impact on the way competition policy is applied both in the USA and beyond. Originally, competition policy focused on the results of market structure and the behaviour of market participants associated with the Harvard School. Increasingly, the so-called Chicago School of anti-trust economics, focusing on efficiency, price effects and the self-policing nature of the market (Posner 1976), has become the new mainstream of industrial organization, and hence of much analysis underlying competition policy (Scherer and Ross 1990). In addition, game theoretic approaches are used increasingly – for example, to deal with problems of collusion and joint dominance in oligopolistic markets (Phlips 1995). EU competition policy has followed these trends to varying degrees, modified in particular by the intervening variable of its overriding integration objective (Peeperkorn and Verouden 2007). It is now thought to be guided by insights of the post-Chicago School of competition policy (Langer 2007). A home-grown economic influence has been that of the Freiburg School or *Ordo*liberalism (Gerber 2001). The proponents of this school accepted the main ideas of classical liberalism, but they also extended the classical views by arguing that individual freedom should be protected not only against governmental interference, but also against private economic power.

Today, the market mechanism is broadly seen as the most efficient instrument to set prices and thereby allocate resources. To a large extent, the success of markets at doing this is determined by the degree of competition in the market involved. However, perfect competition, which presupposes homogeneous products and full transparency of prices and costs, as well as the absence of entry barriers, economies of scale and scope, and learning effects, is not a real-world phenomenon. Instead, market imperfections, or market failures, are likely to lead to restrictions of competition that produce sub-optimal results. Firms also have economic incentives to collude and to exclude competitors. Consequently, the role of competition policy is to substitute for competitive pressure by ensuring that restrictions on competition between undertakings that are harmful to the competitive process (rather than to individual competitors) are prevented or removed. Because pure market outcomes are likely to be theoretically sub-optimal in many cases, this leaves ample room for disagreement on what amounts to a restriction of competition that merits policy intervention.

In the context of EU competition policy, the key concept in this regard is that of maintaining 'effective competition' or 'workable competition'. In the *Metro* v. *Commission* case of 1977, the ECJ appealed to the concept of workable competition as the effective type of competition to realize the economic objectives of the EC Treaty. The court stated that: '[t]he requirement contained in Articles 3 and [101, TFEU] that competition shall not be distorted implies the existence on the market of workable competition, that is to say the degree of competition necessary to ensure the observance of the basic requirements and the attainment of the objectives of the Treaty, in particular the creation of a single market achieving conditions similar to those of a domestic market'.

There is debate about whether effective competition concerns the process of competition as such, or the outcome that markets produce in terms of improving consumer welfare – generally equated with efficiency. In any event, it is by now well established that effective competition is seen in terms of preventing harm to competition as such, not to particular competitors (Bishop and Walker 2002).

This was highlighted by Advocate General Jacobs in the *Oscar Bronner* v. *Mediaprint* case of 1998, when he reminded the court that 'the primary purpose . . . is to prevent distortion of competition – and in particular to safeguard the interests of consumers – rather than to protect the position of particular competitors'. Especially since the start of the tenure of Mario Monti (an academic economist, succeeded by Neelie Kroes, and recently Joaquín Almunia) as commissioner responsible for competition policy in 1999, the promotion of efficiency has been declared to be the core value under competition law alongside promoting consumer welfare. For example, in a speech in July 2001, Monti said that 'the goal of competition, in all its aspects, is to protect consumer welfare by maintaining a high degree of competition in the common market' (Monti 2001). During his tenure, he emphasized the importance of sound economic analysis (creating, inter alia, the office of chief economist).

In practice, whether there is effective competition has to be determined in relation to a specific 'relevant market' that is defined both in terms of the product concerned and geographically. Factors taken into account, such as the existence of market power, the number of competitors, relative market share and degree of concentration, demand and supply substitution, the existence of barriers to market entry and exit, and potential competition, affect both the evaluation of the degree of effective competition in the relevant market and market definition itself (CEU 1997e). Increasingly refined economic analysis is used to define relevant markets.

13.4 General overview of the legal framework

Although EU competition policy is increasingly driven by economic considerations, its origins are found in

European law, and it must evidently operate within the constraints of its legal framework. This legal framework consists of the substantive, procedural and institutional rules that govern EU competition policy (see Chapters 3 and 4). It is important to understand that the framework only applies to 'undertakings' (Wils 2000).

The notion of undertaking is defined in the *Höfner & Elser* v. *Macrotron* case of 1991 as 'every entity engaged in an economic activity, regardless of the legal status of the entity and the way in which it is financed'. The notion of undertaking was further defined in three other cases:

- In the *Poucet & Pistre* v. *Cancava* case of 1993, the ECJ held that an agency charged with managing a social security scheme was not an undertaking within the scope of competition, as the scheme fulfilled an exclusively social function that was based on the principle of national solidarity and was entirely non-profit-making.
- In the *Diego Cali & Figli* v. *Servizi Ecologici del Porto di Genova* case of 1997, the ECJ did not consider a private organization entrusted by the public authorities with anti-pollution surveillance duties in an oil port to constitute an undertaking under the competition rules as it executed a public function.
- More recently, in the *FENIN* case of 2006, concerning the public authorities running the Spanish national health system, which purchased medical goods from an association of undertakings marketing these goods, the ECJ decided that where a public body purchases goods or services that will subsequently be used for social purposes it will not be engaged in economic activity, even in the purchasing market, and consequently will not be an undertaking for the purposes of the competition rules.

The legal basis of EU competition policy is found, first of all, in the TFEU (Treaty of the Functioning of the European Union) itself (101–6 and 107–9). Second, it is found in implementing legislation adopted by the Council and Commission in the form of regulations and directives (see Chapters 3 and 4), which develop in particular the wide-ranging powers of the Commission in this field, notably Council Regulation 1 of 2003 (reforming Council Regulation 17 of 1962 concerning the application of the cartel and dominance abuse prohibitions). Council Regulation 139 of 2004 (reforming Council Regulation 4064 of 1989) provides the framework for merger control by the Commission. In addition, an increasing number of notices and guidelines that are not formally binding provide essential information on the manner in which the Commission intends to apply EU competition policy. An example is the Commission's notice on the definition of the relevant market referred to above (CEU 1997e). By issuing such guidance, the Commission increases the predictability of its policy – allowing undertakings and their legal advisers to take EU competition law constraints into account, while at the same time facilitating the enforcement of EU competition law between private parties and at a national level.

The ultimate arbiter of the various rules, and on whether Commission policy remains within the bounds of its powers, is the ECJ. It decides only on points of law. The ECJ becomes involved either directly, on a 'pre-judicial' reference by a national court, or in judicial review proceedings following a first appeal against Commission decisions to the EU's General Court,[2] which establishes the facts. In principle, the standards applied are those of administrative review of policy – that is, they focus on formal competence to act, on respect for the rights of the defence and enforcing minimum standards of reasoned rationality. The ECJ and General Court have nevertheless on a number of occasions led the way in demanding higher standards of economic argument, rather than more formal reasoning, from the Commission (Korah 2004).

Particularly with regard to merger control, EU courts have scrutinized the Commission's economic reasoning. For example, the General Court concluded in the *Airtours* v. *Commission* case of 2002 that the decision to block the proposed merger, 'far from basing its prospective analysis on cogent evidence, is vitiated by a series of errors of assessment as to factors fundamental to any assessment of whether a collective dominant position might be created'. This indicated that the court requires better economic evidence when reviewing the Commission's decisions, and also addressed the burden of proof, arguing that it was the Commission that had to produce convincing economic evidence of the anti-competitive effects of the proposed merger. Another example in this context is the ruling by the ECJ in the *Tetra Laval* v. *Sidel* case of 2005. The ECJ stressed the importance of 'reviewing the Commission's interpretation of information of an economic nature, especially in the context of a prospective analysis'.

The Commission is the institution that is responsible at EU level for the implementation of EU competition law and policy. It takes most formal decisions by simple majority, as a collegiate body. These decisions are prepared by the Directorate General for Competition, DG COMP, which reports to the commissioner responsible for competition policy; since January 2010 this has been Joaquín Almunia (formerly the commissioner for monetary and economic affairs). Following the abolition of the system requiring notification to the Commission of potentially anti-competitive agreements by the parties to these agreements, the Commission can be apprised of a competition problem by a complaint by an undertaking or an MS, a leniency application by an undertaking trying to come clean, or it can act on its own initiative (*ex officio*) to investigate either specific cases or entire economic sectors (sector inquiries). It has considerable powers to require undertakings to collaborate in its investigations, backed by fines, including the right to obtain evidence by unannounced inspections of company offices (dawn raids). In addition, the Commission can penalize all infringements of the competition rules with significant financial penalties, including fines of up to 10 per cent of the global group turnover of the companies involved, without any absolute upper limit. Fines of well over a hundred million euros have already been imposed in a number of cases.

For example, in 2002 the Commission imposed a total fine of 168 million euros on Japanese video games maker Nintendo and seven of its official distributors in Europe, for colluding to prevent exports from low-priced to high-priced countries – another illustration of its focus on territorial restrictions with their effect on inter-state trade. In 2004, it fined Microsoft over 497 million euros for refusing to supply information necessary for interoperability and for bundling the Windows operating system with Windows Media Player. In 2006 it found that eight suppliers and six purchasers of road bitumen in the Netherlands had participated in a cartel from 1994 to 2002 to fix prices in violation of Article 101. These fourteen companies have been fined a total of 266 million euros and one of the participants was fined more than 100 million euros. In 2009 computer chip manufacturer Intel was fined over one billion euros for various exclusionary practices vis-à-vis its competitors.

Because the treaty prohibitions on restriction of competition (that is, the cartel prohibition of Article 101.1) and on abuse of a dominant position are directly effective, parties may choose to invoke these rules in procedures before national courts of all levels in EU MSs (Komninos 2002).

The *Courage* case of 2001 is interesting in this context. Inntrepreneur Estates Ltd administrated the leased pubs of both Courage and Grand Metropolitan in the UK. The standard form of lease agreement contained the obligation that tenants must order their beer exclusively from Courage. Crehan, one of the tenants, failed to pay for supplied beer. When Courage started proceedings, Crehan claimed that the exclusive purchase obligation infringed the cartel prohibition of the EC Treaty. However, under English law, a claimant cannot rely on his own wrong. The EU's General Court found that the English rule was inconsistent with the long-established direct effect of the treaty prohibitions. The full application of the national rule made it too difficult for the plaintiff to enforce his rights to compensation under Community law, and hence the national rule should not be applied.

Finally, as a result of the modernization exercise (see Section 13.9, page 209), from 1 May 2004 all national competition authorities and national judges in MSs now have explicit powers (and the obligation) to apply the exemption provision of the cartel prohibition as provided for in Article 101.3 of the EC Treaty. Under the old Regulation 17 of 1962, parties could obtain such an individual exemption exclusively from the Commission. Article 9.1 of Regulation 17 conferred 'sole power' on the Commission 'to declare Article [101.1] inapplicable pursuant to Article [101.3] of the Treaty'. Following modernization, Article 101.3 is now directly applicable. This may give rise to increased requests by national courts for the pre-judicial rulings on points of law by the ECJ that are an important mechanism to ensure the coherent application of EU competition law and policy.

13.5 The substantive norms

There are three core substantive norms of EU competition law that are addressed to undertakings:

1. the prohibition of agreements and concerted practices between firms restricting competition;
2. the prohibition of abuse of (single firm or joint) dominance;

3. the obligation to submit mergers and acquisitions for prior clearance under the merger control rules.

In addition, there are specific competition rules that apply to aid by MSs, and to companies privileged in their relation to public authority. These are each discussed in turn.

13.5.1 The cartel prohibition

The prohibition of collusion restricting competition (cartels) is found in Article 101.1 of the TFEU. Prohibited cartel agreements cover, for example, price fixing, market sharing, tying and discrimination.

As far as collusive behaviour is concerned, for example, the ECJ has made clear in the *Sugar Cartel* case of 1975 that undertakings may not knowingly substitute the risk of competition for practical coordination between them that results in conditions of competition that do not correspond to normal market conditions. The court explained that the requirement of independence does not deprive undertakings of the right to adapt themselves intelligently to the existing and anticipated conduct of their rivals, as long as there is no direct or indirect contact between the undertakings that influences the conduct on the market of an actual or potential competitor, or discloses to such a competitor the course of conduct that they themselves have decided to adopt on the market.

By force of Article 101.2, infringement of the prohibition of Article 101.1 triggers the nullity of the restrictive clauses of the agreements involved – that is, they become void, non-existent – which can lead to civil law liability and thereby to claims for damages under national law.

The ECJ addressed the scope of the nullity of an agreement that infringed Article 101 in its above-mentioned *Consten & Grundig* case, as well as in the *Société La Technique Minière* v. *Maschinenbau Ulm* case of 1966, where the court explained that Article 101.2 only applies to 'those parts of the agreement which are subject to the prohibition, or to the agreement as a whole if those parts do not appear to be severable from the agreement itself', and that 'any other contractual provisions which are not affected by the prohibition, and which therefore do not involve the application of the Treaty, fall outside Community law'. This determination is made by the national courts.

As mentioned above, in addition, the Commission can penalize infringements by means of substantial fines. Certain national systems also provide for penal sanctions, and there is an ongoing debate as to whether further criminalization of competition law is desirable.

Whether directed at private undertakings or MSs, EU competition norms are triggered only if constraints on competition are both appreciable and have the effect of distorting trade between MSs (CEU 1997f). This is consistent with the integration rationale of EU competition policy: unless they distort trade flows, restrictions of competition do not hamper integration, and consequently do not concern the EU. However, the integration rationale also means that certain types of territorial protection are prohibited that might not otherwise be particularly objectionable from an economic perspective. This still leaves EU competition policy a broad scope, which has often made it difficult to enforce effectively.

For example, in the *Distillers* case of 1978, the Commission condemned the export deterrent created by Distillers' dual pricing system for the UK and the rest of the EU. In the *Zanussi* case of 1979, the Commission objected to a system of aftersales guarantees that did not apply to washing machines used in a different MS from the one in which they had been bought. In 1998 the Commission fined Volkswagen heavily for setting up a system with its Italian dealers whereby final consumers in MSs other than Italy were unable to order VW cars from Italian dealers.

13.5.2 The prohibition of abuse of dominant position

The prohibition of abuses of dominant position (monopolies and oligopolies) in Article 102 of the TFEU focuses on 'abusive' (that is, anti-competitive) behaviour associated with market power, rather than on securing of high market shares as such. Although it is not illegal to be dominant, provided dominance achieved is based on legitimate commercial advantage won in the market, there are no exemptions for abuse. Like the restrictions of competition covered by the cartel prohibition, possible abuses of dominance include unfair – for example, excessive or predatory – pricing, discrimination and tying. The key difference is that abuse of dominance is typically carried out by a single company, whereas cartels involve explicit coordination between competitors. Abuses are often qualified as either exploitative (of consumers and customers), exclusionary (foreclosing competition from the market) or discriminatory (between consumers, competitors or downstream operations and competitors) in nature. Unlike the cartel prohibition, which in principle applies to all undertakings, the prohibition of abuse of dominance is asymmetrical in nature: it only applies to those firms that can afford to behave independently.

The definition of a dominant position was established in the *Hoffmann-La Roche* case of 1979. The court stated the following: 'The dominant position thus referred to in [Article 102] relates to a position of economic strength enjoyed by an undertaking which enables it to prevent effective competition being maintained on the relevant market by affording it the power to behave to an appreciable extent independently of its competitors, its customers and ultimately of the consumers.'

The prohibition of abuse of dominance is intended to force such firms to behave as if they were subject to effective competition by abstaining from anticompetitive behaviour. In order to establish a breach of Article 102, the relevant market must first be established. The relevant market has a product and a geographic dimension. The product market consists of all products or services that are interchangeable or substitutable by the consumer, by reason of the products' characteristics, their prices and their intended use. The geographic market for the stated product is the area in which the conditions of competition are sufficiently homogeneous. Next, the existence of dominance in that relevant market should be established, and finally, the existence of an abuse must be shown, as well as an effect on trade between MSs. If markets are defined narrowly, the chances of finding dominance increase – and if they are defined broadly, the reverse holds. Hence market definition is strongly contested in most dominance cases.

The legal test for abuse was also set out in the *Hoffmann-La Roche* case and later restated in the *Michelin* case (2002). The court defined abuse as follows:

In prohibiting any abuse of a dominant position on the market in so far as it may affect trade between MSs, Article [102] covers practices which are likely to affect the structure of a market where, as a direct result of the presence of the undertaking in question, competition has been weakened and which, through recourse different from those governing normal competition in products or services based on trader's performance, have the effect of hindering the maintenance or development of the level of competition still existing on the market.

This indicates that residual competition is valued highly.

13.5.3 Merger control

Unlike the prohibitions on cartels and abuse of dominance, which are normally enforced after the alleged infringement occurs (or *ex post*), EU merger control is based on a system of pre-notification (or *ex ante* control) that is elaborated in the Merger Control Regulation. This system is intended to provide legal certainty to firms before they implement their transaction, and to allow the Commission to vet all such transactions of a certain size (or Community dimension), based on a complex system of multiple turnover thresholds. Merger control aims at preserving 'effective' or workable competition, based on an assessment of the structural characteristics of the relevant product and geographic markets. As elsewhere in EU competition policy, market definitions are essential here: if wide product and geographic market definitions are used, mergers are evidently less likely to be considered problematic than if narrower markets are concerned. In principle, mergers are considered useful to allow undertakings to realize potential efficiencies of scale and scope in contestable markets. They can also promote economic integration. However, above a certain size mergers cannot normally be executed until they have been formally approved. Such approval may be given subject to structural remedies – for example, divestiture of assets such as brands and intellectual property rights, as well as production facilities – and frequently is. An early example is the *Nestlé/Perrier* case (1992), which, according to the Commission, could have led to single firm dominance in the French bottled water market (and duopolistic dominance if only one brand, Volvic, had been spun off to the next biggest operator who already owned Evian). In this case, Nestlé eventually offered commitments to sell to a credible competitor not one but four of its established water brands, as well as the relevant water sources, and to provide a minimum water capacity for them. Nor would it be allowed for a period of five years to acquire other bottled water producers in France accounting for more than 5 per cent of the market. On these conditions, the Commission declared the merger compatible with the common market.

In addition, behavioural remedies such as non-discrimination obligations are sometimes considered (Jones and Gonzalez-Diaz 1992), although they are difficult to monitor and enforce effectively. An example of a failed structural remedy is *Vodafone/Mannesmann* (2000), where the resulting mobile phone giant was not allowed to offer its business users seamless use of their telephones abroad (roaming) for a single pan-European tariff unless it gave its competitors access at the same rates. This was intended to give competitors a chance to catch up, but rather than promoting competition it caused Vodafone to postpone its product innovations and encouraged all other operators to lean back and price-gouge their roaming customers instead. This situation was only (so far partially) resolved based on specific, EU-level roaming legislation in 2007 (Council and Parliament Regulation 2007,[3] the legality of which was confirmed by the ECJ in 2010).

The EU was long denied merger policy powers, because its MSs preferred to vet themselves, or indeed to supervise, the creation of national 'industrial champions', in a wide and often ill-defined set of industries (ranging from aerospace to yoghurt making) considered to be of strategic or political importance (see Chapter 14). The failure of such mutually exclusive national strategies, the increasing desire of businesses to merge across national borders without engaging in multiple notifications subject to different rules, and the merger boom triggered by the 1985 internal market initiative, were all instrumental in finally convincing the MSs to adopt the Merger Control Regulation in 1989 (Neven *et al.* 1993a, b). Since then, merger control has become widely acclaimed as a model for EU competition policy generally. The main reasons for this success are strict rules and deadlines that force the Commission to produce binding decisions within a limited timeframe (if they fail, the merger is cleared automatically), and undertakings to collaborate fully in the process of preparing these decisions. The scope of Community competence in this area – determined by the above-mentioned turnover thresholds – remains politically sensitive.

The reform of the Merger Control Regulation by Council Regulation 139 of 2004 has improved the system of referrals between the EU and national jurisdictions, and introduced a number of procedural changes. More importantly, the reform clarified the concept of dominance – that is, the substantive test applied – as including collective dominance in tight oligopoly situations (Stroux 2004). The Commission had earlier tried to pursue such a case (albeit unsuccessfully) in *Airtours* (2002; mentioned above, page 200). The ECJ set out the three-pronged test that would have to be met: first, the members of the oligopoly must be able to observe and monitor each other's behaviour; second, coordination must be sustainable over time, based on the possibility of retaliation against deviation from the common course; and third, the actions of consumers or competitors cannot successfully challenge this behaviour.

The regulation now applies a so-called SIEC test, meaning that a merger that 'significantly impedes effective competition' should be blocked or only be cleared after the acceptance of remedies. The SIEC test is codified in Article 2.3 of the Merger Regulation. This provision reads as follows: 'a concentration which would significantly impede effective competition, in the common market or in a substantial part of it, in particular as a result of the creation or strengthening of a dominant position, shall be declared incompatible with the common market'.

13.5.4 Public undertakings

In addition to the rules that apply to undertakings in general, the TFEU includes specific provisions governing the application of competition rules for undertakings that are controlled, favoured or charged with executing key economic tasks by public authorities. Article 106 of the TFEU provides rules concerning state-owned undertakings, undertakings that benefit from certain legal advantages and undertakings charged with tasks in the general economic interest, such as utilities – for example, in the energy, transport and communications sectors. Article 106.1 is addressed to MSs, not to undertakings. It prohibits MSs from enacting or maintaining in force any measures in relation to public undertakings and undertakings to which they have granted special or exclusive rights that are contrary to the rules of the treaty. Conversely, Article

106.2 is addressed to undertakings themselves. It states that the competition rules apply to public undertakings charged with services in the general economic interest without limitation, unless this makes it impossible for such companies to carry out their duties.

The *Höfner & Elser* v. *Macrotron* case of 1991 provides an example of the anti-competitive exclusive rights scenario. In Germany, a public agency called *Bundesanstalt für Arbeit* had the exclusive right of employment procurement – that is, headhunting. Höfner and Elser were recruitment consultants who contracted with Macrotron to find the latter a sales director. When Macrotron did not approve their candidate and refused to pay, Höfner and Elser started proceedings. In its defence, Macrotron claimed the recruitment contract was void as it breached the agency's exclusive right of employment procurement. The German court dealing with the case turned to the ECJ, which ruled that an MS is in breach of the prohibitions of Articles 106 in combination with Article 102, if an undertaking with a certain legal advantage, merely by exercising the exclusive rights granted to it, cannot avoid abusing its dominant position. According to the court, there was an infringement in this case as the agency was manifestly incapable of satisfying demand. An example of services of general economic interest is found in the *Corbeau* case of 1993. Here a local competitor to the Belgian postal monopoly was charged with having infringed the latter's exclusive rights. The Court found that the operation of a universal postal service throughout the national territory could be covered by a service of general economic interest, and in fact it might cover such cross-subsidies as necessary for the financial balance of the service. It left it to the national court to decide whether these criteria were met.

Article 106.3 concerns the policing and legislative powers of the Commission. First, it provides that the Commission may address decisions to MSs to ensure the observance of Article 106. Second, it gives the Commission power to issue directives to the MSs to ensure the application of this Article. Exceptionally for legislation, such rules do not require approval by the European Parliament and Council. The importance of Article 106.3, long a dormant provision of the TFEU, has increased markedly since 1988, when it was used to abolish exclusive rights in the telecommunications equipment sector. This is because 'natural monopoly' arguments that were long held to apply to public utilities have become contested, and public ownership is increasingly seen as inefficient. The TFEU itself, however, remains formally neutral concerning public and private ownership, by force of its Article 345.

13.5.5 State aid

Finally, in its Articles 107–9, the TFEU contains rules on restrictions of effective competition that result from MSs' authorities at any level favouring some companies over others by means of subsidies – that is, state aid (Quigley and Collins 2004; see also Chapter 14). Illegal state aid covers subsidies in any form, including outright financial subsidies as well as tax advantages or exceptions, favourable loan terms, credit guarantees, the sale or lease of goods and real estate below market prices, and many other forms of discrimination by public authorities between undertakings. Some types of state aid, however, are acceptable. Hence state aid is governed by a rule in Article 107.1 prohibiting aid that distorts competition, and two possible exceptions to this rule: first, aid that is by definition considered compatible with the internal market (see Chapter 7), as listed in Article 107.2 – for example, social aid to consumers and disaster relief; and second, aid that the Commission may clear by decision, following mandatory notification, as listed in Article 107.3 – for example, certain regional and sectoral aid. In this area, then competition Commissioner Kroes announced in 2005 that more weight should be given to market failures. Only when market failures exist is there a potential argument for intervention by means of state aid.

13.6 Enforcement

The Commission's relatively limited human resources have long focused on the enforcement of the prohibition of anti-competitive agreements contained in Article 101 of the TFEU (although, gradually, the relative weight of state aid policy did increase). This is the result of interrelated, systemic, political and practical constraints.

In spite of a recent spate of court decisions supporting the Commission's findings concerning *Deutsche Telecom* (2008), *France Telecom* (2009) and the celebrated *Microsoft* judgment (2007), Article 102 decisions remain relatively rare. This is in large part due to the high burden of proof that the European courts have imposed on the Commission, which is explained by the inherently intrusive nature of this prohibition: based on their size, it bars individual behaviour by companies that would otherwise be acceptable business practice. A clear indication of the difficulties involved is that over the period of almost forty years during which the Commission has actively applied the competition rules, it has adopted only forty-odd decisions: evidently, it is likely that in reality significantly higher numbers of grave abuses of dominance occurred over this period. Since 1989, however, effective EU merger control may also have played a role in preventing dominant positions from emerging in the first place. Meanwhile, the Commission is trying to revive and rationalize its approach to dominance abuse. In December 2008 the Commission (CEU 2008e) published guidance on its enforcement priorities in applying Article 82 (EC) to abusive exclusionary conduct by dominant undertakings (officially recorded in CEU 2009j). This guidance focuses on conduct that risks weakening competition in a market by various means of foreclosure, such as rebates, refusal to supply and tying.

The manner in which the system of Article 101 was implemented until the 2004 modernization effort, on the other hand, was clearly biased in favour of attracting cases to the Commission. Article 101.1 of the TFEU prohibits agreements and parallel behaviour that restrict or distort competition within the common market. However, it is not always clear whether restrictions capable of affecting trade are involved, and in any event the benefits of such restrictions may be more significant than their negative effects (Odudu 2006). In practice, there are therefore many agreements, which are at face value restrictive, but that ought not to be prohibited. Because under Article 101.2 agreements that infringe the prohibition of Article 101.1 are automatically void, it was long held that undertakings require prior assurances that their prospective agreements are not caught by this prohibition. Under the key implementing Regulation 17/62 (Council 1962), only the Commission could provide exemptions to the prohibition on policy grounds, because notification to the Commission of the agreements involved was a precondition for obtaining an exemption. However, this resulted in a flood of notifications which the Commission has never managed to handle in a timely manner, due to capacity constraints. Moreover, the effectiveness of this system was low: harmful cartels are unlikely to be caught in this manner, as they are carefully kept secrets. In over thirty-five years of the application of the notification system, the Commission adopted only nine decisions prohibiting agreements based on notifications, without a complaint having been lodged against them in addition (CEU 1999f).

The most important instrument providing a collective negative clearance was the *de minimis* (see page 220) notice, concerning agreements of minor importance – that is, with negligible effects on trade between MSs or on competition (CEU 2001k). Aside from agreements covered by the *de minimis* notice, few agreements benefited from a negative clearance, largely because the Commission traditionally preferred to perform its anti-trust analysis under Article 101.3 (EC) – and it appears to continue to do so following modernization. This approach has long been criticized by advocates of a 'rule of reason' approach under Article 101.1 (Wesseling 2005). Under Article 101.3, an agreement that is in principle prohibited under Article 101.1 may, if its effects are on balance considered beneficial to competition, obtain a waiver, or 'exemption' from this prohibition, potentially subject to structural and behavioural conditions, and limited in time. This process was streamlined by means of collective, or 'block' exemptions (see Section 13.8, page 208).

Its monopoly on exemptions from the prohibition on restrictive agreements set out in Article 101.1 gave the Commission sole control of key levers of competition policy. The resulting centralization of EU competition law enforcement in the hands of the Commission had considerable benefits in terms of consistency and credibility, and was probably indispensable in order to allow a fully-fledged EU competition policy to develop. In fact, with few exceptions (notably Germany), in the EU a true competition policy was long pursued only at Community level.

In recent years, however, this situation has changed fundamentally. All MSs now accept, at least in principle, that state intervention and tolerance or promotion of private cartel arrangements are poor substitutes for the market allocation of resources. Hence, in a process of 'spontaneous harmonization', most MSs have adopted national competition rules based on the EU model, and have moved towards effective enforcement of these rules. At the same time, it became clear that in order to further advance competition policy, the

Commission would have to focus on new problems, such as those that arise in recently liberalized markets, in oligopolistic markets and in markets that extend beyond the EU. Likewise, to ensure proactive enforcement, it would have to focus more on complaints, and on labour-intensive, own-initiative actions to pursue the gravest cartel and dominance abuses. Meanwhile the adoption of a 'leniency notice' (CEU 2002l) led to a steep increase in the number of applications for a reduction of fines in cartel cases by undertakings 'coming clean' about cartel abuses in which they were involved, and providing the necessary evidence against their co-conspirators. Following up these cases in a timely and effective manner now requires increased resources. Together, these constituted compelling reasons to decentralize and modernize the system of enforcement.

Even prior to the adoption of the key modernization Regulation 1 of 2003, the Commission started rationalizing its existing Article 101.3 practice by streamlining and consolidating its block exemptions, and by moving towards an approach that relies more on economic analysis, in particular in the area of vertical restraints. Likewise, at an earlier stage, following the momentum generated by the 1992 internal market programme (see Chapter 7), the Commission had started focusing its competition policy more on public undertakings and state intervention. These three developments are each discussed below.

13.7 The public turn

During the first three decades of its competition policy, the Commission focused on the basic task of enforcing the Article 101 (EC) and Article 102 (EC) prohibitions against private undertakings. This required it to elaborate implementing rules (the procedural regulations and block exemption regulations mentioned above) and to develop its practice concerning a range of standard competition policy problems in this area. After consolidating this part of its competencies, the Commission started expanding the scope of its enforcement efforts, to cover the politically more delicate areas of the public sector and state aid, over the course of the 1980s and 1990s. This trend has been defined as the 'public turn' of EU competition law (Gerber 2001).

In the first place, the Commission began more active enforcement of the competition rules against public undertakings, and undertakings that enjoy special and exclusive rights, such as legal monopolies, as well as licences or concessions limited in number and awarded on discretionary grounds – for example, the early licenses to operate mobile telephony or port landing rights.

Second, the Commission's policy on state aid has matured, in particular following the completion of the internal market programme. This policy has included: targeting aid to public enterprises; the elaboration of the 'market investor test', which means aid is not acceptable unless private investors might have taken similar investment decisions; and enforcing the repayment of illegal aid (see Chapter 14).

The market investor test emerged from the case law. In the *Spain* v. *Commission* case of 1994, Advocate General Jacobs regarded aid as being granted whenever a state made funds available to an undertaking, which in the normal course of events would not be provided by a private investor applying ordinary commercial criteria and disregarding considerations of a social, political or philanthropic nature. This approach was adopted by the Court itself in the *SFEI* v. *La Poste* case of 1996, where it held that, in order to determine whether a state measure constitutes aid for the purposes of Article 107, it is necessary to establish whether the recipient receives an economic advantage that it would not have obtained under normal market conditions.

At the same time, the belief that state control over the economy is inversely related to its performance became widely shared by policy-makers at national level. This realization was reinforced by the move to economic and monetary union (EMU), which imposes budgetary constraints that make MSs reluctant to expose themselves to the significant potential liabilities represented by public investment that is not guided by efficiency considerations, and indeed by public ownership as such (Devroe 1997; see also Chapters 11 and 12). The degree to which the system of state aid checks has become engrained in the policy process is illustrated by the fact that when the financial crisis caused numerous MSs to rescue ailing financial institutions, EU state aid control over this process continued unabated.

An important new category of state aid cases concerns services of general economic interest (Sauter 2008). The *Altmark* case of 2003 states the main principles for financing services of general economic interest. In that case, the court concluded that payments made by governments to companies providing essential services – for example, public transportation – should not be classed as state aid as long as the following criteria are satisfied. First, the recipient must actually perform a predefined public service obligation. Second, the parameters on the basis of which the compensation is calculated must be established in advance in an objective and transparent manner. Third, the compensation cannot exceed what is necessary to cover all or part of the costs incurred for supplying the public service. Fourth, where the undertaking that performs the public service obligation is not chosen on the basis of a public procurement procedure, the level of compensation needed must be determined on the basis of an analysis of the costs that a typical well-run undertaking in the same market would have incurred. Taken jointly, this means that the undertaking would have provided a public service in proportionate exchange for consideration, and hence was not conferred an unfair advantage, so no aid was given.

Although the developments that constitute the 'public turn' of EU competition policy can certainly also be seen as a form of modernization and rationalization, they still remain distinct from these changes to its traditional core anti-trust enforcement. In the utilities sectors, where traditional monopoly markets must be opened up to competitive entry, sector-specific competition rules enforced by independent sector regulators will continue to play an important role at least in the medium term, until competition becomes sufficiently effective for application of the general (or horizontal) competition rules to suffice. Meanwhile, the existence of such sector-specific national regulators helps to relieve the burden on the competition services of the Commission, and to spread an understanding of how the process of competition may be protected in often technically complex (and politically sensitive) fields, such as electronic communications, energy and transport. The rules on state aid will of course not be phased out, as the need to distinguish legitimate public measures from illegal aid will persist as long as public authorities are tempted to interfere in markets. Moreover, unlike the antitrust provisions, the state aid rules are, by definition, not suited to decentralized application, and no such rules exist at

national level (although EU rules can be invoked in some cases by complainants before national courts). Therefore, they must be enforced in a centralized manner.

In sum, there is a clear case for Commission services to focus on state aid, mergers and other cases with a significant Community interest due to the size and transnational nature or precedent value of the problems involved, while leaving the great majority of competition cases to national competition authorities and sector-specific regulators. A significant Community interest or dimension was arguably not involved in the bulk of competition cases so far examined under Article 101. Accordingly, Regulation 1 of 2003 empowered national authorities to deal with such cases. In addition, limiting the scope of the prohibitions to cases where economically significant effects and market power are concerned would help to allow a clearer focus on more serious competition problems at both the national and EU levels. The developments in the area of vertical restraints and modernization indicate a clear policy trend in this direction.

13.8 Rationalization

Many commentators have criticized EU competition policy for its lack of economic analysis, in particular in relation to restraints on competition under Article 101 (Hildebrand 2002; Korah 1998). In part, the Commission's approach, with its focus on formal and territorial restraints, was a logical consequence of the integration objective. Yet even when it tried to accommodate economically advantageous vertical agreements, the system of parallel block exemption regulations adopted for similar types of agreement led to inconsistencies and, in combination with the practice of identifying exempted restrictions, rather than just those restrictions held to be illegal, to 'straitjacket' effects. Moves towards consolidation and reform started in 1996, when the Commission adopted a single block exemption for technology transfer agreements, replacing previously separate regulations concerning patent and know-how licences. Since then, EU competition policy has shifted away from an approach based on legal form towards one based on market power and economic effects: it is this process that can be described as rationalization.

One of the reasons for this cultural change may have been the integration of economists at DG COMP. There has been a large increase in the number of economists working at DG COMP: around 200 out of over 700 officials have an economics or business background. About twenty of them have a PhD in economics, ten of whom are currently working in the Office of the Chief Economist. The Office of the Chief Economist was created in 2003 as a separate and independent division of DG COMP that mainly consists of economists (presently chaired by Professor Damian Neven). The Office's members work closely with the case teams, getting involved early on in the investigation and providing economic guidance and methodological assistance.

The most important examples so far concern the Commission's approach to vertical and horizontal restraints. In 1999 it adopted a single block exemption regulation for vertical restraints, replacing the formerly separate legal instruments concerning exclusive distribution, exclusive purchasing and franchising agreements. In addition, the new block exemption covers selective distribution agreements, which were previously dealt with under individual decisions (CEU 1999e). In 2000 the Commission adopted 'horizontal' block exemption regulations for specialization agreements and for research and development agreements (CEU 2000g, h), followed by a notice on horizontal cooperation agreements (CEU 2001l). With regard to both vertical and horizontal agreements, the emphasis is now on undertakings with some significant measure of market power. Only the vertical block exemption is discussed in more detail here.

Vertical agreements are entered into between undertakings operating at different levels of the production or distribution chain that relate to the purchase, sale or resale of certain goods and services. The restraints involved in such agreements typically cover various forms of exclusivity and non-competition clauses, as well as branding and pricing constraints that may foreclose market entry, reduce intra-brand competition especially, and obstruct market integration. Especially for the latter reason, vertical restraints have traditionally been frowned on in EU competition law, and a systematic policy recognizing the potential benefits of vertical agreements has been slow to develop. However, as the various specific block exemptions testified, these potential benefits can be significant: vertical agreements can improve economic efficiency by reducing the transaction and distribution costs of the parties involved, and can lead to an optimization of their respective sales and investment levels, in particular where there is effective competition between different brands. Most important from an integration perspective, vertical agreements also offer particularly effective ways of opening up or entering new markets. The objective of the vertical block exemption is to secure these positive effects, turning away from the earlier focus of EU competition law on integration through protecting inter-brand competition (Peeperkorn 1998).

The block exemption for vertical restraints is based on a general exemption, subject only to a prohibition of a limited number of blacklisted clauses (such as resale price maintenance and most territorial constraints), leaving broader freedom for commercial contracts (Korah and Sullivan 2002). Unless the undertakings involved enjoy market power (or where there are networks of similar agreements stifling the market), the block exemption creates a presumption of legality for vertical agreements concerning the sale of goods and services that are concluded by companies with less than 30 per cent of market share. Only cases involving undertakings that are above this threshold require separate analysis. In a move towards decentralization, national authorities are empowered to withdraw the benefits of the block exemption if vertical agreements have effects incompatible with Article 101.3 on a geographically distinct market within their jurisdiction. The vertical block exemption is now under review, especially its prohibition of retail price maintenance.

13.9 Modernization

For more than thirty-five years, following the Council's adoption of the key procedural Regulation 17 in 1962, the Commission was responsible for the administration of a highly centralized authorization system for exemptions to the cartel prohibition of Article 101.1. This system rested on the notification requirement and exemption monopoly introduced by Regulation 17. It has facilitated the uniform application of EU competition law, which in turn fostered a 'culture of competition', now shared with national competition authorities in all twenty-seven MSs, a majority of which obtained authority to apply national competition laws inspired by Community law even prior to modernization (Temple Lang 1998). However, this success came at significant cost to effective enforcement: mass notifications overburdened Commission services, leading to administrative solutions that did not provide adequate legal certainty for undertakings, but which nevertheless used to trump national courts and competition authorities in their own enforcement of the directly effective cartel prohibition (Wils 2003).

Over time, the Commission came to share many elements of the widespread criticism of this system. In addition, it identified the impending further EU enlargement (see Chapters 2 and 19), the effects of economic restructuring following EMU, and the need to reallocate resources to respond adequately to the broadening geographic scope of various anti-competitive practices as the result of economic globalization, as reasons to adopt a programme of far-reaching modernization and reform of the manner in which Article 101 is applied. In its modernization White Paper of 1999 (CEU 1999f), the Commission set three objectives for this exercise: ensuring effective supervision; simplifying administration; and easing the constraints on undertakings while providing them with a sufficient degree of legal certainty (Wesseling 2000). Subsequently, the Commission's proposals resulted in the adoption of the new Council regulation on the implementation of Articles 101 and 102, which came into force on 1 May 2004, coinciding with EU enlargement.

The key element of this modernization exercise is that it replaces the mandatory notification and authorization system with a directly applicable legal exception system. This constitutes a shift from a system of *ex ante* control to a system of *ex post* supervision that relies more on direct effect, and hence on enforcement by national authorities and in private court actions by interested parties. Undertakings are now required to assess for themselves whether their contemplated agreements are likely to infringe the prohibition of Article 101.1, and, if they do, whether they remain within the scope of the legal exception of Article 101.3, because the restrictions involved are limited to the minimum that is necessary to realize legitimate economic benefits shared with consumers, consistent with established EU competition policy practice.

It is important to note that this self-assessment remains subject to challenge before national courts and by the competition authorities both at national and at Community level. The enforcement at national level is facilitated by Commission guidance. In its own handling of such cases, the Commission has announced that it will limit the scope of its review to undertakings with market power. Hence, as with the approach concerning vertical restraints, market shares will come to play a key role. Under the modernized system, all national competition authorities are not only to be empowered but also obligated to apply Articles 101 and 102 in cases where there is an appreciable effect on trade between MSs. This considerably reinforces the decentralized application of EU competition law.

National competition authorities have to keep the Commission informed of their intentions in such cases, and must submit substantive decisions to prior Commission scrutiny. Since the Commission retains the right to take over cases where this is deemed to be in the Community interest, there will also be an increase in coordination at Community level. The ambition is that DG COMP will become the linchpin of a system based on a seamless network of closely cooperating competition authorities at national and EU level (Ehlermann 2003; Temple Lang 2004).

The role of national authorities was at issue in the *Consorzio Industrie Fiammiferi* (CIF) case of 2003. CIF was an Italian consortium of domestic manufacturers of matches. The CIF had been established by royal decree in 1923, and enjoyed a commercial and fiscal monopoly that ended in 1994. Subsequently, the Italian state undertook to prohibit the distribution of matches that had been produced by non-CIF members. In return, CIF promised to ensure that its members paid the excise duty on matches. The Italian competition authority declared the relevant national legislation to be contrary to the good faith clause and Article 101 of the TFEU, as it required the CIF to engage in anti-competitive conduct. Remarkably, the EU General Court agreed with the competition authority and held that the duty to disapply national legislation that contravenes Community law applies not only to national courts, but also to 'all organs of the state', including both national competition authorities and sector-specific regulators.

The complexity of the role of the national courts was brought out in the *Masterfoods* v. *HB Ice Cream* case of 2000. HB had supplied retailers in Ireland with freezer cabinets for no direct charge, provided that the cabinets were exclusively used for stocking and displaying HB ice-cream products. In 1989 Masterfoods, a subsidiary of Mars, Inc., entered the Irish market, and some retailers started stocking Masterfoods products in their HB freezer cabinets. When HB strongly objected to this practice by enforcing the exclusivity provision of its distribution agreements, Masterfoods brought an action before the Irish High Court, as well as a parallel complaint with the Commission, claiming that the HB exclusivity clause infringed Articles 101 and 102. The Commission found that the exclusivity clause did infringe Community rules on competition and HB appealed to the EU General Court. In the parallel national proceedings the Irish High Court held the reverse and Masterfoods appealed to the Irish Supreme Court, which addressed the ECJ. The ECJ held that where a national court is considering issues that are already subject to a Commission decision, the court may not reach a judgment conflicting with the decision of the Commission, irrespective of the fact that the Commission decision in question had been appealed to the General Court. The court further stressed that it is for the national court to decide whether to stay proceedings pending final judgment or in order to address a preliminary reference to the ECJ.

It is clear that new dynamics involving national regulators and courts are evolving. Because ending formal centralization gives rise to an increased need for coordination, it is by no means certain that the Commission's ambitions to refocus its own enforcement activities on intensified *ex post* control – including that against the gravest cartels – can be realized without additional resources. Whether sharing responsibility for competition law enforcement more broadly will create momentum in favour of providing the necessary means remains an open question. At a minimum, however, it will provide the Commission with increased flexibility in reordering its priorities.

13.10 Conclusion

Following its initial system-building efforts, EU competition policy became increasingly hampered by a mismatch between the formal scope of the Commission's powers and its actual capacity for effective enforcement.

To some extent the Commission fell victim to its own success at centralizing its competence in order to secure its key mission of promoting market integration. Nevertheless, its efforts eventually spawned both the spontaneous harmonization of competition policy and an increasingly effective enforcement culture at national level, which are now considered key to modernization.

EU competition policy is in a process of rationalization and modernization that involves imposing increasingly stringent curbs on public intervention, and it is moving away from its former primary focus on the integration objective towards increasing reliance on economic logic and on enforcement at national level.

Although significant advances have already been made concerning previously privileged economic sectors, state aid and revising the block exemptions, the ongoing review of EU competition policy instruments is not complete: a full review of policy on market power and dominance, including approaches to dominance and collusion in oligopolistic markets, remains to be worked out. The process of decentralizing the enforcement of the principles established so far forms a precondition for such further modernization, which has only recently begun. Methods and principles for case allocation and cooperation within the network of European competition authorities are being tested in practice. The state aid machinery is likely to be reformed further. Finally, setting priorities may be necessary to manage a growing flow of cartels subject to leniency applications. Nevertheless, the outline of a fully-fledged market power and effects-based 'second-generation' system of EU competition law is now clear.

Summary

- EU competition law is one of the key instruments of the SEM and thereby of European integration. Although it is based on common concepts of antitrust and law and economics first developed in the USA, it has a typically European dimension. Historically this can be traced back to German *Ordo*liberalism in the 1940s and 1950s, but even more important is the aspect of promoting integration that can be found, for instance, in the approach to parallel trade and vertical restraints (long regarded with scepticism).

- The three main dimensions normally associated with EU competition policy (CP) are the prohibitions on cartels and dominance abuse, and merger control. In addition, there are policies on public undertakings and on state aid, which do not concern the relationships between undertakings as such, but between undertakings and the MSs – for example, exclusive rights or subsidies. These rules are complementary and aim at achieving effective (not perfect) competition in the SEM. The comparatively more recent attention for the role of the state in this context has been called the 'public turn' of CP.

- Finally, the rationalization and modernization of EU CP policy are discussed:

  1. Rationalization largely equates integrating the use of more (up-to-date) economic analysis in CP. A notable example has been the revised policy towards vertical restraints.

  2. Modernization is the most recent trend and revolves around the decentralization of CP to the network of competition authorities in the MSs, coordinated by the Commission, and replacing the centralized exemption procedure with a legal exception based on self-assessment.

  At the same time, hard-core restrictions are combated more vigorously.

Questions and essay topics

1. Why is there an EU CP?
2. What is effective competition and how does it differ from perfect competition?
3. What is the relevant market and why is it important in EU CP?
4. Define an agreement/concerted practice between firms that restricts competition.
5. What are vertical restraints and why are they considered differently from horizontal restraints?
6. What is a block exemption?
7. Under what circumstances would a company be in a dominant position in the EU?
8. Why is it abuse, not dominance, that is a problem under EU CP?
9. What determines whether a merger comes under EU jurisdiction?
10. Under what circumstances will a merger be banned by the EU?
11. What is state aid?
12. Why is EU control of state aid necessary?
13. Explain the position of public enterprises under EU CP.
14. Discuss the goals of EU CP and how they differ from those of another jurisdiction, such as the USA.
15. Why was it necessary to extend EU CP to mergers?
16. What is meant by the modernization of EU anti-trust policy? In this context, explain the importance of the legal exception and the exemption system.
17. Why has EU CP taken a public turn? Consider the form this change has taken.
18. Discuss the relevance of economics to anti-trust in the EU.
19. It has been necessary to modernize EU CP. Consider the forms this modernization has taken.

FURTHER READING

Cini, M. and McGowan, L. (2008) *The Competition Policy in the European Union*, Palgrave Macmillan, Basingstoke.

Elhauge, E. and Geradin, D. (2007) *Global Competition Law and Economics*, Hart Publishing, Oxford.

Faull, J. and Nikpay, A. (eds.) (2007) *The EC Law on Competition*, 2nd edn, Oxford University Press.

Geradin, D., Layne-Farrar, A. and Petit, N. (2010) *EC Competition Law and Economics*, Oxford University Press.

Gerber, D. J. (2001) *Law and Competition in Twentieth Century Europe: Protecting Prometheus*, Oxford University Press.

Monti, G. (2007) *EC Competition Law*, Cambridge University Press.

Motta, M. (2004) *Competition Policy: Theory and Practice*, Cambridge University Press.

van Bael & Bellis (2009) *Competition Law of the European Community*, 5th edn, Kluwer Law International, Deventer.

van den Berg, R. J. and Camesasca, P. D. (2001) *European Competition Law and Economics: A Comparative Perspective*, Intersententia Publishing, Mortsel, Belgium.

NOTES

1 Cases from 17 June 1997 are available at http://curia. europa.eu/jurisp/cgi-bin/form.pl?lang=en; earlier cases are available on the subscription service EUR-Lex.
2 Until 2009 this was known as the Court of First Instance.

3 Regulation (EC) No. 717/2007 of the European Parliament and the Council of 27 June 2007 on roaming on public mobile telephone networks within the Community and amending Directive 2002/21/EC, OJ 2007 L171/32.

14 Industrial and competitiveness policy: the Lisbon Strategy

BRIAN ARDY

14.1 Introduction

Industrial and competitiveness policy (ICP) can be defined as government policy designed to improve a country's economic performance. This includes a very broad range of government policies, both horizontal, to provide a supportive environment for business (fiscal, competition, regional, social, labour and environmental policies), and vertical, designed to favour particular sectors of the economy.

ICP has fluctuated over time. From 1950 to 1979 the prevailing orthodoxy was that government could and should correct market failures, so microeconomic intervention in specific industrial sectors was normal. Thus in the 1970s the response to structural change in the world economy was protection of companies and industries in difficulty, and European industrial policies 'aimed to create European super-firms to compete with the US giants' (Geroski and Jacquemin 1989, p. 299). The failure of these policies to raise EU industrial performance[1] meant that by the 1980s the effectiveness of government action was increasingly questioned. By the early 1990s, in the Commission's view, ICP 'should promote adaptation to industrial change in an open and competitive market' (Bangermann 1994). So company and sector-specific policies were viewed with suspicion, and ICP supported competitive markets in general. Today the consensus is between these extremes of extensive intervention and relying on market forces: ICP can be a helpful tool to improve economic performance, provided it is used sparingly and carefully (Buigues and Sekkat 2009; Lin and Monga 2010).

Competition policy (CP) is really part of ICP, because decisions affect the structure of industries by controlling mergers, joint ventures and preventing cartels. CP is covered in Chapter 13, but Section 14.4 (page 217) discusses the control of state aid to industry because it is an important part of EU ICP.

This chapter begins by examining ICP instruments. It then discusses ICP's intellectual foundations and analyses EU policy. This is followed by a discussion of the control of state aid; and a consideration of the support for research and development (R&D). Then the overarching EU policy seeking to improve competitiveness, the Lisbon Strategy, is examined.

14.2 ICP instruments

Traditional industrial policy uses subsidies/tax breaks, protection, regulation and public procurement. ICP also includes deregulation, education reform, subsidization of infrastructure and research. Over time, with the tightening of trade rules in the GATT/WTO and within the EU, ICP instruments have shifted from tariffs to non-tariff barriers (NTBs). ICP measures either permit local firms to raise their price to enjoy a hidden subsidy, or offer them subsidies that directly reduce the cost or raise the quality of their inputs, such as labour and research. Regulations can be implicit or explicit instruments of ICP – for example, the adoption of the GSM standard for mobile phones helped EU firms to an early dominance of this industry.

The EU has a role in all these areas of industrial policy. It is the major actor in external trade policy (see Chapters 2 and 24), and it has a shared but growing competence over regulatory policy, supervision of state aid and limited but increasing subsidies in such areas as research, plus competition policy.

14.3 ICP: theory and evidence

The economic case for ICP is based on market failure: externalities and uncompetitive markets. For example, the market may under-supply scientific and industrial knowledge because it is a public good – hence public funding of R&D. This is the basis for horizontal industrial policy. With sector-specific ICP, however, the case for market failure is much harder to make, because the underlying assumption is that the government is better at allocating resources than the market.

Externalities are costs and benefits that arise in production or consumption but which do not directly affect the producer or the consumer – that is, they are suffered without compensation or enjoyed free of charge by third parties. There are three types of externalities that are important for ICP: knowledge creation, network interactions and agglomeration/localization. In imperfectly competitive markets new entrants may struggle to be competitive and ICP can help.

14.3.1 Imperfect competition

In the 1980s trade theory turned to models of imperfect competition to explain phenomena such as intra-industry trade between developed countries (Krugman 1979). From this exercise there emerged a policy prescription that looked remarkably like the old infant-industry argument dressed up in modern clothes. Imperfectly competitive markets are characterized by large, profitable firms and high technology, which interact with economies of scale, positive feedbacks/spillovers and path dependence. This makes it very difficult for the 'infant' industry operating below optimum size to compete with established firms. What is perhaps new is the idea that comparative advantage is no longer a matter of traditional factor endowments, but can be *consciously shaped* by judicious ICP (Brander and Spencer 1983).

In a world where technology determines the competitiveness of firms and where location is no longer a question of hard geographic facts, but rather proximity to other firms in the same sector, economic activity is 'footloose'. Attracting specific sectors to particular locations therefore becomes a feasible object of public policy. The market failures are the same as before: first-mover advantages, barriers to entry due to economies of scale, and perhaps lack of appropriate general infrastructure (high-speed communication networks, universities, publicly funded research laboratories, and so on). The problem, as always, lies in whether the response to the observed market failure is to be selective or general.

14.3.2 Network interaction

Network externalities occur where consumer satisfaction increases with the number of people using a particular good. Thus the advantage the iPhone possesses is not just the quality of the product itself, but the fact that the large use of the phone has led to the development of a large number of 'apps'. For ICP, the crucial issue is the adoption of standards which can confer a crucial competitive advantage. Measures can vary from coordination of producers across the EU, financing the development of standards and legislation on standards. In this, as in other forms of ICP, success is not guaranteed; the EU's attempt to develop HDTV standards was a spectacular failure.

14.3.3 Industrial agglomerations

The failure of old-style regional policy to create viable industries in blighted areas, as well as the astonishing success of Silicon Valley, has led to a renewed interest in the economics of agglomeration (Fujita and Thisse 1996). Agglomerations are conducive to technological change; information and ideas circulate informally within an agglomeration, speeding up the process of product development (Lucas 1988). The emphasis on agglomeration has been reinforced by evidence that even for technology the spillovers are concentrated locally (Keller 2002). The notion that people following the same skilled trade derive advantages from proximity because of lower factor prices and economies of scale is old (Marshall, 1920); a modern version is provided by Porter (1990).

The 'pull' factors that reduce costs for members of an agglomeration include: positive externalities based on mass production of specialized inputs (that is, access to lower costs from efficient suppliers); access to specialized labour, specialized services, shared consumers, shared infrastructure (especially universities); and the flow of information (especially tacit and informal information) (Cohen 2006). This reflects the sheer efficiency of markets as coordinating agents (as compared with the corresponding inefficiency of hierarchical management as a method of coordination beyond a certain degree of complexity). An agglomeration reduces costs by allowing firms to contract out all but their core activities, but this is only efficient if the specialized suppliers can themselves operate on a large enough scale, thus offsetting market transaction costs. For outsourcing to work well, it requires many buyers and many service providers to offer similar (but often subtly differentiated) specialized services. The spectacular benefits come when specialization and economies of scale, in turn, hit the service supply industry as well, spreading pecuniary externalities (Scitovsky 1954) throughout the agglomeration and creating a Silicon Valley effect.

One important implication for industrial policy is that while the agglomeration may be very large, most of the firms of which it is composed will be small. In fact, the economies of agglomeration can be interpreted as being both substitutes for and complements of technical economies of scale. Thus an agglomeration of a dense network of small, specialized suppliers and subcontractors might compete head-on with a large, vertically integrated corporation, or be complementary to a less integrated large firm. The competition is keeping costs and prices down, and variety and innovation up.

These factors have led to a range of government policies from science parks, export processing zones and growth poles, which have proliferated with varying results. The ingredients of success remain elusive, partly because they are bound up with R&D research and SMEs which are difficult to foster, for reasons that are considered in the next two sections.

14.3.4 Research and development

The importance of technological change in explaining economic growth has long been recognized (Solow 1957; Denison 1974). In Solow's neoclassical growth model technology is exogenous, but with Romer's (1990) seminal contribution, models where technological change is endogenous have been developed. With innovation as a good, its production is driven by profit, but innovation has peculiar characteristics. Inventions are subject to increasing returns to scale because there are large fixed costs. Firms will only invest heavily in R&D if they can appropriate for themselves the new knowledge they have created. Innovations are non-rival: once an iPad has been developed, its technology and design can be copied relatively easily. This limits firms' incentive to innovate because other firms will copy expensively acquired knowledge – this is the free-rider problem.[2] This market failure is met by patents and by providing public funding of basic research and education so that ideas can be developed and implemented.

Public funding of R&D can be selective and part of vertical ICP. This is less risky than 'picking the winners' directly – for example, funding investment in new production facilities – since the new knowledge thus created might spill over into other areas and be generally useful. For instance, the Apollo space programme is often credited with having developed the transistor, the grandfather of the silicon chip. But there is still the risk of governmental failure (see Section 14.3.6, page 218). Technological loops, linkages, feedbacks and spillovers are at the heart of the argument. They help to translate scientific knowledge into commercially useful innovations, and vice versa. Industrial research by one firm takes known science, applies it to solving a particular problem, and in the course of this adds to general scientific knowledge, which can be exploited by other firms and perhaps find its way back to the universities. Thus the creation of new knowledge by one firm is assumed to generate positive externalities for other firms (Grossman and Helpman 1991). The ability to assimilate existing technologies and generate new ones is by no means universal, but has to be cultivated. Countries in which technological research is carried out acquire a *comparative advantage in the form of human capital resource endowments that may persist for some time* (Ruttan 1998). In turn, this human capital resource can be encouraged by government policy, especially as this seems to be crucial in determining growth (Temple 1999). It is also plausible that pure science will remain economically inert unless society possesses a steady supply of entrepreneurs to convert it into marketable products. More generally, the importance of the institutional setting to economic performance has been increasingly stressed (Gwartney *et al.* 2006).

There is general agreement that R&D should have public support, but how much, in what way and at what stage? The process of transforming general scientific knowledge into commercial applications can be viewed as a pipeline, running from academic institutions where much scientific knowledge is created but few innovations emerge, to the more focused development of prototype products or processes in commercial engineering laboratories, on to small-scale testing of innovations, and finally to full-scale commercial development and marketing. New knowledge is created at each stage in the process. But which stage is the most deserving of public support? Generally speaking, the further away from 'the marketplace' and the more general the type of research, the more appropriate it is for public funding. In this way, the targeting of public funds to particular firms can be avoided. For this reason, the EU promotes 'pre-competitive' R&D – that is, in principle, it does not fund the development of anything 'too close' to the market.

14.3.5 Entrepreneurship: small and medium-sized enterprises

The results of research have to be transformed into marketable innovation and this process emphasizes the role of entrepreneurs and SMEs. It was Joseph Schumpeter (1934) who emphasized the dynamism of capitalism as creative destruction, with innovations embodied in new firms, with the entrepreneur as the agent of change developing the commercial potential of the new idea. This new firm and its imitators would take over the market, displacing existing products, methods and jobs. Thus the ability to innovate depends on entrepreneurs' willingness to take risks. This suggests that the economic growth of a country will depend on the supply of entrepreneurs and their ability to turn their ideas into new enterprises.

Entrepreneurs and SMEs have become more important with changes in the world economy. From 1900 until 1970 economic conditions favoured concentration and the centralization of production (Chandler 1990; Scherer and Ross 1990), as technology and production were characterized by economies of scale and incremental innovation that could be undertaken by large firms. Since 1970 conditions have altered: technological change, outsourcing, globalization, deregulation and variety in demand have increased volatility and uncertainty, encouraging lower concentration and decentralization (Audretsch *et al.* 2001). The evidence suggests that SMEs have become increasingly important, but the extent of this change varies across countries (Loveman and Sengenberger 1991; Acs *et al.* 1994). The link between entrepreneurship and SMEs and economic performance is confirmed by Audretsch and Thurik (2001), who find that increases in the relative share of economic activity accounted for by small firms and the self-employment rate are associated with higher rates of growth and a reduction of unemployment.

14.3.6 Government failure

That markets fail is indisputable, but government intervention will not necessarily improve matters: governments may not have the knowledge and ability to take action. Once government becomes involved, political and bureaucratic processes come into operation, with all their problems. Markets generate and use enormous amounts of knowledge, hence effective government policy requires a range of knowledge: the problem and its causes; and potential instruments and their effects. This information may not be available. Industrial policy may conflict with other policies, most notably competition policy and trade policy. Providing help to particular firms or sectors is an obvious distortion of competition, especially where this is national policy within a Single European Market (SEM). Aid to domestic firms is a protectionist policy and could encourage inefficient production, which is not viable in the long term. But perhaps the most important problem with ICP is the politicization of the process. Decisions on industrial policy are long term, but politics is driven by a short-term electoral cycle, so decisions may be influenced by immediate considerations. Even the attempt to ensure that this is not the case via accountability may lead to increased costs (Dewatripont and Seabright 2006). Governments do not take decisions about ICP in a vacuum; they acquire advice and are lobbied, especially by industry. This process may lead to capture, with the policy furthering the industry interest rather than the public interest (Laffont 1996). For example, researchers may end up influencing decisions so that it is their pet projects rather than those in the interests of society that are financed. In addition, there is a positive correlation between research expenditure and researchers' incomes (Goolsbee 1998). A further potential problem with government policy that is likely to be a particular problem for ICP is corruption. So far, ICP faces significant problems of government failure, which can easily offset the benefits that might otherwise be achieved.

14.4 The control of state aid

The 1957 EEC Treaty did not provide for a common industrial policy. Common policies were necessary in areas where government intervention at the level of the member state (MS) was so extensive that freeing markets could only produce a distorted outcome and policy competition. Where these loomed large, and the political will was present, the problem was elevated to Community level and a 'common' policy was born. ICP was limited to Commission powers of supervision to ensure that state aid did not distort competition in the common market: 'Save as otherwise provided in this Treaty, any aid granted by a [MS] or through State resources in any form whatsoever which distorts or threatens to distort competition by favouring certain undertakings or the production of certain goods shall, in so far as it affects trade between [MSs], be incompatible with the common market' (Article 107).[3]

Apart from the introductory caveat, this is a sweeping prohibition. Its purpose is to prevent MSs' industrial policies from undermining the SEM. However, some industrial aid may be compatible with the common market: regional policy, 'important projects of common European interest', aid for 'certain economic activities' (shipyards are given as an example) and 'such other categories specified by decisions of the Council'. Thus the Commission was given considerable leeway in developing a policy with regard to state aid.

Article 108 empowers the Commission to 'keep under constant review all systems of aid' in MSs. It was some time before the Commission developed these powers into a 'policy', since the role of gendarme was not an easy one to assume when the miscreants were MSs. The 1960s and early 1970s were good years and ICP was not a big issue. The Commission's *First Report on Competition Policy* (CEU 1972) found that competition-distorting state aid was only significant in problem sectors such as shipbuilding, textiles and film production, and the Commission limited itself to exhortations to keep national aid within rather vague 'guidelines'. General aid schemes to promote investment were approved, and even dowries for industrial weddings in the French electronics industry (Machines Bull and CII) were passed without difficulty.

In the prolonged recession of the 1970s, characterized by high rates of inflation and unemployment, traditional macroeconomic policies were powerless to cope with this hitherto unprecedented combination. Firms continued to fail, unemployment to rise and exchange rates gyrated. Many EC MSs resorted to the direct subsidization of loss-making firms. To begin with, the Commission did not appreciate the

danger. It found that MSs, 'in an attempt to protect employment, were justified in boosting investment by granting firms financial benefits . . . it agreed to financial aid being granted to ensure the survival of firms which have run into difficulties, thereby avoiding redundancies' (CEU 1976, para. 133). The list of sectors 'in difficulty' expanded to include automobiles, paper, machine tools, steel, synthetic fibres, clocks and watches, and chemicals. The number of subsidy schemes notified to the Commission rose from a handful in the early 1970s to well over one hundred by the end of the decade.

Finally waking up to the danger, the Commission decided to take a less lenient view of subsidies (CEU 1979a, paras. 173–4), putting more emphasis on the 'need to restore competitiveness' and to 'face up to worldwide competition'. Thus a period of leniency, when subsidies were allowed, was followed by a crackdown, when the Commission vetted state aid much more closely. This coincided with an improvement in the economic situation and with MSs learning what was acceptable and unacceptable in state aid. So the number of formal investigations steadied, despite a rising number of cases, but the level of investigations is related to the business cycle, rising again with the slowdown after 1999. The rise in the number of cases and objections in 2004 is associated with cases in the new member states (NMS).

The change from the Commission permitting, under supervision, the continuing subsidization by MSs of 'sectors in difficulty' (coalmines, shipyards, textiles, and so on), to a more restrictive policy was associated with SEM development (see Chapters 2 and 7). This made it more important than ever that MSs should not thwart the competitive process by extensive use of state aid. The first step was to evaluate the extent of the problem, with a general report on state aid every three years.

The level of state aid[4] has been decreasing with changing attitudes towards it, Commission policy and peer pressure. State aid in the EU15 fell from 3 per cent of GDP in the 1980s, to 0.9 in 1992 and to 0.4 per cent in 2003, where it stabilized (CEU 2009g). All countries have participated in this trend, the most spectacular declines being registered by Belgium, Ireland and Italy, with most of the reductions taking place in the 1980s. Total aid in the EU15 in 2008 varied between 0.9 per cent in Portugal and 0.2 per cent in the UK (see Figure 14.1); in NMSs aid is generally higher, but more

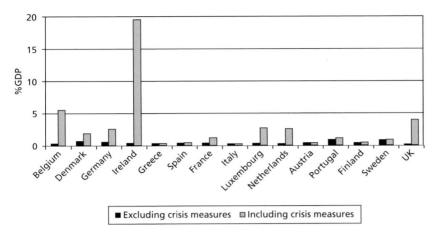

Figure 14.1 EU15 state aid 2008 *Source:* CEU 2009g

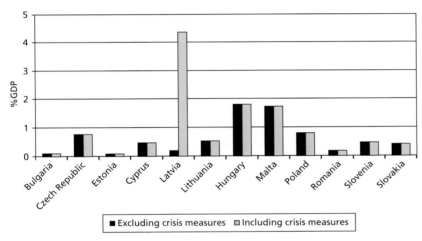

Figure 14.2 NMS state aid, 2008 *Source:* CEU 2009g

variable, with aid only 0.1 per cent in Bulgaria and Estonia, but 1.7 per cent in Malta (see Figure 14.2).

The breakdown of state aid by objective is changing over time. Sectoral aid is cyclical; in the 1980s and 1990s it fluctuated between 40 and 60 per cent of total aid, but since 1997 it has been on a downward trend, accounting for only 4.4 per cent in 2007. This fall in total aid is the result of falling aid to sectors such as steel and shipbuilding, as countries have accepted the diminished size of these industries and changing attitudes towards state aid. With the changing view of the government's role in ICP, the importance of horizontal programmes has increased to 82.5 per cent of the total in 2007,[5] but within this category there have

been changed priorities. Areas associated with competitiveness, such as employment and training, R&D and SMEs, along with the environment (another priority; see Chapter 18), have become more important. Regional aid has declined (see Chapter 22). The distinction between sectoral and horizontal is not clear-cut. The restructuring of East German industry after reunification, under the Treuhand, gave rise to a large number of firm-specific subsidies. Similar ad hoc company rescues have occurred in other countries. These were damaging to the SEM and to the Commission's reputation for maintaining fair competition. The Commission published guidelines in an attempt to contain the problem (CEU 2008b). *Rescue* aid must be given on a 'one time, last time' basis; it must be no more than a short-term holding operation and must take the form of transparent loans or loan guarantees. *Restructuring* aid must be justified by a detailed corporate plan to restore commercial viability. It is difficult to believe that R&D aid is available on demand without any of these limited restrictions.

Policy on state aid for R&D has developed from the first Framework on State Aid for Research and Development in 1986. This was generally favourable, but warned of the dangers of fruitless duplication of effort, pointed to the need for proper coordination by the Commission and required the notification of large R&D subsidies. Current rules require notification of aid of 5–20 million euros, depending on the type of aid.

The change in rules on R&D contributed to an increase in the number of cases investigated by the Commission from 1987 onwards. Other factors included the increase in EU membership and greater efforts to track such aid. Because of the growing caseload, a regulation to grant group exemptions for certain categories of state aid deemed compatible with the treaties was agreed (Council 1998b). The exempt categories are: horizontal aid (in particular, aid to SMEs, R&D, environmental protection, employment and training), regional aid and *de minimis* aid (aid so small as to have no discernible effect on competition; see page 206). This follows current thinking in allowing general aid and, in particular, aid to SMEs and R&D.

This picture of diminishing state aids was brought to an abrupt halt by the financial and economic crisis which began in 2007. This required not only unprecedented aid to the financial sector, but also to other sectors in difficulty as a result of the recession. Many of the measures used to support financial institutions were subject to state aid rules; the Commission recognized the need for fast action, but still needed to ensure that the measures were proportionate and did not unduly distort competition. Requirements for aid for banks were that it should be: non-discriminatory; time-limited; defined and limited in scope, including contributions from the private sector; containing rules to prevent use of state backing for market advantage; and requiring structural adjustment/restructuring of the institutions involved. Although aid was provided for individual banks, it was targeted at the whole financial sector to prevent contagion, so it came within the provision of Article 107(b) 'to remedy a serious

disturbance in the economy of a [MS]'. The extent of the problems of financial institutions was such that further detailed guidelines on recapitalization were issued in December 2008. The effects on the real economy were recognized by the Temporary Framework for State Aid supporting access to finance more generally. The need for state aid in clearing 'toxic assets' from bank balance sheets was recognized in the Communication on Impaired Assets in the Community Banking Sector. Finally, the Restructuring Communication laid out Commission criteria to ensure the long-term viability of financial institutions (CEU 2009h). The 2008 crisis expenditure raised total state aid in the EU15 from 0.4 per cent of GDP to 2.2 per cent, but it was not evenly spread: Ireland suffered worst, but there was also heavy expenditure in Belgium, Germany, Luxembourg, the Netherlands and the UK (see Figure 14.1, page 219). With the exception of Latvia, which, like Ireland, suffered from a collapse of its housing markets, NMSs did not require additional state aid to deal with the crisis (see Figure 14.2, page 219).[6]

The Commission has been gradually exerting its control over state aid, but national governments find it difficult to relinquish this policy instrument. The Commission still has problems enforcing discipline on MSs, but this is within the context of a declining overall level of state aid. There does seem to be a permanent improvement, associated with changing views on ICP. This is reflected in the growth of the EU's R&D programme and the Lisbon Strategy, to which the analysis now turns. The financial crisis has presented a challenge to state aid policy, but the Commission has managed to combine the speed and flexibility necessary for the emergency measures with a retention of control, especially of aid to non-financial companies.

14.5 Research and development policy

EU R&D policy is inspired by the idea that Europe fails to realize its full scientific and technological potential because its research efforts are dispersed, expensive and given to wasteful duplication. Much is made of the 'technology gap' which separates Europe from the USA and Japan. The answer, in the Commission's view, is to create a 'European research area' by fostering long-term collaborative ventures between Community firms; between European firms and publicly funded research institutions; and between universities at a European level. To this end, the EU uses two broad policy instruments: a dispensation from Article 107 for R&D collaborative agreements between large firms, and direct subsidies to encourage research.

14.5.1 Competition and trade aspects of research and development policy

The 1957 EEC Treaty makes provision for private sector cooperative R&D that 'contributes to improving the production or distribution of goods or to promoting technical or economic progress' (Article 107.3). In 1968 Commission guidelines permitted agreements between firms (even large ones) for the exclusive purpose of developing joint R&D, provided the cooperation remained 'pre-competitive' – that is, did not extend to actual production – and that the results of R&D were freely available to the members of the consortium, and preferably also to outsiders on a licensing basis (CEU 1972, paras. 31–2). In 1984 the Commission extended this to a block exemption for cooperative R&D schemes, which no longer had to be individually notified and could extend downstream to the joint exploitation, including the marketing, of the results. This represented a considerable shift in policy for which European industry had been lobbying, on the grounds that it made little sense to pool R&D efforts if, once they were successful, competition between the members of the pool wiped out all the potential monopolistic rents: under such circumstances, firms would prefer not to pool R&D resources at all, but take the risk of going it alone. This dispensation from normal anti-trust rules to permit long-term collaborative research agreements does not prejudge the sectors that will avail themselves of the opportunity; therefore it is horizontal industrial policy. The Commission effectively gave up investigating R&D state aid after it was subject to this exemption (Council 1998b).

In 1996 the Commission issued a new set of guidelines for state aid to R&D (CEU 1996l) to bring Community practice into line with new WTO obligations. In particular, the Commission highlighted the distinction between WTO-compatible support for R&D (squarely in the pre-competitive box) and illegal R&D support (aid for the commercial introduction of industrial innovations or the marketing of new products). Currently the Commission is notified about most aid,

limits are set on the intensity of aid dependent on the type of research and the size of enterprise, and thresholds are set for the different types of aid which trigger detailed assessment (CEU 2008b).

14.5.2 EU research and development policy[7]

The EEC Treaty had no provision for R&D policy and MSs were reluctant to cooperate in research, particularly as the experience of pooling nuclear research had not been a happy one (Guzzetti 1995). The origins of EU R&D policy lie in the problems of the European economy in the 1970s; by contrast, both the USA and Japan recovered quickly from their recessions. The EC's response, organized by Commissioner Viscount Davignon, was two-pronged: 'crisis cartels' in declining industries and support for 'sunrise' industries. He believed that there was a case for European high-technology firms to pool their R&D efforts, to avoid duplication and to benefit from trans-European synergies. Following Servan-Schreiber (1967), he and others were upset by the tendency of European firms to form technological alliances, if they did so at all, with American or Japanese partners, rather than with European companies.

Gradually a strategy emerged, linking universities, research institutes, the major European companies and some SMEs in an effort to narrow the 'technology gap' between Europe and the USA in electronics and information technology. A pilot programme in 1981 led to the first multi-annual framework research programme, an important component of which was the European Programme for Research in Information Technology (ESPRIT), which provided 750 million ECU of Community funding between 1984 and 1988, matched by private funding from the participating companies (Peterson and Sharp 1998). Calls for research proposals produced over 900 projects, only 240 of which were finally approved. This was followed by programmes in telecommunications research in advanced communication technologies for Europe (RACE) and basic research in technologies for Europe raw materials and advanced materials (BRITE/EURAM), launched in 1985, and a host of other programmes.

The Single European Act (SEA; 1987) provided a treaty basis for 'research and technological development', with the new aim 'to strengthen the scientific and technological bases of Community industry and to encourage it to become more competitive at the international level'. This led to a multi-annual framework programme of research funding. The Treaty on European Union (TEU; 1992) widened the policy to 'all the research activities deemed necessary by virtue of other Chapters of this Treaty' (Article 179). So research funding has been extended beyond the competitiveness of European industry to basic science and research connected with social objectives.

Although it is difficult to make comparisons because of the shifting categorization of the research programme, some trends are clear. Expenditure on research accounted for an increasing share of GDP between 1982 and 1994. From then until 2007, with budgetary tightening, the share stagnated. The new budgetary perspective has led to a significant increase in expenditure, but total research expenditure was still less than a fifth of agricultural market expenditure in 2009 (CEU 2010a, p. 72). Over the course of seven Framework Programmes (FP), EU R&D priorities have changed: FP1 and FP2 were dominated by energy and information and communications technology (ICT); while these remain priorities, they have become less important (CEU 2005f, 2009i). Industrial technologies, the third priority in the first four programmes, have been dropped. Life sciences (now health) have become more important, and new priorities have emerged, such as the environment and nanotechnology. The share of expenditure devoted to specific industrial priorities has declined and that on developing capacities has grown: 'ideas' (individual peer-reviewed projects); 'people' (the development researchers); and 'capacities' (the development of research infrastructure, encouraging research in SMEs, and research clusters). This changing distribution of research expenditure reflects changes in ideas about the priorities for research and how it should be fostered. In particular, the gradual reduction in the role of industrially targeted research is the result of a growing emphasis on developing capacities rather than targeting the shift from old to new ICP. There is also some concern that what is happening here is the capture with ever larger sums of money of projects close to the heart of industry and the research community. Yet EU expenditure on R&D remains relatively modest: it has risen from 2.3 per cent of national government research expenditure in 1985 to 9.6 per cent in 2002 (CEU 2004d, 2010a; Eurostat 2010d).

FP7 is also trying to create a European Research Area (ERA) to better coordinate European research. The Commission's contribution is the 'benchmarking of national research policies', and studying, comparing and evaluating individual MSs' R&D policies to identify 'best practices'. ERA is to prevent overlap, to make limited research funds go further and to ensure that a sufficient scale of activity can be financed (CEU 2009c). However, like all research policy, the problem is to reconcile the quirkiness of the unknown within a 'strategic' approach.

14.5.3 R&D policy: an assessment

EU ICP has come a long way from selective support to 'sunset' sectors and 'sunrise' industries to a policy designed to raise the EU's competitiveness more generally. The verdict on R&D policy is less clear-cut. The EU has tried hard to avoid the trap of 'picking the winners' by supporting only 'pre-competitive' R&D but funding has gone far beyond this. The fundamental problem remains the difficulty of identifying potentially successful projects. Inevitably the process is politicized, with countries increasingly concerned about their share of the funding (Peterson and Sharp 1998). There have been successes and failures – HDTV was a fiasco (European Court of Auditors 1995, paras. 9.12–9.49) – but clearly support for telecommunications research has paid off, since the European Global System for Mobile communications (GSM) proved to be a huge commercial success, and some of this success is perhaps attributable to the ESPRIT and BRITE programmes. It is still early to assess FP7; the evaluation of FP6 concluded that 'FP6's large investment in R&D produced high-quality research and results of scientific, industrial, social and policy interest' (Rietschel 2009, p. 46). The problem is that it is impossible to know what the *anti-monde* (see Chapter 9) would have been. The sums are huge, the opportunity costs are enormous, and the probability of a massive improvement on what markets would have achieved is small.

It is clear that EU R&D is becoming more involved with objectives other than competitiveness, such as the environment and regional policy. Is this to be welcomed or deplored? Care must be taken that a lack of focus does not lead to ineffectiveness and capture by interest groups.

14.6 EU economic reform and competitiveness

The development of EU ICP could be characterized as moving from support of specific initiatives to a general improvement of EU competences. This switch reflects changing views on the way to improve economic performance. The conventional wisdom is that the improvement of individual aspects of economic policy is not enough and interaction between policies is crucial – for example, reform of labour policies works more effectively when product markets are reformed. This leads to the idea that the competitiveness of the economy requires a very broad range of policies. Since the late 1990s internal and external factors have led to economic reform in this general sense becoming one of the key items on the EU's policy agenda. Economic reform is seen to be urgently required if the EU is going to be able to meet the social and economic aspirations of its citizens and fulfil its global obligations.

14.6.1 Reasons for economic reform

The EU was perceived to be 'confronted with a quantum shift from globalisation and the challenges of a new knowledge-driven economy' (European Council 2000a). The EU needed to ensure that its economy and society are able to meet new challenges and to maintain/improve its global competitiveness. EU productivity and employment are significantly below the USA's. In 2009 GDP per head was 75.1 per cent of the USA's level, partly due to the lower employment rate, and 5.5 per cent fewer hours worked (see Table 14.1). Strong pressure was exerted by some MSs – for example, Spain and the UK – to move forward on the liberalization agenda. The introduction of the euro in 1999 strengthened the argument for more flexibility in the labour, product and capital markets, and introduced a new sense of urgency to reform.

14.6.2 The development of the Lisbon Strategy

The Lisbon Strategy (LS) was the culmination of a number of EU developments. The introduction of an 'Industry' title in the TEU (1992; Article 173) gave the Community a broad mandate to promote the competitiveness of European industry by improving its

Table 14.1 Productivity and employment in the EU15 and the USA, 2009

	GDP per head	Employment rate	GDP per worker	Hours worked
EU15	75.1	67.5	80.4	94.5
USA	100.0	71.2	100.0	100.0

Source: OECD 2010b

ability to adjust to structural change, encouraging SMEs, favouring cooperation between enterprises and increasing the effectiveness of EC R&D. The Treaty of Amsterdam (1997) provided the legal base for 'developing a coordinated strategy for employment and particularly for promoting a skilled, trained and adaptable workforce and labour markets responsive to economic change' (Article 145). These objectives are to be achieved by the 'open method of coordination' (see Chapters 4 and 23). Under the UK's presidency, the Cardiff European Council agreed that the Broad Economic Guidelines introduced under the EMU process should be developed as a key tool for economic recovery and self-sustaining, non-inflationary growth (European Council 1998; see Chapters 11 and 12). This council also highlighted the need for fresh initiatives to promote entrepreneurship and competitiveness, especially encouraging small businesses and innovation, improving the skills and flexibility of the labour market, and making the capital market more efficient. The Cologne European Council shaped the agenda for the planned Lisbon Council by arguing that 'the jobs of the future will be created by innovation and the information society' (European Council 1999b).

The Lisbon European Council brought together these initiatives in a comprehensive policy strategy. There was a new strategic goal for the next decade: 'to become the most competitive and dynamic knowledge-based economy in the world, capable of sustainable economic growth with more and better jobs and greater social cohesion' (European Council 2000a).

Achieving this goal requires an overall strategy that aims to:

- prepare the transition to a knowledge-based economy and society by better policies for the information society and R&D, as well as by stepping up the process of structural reform for competitiveness and innovation and by completing SEM;

- modernize the European social model, investing in people and combating social exclusion;
- sustain the healthy economic outlook and favourable growth prospects by applying an appropriate macroeconomic policy mix (European Council 2000a, I5.5).

To say that the LS was all-embracing is an understatement. It encompassed new technologies, particularly ICT; research and innovation; encouraging entrepreneurship and SMEs; a fully operational SEM, including services; liberalization of network industries; integrated financial markets; promotion of competition and reduction of state aid; coordination of macroeconomic policy; fiscal consolidation; reform of tax and benefit systems to improve employment; more and better jobs; modernizing the European social model; lifelong learning; increasing physical and human capital; equal opportunities; work–life balance; improved childcare provision; and promoting social inclusion. There are three reasons for the breadth of this agenda. The first is the belief that improving economic performance requires a wide range of interrelated measures. The second is that this is the result of a bargaining process to achieve unanimity where individual national leaders ensured that measures particularly important to them were included. And the third is that it is a reflection of the fact that there is considerable disagreement over how economic performance should be improved. One group of countries, led by the UK, believed that liberalization, particularly of the labour market, was essential, while others were keen to retain their high levels of protection of workers. There was therefore a need to include in the LS elements of the European social model. Thus the LS contained twenty-eight main objectives, 120 objectives and 117 indicators. This wide and somewhat contradictory LS, differing attitudes (Boeri 2005) and the reliance on an open method of coordination (see Sections 23.2, 23.5.1, page 364 and 370) undermined its effectiveness.

The LS operated during 2000–2010 and a mid-point evaluation was very critical: 'Lisbon is about everything and thus nothing' (Kok 2004, p. 16). The mid-term review of the policy (CEU 2005g) recognized these problems and sought to make the policy more focused and raised its status. Lisbon 2 had three priorities, concentrating on growth and jobs: making Europe a

more attractive place to invest and work, completing the SEM and business-friendly regulation; knowledge and innovation for growth: raising expenditure on R&D; and creating more and better jobs, by raising the labour force's adaptability, education and skills. Even this slimmed-down agenda involved a multiplicity of objectives, which widened further when concerns over the downgrading of environmental and social aspects led to their being re-emphasized in the agreement on the revised agenda (European Council 2005a). The Commission also tried to achieve more by 'bending' other policies, such as competition and structural policy, to achieve the LS's objectives.

The Commission has proposed a new Strategy, 'Europe 2020: A strategy for smart, sustainable and inclusive growth' (CEU 2010b), which has been adopted by the European Council (2010c). This looks awfully like Lisbon 3, with targets for an employment rate of 75 per cent,[8] R&D at 3 per cent of GDP, the environment, education and reductions in poverty. To overcome some of the LS's problems, national targets will vary according to starting points and there will be closer monitoring. But doubts remain whether this will be sufficient to overcome the weaknesses of the LS (Euractiv 2010).

14.6.3 The outcomes of the Lisbon Strategy

The LS can be judged on two levels: whether it has changed MS policies and whether these changes in policy have improved EU performance. There has been reform, tax burdens have been reduced, regulations eased and labour markets liberalized, but the changes have not been sufficiently widespread, comprehensive or deep. The policy reform has been no greater than that achieved by non-EU OECD members, so the LS does not seem to have had much impact on policy (Tilford and Whyte 2010).

The LS does not seem to have had much impact on the EU's economic performance. The familiar adverse comparison with the USA is confirmed by Table 14.2. Economic growth of real GDP in the EU15 was marginally higher from 1998 to 2007, at 2.4 per cent, than it was from 1988 to 1997, when it was at 2.3 per cent. Higher growth was achieved by the USA and a group of comparable OECD countries, comprising Australia, Canada, New Zealand and Switzerland (ACNZS), with

Table 14.2 Growth of real GDP in the EU15, the USA, Japan and ACNZS, 1978–2009

	Annual % growth rate				
	1978–87	1988–97	1998–2007	1998–2008	1998–2009
	Real GDP				
EU15	2.2	2.3	2.4	2.2	1.7
USA	3.1	3.0	3.0	2.8	2.4
Japan	4.2	2.9	1.2	0.9	0.4
Australia, Canada, New Zealand and Switzerland (ACNZS)	2.5	2.2	3.1	2.0	1.5
	Real GDP per person employed				
EU15	1.8	1.8	1.3	1.2	0.9
USA	1.2	1.4	2.1	2.0	1.9
Japan	3.4	2.0	1.6	1.4	1.0
ACNZS	0.9	1.0	1.1	0.9	0.8
	Real GDP per hour worked				
EU15[1]	2.2	2.3	1.7	1.5	1.3
USA	1.2	1.4	2.3	2.2	2.2
Japan	3.6	3.2	2.1	1.9	1.7
ACNZS	1.2	1.2	1.4	1.2	1.1

Note:

[1] EU15 excluding Greece, Luxembourg and Portugal 1978–87, and excluding Austria 1978–97.

Source: CEU 2010c; OECD 2010b; own calculations

this group marginally worse than the EU15 during 1988–97. Japan's growth rate was high until the early 1990s, when economic problems led to very low growth which continues.

Overall GDP growth depends not only on changes in productivity but also on changes in the inputs used: the amount of labour and capital. Calculating the growth of real GDP per person in employment provides a macro measure of productivity. Using this measure, a different picture emerges: EU15 productivity growth was significantly higher than the USA's from 1978 to 1997, but EU15 productivity growth slowed significantly after 1998, while US productivity growth rose. This slower productivity was associated with faster employment growth (see Chapter 23), but the USA managed to combine employment growth with rapid productivity growth. ACNZS productivity growth remained below that of the EU15 throughout, but the gap narrowed in the later period. Japan had higher productivity growth in all periods, but suffered a greater reduction in the rate.

The amount of labour available for production is dependent not only on the number of workers, but also on how many hours they work, and trends differ between countries: the average number of hours worked in the EU15[9] declined by 9.5 per cent between 1978 and 2007, but by only 2.5 per cent in the USA. Taking account of these changes in hours of work by calculating GDP per hour worked: the EU15 had faster growth of GDP per hour worked than the USA during 1978–97, but then productivity growth slowed while the USA's productivity rose. The EU15 had superior productivity growth to ACNZS over the whole period, but the difference narrowed after 1998. Japan's growth in productivity per hour worked was higher than the EU throughout, but the rate was declining.

So far the discussion has been about the period up to 2007, before the economic crisis and its associated recession. This is appropriate because the issue is long-term, but to a significant extent recent trends were driven by factors leading to the crisis; some recent growth was the result of 'bubble' activity, particularly in finance and housing. Whether this will alter the conclusions on productivity growth we do not know. The long-term results will also depend on the recovery from the crisis. Europe has responded with fewer job losses and a loss of productivity, while the USA has maintained productivity growth but shed workers – which will prove more effective, only time will tell.

To summarize, the EU15's productivity growth was relatively good from 1978 to 1997, but since 1998 it has declined as higher employment growth has been at the expense of productivity. The USA managed to raise productivity growth and combine it with employment growth. The EU15's productivity problem is well documented (Sapir *et al.* 2003b; Denis *et al.* 2005; Palazuelos and Fernandez 2010) and is seen to be associated with retaining significant production in low- and medium-technology industries, an ICT sector that is too small and a failure to achieve the productivity benefits of ICT, especially in service industries (Gordon 2004; Inklaar *et al.* 2005).

14.6.4 Assessing the Lisbon process

Most of the objectives and policy measures contained in the LS were not new. They were brought together in a high-profile package to demonstrate the EU's determination to embrace the reform agenda. This was to raise the public profile of the reform agenda in order to encourage national government action. The LS's political importance was recognized by the central role played by the heads of state and government, who were involved in an annual cycle of reports and meetings, which helped to maintain momentum, but there is frustration at the slowness to translate fine-sounding slogans into concrete reforms.

The Lisbon commitment is rhetorical and was agreed at the height of the dotcom boom. The breadth of the policy reveals the difference in priorities between MSs. Some are only committed to parts of the LS: the policy is not really owned by the governments which had to drive it forward. These problems have meant that there has been a failure to agree and implement measures. The policy lacked financial incentives to encourage compliance. The EU has made only limited progress on the core commitments, and the economic achievements have been limited.

14.6.5 A radical view of the Lisbon strategy

Do we really want to be the world's most productive economy? Economists are increasingly questioning the link between material living standards and happiness. Becoming the world's most competitive economy might require long working hours and very rapid structural change in the economy. EU countries have consistently shown in the choices they have made – for example, over their welfare systems – that this is not what they really want. The USA enjoys a higher level of GDP than the EU average, but in the USA hours of work are longer, holidays are fewer, retirement is later and inequality is much greater. The EU has problems over unemployment among the young, early retirement and the sustainability of pensions systems, but to many the US model does not seem attractive.

Is it necessary? There is an implicit assumption that failure to be the best in the world implies declining living standards and general deterioration. Countries such as the UK failed to keep up with the growth of other countries for at least one hundred years, while still enjoying rising living standards and retaining an important role in the world. There is a false analogy between the competitiveness of companies and the competitiveness of countries. If companies are not competitive they will become bankrupt and will cease to exist. If countries do not maintain their competitiveness relative to other countries, their relative living standards will decline, but they will not go bankrupt, since they can still enjoy reasonable standards of living.

Do we really know how to raise overall economic performance? Countries succeed with very different economic institutions and policies. While there is general agreement that sound macroeconomic policies, the rule of law and good institutions are essential, there is little agreement beyond this. Indeed appropriate policies may vary between countries, so the policy choices are not clear-cut, otherwise governments would be likely to follow them anyway.

14.7 Conclusion

The development of ICP in the EU reflects changing economic circumstances and ideas about the appropriate role of government. But the one constant has been the desire of governments to improve economic performance, first in narrow problem areas, but then more generally. The principal shift has been from intervention to encourage national champions or sunrise sectors, to more generally providing a suitable environment for the private sector to flourish. The understandable desire to help particular companies/industries in trouble remains, and so do some vestiges of interventionist industrial policy in the form of strategic sectors. With these developments the EU's role has changed and the 1975 EEC Treaty powers to control state aid have gradually evolved to become more effective. In addition to merely overseeing MSs' ICP, the EU has gradually developed a role in ICP. At first this was in relation to R&D policy, where the EU was viewed as a way of enhancing national policies; this has developed to become an important part of the EU's overall research effort. With the simultaneous processes of globalization and Europeanization, national power over economic policy has diminished, and concern has mounted over the performance of EU economies and the ability to sustain European standards in relation to employment, pensions and the environment. The response to this has been the development of a widening European economic policy agenda, encompassed in the LS and economic policy coordination.

ICP has always suffered from the ability of interest groups to exploit policy so that their interests rather than the public good are served, and this problem remains. The developing EU ICP also suffers from two other major problems. The first is the difficulty of achieving a coherent policy when so many conflicting views have to be reconciled. The second is the difficulty of ensuring that the policy is implemented when major elements remain national responsibilities. The first problem led to the rather ramshackle edifice of the LS, which tried to be all things to all people. Furthermore, it is difficult to achieve the consistency required of a policy which seeks to change long-term economic performance. The second problem is one of delivery: the implementation of LS policy is largely in the hands of MSs whose policies do not seem to have been significantly changed by the LS. One cannot be optimistic that the Europe 2020 initiative will be any more successful.

Summary

- ICP is designed to improve the long-term performance of the economy – that is, economic growth and employment, which encompasses a wide range of policies.
- Instruments used include: subsidies/tax breaks, regulation/deregulation, public procurement, education reform, subsidization of infrastructure and R&D.
- The theoretical justification of ICP is based on externalities and imperfect competition.
- In imperfectly competitive markets, characterized by first-mover advantages, barriers, including economies of scale, and particular infrastructure requirements there may be a case for ICP to shape national competitiveness.
- Externalities in networks, agglomerations and R&D may justify ICP.
- The government may also have a role in encouraging entrepreneurship and SMEs.
- Views over ICP have changed over time: in the early post-war period there was perceived to be an important government role in enhancing the growth of the economy, encouraging new (sunrise) industries and managing the decline of old (sunset) industries.
- It is now accepted that government intervention also has problems of knowledge, capture and corruption, so the current view is that ICP interventions need to be considered very carefully.
- EU state aid policy has followed a similar trajectory, from a generally laissez-faire attitude to tight monitoring and control of government help to industry, contributing to a downward trend of such intervention.
- The financial and economic crisis led to very high levels of aid to the financial sector and threatened to undermine this EU control of state aids, but the Commission managed to combine sufficient flexibility and speed with continued control.
- The EU has developed a very significant R&D policy, which seeks to encourage cooperation across national boundaries and to reduce wasteful duplication. This policy has moved more towards the development of research competences.
- In 2000 the Lisbon Strategy was introduced, 'to become the most competitive and dynamic

knowledge-based economy in the world, capable of sustainable economic growth with more and better jobs and greater social cohesion'.

- The results have been disappointing: the policy was overambitious, too wide-ranging and with only a limited commitment from MSs that would have to carry out the measures.
- The LS has not improved the EU's productivity performance.
- The LS operated from 2000 to 2010; a similar strategy, Europe 2020, has now been introduced for the period 2010–20.
- It is argued that the LS is misconceived and its objective and methods can be questioned.

Questions and essay topics

1. What is ICP? What government policy measures does it cover?
2. Why might ICP be necessary if markets are imperfectly competitive?
3. Explain what is meant by network externalities.
4. Explain what is meant by agglomeration economies.
5. Explain what is meant by R&D externalities.
6. Consider how ICP can adjust for these externalities.
7. Explain the idea of government failure in relation to ICP.
8. Why are entrepreneurship and SMEs particularly important for economic performance?
9. What aspects of ICP can be used to increase entrepreneurship and the development of SMEs?
10. What are the main elements of EU state aid policy?
11. Consider how state aid policy has developed since 1958.
12. Why did the financial and economic crisis that began in 2007 pose particular problems for state aid policy?
13. Evaluate how effectively DG COMP responded to this challenge.
14. Examine the case of EU R&D policy.
15. Describe the way in which EU R&D policy has developed.

16. Evaluate the success of EU R&D policy.
17. What was the Lisbon Strategy (LS)?
18. Why was it difficult to get LS measures implemented?
19. Assess the impact of the LS.
20. Do you think Europe 2020 resolves the LS problems?
21. Was the LS appropriate and necessary?

FURTHER READING

Buigues, P.-A. and Sekkat, K. (2009) *Industrial Policy in Europe, Japan and the USA: Amounts, Mechanism and Effectiveness*, Palgrave Macmillan, Basingstoke.

Tilford, S. and Whyte, P. (2010) *The Lisbon Scorecard X: The Road to 2020*, Centre for European Reform, London.

NOTES

1 As well as the failure of individual companies, illustrated vividly in 2005 by the final demise of Rover, the supposed national champion of the UK motor vehicle industry.

2 Innovation is still possible without patent protection because the innovator will enjoy benefits until the innovation is copied. There may also be first-mover advantages.

3 Article numbers refer to the latest version of the Consolidated Treaty (CEU 2008a).

4 Total aid, excluding agriculture, fisheries, transport and, in 2008, crisis measures.

5 Because of the decline in overall aid, even expenditure on horizontal objectives has declined in real terms.

6 Although the effect on their real economies was significant and in some cases severe.

7 EU research programmes are supplemented by the Eureka (European Research Coordinating Agency) programme launched in 1985, which today encompasses forty European countries which cooperate on research. In the early 1990s Eureka expenditure was almost as large as Framework Programmes, but today Eureka is much smaller than FP. Eureka concentrates on near market research and so is complementary to FP pre-competitive research.

8 For 20- to 64-year-olds.

9 See Table 14.2, note 1.

15 Tax harmonization

BRIAN ARDY AND ALI EL-AGRAA

15.1 Introduction

Tax harmonization has been a very thorny issue for the EU: witness the vehement argument in the 1980s when Margaret Thatcher, British prime minister, flatly declared that tax harmonization was not EU business, only to be told by Helmut Kohl, German chancellor, and Jacques Delors, Commission president, that it was indispensable for EU integration. Such a bold statement cannot be treated lightly, since tax harmonization remains one of the few areas where new EU legislation requires unanimity: hence a single EU member state (MS) can frustrate any new initiatives in this domain.

Tax harmonization is the agreement and application of common rules for taxation across the entire EU. This involves three separate aspects: the object of taxation – that is, what is to be taxed; the tax base – that is, agreement on the calculation of what is to be taxed; and harmonization of rates. The first purpose of this chapter is to clarify what they mean. The second is to consider to what extent tax harmonization is necessary for the EU. And the third is to assess the progress the EU has achieved in this respect. The chapter finishes with conclusions.

15.2 Why is tax harmonization necessary?

Tax harmonization is the agreement and application of common rules for taxation across the EU. This involves three separate aspects: first, the object of taxation – what is to be taxed; second, the tax base – agreement on the calculation of what is to be taxed; third, harmonization of rates. Tax harmonization in the EU so far has been very limited, with an agreed base for the Value Added Tax (VAT), and minimum rates for VAT, alcohol, cigarette and energy taxation, plus some agreements to limit unfavourable interaction between national tax systems.

The government plays a very important role in modern economies: in 2008 tax revenue accounted for 39.3 per cent of EU27 GDP.[1] Normally tax and government expenditure is primarily the responsibility of the highest tier of government, the federal or central government. As is demonstrated in Chapter 19, this is not the case in the EU, since MSs control most tax revenue and are responsible for most government expenditure. This makes the EU unusual because there is a large variation of taxes and government expenditures in a single market.

There are two basic types of taxation: direct and indirect. Direct taxes, such as income and corporation taxes, are levied on wages and salaries (income taxes), or on the profits of business (corporation taxes; CT). Direct taxes are not intended to affect the price of commodities or professional services.[2] Indirect taxes are levied specifically on consumption and are therefore, in a simplistic model, significant in determining the pricing of commodities.

Taxes can act as non-tariff barriers (NTBs) to international trade (see Chapters 2, 6 and 7), as well as affecting the international movement of factors of production (Bhagwati 1969; Johnson 1965a; and Chapter 8). Therefore, to complete the Single European Market (SEM), and to realize the four freedoms for the movement of goods, services, persons and capital, some degree of tax harmonization is required in the EU.

The other reason for tax harmonization is that the ability of national tax systems to raise revenues, and the efficiency effects that they have, are affected by the tax regimes in the other MSs – for example, the revenue from tobacco taxation will depend on the rates of taxation in neighbouring MSs. Thus there can be positive or negative spillovers/externalities between MSs' tax systems. The movement of factors of production can be influenced by government tax and expenditure policies. The administrative and compliance costs for the government and taxpayers may be affected, and the ability of national governments to pursue redistributive policies is constrained. Tax harmonization in the EU is the alignment of tax bases, rules and rates to reduce the harmful interactions between different MSs' tax systems.[3]

15.3 The principles of tax harmonization

Three criteria should inform tax harmonization: *jurisdiction*, *distortion* and *enforcement*.

Jurisdiction is the determination of who should receive the revenue from a particular tax. With EU taxation tightly controlled, MSs are the jurisdiction for the overwhelming majority of tax revenue, but this sovereignty has to be pooled for the effective operation of national tax systems in the SEM. Transparency is required, with clear definitions of tax bases and regulations. The operational independence of national tax systems should be possible within agreed rules; cooperation and information exchange should not be part of the day-to-day operation of the tax system. The clearest example of the jurisdictional principle applies to consumption taxes and the choice between the destination and origin principles (see Section 15.4, page 232). Labour taxes are usually paid in the country of *residence*, which is normally the same as the *source* country where the income is earned. Income from capital is taxed at source in the case of CT, but income is also subject to residence-based tax. Where more than one tax jurisdiction is involved, the interaction between national tax systems becomes important.

Distortion concerns the avoidance of tax-induced inefficiency in the operation of the SEM. Spillover/externalities can occur as a result of the operation of tax systems. The most common externality is tax competition, which will tend to lead to lower tax rates, because governments fear the loss of the tax base to countries with lower rates. This will reduce tax revenues overall and increase the marginal cost of public funds.[4] Tax competition encourages the taxation of less mobile tax bases and may cause lower provision of government services. Whether this is a problem is debatable; it can be argued that tax competition acts as a necessary discipline on government fiscal profligacy.

The extent of the problem of distortion depends on the type and rate of tax. There are particular problems with excises on products such as alcohol and tobacco, with enormous differences in rates. Tax competition is not a significant problem with labour taxation because of the very low degree of international mobility in the EU[5] (Braunerhjelm *et al.* 2000, pp. 46–59; Chapter 8). High-tax countries would also tend to offer a higher provision of public services, offsetting the higher taxes. The high mobility of capital, especially in an economic and monetary union (EMU), means that capital will tend to move to where taxation is lowest. This process will continue until differences in the return on capital offset differences in taxation and returns on immovable factors, labour and land prices are accordingly depressed in high capital tax countries.

Enforcement is the ability to ensure that the agreed rules apply in practice. Large differences in excise taxes on cigarettes are difficult to enforce in the absence of borders. Taxes on labour are usually withheld by employers at source and so are relatively easy to enforce. CT poses particular enforcement problems. If the tax is based on the source of the income, this requires separate national accounting for each MS, but this is not possible for multinational corporations (MNs), so unsatisfactory, ad hoc arrangements are necessary. The location of profits can also be shifted by the manipulation of transfer prices[6] and other methods. Taxes based on residence also face problems associated with the need to allow for taxes paid elsewhere.

National tax independence within the EU necessitates a significant degree of tax coordination to ensure the effective operation of tax systems. The analysis now turns to the four principle areas of harmonization: VAT, excise duties, energy taxes and CT (see Table 15.1).

15.4 Value added tax

In the 1957 EEC Treaty tax harmonization is solely concerned with indirect taxes. Harmonization was seen as vital for preventing indirect taxes from acting as NTBs on intra-EU trade. However, the treaty only required the harmonization necessary to ensure the establishment and functioning of a single market. The treaty is rather vague about what it means by harmonization, but this is normal; treaties lay down the objective, while further negotiations lead to detailed legislation.

Table 15.1 EU27 tax structure, 2008 (% of GDP)

	Personal income tax	Corporation tax	Social contributions	VAT	Excises	*Total tax revenue*
Belgium	12.6	3.3	13.9	7.0	2.1	44.3
Denmark	25.3	3.4	1.0	10.1	3.2	48.2
Germany	9.6	1.1	15.1	7.0	2.5	39.3
Greece	4.7	2.5	12.2	7.1	2.3	32.6
Spain	7.5	2.9	12.3	5.3	2.1	33.1
France	7.7	2.8	16.1	7.0	2.0	42.8
Ireland	8.2	2.9	5.3	7.1	2.4	29.3
Italy	11.7	3.2	13.4	5.9	1.9	42.8
Luxembourg	7.7	5.1	10.1	6.0	3.5	35.6
Netherlands	7.2	3.4	14.5	7.3	2.4	39.1
Austria	10.4	2.6	14.4	7.8	2.5	42.8
Portugal	5.8	3.7	11.9	8.7	2.8	36.7
Finland	13.3	3.5	12.1	8.4	3.4	43.1
Sweden	14.2	3.0	11.3	9.4	2.8	47.1
UK	10.7	3.6	6.8	6.3	3.2	37.3
EU15 average[1]	**10.4**	**3.1**	**11.4**	**7.4**	**2.6**	**39.6**
Bulgaria	3.0	3.3	8.1	11.5	6.1	33.3
Czech Republic	4.0	4.4	16.2	7.1	3.4	36.1
Estonia	6.3	1.7	11.8	8.0	3.3	32.2
Cyprus	5.0	7.1	7.7	11.3	3.3	39.2
Latvia	6.3	3.1	8.2	6.6	3.2	28.9
Lithuania	6.6	2.8	9.0	8.1	3.1	30.3
Hungary	7.7	2.6	13.8	7.8	3.4	40.4
Malta	5.8	6.8	6.2	8.0	3.1	34.5
Poland	5.4	2.7	11.4	8.0	4.4	34.3
Romania	3.4	3.0	9.3	7.9	2.7	28.0
Slovenia	5.9	2.5	14.1	8.4	3.4	37.3
Slovakia	2.8	3.1	12.0	6.9	2.7	29.1
NMS10 average[1]	**5.2**	**3.6**	**10.7**	**8.3**	**3.5**	**33.6**
EU27 average[1]	**8.1**	**3.3**	**11.0**	**7.8**	**3.0**	**37.0**

Note: [1] Arithmetic average
Source: Eurostat 2010c

At EEC inception there were four types of sales, or turnover, taxes operating in Western Europe (Dosser 1973; Paxton 1976). One was the *cumulative multi-stage cascade system* (West Germany, Luxembourg and the Netherlands), where the tax was levied on the gross value of the commodity at each stage of production, without any rebate on taxes paid at earlier stages. Another was the *value added tax* (VAT; in France), levied at each stage of production as a percentage of the value of sales less tax levied at earlier stages of production.[7] A third was *mixed* systems (Belgium and Italy). The fourth was the *purchase tax* (UK), a single-stage tax charged at the wholesale stage by registered manufacturers or wholesalers, which meant that manufacturers could trade with each other without paying tax.

Although all these tax systems had a common treatment of trade, with no tax paid on exports, and tax levied on imports at the point of entry, the cumulative systems involved distortions. Since the amount of tax in cumulative systems varied with the number of transactions in the supply chain, the precise amount of tax to be remitted on exports could not be calculated accurately, and nor could the tax on imports; this meant that these taxes could be used as NTBs.[8]

The EEC adopted VAT as its turnover tax and a common base[9] was agreed. Having chosen the tax and the tax base, the EEC had to decide on the tax jurisdiction, using either the 'destination' or 'origin' principle. Under the destination principle, tax revenue would be attributable to the country of final purchase. For example, if the UK levies VAT at 8 per cent and France at 16 per cent, a commodity exported from the UK to France would be exempt from UK tax but would be subject to the tax in France. Hence France would collect the tax revenue and the UK's exports would compete on equal terms with French products in the French market. Under the origin principle, tax revenue would be distributed according to the value added in each country. Hence a commodity exported by the UK to France would pay UK tax (8 per cent), and in France additional tax would be levied to bring the overall tax on the commodity to 16 per cent. Under strict conditions, equivalence would apply: tax revenue and its distribution would be the same under the destination and origin principles. These conditions are that the tax systems in both countries must be exactly the same in terms of base, rules and rates, and trade should be balanced. In this situation the tax collected from foreign countries on exports would be the same as the tax paid to foreign countries on imports. In the absence of these conditions, the destination and origin principles will lead to an uneven distribution of the tax burden between countries. The destination principle requires border tax adjustments, so it was argued that a borderless EU needed a shift to the origin principle (Shibata 1967). In the absence of the equivalence conditions, both systems involve potential jurisdiction and distortion problems, so it is practical issues that will decide the choice of system (Bovenberg 1994; Lockwood et al. 1994). The EEC decided to use the destination principle, which is consistent with undistorted intra-EU trade, provided that customs controls remain. This decision ensured that the EEC continued to have separate national markets divided by physical borders. Changes were needed once these physical borders were eliminated by the SEM.

There are three fundamental problems with VAT: first, the definition of the tax base; second, the widespread use of multiple rate VAT; third, the treatment of cross-border trade. Under current legislation (Council 2010a), exemptions from VAT include: activities such as healthcare, education, social services, cultural services, public broadcasting, postal services, leasing/letting property, insurance, financial transactions and gambling; and organizations, public bodies, small business and farmers. Public bodies are exempt because it seems strange for the government to tax itself, but recent experience of privatization and contracting out has indicated that there is no clear division between public and private activities. The exemption of small business is the result of the high, largely fixed cost of operating VAT, which would function as regressive tax on small business.[10] The compliance costs of VAT are estimated to be 2 per cent of turnover for small businesses (turnover below 60,000 euros), but only 0.3 per cent for large companies (turnover greater than 1 million euros) (Sandford et al. 1989). The problem with exemptions is that they can lead to distortions in prices, reduce the efficiency of tax collection and increase compliance and administration costs. A wider tax base with fewer exemptions is desirable.

The EU is still a long way from achieving the approximation of VAT rates envisaged in the SEM White Paper (CEU 1985a). All countries respect the minimum standard rate of 15 per cent, with a range from 15 per cent in Luxembourg and Cyprus to 25 per cent in Denmark and Sweden (see Table 15.2). Lower rates vary between 0 and 10 per cent, with the majority of countries operating multiple-rate VAT. A long list of exceptions complicates the system considerably.

The extent to which the variation in rates represents a problem with regard to cross-border shopping is arguable. Evidence suggests that its magnitude diminishes rapidly with distance, and differences in excises seem to be more important, accounting for two-thirds of the value of cross-border shopping (Bygrä et al. 1987; Fitzgerald et al. 1988). Similarly, Commission studies find that the abolition of border controls has not led to significant changes in cross-border shopping patterns, distortions of competition or changes in trade, due to differences in VAT rates (European Parliament 2001b). So there does not seem to be any great need to further harmonize VAT rates to reduce distortions caused by cross-border shopping.

The existence of multiple rates is much more questionable. The major reason for special exemptions and

Table 15.2 VAT in EU member states, 2008

	VAT rates (%)		VAT revenue (%)	
	Standard	Other	Total tax revenue	GDP
Single rate				
Denmark	25.0	–	21.0	10.1
Dual rate				
Bulgaria	20.0	7.0	34.5	11.5
Czech Republic	19.0	9.0	19.5	7.1
Germany	19.0	7.0	17.9	7.0
Estonia	18.0	5.0	24.9	8.0
Hungary	20.0	5.0	19.3	7.8
Latvia	18.0	5.0	23.0	6.6
Malta	18.0	5.0	23.3	8.0
Netherlands	19.0	6.0	18.6	7.3
Austria	20.0	10.0	18.2	8.0
Romania	19.0	9.0	28.2	7.6
Slovakia	19.0	10.0	23.6	6.9
Slovenia	20.0	8.5	22.6	8.4
UK	17.5	5.0	17.0	6.3
Multiple rate				
Belgium	21.0	6.0/12.0	15.8	7.0
Greece	19.0	4.5/9.0	21.8	7.1
Spain	16.0	4.0/7.0	15.9	5.3
France	19.6	2.1/5.5	16.4	7.0
Ireland	21.0	4.8/13.5	24.4	7.1
Italy	20.0	4.0/10.0	13.8	5.9
Cyprus	15.0	5.0/8.0	28.9	11.3
Lithuania	18.0	5.0/9.0	26.6	8.1
Luxembourg	15.0	3.0/6.0/12.0	16.8	6.0
Poland	22.0	3.0/7.0	23.4	8.0
Portugal	20.0	5.0/12.0	23.6	8.7
Finland	22.0	8.0/17.0	19.4	8.4
Sweden	25.0	6.0/12.0	20.0	9.4
Arithmetic average EU15	**19.9**		**18.7**	**7.4**
Arithmetic average NMS10	**18.8**		**24.8**	**8.3**
Arithmetic average EU27	**19.4**		**21.4**	**7.8**
Minimum rates	*15.0*	*15.0*		

Source: Eurostat 2010a

reduced rates is to limit the regressive impact of VAT,[11] but the major beneficiaries of such exemptions are not the poor. The conclusion of a 1988 study, which has been supported by subsequent evidence,[12] was that the distribution of the tax burden was not very different if products were zero-rated (the UK), taxed at a reduced rate (the Netherlands) or even at the same rate as other goods and services (Denmark) (OECD 1988b). Thus, although expenditure on food is proportionally higher for poorer groups, the better-off spend more in absolute terms, thus the improvement in the progressivity of the tax system is minor. 'Differentiated VAT rates are an ineffective, ill targeted instrument for eliminating the impact of the tax on the poor' (Cnossen 2002, p. 492).

Multiple rates are also not without cost, since they increase the administrative complexity of the system and cause problems of compliance. One study suggested that UK firms found that having multiple rates rather than a single rate doubled compliance costs (Hemming and Kay 1981). Imposing an additional VAT rate also reduces the compliance rate by 7 per cent (Agha and Houghton 1996). This is not surprising when one realizes that the following factors need to be considered in applying the zero rate to food in the UK: 'place of consumption, timing of consumption, temperature, saltiness, number, volume, concentration, sugar content, use of fingers in consumption and alcoholic content' (Cnossen 2002, p. 493). There is, therefore, no economic or social justification for the continued use of multiple rates.

The EU responded to the abolition of fiscal borders in the SEM with a transitional regime of cross-border trade on a deferred payment or postponed accounting basis. Under this system exports are free of VAT, but the exporter must inform the fiscal authorities in the country it is exporting to. Importers must declare imports and pay VAT at the local rate. A VAT Information Exchange System (VEIS) reinforces checks by requiring registered businesses to file quarterly reports of exports and imports. In the past the Commission has argued that the deferred payment system is bureaucratic, creates additional administrative burdens for companies and is subject to fraud. The European Parliament (2001b, p. 44) suggests that the identified 1,300 million euros of VAT fraud is merely 'the tip of the iceberg'. The Commission wanted to shift to the origin system (CEU 1985a), but it has now accepted that this is politically too difficult and has sought to improve the transitional regime. This has become more urgent with the escalation of missing trader/carousel fraud. This occurs where fraudsters set up bogus companies to import high-value items (mobile phones and computer chips) that are VAT-free, then sell them on to other bogus companies, charging VAT, but not paying it to the tax authorities. The goods are then exported and the VAT that has not been paid is reclaimed. The process can then start over again, hence the term carousel. When the tax authorities seek to claim the VAT, they are unable to trace the owners/officers of the companies involved. With organized crime involved, the losses are very high: 10 per cent of VAT revenue (*The Economist* 2006, p. 5). The suggestions for controlling this problem

vary from tightening up the administrative arrangements to altering the VAT system – for example, by not charging VAT on business-to-business transactions or charging VAT on intra-EU trade. Such measures could be limited to certain items likely to be involved in carousel fraud. However, this could weaken self-policing elements of the system and complicate and increase the costs of policing and compliance.

This analysis leads to the conclusion that VAT reform should extend the tax base and eliminate multiple rates. Eventually the problem of fraud may give MSs the incentive to finally achieve sufficient harmonization of rates to enable a move to the origin system to take place.

15.5 Excise duties

There are large differences in rates between MSs, and excise duties are important for EU governments, being the fifth most important source of revenue (see Table 15.1, page 231). Thus the importance of excises varies substantially between MSs, from 18.3 per cent of tax revenue in Bulgaria to 4.5 per cent in Italy in 2008.

The EU position on tobacco duties is a compromise between the southern and northern MSs. The south favoured taxation based on the value of the product to protect their cheap, home-grown tobacco. The north preferred specific taxes based on volume rather than value to discourage tobacco smoking. This led to wide differences in rates and in the total tax burden on cigarettes.[13] This widened still further with low tax and low cigarette prices in the new member states (NMSs; see Table 15.3). EU regulations (Council 1992b, 1995a) have had to accommodate this wide variation. Thus the EU requires that the specific and *ad valorem* excises plus VAT must not be less than 57 per cent of the retail price and 64 euros per thousand cigarettes; these are to be raised to 60 per cent and 90 euros in 2014 (Council 2010b). The total tax on a pack of twenty cigarettes varies between 1.28 euros in Poland to 5.21 euros in Ireland (see Table 15.3). With such a disparity of tax and consequent variation in prices, it is not surprising that high-tax countries are suffering a substantial loss of revenue as a result of personal purchases overseas and small- and large-scale smuggling. It is estimated that 25 per cent of the cigarettes smoked in the UK are smuggled (Public Accounts

Table 15.3 Cigarette taxation in EU member states, 2010

| | % retail selling price | | | € | |
	Specific	Ad valorem	VAT	Total	Total[a]
Belgium	6.58	52.41	17.36	76.34	2.84
Denmark	34.04	20.80	20.00	74.84	2.73
Germany	33.43	24.66	15.97	74.06	2.87
Greece	8.57	58.43	18.70	85.70	2.14
Spain	6.00	57.00	15.25	78.25	2.14
France	6.03	57.97	16.39	80.39	3.58
Ireland	43.16	18.25	17.36	78.77	5.22
Italy	3.76	54.74	16.67	75.17	2.16
Luxembourg	9.18	47.84	13.04	70.06	2.10
Netherlands	36.48	20.52	15.97	72.97	2.88
Austria	13.35	43.00	16.67	73.02	2.25
Portugal	38.62	23.00	18.03	78.97	2.15
Finland	7.95	52.00	18.70	78.65	4.40
Sweden	12.40	39.20	20.00	71.60	4.91
UK	37.85	24.00	14.89	76.74	6.91
EU15 average[a]	**19.83**	**39.59**	**17.00**	**76.37**	**3.29**
Bulgaria	49.03	23.00	16.67	88.70	2.11
Czech Republic	33.97	28.00	16.67	78.64	2.48
Estonia	32.91	33.00	16.67	82.57	2.04
Cyprus	14.54	44.50	13.04	72.08	2.82
Latvia	29.61	34.50	17.36	81.46	2.15
Lithuania	34.78	25.00	17.36	77.09	2.20
Hungary	30.63	28.30	20.00	78.93	2.26
Malta	11.00	50.00	15.25	76.25	4.00
Poland	36.94	31.41	18.03	86.38	1.87
Romania	41.83	22.00	19.35	83.18	2.32
Slovenia	15.17	44.03	16.67	75.87	2.50
Slovakia	43.32	24.00	15.97	83.29	2.42
NMS10 average[b]	**31.14**	**32.31**	**16.92**	**80.37**	**2.43**
EU27 average[b]	**24.86**	**36.35**	**16.96**	**78.15**	**2.91**

Notes: [a] per 20 cigarettes; [b] arithmetic average

Source: CEU 2010h, p. 7

Committee 2002). Tobacco smuggling is not simply a UK problem; it is an EU-wide and global problem (Cnossen and Smart 2005). With internal harmonization of tobacco duties problematic and the threat of external smuggling, governments in high-tax countries are faced with a difficult choice between lower duties and revenue loss.

Excises on alcoholic drink are based on relative alcohol content as a result of a judgment by the European Court of Justice (1983), which was necessary to avoid taxation distorting trade between MSs. Thus the most flagrant discrimination in favour of local producers has been eliminated (Cnossen 1987), but national beverages are still protected – for example, by applying different excises to still and sparkling wine. Some convergence of rates has occurred as MSs have moved towards the lowest rate: seven MSs levy no excises on wine, and in France it is only 3 euro cents a litre. Some high rates persist, with large differentials remaining: the excises on wine vary from 0

Table 15.4 Alcohol taxation in EU member states, 2010 (per litre)

	Specific excise (euro)			VAT (%)
	Beer	Still wine	Spirits	
Belgium	0.017	0.471	17.522	21.0
Denmark	0.068	0.825	20.148	25.0
Germany	0.008	0.000	13.030	19.0
Greece	0.026	0.000	24.500	23.0
Spain	0.075	0.000	8.303	18.0
France	0.027	0.036	15.130	19.6
Ireland	0.157	2.622	31.130	21.0
Italy	0.024	0.000	8.000	20.0
Luxembourg	0.008	0.000	10.411	15.0
Netherlands	0.055	0.706	15.040	19.0
Austria	0.020	0.000	10.000	20.0
Portugal	0.087	0.000	10.093	21.0
Finland	0.260	2.830	39.400	22.0
Sweden	0.163	2.118	49.211	25.0
UK	0.190	2.470	26.129	17.5
EU15 average[a]	0.079	0.8052	19.8698	20.4067
Bulgaria	0.008			20.0
Czech Republic	0.013	0.000	8.954	20.0
Estonia	0.026	0.731	9.715	23.0
Cyprus	0.048	0.000	6.107	15.0
Latvia	0.031	0.635	9.050	21.0
Lithuania	0.025	0.573	9.268	21.0
Hungary	0.023	0.000	8.801	25.0
Malta	0.008	0.000	23.288	18.0
Poland	0.018	0.372	11.611	22.0
Romania	0.007	0.000		24.0
Slovenia	0.100	0.000	6.951	20.0
Slovakia	0.017	0.000	7.284	19.0
NMS10 average[a]	0.027	0.210	10.103	20.667
EU27 average[a]	0.056	0.553	15.963	20.522

Note: [a] arithmetic average
Source: CEU 2010h

to 2.73 euros a litre and on spirits from 6.45 to 15.45 euros (see Table 15.4). A directive on minimum rates was agreed in 1992 (Council 1992c); the minimum was set at a low level, and since then it has been eroded by inflation so now it does nothing to reduce the differences in taxation. The taxation of alcohol is also excessively complicated.

Substantial smuggling and cross-border purchases occur; it is estimated that about a quarter of the spirits consumed in Denmark and Sweden are purchased outside the consumers' own MS (European Parliament 2001b, p. 39). Harmonization of rates and a similar basis of taxation across drinks is required, reducing rates in northern Europe, leading to some increase in consumption, and raising rates in the south, causing some inflation.[14] These largely transitional problems are a price worth paying to eliminate the difficulties caused by current large differences in rates (London Economics 2010).

Table 15.5 Taxes on petrol and diesel fuel, 2010			
	Unleaded petrol excise duty (euros per litre)	Diesel fuel excise duty (euros per litre)	Diesel and gasoline VAT (%)
Belgium	0.614	0.580	21.0
Denmark	0.567	0.426	25.0
Germany	0.670	0.655	19.0
Greece	0.670	0.440	23.0
Spain	0.425	0.316	18.0
France	0.607	0.417	19.6
Ireland	0.543	0.449	21.0
Italy	0.564	0.337	20.0
Luxembourg	0.465	0.330	15.0
Netherlands	0.714	0.421	19.0
Austria	0.442	0.355	20.0
Portugal	0.583	0.308	21.0
Finland	0.627	0.391	23.0
Sweden	0.374	0.425	25.0
UK	0.628	0.628	17.5
EU15 unweighted average	0.566	0.432	20.5
Bulgaria	0.350	0.307	20.0
Czech Republic	0.505	0.431	20.0
Estonia	0.423	0.330	20.0
Cyprus	0.359	0.330	15.0
Latvia	0.380	0.330	21.0
Lithuania	0.434	0.330	21.0
Hungary	0.444	0.460	25.0
Malta	0.459	0.352	18.0
Poland	0.391	0.429	22.0
Romania	0.348	0.376	24.0
Slovenia	0.485	0.165	20.0
Slovakia	0.515	0.481	19.0
NMS10 unweighted average	0.424	0.360	20.4
EU25 unweighted average	0.503	0.400	20.4
Agreed minima	**0.421**	**0.330**	

Source: CEU 2010h

15.5.1 Energy taxes

Energy taxes vary significantly between forms of energy, where the energy is used and among EU countries (Kouvaritakis *et al.* 2005). The most heavily taxed is fuel for transport. Although the tax on unleaded gasoline varies from 0.35 euros in Romania to 0.713 euros in the Netherlands, there is little possibility of cross-border shopping or smuggling, so this does not raise issues for tax harmonization. Differences in the excise duties on commercial diesel fuel can affect competition in road transport, where goods in one country can be transported by lorries buying their fuel in another. The extent of such problems has been limited by a reasonable degree of similarity of rates: twenty-two MSs have rates between 0.307 and 0.449 euros per litre of normal diesel fuel (see Table 15.5). Belgium, Germany and the UK are out of line, with rates of 0.58, 0.655 and 0.628 euros per litre respectively. Since these countries are exceptions, the solution seems to lie in their own hands.[15]

While the heavier taxation of road transport can be

justified as a means of paying for roads, concentrating tax on one energy use makes little sense in a wider environmental context. To reduce distortions caused by the haphazard taxation of energy, a directive applying minimum tax rates to all energy products was agreed in 2003 (Council 2003d). This applies to fuel used for transport or heating, not when used as raw materials, and it allows differential taxation between private and commercial use. While it irons out some distortions and encourages energy efficiency, this is very far from a comprehensive carbon tax (considered in Chapter 18).

This indicates that further reform of indirect taxes in the EU is desirable. The operation of VAT is complicated by multiple rates, which seem to have little merit. The transitional regime for the collection of VAT worked reasonably well, but is now under pressure from growing fraud, and tackling this will either complicate the existing system or require more fundamental change to the origin system. Differences in excise rates are a cause of substantial smuggling from both within and outside the EU. Further harmonization, with reductions, particularly in the highest rates, seems to be the only answer here.

15.6 Corporation tax

CT is a tax on company profits and thus on capital. Since capital is potentially mobile there are concerns that the movement of capital will undermine national CT and governments' revenue.[16] The received wisdom that tax competition would inevitably lead to a race to the bottom, however, has been questioned on both theoretical and empirical grounds. Not all capital is mobile and governments have consequently sought to tax immobile corporations while reducing burdens on mobile capital. The widening of the CT base and the lowering of rates can be seen as a move in this direction (Devereux *et al.* 2002). In addition, CT is only one of the factors affecting choice of location, and if there are offsetting benefits then CT can still be collected. These benefits could be agglomeration economies leading to a differential return on capital (Baldwin and Krugman 2004). Alternatively, the benefits could derive directly from the effects of government expenditure on productivity (Wooders *et al.* 2001). If this view is taken, then tax competition has the benefit that it encourages

government expenditure, which benefits the economy while constraining wasteful expenditure.[17]

Unfortunately, this theoretical ambiguity cannot easily be resolved by empirical analysis. This is bedevilled by the complexity of CT and the lack of aggregate measures of corporate profits. The complexity of the tax stems from the variation in the way in which profit is measured for tax purposes (depreciation of investment, treatment of research and development expenditure, and so on), the interaction with the personal tax system, the treatment of overseas earnings, and so on. There are substantial differences between the statutory and implicit rates[18] (Eurostat 2010a; Nicodème 2001). Thus statutory CT rates are poor indicators of the actual rate of tax on profits; estimates of implicit CT rates take into account the differences in tax legislation between countries (Devereux *et al.* 2002). However, these estimates are sensitive to assumptions that have to be made relating to tax policy, economic conditions and investor behaviour.

Given these problems, it is not surprising that the empirical evidence on globalization and corporate tax revenue is ambiguous. Some studies actually suggest a positive relationship between the two (Garrett 1995b; Swank 1998), but the relationship was found to be negative when implicit CT rates were used (Bretschger and Hettich 2002; de Mooij 2005). CT rates have been reduced in the EU, with the average top rate in the EU27 falling from 35.3 per cent in 1995 to 23.2 per cent in 2010; however, this is not necessarily the result of tax competition. Rates may have been reduced and bases widened to improve the efficiency, equity and simplicity of the tax system; the implicit CT rate rose from 1995 to 2007, so there is no evidence of a downward trend in CT revenue in the EU.[19] Microeconomic evidence does seem to suggest that CT is a factor affecting MSs' location decisions: head offices and foreign subsidiaries are attracted to low-tax jurisdictions (Buettner and Ruf 2007; Barrios *et al.* 2009). There is also evidence of significant shifting of profit from high- to low-tax jurisdictions (Huizinga and Laeven 2008) and that it occurs within the EU (Huizinga *et al.* 2008).

Perhaps even more than with other taxes, the bewildering complexity of the different national systems is an issue. In addition to great variation in what can and cannot be deducted in the calculation of profit, CTs vary in the extent of personal income tax liability on dividend income (distributed profits). There are

Table 15.6 EU25 corporation tax, 2010

	System	Main rate	Implicit rate[a]
Belgium	Special personal tax rate	34.0	21.4
Denmark	Special personal tax rate	25.0	24.9
Germany	Special personal tax rate	15.0	n.a.
Greece	Dividend exemption	25.0	18.6
Spain	Imputation	30.0	34.0
France	Imputation	33.3	29.1
Ireland	Classical	12.5	7.6
Italy	Imputation	27.5	31.5
Luxembourg	Classical	22.0	n.a.
Netherlands	Dividend exemption	25.5	11.9
Austria	Special personal tax rate	25.0	26.1
Portugal	Imputation	25.0	22.6
Finland	Imputation	26.0	19.3
Sweden	Classical	26.3	23.2
UK	Imputation	28.0	22.2
Bulgaria	Classical	10.0	20.0
Czech Republic	Classical	19.0	25.7
Estonia	Dividend tax	21.0[b]	8.3
Cyprus	Classical	10.0	37.3
Latvia	Exempt	15.0	15.2
Lithuania	Classical	15.0	11.1
Hungary	Classical	19.0	19.9
Malta	Imputation	35.0	n.a.
Poland	Imputation	19.0	20.0
Romania	Classical	16.0	n.a.
Slovenia	Classical	20.0	27.4
Slovakia	Classical	19.0	20.7

Notes: [a] 2008; [b] no tax on retained profit
Source: Eurostat 2010a

two extreme systems: the classical and imputation systems. Under the classical system, corporations pay tax on their profits, but there is no allowance for this tax against personal taxation (PT). Under the imputation system, the whole or part of the corporation tax can be used to offset PT liability on dividends. Another possibility is subjecting dividend income to a separate lower rate of PT. EU enlargement has added yet another variant – only taxing dividends, not retained earnings. At present, CT systems in the EU run the whole gamut, with four different systems in operation and a range of rates from 10 to 34 per cent (see Table 15.6). Higher

rates may be offset by other characteristics of the CT system, but there are large differences in implicit rates. NMSs generally have low nominal CT rates, but their simpler systems with few allowances mean that differences between nominal and implicit rates are usually small.

CT has other economic effects: the higher rate on dividends favours profit retention. Since interest can be allowed as a cost before the calculation of profit, CT encourages the use of debt rather than equity for finance; this is reinforced by financial innovation blurring the distinction between equity and debt. This will tend to make it more difficult for new firms to raise capital, because profit will be retained by existing firms rather than recycled via dividends. Also, the limited credit history and asset bases for collateral of new firms make it difficult for them to borrow. Devereux and Griffith (2001) calculate effective average CT rates on hypothetical investment projects using the rates and rules in current legislation, showing that retained earnings have an effective CT rate on average 10 per cent higher than that on debt.[20]

This analysis of the effects of CT suggests that the distortions can extend across EU borders. The CT system favours incumbent as opposed to new firms, limiting competition and reducing SEM dynamism. It also favours markets where shareholder involvement in the company is more direct, such as in Germany, where banks typically have large holdings and where the need to satisfy shareholders with dividends is lower. The lower taxation of debt finance is to the advantage of MSs with large firms that are creditworthy; where there are close links between banks and companies it can protect against foreign takeovers, because foreign firms do not have the same access to local bank finance. The favourable tax treatment of debt finance is reinforced by internationalization and liberalization of capital markets. With withholding tax on cross-border interest payments very low, a large part of interest income escapes taxation (Huizinga 1994).

The requirement that profits for CT should be calculated separately for each MS creates problems for pan-European business. Tax losses in one MS cannot be offset against profits in another, and assets transferred between MSs may be subject to capital gains tax. This discourages cross-border mergers and takeovers and constrains the operation of MSs within the EU. The administrative costs of complying with different CT regimes can also be high.

The Commission's Bolkestein Report (CEU 2001g) scrutinized two approaches to these problems: first, piecemeal changes to legislation to correct particular distortions – for example, improving double taxation conventions; second, general measures to establish a common tax base for EU activities. There are three possibilities for a common tax base: an EU CT, common base taxation (CBT) and home state taxation (HST). An EU-wide CT would be difficult to agree, given the requirement for unanimity. CBT would harmonize rules for calculating taxable profits on cross-border operations (national rules would remain for domestic operations). HST means that MSs would only be taxed in the MS in which their headquarters is located. With both systems, one set of consolidated accounts would be produced, and a formula using shares of sales, payroll and property would be used to apportion profit,[21] to which MSs would apply their tax rates. The Commission is supporting the development of a CBT (CEU 2007c).

CBT is not without problems; it would tend to increase tax competition due to greater transparency, because differences in tax paid would depend solely on rates. Distortions between MSs caused by national distortions, such as the favouring of debt over equity finance, are not dealt with: 'the elimination of in-state distortions is a prerequisite to the elimination of inter-state distortions' (Cnossen 2002, p. 531). Although one of the objectives is to make cross-border mergers easier, tax considerations will become a factor influencing such mergers. Formula apportionment of profit would lead to further distortions of the location of production. The problems are such that some commentators doubt whether CBT or EU CT are worth the effort (Mintz 2002). Whether such proposals would carry sufficient support to be agreed is questionable in any case.

Another problem is that of interest and dividend payments to foreign holders, who can avoid income taxation: a withholding tax was proposed to deal with this issue. This tax would have to be accepted to offset income tax liability in the MS of residence. In liberalized financial markets, an EU withholding tax would encourage an outflow of funds from the EU and the City of London in particular. Instead, the EU and 15 other states have agreed on the exchange of information on assets held by residents of other MSs, so as to enforce residence-based taxation (Council 2003a).[22] The directive does not seem to have affected saving behaviour, but this may reflect the paucity of the available data and loopholes in the legislation (Hemmelgarn and Nicodème 2009). A review (CEU 2008c) concluded that the legislation was operating satisfactorily, but some tightening of the rules was needed and an amended directive is now going through the legislative procedure.

15.7 Conclusion

It should not come as a surprise that tax harmonization continues to be a difficult issue for the EU: a sensitive area of national sovereignty that remains the prerogative of MSs collides with the need to avoid distortions to trade and investment in an increasingly integrated SEM. Therefore, tax harmonization involves a trade-off between national sovereignty over tax, and the difficulties caused by variations in rates and systems. The limited degree of tax convergence achieved so far indicates that tax competition cannot be relied on to achieve spontaneous harmonization. Tax competition moves rates to lower levels, but this is not always undesirable: it may act as a restraining influence on taxation. Tax harmonization, therefore, may be regarded as a way of maintaining the level of taxation. There are some areas, however, where harmonization could achieve significant potential benefits (excise duties), but given the law of unintended consequences, which seems to hold sway in tax matters, a gradualist approach to harmonization is both practical and preferable.

Summary

- EU tax harmonization is the agreement and application of common rules for taxation across the EU. This involves three separate aspects:
  1. the object of taxation – that is, what is to be taxed;
  2. the tax base – that is, agreement on the calculation of what is to be taxed; and
  3. harmonization of rates.
- Tax harmonization in the EU so far has been very limited to:
  1. an agreed base for VAT;
  2. minimum rates for VAT, alcohol, cigarette and energy taxation; and
  3. some limits to unfavourable interaction between national tax systems.
- Tax harmonization is necessary because in the SEM different tax systems:
  1. can cause distortions; and
  2. can undermine the ability of national governments to raise revenue.
  This process needs to consider:
  3. jurisdiction – that is, who is to receive taxes;

4. distortion – that is, the effects of the taxes on the economy; and
5. enforcement – that is, how the tax rules are applied.

These will guide the tax harmonization process, which involves the narrowing or elimination of differences of the tax base and tax rates. The need for these adjustments and for tax harmonization is principally in relation to taxes on consumption and on capital.[23]

- Of the consumption taxes, VAT presents limited problems:
  1. the tax base of consumption is relatively immobile and consumers are not very sensitive to differences in rates;
  2. the tax is relatively cheap to collect and it is difficult to evade.

The principal difficulties with VAT are associated with exemptions, multiple rates and their administrative costs. There is a good case for making the tax base as wide as possible and for the abolition of multiple rates. The transitional regime on cross-border trade has worked satisfactorily, but is now under increasing pressure from fraud; this calls into question the continued use of the destinations system of taxation.

- Excise duties on cigarettes and alcohol do present substantial problems because of the enormous differences in rates that persist. This encourages a substantial illegal market, with suppliers ranging from small-scale smuggling to organized crime. These problems can probably only be dealt with effectively by harmonization of rates. Energy is an area where there are good arguments for increasing taxation, but where, with the exception of vehicle fuel, rates are low.

- Taxation of capital presents difficulties because of the mobility of the tax base and the spread of corporate activities across states. This means that the taxation jurisdiction is somewhat arbitrary and the taxes levied will have considerable cross-border effects. Corporation tax is also notable for its complexity, which is not helped within the EU by differences in its bases, rules and rates. The system at the moment distorts the choices of retaining and distributing profits, and encourages financing by debt rather than equity. These distortions within MSs also have cross-border effects on investment and business restructuring. The Commission's suggested common base taxation is not without problems.

Questions and essay topics

1. Is tax harmonization necessary in the EU?
2. Why is tax harmonization so difficult in the EU?
3. Explain what is meant by the following terms: jurisdiction, distortion and enforcement. Consider why they are important for tax harmonization.
4. Distinguish between origin and destination VAT systems. Explain how the EU has managed to continue with the origin system in the SEM.
5. Explain the problems caused by differences in VAT between EU MSs.
6. Why are differences in excise duties on cigarettes and alcohol so large in the EU?
7. Why has it proved so difficult to harmonize excise duty on cigarettes and alcohol?
8. Why do differences in excise duties on commercial diesel fuel cause problems in the SEM?
9. What economic effects could differences in corporation tax (CT) between MSs have?
10. Why is CT harmonization particularly complicated?
11. Why has the Commission argued that a common CT base is necessary?
12. How would you explain the fact that while the statutory rate of CT has fallen, the implicit rate has risen?

FURTHER READING

Cnossen, S. (2003) 'How much tax coordination in the European Union', *International Tax and Public Finance*, vol. 10.

Griffith, R., Hines, J. and Sørensen, P. B. (2008) *International Capital Taxation*, Institute for Fiscal Studies (www.ifs.org.uk/mirrleesreview/press_docs/international.pdf).

Keen, M. and de Mooij, R. (2008) 'Tax policy and subsidiarity in the European Union', in G. Gelauff, I. Grilo and A. Lejour (eds.) with M. Keen (2008) *Subsidiarity and Economic Reform in Europe*, Springer, Berlin.

NOTES

1 Eurostat 2010a. All other taxation statistics in this chapter are from this source unless otherwise indicated.
2 This is formal incidence; the legal responsibility for paying the tax, the real incidence, who really bears the burden of the tax, can be very different. Thus social security payments made by employers may be effectively borne by employees as reductions in their wages.
3 Government expenditure can cause analogous effects to differences in taxes. These effects are dealt with by internal market legislation (Chapter 7) and, for industrial subsidies, by competition policy (Chapter 13).
4 Tax competition means that a higher rate of tax is needed to raise funds, increasing tax-induced inefficiency.
5 The main people affected will be very high income earners, who would in any case be attracted by tax havens, which offer extremely low rates of tax.
6 This is the intra-company price for international trade that takes place within the company.
7 Thus the tax paid equals the rate of tax multiplied by the value added at that stage of production.
8 Such taxes also had variable effects on prices and encouraged the vertical integration of companies.
9 See Council 2010a for the latest version.
10 This is the reason for the exemption of farmers, although they receive flat rate compensation for tax on agricultural inputs.
11 Some countries also use lower rates for labour-intensive services as an employment measure.
12 For example, the Australian Society of CPAs (1998) estimated that only 15 per cent of the benefit of a zero rate on food in New Zealand would go to households with the lowest 20 per cent of income.
13 Ninety-five per cent of total tobacco consumption.
14 Although additional revenue could be used to lower other indirect taxes, eliminating the inflationary effect.
15 Part of the justification for high vehicle taxes is to reduce emissions for environmental reasons. The Commission's proposal for a carbon tax was not approved, but some member states have introduced carbon taxes (see Chapter 18).
16 The problem of tax avoidance on interest by the use of accounts in another EU country has been dealt with by an agreement to exchange information on such accounts (Council 2003e).
17 This, of course, could constrain government expenditure considered desirable by the population.
18 The implicit or effective rate is the tax revenue divided by the tax base.
19 Since a lot of corporation tax was collected from the finance sector, this downward trend may reflect the unusual circumstances of this period.
20 Excessive leverage was a causal factor in the financial crisis, so CT reform should be part of the general recasting of the economic system to avoid excessive debt.
21 This is the system widely used in the USA and Canada.

22 Some non-EU countries operate withholding taxes rather than exchange information, and this includes Switzerland; given that this tax was at the relatively low rate of 15 per cent, this limited the effectiveness of the measure.

23 Since income taxes present few independent cross-border problems, they are not considered here.

16 Transport policy

KENNETH BUTTON

16.1 Introduction

Transport is an integral part of any economic or social structure. Military conquests in the past were largely along well-defined, natural transport corridors or, in the case of the Roman Empire, along man-made infrastructure. In terms of lifestyles, the growth of cities has mainly been at important junctions in transport networks. Technology advances and changes in political ambition, as well as new economic conditions and institutional developments, have altered the nature of this link, but its fundamental importance remains. The role of transport as a lubricator of economic reconstruction was appreciated in the post-Second World War period. Institutions such as the European Conference of Ministers of Transport (ECMT),[1] were set up under the Marshall Plan (1948) to assist in reconstructing transport infrastructure, while the European Coal and Steel Community (ECSC, 1951) devoted energies to improving the efficiency of the European rail transport system. It was even more transparent in the formation of the European Economic Community (EEC, 1957), whereby the explicit creation of a Common Transport Policy (CTP) was mandated (see Chapters 2 and 17**).**

Transport is also a major industry. It directly employs about 7 per cent of the EU's workforce, accounts for 7 per cent of EU GDP and for about 30 per cent of final energy consumption (see Chapter 17). But this is perhaps not really the important point. From an economic perspective, the crucial point about transport is its role in facilitating trade and allowing individuals, companies, regions and nation states to exploit their various comparative advantages. Early debates concerning the merits of free trade tended to assume away the friction associated with moving goods to markets, and the analysis of migration patterns exhibited similar tendencies to assume transport costs to be negligible. Some economists did take account of transport costs when trying to explain land use patterns, but such explicit consideration of space and the problems of traversing it was exceptional. The situation changed with the advent of new transport technologies in the mid-nineteenth century and as countries appreciated that manipulation of the transport system could influence their economic conditions. However, the manipulation of transport rates and the strategic design of infrastructure networks were used to protect domestic industries in ways akin to tariff and non-tariff trade barriers (NTBs; see Chapter 6).

The contemporary upsurge of interest in supply chain management, just-in-time production and the like has led to a wider appreciation of the general need to enhance the efficiency of European transport if the region as a whole is to compete successfully in the global economy. The concern is that the effectiveness of transport logistics in the EU should be at least comparable with those elsewhere, to ensure that the labour, capital and natural resources of member states (MSs) can be exploited in a fully efficient manner.

It was against this broad background that the EU initially sought to develop a transport policy, of which the CTP is now but one element, designed to reduce artificial friction. It has taken time for the CTP and other elements of policy to come together to represent anything like a coherent strategy. There have been shifts of emphasis since the signing of the EEC Treaty and frequent changes in the types of policy deemed appropriate to meet these moving objectives. This chapter provides details of the underlying issues that have been central to these efforts and charts some of the paths that have been pursued to confront them.

16.2 The European transport system

Problems with CTP creation began early. The EEC Treaty contained an entire chapter on transport, although limiting itself to movement of freight by road, rail and inland waterways. Strictly, the treaty said: 'The Council may, acting unanimously, decide whether, to what extent and by what procedure appropriate provisions may be laid down for sea and air transport'.

While the treaty gave indications of what national obligations should be, it was not until 1961 that a memorandum appeared setting out clear objectives, and not until the following year that an Action Programme was published. The emphasis of these initiatives was to seek means to remove obstacles to trade posed by the institutional structures governing transport, and to foster competition once a level playing field of harmonized fiscal, social and technical conditions had been established. It has subsequently taken over forty years to make significant progress towards a CTP.

Examination of an EU map provides information on some of the problems of devising a CTP. Even when the Community consisted of only six MSs, the economic space involved hardly represented a natural market. Ideally, transport functions most effectively on a hub-and-spoke basis, with large concentrations of population and economic activity located at the corners and in the centre, with the various transport networks linking them. The central locations act as markets for transport services in their own right, but also as interchange and consolidation points for traffic between the corner nodes. In the six MSs, however, the bulk of economic activity was at the core, with limited growth at the periphery. The accession of such states as Finland, Ireland, Greece, Portugal and Sweden added to the problems of serving peripheral and often sparsely populated areas, and subsequent enlargements have complicated the diversity of transport considerations further. The geographical separation of some MSs and the logical routeing of traffic through non-MS countries, together with the island nature of others, pose further problems.

Also, the CTP was not initiated with a clean slate: MSs had established transport networks and institutional structures that could not be changed rapidly. At the outset, countries such as France and West Germany carried a significant amount of their freight traffic by rail (34 and 27 per cent by tonne-kilometres respectively). Others, such as the Benelux nations and Italy, relied much more on road transport, the average length of domestic hauls being an important determining feature. The resultant differences were not simply physical

(including variations in railway gauges, vehicle weight limits and different electricity currents); they also reflected fundamental differences in the ways transport was viewed.

At a macro, political-economy level there are two broad views on the way transport should be treated. Following the continental philosophy, the objective is to meet wide social goals that require interventions in the market involving regulations and public ownership. This approach dominated much of twentieth-century transport policy thinking in continental Europe. Its place has been taken in recent years by a wider acceptance of the Anglo-Saxon approach to policy. This treats the transport sector as little different to other economic activities. Transport provision and use should be efficient in its own right. Efficiency is normally best attained by making the maximum use of market forces. Of course, the extremes of the alternative approaches have never been employed; it has been a matter of degree. Even in countries such as the UK that had in the past been seen as a bastion of the Anglo-Saxon ideology, there existed extensive regimes of regulation and large parts of the transport system have been in state ownership. There have been shifts in the importance of the approaches. The interventionist positions of Germany and France were initially set against the more liberal approach of the Netherlands. With Denmark and the UK's accession in 1973, interventionist thinking was weakened. Subsequent enlargements, combined with a more generic movement away from interventionist policies, added to the impetus for less regulation of transport markets.

Views on efficiency have also changed. The approach until the 1970s was to treat efficiency largely in terms of maximizing scale efficiency, while limiting any deadweight losses associated with monopoly power. Most transport infrastructure was seen as enjoying economies of scale that could only be exploited by coordinated and, *ipso facto*, regulated and often subsidized, development. State ownership was common. Many aspects of operations were also seen as potentially open to monopoly exploitation and in need of oversight. This situation changed from the late 1970s. The high levels of subsidies enjoyed by many elements of the transport sector became politically and practically unsustainable, and economists began to question whether the regulations were actually achieving their aims. They may have been captured by those that are intended to be regulated or manipulated to the benefit of individuals responsible for administering the regime. Government failures, it was argued, were larger than the market failures that interventions were trying to correct.

New elements also came into play in the 1970s, concerning the wider environmental implications of transport. To some extent this has been part of a wider effort within the EU to improve the overall environment (see Chapter 18) and to fulfil larger, global commitments on such matters as reducing global warming gas emissions (CEU 1992b). Transport impacts the environment at the local level (noise, carbon monoxide, and so on), at the regional level (for example, nitrogen oxide emissions and maritime pollution) and at the global level (carbon dioxide). It is this diversity of implications and the trade-offs between them, as well as the absolute scale of some of the individual environmental intrusions, that make policy formulation difficult. Local effects have largely been left to the individual MSs, but as the implications of regional and global environmental intrusions have become appreciated, so EU transport policy has become proactive. The main problem with these types of environmental issue is that their effects are often trans-boundary, offering little incentive for individual action by governments.

A new focus of attention since the 2001 terrorist attacks on the USA has been the security of the European transport supply chain for passengers, freight and third parties. This has involved interactions not only between MSs, but also with external bodies, including the UN's International Civil Aviation Authority and the International Maritime Organization. The measures taken have imposed costs not only directly on those supplying transport services, but also on the users of these services, with inevitable consequences for the way the system performs. This is a matter that overlaps with international relations and defence and is not considered in any great detail here.

16.3 The initial development of a CTP

The past forty years have seen important changes in the ways in which transport is viewed. There have always been periodic swings in transport policy, but the period since the late 1970s provides a watershed that has permeated EU thinking. The change has been dramatic and transcends national boundaries and modes. The liberalization of transport markets throughout the world and the extension of private sector ownership have had an influence too, providing important demonstration effects to other sectors, which, in turn, have also been liberalized (Button and Keeler 1993).

The early thinking regarding the CTP centred on creating a level playing field on which competition would be equitable. The ECSC had initiated this approach in the early 1950s, and it continued as EU interest moved away from primary products. The ECSC had removed some artificial tariff barriers relating to rail movements of primary products, and the CTP initially attempted to expand this idea in the 1960s to cover the general carriage of goods, and especially those moved on roads. Road transport was viewed rather differently to railways. It was perceived that the demand and supply features of road haulage markets could lead to excessive competition, as well as supply uncertainties for periods and shortages at others, with the potential of monopoly pricing.

The early efforts involved seeking to initiate common operating practices – for example, relating to driving hours and vehicle weights – common accounting procedures and standardizing methods of charging. A forked tariff regime for trucking, with rates constrained between officially determined maxima and minima, was aimed at meeting the problem period swings between excesses and shortages of supply. Maximum and minimum rates on international movements within the EU were stipulated and statutory charges established. Practically, there were problems in setting the cost-based rates, but besides that, questions were raised concerning a policy that was aimed at simultaneously tackling monopoly and excess competition (Munby 1962). Limitations on the number of international truck movements across borders were marginally reduced by the introduction of a small number of Community Quota licences – authorizing the free movement of holders over the entire EU road network (Button 1984).

The 1973 EC enlargement to nine MSs stimulated renewed interest in transport policy. The new MSs (Ireland, Denmark and the UK) tended to be more market oriented in their philosophies. Also, there was inevitable horse-trading across policy areas, and with enlargement came the opportunity to review a whole range of policy areas. At about the same time, the

Commission raised legal questions concerning the inertia of the Council to move on creating a genuine CTP. It also followed a period of rapid growth in trade within the EU, with a shift towards greater trade in manufactures. As a result, infrastructure capacity issues were coming to the fore and the case for more flexible regulation of road freight transport was being argued (Button 1990).

The outcome was not dramatic, although new sectors entered the debates, most notably maritime transport, and wider objectives concerning environmental protection and energy policy played a role. Overall, the Action Programme carried through between 1972 and 1974 involved a gentle move to liberalization by making the quota system permanent, and expanding the number of licences increased international intra-EU road freight capacity. The option of using reference tariffs rather than forked tariffs was a reflection of the inherent problems with the latter. A major initiative involved seeking to improve decision-making regarding infrastructure provision and to appropriate ways of charging for its use. The importance of transport links outside the EU, but as part of a natural European network, also began to play a part in policy, with the development mechanisms for their planning and financing.

The second/third EU enlargements (Greece, then Portugal and Spain) had little impact on the CTP, which essentially remained piecemeal. The only significant change prior to major developments in the early 1990s was the gradual widening of the modes covered. There were, for example, moves to bring maritime and air transport policy in line with EU competition policy.

The accession to the EC in the 1970s and early 1980s of the UK and Greece, with established shipping traditions, brought maritime issues to the table, and then the Single European Act (SEA) of 1987 provided a catalyst for initiating a maritime policy (Erdmenger and Stasinopoulos, 1988). A series of measures was introduced aimed at bringing shipping within the EU's competition policy framework. Technical shifts, such as the widespread adoption of containerization, had begun to influence the established cartel arrangements that had characterized scheduled maritime services; these initial arrangements were 'conferences' that coordinated fares and sailings, but later were more integrated 'consortia'. Conferences had been permitted in most European countries since the late nineteenth century, because they offer scheduled services of less than a shipload at relatively stable rates. The ability to discriminate in relation to price enjoyed by these cartels, however, was beginning to be eroded as it became more difficult to differentiate cargoes. Action by the UN to limit the power of these cartels in the 1970s, aimed at protecting developing countries, was also in conflict with the national policies of some EU MSs, but others ratified it. Concerns were reinforced in the 1980s as the size of the EU's shipping sector declined significantly in the face of competition from Far East and Communist bloc fleets. Taxation and policies on such matters as wages and technical standards were adding to the problem by stimulating operators to 'flag out' and register in non-MSs. A need for a more coordinated EU maritime policy thus emerged (Brooks and Button 1992).

The First Package in 1985 sought to improve the competitive structure of the EU's shipping industry and its ability to combat unfair competition from third countries (CEU 1985c). It gave the Commission power to react to predatory behaviour by third party shipowners. The measures also allowed block exemptions for shipping cartels, albeit with safeguards to ensure that the exemption was not exploited (see Chapter 13). In 1986 a Second Package – the Positive Measures Package – was initiated, aimed at addressing the decline in the competitiveness of the EU's fleets, as well as covering safety and pollution issues, and a common registry was proposed. It was not a success, however, and fleet sizes have continued to decline, bringing forth new ideas for capacity reduction from the Commission. As part of the general effort to liberalize the EU's market and enhance efficiency, agreement on cabotage (the provision of a domestic service within a country by a carrier from another nation) was reached, with exceptions in some markets – for example, Greek Islands.

Compared to shipping, ports policy can best be described as ad hoc. Initial concerns in the early 1990s centred on modernization and the assurance that there was port capacity to handle the larger ships that were being introduced. Progress was relatively slow until 2000, when sea and inland ports were incorporated into the Trans-European Networks (TENs) initiative, with the objective of integrating and prioritizing investment in transport infrastructure. In 2001 the notion of 'motorways of the seas' was introduced as part of the initiative.

Globally, air transport policy, since the USA had

liberalized its domestic passenger and freight markets in the 1970s, had been moving away from a tradition of regulation (Button *et al.* 1998). And until the early 1980s, it had also generally been thought that aviation policy was outside the jurisdiction of the Commission and a matter for national governments. This changed, following a number of legal decisions by the European Court of Justice (ECJ) regarding the applicability of various aspects of EU competition rules to air transport.

The EU's bilateral system of air service agreements covering scheduled air transport between MSs was tightly regulated, as was the case in other parts of the world; typically, only one airline from each country was allowed to fly on a particular route, with the capacity offered by each bilateral partner restricted, revenues pooled, fares approved by the partners, and designated airlines substantially state-owned and enjoying state aid. Domestic air markets were also tightly controlled. The charter market, largely catering for holiday traffic from northern Europe to southern destinations, represented about 50 per cent of the revenue seat miles within the EU and was less strictly regulated, but such services seldom met the needs of business travellers.

A change in the policy climate began in 1979, when the Commission put forward general ideas for regulatory reform (CEU 1984a) following the ECJ decision. The Council subsequently decided that the best way to regain control was to agree to introduce deregulation, but of a kind and at a pace of its own choosing – hence the 1987 First Package. The basic philosophy was that deregulation would be phased, with workable competition being the objective. A regulation was adopted that covered interstate operations, enabling the Commission to apply the anti-trust rules directly to airline operations. Certain technical agreements were left untouched. The Council also adopted a directive (see Chapters 2 and 4) designed to provide airlines with greater pricing freedom. While airlines could collude, the hope was that they would increasingly act individually. MSs' authorities approved applications for airfare changes. While conditions were laid down that reduced national authorities' room for manoeuvre in rejecting changes in airfares, they could still reject them, but if there was disagreement, the disagreeing party lost the right of veto under arbitration.

In 1987 the Council adopted a decision that provided for a deviation from the traditional air services agreement that set a 50/50 split on traffic between two countries. MSs were required to allow competition to change the shares up to 55/45 until 30 September 1989, and thereafter to 60/40. Fifth freedom (also called 'beyond rights', which means granting an airline the right to carry revenue traffic between foreign countries as part of a service connecting the airline's own country) traffic was not included in these ratios, but was additional. There was also a provision in which serious financial damage to an air carrier could constitute grounds for the Commission to modify the shift to the 60/40 limit. The decision also required MSs to accept multiple designations on a country-pair basis by another MS. An MS was not obliged to accept the designation of more than one air carrier on a route by the other MSs unless certain conditions, which were to become less restrictive over time, were satisfied. The decision also made a limited attempt to open up the market to fifth freedom competition.

The 1989 Second Package involved more deregulation. From the beginning of 1993, a system of double disapproval was accepted. Only if both MSs refused to sanction a fare application could an airline be precluded from offering it to its passengers, and the system of setting limits on the division of traffic between the bilateral partners disappeared in a phased manner. MSs also endorsed the principle that governments could not discriminate against airlines provided they met safety criteria. In terms of ownership rules, in the past, an airline had to be substantially owned by an EU MS before it could fly from that country, but the Council abolished this rule over a two-year period. Air cargo services were liberalized so that a carrier operating from its home MS to another MS could take cargo into a third MS or fly from one MS to another and then to its home state. Cabotage between two freestanding MSs was not liberalized.

16.4 The Single European Market effect

The creation of the Single European Market (SEM; see Chapters 2 and 7) in 1992 and subsequent moves towards greater political integration have brought important changes to the CTP and related policies (Button 1992). Broadly, the 1987 SEA stimulated a concerted effort to remove institutional barriers to free trade in transport services. At about the same time, efforts at further political integration led to major new initiatives to provide an integrated EU transport infrastructure – for example, TENs (CEU 1989b). These strategic networks are aimed at facilitating higher levels of social and political integration at the national and regional levels, as well as having purely economic objectives. The broad basis of EU transport policy was established in the Commission's White Paper on *The Future Development of the Common Transport Policy* (CEU 1992b). This sets as a guiding principle the need to balance an effective transport system with a commitment to the protection of the environment. The environmental theme was also expanded (CEU 1992a). This is set in the context of defending the needs and interests of individual citizens as consumers, transport users and people living and working in areas of transport activity.

Even if these effects were not present, questions arose at the time regarding the ability of regulators to serve the public interest with the information they had. The development of economic theories involving such concepts as contestable markets (where potential competition could be as effective as actual competition in blunting the power of monopoly suppliers), were central to several EU initiatives. There was also a switch away from concern about problems of optimal scale and monopoly power that had been the intellectual justification for state ownership and regulation, to attempts at seeking to create conditions favourable to X- and dynamic efficiency. This was largely, but not exclusively, a concern with reducing costs, replacing that of containing consumer exploitation. In particular, there was mounting concern that the costs of regulated transport were having macroeconomic implications for inflation and EU growth. Transport was neither being provided with services at minimum costs for the technology they were using, nor moving forward to adopt lower-cost technologies. The approaches to attaining this varied by sectors.

16.4.1 Road transport

Road transport is the dominant mode of both freight and passenger transport in the EU. Since 1970, the total EU freight tonnage has increased 2.5 times, and the share of this going by road has risen from 48 to 74 per cent. The initial efforts to develop a CTP regarding road transport proved problematic, as we have seen. Technical matters were more easily solved than those

of creating a common economic framework of supply, although even here issues concerning such matters as maximum weight limits for trucks have tended to be fudged. Economic controls lingered in countries with less efficient road haulage industries, which sought to shelter themselves from the more competitive fleets of countries such as the Netherlands and the UK.

The SEM initiative, later influenced by the potential of new trade with the post-Communist Eastern and Central European countries (CEECs; see Button 1993), resulted in significant reforms to economic regulation. From the industrial perspective, road freight transport offers the flexibility that is required by modern, just-in-time production management, but from the social perspective it can be environmentally intrusive, and, in the absence of appropriate infrastructure pricing, it can contribute to excessive congestion costs.

The long-standing bilateral arrangements for international licensing of road haulage had led to high levels of economic inefficiency; not only did they impose an absolute constraint on the number of movements, but also cabotage was not permitted and combinations of bilateral licences permitting trucks to make complex international movements were difficult to obtain, leading to a lot of empty running. The system also added to delays for document checks at borders. Besides leading to the gradual phasing out of bilateral controls and the phasing in of cabotage rights, the 1992 initiative also led to considerable reductions in cross-border documentation.

Passenger road transport policy has largely been left to individual MSs, although in the late 1990s the Commission began to advocate the development of a citizens' network and more rational road-charging policies (notably systems of congestion pricing). Perhaps the greatest progress has been made regarding social regulations on such matters as the adoption of catalytic converters in efforts to limit the environmental intrusion of motor vehicles. It has taken time to develop a common policy regarding public transport, despite efforts in the 1970s to facilitate easier cross-border coach and bus operations.

16.4.2 Railways

Rail transport, while largely filling a niche market in many countries, is an important freight mode in much of continental Europe and provides important passenger services along several major corridors. At the local level, it serves as a key mode for commuter traffic in larger cities. The earlier phase had initially sought to remove deliberate distortions to the market that favoured national carriers, but from the late 1960s and 1970s had shifted to the rationalization of the subsidized networks through more effective and transparent cost accountancy. However, the exact incidence of subsidies still often remained uncertain. The EU has also instigated measures aimed at allowing the trains of one MS to use the track of another, with charges based on economic costs. The aim of the EU directive 91/440 was to develop truly EU networks, but open-access rules did not explicitly apply to the new high-speed rail lines, such as the French and Belgian *Lignes à Grande Vitesse* and the German *Neubaustrecken* networks. The implementation of the open-access strategy has been slow and has had limited impact (Vickerman 1997).

The EU has traditionally found it difficult to devise practical and economically sound common pricing principles to apply to transport infrastructure, despite the proposals of the Oort Report (Oort and Maaskant 1976). With regard to railways, the gist of the overall proposals is for short-run marginal costs (which are to include environmental and congestion costs, as well as wear on the infrastructure) to be recovered. Long-run elements of cost are only to be recovered in narrowly defined circumstances and only in relation to passenger services. This clearly has implications, especially on the freight side, if genuine, full, cost-based competition is to be permitted with other transport modes. Rail transport has also received considerable support from the Commission as an integral part of making greater use of integrated, multi-modal transport systems – essentially, the use of containers. Such systems would largely rely on rail (including piggyback systems and kangaroo trains) or waterborne modes for trunk haulage, with road transport used as the feeder mode. This is seen as environmentally desirable and as contributing to containing rising levels of road traffic congestion in the EU.

The success of some of the French TGV services, and especially that between Paris and Lyons, where full cost recovery has been attained, has led to a significant interest in this mode. In 1990 the Commission set up a high-level working group to help push forward a common approach to high-speed railway development. A master plan for 2010 was produced. The EU's efforts to harmonize the development of high-speed rail has not been entirely successful and there are significant technical differences – for example, between the French and German systems. Indeed, both countries actively market their technologies as superior (Viegas and Blum 1993).

The difficulties that still remain with rail transport are the technical variations in its infrastructure and the working practices of individual MSs that are only slowly being coordinated. Some MSs, such as the Netherlands, Sweden and the UK, have pursued the broad EU liberalization philosophy and gone beyond the minimal requirements of the CTP, but in others rigidities remain and the rail network still largely lacks the integration required for full economies of scope, density and market presence to be reaped.

16.4.3 Inland waterway transport

Inland waterway transport was already an issue in the early EU days. This is mainly because it is a primary concern of two founder MSs, Germany and the Netherlands, which in 1992 accounted for 73.1 per cent of EU traffic. Belgium and France also had some interest in this mode of transport. Progress in formulating a policy has tended to be slow, in part because of historical agreements covering navigation on the Rhine – for example, the Mannheim Convention – but mainly because the major economic concern has been that of overcapacity, which in 1998 was estimated at between 20 and 40 per cent at the prevailing freight rates. Retraction of supply is almost always difficult to manage, both because few MSs are willing to pursue a contraction policy in isolation and because of the resistance of barge owners and labour.

As in other areas of transport, the EU had begun seeking technical standardization and principles for social harmonization from 1975 (CEU 1975, 1979b), but economic concerns took over in the 1990s. In 1990 the EC initiated the adoption of a system of subsidies designed to stimulate scrappage of vessels. Subsequent measures only permitted the introduction of new vessels into the inland fleet on a replacement basis. Labour subsidies operated in Belgium, France (the rota system that provides minimum wages for bargemen) and the Netherlands have also been cut back in stages. They were removed entirely in 2000.

These measures were coupled with an initiative

in 1995 to coordinate investment in inland water-way infrastructure (the Trans-European Waterway Network), designed to encourage, for environmental reasons, the greater use of waterborne transport. More recently, in *European Transport Policy for 2010: Time to Decide* (CEU 2001e), the Commission has emphasised its Marco Polo programme on integrating inland water-ways transport with rail and maritime transport for the movement of bulk consignments within an intermodal chain.

16.4.4 Maritime transport

Much of the emphasis of EU maritime policy in the late 1990s was on the shipping market rather than on pro-tecting the EU's fleet; it was user rather than supplier driven. In the 1990s the sector became increasingly concentrated as, first, consortia grew in importance, mergers took place – for example, P&O and Nedlloyd in 1997 – and then the resultant large companies formed strategic alliances; in 1999 all shipping companies, with the exception of two of the world's largest, were part of alliances. An extension of the 1985 rules cover-ing consortia was initiated in 1992 and subsequently extended, as the nature of maritime alliances became more complex. In 2008, the protection that some alli-ances had enjoyed was repealed, and EU competition law was applied to the industry.

In 1994 the Commission acted to ban the Transatlantic Agreement reached the preceding year by the major shipping companies to gain tighter con-trol over the loss-making North Atlantic routes. It did so on the grounds of capacity and rate manipulations, and because it contained agreements over pre- and on-carriage over land. In the same year it fined fourteen shipping companies that were members of the Far East Freight Conference for price fixing. The main point at issue was that these prices embodied multi-modal carriage, and while shipping per se enjoyed a block exemption on price agreements, multi-modal services did not.

Ports also attracted attention in the 1990s. Ports handled about 24 per cent of the world's tonne equiva-lent units in 1994, but shipping companies had moved to hub-and-spoke operations, leading to congestion problems. The EU's main ports have capacity utiliza-tion levels of well over 80 per cent, and some are at or near their design capacity. Whether this is a function of a genuine capacity deficiency or reflects inappropriate port pricing charges that do not contain congestion cost elements is debatable. The Commission has pro-duced further proposals for coordinating investment in port facilities (CEU 1997d). In 2001 the Commission launched an initiative to improve the quality of services offered by ports. This involves tightening access stand-ards for pilotage, cargo handling, and so on, and making more transparent the rules of procedure at ports, with the particular aim of bringing ports more fully into an integrated transport structure (CEU 2001e).

16.4.5 Air transport policy

The air market was still heavily regulated at the time of the Cockfield Report that heralded the SEM. The final reform – the Third Package – came in 1992 and was phased in from the following year. This led to a market similar to that for the USA's domestic aviation by 1997 (Button and Swann 1992). The measures removed significant barriers to entry by setting common rules governing safety and financial requirements for new airlines. After January 1993, EU airlines were able to fly between MSs without restriction, and within MSs (other than their own) subject to some controls on fares and capacity. National restrictions on ticket prices were removed; the only safeguards related to excessive falls or increases in fares. Since 1997 full cabotage has been permitted, and fares are generally unregulated. Additionally, foreign ownership among EU carriers is permitted, and these carriers have, for EU internal pur-poses, become EU airlines. There has been an increase in cross-share holdings, and a rapidly expanding number of alliances among airlines within the EU. This change did not apply initially to extra-EU agreements, where national bilateral arrangements still dominate the market. A ruling by the ECJ in November 2002, however, gave the Commission power to undertake such negotiations. This initially brought into question some existing bilateral agreements between individual MSs and third parties, but in 2003 the Council gave powers to the Commission to negotiation with the USA on liberalizing the transatlantic market. Efforts to develop a free market across the Atlantic proved dif-ficult to negotiate, in part because of matters involving access to the respective domestic markets in the USA and the EU (Button 2009). An initial agreement was signed, however, in 2007, effective the following year, that provides free access to USA/European Common Aviation Area (ECAA) routes across the Atlantic, but precluded cabotage on either side of the ocean, and limited 'foreign' ownership of airlines. A second phase was agreed in 2010.

Early analysis of EU airline regulatory reforms by the UK Civil Aviation Authority (1993) and the Commission indicated that the reforms of the 1990s produced greater competition on both EU domestic routes and international routes within the EU. The Commission, in examining the impact of the Third Package, found that the number of routes flown within the EU rose from 490 to 520 between 1993 and 1995, that 30 per cent of the EU's routes were served by two operators and 6 per cent by three or more, that eighty new airlines have been created and only sixty have disappeared, that fares have fallen on routes where there are at least three operators, and that overall, when allowance is made for charter operations, between 90 and 95 per cent of passengers on intra-EU routes are travelling at reduced fares, albeit with significant variations in the patterns of fares charged across routes. Much of the new competition was on domestic routes, where those routes operated by two or more carriers rose from 65 in January 1963 to 114 in January 1996. A subsequent study (BAE Systems 2000) found that while promotional fares fell between 1992 and 2000, there were rises in business and economy fares in nominal terms, with regional differences in the patterns of fare changes.

The conditions after 11 September 2001 have led to more volatility in the market that extends beyond the demise of Sabena and Swissair in 2002. In terms of the scheduled market, from September 2001 to May 2002, seventeen airlines withdrew and there were fourteen start-ups. In the French market the number of airlines fell from a peak of twenty-six in 1996 to twelve at the end of 2000, and to six by mid-2002. There were also significant turnovers in Greece and Sweden. The traditional, full-cost flag carriers have been forced to restructure their operations as new, low-cost carriers; while the traditional EU airlines carried 325.7 million passengers in total in 2009, the low-cost carriers Ryanair, easyJet and Air Berlin moved 48.7 million, 45.2 million and 21.6 million respectively within the EU.

Some of the more significant recent EU air transport policy initiatives have involved both intra-European air transport infrastructure coordination (Button 2007) and the environment. This has involved the privatization or corporatization of airports, following on from the UK in 1987, where the major airports were privatized as the British Airport Authority. Access to airport take-off and landing slots has also been modified by a series of measures initiated in 1993 to allow easier access by non-incumbent carriers. The aim has been to introduce incentives for more efficient management and open new channels for finance (Button 2010a). The Chicago Convention of 1994 gave individual nations responsibility for the air space above their territories, and, as a result, the EU has a plethora of different national air navigation providers, each with its own technologies and operating arrangements. The notion of a European Single Sky is that air traffic control should be reorganized to reduce the excessive fragmentation of the current system, to update the technology used and to be operated under common ECAA rules. The initial aim was to begin working to achieve this in 2004 (CEU 2001e), but progress has been slow, with continuing important differences in the ways that national air traffic control systems perform (EUROCONTROL Performance Review Commission 2010). In 2008 a new schedule for implementation was drawn up.

Air transport globally contributes about 3 per cent of climate change gas emissions. A problem with developing a policy to handle any external costs of this is that much of the air traffic in EU air space involves foreign airlines; also, EU-owned aircraft can refuel outside of the EU when engaged in transcontinental flights. In 2008 the EU initiated a carbon trading scheme whereby airlines must reduce CO_2 emissions by 10 per cent when they join the EU's carbon cap-and-trade scheme in 2012; 85 per cent of emissions allowances will be allocated to airlines for free, with 15 per cent to be auctioned off. The policy has met with opposition from non-EU countries, and the USA has warned that it could take legal action in the World Trade Organization if the EU goes ahead.

16.5 The 2004 and 2007 enlargements

The 2004 and 2007 enlargements of the EU have impacted on the demands placed on the existing transport systems of established MSs and those of the new member states (NMSs). Change has perhaps been less dramatic than some had feared, partly because trade had already expanded considerably between the accession of NMSs in 2004–7 and the EU15 over preceding eras. NMSs had also considerably reformed their economic structures – important for influencing what is transported and where – and their transport systems prior to joining the EU. Nevertheless, the difficulties to be overcome have not been trivial and challenges continue, especially since enlargement comes as part of a wider set of developments:

- *Geographic.* Enlargement has had implications for the economics of the operation of long-haul transport, as well as necessitating investment in infrastructure. It has opened up new markets for trade, and with this have come new demands for transport services internal to all MSs as well as between them. What the enlargement has not done is to create a 'natural' geographic market for transport services. The spatial distribution of economic activities, for example, still does not have the structure of the US market. There, the locations of centres of population and economic activities at the corners and in the centre of the country results in efficiency benefits from long-haul carriage and hub-and-spoke structures. In the EU economic activity is dichotomously distributed and enlargement has, at least in the short term, added to the central/peripheral nature of the EU; the addition of further island economies such as Cyprus and Malta adds to this phenomenon. The USA's transport market has also evolved gradually, but in an integrated manner, whereas there were quite distinct differences in the way the transport networks of Western Europe and the former Soviet Union evolved, with limited connectivity between them.
- *Legal.* The Constitutional Convention sought to develop a longer-term basis for the EU (see Chapter 2). Issues concerning the nature of central legal responsibilities and the degree of local national autonomy inevitably arose, and enlargement adds to such challenges. One of the outcomes of adopting the Constitutional Treaty would have been a more structured way of shaping the wider legal framework within which macroeconomic policies regarding transport could be formulated. It would also have influenced the external policies of the EU – important for transport in a world of global economies and global trade. The failure to ratify the treaty

leaves the situation in limbo regarding these policy areas in many fields, including that of transport.
- *Economic.* In 2002 the Commission raised the issue of the need for a more sophisticated common fiscal policy within the EU, or at least that part of it in the Eurozone. The recent global economic recession, beginning in 2007, has led to further concerns about the lack of a common fiscal framework. Economists have long understood that a common currency requires a common fiscal policy as a concomitant (see Chapters 10–12,15 and 19). A common policy would involve the centre having responsibility for fiscal transfers above those now controlled by Brussels. While the exact amount of control is debated, and depends on the extent to which the centre considers distribution as well as macroeconomic stabilization as part of its function, it may well be considerable. This would take away much national autonomy over major infrastructure works and influence short-term public expenditure patterns. The rejection of the Constitutional Treaty, at least in the short term, has made it more difficult to develop an EU-wide framework of any substance.
- *Security.* The attacks on the USA's national edifices in 2001, and subsequent terrorist attacks in EU countries such as Spain and the UK, have led to increasing concerns over the security of the transport networks in the EU. Individual MSs have developed their own strategies, but EU-wide actions have also been important, at the sectors level, but also under the common security and defence policy. The EU has also been active with multilateral agencies such as the UN (CEU 2004j). The associated measures have an impact on the cost of supply of transport services, and, because of the standard nature of many of the regulations, inspections and other measures hit the newer, lower-income MSs the hardest.

In the context of the former Soviet states, the situation has not been one of combining two static blocks, but rather of bringing together two units that started from different places and were moving forward at different speeds. The nature of the economies of the transition states, and their relationships to the EU changed considerably after 1989. European agreements had fostered trade and provided various forms of aid (see Chapter 25). The EU, and some MSs unilaterally, had been involved in improving the communications systems within transition states. The EU *Agenda 2000* (CEU 1997b) had identified some 19,000 kilometres of road, 21,000 of rail and 4,000 of inland waterway, forty airports, twenty seaports and fifty-eight inland ports as key links for transport networks. With the exception of Bulgaria, all NMSs experienced increases in their euro trade between 1989 and 1999, and their industrial structures were gradually changing in the light of domestic reforms, exposure to international markets and access to more extensive sources of finance. Nevertheless, there were numerous ways in which their transport systems differed from those in the EU. The former Soviet bloc countries are largely distant from the EU core, meaning that railways become a potentially viable mode for long-distance freight movements. Indeed, the physical area of an enlarged EU offers the prospect of haul lengths comparable with the USA's, where deregulated railways have at least been maintaining their market share. However, the rail networks that currently carry 40 per cent of freight by tonne-kilometre within former Soviet bloc economies were largely based on dated technologies and were not designed to meet transport demands for movements to/from the EU (Suchorzewski 2003). They were also excessively labour-intensive and often served as job creators rather than transport suppliers.

Car ownership is considerably lower in most NMSs than in the established EU, although this is changing. While several of the national car markets within the EU15 are reaching maturity, markets are expanding rapidly in most NMSs, putting strains on their urban infrastructure and posing mounting environmental problems. Smaller MSs, and some regions within the larger MSs, now find themselves subjected to significant transit traffic flows. This raises issues of infrastructure capacity and environmental degradation, but also raises matters of charging and pricing – a subject the EU itself has been singularly poor at addressing. Many NMSs also joined with poorly maintained transport networks, ill-suited to the needs of modern, just-in-time production and the increasing availability of road infrastructure links to the major markets in Western Europe.

NMSs with maritime access and inland waterways make considerable use of them, with about 40 per cent of tonnage moved by water. Enlargement, however, comes at a time of technical change in maritime transport, with the increasing deployment of a post-Panamax[2] fleet exploiting scale economies and mounting pressure for more hub-and-spoke operations and fleet rationalization. Nevertheless, given the environmental advantages of waterborne transport, the EU is fostering its use.

NMSs have not generated sufficient resources to enhance their networks in line with anticipated demands resulting from membership. The EU has provided some resources to supplement those of the new entrants – pre-accession sums of €520 million per annum (see Chapters 19 and 22). But these are relatively small. Loan finance has been suggested and discussed in *European Transport Policy for 2010: Time to Decide* (CEU 2001e). Essentially, the loans would be financed from user charges. A difficulty is that this is not the way that transport infrastructure has traditionally been financed elsewhere in the EU. The majority of networks have been constructed from non-dedicated general taxation revenues and direct subsidies. Measures to make transport users more aware of their costs have been discussed, and limited efforts to introduce them made in the EU15, but the situation is still not one of a user-pays-principle along the lines suggested for NMSs.

Enlargement has inevitably been accompanied by a transition period, and transport has been included within this. This may be seen as reflecting the time needed for NMSs to adjust their transport systems, if not completely, at least largely to the needs of an integrated, EU-wide, single market. In practice, this seems to be much less of a physical problem than one of psychology. There have already been major shifts in the way in which goods are transported in NMSs, as new entrepreneurial talent has come on to the scene, in particular in the trucking sector. There has also been some consolidation in rail networks, albeit still not large by the scale of the likely cuts required.

The EU's 2001 White Paper on transport policy offers a potpourri of ideas on what the future may look like for the larger NMSs and the transition economies in particular. The concern is very much to make use of the 'extensive, dense network and of significant know-how' in these countries to rebalance the transport modes in the EU – in other words, to maintain the modal share of the railways in NMSs and have 35 per cent of freight moved by rail. Interim assessments (for example, CEU 2006r), however, indicated that progress had been slower than had been hoped for. Congestion continues to be a major problem for many parts of the EU's transport network, and efforts to reduce it, outside of a few cities acting independently of any EU initiative, have produced no positive results. This is despite the manifest and transparent positive results in places like London, Stockholm and Valetta that appropriate economic pricing offers a tractable remedy. Infrastructure remains deficient in many places and efforts to improve it have not been entirely successful. The money available from the Commission for the TENS 2004 revised programme of seventy-five projects, initially budgeted at €21 billion, for example, was reduced to €7 billion. Equally, the goal for achieving environmentally cleaner transport has only partially been fulfilled. Much of the difficulty in these areas lies in the political unwillingness of the EU to consider applying the most elementary economic principles to what are largely economic problems. The power of coalitions of vested interests, both in the public and the private sectors, has partially stymied policy initiatives.

16.6 Conclusion

Papers written in the early 1990s were extremely pessimistic about the prospects for any viable transport policy being initiated within the EU. That transport was important was seldom questioned, but prior attempts to do anything other than tinker with the prevailing, largely national driven, transport policies had proved disappointing. Early efforts in the 1960s to draw up what essentially amounted to a master plan or blueprint policy had failed. The problems of continued EU enlargement, coupled with fresh, often radical thinking on how transport as a sector should be treated, seemed to pose almost insurmountable problems for policymakers in the 1970s and 1980s. These problems were not helped by mounting concerns over physical and institutional bottlenecks in the EU's transport system that were manifestly an impediment to any radical shift towards a more rapid phase of economic integration.

At the time of writing the picture is entirely different. Certainly, many issues remain to be resolved (CEU 2006r), such as the initiation of more rational pricing for most modes, but by and large transport inadequacies are no longer seen as a major threat to further economic and political integration within the EU. There is broad agreement that transparency and market-based systems afford an efficient way to meet EU transport needs. While there has been much wasted time and effort, and significant economic, social and political costs are inevitably associated with this, the current phase of transport policy formulation can be seen as one of the important recent successes of the EU.

Summary

- Transport is a major EU industry, facilitating trade and personal mobility, as well as being a large employer of labour, consumer of energy and creator of infrastructure. MSs have traditionally focused on domestic networks, often paying scant attention to international transport gateways or corridors within the continent, and, for military reasons, even consciously limiting cross-border movements.

- The importance of having some form of CTP as an integral part of EU economic and political integration goes back to the ECSC in 1951. The development of such a policy has been slow, spasmodic and incomplete. National interests, geography, established institutions, new technologies, available infrastructure and changing demand patterns have hindered progress. While a CTP was one of the two major common policies in the EEC Treaty of Rome in 1957, little of substance happened for three decades.

- The EU's focus on transport policy has shifted with time. The ECSC was concerned with the efficiency of freight railways because of its importance in the carriage of bulk commodities, but after the EEC Treaty, trucking became the main concern because of its role as a mover of manufactures; air transport grew in relevance as globalization increased from the 1990s; and more recently attention has turned to less environmentally intrusive transport and to fuel efficiency. With these shifts in modal priorities have come accompanying changes in the types of policy areas given priority, with, in broad terms, concerns about subsidies and economic pricing of operations shifting to matters of market access and economic regulation, and then to challenges in the provision and pricing of infrastructure, and recently to more socially oriented subjects.

- The major movement forward in EU transport policy

came with the creation of the SEM in the 1990s that allowed free supply of transport services across the borders of MSs, and the subsequent support of the development of Trans-European Networks that have begun to provide the infrastructure to physically allow more intra-EU transport. The more recent trends in policy have included, first, taking more account of the social and environmental implications of transport in such things as pricing, regulation and investments, and second, beginning to develop policies to improve the efficiency of extra-EU transport by giving the Commission powers to negotiate with non-MSs.

Questions and essay topics

1. What factors initially limited the development of an EU CTP?
2. What were the main gains to the EU's economy due to the freeing up of the internal transport market after the initiation of the SEM?
3. Why did the EU pursue a phased approach to airline liberalization, as opposed to the USA's 'big bang approach'?
4. How have the various EU enlargements stimulated reforms in transport policy and how have they stymied them?
5. What are the Trans-European Networks?
6. What are low-cost airlines and why are they important?
7. Put the case against the Commission getting involved in the detailed pricing of transport services.
8. Why was it so problematic for the first 30 years after the signing of the Treaty of Rome in 1957 to develop a CTP?
9. How should the EU approach developing an extra-European transport policy?

FURTHER READING

Banister, D., Stead, D., Steen, P., Akerman, J., Dreborg, K., Nijkamp, P. and Schleicher-Tappeser, R. (2000) *European Transport Policy and Sustainable Mobility*, Spon, London.

Button, K. J. (2000) 'Transport in the European Union', in J. B. Polak and A. Heertje (eds.) *Analytical Transport Economics: An International Perspective*, Edward Elgar, Cheltenham.

(2005) 'The European market for airline transportation and multimodalism', in European Conference of Ministers of Transport, *Airports as Multinational Interchange Nodes*, ECMT, Paris.

(2010) *Transport Economics*, 3rd edn, Edward Elgar, Cheltenham.

Chlomoudis, C. I. and Pallis, A. A. (2002) *European Union Port Policy: The Movement Towards a Long-Term Strategy*, Edward Elgar, Cheltenham.

Eno Transportation Foundation/European Commission (2002) *Intermodal Freight Transport in Europe and the United States*, Eno Foundation, Washington D.C.

Leinbach, T. R. and Capineri, C. (eds.) (2007) *Globalized Freight Transport: Intermodality, E-Commerce, Logistics, and Sustainability*, Edward Elgar, Cheltenham.

Lepori, C. (2010) *Sustainable Intermodal Freight Transport in Europe: Motorways of the Sea Services and Innovative Railway*, AP Lambert Academic Publishing, Saarbrücken.

Ross, J. (1998) *Linking Europe: Transport Policies and Politics in the European Union*, Praeger, Westport, Conn.

NOTES

1 Now the International Transport Forum.
2 Panamax and New Panamax are widely used terms referring to the size of ships passing through the Panama canal.

17 Energy policy and energy markets

STEPHEN MARTIN AND ALI EL-AGRAA

17.1 Introduction

Energy has been central to the European Union (EU) ever since its inception: witness the creation of the European Coal and Steel Community (ECSC) in 1951, and the European Atomic Energy Community (Euratom) in 1957. The details of these treaties (and their rationales) are covered in Chapter 2, but their significance for energy policy is clear enough. The ECSC reflected the dominance of coal in the energy balance of member states (as well as its role in the steel industry): by tackling coal, most European Community (EC) energy supply and demand issues were addressed. Euratom sought to foster cooperation in the development of civil nuclear power, then perceived as the main source of future energy requirements (Lucas 1977). Moreover, in principle, both were geared towards the creation of free and integrated markets in these sectors: the ECSC, being a common market (CM; see Chapter 1), sought to abolish all barriers to trade between the Member States (MSs), while controlling subsidies and cartel-like behaviour among producers, and Euratom aspired to do likewise for nuclear products.

A CM for other energy sectors was addressed in the EEC Treaty. While the EEC was oriented towards more or less competitively structured sectors, it also applied to the more oligopolistic or monopolistic sectors, such as oil, gas and electricity. Accordingly, in addition to being subject to the EEC Treaty's general provisions on opening up markets, these energy industries' special characteristics were covered by the Treaty's provisions on state enterprises and their conduct (see Chapter 13).

The gap between intentions expressed in the treaties and the outcomes, however, has been a large one for energy – more so than for most other parts of the economy. The attempts by the European Commission (Commission) to develop a common energy policy (CEP) of any sort, let alone one reflecting the ideals of the treaties, have proved to be of only limited success. MS governments have grudgingly left energy sectors to the marketplace when energy markets seemed to be working well. When they suffered disorienting shocks – all too often – they intervened directly, or tried to do so. Throughout, the Commission has been true to its vocation, seeking to lay the foundations for a single EU energy market. The results have been mixed in terms of coping with periodic crises, and have impeded the development of an effective CEP.

This chapter considers the EU's role in energy policy, notes past attempts to create a CEP, assesses the factors behind their failure and examines why the EU has been more successful of late in influencing national policies. After discussing the situations in the different EU energy markets, current policy proposals and their context are reviewed. Finally, some of the difficulties the Commission faces in developing a credible CEP, and prospects for the future, are assessed.

17.2 The golden years (mostly)

In the immediate aftermath of the Second World War, Europe faced shortages and rationing of food and fuel. The most pressing concern was to jump-start production. The idea that European coal would go into secular decline would have been inconceivable in the late 1940s. Yet that is what happened. European production took off in the 1950s, as shown in Figure 17.1, and energy consumption went along with it. But the energy that was consumed was generated from crude oil, which was cheaper and cleaner than coal. Most of that crude oil came from the Middle East.

From the 1950s onwards, the Commission or its equivalents sought first to develop a policy for coal and then for energy more broadly (El-Agraa and Hu 1984).

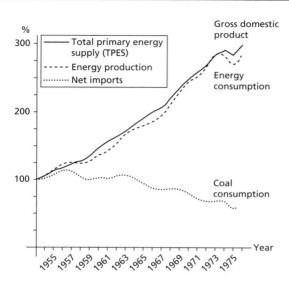

Figure 17.1 Indices of EC6 GDP, primary energy consumption and coal consumption, 1953–1979 (1953 = 100) *Source:* CEU 1977b (Table 1)

On coal, the High Authority of the ECSC was unable to impose the spirit of the treaty on national industries. It was mainly involved in tackling the crises which beset the European coal industry from the mid-1950s onwards (Lindberg and Scheingold 1970), crises triggered by the decline shown in Figure 17.1.

In the sphere of energy generally, initial efforts were made as the negotiations for the EEC were progressing. The Messina conference recommended that the potential for coordinated energy policy be considered, but the Spaak Committee determined that this would not be necessary (von Geusau 1975).

Following the establishment of the new Communities, there was a renewed attempt to develop a CEP. An inter-executive committee on energy formed in 1959 sought to develop a policy focusing on the creation of a common energy market. The main concerns of the committee were the effect of energy prices on industrial competitiveness, and, to a lesser extent, the security of energy supply (Political and Economic Planning 1963). However, governments largely rejected the committee's attempts to gain access to energy policy. Instead, they exercised benign neglect towards the energy sector. This inertia on energy policy reflected the largely untroubled energy markets of the period. Yet when there was concern over supply in the 1950s

and 1960s (such as in the wake of the Suez crisis), governments were keen to retain their autonomy.

The merger of the Communities in 1965 saw the Commission renew its efforts to develop a CEP. In its *First Guidelines Towards an EC Energy Policy* (CEU 1968b), the Commission noted continuing barriers to trade in energy, stressed the need for a common energy market and proposed three broad objectives: a plan for the sector involving data collection and forecasting as a means of influencing members' investment strategies; measures to bring about a common energy market (tackling issues such as tax harmonization, technical barriers and state monopolies); and measures to ensure security of supply at lowest cost.

The proposals proved difficult to put into practice, partly because of the scale of objectives and contradictions between the substance of different goals, but mainly because of the resistance of MSs. Even though the Council approved the strategy, it ignored most of the Commission's subsequent attempts to enact the proposals. The principal measures adopted in the wake of the Commission's proposals concerned oil stocks (following OECD initiatives) and some requirements for energy investment notification. These actions owed more to growing concern about security of supply than to the creation of a common energy market, and presaged a wider shift in MS perceptions of the priorities of energy policy.

17.3 Oil shocks and afterwards

The golden age of cheap oil and well-functioning energy markets came to an end with the oil shocks of 1973 and 1979. These shocks triggered downturns in worldwide economic activity.

Energy demand responds to price changes, but with a lag, reflecting the time needed to develop energy-efficient production techniques and install the physical capital required to put those techniques into effect. EU energy use became more efficient after the oil crises of the 1970s. Thirty years later, the EU economy consumes less primary energy and less oil per unit of gross domestic product (GDP). Electricity consumption per unit of GDP, much of it generated using natural gas, levelled off in the mid-1980s.[1] At the same time, reliance on imported energy fell from the mid-1970s to the mid-1980s. In the early twenty-first century there has been a gradual decline in production of primary energy, and a gradual increase in energy imports (Eurostat 2010f, p. 10).

In the midst of the first oil shock, the EC attempted a crisis management role, but failed even to provide a united front vis-à-vis OAPEC over an oil embargo of the Netherlands (Daintith and Hancher 1986). MSs pursued their own policies or worked through the International Energy Agency (IEA). Formed in 1974, the IEA overshadowed the EC, both in breadth of membership (covering all OECD countries except France) and in terms of its powers on oil sharing in a new crisis (van der Linde and Lefeber 1988).

Even so, the shock of oil price increases prompted the reassessment of energy policies by MSs and the Commission. The Commission attempted to develop a more strategic approach to the management of energy supply and demand. The 'New Strategy' (*Bulletin of the European Communities,* Supplement 4/1974), which was only agreed after much wrangling and dilution (a proposal for a European energy agency was abandoned after MS opposition; see Lucas 1977), envisaged a number of targets to be met by 1985. These included the reduction of oil imports, the development of domestic energy capabilities (notably nuclear power) and the rational use of energy. The policy, while only indicative, mobilized resources for R&D and promotional programmes on energy, covering conventional and nuclear technologies, but also (albeit to a limited extent) renewables and energy-efficiency technologies. The new strategy was the basis for a handful of directives designed to restrict the use of oil and gas.

The New Strategy clearly entailed a shift in emphasis. The goal of a common energy market was demoted, although it was alluded to in areas such as pricing policies and some measures directed at the oil sector (see page 262). Overall, policy was concerned with changing the structure of energy balances rather than the structure of energy markets. The condition of energy markets (notably after the second oil shock) and concern over energy prices and security in the early 1980s were such that the policy was sustained into the decade. Further rounds of energy policy objectives were agreed in 1979 (to be met by 1990) and 1986 (for 1995). The 1995 objectives included a number of 'horizontal' ones, aimed at more general energy policy concerns, such as its relationship with other EC policies. Each round sought to build on the previous one. Although

in general the goals appeared to be on target, in some cases they reflected a degree of failure either across the EC or in certain member states, and subsequent rounds adopted rather less ambitious agendas (CEU 1984b, 1988d). The objectives approach later reappeared as part of the EU energy strategy (CEU 1996m).

By the mid-1980s, therefore, the Commission had succeeded in establishing a place in energy policy-making, but it was far from being central to MSs' energy policy agendas, let alone sufficiently influential to dictate the development of a common energy market. Instead, its role consisted of information gathering, target setting and enabling activities (the latter had a substantial budget for energy R&D and promotion). While these measures ensured that the Commission had an influence on policy, they were not without problems – some of the objectives showed few signs of achievement, while aspects of the Commission's funding strategies were also open to criticism (Cruickshank and Walker 1981). Moreover, aside from a few legislative measures, the Commission's policy had few teeth. The locus of power remained with national governments, which generally chose to follow their own energy policies, resisting too strong a Commission role.

17.4 Demand and supply: the status quo

Table 17.1 gives a breakdown of primary energy sources for the EU27 for the year 2008. Oil remains the leading source of EU energy, and by far the largest part of that oil is imported.

The trend in energy use is upward (International Energy Agency 2008, p. II.27). This trend is expected to continue. Commission projections are that EU energy consumption in 2020 will be 22 per cent greater than EU energy consumption in 1990 (Council 2001, p. 46). It is also expected that oil and gas will continue to supply the lion's share of EU energy needs (see Table 17.2). The share of natural gas is expected to rise.

The share of imported energy in overall EU energy use is expected to rise from the current near 50 per cent to 70 per cent (EU15; see Table 17.2). The anticipated increasing share of oil imports reflects in part the decline in output of North Sea oil, which peaked in 1999. The rate of decline has been slowed by technological advance, but will continue.

Table 17.1 Composition of primary energy supply (millions of tonnes of oil equivalent), EU27, 2008

	Production	Imports	Exports	Net supply	% TPES[1]
Coal, lignite, peat	177.35	153.04	–	330.39	17.79
Oil and oil products	107.35	955.85	357.21	705.99	38.00
Gas	168.12	347.37	72.88	442.61	23.83
Nuclear	241.76	–	–	241.76	13.01
Combustible, renewable, waste	102.32	–	–	102.32	5.51
Electricity (includes hydro)	28.15	26.19	24.77	29.57	1.59
Other	17.66	15.66	28.79	4.53	0.24
Total	842.71	1498.11	483.15	1857.67	100.00

Note: [1] Total primary energy supply

Source: Eurostat 2010f, p. 10

17.5 Current energy policy agenda: sustainability, security, competitiveness

The Commission's 2007 *An Energy Policy for Europe* (CEU 2007a) paved the way for the 2009 Third Energy Package. It highlights the three facets of EU energy policy: sustainability, security of supplies and competitiveness.

17.5.1 Sustainability

The Commission's interest in environmental issues is not new. The formal EC commitment to environmental policy dates from early 1972, when, in the wake of the Stockholm conference, the Council agreed a programme of action. Some measures on environmental problems predated even this initiative (Haigh 1989). While the Commission's concerns on the environment are very wide-ranging (see Chapter 18), covering issues such as chemical waste, water quality and noise pollution, the consequences of energy choices are a major part of the policy.

The importance of EC environmental policy for the energy sector has paralleled the ascent of the issue up the political agenda in an increasing number of MSs, particularly as the Greens have become a political force. In those cases where governments have been obliged to introduce new controls on pollution, they have sought to have them accepted across the EC so as not to lose competitiveness. The best example was

Table 17.2 Projected oil and gas consumption, share of imported energy in EU energy consumption, 1998–2030

	Projected share of oil and gas in total EU energy consumption (%)		Projected import dependence (%)	
	EU		EU	EU30
1998	64	61	49	36
2010	66	63	54	42
2020	66	65	62	51
2030	67	66	71	60

Source: CEU 2001h, p. 67

the acid rain debate, when the German government, forced to introduce major controls on domestic emissions from industrial and electricity plants, pressed for similar controls in all MSs (Boehmer-Christiansen and Skea 1990). These were agreed in 1988, setting targets for emission reduction into the next century.

The emergence of the environment has given the Commission a higher profile in energy matters and another, more robust, lever on energy policy (Owens and Hope 1989). The importance of the issue to energy policy was demonstrated in the 1995 objectives, where environmental concerns were identified as a major consideration in policy. The status of environmental issues overall was confirmed in the Single European Act

(SEA; see Chapter 2), where it was given its own provisions (allowing it to enforce decisions on a majority vote). The Single European Market (SEM; see Chapter 7) proposals also identify the need for high standards of environmental protection in the EC, and this has impacted on the internal energy market debate.

Integrating environment and energy has not been easy for the Commission; a document on the issue was apparently the focus for considerable dispute within the Commission because of the different perspectives of the Directorates for Energy and for the Environment (CEU 1989c). However, the issue that has brought the environment to the centre of Community energy policy-making and exposed the tensions between the two policies most starkly has been the greenhouse effect.

The Commission has sought to coordinate a common European response to the threat of global warming. In 1991, with the exception of the UK, MSs agreed to stabilize emissions of CO_2 by the year 2000. In the following year it produced proposals for decreasing emissions of greenhouse gases, particularly CO_2 (CEU 1992c). These comprised four elements: programmes to encourage the development of renewable energy sources (which have zero or very low carbon dioxide emissions) and of energy efficiency, a monitoring system, and a carbon-energy tax to discourage the use of fossil fuels.

The Commission's 2007 *Energy Policy* (CEU 2007a) proposes an EU goal of a 20 per cent reduction of greenhouse gases, from the 1990 level, by 2020. The EU's 'cap and trade' emissions control system, which limits aggregate emissions and allows covered emitters to trade allowances within the limit, is central to plans to achieve this goal. Another element is the 2006 Energy Efficiency Action Plan, which seeks to promote efficient energy use in transportation, buildings, and the generation, distribution and use of electricity. In recognition of the value of market incentives, part of the Action Plan is 'ensuring that the true costs of transport are faced by consumers' (COM (2007) 1 final, p. 13).

The Commission reaffirmed the objective of increasing reliance on renewable energy, setting the ambitious goal of a 20 per cent share of renewables in EU energy use by 2020. It acknowledged that previous efforts had fallen short of their goal, which it attributed to the relatively high cost of renewable energy and the absence of a stable, long-term EU policy framework. It pledged to reduce reliance on fossil fuels.[2] It noted both the cost

advantages of and the controversy surrounding the generation of electricity from nuclear reactions. Here the decision is left at MS level; the Commission sees its role as ensuring 'the most advanced framework for nuclear energy in those [MSs] that choose nuclear power, meeting the highest standards of safety, security and non-proliferation' (COM (2007) 1 final, p. 18).

17.5.2 Security

The security situations regarding crude oil and natural gas supplies are different. The market for crude oil is a world market. Before 1973 it was a large-numbers oligopoly, the most important operators on the supply side being the Seven Sisters.[3] The rise of OPEC, itself a large-numbers oligopoly, cut the vertically integrated majors loose from their crude supplies. The majors' distribution networks remained valuable assets, and oil provinces outside OPEC proved only too willing to hire the majors to develop their own oilfields. The majors thus integrated backwards, by ownership or contact, into production, and developed new oil supplies.

As the shares of output and proven reserves outside OPEC control rose, OPEC members learned the hard lesson that a business's most important asset is its customers. OPEC national oil companies integrated forwards into refining and distribution. The world oil market continues to be a large-numbers oligopoly, and the numbers are larger than they were in 1973.

Table 17.3 shows regional data on production and proven reserves of crude oil for the year 2008. Table 17.4 (page 263) shows similar data for natural gas. The figures for proven reserves should be interpreted with caution, for at least three reasons. The first is that reported figures for proven reserves in the Middle East are widely believed to be understated. The second is that not all proven reserves are created equal: what one would really like, for each region, are not figures for total supply, but rather a kind of cumulative marginal cost curve: how much could be extracted at a cost less than x per barrel (per million BTUs, in the case of natural gas), how much at a price of $x + 1$ per barrel, and so on. The third, related to the second, is that the march of technological progress continually expands the amount of crude oil and natural gas that it is profitable to extract from known oilfields. Even if no new fields are developed, proven reserves next year are not proven reserves today minus production during the year. Proven

Table 17.3 World proven production, crude oil reserves, by region, 2008

	Production		Proven reserves	
	1,000 barrels per day	% world total	Million barrels	% world total
Middle East	23,125.5	32.1	752,258.0	58.1
Eastern Europe	12,028.9	16.7	128,979.0	10.0
Latin America	9,811.1	13.6	210,507.0	16.3
Africa	9,323.7	12.9	122,041.0	9.4
Asia and Pacific	7,397.7	10.3	40,278.0	3.1
North America	6,303.5	8.8	26,217.0	2.0
Western Europe	4,037.9	5.6	14,805.0	1.1
Total world	72,028.3	100.0	1,295,085.0	100.00
OPEC	33,093.0	45.9	1,027,383.0	79.3

Source: OPEC 2009, pp. 20, 22

reserves next year are proven reserves today, minus production during the year, plus the additional deposits that it becomes profitable to produce from known oil-fields as extraction technology improves.[4]

By luck of geology, most of the world's crude oil reserves are located in the Middle East. All evidence is that these deposits are much less costly to extract than oil deposits located elsewhere in the world.

Production of crude oil is much less geographically concentrated than are proven reserves. Middle Eastern producers, more generally OPEC member states (members), could easily supply most of the world's oil – at a lower price than they would like. By attempting to restrict their own output, OPEC members (through their national oil companies) set two forces in motion.

First, OPEC as a group creates incentives for each individual OPEC member, acting in its own immediate interest, to produce more than its OPEC quota output. Indeed, OPEC members consistently produce more than they have agreed to produce. The interests of the various OPEC members, not only those in the Middle East and those located elsewhere, but also those located in the Middle East taken as a group, are simply too diverse to expect most OPEC members to pay more than lip service to agreed output levels.

Second, to the extent that OPEC succeeds in raising the price of crude oil, it makes it economical to exploit deposits that would otherwise remain in the ground for decades. This second effect works with long lags, and it is to those lags that OPEC owed the momentary market

control it enjoyed in the 1970s. The effects of induced entry are also long-lasting. Given the high ratio of fixed to marginal cost in developing oilfields, and the fact that fixed investments are also largely sunk,[5] once higher-average-cost oilfields come on line they tend to produce as long as price remains above a level of marginal cost that is far lower than average cost.

Thus, from Table 17.3, North America's share of world oil production in 2008 was 4.4 times its share of proven oil reserves. Western Europe's share of world oil production in 2008 was 5.1 times its share of proven oil reserves. It would be easy, and simplistic, to conclude that, at 2008 production rates, Western Europe will have completely exhausted its oil supplies in about ten years, and North America in about eleven years, at which point OPEC will have those regions over a barrel, so to speak. Long before physical supplies are exhausted in the old oil provinces of North America and Western Europe – indeed, long before the world price of crude oil would make it profitable to exhaust those supplies – new oil provinces will come online. Supplies from those provinces will be available in North America and Western Europe, not out of good will, but because international trade based on comparative advantage is mutually beneficial.

Neither OPEC nor the core of Middle Eastern OPEC members were able to stop the rise in the spot market price of crude oil to above $131 per barrel at the end of June 2008, or its fall to under $35 per barrel at the start of January 2009.[6] Oil-producing states take such

Table 17.4 World proven natural gas reserves and marketed production, by region, 2008

	Production		Proven reserves	
	Million standard m^3	% world total	Billion standard m^3	% world total
Eastern Europe	832,790.0	27.3	55,000.0	30.1
North America	749,100.0	24.5	9,168.0	5.0
Asia and Pacific	410,580.0	13.4	15,394.0	8.4
Western Europe	282,750.0	9.3	5,292.0	2.9
Middle East	382,511.0	12.5	75,298.0	41.2
Latin America	194,230.0	6.4	8,007.0	4.4
Africa	202,110.0	6.6	14,692.0	8.0
Total world	3,054,071.0	100.0	182,842.0	100.0
OPEC	565,461.0	18.5	93,347.0	51.1

Source: OPEC 2009, pp. 20, 24

advantage as they can of fluctuations in the crude oil market, but they do not control those fluctuations.

The security issue with natural gas is not so much that EU MSs import a substantial portion of their natural gas; it is that a good deal of this natural gas is imported from Russia, a government whose understanding of the market mechanism must at present be held to differ from that of longer-established capitalist countries. The share of natural gas imports from Russia for EU MSs listed in Table 17.5 varies from 24.8 to 100 per cent, with many of the Eastern MSs critically dependent on Russian supplies.

The difficulties inherent in this relationship became clear in January 2006, and again in January 2009, when the Russian firm Gazprom reduced previously contracted deliveries of natural gas to Ukraine. Nominally, the motive was to impress on Ukraine that it was reasonable to agree to pay prices closer to world market levels. It was widely believed that Russian government displeasure over Ukraine's political shift toward the West also played a role in the interruption of natural gas supplies. Be that as it may, the bulk of EU natural gas imports from Russia passes through Ukraine, and the Russian action disrupted deliveries to major EU customers as well as to Ukraine.[7]

The 2007 *Energy Policy* highlights the need to diversify supplies of natural gas, which it proposes to do by setting up new gas hubs in Central Europe and the Baltic states, constructing new natural gas terminals, and investing in storage facilities and strategic gas

Table 17.5 Natural gas imports of selected EU members states from the Russian Federation, 2009 (billion cubic metres)

	Imports from Russia	Total imports	% from Russia
Austria	5.44	7.98	68.2
Czech Republic	9.40	9.40	100.0
Estonia	0.71	0.71	100.0
Finland	4.10	4.10	100.0
France	8.20	49.06	16.5
Germany	31.50	88.82	35.5
Greece	2.05	3.29	62.3
Hungary	7.20	8.10	88.9
Italy	20.80	66.41	31.3
Latvia	1.19	1.19	100.0
Lithuania	2.77	2.77	100.0
Netherlands	4.26	17.21	24.8
Poland	7.15	9.15	78.1
Romania	2.05	2.05	100.0
Slovakia	5.40	5.40	100.0
Slovenia	0.51	0.89	57.3

Source: BP 2010, pp. 33–4

reserves. New natural gas pipelines have been put in place in Central Europe.[8] If it is completed, the proposed Nabucco pipeline would carry Turkish natural gas to Austria from 2015.

17.5.3 Internal energy market

Energy prices stabilized and faltered in the early 1980s and continued to weaken until the 1986 oil price collapse. The reasons for this were more fundamental than the rows within OPEC that precipitated the fall in prices. The price increases of the early 1980s had had the effect of boosting output in OPEC countries, as well as fostering exploration and production in the rest of the world. Furthermore, many countries had sought to improve energy efficiency and diversify sources of energy (if not to the levels sought by the Commission). The economic recession of the 1980s dampened demand. The combined effect of these factors was overcapacity in supply and minimal demand growth, which forced down prices. The effects were not confined to oil: gas and coal were in equally plentiful supply, while past over-investment in electricity capacity also boosted the energy surplus.

The combined effect of these developments was to weaken the scarcity culture that had prevailed among suppliers, consumers, governments and the Commission. As prices fell and markets appeared well supplied, policy focused less on energy supply per se and more on prices and the existence of obstacles to good market performance.

This change in market conditions made it difficult to sustain energy policies fostering conservation or diversification from high-price fuels. In some countries, governments abandoned traditional approaches to energy policy. The UK was the most notable example, moving explicitly to reliance on market forces for determining supply and demand. A major plank of that policy was deregulation, with attempts to introduce competition to gas and power, and privatization, including the sale of oil interests and then the gas and electricity industries (Helm *et al.* 1989). Shifts in policy were under review in other parts of the EC (Helm and McGowan 1989), although these were often conceived at a less ambitious level or pursued for rather different reasons.

The deregulatory thrust was not confined to the energy sector; indeed it was probably initially more widely spread in other areas of the economy. It was at the forefront of the Commission's plans for the SEM (see Chapters 2 and 6), as covered in the White Paper (CEU 1985a). Partly due to past energy policy failures, the Commission did not include energy in the initial agenda for the SEM. However, areas where energy was affected indirectly by more general SEM measures (such as indirect taxation and procurement policies) meant that the sector was not untouched by the proposals.

Indeed, there were already some signs of a different policy towards energy. The issue of price transparency was extended across the energy industries, with attempts to agree a directive (see Chapter 2 for definition) on the issue. While the moves failed, they indicated a greater interest in the issue by the Commission. The Commission was also taking a greater interest in energy subsidies (as in the case of Dutch support to its horticultural industry through the provision of cheap gas). Other indications of change included moves to tackle state oil monopolies and the types of support given to the coal industry in a number of MSs.

The potential for more radical action was indicated by a number of moves taken by the Commission's Competition Directorate towards other utility industries. It sought the introduction of more competitive arrangements in the civil aviation industry, and was able to threaten the use of legal powers to this end. In telecommunications it sought (using powers under Article 90) to open access for equipment and service sales (see Chapter 13). These moves demonstrated not only a willingness to act, but also a range of mechanisms that could be used in other sectors. The further the policy went in one industry, the more likely it was that it would be applied to others.

This changing agenda meant that the idea of an internal energy market (IEM) was once again an issue for the EC. While the 1995 goals were largely flavoured by energy security concerns, one of the 'horizontal' objectives was the creation of an IEM. As the prospect of the SEM became realizable with the '1992' campaign, the idea of extending it to energy took root, and in 1987 the Energy Commissioner, Nicolas Mosar, announced a study of the barriers to an IEM.

The Commission's thinking was revealed in *The Internal Energy Market* (CEU 1988e), a review which set out the potential benefits of and obstacles to an IEM. An IEM would cut costs to consumers (particularly to energy-intensive industries), thereby making European industry as a whole more competitive; it would increase security of supply by improving integration of the energy industries; and it would rationalize the structure of the energy industries and allow for greater complementarity among the different supply and demand profiles of MSs. The benefits would stem from a mixture of cost-reducing competition and the achievement of scale economies in a number of industries. Taken together these would more than recover the 0.5 per cent of EC GDP that the Commission claimed was the 'cost of non-Europe' in the energy sector (although, as noted, energy was not part of the original SEM debate, nor of the 'cost of non-Europe' exercise that assessed the benefits of the SEM; see Cecchini 1988; Emerson *et al.* 1988; and Chapter 7).

According to the Commission, the obstacles to an IEM were to be found in the structures and practices of the energy industries. These ranged from different taxation and financial regimes to restrictive measures that protected energy industries in particular countries, and conditions that prevented full coordination of supplies at the most efficient level (the latter applying to the gas and electricity industries). However, as the Commission admitted, the effects of particular practices were difficult to assess given the special nature of the energy industries. Indeed, in certain cases, the Commission appeared hesitant over the extent of an IEM. Nonetheless, the document demonstrated that the Commission was committed to implementing an IEM and would examine all barriers to its development. It has followed up that commitment with measures to implement the White Paper proposals (on taxation and procurement) and to apply EC law to the sector.

The historical choice for the organization of electricity and natural gas supply has been the vertically integrated, often publicly owned, regional monopolist, with the regional monopoly covering part or all of the MS concerned. Vertical integration was justified, if it was not simply regarded as the obvious choice, on the grounds that transmission was a natural monopoly (more on this below), and that, particularly in the case of electricity, the precise coordination between supply and demand required to make the system work made integration the only practical option.

The consensus behind the public firm/public utility model unravelled in the 1980s.[9] One contributing factor was the oil shocks of the early and late 1970s, which rendered invalid the projected increases in demand on which energy-sector capacity plans had been based. Nuclear power also turned out to be more expensive than anticipated. Heightened public awareness of the environmental implications of nuclear and

carbon-based power generation effectively internalized some costs that had hitherto been ignored or treated as external in energy-sector planning. In some EU MSs, public firms had been directed to alter business behaviour in order to meet policy goals (hold down rates to fight inflation; maintain coal-fired generators to support the coal sector), with the effect of raising costs and, directly or indirectly, imposing burdens on the national budget. While the UK under Margaret Thatcher led the way (Newbery 1999a, pp. 6–24), the SEA of 1986 (see Chapter 2) inevitably called the position of energy-sector MS monopolists into question. Further, the macroeconomic constraints adopted by MSs in connection with the introduction of the euro created incentives to balance energy-sector operating accounts and get them off government budgets.[10]

The supply-side structures of all industries are shaped by the technologies they employ. However, the impact of the laws of nature on the organization of the electricity industry is distinctive, and only slightly less so on the natural gas industry.

The electricity supply chain can be broken down into generation, transmission, distribution and retailing (Jamasb and Pollitt 2005, p. 12; Green 2006, p. 2533). Transmission takes place over a grid. Electricity cannot be stored in a cost-effective way, and the electrons delivered to the grid by one generator are indistinguishable from those delivered by any other. The physical task of grid management is a daunting one (Green 2001, p. 330):

> Power flows from generators to consumers cannot be directed, but will be distributed along every line in the network, according to physical laws. If too much power attempts to pass along a given line, or through a particular transformer, that component of the network will fail. Following a failure in the network, the power flows will instantaneously redistribute themselves across the remaining circuits. If any of these are now overloaded, they in turn will fail. Millions of consumers can be blacked out in seconds. To minimize the risk of this, the grid controllers must run the system in such a way that power flows will be within safe limits, not just given the present state of the network, but if any link in it suddenly fails. This implies leaving a margin of spare capacity on every part of the network.

To these physical challenges are added economic challenges. To achieve good economic performance, lower-cost generators should be used before higher-cost generators. The price received by generators should reflect the marginal cost of production, to give proper signals about the nature of maintenance and new capital investment needed for the future. At the same time, price must cover the average cost of suppliers efficient enough to stay in business over the long run. Further, the prices paid by final consumers should reflect the marginal cost of production, to give proper signals about the scarcity of electricity relative to other energy sources and about the overall cost of energy, and thereby to encourage efficient consumption of energy.

These considerations suggest that transmission should be treated as a natural monopoly. In markets of reasonable size – and this includes both the EU and larger EU MSs – electric power generation is not a natural monopoly. Technological progress has made it possible to organize distribution in ways that permit rivalry, if not perfect competition in the classroom sense. The critical element in the introduction of an element of rivalry to distribution is the organization of access to the transmission grid, which is an essential facility standing between generation and distribution. Much the same role is played by the pipeline grid in the market for natural gas.

To promote competition where it was technically feasible, and effective regulation where it was not feasible, the Commission issued draft directives for the completion of the internal market in electricity and gas in 1992.[11] The Commission sought 'to introduce competition in the generation of electricity, the possibility to construct transmission and distribution lines (and the right to hook these up to the network) and third-party access to the network. These three measures effectively eliminate the exclusive rights which currently exist in each of these areas' (Argyris 1993, p. 34).

The question of access to transmission facilities proved to be a thorny one. The Commission first proposed a system of regulated third-party access, under which generators and retail distributors could use the grid to carry out contracts, subject to capacity constraints, at public and regulated rates. The idea of regulated third-party access was criticized by industry groups (Argyris 1993, p. 39) and in the European Parliament (Hancher 1997, p. 94). In later proposals the Commission added the option of *negotiated* third-party

access to transmission facilities, under which generators and retail distributors would work out contracts directly and the generator would negotiate the rate to be paid for use of the grid with the grid manager. At the insistence of France, an insistence that was widely interpreted as reflecting a reluctance to expose Électricité de France to competition, the first Electricity Directive[12] included the single buyer (SB) model for managing grid access. The SB model left consumers free to turn to independent suppliers, but delivery had to pass over the SB grid (Whitwill 2000).

In the event, SB was not adopted in its pure form by any MS. Most MSs opted for regulated third-party access. Germany chose negotiated third-party access. Italy and Portugal chose a combination of regulated third-party access and the SB model.[13]

Article 19 of the Electricity Directive included a detailed specification of the pace of liberalization. It also included a reciprocity clause: MSs could block access to their market of firms from other MSs that had liberalized to a lesser degree (Pelkmans 2001, p. 445, footnote omitted):

> The political background of this provision is the monopoly of Electricité de France (EdF), a fully integrated company, also fully state-owned . . . The reciprocity clause follows from the disparate progress in electricity liberalization among [MSs]: with a range of countries going faster than . . . EU calendar . . . the fear was that some countries, but in particular France, would stick to the minimum obligations, and otherwise exploit the many loopholes in the 1996 directives.

The reciprocity clause did not have the desired effect of ensuring that market opening went forward at a comparable rate across MSs. EdF made acquisitions in eleven other EU MSs, two of the EU candidate countries and in South America (CEU 2001c, p. 75), while the French market remained essentially closed to generators located in other MSs.

The Commission returned to the charge in 2003, with the second Electricity[14] and Gas[15] Directives, which seek 'to achieve, by July 2007 at the latest: (i) unbundling of transmission system operators (TSOs) and distribution system operators (DSOs) from the rest of the industry, (ii) free entry to generation, (iii) monitoring of supply competition, (iv) full market opening, (v) promotion of renewable sources, (vi) strengthening the role of the regulator, and (vii) a single European market'

(Jamasb and Pollitt 2005, p. 17). The Commission's own assessment of progress toward the creation of internal electricity and gas markets is glum: as of November 2005 (CEU 2005i, p. 2), 'electricity and gas markets remain[ed] national in scope'.[16]

For the Commission, factors contributing to the slow pace of market integration included the lacklustre pace at which MSs transposed the directives into national law (CEU 2005i, p. 4) and (for electricity in particular) constraints on interconnection capacity across MS boundaries (CEU 2005i, p. 5). The Commission also noted a trend of mergers and increasing horizontal concentration of gas and electricity.[17]

On the one hand, consolidation is to be expected as market size increases and firms seek to take advantage of economies of large-scale operation. Indeed, this is one source of gains from market integration – lower average cost. But if concentration goes too far, more efficient surviving firms may refrain from vigorous competition (Green 2006, p. 2540):

> The pattern is clear – Europe's larger electricity companies have been growing larger, acquiring footholds in new markets. These footholds could be used to compete aggressively across Europe, but the relatively limited number of really large companies, and the theory of multi-market contact, suggest a more worrying alternative, that the European electricity industry would become dominated by a few firms with little incentive to compete.

A 2007 Commission Communication renews the call for integrated, interconnected and competitive energy markets. It calls for unbundling either the ownership or the management of vertically integrated energy companies, on the ground that 'If a company controls the management of networks as well as production or sales, there is a serious risk of discrimination and abuse. A vertically integrated company has little interest in increasing the capacity of the network and thereby exposing itself to increased competition on the market and a consequent fall in prices.'[18]

The road to competitive energy markets will continue to be a rocky one. In July 2009 DG COMP, the administrator of EU competition policy, fined the French and German energy companies Gaz de France and E.ON €1.1 billion over an agreement that neither would compete in the other's market. The Commission later accepted commitments from Gaz de France and

E.ON to open up access to their gas transmission network, as a way of closing investigations into possible abuse of a dominant position.[19] To smooth the way, one element of the Third Energy Package is the Agency for the Cooperation of Energy Regulators, established by Regulation 713/2009,[20] to facilitate interactions among MS regulatory bodies and monitor the conduct of transmission system operators.

17.5.4 Infrastructure investment

The Commission has announced its intention to put forward an Energy Infrastructure Package (EIP) in November 2010. The EIP will promote the goals of completing an IEM, guaranteeing energy supply security, and ensuring compatibility of interconnected national gas and electric grids, with the goal of increased reliance on renewable energy (Vinois 2010). To this end, it is expected that an EIP will be accompanied by financial measures allowing for EU subsidies in the order of €15 billion for infrastructure investment.

17.6 Conclusion

The EU will increasingly rely on sources of primary energy located outside its borders. Efficient energy use, the development of alternative energy sources, and the geographic diversification of sources of supply can ensure long-run energy security. Strategic reserves are a way to insure against short-run disruptions of primary energy supplies.

Market integration is a process that brings short-run adjustment costs and promises long-run benefits. EU energy-sector integration will bring greater efficiency and reduced costs for what is an essential input to virtually all EU economic activity. The long-run benefits of energy-sector integration are immense. Political pressures rooted in the short-run adjustment costs that come with market integration slow down the process. Commission proposals for energy integration date back to 1992; full freedom of choice of supplier came into effect on 1 July 2007. The realization of the internal energy market will come after that. The internal EU energy market is not yet complete; that it will be completed is not in doubt.

Summary

- Energy has been central to the EU since its inception. This is attested to by the creation of the ECSC in 1951, and Euratom in 1957.
- The ECSC reflected the dominance of coal in the energy balance of MSs (as well as its role in the steel industry). By tackling coal, most EC energy supply and demand issues were addressed.
- Euratom sought to foster cooperation in the development of civil nuclear power, then perceived as the main source of future energy requirements.
- Both the ECSC and Euratom were, in principle, geared towards the creation of free and integrated markets in the relevant sectors: the ECSC, being a CM, sought to abolish all barriers to trade between MSs, while controlling subsidies and cartel-like behaviour among producers, and Euratom aspired to do likewise for nuclear products.
- Also, a CM for other energy sectors was addressed in the EEC Treaty. While the EEC was oriented towards more or less competitively structured sectors, it also applied to the more oligopolistic or monopolistic sectors, such as oil, gas and electricity. Accordingly, in addition to being subject to the EEC Treaty's general provisions on opening up markets, these energy industries' special characteristics were covered by the treaty's provisions on state enterprises and their conduct.
- The gap between the intentions expressed in the treaties and the outcomes, however, has been a large one for energy – more so than for most other parts of the economy:
  - (a) The Commission's attempts to develop a CEP of any sort, let alone one reflecting the ideals of the treaties, have proved to be of only limited success.
  - (b) MS governments have grudgingly left energy sectors to the marketplace when energy markets seemed to be working well. When they suffered disorienting shocks – all too often – they intervened directly, or tried to do so.
  - (c) Throughout, the Commission has been true to its vocation, seeking to lay the foundations for a single EU energy market. The results have been mixed in terms of coping with periodic crises, and have impeded the development of an effective CEP.

Questions and essay topics

1. In the midst of the first oil shock, the EC attempted a crisis management role, but failed even to provide a united front vis-à-vis the OAPEC. Why was that?
2. By the mid-1980s, the Commission had succeeded in establishing a place in energy policy-making, but it was far from being central to MSs' energy policy agendas, let alone being sufficiently influential to dictate the development of a common energy market. Can you explain why?
3. Given the diversity of energy supplies in the individual EU MSs, would it not be more rational to let each devise its own ways for dealing with any problems in the sector?
4. 'The Commission's 2007 *An Energy Policy for Europe* highlights the three facets of EU energy policy: sustainability, security of supplies and competitiveness.' Explain and discuss.
5. Discuss the proposition that the EU's attempts at creating a CEP are at best feasible.

FURTHER READING

CEU (2007) *An Energy Policy for Europe* (http://europa.eu/legislation_summaries/energy/european_energy_policy/l27067_en.htm).

NOTES

1 International Energy Agency (2008, p. II.27). Here and below, IEA statistics are for European countries that are members of the OECD.
2 See also COM (2006) 843 final: 'Sustainable power generation from fossil fuels: aiming for near-zero emissions from coal after 2020'.
3 The Seven Sisters were five USA-based firms (Exxon, Gulf, Texaco, Mobil, Socal), plus British Petroleum and Royal Dutch/Shell; they are now consolidated into four firms (ExxonMobil, Chevron-Texaco, BP and Royal Dutch/Shell). Compagnie Française des Petroles (later Total, and later still TotalFinaElf) was sometimes listed as an eighth 'Seven Sister'.
4 Thus Table 17.3 shows proven reserves outside OPEC control in 2008 of 267,702 million barrels. In 1970 world proven reserves were 548,452 million barrels, of which OPEC held 72.8 per cent; proven reserves outside OPEC control were 149,707 million barrels. Despite thirty-five years of consumption, OPEC and

non-OPEC nations have substantially more proven reserves in 2008 than they acknowledged in 1970. Similarly, in 1970 there were 28,739 billion standard cubic metres of proven gas reserves outside OPEC control, versus 89,495 in 2008.

5 Literally as well as financially.

6 Likewise, the Russian firm Gazprom, which came to dominance in the supply of natural gas to Europe by contracting with Central European suppliers to buy natural gas at $340 per 1,000 cubic meters in 2009, could not stop European prices from falling to $280 per 1,000 cubic meters (Kramer 2009).

7 The projected Nord Stream pipeline, which is to lie under the Baltic Sea, will free Russian natural gas from the need to pass through Ukraine to reach the EU.

8 The Economist, 'United in the cause of undermining Russian pipeline monopolies', 4 March 2010, internet edition.

9 See Doyle and Siner 1999, pp. 1–3; Newbery 1999a, Chapter 1; Johnston 1999.

10 It is also fair to note that the one-off injections of cash resulting from privatization were a welcome element to MS governments.

11 CEC 1991d; Argyris 1993, p. 34. The Transit Directive of 1990, Council Directive 90/547/EEC, 29 October 1990, sought to promote the construction of electricity and gas networks linking MS networks, a matter that remains on the front burner.

12 EC Directive 96/92 concerning common rules for the internal market in electricity, *OJ L* 27/20, 30 January 1997, adopted 19 December 1996, with effect from 19 February 1997 (and with delays for Belgium, Ireland and Greece). The first Gas Directive was EC Directive 98/30 concerning common rules for the internal market in natural gas, *OJ L* 207 21 July 1998, adopted 22 June 1998, with effect from 10 August 1998.

13 On the Italian case, see Valbonesi (1998).

14 Directive 2003/54/EC of the European Parliament and of the Council of 26 June 2003 concerning common rules for the internal market in electricity and repealing Directive 96/92/EC *OJ L* 176, 15 July 2003, pp. 37–56.

15 Directive 2003/55/EC of the European Parliament and of the Council of 26 June 2003 concerning common rules for the internal market in natural gas and repealing Directive 98/30/EC *OJ L* 176, 15 July 2003, pp. 57–78.

16 On the Italian case, see Valbonesi (1998).

17 For details of gas and electricity mergers, see Codognet *et al.* 2002; Green 2006.

18 Communication from the Commission to the European Council and the European Parliament of 10 January 2007, 'An energy policy for Europe' COM(2007) 1 final' (http://europa.eu/legislation_summaries/energy/european_energy_policy/l27067_en.htm).

19 In February, April and May 2010 the Commission, in closing abuse-of-dominance investigations, accepted commitments by the Italian energy firm ENI, by Électricité de France, and by the Swedish power grid operator Svenska Kraftnat, respectively, to open up their markets to competition.

20 *OJ L* 211/1 14.8.2009. Companion regulations 714/2009 and 715/2009 deal with access to electricity and natural gas networks, respectively.

18 Environmental policy

IAN BARNES

18.1 Introduction

Concern about the state of the environment is not a new phenomenon. There have been attempts to address specific problems for generations, many of which involved dealing with public health issues, such as the need to improve the quality of the water system, but inevitably had an impact on the wider environment. Industrialization, population growth and the pace of urbanization had inevitable consequences for the state of the environment, with the health of populations suffering as a consequence. Neither of the two economic systems that emerged after the Second World War, communism and the free market, performed well in terms of environmental protection. The emphasis in the late 1940s and early 1950s was promoting recovery and material progress. There was no specific reference to environmental protection in the EEC Treaty of Rome. It was not until the inclusion of the environmental chapter in the Single European Act (SEA) in 1987 that the legal basis for an EU environmental policy was fully established.

The subsequent development of environmental policy was substantial, spurred by the accession of Austria, Finland and Sweden in 1995, which saw the EU embrace three states with a high-level commitment to environmental protection. However, the enlargements of 2004 and 2007 included ten Central and Eastern European countries (CEECs) with significant environmental problems. The scope and influence of the EU has grown at the same time as recognition that more needs to be done to protect the environment. The public believes that protecting the environment is an important issue, and therefore action in this area is likely to be popular and gain support for the EU. In a special Eurobarometer (2008) poll, 96 per cent of those asked across the EU27 said they thought that protecting the environment was important to them (64 per cent very important and 32 per cent fairly important). Also, 78 per cent thought that environmental problems had a direct effect on their daily life.

In this chapter the economic basis of EU environmental policy will be examined. Account will be taken of the EU's very limited powers to operate the desired economic levers directly and the fact that environmental policy is an area of shared competence. It will analyse the case for Member State (MS) and EU intervention in environmental issues and the way that the policy area has developed, in particular, the movement from the use of environmental rules as a tool to complete the internal market, to the attempt to create a comprehensive regime, involving global partners, to deal with the perceived major threat of global warming.

18.2 The nature of EU environmental policy

Environmental protection is only one aspect of the EU's actions to move towards the broader and more wide-ranging strategy to achieve the goals of sustainable development. The 1999 Treaty of Amsterdam provided an explicit reference to sustainable development for the first time (Council 1997d, Article 1.2). The 2001 European Council in Göteborg adopted the EU's first Sustainable Development Strategy (SDS). An external dimension to this was added by the European Council in Barcelona in March 2002, in anticipation of the World Summit on Sustainable Development in Johannesburg in September 2002. A revised strategy was adopted by the European Council in June 2005 (European Council 2005a). As a consequence, the SDS

I wish to thank Alan Marin for helpful comments and suggestions.

commits the EU and its MSs to actions that will safeguard the earth's capacity to support life, offering a high level of environmental protection, and respect the limits of the planet's natural resources. Other objectives included social inclusivity, with a healthy and just society running a competitive, eco-efficient economy and meeting international commitments. The guiding policy principles thus place human beings at the centre of policy, through promoting public awareness and the involvement of business and social partners in making sustainable choices.

In an area as complex and diffuse as the environment, the promotion of policy coherence at the different levels of governance was considered as important as the policy integration. The core economic principles on which the EU's environmental policy is founded are:

- the use of best available knowledge;[1]
- the application of the precautionary principle, which suggests that it is best to take action to deal with potential environmental problems on the best available information, since it might well be too late if problems such as extreme climate change are left until the actual disaster arrives;
- decoupling resource use from economic growth; and
- making the polluters pay for the damage they cause.

The Treaty of Lisbon (formally the Treaty of the Functioning of the European Union, TFEU) firmly embeds sustainability into the treaties. The consolidated Treaty on European Union (TEU) states that the EU 'shall establish an internal market. It shall work for the sustainable development of Europe based on balanced economic growth and price stability, a highly competitive social market economy, aiming at full employment and social progress, and a high level of protection and improvement of the quality of the environment. It shall promote scientific and technological advance' (Article 3.3). Also, the TFEU stresses that sustainable development applies across the whole range of EU policies (see Chapter 25): 'Environmental protection requirements must be integrated into the definition and implementation of [EU] policies and activities, in particular with a view to promoting sustainable development' (Article 11). Environmental policy should therefore be seen in the context of a greater integration of EU policies within a wide spectrum of policy and mission.

18.3 The rationale for intervention

At its outset the EU was based on the idea of promoting economic activity, which almost invariably involves the use of resources and has an impact on the environment. In the early EU years it was clear that the focus of action was the promotion of the wider market access across Europe (indeed the organization was frequently called the common market), without taking environmental impacts into account. Intervention was driven by the need to promote trade: the gains from increased cross-border trade leading to greater economic welfare, reflecting a neoclassical economist's perspective for concern with individual welfare. However, it became clear over time that unregulated markets do not deliver an acceptable level of environmental protection. At the same time, the rationale for certain aspects of environmental policy goes beyond just the economic and pollution control and specific remedies. It is concerned with conservation, the protection of habitats and issues such as the maintenance of biodiversity.

The unregulated market mechanism fails to take account of the degradation of the environment caused by the existence of public goods and externalities (spillover effects; see Box 18.1). The basic feature of public goods is that it is difficult to prevent additional users from exploiting them (non-excludability), and additional users do not add to the cost (non-rivalness). Therefore many users are tempted to exploit the environment without contributing to its maintenance. Left to the free market, there is a tendency towards overproduction of pollutants and an under-availability of clean water. Even if environmental conditions are often poor, additional users are often tempted to 'free-ride', because refraining from doing so may simply add to costs reducing competitiveness. Examples of this include pumping toxic gases into the atmosphere and dumping waste into the sea.

If we compare the marginal private cost[2] (MPC) to the marginal social cost[3] (MSC) of production in a competitive industry that causes pollution, we can see in Figure 18.1 that the market equilibrium level of output and price level differs from the socially optimal level. Left to the free market the price of goods (P1) is too low and consumption is too high (Q2). When the cost of environmental damage is included to take account of environmental damage caused by producing the product, we can see that the price of the product should

Box 18.1 Externalities

Externalities occur when the actions taken by one economic agent (individual or firm) affect others, but where there is no feedback mechanism leading the agent to take correct account of the effects on others. Thus there are social benefits or they impose social costs on people other than the economic decision-takers. It is not the existence of an effect on others that constitutes an externality, but the lack of incentive to take full account of it. Every economic action may affect others, but in a well-functioning system the price mechanism provides incentives to take account of the effects. Externalities are a by-product that impacts on people or the environment that is not reflected in the market price, and this frequently means that commodities such as clean air and pure water are not available in the quantities that society may wish them to be.

If an individual's car pollutes the air and causes annoyance, or more serious harm, to others, the car owner could be said to be using up another scarce resource (quiet and clean air), but they do not have to pay for it. Hence, there will be times when using the car gives benefits to the individual that are less than the true cost to society – that is, the sum of the costs that the individual takes into account (the fuel) plus those that the individual does not consider (the pollution); the result is therefore not optimal. Thus another, exactly equivalent, way of expressing an externality is to define it as when the marginal private cost is not equal to the marginal social cost.

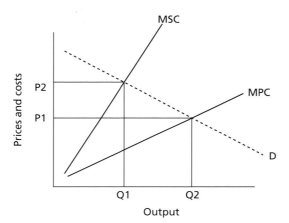

Figure 18.1 Market versus social equilibrium

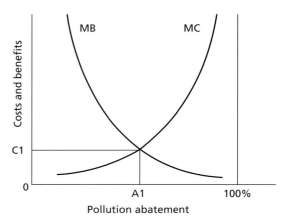

Figure 18.2 The optimum level of pollution abatement

rise to P2 and output should decline to Q1. One way to achieve a socially desirable level of output might be to impose a tax so that prices would reflect the social as well as the private cost, so as to achieve the ideal level of output.

While Figure 18.1 suggests that there is a problem of the prices being paid by the consumer being too low, it is easy to see how there might be disagreement about this by businesses who are driven by the profit motive, and their workers who may fear that their jobs will be sacrificed if social costs are fully included.

The total of individual business decisions is also important when the impact of environmental damage is considered. While it is desirable to remove highly

toxic pollution, which has an immediate impact on life forms of all types, it is not normally desirable – that is, efficient – to remove all forms of pollution, simply because it would be too expensive to do so relative to the benefits, especially as, in some cases, the environment can cope with this. The earth's biological systems, its so-called carrying capacity, give it the ability to deal with many of the challenges that man and nature throw at it, although it is important to remember that this is not infinite and pollution can be harmful, even if it is not dangerous. In Figure 18.2 the optimum level of pollution abatement is A1 and the cost to society is C1. This is where the marginal benefit (MB) of further pollution abatement is equal to the marginal cost (MC) of abatement. The marginal benefits will be the avoidance of certain costs and nuisances such as health risks. The marginal costs include the provision of additional treatment plants and other processes, which put a financial burden on companies and the state. The marginal (additional) benefits decline as more pollution is abated, hence the downward slope of the line from left to right. Costs increase as the level of pollution declines towards zero, so in most cases it is not possible or necessary to achieve 100 per cent abatement. If legislation proposes that there is to be 100 per cent abatement, the cost may well be prohibitive and there could be a greater risk of significant non-compliance.[4]

While individuals can act independently, they seldom have the power to counteract the activities of the polluters. In most cases individuals do not own the environment, and it is lack of ownership that encourages free-riding. One way forward might be to regard the environment as property, in the same way as a house or a car, but such an approach has its limitations. The issue of property rights and their ownership is of course highly contentious. Polluters cause the damage – for example, pumping smoke into the environment – because they feel that they are entitled to do so; perhaps they have been behaving like this for generations. At the same time, the victims of the poor quality air may claim that they are entitled to have clean air. The market fails because both parties feel that they have property rights, in which case it is up to the legal system to decide who actually owns them; however, by default, rights otherwise lie with the polluter. Once this is established, either the polluter or the victim, depending on who has the property rights, could pay to modify the behaviour of the other. This is a variant of the Coase theorem (Coase 1960), which suggests that it may be possible to bargain between the two parties to achieve a result. However, the idea of polluters being paid not to pollute flies in the face of the environmentalist's view of the world. The general view of the EU is that it is the polluter who should pay in almost all circumstances (see Section 18.7, page 277).

The property rights approach does not take into account the cost of environmental degradation on future generations. Although it might seem reasonable that each generation should attempt to leave the environment in an improved state for future generations, the public tends to place a very high value on consuming now and a very low value on benefits in the future.

When we are looking at the problem of global warming, for example, it is easy to dismiss the likely costs on the grounds that they are uncertain and may occur at some indeterminate time in the future. But global warming is something on which we may need to take action now if we are to prevent significant problems for the future.

We are now in an era when many more countries have gone through the industrialization process and we have massive globalized enterprises. In many cases the polluters may also have the backing of national governments, but not the international community. The failure of markets provides a rationale for collective action. Sometimes this can be organized by the state, by national laws or interventions, but the reality is that there is a high degree of interdependence across the boundaries of states. Acid rain from UK power stations has been thought to be the cause of dying forests in Scandinavia and Germany. The savings made by polluting the environment came to UK power plants, while the cost of dealing with the problem fell on others.

Two specific events demonstrated the problem of the spread of pollution across borders. The first was the explosion on 27 April 1986 at the nuclear plant at Chernobyl, which is now in Ukraine. Not only was there a huge amount of fallout in the immediate area, but the nuclear cloud spread across Europe, to places in Scandinavia and even to Wales. Although the number of immediate deaths was relatively small, there are still people dying today as a result of the longer-term effects of exposure. A second example also comes from 1986, when, on 1 November, there was an explosion and fire at the Sandoz Chemical plant in Basle, Switzerland. The efforts to extinguish the fire resulted in huge quantities of toxic compounds being washed into the Rhine. These pollutants did not kill humans, but killed off thousands of fish and water birds. Once the pollutants were in the river, there was nothing to be done to prevent the disaster unfolding, but lessons were learnt about the containment of pollution. The aftermath of both these disasters was that there was concerted action to prevent similar occurrences. Nuclear safety has remained a priority, especially after the 2004 EU enlargement, when Eastern European states joined with the older nuclear plants of the Chernobyl type.[5] In the case of the Sandoz accident, EU legislation put in place after the Seveso disaster in Italy (1976) was improved. The objectives of the Seveso II Directive (Council 1996) were to prevent major accidents involving dangerous substances, and to ensure that when accidents did occur, the consequences of these were limited for both man and the environment.

What the above illustrates is the importance of having an internationally coherent response to environmental disasters. But in the past international agreements have proved to be weak, because of a lack of an adequate means of enforcement. The EU, on the other hand, is well placed to construct an agreement that can be enforced throughout its territory. Increased commitments to environmental standards within the EU have also become a catalyst for actions in other areas of the world that seek trade agreements or development aid from the EU.

18.4 Standards and thresholds

Although Figures 18.1 and 18.2 seem to indicate a degree of precision regarding the extent of action needed to reduce the level of pollution, it is often unclear what the exact extent of environmental damage is, in part because it is unethical to conduct certain experiments, since we would be dealing with human beings or vulnerable species. Also, it can take many years for the full effects of toxicity from pollution to become apparent – for example, evidence in the case of forests that die back. The cause may be a local one, but even if it is caused by acid rain, the route of the pollution will depend on the prevailing winds and climatic conditions, which are difficult to predict. This has led the EU to try to collect reliable data on a variety of pollutants so that it is possible to enable statistical studies relating health issues to pollution. The earliest requirements were for data related to smoke and sulphur dioxide (1975 onwards) and water pollution (1977 onwards), and since 1987 there has been an attempt to gather systematic data on damage to trees.

Added to the problem of a lack of clear understanding of the damage caused by pollution is that many of the standards that are adopted are the result of a political process, and they are disguised as scientific standards (see Section 18.12, page 283). Each national government finds itself under constant pressure from vested interests to raise or lower standards. In the negotiation process the national position is, of course, always said to be fully supported by scientific evidence.

It may be that there is a limit to the extent that

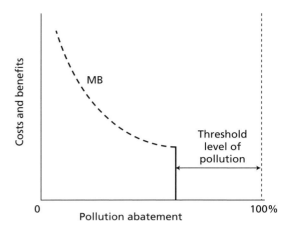

Figure 18.3 Pollution threshold

individuals or society can cope with pollution, but above which harm might start. In the policy process it is tempting to look for a threshold level of abatement, because it adds a degree of precision to policy positions. In the case depicted by Figure 18.3, it might be best to adopt the threshold as a standard. Only if the marginal cost curve cuts the marginal benefit curve to the left of the threshold would less abatement (higher pollution) be justified. This kind of threshold, however, if it is for society as a whole, may not fully encompass the needs of the vulnerable in society, such as the very young and the elderly. The fact that tolerance of pollution does vary means that the threshold level of pollution will continue to be debated. Mostly, society's tolerance of pollution tends to go down, perhaps a feature of a more affluent society (Pearce and Barbier 2002), implying that the whole MB curve shifts to the right.

The standards that have been set are rarely attainable instantly. It takes time for directives to be translated into national law (see Chapters 3 and 4), and it takes time for the investment to be made. So much so that, as we shall see in the case of the Bathing Water Directive (BWD), it took decades before there was an acceptable quality of water in some locations (Commission of the European Union and European Environment Agency 2010). Where standards are not achieved within a reasonable time, MSs concerned need to report this to the Commission on the basis of the time schedule set out in the legislation. At this point the Commission considers if it is reasonable to grant a longer time period or takes legal action for non-compliance. If MSs take too long to comply with standards or are granted derogations without reasonable justification, those that do comply may justifiably complain about unfair competition.

18.5 The legislative approach

The traditional way of dealing with environmental problems is to pass legislation that attempts to mitigate the cause of the problem. Command and control policies can be an effective way of developing minimum environmental standards – for example, setting minimum standards for energy efficiency and how they are to be achieved. By doing so it is possible, with effective monitoring, to ensure how the process of managing pollution takes place. Under this approach, pollution targets are set and enforced, but the method of achieving these targets may vary. An example of this kind of approach is the 1976 BWD (Council 1975), which aimed to set minimum standards for the quality of all places where bathing was permitted and was taking place. Its introduction followed growing concern about public health arising from bathing in areas that should have been safe, but were in fact polluted. Clean bathing water is not only important for public health, but is an important pillar of the tourism industry.

BWD set minimum quality standards for areas where coastal and inland bathing took place. By using the approach allowed by directives, it meant that each MS or regional authority could determine the best way to achieve this standard. For example, the approaches required in the Mediterranean, a closed sea with little movement of water, vary significantly from what might be required for the waters on the Atlantic coast. The directive allowed for certain derogations – for example, if there were problems with respect to flooding – but only if the Commission was informed of the full circumstances. There were drawbacks. The definition of what was a bathing area was not always clear, which caused some MSs to delay effective implementation. Also, the huge cost of upgrading bathing water quality meant that the benefits were spread over a number of years. Upgrading sewage disposal on the coast and inland is a burden that falls on local communities, many of whom feel that the benefits of such schemes go to the tourist industry and not to local taxpayers.

BWD has been regarded as a success, with the quality

Box 18.2 The European Environment Agency (EEA)

The European Environment Agency (EEA) is based in Copenhagen and has been in operation since 1994. It helps the EU and MSs to make informed decisions about improving the environment, integrating environmental considerations into economic policies and moving towards sustainability. The EEA, and the European Environment Information and Observation Network (Eionet), which it coordinates, has the task of providing its thirty-two members and their citizens with objective, reliable and comparable information.

of bathing water improving over the years. BWD was revised in 2006 (Council 2006), with the aim of simplifying the process of determining the suitability of bathing water, but at the same time raising standards. There were concerns in the early debate about the revised BWD that standards might be set too high and their implementation might become too burdensome. In particular, some of the benefits of the earlier proposals to revise BWD were called into question, while the costs were thought to be underestimated (House of Lords 2003). Agreement was reached so that the new directive included four categories of water: excellent, good, sufficient and poor. Authorities are expected to ensure that all beaches meet at least the sufficient standard by 2015. There are to be only two parameters by which the water is to be judged: intestinal enterococci and Escherichia coli.

The use of public engagement is important in a policy area like this, where there is potential to offer the public a direct benefit in terms of an improved leisure experience. Each year the European Environment Agency (EEA; see Box 18.2) and the Commission present a bathing water report, which assists citizens in making informed choices about the bathing sites they might wish to visit (Commission and European Environment Agency 2010). The report assesses bathing water quality in all 27 EU MSs, based on the finding from the previous year, and it is made available at the start of the new holiday season. A total of 20,000 bathing areas were monitored throughout the EU in 2009, with about two-thirds being on the coast. The number of coastal sites meeting the minimum standard rose from 80 per cent in 1990 to 96 per cent in 2009. The number of inland areas meeting the standard rose from 52 to 90 per cent in the same period.

18.6 The Single European Market and environmental controls

As the EU has grown, so has the diversity of the organization, with some MSs taking the role of environmental champions. Other states have yet to fully buy into the environmental agenda, and they feel that their economic development needs must come first. At the time of the 2004/2007 enlargements, there were around 200 pieces of legislation in the environmental acquis; although some were in force from the point of accession, there were many with derogations for some new members lasting until 2017.[6] Given that environmental policy is a shared competence, there is considerable scope for a variation in approach to environmental matters, which can lead to a distortion in trade within the Single European Market (SEM; see Chapters 2 and 7). Without intervention, these distortions in the market arise because of differing taxation and subsidy regimes, although it should be remembered that some states may have lower environmental costs, which can be exploited when dealing with national environmental issues. Now that the SEM for energy is in place, the environmental costs should ideally be calculated on a common basis. The environmental cost of producing electricity from wind power is generally believed to be small, while the use of coal can create considerable environmental damage (CEU 2003k). In these circumstances, coal trades at a considerable advantage because of the absence of a common system of environmental taxes. This is the reason why the introduction of a carbon tax, based on the actual level of pollution caused, is believed to be a priority by the Commission. Similar arguments can also be made with respect to a whole range of dirty industries that exist in some countries and not in others.

The lack of standardization of environmental rules may lead to some MSs being in a situation where their cleaner industries might be at a competitive disadvantage, causing market distortion. Even where there are common rules in place, there is a possibility of markets being distorted by different levels of enforcement. If EU rules are not applied on a common basis,

some industries may be able to take advantage of a lax enforcement regime.

Without EU policy on the environment, it is easy to see how it is possible to have a 'race to the bottom', with companies facing severe international competition lobbying for lower standards. The argument is that governments might be under pressure to lower standards to prevent firms moving to those places where standards are lowest. Or, in the case of the public sector, the cost of achieving the highest possible standards might be thought to be excessive. More costly environmental schemes might not be embarked on, or there may even be a dismantling of existing commitments to environmental protection in order to save money. While lobbyists frequently make such proposals, the public would generally prefer standards to be higher rather than lower. Few places inside or outside the EU would welcome the arrival of more polluting industry.

At the other end of the spectrum there is a problem of a 'race for the top'. This is where higher environmental standards are demanded in one MS than are common throughout the EU. Higher standards should generally be welcomed, but they can impose unjustifiable costs on others and may even be a source of protectionism because only national producers can compete. If standards are set too high, they can undermine others' sovereignty by enforcing compliance to unjustifiably high standards. In this case, the EU has tried to ensure that there is flexibility, so that higher standards can be achieved, but not at a disproportionate cost. The TFEU's Article 114 allows MSs to upgrade existing legislative standards on the grounds of new scientific evidence or to address a specific problem faced by that MS. But the Commission must be informed and must approve of the revised standard, and must be sure that the new standard is not simply arbitrary discrimination and a disguised obstacle to SEM functioning.

In practice, it is very difficult to stop all cases of environmental protectionism. An example of this was the Danish bottles case. In 1981 the Danish government introduced legislation concerning a deposit and return scheme for bottles used for beer and soft drinks, which meant that manufacturers had to package their goods in approved reusable containers. In order to ensure that they were recyclable, prior approval of the containers had to be granted by the Danish Environmental Agency. The Commission requested that the legislation be amended, because it made it difficult for drinks manufacturers to sell their products in that market. This failed, so the case was referred to the European Court of Justice (ECJ 1998). The result was that the deposit and return scheme was approved by the ECJ because the protection of the environment was considered to be an essential EU objective and was therefore not a disproportionate response to a problem. In contrast, the national approval of the containers was struck down as being disproportionate and therefore unacceptable. The effect of the judgment was to permit a barrier to trade, because Danish law still required that foreign manufacturers set up schemes to collect empty bottles. In many cases it would be difficult to do this because of the small size of the market and, in some cases, manufacturers' minimum presence. The need to enhance EU legislation in the area of waste and recycling led to the 1994 Packaging and Packaging Waste Directive (Council 1994) being put into place to try to avoid some of the cross-border internal market issues.

18.7 The polluter pays principle

One of the guiding principles of EU policy towards the environment is the idea that the persons or organizations causing the pollution will pay for the costs of either preventing the pollution or mitigating the harm, up to the required levels. The polluter pays principle (PPP) is designed to ensure that environmental damage is either remedied or prevented. Article 191 of the TFEU states that:

> Union policy on the environment shall aim at a high level of protection taking into account the diversity of situations in the various regions of the Union. It shall be based on the precautionary principle and on the principles that preventive action should be taken, that environmental damage should as a priority be rectified at source and that the polluter should pay.

PPP means that firms should meet the costs of achieving environmental standards once they have been set. Of course, that still gives businesses some leeway because firms do not have to meet the costs of eliminating all damage. (As the earlier analysis implied, businesses will generally not be required to eliminate all damage – that is, MB and MC cross at less than 100 per cent abatement.) In the longer term, PPP should be internalized within the firm's costs, and should be

taken into account in deciding all production processes and the price being charged to the consumer. So prices should take into account the full costs of production, and firms will deal with environmental problems in a more cost-effective way. The benefit of internalizing environmental costs is that it may deter market failure and lead to a situation where output is at a social optimum rather than just a market optimum.

Implementing PPP has proved to be difficult for a number of reasons:

- It is not always clear who the actual polluter is, especially in areas like agriculture, where pollutants seep into the soil.
- Sometimes pollution comes from a number of different sources – for example, greenhouse gases (GHGs).
- Some industries may be hit by the costs associated with PPP and be unable to compete, especially where trading partners are not subject to charges.
- Industrial lobbyists are often very adept at reducing the impacts of policies designed to make the polluter pay.

The idea that the polluter should pay was first incorporated directly into EU law with the Environmental Liability Directive (Council 2004c), which came into force in April 2007 (there were significant delays in transposing this legislation into national law). The directive established a framework for environmental liability, which helps to ensure that damage to species and their habitats is either prevented or remedied by those who cause the damage. The directive is an incentive for firms to take a great deal more care about their activities and to consider adequate insurance in the case of an accident.

18.8 Market-based instruments

The EU has increasingly favoured the use of market-based instruments (MBI) to enhance environmental performance. Such economic instruments include:

- *pollution charging*, which can be used as an instrument in areas such as water pollution, either for cleaning up the related pollution or, as in more recent times, as a way of encouraging an improved environmental performance;

- *indirect taxation*, to be applied depending on whether the production or use of a good is environmentally friendly or not;
- *subsidies*, to be used as incentives to improve environmental performance, which can take the form of direct payment, tax allowances or the provision of low-cost services (their use tends to be limited because subsidies run counter to PPP);
- *financial penalties*, which are related to the enforcement of environmental laws whereby a failure to comply can lead to a fine, ideally at least as high as the benefits gained from damaging the environment;
- *creating artificial markets* by using tradable permits, which include the use of emission trading schemes; and
- *deposit schemes*, which involve charging customers for items such as packaging, but then give a refund on their return in order to encourage recycling.

Many businesses and legislators prefer regulation because it offers a more consistent approach to environmental standards and, unlike most MBIs, firms do not pay for remaining pollution emissions once they meet the required standard. But MBIs are believed to be more flexible and effective because they offer an incentive to achieve improved environmental outcomes. MBIs can:

- take account of the fact that where different polluters have different marginal costs of abatement, they can minimize the total cost of achieving the desired reduction in abatement;
- offer an incentive to innovate such that both the production process and the environmental standards are improved;
- allow choices to be made about the cost of intervention and the environmental benefits that can be gained;
- avoid excessive government interference into the business of private companies;
- avoid many of the burdens of environmental protection falling on the public purse; and
- present governments with a way of raising money.

Of course, measures that are presented as being motivated by the desire to protect the environment may be nothing more than a means of raising government revenue. Raising excise duties on petroleum can be an incentive to develop and buy more fuel-efficient cars in the medium term, but if the quality and frequency of public transport is not improved, much of the public will feel cheated. In an era when budgets are under pressure, there is a temptation to maximize the revenue for budgetary purposes and, wherever possible, save on the provision of alternative services.

MSs' power over fiscal matters means that the EU needs to continue to try to persuade them to cede more of them to the EU. MSs are concerned with revenue raising and preserving their taxation rights, but they could, of course, collect an agreed tax, so avoiding an increase in the size of the EU's budget (see Chapter 19). The different economic structures across the EU mean that the impact of taxes will vary, particularly in areas like employment. Improved efficiency as a result of taxation structures tends to benefit those MSs that already have a lead in this area. Those MSs with well-developed 'green technology' are normally those with the highest living standards.

18.9 The EU's developing environmental perspective

When the EEC was launched in 1957, concerns about the state of the environment were heavily constrained by the need to complete the task of post-war reconstruction and to move the European economies onwards to greater prosperity.[7] So the 1957–72 period was characterized by limited Community action with respect to the environment, although MSs introduced their own initiatives. Only nine directives and one regulation were passed in the environment area. This legislation was designed to deal with trade-related issues and was driven by an economic imperative rather than an environmental one. In 1973 Directorate General (DG) 11 was created, which was responsible for the environment and nuclear safety. This was originally known as the environment and consumer protection service and it had only twenty permanent officials. It is now many times larger, reflecting EU enlargements and the growing importance of the policy area. Paradoxically, the chain of command has become somewhat more complex in the new millennium, with the creation of a high-profile DG for climate action as part of the second Barroso Commission. This means that three DGs are involved in dealing with important aspects of the policy agenda: DG Environment, DG Energy and DG Climate

Action. The three DGs must also work with other parts of the Commission, such as DG Taxation, to create a common environmental agenda.

The public's thirst for economic development at any price began to wane in the late 1960s. There was increasing concern that long-term environmental damage was being done in the name of progress, not only within the Community but also internationally, in countries like Sweden and the USA. It was recognized that economic growth could not be an aim in itself and that there needed to be measures to improve the quality of life. There was a concern especially that excessive use of pesticides in agriculture, for example, might cause damage to human health. There was also an awareness that environmental damage might spread across national boundaries.

The first step towards creating a broader policy came in 1972, with the First Environment Action Programme (EAP) for 1973–6. This was the first attempt at a strategic approach to environmental action across the EU, but in reality it only contained very limited environmental priorities for the next three years. The Second EAP (1977–81) continued in a similar vein, but it did emphasize preventative measures. The Third EAP (1982–7) built on the success of the earlier programme. It aimed to harmonize national environmental policies to a greater extent. Importantly, the introduction of PPP (see page 277) was a feature of this programme, which was an attempt to bring the market mechanism into play to encourage restricting industry in line with environmental objectives. (The OECD had already adopted PPP as an agreed policy.) Other important features were that action should be taken at the most appropriate level, prevention was better than a cure and, wherever possible, attempts should be made to restore environmental damage.

The Fourth EAP (1987–92) was scheduled to run at the same time as the programme to complete the SEM. It was recognized that the ability of national governments to contain environmental damage would be limited by the removal of border controls and the increasing extent of economic integration. So, for example, hazardous waste would be relatively free to cross national borders, creating potential dangers even for those countries that were not responsible for generating the waste. At this time, the legal basis of the environmental action was also established with the adoption of a new treaty, the SEA in 1987. The EAP included the principle of shared competence for environmental policies between MSs and authorities within them and the EU. The issue of not allowing national environmental policies to distort markets was also a concern of the programme and of earlier directives.

The Fifth EAP (1993–2002), named 'Towards Sustainability', was designed to be a longer-term strategy and reflected increased concern about sustainable development. The Brundtland definition (WCED 1987) of sustainable development was used in this EAP – that is, that development should meet the needs of today, without compromising the outlook of future generations. In practice, sustainable development proved somewhat difficult to define in a purely legalistic sense, and the Fifth EAP is regarded as just the starting point of the process of tackling the problem. It was an attempt to recognize that the EU had a greater responsibility than just economic development.

Importantly, the Fifth EAP sought to integrate an environmental dimension into all major areas of policy, reflecting the reality that environmental issues are both wide-ranging and multi-sectoral. Second, the command and control approach to the environment was to be replaced with a philosophy of shared responsibility between the actors, such as governments, the EU and business. This recognized the importance of a more democratic approach to environmental issues, where everyone sees it as their role to be involved in the improvement of the environment, rather than just accepting passively instructions sent down from above, as in the command and control approach. This approach should have led to greater monitoring of environmental issues by the public, if, of course, they were adequately informed and felt interested in the issue. The strategy involved the use of legislation to set minimum environmental standards and to meet international obligations. A broader range of instruments was to be introduced to encourage the meeting of these standards and environmentally friendly production. In particular, the use of financial incentives – for example, the structural funds (see Chapters 19 and 22) – were seen as a way of investing in environmental improvements, while the focus on economic instruments could be used to ensure that the true cost of the use of the environment was reflected in the prices of goods.

The Fifth EAP targeted sectors where there were particular environmental concerns. In the case of industry, it was considered that the need was to adopt appropriate standards while avoiding the distortion of competition (see Chapter 13). For the energy sector, the focus was on promoting greater efficiency and reducing the dependence on fossil fuels. The completion of the SEM would place increased demands on the transport sector, and there was therefore a need for improved efficiency promoting public transport (see Chapter 16). The intensity of agricultural production was an issue, along with the overdependence on fertilizers and pesticides (see Chapter 20). Finally, the accommodation of mass tourism was seen as a problem because of the issue of transportation, waste disposal and over-utilization of tourism assets. The problem with this sectoral approach is that it lacked coherence and, in many cases, the EU had little control over the industries concerned. It was therefore difficult to achieve substantive results in some cases.

The absence of a meaningful eco tax was the major weakness of the Fifth EAP. Advocating the use of economic instruments to promote environmental objectives was a central plank of the EAP. But EU powers in the area of taxation are weak. MSs control this agenda because unanimity was (is) required in the Council (see Chapter 2), so that all that has been agreed is a minimalistic harmonization of tax rates (see Chapter 15). At the national level, taxes on petroleum products are one area where MSs have stimulated efficiency, even if the motoring public suspect that such measures are primarily driven by the need to raise revenue.

The Sixth EAP (2002–12) picked up many of the ideas in past programmes, but of course the emphasis changed as different concerns moved up the policy agenda, in particular the concern over the issue of global warming (CEU 2001m). The problem for the Sixth EAP was that the proposals came at a time when a major priority for the EU was the Lisbon growth and jobs agenda (see Chapter 23). Although environmental issues became part of the Lisbon agenda, they had to compete for a place in the overall scheme of priorities. Unlike previous EAPs, it did not propose new quantifiable targets or related timetables. It represented the environmental dimension of the EU's SDS (see page 270) and provided a link between the strategy for growth and competitiveness and employment. The strategy focused on four issues:

- climate change;
- nature and biodiversity;

- health and quality of life; and
- natural resources and waste.

The Sixth EAP aimed to modernize environmental policy-making by taking a broader approach. It introduced 'thematic strategies', which built on the existing regulatory framework and focused on a more integrated approach and implementation issues. In particular, taking into account the overspill effects of adopting one policy initiative on other sectors was to be part of the EU's overall better regulation strategy (CEU 2009e). This aimed at simplifying existing legislation and cutting bureaucracy, as well as ensuring more effective and efficient methods of the correct application of EU law. The thematic strategies covered:

- air;
- waste prevention and recycling;
- marine environment;
- soil;
- pesticides;
- natural resources; and
- urban environment.

The fact that the Sixth EAP avoided much of the detail of its predecessors indicates that it has a more cautious approach. As time goes on, the tendency towards over-ambition means that disappointment tends to creep in as it is realized that targets will not be reached. This has not stopped criticism of the Sixth EAP. In its mid-term review of the Sixth EAP, the Commission (CEU 2007e) believed that there had only been limited progress towards integrating environmental concerns into other policy areas. Also, it thought that at that time, GHG emissions were increasing and the threat from the loss of biodiversity had become more serious. Pollution was still a major threat to public health and climate change was one of the most pressing environmental challenges. Therefore the main task was to ensure that implementing and building on the Sixth EAP would be at the centre of their work.

Typically, a variety of other views were expressed; the Union of Industrial and Employers' Confederations of Europe (UNICE; EurActiv 2007) wished to see a concentration on implementing existing legislation rather than bringing in new laws. UNICE's main concern was with the implementation gap, with more and more legislation being introduced without the existing legislation being properly applied and evaluated. With better regulation and implementation there would be less need for eco taxes. The employers were concerned that the costs of environmental measures should become more apparent and they also hoped for fewer fiscal instruments and a more voluntary approach to achieving the aims of the programme. Similarly, the European Association of Craft, Small and Medium-sized Enterprises (UEAPME) preferred a more voluntary approach, with fewer eco taxes. They stressed the need to balance the concerns of business with those of the environment. The European Environmental Bureau (EEB) preferred more targets as part of the programme in order to give the whole thing more teeth; they favoured more ambitious use of environmental taxes and the abolition of perverse subsidies. Stavros Dimas, the Environment Commissioner (2004–9), suggested that the EU would not lose its environmental ambitions, despite claims that these might cause job losses. He also suggested the need for new instruments, including the greater use of market-based instruments and fiscal reform.

18.10 Global warming strategy

GHGs have the ability to trap the heat in the world's atmosphere in a way that helps to maintain life. Because of man's activities, GHG levels have risen and they are thought to be causing the phenomenon known as global warming. This is where the temperature of the world is rising at a faster rate than can be explained by natural phenomena, with the result that sea levels are rising and we are experiencing climate change. As Table 18.1 shows, the two largest sources of GHGs are the energy and transport sectors.

Global warming is a gradual rise in the earth's average temperature which has the potential to significantly damage the way man exists on this planet. If global temperatures rise by 2–3 degrees centigrade, as they may, without intervention this could lead to rising sea levels and flooding of low-lying areas, as well as increased desertification. This will have major economic, social and environmental consequences. There is a widespread belief that man's activities are the cause of climate change and therefore there needs to be joint action to try to avert the crisis, which may impact most seriously on future generations. The EU has attempted to work globally to introduce a strategy based around its Emissions Trading System (ETS) to mitigate climate

Table 18.1 Main sources of greenhouse gases by sector for the EU 27, 2008

Sector	%	Sector	%
Energy production	31.1	Agriculture	9.6
Transport	19.6[1]	Industrial processes	8.3
Household services	14.5	Waste	2.8
Manufacturing and construction	12.4	Fugitive fuel emissions	1.7

Note: [1] Excludes international shipping and aviation, which is 6 per cent of total GHG emissions.
Source: EEA 2010

change, as well as agreeing action by MSs. The major cause of the rise in global temperatures is believed to be the emission of carbon dioxide and other GHGs into the atmosphere. The Stern Review (Stern 2007) suggested four ways of cutting GHGs:

- reducing the demand for goods and services that generate a high level of emissions;
- increasing efficiency, which can save both money and emissions;
- taking action to avoid harmful things such as deforestation; and
- moving to low-carbon technologies for power, heat and transport.

These could be achieved with carbon pricing, technology and measures to overcome barriers to behaviour change. In addition, measures were required to promote sustainable land use and to adapt to climate change where the effects can no longer be prevented.

The 1992 United Nations (UN) Framework Convention on Climate Change (UNFCCC) was an important step forward in the global environmental agenda, and added to this was the Kyoto Protocol (KP), which was agreed in 1997. The distinction between the two was that the UNFCCC encouraged industrialized countries to stabilize GHG emissions; the KP committed them to doing so. KP came into effect in 2007 and set binding targets for thirty-seven industrialized countries averaging 5.2 per cent against 1990 levels over the five-year period 2008–12. It is notable that the USA did not ratify the KP. The KP suggested that the targets should be carefully monitored and three types of MBI might be introduced: emissions trading (known as the carbon market); a clean development mechanism (CDM); and joint implementation. The latter two schemes gave carbon credits for projects in third countries which could be offset against targets. These schemes offered flexible environmental and technological benefits for the participants. By the middle of 2010, eighty-four states, plus the EU, had signed the KP.

A further UN climate change conference (COP15)[8] was held in Copenhagen, during 7–9 December 2009. Great things were hoped for from this gathering, as the Obama administration had committed the USA to engaging in the process. There was an acceptance that something needed to be done to reduce the causes of climate change. From an EU perspective, the outcome of the conference was a disappointment, because there was no binding agreement to cut emissions. Most participants saw the problem from a purely national perspective. While the potential benefits of policies to reduce GHGs were clearly understood, many countries are happier to free-ride on the benefits of others' policy initiatives, rather than take action themselves which might damage their economic performance. Others felt that there was little to be gained in any case, because their individual efforts would be overwhelmed by the actions of others.

COP15 came at a poor time for the EU. The TFEU had only just been ratified and the Commission was on an extended mandate, waiting for a new set of commissioners to be appointed. At the European Council in December 2008 (Council 2009a) there was confirmation that the EU's target would be a 20 per cent reduction in GHGs from the 1990 levels by 2020; the EU's strategy was also for a 20 per cent reduction in primary energy consumption, and a 20 per cent target for renewable energy sources in the energy mix by 2020. The EU's aspiration was for a 30 per cent reduction in GHGs if other industrialized countries, including the USA, would make comparable commitments at Copenhagen. A contribution to an enhanced target was also expected from advanced developing countries like China and India. However, within the EU there was a lack of agreement. The 30 per cent reduction in GHGs implied a heavier burden on MSs at very different stages of development, so there was not a united front. It is therefore not surprising that the proposal did not progress far at that time. Without the agreement of all concerned, the free-rider problem remained. Any reduction by the EU or any of the other international entities risked not being reciprocated.

The aspiration to reduce GHGs by 30 per cent remained at the centre of the EU's strategy post-Copenhagen (CEU 2010b) because the circumstances had changed. EU emissions of GHGs had been reduced by 7–10 per cent below the 1990 levels during 2005–8. Between 2008 and 2009 emissions were further reduced by higher energy prices and the recession, so that in 2009 the EU was emitting 14 per cent less GHGs than in 1990. With economic recovery, high energy-using industries such as steel might be expected to reverse some of this reduction, indeed many renewable technologies such as wind turbines use a great deal of high quality metals. Overall it was thought that the cost of meeting the original 20 per cent target by 2020 had probably fallen from €70 billion a year to €48 billion per year. The reasons for the fall in the expected costs of meeting the 20 per cent target were:

- lower economic growth;
- higher oil prices; and
- the expected low carbon price, due to allowances not used in the recession being carried forward.

The additional cost to move forward to the 30 per cent reduction in GHGs was estimated to be €33 billion per year, or 0.2 per cent of GDP. So the Commission estimated that the total cost of a 30 per cent reduction in GHGs would be €81 billion per year, or 0.54 per cent of GDP. The benefits of better environmental conditions if these targets could be met are clear, but the overall issue is still that of burden sharing. The cost of achieving these targets will still fall disproportionately on the poorer MSs and there may be a lack of willingness of wealthier MSs to assume additional burdens if economic growth remains slow and it is difficult to balance national budgets. Finally, without any meaningful global commitment to binding targets, the purpose of such reductions is not clear.

18.11 The carbon tax

In 1990 the Council undertook to restrict carbon dioxide (CO_2) to 1990 levels by 2000. One of the main instruments in the EU's armoury of weapons against excessive CO_2 emissions was the 1992 proposal for a carbon tax (CEU 1992c). This is a levy on the energy sources that emit carbon based on their carbon content (see Chapter 17). A carbon tax is a broadly based tax that is designed to promote emission reductions and would have been paid by almost all citizens who consumed petrol, heating oil and aviation fuel. Emissions trading, which we will look at later, is an initiative that is restricted to the corporate sector. The benefit of a carbon tax is that it is predictable and can be simple and quick to implement once it has been agreed to. The revenue raised can either be used for general budgetary purposes or be recycled back into environmental projects. In this sense it can be a revenue neutral tax, because it taxes something that is bad for the environment and, potentially, the taxes on things that are good for the environment can be reduced. This tax neutrality is important because it can be seen as a way of retaining the international competitiveness of the economy. The existence of the tax is one way of encouraging greater efficiency on a permanent basis, because the lower the carbon usage, the lower the total taxation bill.

Carbon taxes are not generally well liked by the general public because they are taxes. For this reason they can become highly politicized, with decisions being delayed because of protests. They can also be regressive, because they may place an increased burden on poorer households, who tend to spend a higher percentage of their incomes on heating than the more affluent.

The 1990 proposal for an EU carbon tax was not successful and was withdrawn by the Commission in 2001 because of the combined opposition of key MSs and industrial lobbyists. It is tempting to see this outcome as demonstrating, once again, that the need for unanimous agreement on taxation can frustrate fiscal innovation; however, there may not even have been a qualified majority of states in favour of the initiative because of a widespread view that raising taxes remains the business of MSs. By 2009 carbon taxes were being discussed again and the new Commission, which came into office in 2010, relaunched the idea of a minimum carbon tax in June 2010. This initiative illustrates the complexity of the policy process, with Algirdas Šemeta, Commissioner for Taxation, leading the proposal, but with support from Connie Hedegaard, Commissioner for Climate Action, and Janez Potočnik, Commissioner for Environment. While there was support from some

MSs for the idea, notably the Nordic MSs who had a national carbon tax, the requirement for unanimity in the Council remains a major hurdle. It was suggested that the tax would cover motor fuel and energy for heating and would apply to households and sectors not covered by the ETS. Predictably, the car industry was quick to respond to the threat to raise the price of diesel, which is taxed less than petrol in some MSs. Other industrial groups were also concerned that such a proposal would impact on their overall competitiveness. What might keep the issue on the political agenda is the growing number of MSs thinking of raising their own carbon taxes and the need to harmonize these initiatives. Also, many MSs may see a national carbon tax as a way of raising additional revenue, and so may be less concerned about tax neutrality issues.

18.12 The EU's Emissions Trading System

The release of GHGs is a classic example of market failure associated with a public good, where the atmosphere exhibits both non-rival and non-excludable features – that is, additional users of the atmosphere do not impact on fellow polluters and it is difficult to exclude polluters, unless specific action is taken against them. The EU has attempted to control emissions by allowing polluters who own permits to 'use' the environment, but at a price (Council 2003f). If they do not have sufficient permits to meet their needs, they must purchase them from other producers who have a surplus. Over time, the number of permits will be reduced, forcing up their price, encouraging businesses to reduce their level of emissions. This so-called cap-and-trade system accepts that there will be pollution, but the extent of the damage must be reduced by charging a price for the environment so that firms internalize a social cost within their pricing system, something that was regarded as free in the past. The advantage of the EU Emissions Trading System (ETS) is that there is a market for permits which allows those businesses that can reduce their emissions cheaply to trade surplus permits to those who cannot. So heavy polluters must pay if they are less efficient or have less scope to reduce emissions. The idea behind the scheme is to create a scarcity of permits, so that those companies that reduce their emissions can sell them to others who do not find it cost-effective to reduce their pollution. In the longer term, even businesses that find it expensive to reduce emissions may choose to invest in improved technology.

The permits to allow emissions can be: allocated for free; assigned on the basis of historical usage or technological benchmarking; or auctioned. The highest bidders should be businesses who find it most difficult to reduce their emissions. The problem of such schemes comes in deciding who will have the permits in the first place. Many of the allocations tend to be based on historic pollution records, but records have tended to be poor at an industry level, in part because the EU has enlarged and its industrial structure has changed a great deal since the late 1980s. Issuing permits rewards those businesses or industries that have performed worst in the past. In such circumstances, lobbyists have proved adept at defending industries that have often had a poor pollution record. Particularly in the period prior to the introduction of such schemes, there was an incentive to do little to improve emissions, because this will take away the rewards of reducing emissions once the scheme is in operation.

The UK ran a voluntary ETS during 2002–6 as a pilot prior to the mandatory EU scheme that is now in place. Participants were allowed a discount from the Climate Change Levy if they made reductions while participating in the scheme. At that time carbon trading was something of a novelty, and it allowed for some of the practical lessons of operating such a scheme to be discovered. The EU's ETS, which began operations in January 2005, is the centre of its strategy to combat the threat of climate change. Initially there were 2 billion tradable permits issued per year. There are over 10,000 installations in the industrial and energy sector participating in the scheme. Collectively, these cover nearly 50 per cent of the EU27's carbon dioxide emissions and 40 per cent of its GHG emissions, making this the world's largest multi-country, multi-sector GHG ETS. The scheme has been planned to operate over three phases. The first phase covered the period 2005–7. In the second phase (2008–12) the scheme's scope was expanded. In the third phase (2013–20) there are proposals to set more ambitious targets; aviation emissions are expected to be covered in this phase. The scheme was amended in 2009 (Council 2009b).

A way of evaluating the ETS is to try to project what might have happened if the scheme had not been introduced – what the UK government has called 'business as usual' (BAU; House of Commons 2007). But of course these projections are based on estimates that build on past trends, but the counterfactual case can only be speculative; indeed there may be a range of potential outcomes. Overestimates for BAU have the effect of exaggerating the success of the ETS and increasing the initial level of credits. Also, the purchase of carbon credits may not actually lead to carbon reductions – for example, if the reduction would have happened anyway, without being able to sell the credit onwards, or if a company was awarded credits for a plant that was due to close. In this case, the money received for the carbon credits would not be used to fund a reduction, but would amount to buying 'hot air'. In other cases, it has been possible for steel manufacturers to import semi-finished steel from outside the EU, which means that the reduced internal EU emissions are not real, because the main industrial process takes place elsewhere.

Since the launch of the ETS there have been doubts about its effectiveness. The ETS is complex and difficult to understand in an operational context, leading to a degree of inefficiency. As the ETS has operated over time, there have been a number of cases of fraud, involving as much as €5 billion. This fraud undermines the ETS's integrity and suggests that more needs to be done to make the operation of the ETS transparent.

The ETS has been criticized for being too generous, with free permits giving the potential of a windfall to polluters. Schemes such as the ETS always have problems dealing with volatile demand patterns, which can affect the price of permits significantly. The ETS did not deal well with falls in demand for permits: many of the permits were not used due to the recession that hit Europe, so the price of permits actually fell, thus reducing the potential incentive to reduce pollution. The fall in price could have taken away a signal to improve efficiency, had it not been for relatively high fuel prices. Permits are bankable, so, in the longer term, surplus permits could be sold at a huge profit or kept for later use. Some estimates suggest that there may be as much as 700 million tonnes worth of permits to carry over to the post-2012 period. This means that the market for permits is likely to remain highly liquid for some time, and therefore it is more likely to be subject to volatility. Also, if the credits are too cheap, the impact of the trading process on emissions will be limited. But perhaps this may not matter too much if oil prices are high, in the sense that efficiencies may come about anyway because of market conditions.

The failure of the ETS to operate as effectively could weaken the EU's aim to offer global leadership in the fight against climate change. It could also make the prospect of a global carbon market a more distant prospect. If the price of carbon permits is too low, then the EU might consider placing a minimum floor price for permits or actually withdrawing permits from the market. If, on the other hand, prices for permits are too high in the EU, then industrial competitiveness might suffer and some industries might consider moving production overseas. Schemes like the ETS take time to refine, and operate best in fairly stable and predictable environments. If the ETS fails to verifiably reduce carbon emissions on its own account and does not deliver a stable price for carbon to be traded, it cannot be viewed as a success.

A significant anomaly with respect to the ETS was the exclusion of aviation from the original scheme (see Chapter 16). The aviation sector is international and there are problems with enforcing the ETS and its like. Aviation taxes are a popular way of raising money at a national level, but do not appear to have dampened enthusiasm for flying. While there has been a fall in the total level of EU GHG emissions, international aviation grew by 100 per cent during 1990–2006. This is despite the introduction of modern and efficient fleets of aircraft. As of 2012, airlines will be included in the ETS, but, not surprisingly, there were protests from nearly 4,000 companies, including commercial airlines and private jet operators, which are expected to take part. This is especially the case in those countries where there is already a passenger-based tax, but this particular tax is more concerned with revenue raising than improving environmental performance. There is also a sense of grievance from those airlines that are based outside the EU, but appear to be trapped into participating in the ETS. The scheme caps airline emissions at 97 per cent of their 2004–6 levels in 2012, falling to 95 per cent in 2013. Although 85 per cent of the permits will be free, they will have to buy 15 per cent of the permits through auction, which means that the ETS will raise money. The base year for allocating the licences was 2010, a year when a large number of flights were cancelled because of the eruption of a volcano in Iceland, which illustrates the problem of setting allowances – no year is ever a normal year. Many airlines lost money during the 2008–9 recession, so the fear is that the ETS might cause further financial problems to the sector.

18.13 Conclusion

The EU's environmental policy now makes a substantial impact on the life of EU citizens and has helped to address many very pressing problems, which can only be dealt with via international cooperation and enforcement. The sharing of responsibility with MSs has had a positive impact in terms of raising standards and promoting policy innovation. There is now a far greater range of policy instruments to deal with environmental concerns than ever before. But despite much rhetoric about the use of economic instruments as the most effective way of implementing policy, examples of these at a community level are still limited. MSs are unlikely to cede significant fiscal powers to the EU at any time in the near future. Similarly, the integration of environmental objectives into other policy areas will remain a difficulty because of the EU's style of decision-making. However, recovery from the 2008–9 recession, and the resulting higher energy prices, have re-emphasized the importance of environmental policy. Finally, the EU has tried to make a major contribution to leadership of the global warming debate. The extent of the EU's impact as a global leader will depend on greater policy coherence within the EU itself.

Summary

- Environmental policy was not part of the original EU treaties and is an area of shared competence with MSs.
- Environmental policy was introduced initially because of the operation of the SEM and competition policy. However, incidents of cross-border pollution caused alarm in the 1970–1980s, and it became clear that a focus on broader environmental policy would be desirable on both economic and social grounds.
- The unregulated markets mechanism fails to take account of the degradation of the environment caused by the existence of public goods and externalities (spillover effects).

- The optimum level of pollution abatement is where marginal benefit equals marginal cost.
- There is a strong case for focusing on the use of market-based instruments (MBIs) as an incentive to improve environmental performance, rather than just relying on legislation to set minimum standards.
- Central to policy is the aim of sustainable development and the view that it is the polluter who should pay (PPP) for the cost of either preventing pollution or mitigating the harm that it causes.
- The EU's policy has developed through a series of Environment Action Programmes.
- The EU has only had limited success in helping to develop a global strategy to prevent further global warming.
- The prospect of global warming led to the introduction of the EU's greenhouse gas Emissions Trading System, where permits are traded.
- An alternative to emissions trading is the introduction of a carbon tax.

Questions and essay topics

1. What is meant by the producer pays principal?
2. What is the role of the European Environment Agency?
3. What are externalities?
4. Why is it unlikely that pollution will be reduced to zero?
5. What were the recommendations of the Stern Review?
6. What are the advantages of using MBIs to limit environmental damage?
7. What is meant by sustainable development?
8. What is the Kyoto Protocol?
9. Consider the case for abandoning carbon trading for a European-wide system of carbon taxation.
10. Critically examine the arguments for the EU taking an even greater role in developing environmental policy.
11. Why has it been so difficult to introduce an EU-wide carbon tax?
12. Examine the case for and against the use of a legislative approach to controlling environmental damage.
13. Why is the adoption of MBIs regarded as a superior option for controlling pollution?
14. Why is it sometimes very difficult to make the polluter pay for the environmental damage they cause?
15. How might differing environmental standards in MSs impact on the SEM's successful operation?

FURTHER READING

Carmin, J. A. and Stacy, D. (2004) *EU Enlargement and the Environment: Institutional Change and Environmental Policy in Central and Eastern Europe*, Routledge, Abingdon.

Golub, J. (2007) *Global Competition and EU Environmental Policy*, Routledge, Abingdon.

Helm, D. and Hepburn, C. (eds.) (2009) *The Economics and Politics of Climate Change*, Oxford University Press.

Jordon, A., Huitema, D. and van Asselt, H. (2010) *Climate Change Policy in the European Union: Confronting the Dilemmas of Mitigation and Adaptation?* Cambridge University Press.

NOTES

1 This is not the same as best available technology, which is limited by costs.
2 The cost of producing additional output which excludes the cost of environmental damage.
3 The cost of producing additional output which includes the cost of environmental damage.
4 Non-compliance can be a risk at any proposed level of abatement, depending on the balance between the cost versus the sanctions in place for non-compliance.
5 Even in 2009 there were still eleven Chernobyl type reactors in operation (Cragg 2009).
6 Poland, for example, had a derogation until 2017 on the directive related to air pollution on large combustion plants.
7 For a detailed account of the development of EU environmental policy, see Barnes and Barnes 1999.
8 This was the 15th Conference of the Parties (COP15) to the UNFCCC and the 5th Meeting of the Parties (COP/MOP5) to the KP.

Part V   EU budget and structural policies

Part V of this book covers all EU policies that address certain structural aspects of the EU economy and society. The EU affords special treatment to those in the agricultural sector, the fishing industry and depressed regions, as well as dealing with EU-wide social problems, especially unemployment, and hence employment. These areas are not only financed by the EU general budget, but also claim the bulk of its general budgetary resources. Thus this part of the book begins with a chapter on the budget and follows on with chapters on each of the mentioned areas.

19 The general budget

BRIAN ARDY AND ALI EL-AGRAA

19.1 Introduction

The general budget of the EU (EU budget)[1] has always been an issue of high political salience. Member states (MSs) are naturally concerned with their contributions to and receipts from it. Until 1988 the political significance of the EU budget was also heightened by inter-institutional rivalry within the European Community (EC). The right to approve the EU budget, one of the more significant powers of the European Parliament (EP), was used as a lever to force concessions from the Council (see Chapter 3). This problem has been resolved by gradually increasing EP powers by making it more directly involved in EU budgetary planning.

The EU budget is also a window on the EU as a political and economic institution. In the early years the EU budget was very small and financed from national contributions. With the development of EU policies, in particular the Common Agricultural Policy (CAP; see Chapter 20), expenditure rose and 'own resources' were introduced in 1970. There followed a period of expenditure growth, principally on agriculture. The late 1970s and early 1980s were plagued by disagreements over the EU budget between the institutions and in relation to the UK's contribution. The resolution of this British problem was accompanied by measures to control agricultural expenditure, and was one of the factors that facilitated the development of the Single European Market (SEM; see Chapters 2 and 7). The SEM and the EU's Mediterranean enlargement led in 1988 to the Delors I budgetary package. This was a comprehensive revision of the EU budget which increased expenditure (European Council 1988). Following agreement on the Treaty on European Union (TEU), the budget was further modified by the Edinburgh Agreement (European Council 1992b), the Delors II package. This was accompanied by a radical CAP reform and further expanded budgetary resources to accommodate

more expenditure on structural policies, internal policies (particularly research) and on external action, recognizing the impact of the changes in Central and Eastern Europe. The reduced dynamism in the EU in the second half of the 1990s is reflected in budgetary developments. Thus it took eight years to agree relatively modest financial resources for enlargement (European Council 2005a).

This chapter commences with a survey of the economic theory of the state, then goes on to consider fiscal federalism and its application to the EU. Consideration of the EU budgetary system follows. Then the EU budget revenues and expenditures are analysed and the problems facing the budget are examined: net contributions and equity, and enlargement. The chapter finishes with conclusions.

19.2 The economic theory of the state

In his classic public finance text, Richard Musgrave (1959) delineates the role of the state into three branches: allocation, distribution and stabilization. These days the regulatory role of the government would also be stressed (Bailey 2002).

The government's role in allocation is the result of externalities, which are costs and benefits that arise in production but which do not directly affect either the producer or the consumer – that is, they are suffered without compensation or enjoyed free of charge by third parties. Air pollution is an externality: when coal was the major source of energy, households and firms burnt coal without thinking of its effects on the atmosphere. It took government intervention in the UK, in the form of Clean Air Acts, to encourage the burning of smokeless fuel to solve this problem of urban air pollution (see Chapter 18). What is crucial about externalities is that in the absence of government intervention their costs/benefits are non-rival and non-excludable. Non-rivalry occurs where one person's benefit/cost from a service does not limit other people's enjoyment/suffering. Such non-rivalry implies that access to benefits should not be limited by price or other means. If it is not possible to prevent access to a service to individuals who have not paid, then the service is non-excludable: it is generally not possible to finance the service privately because it cannot be charged for – the free-rider problem. With public goods such as defence, all the benefits are non-rival and non-excludable, so governments finance them from general taxation. The allocative role of government involves the provision or subsidization of services where externalities are significant.

The regulatory role of the state overlaps with that of allocation, by setting rules in markets to make them work in society's interests. So regulation encompasses competition policy (see Chapter 13), the rules for natural monopolies (see Chapter 17), the safety of products, financial services, and so on. The reason for government regulation is either that there are problems with the operation of markets, with competition, or that there are informational problems. For example, with financial services there is a case for regulation because of systemic risk: the government has to ensure the viability of key financial institutions in a crisis, while avoiding moral hazard[2] in its underwriting of banks in difficulties. Financial services also need to be regulated because of information problems related to the complexity of the product, so consumers need to be protected from fraud and misrepresentation.

The distributive role of government recognizes the fact that markets are compatible with very unequal distributions of individual income levels, which are unacceptable to modern societies. Redistribution occurs as a result of equity, insurance and special interest. Equity justifies the redistribution of income from rich to poor in accordance with society's views on fairness. Insurance is a payment to people with particular adverse circumstances: unemployment, sickness and retirement. The political power of special groups may also enable them to obtain redistribution in their favour, which is the case with farmers in the EU. Redistribution takes place via a progressive tax system,[3] a progressive benefit system and the provision of public services that are subsidized or free of charge. Central governments also redistribute income among regions. Part of this is explicit through grants and transfer mechanisms,

but most occurs via the operation of national taxation, social security systems and the provision of government services (CEU 1977a; Sala-i-Martin and Sachs 1992). Governments provide insurance against unemployment and sickness and pensions for the elderly, even though this can be purchased privately. However, market provision is unlikely to cover all eventualities – for example, long-term unemployment – and many individuals, particularly those at greatest risk, would be unable to pay the necessary premiums. Thus the government provides social insurance partly as an allocative measure because of gaps in the market, but largely for redistributive reasons.[4]

The government's stabilization role is the use of monetary and fiscal policy to try to achieve the objectives of full employment, price stability, economic growth and balance of payments equilibrium. Today there is much less confidence in government's ability to stabilize the economy than there was when Musgrave's book was published. Many governments have delegated authority over monetary policy to independent central banks, because it is believed that better decisions will result from technocratically driven decisions, freed from short-term political considerations. Similarly, difficulties with the accurate timing and magnitude of discretionary fiscal policy have led governments to rely on automatic stabilization (see Chapters 10 and 12).

Although these arguments provide a clear justification for state intervention in the economy, its extent is subject to discretion, with the size of the public expenditure and the extent of public services varying widely among nation states. While part of this variation is due to differences in the level of development, much is the result of history, national values and institutions.

19.3 Fiscal federalism

Choices have to be made not only about the extent of the public sector, but also about the level of government at which the activity takes place. The traditional theory of fiscal federalism (Oates 1999) examines the factors that will determine the choice of the level of government, which will undertake the various economic tasks of the state.[5] The theory assumes that each level of government cares exclusively about the welfare of its constituents. An efficient system of fiscal federalism would then balance the advantages and disadvantages of provision at various levels of government, and allocate competences accordingly.

The principal advantage of decentralization is that the lower the level of government, the easier it is to assess the preferences of local residents, so the provision of services can be better tailored to their requirements. The existence of different sub-national units of government (regions) means that levels of taxation and public services can be varied. Central government not only has informational problems, it also has a limited ability to differentiate policies across jurisdictions.[6] Democratic accountability is also best achieved with decentralized government, where the correspondence between those who benefit from public expenditure and the taxpayers who fund it is most apparent (Oates 1977).

Centralized public services may offer benefits provided the preferences of citizens in different jurisdictions are similar. The policies of one region may have effects on other regions (spillovers) and central government can take account of these interactions. When there are economies of scale – that is, where the cost per unit diminishes with the volume of the service produced, central government provision may be more efficient.[7] Centralization can be used to achieve uniformity in public provision, which may be regarded as important for equity and efficiency – for example, in health and education. There are also advantages of centralization in relation to taxation; generally, immobile tax bases should finance state/local government. Since mobility is potentially a problem with the major sources of taxation – personal income, corporate profits, social security and, to an extent, the taxation of consumption (see Chapter 15) – state/local government financial autonomy is limited. Local variation in taxation is possible, however, provided that differences in rates are not too great and where sub-national jurisdictions are large. The ability to finance public services, therefore, will vary across jurisdictions; the national government can reduce these inequalities to acceptable levels. Redistribution is difficult to achieve at the local level because the rich would tend to migrate to low-tax jurisdictions (the poor might migrate to high-benefit localities).

If the assumption of a benevolent government is relaxed, governments may also pursue their own ends, which will not always coincide with society's. Governments have considerable discretion because parliamentary oversight is imperfect and elections

Table 19.1 Expenditure at different levels of government in federal states (% of GDP), 2007

	Level of government			
	Federal	State	Local	Total
Australia	22.6	12.4	1.5	36.4
Canada	17.8	20.7	7.1	45.7
Germany	28.9	12.2	7.4	48.4
Switzerland	17.3	11.7	8.6	37.6
USA[a]	20.0	11.6	10.4	42.0
EU15[b]	1.0	30.2[b]	15.8[c]	47.0

Notes: [a] 2006; [b] federal/central government; [c] state and local

Sources: International Monetary Fund 2010c; Eurostat 2010c; CEU 2010a

infrequent. If this is the case, decentralization may be advantageous because it increases the options available to citizens (moving to a different jurisdiction), promoting competition between jurisdictions and providing an additional mechanism for achieving efficiency in the provision of public services. This argument is particularly strong in relation to the EU because of the strength of national democracy and concerns over EU democratic deficit.

The Commission has examined the implications of fiscal federalism for the EU on three occasions, all related to EMU (CEU 1977a; Padoa-Schioppa *et al.* 1987; CEU 1993a). These reports mark a gradual retreat from a significant public finance role for the EU. In its last assessment the Commission (CEU 1993a) downgraded the importance of redistribution, emphasized decentralization and subsidiarity and suggested that a budget of 2 per cent of GDP was sufficient for EMU.

The large gap between public finances in the EU and existing federations is indicated by a comparison of EU and federal expenditure. Even in the leanest federation, Switzerland, federal government expenditure amounts to 17.3 per cent of GDP, compared with just 1.0 per cent in the EU (see Table 19.1). The EU has significant responsibility in relation to only one area important to federal government expenditure: economic affairs (agricultural, industrial and regional policy, R&D); in the other important areas of defence, education, health and social security it has virtually no role (see Table 19.2, page 292). Interest payments do not arise for the

Table 19.2 Federal government expenditure by main function (% of GDP), 2008

	Defence	Education	Health	Social security	Debt interest	Economic affairs	Other functions
Australia	1.3	1.5	3.4	8.8	0.4	1.2	6.0
Canada	1.5	0.5	2.1	6.2	2.6	0.7	4.2
USA[a]	4.3	0.6	4.6	5.3	1.8	1.4	2.6
EU15	0.0	0.0	0.0	–	–	0.8	0.2

Note: [a] 2002

Sources: ABS 2010; Statistics Canada 2010; EOPUS 2010; CEU 2009c

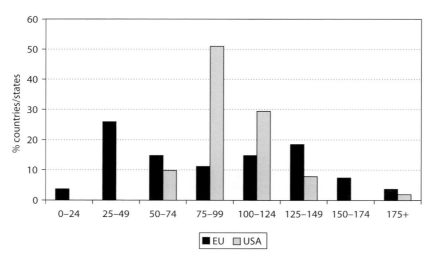

Figure 19.1 GDP per capita in the EU27 and US states, 2008 *Source:* CEU 2010c; BEA 2010

EU; since the EU cannot run deficits (see Section 19.5), it does not have debt to service.

These comparisons indicate that the EU is currently very far from even a decentralized federation like Switzerland. Given the crucial differences between the EU and other federations, the latter are unlikely to provide an appropriate template. The next section considers the characteristics of the EU that will affect its economic role and what that role should be.

19.4 The EU and fiscal federalism

The EU is not a nation state; it is made up of individual MSs, each with its own institutions, history, culture and languages. Thus the evolving EU constitution is very different from that of national federal states, and

it is probable that the economic role and budget of the EU will remain distinct. One aspect of EU distinctness is the difference in income levels between EU MSs (see Chapter 5), which is important for the provision of public services, especially social security. The non-economic differences between MSs present problems for common policies in other areas, such as defence/security and education.

The dispersion of income levels is much wider in the EU than in the USA (see Figure 19.1), which makes it unlikely and undesirable that the EU could have a significant distributional role. It is unlikely because redistribution would involve taxpayers in one MS supplementing the income of citizens of another MS. Besides the questionable political acceptability, the practical difficulties are immense – for example, how much should differences in income be reduced?

Where does this leave the EU's current redistributional role in the structural policies? The political stability of the EU in general and EMU in particular is dependent on a reasonable degree of cohesion in the EU. While this probably does not require equality of income levels,[8] what is needed is that the poorer countries are at least converging on the rich. Convergence in income levels is not automatic (Ardy *et al.* 2002, pp. 46–50), so some effective aid policy can be justified.[9]

There is no compelling externality or economies-of-scale argument for significant EU involvement in health and education. With regard to defence a more compelling case can be made for a larger EU role. Defence is the classic public good, and with war in the EU increasingly unlikely, defence is against external threats to the EU as a whole, or is related to peacekeeping/making beyond the EU. There is public support for the development of an EU defence policy (CEU 2009d, p. 10). There are a number of obvious difficulties, such as the reluctance of governments to cede sovereignty over such a sensitive area, whether the public would be supportive of European armed forces, and the role of EU neutral countries. Similarly, there are strong reasons for an important EU role in fighting organized crime and terrorism, where there is again public support (CEU 2009d, p. 10).

Beyond these areas,[10] the EU economic role would seem to be confined to competences that are already part of its responsibilities, such as overseeing the SEM, operating competition policy and regulation more generally, and also R&D policy, where EU programmes are justified because there are potentially important economies of scale (Sapir *et al.* 2003b). External action is really part of foreign policy and related increasingly to defence. The current EU role in agricultural policy is more questionable; there seems little reason for the EU to be paying direct agricultural subsidies (see Section 19.7, page 296, and Chapter 20), so agricultural expenditure could shrink, with the EU's role confined largely to regulation and trade policy. These arguments tend to suggest that there is a case for some limited expansion of the EU budget, if the EU were to acquire a significant defence role. It would, however, remain small – much smaller than that of existing federations. The conclusion must be that, at the present stage of development, a limited budget seems well suited to EU requirements. The EU still has to ensure that the operation of this limited budget is fair and efficient. These are the issues to which this chapter now turns.

19.5 Budget rules and procedure

There are five basic principles derived from the treaties under which the EU budget operates:

1. *Annuality* – the budget is only for the one year, so expenditure has to be made in that year. This prevents the build-up of long-term commitments, but has caused some problems because much EU expenditure is now on multi-annual programmes. The practical resolution of this problem has been the use of commitments for future years, which strictly do not have to be honoured, but which in practice usually are.

2. *Balance* – revenues must cover expenditure, and deficit financing is not possible. If expenditure is going to exceed revenue, additional resources have to be raised by supplementary or amending budgets in the current year. Surpluses at the end of the year are carried over to the next year as revenue.[11] The EU is not allowed to borrow to finance its own expenditure, but can use its triple-A credit rating to borrow for loans.[12] Most of these loans take place via the European Investment Bank (EIB; see Chapter 3). These capital transactions are financially self-supporting and do not breach the principle of EU budgetary balance.

3. *Unity* – all expenditure is brought together in a single budget document.

4. *Universality* – all EU revenue and expenditure is to be included in the budget, and there are to be no self-cancelling items.

5. *Specification* – expenditure is allocated to particular objectives to ensure that it is used for the purposes the budgetary authority intended. There is some possibility for transfers between categories for the effective execution of the budget.

These rules indicate the extent to which MSs wanted to limit EU competence in this sensitive area of government activity. So they ensure maximum control by MSs and minimum discretion for the EU.

The budgetary procedure laid out in the 1971 Budget Treaty[13] contained the seeds of discord in decision-making. This treaty granted the EP responsibility for the final approval of the budget[14] (see Chapter 3), a power the EP was determined to use. So in the early 1980s the annual budgetary cycle was one of frequent disputes between the institutions (Lindner 2006, Chapter 3). Two developments resolved this situation: first, the increased EP powers, which commenced with the Single European Act (SEA) in 1987; second, new budgetary procedures introduced with the 1988 Delors I package. This contained two innovations that continue to this day: a multi-annual financial perspective and an inter-institutional agreement on budgetary procedure. The Treaty of Lisbon (formally the Treaty on the Functioning of the European Union, TFEU) shifted these procedures from soft to hard law, so that the Council and the EP agree the budget in a co-decision type of procedure and the budget perspective has legal force.

The current financial perspective 2007–13 (European Council 2005b) contains agreed ceilings on broad categories of expenditure and for the budget overall. Actual levels of expenditure are set by the annual budget, which must be within the financial perspective limits. This budget has to be accepted through the procedure laid down in the treaties: preliminary draft budget from the Commission; co-decision; and, if necessary, conciliation between the Council and the EP (see Chapter 3). With the broad parameters of the financial perspective, the agreement of the annual budgets since 1998 has been straightforward. The decisions on the financial perspective, however, are far more hard fought.

19.6 EU budget revenue

Tax systems should be fair, efficient and transparent. Fairness can only be evaluated on the basis of consistent principles to decide tax liability.[15] There are two dimensions of fairness or equity – horizontal equity and vertical equity. Horizontal equity – the identical treatment of people in equivalent positions – implies that those with the same level of income and similar circumstances should pay the same amount of tax. Vertical equity requires the consistent treatment of people in different circumstances. In general, equity is taken to imply a progressive tax system. Depending on how the EU raises its revenues, this could apply to taxes on individuals or it could apply to MSs.

Efficiency requires that the tax system should

Table 19.3 Tax revenue of different levels of government in federal states (% of GDP), 2008

	Level of government			
	Federal[a]	State	Local	Total
Australia	27.8	4.2	0.8	32.8
Canada	16.7	11.3	3.0	31.0
Germany	27.4	8.8	3.2	39.4
Switzerland	16.1	7.1	4.6	27.8
USA	17.3	7.0	6.5	30.8
EU15[b]	0.1	33.7[c]	6.9[d]	40.7

Notes: [a] including social security contributions, 2001; [b] traditional own resources, agricultural and customs duties; [c] national central government; [d] state and local *Sources:* International Monetary Fund 2010a; Eurostat 2010c

minimize harmful market distortions. Low collection and compliance costs are important additional aspects of tax efficiency. Transparency requires that the tax system should be simple to understand, so that taxpayers are aware of their tax liability and how this is determined. This requirement of transparency is essential for democratic accountability. This section will consider the development of the EU revenue system and how it matches up to these requirements, but first a comparison will be made between the EU revenue system and those of federal governments.

As Tables 19.3 and 19.4 clearly demonstrate, the EU does not have a financing system like that of federal states. The amount of truly independent tax revenue is extremely low and taxation remains predominantly under the control of MSs in the EU15. Federal governments typically raise a large part of their revenue from taxation of income directly through the personal income tax system or indirectly through the social security system (see Table 19.4). Corporation tax, VAT/general sales taxes and excises are other important sources of tax revenue for federal government. None of these revenue sources is available to the EU.

The EEC was initially financed, like other international organizations, by fixed national shares, but the EEC Treaty provided for the development of a system of 'own resources'. The significance of this was that the EEC would have financial autonomy, by acquiring financial resources distinct from those of MSs. This

Table 19.4 Tax systems: federal states and the EU (% of GDP), 2008

	Personal income tax	Corporation tax	Social security	VAT[b]	Excises	Total
Australia	10.2	6.3	0.0	3.7	1.9	27.8
Germany	4.5	0.7	15.3	3.7	2.5	28.5
Switzerland[a]	2.2	1.1	6.5	3.6	1.4	17.9
USA	9.9	1.8	6.9	2.1	0.9	21.6
EU15	–	–	–	–	–	0.1[c]

Notes: [a] 2007; [b] general sales taxes or VAT; [c] traditional own resources
Source: International Monetary Fund 2010c

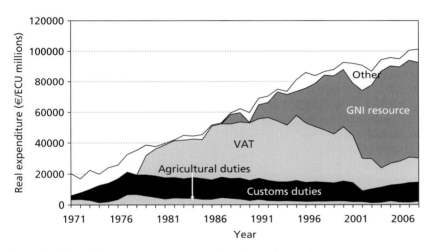

Figure 19.2 EU budgetary revenue resources, 1971–2008 *Source:* CEU 2009c

proved controversial and it was not until April 1970, just before negotiations opened for the first enlargement, that agreement was reached. This provided for the EEC to be financed by duties on agricultural imports and sugar production, revenue from the Common Customs Tariff (CCT; the CETs of Chapter 1) and VAT up to 1 per cent of the harmonized base (see Chapter 15). The traditional own resources (TOR), agricultural levies and customs duties are naturally EU revenue because they arise from EU policies: the Common Agricultural Policy (CAP) and Common Commercial Policy (CCP; see Chapters 1, 20 and 23). In a common market it is difficult to assign these revenues to individual MSs, because goods imported through an MS where the duties are paid may then be sold in another where the actual burden or incidence of the tax occurs.[16] As MSs

have not used the harmonized base, the VAT contribution has always rested on an 'artificial' calculation (Begg and Grimwade 1998, pp. 41–2), so it amounts to being just a particular way of calculating a national contribution.

The original own resources system had a number of problems as a system of finance for the EEC. At first, revenue expanded as the call-up rate of VAT increased, but once the 1 per cent limit was reached, revenue grew comparatively slowly (see Figure 19.2). TOR revenue was constrained by falling agricultural imports, as EEC food self-sufficiency levels increased (see Chapter 20), decreasing tariff rates, expanding membership of the EC and the extension of preferential trade agreements with third countries (see Chapters 23 and 24). The VAT base also grew slowly because it excluded government expenditure and savings, which tend to expand over time. It was regressive because these elements tend to increase with income. So the system was not equitable; contributions to the budget were not related to income per capita. The UK, in particular, seemed to be contributing more than its fair share, because of its high level of imports from outside the EU, and a relatively low level of government expenditure and savings.[17] Raising the VAT limit to 1.4 per cent in 1984[18] increased revenue, but this was only a temporary solution, which did not address the problems of lack of buoyancy or of equity in contributions.

The own resources system was made more equitable and more buoyant by the introduction in 1988 of the fourth resource. The base for own resources is now expressed as a percentage of EU gross national income (GNI), currently 1.24 per cent. EU revenue now comes from the four own resources and miscellaneous revenue:

1. *Duties on agricultural imports and sugar production.* Agricultural duties are tariff revenue on imports of agricultural goods. Sugar levies are a tax on the production of sugar beyond quota limits.
2. *Common Customs Tariff* (CCT). This is the revenue from EU taxes on non-agricultural imports, the importance of which has diminished due to the general lowering of tariffs (see Chapter 22) and, since 1999, when the share retained by national governments to cover the cost of collection rose from 10 to 25 per cent (European Council 1999a).
3. *VAT* revenue of 0.3 per cent of VAT on the harmonized base. To make VAT fairer, since 1992 the VAT base has been capped at 50 per cent of GNI for member states whose per capita GDP is less than 90 per cent of the EU average.
4. *The GNI resource.* The revenue raised from TOR and VAT is subtracted from total EU expenditure and the difference is expressed as a percentage of EU15 GNI, with each MS contributing an amount equal to this percentage of its GNI.[19] With the revenue from other sources diminishing as a percentage of GNI, this resource is becoming the dominant source of EU revenues (see Figure 19.2 and Table 19.5).

This system of finance has ensured that EU revenue grows in line with GNI and is reasonably fair because contributions are roughly proportional to GNI (see Figure 19.3).[20] The exceptions are Belgium and the

Table 19.5 Sources of EU revenue, 2008

	€ million	%
Traditional own resources:	*17,282.9*	*14.3*
Agricultural duties	1,703.5	1.4
Sugar levies	943.8	0.8
Customs duties	20,396.6	16.8
Collection costs	−5,761.0	
VAT resources	*19,007.7*	*15.7*
GNI resources	*74,878.5*	*61.8*
Total own resources	*111,169.1*	*91.7*
Other revenue	*8,537.8*	*7.0*
Surplus from previous financial year	*1,528.8*	*1.3*
Total	**121,235.7**	**100.0**

Source: CEU 2009c

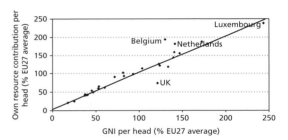

Figure 19.3 EU27 'own resource' contributions and GNI per head, 2008

Netherlands (the Rotterdam problem) and the UK (due to its correction mechanism; see Section 19.8, page 300). The increasing dependence on GNI-based contributions means that the EU has largely gone back to a system of national contributions.

19.7 EU budget expenditure

The development of budgetary expenditure follows the development of EU policies. For a long time the budget was dominated by agricultural expenditure, partly because other policies were underdeveloped, but also because CAP became expensive to operate. Until the late 1980s, agricultural expenditure grew rapidly, but has been stabilized since then (see Figure 19.4) because of CAP reform and limits being placed on agricultural

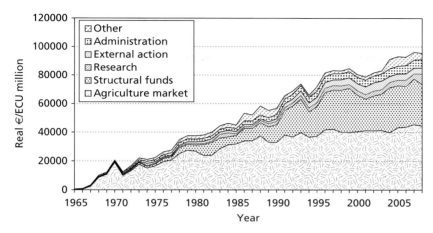

Figure 19.4 Real EU expenditure, 1965–2008 *Source:* CEU 2010c

expenditure (see Chapter 20). As enlargement increased EU heterogeneity, it was felt necessary to introduce a greater redistributive element into the budget by expanding and concentrating expenditure on structural operations (see Chapter 21). Part of this additional expenditure was financed by increased revenue, but the stabilization of agricultural expenditure freed resources for structural policies. Expenditure on research has increased as a result of concerns over EC competitiveness. The ending of the cold war led to increased expenditure as the EU sought to bring stability to Central and Eastern Europe, initially with pre-accession expenditure and subsequently with expenditure on internal policies as they became new member states (NMSs). Agriculture and structural expenditure, however, continue to dominate the budget (see Table 19.6).

Direct payments and market management continue to dominate agricultural and fisheries expenditure; in 2008 this accounted for 71.3 per cent of the total, and most of this, 89.1 per cent, is accounted for by direct payments (CEU 2009c). Rural development expenditure has been growing and if this is added to structural and cohesion expenditure, these now exceed the amount spent on agricultural support. The change in the pattern of agricultural expenditure from price support to direct subsidies and rural development has substantially enhanced budgetary planning and control.

There are substantial variations in CAP guarantee expenditure[21] among MSs, which bear no relation to their GNI per head. In Figure 19.5 EU25 MSs are

Table 19.6 EU expenditure, 2008

	€ million	% EU GNI
Common Agricultural Policy:	53,817.7	46.2
CAP markets	43,288.6	37.1
Rural development	10,529.1	9.0
Structural operations	35,554.8	30.5
Internal policies:	12,361.9	10.6
Research and development	6,494.1	5.6
External action	5,184.0	4.4
Administration	7,292.5	6.3
Pre-accession aid	2,126.7	1.8
Compensation	206.6	0.2
Total	116,544.2	100.0

Source: CEU 2009c

arranged in order of their GNI per head, with the highest to the right. CAP expenditure does not diminish as GNI per capita increases. Denmark, Greece and Ireland receive substantial payments, although Greece is one of the poorest EU15 countries and Denmark and Ireland are among the richest. All NMSs received low levels of CAP expenditure, reflecting the gradual build-up of payments and a lower level of direct payments. With just under half the budget spent on agriculture, it is difficult to achieve an equitable budget with this distribution of CAP expenditure.

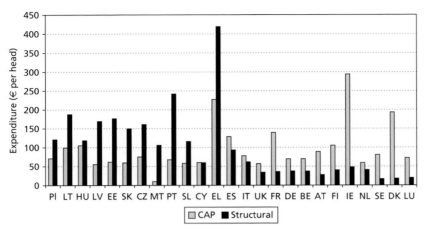

Figure 19.5 EU15 CAP and structural expenditure, 2008
Notes: EE = Estonia, EL = Greece, ES = Spain, SE = Sweden; see page 231, Table 15.1.
Source: EU 2010a; ECA 2009

For farmers, landowners and industries associated with agriculture, EU support of prices and direct subsidies provide substantial benefits.[22] For taxpayers and consumers CAP imposes substantial costs in two ways: first, by the taxation paid to finance the budgetary expenditure; and second, by the additional expenditure on food due to EU prices exceeding world market prices. With the reformed CAP, and the high world prices of recent years, the gaps between EU and world prices have narrowed substantially. For most agricultural products, EU prices are near to world levels, so the additional costs to the consumer are minor. This is not the case for milk products, beef and sugar, but this consumption cost is relatively minor nowadays (Ardy 2002a, pp. 96–7), so measured CAP expenditure provides a reasonable approximation of national benefits from CAP.

The structural funds – the European Social Fund (ESF), the European Agricultural Guidance Fund (EAAGF), the European Regional Development Fund (ERDF) and the Cohesion Fund – were developed to try to achieve greater solidarity within the EU. They were justified, therefore, as a redistributive policy, to encourage political solidarity. Structural expenditure has also been useful as side payments to facilitate agreement between MSs. The expansion of the structural funds and their concentration on poorer regions since 1988 was part of the bargain to achieve agreement on the SEA. This was reinforced by restricting the Cohesion Fund to countries with GNI per head of less than 90 per cent of the EU average. This concentrates

expenditure on poorer countries, but the highest levels of expenditure per head in the EU in 2008 were in Greece and Portugal, and only 28.5 per cent of EU structural expenditure is in NMSs (European Court of Auditors 2009). With structural spending aimed at regional rather than national redistribution, other objectives being pursued and political factors affecting its distribution, its redistributive effect is somewhat uneven. With CAP and structural spending accounting for over 75 per cent of EU expenditure, it is their distribution which largely determines the distribution of expenditure among EU MSs.

The largest element of internal policy expenditure is research and technological development (see Chapter 14), which tries to enhance EU competitiveness. Also significant under this heading are education, vocational training and trans-European networks (TENs). Education expenditure mainly finances grants for study in other EU countries. This expenditure should help forge a greater sense of EU identity and could have beneficial effects on SEM by encouraging labour mobility. Expenditure on TENs is very similar to ERDF expenditure, financing cross-border networks of roads, railways and energy and telecommunications grids. Such networks are important in fostering competition in the SEM, and, since they are cross-border, EU involvement is probably desirable to encourage their development.

EU external expenditure is concentrated on three groups of countries:[23] African, Caribbean and Pacific (ACP) countries, the Middle East and the southern

Mediterranean (see Chapters 23 and 24), and there is still some enlargement expenditure for the western Balkans. Pre-accession aid for the candidate and potential candidate countries[24] is a separate budget category, to protect this expenditure if there is pressure on the budget and underlining the passage of relations with these countries from external to internal. Russia and Commonwealth of Independent States (CIS) countries have not been offered EU membership, but the development of a closer political and economic relationship and economic aid are an important part of this process.

Aid to Mediterranean and Middle Eastern countries again tries to increase the stability of another volatile region close to the EU. Economic development in this area would also help to reduce the pressure for migration to the EU. Aid to ACP countries reflects obligations and ties to former colonies. The EU channels aid both via the budget and by a separately financed European Development Fund (EDF), which is responsible for most EU aid to ACP countries. Expenditure under the EDF is decided separately from the budget by the Council and is financed by fixed national shares. There are concerns about the effectiveness of aid programmes (see Chapter 25), as well as about individual elements of aid. For example, food aid accounts for around 20 per cent of budget expenditure on aid; this has sometimes been little more than an extension of CAP, facilitating the disposal of surpluses, with problematic consequences for recipient nations (Cathie 2001).

Although there is public support for foreign aid, the EU's role is not well understood, nor is it differentiated from national government aid programmes. The necessary scale of the operations, and the need to avoid wasteful duplication, justifies EU aid, but the continuance of national government programmes undermines the development of a clear role for the EU.

The least understood element of EU expenditure is that on administration. Constant press references to the Brussels bureaucracy, their gravy-train lifestyle and pictures of enormous edifices in Brussels and Strasbourg, suggest a vast and expensive bureaucracy. Thus administrative costs were selected by the public as the largest item in the budget (CEU 2010i, p. 210). This is a very distorted picture: the number of people employed by EU institutions is relatively small – 32,181 in the Commission in 2010 (CEU 2010g). This is

modest compared to national and local governments: in 2008 US federal government had 2,016,800 employees (Bureau of Labour Statistics 2010, Table 3). So the depiction of the Commission as a vast and unwieldy bureaucracy is completely false. The small Commission size is the result of the limited policies for which the EU is responsible, and the way in which these policies are operated. Government policies with large numbers of employees, such as health, remain the responsibility of national governments. National governments and their employees largely operate EU policies. Administration has remained a small and stable proportion of total EU expenditure as a result of the continued limitation of EU powers and responsibilities.

Concerns over administration also relate to issues about administrative competence and corruption; three aspects of the EU and its administration are important in this respect. First, the multinational character of the administration makes it difficult to devise suitable codes of conduct, because different countries have different ideas of what is acceptable. Thus, the employment of relatives and friends by governments and officials is normal in some countries but not in others. Second, the small Commission size, in relation to its responsibilities, has made it difficult to keep track of expenditure. There have been difficulties with the employment of contract workers, and the supervision of EU programmes is hampered by a shortage of staff. The Commission budget department has had particular problems. The European Court of Auditors (ECA) has noted progress, but there are still problems in rural development, cohesion, research, energy and transport,[25] external aid, development and enlargement (European Court of Auditors 2009, p. 12). Third, MSs have the primary responsibility for monitoring most programmes. The Commission has a rather ambiguous managerial and supervisory role, but generally no powers to carry out investigations in MSs.

Administrative expenditure is heavily concentrated in Belgium and Luxembourg, but the extent of the benefits this confers on these countries is limited. With other areas of expenditure it is possible to argue that EU expenditure is largely for activities that would have occurred anyway, so it is a net addition to GNI. Administrative expenditure either involves the use of resources such as labour, capital and land, or pays for individuals who are citizens of other MSs. While Belgium and Luxembourg undoubtedly enjoy

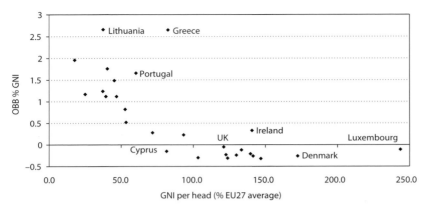

Figure 19.6 Operating budgetary balances and GNI per head, EU27, 2008 *Source:* CEU 2009c, 2010c

multiplier and balance of payments effects, this benefit is far less than the total amount of administrative expenditure in their countries.

19.8 Operating budgetary balances

An MS's operating budgetary balance (OBB) is the difference between the amount it pays in own resource revenue and the amount it receives from allocated expenditure.[26] The Commission's position on OBBs has changed: it used to argue that national concerns with OBBs were mistaken, and that the budgetary costs and benefits were an inaccurate measure of the costs and benefits of EU membership.[27] While this is true, it is irrelevant; whatever the overall costs and benefits of membership, the EU should be equitably financed. Another frequent observation is that the budget is too small to matter. However, the amounts involved are very large: EU expenditure is greater than the GNI of ten EU MSs. Unlike national budgets, which are largely transfers from one group within the national economy to another, payments to the EU represent imports and reductions in GNI, and receipts from the EU represent exports and additions to GNI. The Commission now accepts that OBBs can be unfair and there needs to be a correction mechanism (CEU 2004g).

Figure 19.6 plots OBBs for 2008 against GNI per head, revealing a weak negative relationship between them. All NMSs, except Cyprus, are net recipients from the budget; however, considering their low level of GNI per head, they are treated less generously than Portugal and Greece. Ireland, with the fifth-highest GNI per head in the EU, received net benefits from the budget.[28] Luxembourg, the EU's richest MS, makes rather small net contributions to the budget, even if its substantial administrative receipts are ignored. Thus the EU's twelve richest MSs, with GNI per head between 103 and 244 per cent of the EU average, have OBBs between 0.33 and −0.32 per cent of GNP. The budget thus has a rather haphazard impact: overall it is redistributive, but the relationship between OBBs and GNI is weak, as is the budget's redistributive effect (de la Fuente and Domenesh 2001; Asdrubali and Kim 2008).

National governments are very well aware of their OBBs, and if they think they are being treated unfairly they will demand that the situation be resolved. The most infamous example of this is the British problem, a recurrent issue from 1973, when the UK joined the EEC, until its resolution in 1984, unfortunately with a rebate specific to the UK. The UK's correction for budgetary imbalances is calculated as follows: in the current year, the correction is calculated on the basis of the imbalance in the previous year, equal to the percentage share of the UK in VAT and GNI payments, minus its share in total allocated expenditure, multiplied first by total allocated expenditure and then by 0.66.[29] The correction is financed by increasing the own resource contributions from other MSs, and not surprisingly this is strongly resented. The UK's position within the EU has also changed substantially: when the rebate was agreed in 1984 the UK was the fourth poorest of ten MSs; today it is the eleventh richest of twenty-seven, a point emphasized by the fact that NMSs with very low levels of GNI per capita are contributing to the UK rebate. Nevertheless, without the rebate the UK would be the second largest proportional net contributor to the EU budget.[30]

There has been a hardening of attitudes towards the OBBs budget. Two developments have been crucial: the changing situation of Germany and EMU. German unification has put tremendous pressure on the federal government's budget, with a net transfer of 4 per cent of GDP from West to East Germany (CEU 2002c, p. 2). Germany is therefore no longer willing or able to act as the paymaster for the EU; indeed it wants to reduce its net contributions. The change in German attitudes has been mirrored by Austria, the Netherlands and Sweden calling for reductions in their net contributions. For Eurozone MSs, EMU budgetary restraint is also a problem (see Chapter 12). Net contributions to the EU budget of 0.5 per cent of GNI do not seem very significant compared to government budgets of 30 to 50 per cent of GNI. But these net contributions loom much larger in relation to the Stability and Growth Pact's upper limit for public sector deficits of 3 per cent of GDP, and the medium-term requirement for the budget to be close to balance or in surplus. With monetary policy determined by the ECB on the basis of Eurozone conditions, national fiscal policy remains the one flexible short-term element of macroeconomic policy in national governments' hands. Net contributions to the budget eat into this national margin for flexibility and so have become a much more salient political issue. The widening of government deficits in the economic crisis is likely to intensify the desire of governments to restrict their net contributions to the EU budget.

With the current range of revenue resources and expenditure, it is difficult to achieve a fair distribution of budgetary costs and benefits. Over time the complexity of the revenue system is increasing, as more and more adjustments are made to make the system more equitable. Policy reform could achieve a fairer outcome, but to conflate reform and equity could compromise the objectives of reform. In the absence of reform, net contributions can be restricted by limiting budgetary expenditure, and this is what has happened. A much better solution would be a redistribution mechanism that would ensure a fair distribution of net contributions (de la Fuente and Domenesh 2001). Such a system would have the enormous advantage that each MS would feel the effects of new expenditure commitments on its OBB, and thus budgetary considerations would not bias policy-making.[31]

19.9 The EU budget and enlargement

When countries join the EU they will make contributions to the EU budget and be recipients of EU expenditure. So enlargement involves negotiations among existing MSs over the budgetary arrangements that will prevail after enlargement. These will have to take some account of NMSs, because after membership they will be involved in further budgetary negotiations.[32] The Original Six had relatively similar income levels, but enlargement has substantially increased the number and importance of relatively poor MSs. This is particularly the case in the 2004/7 enlargements, which placed large potential demands on the budget because of three characteristics of the countries involved: low income levels, the large total size of their populations and the importance of agriculture. Since contributions to the budget are roughly related to GNI (see Section 19.8), only a small amount would be added to EU revenue from own resources, but EU expenditure with unchanged policies would have risen significantly because of the demands on the structural and agricultural budgets. EU15 MSs were unwilling to finance this by increasing contributions and against large reductions in their EU expenditure receipts. So additional expenditure in NMSs was limited and expenditure in other areas was to be tightly controlled.

The Brussels Agreement (European Council 2002b) finalized the financial arrangements for enlargement. It contained four principal elements. First, there was to be no extra expenditure for enlargement; second, direct agricultural payments are to be extended to NMSs; third, CAP guarantee expenditure from 2007 to 2013 is to be kept below that for 2006, plus 1 per cent per annum. Fourth, if forecast cash flow under the EU budget is less than in 2003 for any NMS, compensation will be offered.

This was the starting point for the negotiations on the 2007–13 financial framework, which required unanimous agreement among EU25 MSs. These negotiations needed to reconcile four contradictory demands: first, additional 'enlargement expenditure'; second, extra expenditure in new priority areas; third, for large net contributions to be reduced; fourth, unwillingness among EU15 MSs to increase their net contributions, or to reduce their net benefits. The only area of near unanimity was that the UK's rebate should be reduced, a concession the UK was only prepared to make in conjunction with CAP reform. The Commission's initial proposals were for a modest expansion of expenditure (CEU 2004e) of 15 per cent in real terms over the 2007–13 period, compared to 2006. Under the new categorization of expenditure by objective rather than by policy, the greatest absolute expenditure increase was in sustainable growth, competitiveness (mainly R&D) and cohesion; also expenditure on external action was to increase substantially. On the revenue side a generalized correction mechanism was proposed (CEU 2004i, p. 70).

The deal reached (European Council 2005b) followed the familiar pattern of expenditure restriction, limited reform, side payments, the postponement of difficult issues, plus the adjustment of the UK's rebate. The overall growth of the EU budget was reduced substantially, so that instead of the proposed 15.6 per cent increase, real expenditure on average for 2007–13 is to be only 2.7 per cent higher than in 2006. All categories of expenditure are to be reduced, with the largest cuts in competitiveness, citizenship and the EU as a global partner (see Table 19.7). The two largest items of expenditure – agricultural market and cohesion expenditure – fare better, with only marginal cuts in agriculture. The cohesion budget was to grow significantly. There was a further marginal modification when agreement was reached on a limited budgetary response to the economic crisis, with the European Economic Recovery Plan, which provided accelerated payments of €5 billion of expenditure on energy interconnections and rural broadband (CEU 2009c).

The demands from Austria, Germany, the Netherlands and Sweden for reductions in their net contributions were partially met by the constraint in overall EU budgetary expenditure. They also benefited from reductions in VAT contributions, and in the case of the Netherlands and Sweden from reductions in their GNI contribution. The positions of NMSs were enhanced by the concentration of structural funds on poorer MSs and poorer regions. These provisions were partially financed by reductions in the UK's rebate, which remained in full on all expenditure except that relating to NMSs, where the UK's maximum extra contribution is 10.5 billion euros, and from 2009 it will contribute fully to the non-CAP market expenditure. The comprehensive reassessment of the financial framework in 2008/9 has not resulted in any changes to the EU budget.

19.10 Conclusion

The last two financial frameworks seem to have established a pattern of a low overall growth of expenditure based on the expansion of GNI. This, together with gradual decline of spending on CAP, permits the growth of expenditure on structural and other priority areas, within tight expenditure constraints, but fundamental budgetary reform eludes the EU budget.

The EU budget faces the challenges of equity and the future development of the EU. The problem of equity is vital because MSs will block future developments with budgetary implications unless the EU financing and expenditure system is fair. CAP reform would help to make the EU budget fairer and would release funds for the expansion of other policies and for expenditure in NMSs. Structural operations can be justified as facilitating convergence and providing a visible EU response in problem regions. Generally, the concentration of funds should be enhanced, but all MSs should continue to receive some structural funding; it would not be desirable to create sub-groups of client and donor MSs within the EU. These changes would make the EU budget fairer, but with the EU likely to continue with a narrow range of financial resources and expenditure policies, equity in the EU budget can only be achieved by a generalized redistribution mechanism. This would ensure that net contributions were related to GNI per head in a consistent and equitable manner. Failure to resolve these issues means that the EU budget is still concentrating on dealing with past CAP and regional problems rather than developing the EU of the future – for example, placing emphasis on R&D and environmental expenditure (Sapir *et al.* 2003a, b, c).

The role of federal budgets in a monetary union is considered in Chapters 10–12. The EU budget cannot have a significant role in fiscal policy because it is too small and it has to balance. The way the budget operates also makes it unsuitable for providing aid for regions badly affected by recessions; regional and cohesion expenditure only adjusts slowly to changing economic circumstances and is targeted on the poorest regions. So the EU budget does not currently fulfil the functions normally undertaken by federal budgets in monetary unions.

That the EU does not have a budget comparable to existing federations is both unarguable and unsurprising. It is unarguable because of the requirement of

Table 19.7 EU financial perspective for 2007–2013

	% change in payment appropriations, 2007–13, compared to 2006			% share of expenditure, 2007–13	
	Commission 2004 proposal	European Council 2005 agreement	2005 agreement	2009 agreement	
1. Sustainable growth	43.5	14.8	44.0	44.8	
1a. Competitiveness for growth and employment	115.9	18.0	8.4	9.1	
1b. Cohesion for growth and employment	27.1	14.2	35.7	35.6	
2. Sustainable management and protection of natural resources	3.3	-4.6	43.1	42.4	
Agriculture – market-related expenditure	-1.6	-3.6	34.0	33.9	
Other expenditure	20.6	-8.2	9.1	8.5	
3. Citizenship, freedom, security and justice	91.6	7.0	1.2	0.8	
4. The EU as a global player	21.7	-35.9	5.8	5.7	
5. Administration	19.0	10.9	5.8	5.7	
Appropriations for payments in 2004 prices	*15.6*	*2.7*	*0.99 GNI*	*1.0%*	

Sources: European Council 2005b; CEU 2004f; European Parliament, Council and Commission 2006; CEU 2009c

balance, its small size, the composition of expenditure and the fact that it is financed largely by national contributions, not its own taxes. It is unsurprising because the EU is very far from a political federation, made up as it is of nation states determined to preserve a significant degree of national sovereignty. Thus the expenditure and revenues of the EU tier of government will continue to develop slowly. The most important areas of federal government activity will remain national, because there are few clear advantages and many problems in moving provision to the EU. This is not to suggest that there should be no further EU-level development of policies. The strongest arguments here relate to internal security and common foreign and security policy. The likelihood, therefore, is that EU budgetary responsibilities will remain limited.

Summary

- The EU budget provides a number of insights:
  1. It indicates that despite its very significant development, the EU is still far from having the powers of a nation state.
  2. MSs retain tight control over EU revenue and expenditure.
  3. There is a strong status quo bias in EU revenues and expenditures.
  4. Distributional issues are very difficult for the EU.
- EU revenue and expenditure are very different from those of national federal governments.
- The EU budget does not have any significant tax discretion; it is largely financed by national contributions.
- EU expenditure remains narrowly concentrated on agricultural and structural and cohesion policies; it has been difficult to achieve significant increases in expenditure in other areas that are regarded as important. With this structure of taxation and expenditure, an equitable distribution of contributions and expenditure between MSs is hard to achieve. The EU has not been able to resolve this issue and this has contributed to the strong tendency of path dependency, evident in the EU budget and in other policy areas.

Questions and essay topics

1. Identify the factors that determine at what level of the administration (local, state/national, federal) government activity should take place?
2. What government activities should be undertaken by the EU?
3. How does EU budget revenue differ from that of national federal governments?
4. How does EU budget expenditure differ from that of national federal governments?
5. Examine why EU expenditure and revenue is so different from that of national federal governments.
6. Consider how the EU's pattern of expenditure has changed over time. How would you account for these changes?
7. What are operating budgetary balances (OBBs)?
8. How do OBBs differ between EU MSs?
9. Consider whether OBBs and their variation between MSs are important issues for the EU.
10. What functions does the federal government budget normally fulfil in a monetary union? Assess the extent to which the EU budget is able to fulfil these functions.
11. Why does EU enlargement pose particular problems for the EU budget?
12. Identify the challenges facing the EU budget and consider how these may be overcome.

FURTHER READING

Begg, I., Enderlein, H., Le Cacheux, J. and Mrak, M. (2008) 'Financing of the European budget', Final Report, Study for European Commission DG Budget (http://ec.europa.eu/budget/reform/conference/documents_en.htm).

Ecorys (2008) 'A study on EU spending', Final Report, Study for European Commission DG Budget (http://ec.europa.eu/budget/reform/conference/documents_en.htm).

NOTES

1 The EU general budget excludes the European Development Fund (see Section 19.7, page 299).
2 Moral hazard is the problem that if the government guarantees the financial viability of banks in a crisis, this may encourage greater risk-taking by banks, which in turn could lead to another crisis.

3 Where the proportion of income paid in tax increases as income rises.

4 There is again a moral hazard problem here: if government provides adequate pensions, this reduces the incentive, particularly among the less well-off, to purchase private pensions.

5 In practice, responsibility for many services are shared between different levels of government. This may allow some of the benefits of centralization and decentralization to be achieved. It may also blur responsibilities and be associated with problems of administration.

6 It would be difficult to justify such variation for policies funded from national taxation; the call is usually for equality of provision.

7 Externalities and economies of scale do not necessarily require central government provision; cooperation among local governments may be sufficient, but this can be problematic (Berglöf et al. 2003, p. 9).

8 Comparisons of income are probably made within rather than between countries, even with the Eurozone.

9 For a different view, see Berglöf et al. 2003.

10 For a discussion of the EU's stabilization role, see Chapters 10–12.

11 Deficits would be carried over as expenditure, but surpluses are normal because planned expenditure (commitment appropriations) is usually underspent, so actual expenditure (payment appropriations) is usually lower.

12 It also guarantees loans.

13 Treaty amending Certain Financial Provisions of the Treaties establishing the European Communities, *OJ L*, 2, 2 January 1971.

14 If the budget is not approved, the EU works with the previous year's budget.

15 The same principles should apply to benefit systems.

16 This is the 'Rotterdam problem', so called because Rotterdam is the port of entry for many goods that are then sold in other MSs, notably Germany.

17 The Netherlands also seemed to be making excessive contributions, but this was largely because of the Rotterdam problem.

18 It was reduced to 1 per cent in 1988, 0.5 per cent in 2002 and 0.3 per cent in 2007. For 2007–13 lower VAT rates apply to Austria, Germany, the Netherlands and Sweden.

19 For the 2007–13 period the Netherlands and Sweden will benefit from a reduction in their GNI contribution.

20 Shown by the fact that countries are near or on the 45 per cent line, indicating that their income relative to the EU average is the same as their contribution.

21 This depends largely on the composition and amount of previous production.

22 But not in an efficient manner: 20–50 per cent of expenditure (depending on the measure) ends up as an increase in farm household incomes (OECD 2003, pp. 54–75).

23 A small element of the external action is operational expenditure on joint actions decided under the common foreign and security policy (CFSP).

24 Candidate countries in 2007 were Croatia, Macedonia and Turkey; potential candidates are Albania, Bosnia Herzegovina, Montenegro and Serbia, including Kosovo (see Chapter 2).

25 But not the Sixth Framework Programme for research.

26 Not all expenditure can be allocated to individual MSs; the categories not allocated are administration for the reasons given (in Section 19.6.5, page 293), external action and pre-accession aid – 9.9 per cent of expenditure in 2008.

27 In addition, there are methodological problems with the measurement of net contributions (CEU 2004h, annex II).

28 This is due to delayed adjustment to Ireland's improved economic circumstances and substantial CAP benefits.

29 Further adjustments are made for the capping of VAT and the increase in MSs' own resource collection costs from 2001. From 2009 the additional expenditure due to the 2004 and 2007 enlargements will be eliminated from the calculation.

30 The UK's 2004 net contribution without the rebate would have been 0.57 per cent and that of the Netherlands 0.65 per cent of GNI.

31 For example, an MS's net contribution can improve significantly as a result of new expenditure commitments because its benefits may outweigh its small share of the costs.

32 The difficulties caused by the UK budgetary situation after the first enlargement indicate the need to accommodate the needs of NMSs.

20 The Common Agricultural Policy

ULRICH KOESTER AND ALI EL-AGRAA

20.1 Introduction

Unlike other regional blocs, the European Union (EU) extends free trade between its member states (MSs) to agriculture and agricultural products. Agricultural products are defined (in both the 1975 Treaty of Rome, creating the European Economic Community, EEC, and 2009 Treaty of Lisbon, formally the Treaty on the Functioning of the European Union, TFEU, Article 38.1) as those of the soil, stock-farming and fisheries, as well as those of first-stage processing directly related to them, although fisheries has developed into a policy of its own, the Common Fisheries Policy (CFP; see Chapter 21). Moreover, both treaties dictate that the operation and development of the common market for agricultural products should be accompanied by the establishment of a Common Agricultural Policy (CAP) among MSs.

One could ask why, in 1957, were the common market arrangements extended to agriculture? Or why agriculture (together with transport) was singled out for special treatment? Such questions are to some extent irrelevant. As mentioned in Chapter 1 (Chapter 1, Section 1.2, page 1), Article XXIV of the General Agreement on Tariffs and Trade (GATT, now managed by the World Trade Organization, WTO) dictates that duties and other restrictive regulations of commerce should be eliminated with respect to substantially all the trade between the constituent territories of a regional bloc. Since agricultural trade constituted a substantial part of the total trade of the founding MSs, especially in the case of France, it should be quite obvious that excluding agriculture from EEC arrangements would have been in direct contradiction of this requirement (see Section 20.2). Moreover, free agricultural trade would have been to no avail if each MS continued to protect agriculture in its own way (see Section 20.3), since that would likely have amounted to the replacing of tariffs with non-tariff trade barriers (NTBs; see Chapter 1) and might also have conflicted with EEC competition rules (see Chapter 13). In any case, an economic integration arrangement that excluded agriculture had a zero success chance. This is because the EEC Treaty represented a delicate balance of national interests of the contracting parties: West Germany favoured free trade in industrial goods since there lay its strength, while France was inclined towards agriculture, given its relative efficiency in the sector.

The purpose of this chapter is to discuss the need for singling out agriculture as one of the earliest targets for a common policy; to specify CAP objectives; to explain CAP mechanisms and their development to date; to evaluate CAP economic implications; and to assess CAP performance in terms of its practical achievements (or lack of them) and its theoretical viability. Before tackling these points, it is necessary to give some general background information about agriculture in the EU at the time of the EEC formation and at a more recent date. The chapter finishes with conclusions.

20.2 General background

The changing role of agriculture in MS economies can be demonstrated on the basis of some salient facts:

1. At the time of signing the EEC Treaty many people in the Original Six (Six) MSs were dependent on farming as their main source of income; indeed, 25 per cent of the total labour force was employed in agriculture – the equivalent percentage for the UK was less than 5 per cent and for Denmark about 9 per cent. The respective share for the EU15 in 2003, the year before the second to last enlargement, was 5.2 per cent.

2. At EEC inception, the agricultural labour force was

worse off than most people in the rest of the EEC – for example, in France about 26 per cent of the labour force was engaged in agriculture, but for the same year the contribution of this sector to French GNP was about 12 per cent.[1] The respective shares in 2003 were 4.4 per cent of the labour force and 2 per cent of GNP. The last figure certainly exaggerates the disparity of agriculturists, as many of them have an additional income from off-farm work and from capital invested outside the agricultural sector.

3. A rapid fall in both the agricultural labour force and in the share of agriculture in GNP occurred between 1955 and 1995,[2] and this trend is being maintained, albeit at a slower pace.

4. The structure of the sector has changed significantly over time. Agriculture used to be one of the most labour-intensive sectors in the early days, but has become one of the most capital-intensive. Consequently, the agricultural sector has become much more heterogeneous over time. Approximately two-thirds of farmholdings were between 1 and 10 hectares (ha) in size in 1957. Nowadays the structure is much more diversified, partly because of enlargement, but also because in the old MSs:

   (i) there is a large, growing farm sector that cultivates an increasing share of land (62.5 per cent of land is in the hands of farm operators, who cultivated more than 65 ha in 2003);

   (ii) there are farms that use the most recent technology (conventional farms) and others that constrain themselves by adhering to the rules of organic farming (organic farms);

   (iii) a fairly high proportion of farms are run part-time (23 per cent in 2003), but their share in total cultivated area is declining over time.

5. Agriculture in the EEC was not well integrated in the overall economy; the share of revenue spent on purchased inputs was less than 40 per cent in the 1960s, but is now well above 50 per cent.

6. The share of income spent on food has declined significantly over time (Engel's law). In the 1960s it was about 40 per cent, but it is now less than 15 per cent in the EU15; it is in excess of 35 per cent in some of the new member states (NMSs) joining since 2004.

7. The policy-makers reacted to these changes by an ever-increasing intensity of regulation. It started mainly with intervention on the markets for temperate zone products (grain, sugar and milk), expanded to the regulation of Mediterranean products (vegetables and fruits), and ended with the regulation of farms by setting constraints on decisions made on farms.

8. It is no surprise that EEC expenditure on agriculture continued to grow over time; the average rate of change during 1960–2003 was 6 per cent; and, despite large reductions, 46 per cent of the EU budget was devoted to agriculture in 2008 (see Chapter 19).

9. In assessing the impact of policy measures one should also take into consideration that ownership in agriculture has changed. In 1957 farms were not only small, but most of the farmers owned the land that they cultivated. However, the growth of individual farms has been more through the rent rather than the purchase of land. Moreover, the enlargements since 2004 have added some agricultural sectors that are mainly based on tenant farming.

20.3 The problems of agriculture

Although most economists praise the advantages of free markets, the agricultural sector in most countries has been more or less regulated by specific policies for centuries. In this section we analyse six reasons for this special treatment: food security, agricultural income, efficiency, stability of markets, food safety and environmental concerns.

20.3.1 Food security concerns

It is well known that there are significant fluctuations in food supply at the regional level. If markets were to function perfectly, such fluctuations would cause no concern as long as the world supply was stable. Regional trade and stockpiling could easily stabilize regional food consumption. However, markets are not perfect. Inter-regional trade may not stabilize consumption, as markets are not perfectly integrated due to high transaction costs. Moreover, specific policies may hinder inter-regional trade flows. Private stockholders may not hold high enough stocks in order to stabilize consumption on the regional level, making stockpiling a risky investment, since future harvests and prices are not known. Market failure and policy intervention may also lead to food security concerns by other nations. Thus most countries have food security included in the list of their agricultural policy objectives. Of course, how governments should intervene in order to achieve the objective would depend very much on the extent of market failure and on available policy alternatives. The more integrated the markets, the better the flow of information and the lower the transport costs. Regional integration schemes with trading agreements mitigate food security concerns at the regional level. EU markets are more integrated than in insulated countries with protectionist policies. The WTO has also helped to integrate agricultural markets by setting rules for trade. Private stockpiling is more effective in stabilizing food consumption if stockholders are not exposed to unpredictable interventions by governments. As far as the EU is concerned, markets are fairly well integrated regionally, so regional fluctuations in production should not lead to food security concerns. Nevertheless, most countries pretend that price support policies are also needed to secure food. Price support will certainly increase food self-sufficiency, defined as the percentage ratio of domestic production over domestic consumption. However, it is highly questionable whether a higher degree of self-sufficiency for food due to protectionist policies really contributes to the achievement of food security. Food security is mainly related to income and availability of food. Poor people may not have the income to buy food. High food prices lower their purchasing power, and thus lead to food insecurity for vulnerable households. Moreover, protection leads to a lower overall income in the economy and makes people poorer. Hence an efficient food security policy should focus on the poor and not just on available supplies on the markets. The latter is a necessary condition to secure food, but it is not sufficient.

20.3.2 Agricultural income

There is a widely held perception that in a growing economy income from farming does not increase as much as non-agricultural income. The argument is based on a closed economy and limited mobility of labour (*L*). The relationship can be clarified using a simple model, where demand is assumed to depend on income and prices:

$$q^D = q^D(Y,B,p) \tag{20.1}$$

where q^D = quantity demanded of the agricultural product, Y = income, p = price of the agricultural product, and B = population size.

Supply is assumed to depend on prices and a supply shifter, which stands for the effect of technological change:

$$q^S = q^S(p,a) \tag{20.2}$$

where q^s = quantity supplied of the agricultural product and a = supply shifter due to technical change.

It is assumed that demand and supply are equated by the prevailing price. Hence:

$$q^D = q^S \tag{20.3}$$

From equations (20.1) and (20.2) one gets:

$$\frac{dq^D}{q^D} = \eta \cdot \frac{dy}{y} + \varepsilon_{q,p}^D \frac{dP}{P} + \frac{dB}{B} \tag{20.4}$$

and

$$\frac{dq^S}{q^S} = \varepsilon_{q,p}^S \cdot \frac{dp}{p} + \frac{da}{a} \tag{20.5}$$

where $\varepsilon_{q,p}^D$ = price elasticity of demand, $\varepsilon_{q,p}^S$ = price elasticity of supply and η = income elasticity of demand.

Equating equations (20.4) and (20.5) and solving for the relative change in P results in

$$\frac{dP}{P} = \frac{1}{\varepsilon_{q,p}^D - \varepsilon_{q,p}^S} \left(\frac{da}{a} - \eta \frac{dy}{y} - \frac{dB}{B} \right). \tag{20.6}$$

From equation (20.6) one draws certain conclusions. Prices will decline if the value in the bracket is positive. It will be positive if the rate of technical change da/a is larger than the product from the rate of change of per capita income in the economy multiplied by the elasticity of income plus the rate of change in population. Hence technical change in agriculture is price-depressing, but only under certain conditions. If there were no technical change, but high population growth without economic growth in the economy ($dY/Y = 0$), prices would go up as predicted by Malthus. The reality of the last fifty years shows that technical change in agriculture has been large enough to offset the price increasing effects of income and population growth worldwide. Indeed, as the elasticity of income declined, with higher income and population growth somewhat flattened, technological progress in agriculture tended to lower food prices even more.

However, even if there were technological progress, farm prices may not have fallen – for example, if the elasticity of demand were infinite, prices would remain unchanged. This situation may materialize for a small, open country,[3] such as New Zealand. The shift in the domestic supply curve due to technical change will not alter prices, as the country is a marginal supplier of food products on the world market. However, for the world as a whole the price elasticity is fairly small and therefore prices come under pressure. Yet even if prices do fall, L income in agriculture may not decline. If L input in agriculture were completely determined by opportunity costs – that is, income that could be earned in alternative occupations, the price elasticity of supply would be high, leading to a lower decline in prices. Hence, price elasticities of supply and demand are crucial for the effects of technical change on agricultural prices and incomes. If sectoral L markets are not well integrated, L income in one sector may deviate from that in others, but if they are integrated, differences in L income will reflect preferences for work, protection of the environment and/or living in the countryside, differences in qualifications, and so on.

The current situation concerning L market integration certainly differs across countries. It can be shown that L markets are more integrated in developed market economies where information is available and transaction costs are low. Hence it was no surprise that Gardner (1992), in his seminal article, proved that there was no income disparity in the USA – that is, farmers' total income from farm and non-farm activities was about the same as that of other people in society.

If policy-makers nevertheless assume that there is a need to support farm incomes by politically setting prices above market equilibrium, they will affect the number of people engaged in agriculture, but not necessarily their income per work unit. Yet in spite of this reasoning, policy-makers in most countries intervene in order to affect farm incomes.

20.3.3 Efficiency in agriculture

Efficiency concerns the use of factor inputs in the agricultural sector. The sector produces efficiently if the ratio of total output to total input – that is, total productivity, cannot be increased by an alternative use of factors. The agricultural sector may lack efficiency for at least four reasons:

1. Individual farms do not employ the most efficient technology. Farmers may lack the know-how to find out about the best technology; they may be conservative and may not want to change; or they may not have their own capital or access to credit allowing them to be in the forefront of change. Hence most governments intervene in order to provide information to farmers, speeding up the use of new technologies.

2. The size of farms is too small to take advantage of economies of scale and economies of size. Individual farmers may like to expand their farms to a more efficient size; however, the growth of some farms has to be accompanied by the shrinking or closing of others, as there is a land constraint in agriculture. In order to improve efficiency, land should move to those farms that generate a higher marginal productivity of land than shrinking or dissolving farms. Optimal use is made of land if its marginal productivity is the same in all uses. The optimum situation will change from time to time as factor prices change in the economy and new technologies can be introduced in agriculture. Consequently, there is a tendency for the marginal productivity of land to differ across farms; hence a transfer of land, from farms where the marginal value of land is lower, to where it is higher, would increase the value of total production.

The optimal allocation of land will materialize only if land markets function perfectly. However, land markets are property-rights-intensive and the transfer of land may incur high transaction costs. The prospective buyer and seller of land have to find out the likely future returns of the land and the likely interest rates. Hence there is great uncertainty on both sides of the market. There may even be an outcome where there are no transactions on the market. The suppliers may have a high reservation price for land, possibly because they consider landownership a hedge against risk, or because they value landownership more than the ownership of other assets and hence ask for a high price. The buyer may only be willing to offer a low price because of the uncertainty of future returns. The result can be that there is no match between supply and demand, with the curves for the former lying consistently above the latter. Indeed, such a situation seems to prevail in some regional markets in transition countries.

3. Farms might also be inefficient in terms of allocation due to lack of access to credit. Transaction costs for creditors may be quite high because the assessment of the creditworthiness of farms might be costly and the risk for the creditor might be high. Such a situation may arise when farmers are not the owners of the land or when land markets are not active. Lack of credit history contributes to limited access to credit in transition and developing countries.

4. The technical efficiency of farms might be considerably smaller in comparison to other sectors. The reasons are again related to the peculiarities of agricultural production. Agriculture experienced a higher rate of technical change, thus making it difficult for many farmers to produce using old technology. Further, the steady L outflow might lead to larger heterogeneity in the quality of the agriculturists, with many farms not achieving their full technical potential. Finally, many restrictions on input use, in combination with tax advantages for keeping up agricultural production and selective investment aids, might lead to a systematic overuse of factors and thus increased technical inefficiency.

In short, market failure on land, L markets and markets for rural finance provide rationales for government intervention in order to improve the efficiency of agriculture. Promotion of research and extension, as well as measures to increase the mobility of land and L, are most often incorporated in the policy package.

20.3.4 Stability of markets

Agricultural markets tend to be volatile. The basic reasoning has already been offered by Gregory King, an English scientist (1648–1712). He found that a 1 per cent change in grain production resulted in more than a 1 per cent change in grain prices. This finding states implicitly that the price elasticity of demand for grain is less than 1.

The reasoning can easily be illustrated with the help of some algebra. Assume that there is a demand function where demand only depends on the price of the product:

$$q^D = q^D(p) \qquad (20.7)$$

Also assume that supply is completely price inelastic – that is, a vertical line in a diagram. Further assume that there is no storage and that all that is produced has to be consumed in the same period:

$$q^S = \bar{q}^s \qquad (20.8)$$

and

$$q^D = q^S \qquad (20.9)$$

Solving this system with respect to the relative change in p results in:

$$\frac{dp}{p} = \frac{1}{\varepsilon_{q,p}} \frac{dq^S}{q^S}. \qquad (20.10)$$

According to equation (20.10), the percentage changes in price resulting from a 1 per cent change in supply will be larger the lower the price elasticity of demand in absolute terms. It is often argued that the price elasticities for agricultural products decline with growing income, and hence fluctuations in prices may become even more pronounced in a developed economy. However, it has to be kept in mind that the model derived above was based on the assumption that total production in a given period of time had to be consumed in the same period. If one allows for storage, market demand in a specific period will depend on demand for consumption purposes in that period and on demand for storage. The latter takes into account expected prices in future periods and storage costs. Hence storage leads to an inter-temporal integration of markets. If expectations are correct, price differences between two points in time should not be higher than storage costs and a reasonable profit to cover risk and interest. As storage costs have significantly decreased over time, the inter-temporal price integration should have become stronger.

The impact of inter-regional trade on the price elasticity of demand points in the same direction. If there were fluctuations in regional production, exporters or importers would step in and link regional prices to those in other regions. Hence the blessing of a good harvest would be spread to other regions and the curse of a bad harvest would be mitigated by imports from other regions. Thus the regional price elasticity of demand not only depends on demand for consumption purposes in the region, but also on prices in other regions and on transport costs. Transport costs have significantly declined over the last fifty years, in particular for shipping. It is cheaper to transport grain from the US Gulf to Rotterdam by ship than from Munich to Hamburg by train or lorry. Hence an open trading economy would help to mitigate fluctuations in regional production. Domestic market policies to stabilize price fluctuations are less needed nowadays than in past centuries.

20.3.5 Food safety concerns

Food safety has become a more important element in agricultural policy for many countries. This development may seem surprising to an outside observer. It is questionable whether food has really become less safe over time: the opposite is more likely. Animals are healthier nowadays than fifty years ago and new technologies in food conservation and preparation have lowered food risk. Nevertheless, there are new developments that have led to food safety concerns. New technologies that are based on biotechnology have created new production processes and new products that are not always safe. Hence control of the food chain is needed. People are aware that food is not a search good where one knows the quality of the product. Instead, many food products are credence goods. The consumer knows neither the quality of the product nor the production process, so has to trust in its quality. However, trust will only be sustainable if food scandals are prevented. Of course, producers and traders have a genuine interest in creating and preserving trust, but the individual producer or trader cannot control the complete marketing chain. Moreover, new products, such as genetically modified organisms in food and feed products, as well as chemical and biological fertilizers and pesticides, have to be tested before they are allowed to enter the market. Hence it is a genuine task for a government to take care of this type of market failure.

20.3.6 Environmental concerns

In general, concern for the environment has increased in most countries over time. Hence the impact of agricultural production on the environment has become of greater interest. Some countries, in particular EU MSs, Japan, Norway, South Korea and Switzerland, emphasize the multi-functionality of agriculture. Agriculture produces not only the typical agricultural products, like food, feed and renewable primary products, but also by-products. By-products can be 'bads', which are non-marketed goods that lower the population's welfare, or 'goods', which are non-marketed goods that increase welfare. Hence policies have to be defined to take care of these by-products. Of course, the policy instruments used have to be different from those employed in the past to raise agricultural income.

The arguments presented may justify governmental interference in agricultural markets. As the importance of individual justifications for intervention has been changed over time, policies should also have changed. However, the change in policies in most countries is not in line with the changes in their rationale. Policies have pronounced path dependencies. Policy instruments that have been introduced in the past cannot easily be removed, as any policy change leads to winners and losers. The loss often materializes in the short or medium term, whereas the gain arises in the long term. Take, for example, a reduction in politically set grain prices. Grain producers will immediately see a loss and lobby against it. Consumers may gain if bread prices eventually decline. However, that will take time, and the gain for the individual consumer is quite small compared to the loss for the individual grain producer. Hence it is much easier to organize producers and to lobby against price reduction than to organize consumers. This fact helps to explain why governments in democratic countries are inclined to be more producer-friendly than consumer-friendly. It also explains why policies are as they are and why present policies are often not in line with economic reasoning. They are constrained by the past. What has been decided in the past is relevant for today even if it is not justified on economic grounds. The agricultural policies that were introduced in the 1930s at the time of the Depression often determined the main policy instruments of recent times. Changes will mainly occur if there are binding budgets or external constraints, such as those of the WTO.

20.4 The birth of CAP and the institutional setting

At the time of its inception, CAP was supposed to be a major engine of European market integration; there was a widely held hope that positive integration in agriculture would force other sectors to follow the same route. However, such expectations have not materialized; the annual price negotiations for agricultural products made evident the divergence in the national interests of EU MSs, with decisions being dominated by compromises between them rather than by EU-wide interests.

Agriculture is a special case in the integration process. As most countries had more or less strong national agricultural policies in the pre-integration phase (see Section 20.2, page 307), they were not willing to let market forces play freely in an integrated economy. Hence positive integration was needed – that is, specific policies for agricultural and food markets were needed at EEC level. In markets for industrial products a major policy decision was made at the beginning of the integration process to dismantle trade barriers without increasing the external level of protection (see Chapters 1 and 23). In contrast, CAP has been regulated through fundamental policy decisions made both at the beginning and throughout this period. Consequently, one can assume that EU agricultural markets have been more affected by policy decisions than by pure market forces.

It is argued in the previous editions of this book that the institutional and organizational CAP set-up was misconceived from the very beginning. Due to this, market forces have played a minor role relative to political decisions in determining CAP development. Due to space limitations, the reader is advised to refer to the last edition of this book; here we concentrate on the salient points.

20.4.1 The foundation of CAP: a crucial policy failure[4]

It is argued at the beginning that European integration was not possible on a political level without the main countries leading the integration process (France and Germany) partly agreeing on some form of CAP. However, that does not imply that without the specifics of CAP that was then created European integration would not have happened, otherwise there would hardly be any reason to discuss the 'misconception' of CAP. This hypothesis can be denied, as the EEC Treaty cannot support it; the Treaty foresaw 'alternatives' for integrating agricultural policy and remained vague as to the nature of CAP. It could consist of common competition rules or of coordination of national market

organizations or of a 'European' market organization. Indeed it was to take nearly three and a half years of argument after the EEC Treaty was signed to settle the basic principles of a common policy, another three years (1962–4) to agree on one of the key questions (a common level of cereal prices) and a further one and a half years to solve the second key question (a long-term agreement on CAP financing).

The fact that agreement was reached reflects a strong political commitment in favour of a common Europe by all MSs. National interests diverged considerably. Possibly owing to Hallstein, the first president of the European Commission (Commission; see Section 3.3, page 40), the price agreement was finally settled in 1964. When the Commission first submitted the proposal for the unification of cereal prices to the Council of Agricultural Ministers (hereafter, Council), the Council rejected it and asked for a modified version, which would more closely match individual national interests. Hallstein, a strong personality, resubmitted the original proposal after only half an hour arguing in favour of the unification of Europe. He asked the Council to either endorse the proposal unanimously or accept the resignation of the Commission. This contributed to the sense that a common Europe dominated national interests. Since then, the Commission has never again fought national interests in favour of Community interests so convincingly and so crucially.

It seems justified to investigate how the organizational and institutional setting created in the first years of CAP has affected CAP evolution. The purpose is to draw lessons for the prospective design of CAP. Moreover, it should be kept in mind that, at the time of designing the policy, the importance of organizations and institutions was less obvious than it is today. Again, due to space limitations, we refer the reader to the previous edition and here highlight the salient points.

20.4.2 A model of the decision-making process

Prescriptive policy decision models assume that policy-makers try to maximize a well-defined objective function, taking economic conditions as a given. It would follow that policies change because objectives and/or economic conditions change. This model does

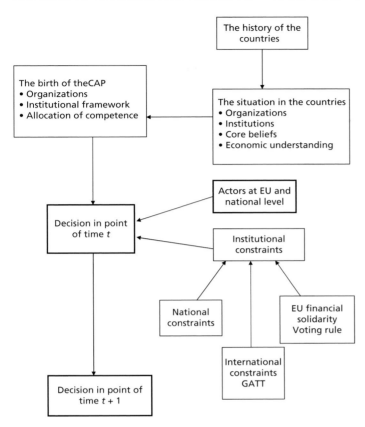

Figure 20.1 The decision-making process: a stylized model

not reflect reality in a reasonable way, particularly as it does not take into account that present choices greatly depend on past decisions. In actuality there is a certain degree of path dependency in policies (see Figure 20.1). Path dependency explains why economic policies change only gradually over time, ratcheting up their effects, unless significant shocks in the economic environment force massive adjustments (like the Great Depression in the 1930s).

Following this basic idea, the status quo of a given set of policies determines the policy decisions in the next period. This assumption is in contrast to the prescriptive policy approach, where policy-makers are seen as newly born in each period and not bound by past decisions or conditions on the political market. According to the underlying assumption in this section, the specific economic and political environment at CAP's birth affects the evolution of CAP in the following years and also determines the influence of MSs.

20.4.3 The main players in European agricultural policy

Market and price policies, which have been the main determinants of developments of CAP, have been the domain of European decision-makers from the very beginning of CAP. Hence, it makes sense to base the analysis on the players foremost at the EU level. However, only those players coming into existence with the foundation of CAP (Council) or deriving their power in the field of agricultural policy from the existence of the specifics of agricultural policies (Commission) need be considered; thus nothing need be said about the European Parliament (EP; see Chapter 3), even though the TFEU foresees an adjusted decision-making mechanism for agricultural issues in the same way as for other sectors. However, given the stated space proviso, we refer the reader to the previous edition and confine ourselves here to just a few sentences.

We begin with the Council, since it is the ultimate EU legislative body. The Council is designed to represent the national interest; hence each minister is naturally expected to act accordingly. But the ministers are, in most cases, more interested in the welfare of the farming population and less in society at large, so they are not likely to behave differently in the Council; hence their decisions cannot be in the EU interest.

The Commission is supposed to balance the national interests in the Council (see Section 3.3, page 40). However, the Commission is a bureaucracy, so it is most likely to follow the general behaviour of a bureaucratic organization. According to the findings of the 'new political economy' (Downs 1957; Buchanan and Tullock 1962), the individual members pursue their own objectives, taking into account the constraints imposed on them. It is generally accepted that bureaucrats prefer policy decisions that lead to more regulations and higher budget expenditure. It would therefore be unusual for the Commission to act otherwise.

20.4.4 Institutions affecting CAP

CAP evolution is not only influenced by the Council and the Commission (players); it is even more dependent on the institutions set in place. According to North, 'institutions are the rules of the game in a society, or more formally, are the humanly devised constraints that shape human interactions' (North 1990, p. 3). It is obvious that the outcome of the game (the shape and performance of CAP in our case) not only depends on the organizations, but also on the allocation of competence among the players and the rules they have to follow. It will be shown that the main institutions put into force at the inception of the common market support the protectionist bias of CAP decisions.

The principle of financial solidarity

The principle of solidarity is considered to be one of the three pillars of the common agricultural market organizations (Tracy 1989, p. 255). Indeed it makes sense to finance common activities such as CAP in solidarity – that is, out of a common budget. However, such a financial scheme may create additional divergences in national interests. Indeed the past and present pattern of financing the EU budget and enjoying the benefits of Community expenditure creates significant divergences in national interests (Koester 1977, pp. 328–45).

First, the welfare of individual countries is affected differently by increases in common prices for individual products. Second, individual countries may have interests that depart from those of the Community for promoting production growth. Third, countries may be more or less inclined to implement Community policies.[5] It should be noted that integration of countries might generally have distributional implications for individual countries, due to differences in their production and consumption patterns. However, CAP financial system distributional effects are policy-made. Any collective that creates institutions increasing the divergence of interests of the individual members weakens the viability of the collective.

The principle of preference for agricultural products

It seemed to make sense to the founders of the agricultural product market organizations to embed the preference for agricultural products in their basic tenets: domestic users should exhaust domestically produced foods before relying on imports. In reality, domestic consumers could do this of their own free will, as they do in many countries for specific food items. However, the founders seemed set against consumers' free choice, preferring external protection as the main instrument for achieving the 'preference', since making imports more expensive does increase consumption of domestic products. Therefore, the preference is tantamount to external protection of domestic producers.

The realization of this principle was most important for CAP evolution. First, together with the principle of financial solidarity, it created additional divergences of interests among MSs as it gave rise to invisible intra-MS income transfers. Second, the principle's implementation created great pressure on the Council and gave it much more political clout than existed in other sectors. It was accepted from the inception of the market organizations that the principle would be enforced by a system of variable levies on the main agricultural products. Strangely enough, the Council was allowed to decide annually about the magnitude of preference given to domestic products, and thus on the magnitude of the external rate of protection.

Due to Council members' interests and the distributional effects of the common financial system, annual decisions on the rate of external protection placed great pressure on the Council to secure agreement,

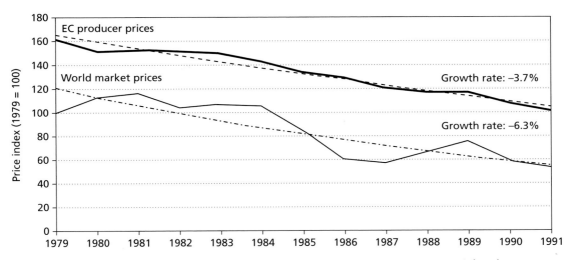

Figure 20.2 Development of EU and world market prices for agricultural products *Source*: CEU 1994b (p. 17).

especially given the divergent interests of the various countries. However, the Council had enormous discretionary powers, which could be exerted in favour of farmers, opening the door for strong lobbying efforts by them. It is true that the overall prices for farm products did fall over time (see Figure 20.2), but up to the mid-1990s by less than the aggregate level of world market prices; hence the nominal rate of protection even increased over time, in spite of growing surpluses. It should be noted that external rates of protection have even been increased for products for which there was already a surplus in the EEC. External protection could hardly have been justified for securing the preference. Indeed the preference played hardly any role in the justification of price proposals and price decisions. It was only the negotiations in the Uruguay Round (1986–94) that imposed binding constraints on the EU price support policy (see page 316). Much more important was the income objective, which leads to a discussion of the misconceived CAP in terms of the allocation of competence between MSs' and Community organizations, our next point.

20.4.5 The allocation of competence between member countries and the EC

The EU continues to be in charge of market and price policy, and since *Agenda 2000* (CEU 1997b; see page 30), partly in charge of rural development policy,

whereas MSs have more freedom in conducting structural policy, although constrained by EU-set rules. Such an allocation of competence makes sense. Market and price policies rely heavily on the rate of external protection, and not only are there good arguments for having a common degree of external protection for all MSs, but, vitally, the Commission is also in charge of the common commercial policy (see Chapters 1, 2 and 24). However, supranationalizing market and price policies can cause problems for the EU if the decision-making body is allowed to set the external rate of protection annually, and if the members of the decision-making body, the Council, bias their decisions in favour of farmers. Even if not supported by the EEC Treaty, market and price policy has been used as a means to achieve the income objective.[6]

It is obvious that national interests diverge significantly on the price changes needed to achieve the national income objective. First, the need to increase national agricultural income is more related to income changes in the national economies and less to farmers' incomes in other countries. Hence differing growth rates in overall national income may result in divergent needs for increasing agricultural income. Second, an increase in institutional prices in EU currency leads to divergent increases in actual farm gate prices among MSs (Colman 1985, pp. 171–87), as the transmission coefficient between institutionalized prices and farm gate prices varies significantly across countries. Allocating the responsibility for the income objective to the EU, and accepting price support as the main instrument to achieving it, necessarily enlarges the divergences in national interests with respect to price policy. It could have been expected that price changes would generally be at the cost of those parties who had no voice in the negotiations – that is, the consumers, taxpayers and foreign trading partners. However, EU policy-makers could not externalize the costs of their decision without any constraints, and it is to these that we turn next. As external protection has declined significantly since the middle of the 1990s, this problem has become less important. However, the birth of the rural development policy has created new divergences between national and EU interests (see Section 20.6, page 328).

The importance of voting rules

Voting rules can be quite important for the behaviour of a collective. Article 148 of the EEC Treaty envisaged that the Council should generally decide by majority rule. However, majority voting is more questionable if voters differ significantly in their preferences and if the individuals are affected to different extents by the collective decision. Accepting the majority rule for every decision would give rise to significant divergences in national interest concerning CAP. Therefore, two years after the first price decision was made, France demanded that decisions be unanimous in cases that could be considered of vital interest for any single country – hence the 'Luxembourg compromise' (see Chapters 2 and 3). Thus, up to 1982–3, the Council made only unanimous decisions, avoiding minority exploitation. However, it is well known that groups are well advised to apply this rule only for cases that are of the utmost importance, because the expected external costs[7] of such decisions are high. Unfortunately, CAP design implied that policy decisions would have quite different effects on individual MSs. Hence it might have been impossible to reach an agreement on the individual elements of a proposal presented by the Commission. There has always been at least one loser, possibly the European paymaster, who would have voted against the proposal. However, due to CAP specifics, a mechanism for discretionary decisions was built into the system, and it was only feasible to decide on packages (logrolling). The outcome was certainly a compromise among Council members and their decisions were generally not in the interests of the Community at large. The move to majority voting

in the 1980s has contributed to an EU ability to change its CAP. The TFEU has further improved the chances for a genuine change of CAP. However, the tendency to externalize the costs of the decision is still prevalent, but less than in the first three CAP decades.

The voting rules are of the utmost importance if policy changes affect the EU financial system. Individual MSs check proposals for changes with respect to national implications. Proposals that may improve the rationale of CAP from an EU perspective would not be likely to be accepted by the Council if some (important) MSs were to lose out. Hence the past reforms of CAP tried to stabilize the already established pattern of national and regional gainers and losers from CAP.

20.4.6 Constraints on CAP policy-makers

Foreign trade restrictions

From the very beginning, agricultural policy-makers had to take into account restrictions imposed by international trade agreements, principally GATT (see Chapter 24). The external rate of protection could not be increased for some feed imports. This constraint had significant implications for the other constraints – that is, budget outlays (CEU 1988b), which will be discussed below. The growth of expenditure for the market organizations for grain and milk depended directly on GATT-imposed constraints.

Actually, GATT could have posed a much more binding constraint on CAP policy-makers, had its Article XVI.3 been taken literally. It states that subsidies to agricultural exports (and other primary commodities) are only allowed provided the exporting country does not capture more than an equitable share of world export trade (see, inter alios, Tangermann 1991, pp. 50–61). However, a clear definition of the term 'equitable share' has never been agreed. After the EEC became self-sufficient for individual products one after another, exports increased more than world trade, leading to an increase in the share in world trade.[8]

Foreign trade constraints became more binding after GATT's Uruguay Round (1986–94) was finalized. Until the late 1970s, the EU and the USA had opposing trade interests. The USA, as the main exporter of temperate zone agricultural products, was from the very beginning interested in high world market prices for them. In contrast, the EU, as an importing region, preferred low prices. However, in the late 1970s the EU turned into an exporter of most of these products. Low world market prices led to negative terms of trade effects and boosted export subsidies, which in turn resulted in complaints by trading partners. Therefore the EU agreed to open a new trade round with the focus on agricultural trade. The outcome of the negotiations was that the EU, like other GATT members, had to accept some significant constraints in its foreign trade regime, the details of which are analysed below.

These restrictions also obliged the EU to change its domestic policies for most agricultural products (see pages 320–2). Further reforms can be expected after agreement is reached on the ongoing WTO Doha Round. CAP experience indicates that the driving force behind policy changes is neither rational economic considerations nor internal budgetary constraints, but rather external trade restrictions.[9]

One may wonder whether these trade constraints might have guided CAP in a more welfare-maximizing direction had they been there at the time of CAP's inception. The answer would most likely be in the negative. The constraint has contributed to non-uniform rates of protection, thus increasing the overall welfare loss incurred from securing for farmers the given income level. The EU, and its main trading partner/ opponent, the USA, could have enjoyed higher welfare had EU protection rates been higher (Koester and Tangermann 1990). It is true that the restrictions on the import side for feed and some vegetable oils made protection for grain and milk more costly in economic terms. However, it is doubtful whether this had a more than marginal effect on the decisions of policy-makers.

Past experience does support the view that the main driving force of domestic policy changes, the foreign trade constraint – more specifically, the pressure of trading partners – has eventually led CAP to adopt a superior resource allocation policy. The Uruguay Round forces CAP decision-makers to accept a cut in import tariffs of 36 per cent on average, to reduce the quantity of subsidized exports, to lower the outlays for export subsidies and to reduce domestic support. These imposed changes required great changes in the application of CAP instruments (see page 320). Some of these changes, such as the move to decoupled direct payments (see page 324), have certainly improved the allocation of resources. However, the institutional constraint due to the principle of financial solidarity did

hinder genuine reform. The birth of the 'second pillar' gave rise to a new set of instruments, which stabilized the distributional flows of EU expenditure and led to some new instruments, in particular concerning environmental constraints, which increased the intensity of regulation and conflicted with the objective of improving resource allocation (see Section 20.6, page 328).

The budget constraint

One of the main domestic constraints faced by agricultural policy-makers is the budget. Even if governmental expenditure is not an adequate indicator for costs and benefits of any policy activity, expenditure plays an important role. First, most governments are restricted in their total outlays due to limited access to tax revenue. Therefore, the individual expenditure items compete with each other. The minister of agriculture has to compete with other government ministers for additional spending. Second, budget outlays are a visible indicator of governmental activity. Increasing expenditure on agriculture seems to convey to the public that the government is intervening more strongly in favour of farmers. Of course, this indicator is not at all adequate for mirroring the total transfer accruing to agriculture. It is well known that European policy-makers relied more on invisible than on visible transfers before the CAP reform of 1992.[10] Nevertheless, the general public is more informed on the visible transfers and hence constrains policy-makers in this respect. It was most likely the budget constraint that led to a more prudent price policy after the EU had passed self-sufficiency for the aggregate of agricultural products at the beginning of the 1980s (see Figure 20.3). The budget constraint became even stronger over time since the setting up of the intermediate Financial Framework, which programmes expenditure for a seven-year period; the present framework runs from 2007 to 2013 (see Chapter 19).

Constraints by non-agricultural pressure groups

Governmental interference in the markets in favour of farmers places both direct and indirect taxes on other sectors of the economy (Koester 1991, pp. 5–17). Surprisingly, there was, at least in Germany, a tacit agreement between the farmers and the industrialists' unions that CAP should be left to the former. The industrialists may have viewed CAP as unimportant,

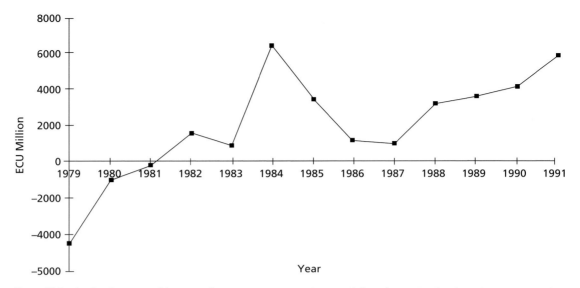

Figure 20.3 The development of the EU trading situation *Source*: CEU 1994b (p. 15) *Note:* Production minus consumption of PSE commodities weighted by 1979 world market prices (ECU million); PSE being an indicator for the value of gross transfers from consumers and taxpayers in favour of producers.

given that they were more focused on the divergence of interests within their own ranks. Some of them profited greatly from CAP. Hence they did not agree on a clear line of opposition to CAP. The attitude of the industrialists' union changed in the 1980s, when it became frightened of the trade repercussions caused by aggressive agricultural export subsidies. It was only then that they published a clear statement demanding a less distortive CAP. This supports the view that foreign trade constraints are most likely the main driving force for domestic policy changes.

One may wonder whether the consumers' unions could play a crucial role in constraining agricultural policy-makers. There is hardly any evidence supporting the role of these interest groups; generally, they seem not to be well represented in most countries. Not being well staffed, they lack the information and the power to push for policy changes.

20.5 The market organizations of CAP

CAP has an extremely complex set of instruments and regulations, which have changed greatly since the days of its inception. Here we concentrate on the present system, but with a flavour of the past; those interested

in how it developed over the years are advised to turn to earlier editions of this book.

From the outset, the main ingredients of CAP were market organizations for individual agricultural products. These organizations are built on external and internal trade regulations. Up to 2007 there were twenty-one common market organizations for individual products or groups of products. As price support, which used to be the most important measure, has become less important since 1993, and has been gradually substituted by direct payments that were not part of the market organizations, in 2007 the Council decided to integrate the twenty-one market organizations into one single market organization. The main positive effect is a reduction in administrative costs. Economic costs remain unaffected, as there was neither a change in policy measures nor in the intensity of their use. Still there is external and internal protection for most agricultural products, and they remain unchanged, although on a lower level.

Farmers often believe that internal market regulations are more important for the performance of markets than external trade regulations. However, that is a fallacy. As the main objective of the market organizations is to provide a higher income for farmers, the main instrument is price support. Domestic prices are higher than import or export prices. A wedge between domestic and world prices can only prevail if there are border measures in place. Hence external trade regulations are more important for the performance of domestic markets. Consequently, the following presentation starts with an analysis of the external trade regulations.

20.5.1 Instruments applied

Import regulations

VARIABLE LEVIES AND SPECIFIC IMPORT TARIFFS In 1957 the EEC was an importer of the main temperate zone agricultural products. Hence the market organizations were set up for import situations. Originally the EEC had set threshold prices for the main agricultural products (individual grains, sugar, milk and beef). These prices were set at the annual price negotiations and hence were politically determined. Under normal conditions, these prices were far above the world market prices (c.i.f. prices – that is, including cost, insurance and freight). The gap between the two prices was made up by variable levies. Variable levies are comparable to duties levied on imports, but as the levy changes with changing world prices, it becomes completely divorced from world market prices. How it functions is clarified with the help of Figure 20.4. Import prices are determined by the c.i.f. world price plus the variable levy. The supply curve on the EU market is equal to the domestic supply curve up to price p_s, and at this price it is equal to the world market supply curve plus the levy. If it is assumed that the EU is a relatively small country that has no impact on the world market price, the supply curve faced by the EU deviates and becomes a horizontal line. The variable levy shifts the world supply curve upwards to the level of the threshold price, which will be the domestic price at the point of entry of the imported product. The EU has set the same threshold prices for a well-defined product for all ports of entry. These prices strongly determine domestic prices at any other location, as regional prices are strongly correlated across different locations. The main difference between local prices and threshold prices are transport costs.

Figure 20.4 shows that the typical market organization at the time of setting up the schemes had positive effects for the budget. The EU could have increased its

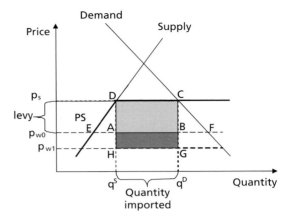

Pw = world market price (cif)
Ps = threshold price
ABCD = budget revenue
EAD = welfare loss on the supply side
BFC = welfare loss on the demand side
PS = producer surplus
ABGH = terms of trade effect

Figure 20.4 The impact of variable levies on domestic prices

so-called own resources (see Chapter 19) by charging variable levies on imports. However, the scheme also had negative welfare effects. Domestic producers received incentives to increase their produced quantity, but incurred higher costs than the EU would have had to pay for imports, resulting in a welfare loss of EAD on the supply side. Domestic consumers would like to have consumed a higher quantity at world market prices, but they are taxed by domestic prices above world market prices. The welfare loss on the demand side is BFC. Thus the figure shows that the budget effects of a specific policy are not identical to welfare effects.

It might have been that the EU could already exert market power on some markets in the first years of its existence – that is, the world supply curve on the EU market would have been upward-sloping. Assuming such a case, the setting up of variable levies that reduced EU demand on world markets led to lower world market prices, generating a positive welfare effect for the EU, a terms of trade effect. The terms of trade effect did generate budget revenue by increasing the levy, and at the same time led to positive welfare gains offsetting parts of the Harberger triangles. The overall welfare impact, however, was probably negative.

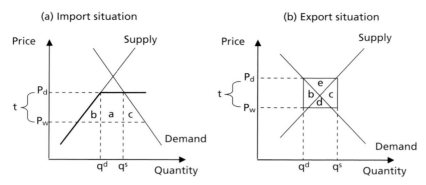

Figure 20.5 The effect of variable levies or fixed tariff rates

The system of variable levies continued until 1995, when the new WTO rules came into force. WTO agreements required that all NTBs to trade, such as variable levies, had to be transformed into tariffs, the term employed being tariffication. The tariff equivalents of 1986–8 had to be lowered by 36 per cent on average, but by at least 15 per cent for individual commodities. Hence tariff rates should not be higher than the new bound-reduced tariff rate. However, as world market prices were very low in the base period, the EU has had no problems in securing the domestic price at the desired level. Anyhow, at the last minute the EU managed to get a special regulation for those grains for which there are intervention prices on the domestic market. According to this regulation, the domestic threshold price is set at 155 per cent of the domestic intervention price. The difference between the threshold price and a hypothetical c.i.f. import price (world market price) is charged on imports. The main difference on the grain market that had to be introduced was the rule concerning the threshold price. It used to be a political price that could be set annually at the Council's discretion. The new rule sets the price in fixed relation to the intervention price, and the EU agreed not to increase the intervention price during the term of the agreement (1995/6 to 2001/2). Of course, the EU is free to lower the intervention price, which it did in the year 2000.

The second rule concerned the definition of the relevant world market price. Prior to the agreement, the EU considered the c.i.f. price to be the relevant offer price of foreign countries at EU borders. This practice caused problems, as imports had declined over time, and hence it was difficult to find the representative c.i.f. price. In the Uruguay Round, EU trading partners

agreed to accept the representative US market price as the representative world market price. Adding costs for insurance and freight results in the hypothetical EU c.i.f. price. As long as this price is lower than the EU's threshold price, and as long as the price gap is smaller than the tariff that the EU could apply according to the agreement, the EU charges the difference between the threshold price and the c.i.f. price. Thus the old system continued almost unchanged up to 2003. The effect of the regulation is clarified with the help of Figure 20.5.

The domestic price is determined for imports in panel (a). Importers can offer at prices p_w plus t, the tariff or levy. The supply curve deviates at price p_d on the domestic market if the importing country is a relatively small country. The country generates revenue equal to $(q^d - q^s) * t$ (the asterisk is used throughout to indicate multiplication). However, the welfare loss for the country is equal to b plus c.

If t is a variable levy, as it used to be for most EU agricultural imports before the Uruguay Round, t varies with the world market price, leaving the domestic price completely divorced ('decoupled', in the jargon) from the world market price. Domestic prices are stable even if world market prices vary. If domestic supply falls short due to a bad harvest, the supply curve shifts to the left, allowing for a greater volume of imports.

In 2002 a further change in the import regulations for medium- and low-quality wheat was introduced. The EU realized that due to high market prices in the USA based on a bad harvest, import levies had to be set at zero. At the same time some Eastern European countries, in particular Ukraine and Russia, had excellent harvests and could offer wheat to the EU even below the intervention price. Hence the EU managed to replace the import regulations for medium- and low-quality wheat and feeding barley by tariff rate quotas (see right column on the functioning of these regulations).

If the country is an exporter of the product under consideration, the tariff or levy will not determine the domestic market price directly. However, a country cannot be an exporter with prices above p_w. Foreign supply would enter the market and drive domestic prices downwards to the world market level. Panel (b) of Figure 20.5 shows that part of the tariff may become redundant. The tariff rate could be lowered without resulting in more imports. The country incurs budget expenditure equal to $(q^S - q^d) * (p_d - p_w)$ – that is, $b + d + c + e$. However, the welfare loss is equal to the triangle below the demand and supply curves, $b + d$ and $c + d$. A comparison of panels (a) and (b) clearly shows that the welfare losses of trade policies are not related to budget effects, but only to the price gap between domestic and world market prices and the price elasticities of demand and supply.

AD VALOREM TARIFF RATES There are a few agricultural products for which the EU charges only an ad valorem tariff – for example, potatoes and tropical products, or in addition to other import restrictions. Ad valorem tariff rates are also used to provide specific protection for EU processing industries. Concerning tropical products, the ad valorem tariff is higher for processed products than for raw materials (tariff escalation), providing additional protection for the domestic processing industry. Ad valorem tariff rates have to be preferred to specific tariffs or variable levies if the products under consideration are heterogeneous, since one levy for a set of highly differentiated products would lead to undesired distortion in trade flows. Take the case of fruit and vegetables, where ad valorem tariff rates are applied. Even a product like cabbage is highly differentiated. If there were one specific tariff for all varieties or one levy, high-quality products would enter EU markets at a lower percentage charge than low-value products. Hence domestic producers of high-quality cabbage would be put at a disadvantage compared to producers of lower-quality cabbage. If the EU were to introduce alternative specific tariff rates for individual qualities, the administrative burden would be very high. Hence it is reasonable to apply variable levies or specific tariff rates only for fairly homogeneous products.

TARIFF RATE QUOTAS Tariff rate quotas are a new element in agricultural trade; they were introduced in the Uruguay Round. WTO member countries have to allow each other minimum access to their markets, amounting to 5 per cent of consumption in the period 1986–8. These imports enter the EU market at a lower tariff rate than is normally applied. In January 2003 such a system was also introduced for some grains (see page 323).

The effect of this import regulation is clarified with the help of Figure 20.5. Panel (a) depicts the situation of an import case. The country charges the tariff t and tariff revenue is $t^* (q^d - q^S)$. If the country has to charge a lower tariff rate for within-quota imports, the tariff revenue forgone is equal to $(t - t_q) * q^*$, where q^* stands for the tariff quota. Thus the country loses revenue and enjoys a lower welfare if the tariff quotas are allocated to foreign exporters. If the quota is auctioned, the loss for the country might be minimal; private traders, whether foreign or domestic, would be willing to pay a price per unit of import quota about equal to the difference between the domestic price and the world market price. The only deviation would arise from transaction costs. Actually, only 12 per cent of tariff quotas are auctioned (Skully 1999). The EU does not apply an auction system for any tariff quota.

Panel (b), which is more important for EU agricultural markets, shows the export case. It is assumed that the domestic price p_d is lower than the world market price p_w plus the tariff rate t. This is a typical EU situation: the tariff was set at the time when the EU was still an importer, but having matured to an export situation there are no more imports. The actual tariff rate could be lowered (by the difference between $p_w + t$ and p_d) without affecting imports – that is, part of the tariff is redundant (in the jargon, there is water in the tariff rates). The EU has actually bound tariff rates which are partly redundant – that is, tariffs can be lowered without giving rise to imports. Allowing tariff quota imports, the EU has to increase subsidies for exports as $p_d > p_w$. These additional subsidies imply a welfare loss for the EU, but only if the tariff quotas are allocated to foreign exporters.

PREFERENTIAL ACCESS It is widely agreed that CAP distorts world agricultural markets. Hence trading partners complained about restricted access to EU markets. The EU's response was to offer

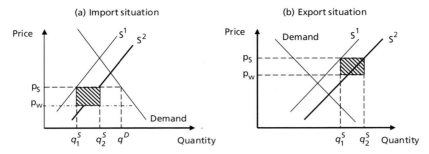

Figure 20.6 The impact of preferential access to EU markets

preferential access to its market. First, trade preferences were granted to some countries which had lost market access to countries that joined the EU (see Chapters 24 and 25) – for example, New Zealand's quota for butter exports to the UK and the USA's quota for maize exports to Spain and Portugal. In 1975 preferential access was granted to some African, Caribbean and Pacific countries (ACP countries; see Chapters 23 and 24) that had former colonial ties to EU MSs. In the 1990s the EU signed the so-called European Agreements, the Association Agreements, with selected Central and Eastern European countries, which granted them import quotas. In 2001 EU markets were opened completely for imports from some Balkan countries and for most imports from the forty-nine least-developed countries (see Chapters 24 and 25). In the latter case, the only restriction was for imports of bananas, rice and sugar, but only for a transition period up to 2009. The effects of these agreements can be clarified with the help of Figure 20.6. The EU supply curve shifts to the right by the amount of the preferential quota or by the unrestricted imports. The EU either loses tariff revenue or has to spend additional amounts on export restitutions (see next page). Hence the welfare loss for the EU is equal to the price gap between domestic prices and world market prices multiplied by the quantity of preferential imports. The indirect impact of the Everything But Arms (EBA) agreement on the common market organization for specific products may be substantial, as the case of sugar illustrates (see next page and Chapters 24 and 25), because unrestricted imports are deleterious for products with binding production quotas in combination with high external protection.

Export regulations

Until the end of the Uruguay Round in 1994, there were no real constraints on agricultural exports. GATT rules did not allow export subsidies on manufactured products. The USA was instrumental in introducing the GATT waiver for agricultural exports, but GATT set the proviso that they should not be used to capture more than an 'equitable share' of world exports of the product concerned (GATT's Article XVI.3). As it was not clear what the term 'not more than an equitable share' actually meant, countries were free to use export subsidies. This waiver was of the utmost importance for the functioning of EU markets up to 1992. The EU developed from an importing to an exporting region for almost all temperate zone products, even with the lowering of the rate of nominal protection. In spite of declining real agricultural producer prices, the shift in the supply curve due to technological change was higher than the shift in the demand curve due to income growth. The EU was not forced to reduce prices in order to avoid surpluses at support prices, as the surplus could be dumped on the world markets. The differences between domestic and world market prices were met by the EU budget. The Uruguay Round Agreement posed a significant constraint on EU policymakers. They had to agree to cut the volume of subsidized exports by 21 per cent (based on 1986–90) and the amount of subsidies paid by 36 per cent (same base period). The impact of these constraints can be illustrated with the help of Figure 20.7.

Depending on the market situation, either quantity or expenditure constraints could become binding. So far, volume constraints have become binding on some markets. As long as EU prices are above world market prices, domestic supply has to be restricted to domestic demand plus the permitted volume of subsidized

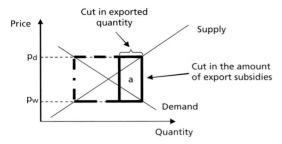

Figure 20.7 The impact of subsidized export constraints

exports minus the quantity imported on minimum market access *s* – this is not in the figure (tariff rate quotas).

Therefore, EU policy-makers were forced to change the market regulations for some commodities; before the agreement was signed, the EU had already instituted drastic cuts in institutional grain prices of 30 per cent (the 1992 MacSharry reform) and enlarged the cut by another 15 per cent in 2000 (CEU 1997a). A further drastic change in market organizations was decided in June 2003, when price cuts for milk and beef were agreed upon, and in 2005 for sugar.

The payment of export subsidies causes more administrative problems than charging imports. If the Commission wants to bridge the gap between domestic prices and competitive export prices, it has to know the relevant export price. However, these prices are not quoted on a market, so instead the Commission has to collect information on prices in importing countries and take into account import charges and shipping costs (freight, insurance and *L* costs). This information is difficult to acquire, in particular for the many differentiated processed agricultural products. Moreover, the Commission has to know how much of the raw material has been used to produce specific processed products. Take the case of pasta. Pasta can be produced on the basis of common wheat and eggs or durum wheat. As the price gap for common wheat is smaller than that for durum wheat, the kind of wheat is important for quantifying the amount of export restitutions – that is, subsidies. Another case is the export of wheat flour. The Commission has to know how much wheat is needed to produce one unit of wheat flour. The necessary information is not easily available; only the flour mills can provide it, but it is naïve to expect them to report it correctly. This may explain why the EU used to be very competitive on the international wheat flour

market, where the EU's share was in excess of 60 per cent for many years. The share of the wheat market was no more than 16 per cent in the 1980s.

Problems were even more pronounced on the meat market, as export restitutions differed for different cuts of meat. They were the lowest for offal and were high for high-quality meat. Hence there was a tendency for false declaration; indeed the European Court of Auditors (ECA) found most fraud to be in meat exports.

Domestic market regulations

INTERVENTION PURCHASES The effect of intervention purchase will be explained for a specific group of products, namely grains. However, the effect is similar for other products.

Intervention prices are prices at which intervention agencies are obliged to buy in unlimited amounts of a specific product like grain or limited amounts under certain conditions. These prices were introduced in order to stabilize markets. Hence these prices, which are politically set, were supposed to be below normal market prices at the time when the market organizations were designed and first implemented. Therefore, these prices are below the import price (p_T) at which international competitors can enter the domestic market. As long as foreign supply was needed to clear the EU grain market at a price related to the threshold price (p_T) (see page 324), the intervention price was not relevant. Actually, buying in took place only in some regions, due to market imperfection as long as the EU was in grain deficit. However, gradually the EU matured to an exporter of grain and the intervention price could become the relevant market price if the EU did not enter the market by paying export subsidies. The situation is shown with the help of Figure 20.8. The domestic demand curve becomes completely elastic at the intervention price if private and official demand does not clear the market at prices above the intervention price. The actual market price will be above the intervention price if the government pays export subsidies. These subsidies raise domestic demand. The effect is that the domestic demand curve will be completely elastic at a price p_I, which is equal to the world price plus the subsidy per unit of export. It should be noted that the effect of an export subsidy on domestic prices does not depend on the quantity exported, but on the subsidy per unit of exports. Even if the EU produces a small surplus on a market, as in the case of

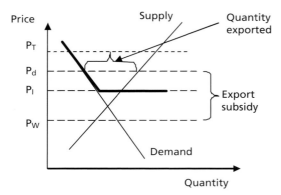

Figure 20.8 The importance of intervention prices

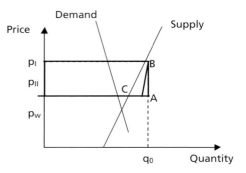

Figure 20.10 Price cuts and direct payments: the case of grains

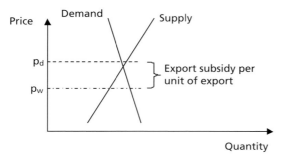

Figure 20.9 The effect of export subsidies on domestic prices

pork with a degree of self-sufficiency of about 103, the price effect of the subsidy can be very high. Figure 20.9 clarifies this point. The volume of exports is fairly small, but the gap between domestic and world market prices is fairly high. Without any foreign trade regulations, the domestic prices would be at p_W.

DIRECT PAYMENTS Direct payments have become a most important element of market organizations since the MacSharry reform. These payments were originally introduced on the grain and oilseeds markets in order to compensate for the cut in institutional prices, attracting the term 'compensatory payments'. The basic idea was to offset the income loss due to the price cut; in order to do this as accurately as possible, payments were linked to the area cultivated under cereals or oilseeds. Figure 20.10 depicts the effects. Grain intervention prices were reduced by 30 per cent. Policymakers assumed that the income loss would be equal to the area $(p_I - p_{II})^* q_0$. The actual lost income was lower,

since it is the negative change in producer surplus (area $p_I p_{II} CB$); hence the overcompensation was area CAB. As the payment was linked to the use of the land (it was paid per hectare of land under grain cultivation), payments were part of the gross margin earned in grain production. Hence the area under grain production did not decline. The effect of lower prices on yields may show up after a long period of adjustment, as a new set of technologies may be needed. So far yields have continued to increase over time. Consequently, total grain production did not decline in spite of the drastic price cut. Due to the direct payments, the supply curve became steeper below the former intervention price p_I. The supply curve may have even shifted to the right, as there was overcompensation leading to an increase of profitability in grain production.

In 1999 the Council decided on a further drop in grain prices by 15 per cent (CEU 1997b), and to reduce beef prices by 20 per cent and dairy prices by 15 per cent. The latter became effective from 2005/6 onwards. The (falsely) calculated income losses are supposed to be compensated by half. In the case of beef, payments were per animal, but in the case of dairy products they were initially linked to the reference quantity – that is, the amount of milk a producer can achieve at high guaranteed prices. Both types of direct premiums have been incorporated in the single farm payment starting from 2005.

CAP reform in the 1990s put more pressure on European farms than the previous policy changes. However, the price cuts leading to a reduction in external protection were widely replaced by direct payments. Figure 20.11 clearly shows that in the aggregate for the OECD and in the main MSs the average level of

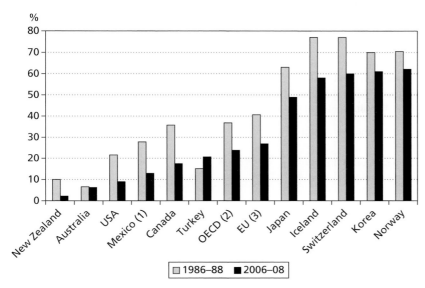

Figure 20.11 Support levels in the OECD and selected member countries in % PSE *Notes*: Data for this figure are available at the source website. (1) For Mexico, data are for 1991–3 instead of 1986–8. (2) Australia, Finland and Sweden are included in the OECD total for all years and in the EU from 1995. The Czech Republic, Hungary; Poland and the Slovak Republic are included in non-OECD member countries. (3) EU12 for 1986–94, including ex-GDR from 1990; EU25 for 2004–6; and EU27 from 2007. *Source*: Authors' calculation based on OECD 2009 (www.oecd.org/document/59/0,3343, en_2649_33797_39551355_1_1_1_1,00.html)

support as measured by producer support estimates (PSE)[11] was fairly stable over time.

The 2003 Council decision introduced a major change in direct payments, the single farm payment scheme. The Commission had proposed simplifying the market and price policy by summing up all the different entitlements of individual farmers by direct payments and introducing one single payment, based on past payments, and completely decoupled from production. Moreover, the proposal foresaw making the entitlement for payments tradable. The Council was not able to reach such a wide-ranging agreement. However, the principle was accepted, but MSs were allowed to introduce some coupled payments for some period or to introduce coupled payments when there is a serious drop in regional production. Moreover, countries can link payment to area and pay a flat rate at the national level, possibly differentiated with respect to arable or grass land. Furthermore, MSs were allowed to introduce limitations on the tradability of the payment entitlements.

The basic idea behind the change was political. It was argued that payments justified as compensation for price cuts could not last for ever. Hence another rationale for carrying on with gifts for farmers was needed. Some politicians, supported by the Commission, hoped that the prevailing form of direct payments could be sold to the public, arguing that these are payments for farmers' contributions to a multi-functional agriculture. It was believed that this reasoning would be more convincing if payments were tied to the condition that farmers use 'good agricultural practice', and if some of these payments were directly linked to participation in environmental programmes.

Unfortunately, the new justification for direct payments would have been convincing only if it had been accompanied by a significant change in the national and regional distribution of payments. Such a change had to follow the national and regional needs for a multi-functional agriculture. However, the distribution of payments across nations has not been changed: a change in the gainer and loser situation across MSs was not acceptable to the Council. Again, this policy decision proves the strong CAP path dependency: policy changes seem to be possible only when the status quo of the present pattern of financial flows between MSs remained almost unchanged. Of course, this reality provides a strong constraint on rationalizing CAP.

PRODUCTION QUOTAS The EU applies production quotas on sugar, milk, starch potatoes and tobacco. The sugar quota was set up at the outset. Production quotas are only considered a reasonable policy alternative if:

- there is a surplus on the domestic market at supported prices;
- budget outlays are high due to a high price differential between domestic and world market prices and a high exportable surplus;
- domestic production is growing, leading to even higher outlays in the future; and
- there is a bottleneck which allows the produced quantities to be controlled at acceptable financial costs.

The first three conditions prevail on many EU agricultural markets, but the bottleneck arises mainly in the selected markets where quotas have been introduced. In the case of sugar, all the sugar beet has to be processed in factories where the quantities can be checked. As to milk, most of it is nowadays delivered to EU dairies (over 95 per cent), but much less than this in NMSs. In Poland it is only about 60 per cent.

The analysis of a quota system will focus on the milk market regime. Quotas were introduced in 1984 because surpluses on the milk market were rising and the price differential between domestic and world market prices was extremely high. The rise in milk production was not expected at the time of the inception of the milk market regime. In 1967/8 cows were mainly fed on domestically produced fodder. Hence milk production was constrained by the domestic capacity to produce feed. However, the situation changed quickly due to some specifics of the trading regime for feed imports. In GATT negotiations the EU had agreed to apply low tariffs on imports of feed in exchange for being allowed to introduce the variable levy system for the main temperate zone products. At that time, feed (soya, tapioca and others) was not imported in sizeable quantities. However, with increased EU grain prices, the willingness to pay for imported feed went up. The decline in shipping rates also contributed to booming imports of feed. A mixture of soya meal or cake and tapioca was used as a perfect substitute for grain. Thus milk production became less dependent on farm-grown fodder and

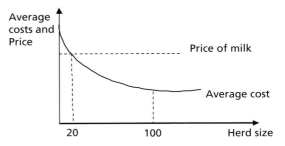

Figure 20.12 Average costs in milk production and milk prices

it expanded heavily. Farmers not only increased milk yield from just over 3,000 kg per cow in 1967 to about 5,000 kg in 1983, but also increased herd size, taking advantage of economies of scale in milk production. Hence it became less feasible to increase the income of milk producers through support prices. The situation is depicted in Figure 20.12. At the given milk price, most of the producers milking fewer than twenty cows did not make a profit, since average costs were above the milk price. However, those farmers milking in excess of twenty and fewer than a hundred cows could make a profit. Hence there was a huge incentive for increasing herd sizes for milking, almost irrespective of the amount of arable and pasture land used on the farm. Thus milk production grew much faster than milk consumption, leading to growing exportable surpluses. EU policy-makers could have lowered prices long before 1984, as the problem was already visible for many years prior to that. However, they postponed making a decision, as they did not dare to provoke farmers. In 1984 drastic measures were needed to correct the problem: a significant price cut by about 12 per cent was considered unacceptable, so the introduction of a quota system was seen as a reasonable alternative.

Policy-makers and bureaucrats generally prefer a quota system to price cuts. Quotas are attractive as they do not lead to an immediate, high income loss. Bureaucrats may even value highly the new control system that has to be instituted as a consequence: the higher the bureaucratic burden, the better the prospects for job promotion. In contrast, economists generally oppose quota systems because of misallocation of resources. An efficient farmer cannot expand production without gaining additional quotas. If they were tradable, the farmer would buy them, but the costs of expanding production would increase. Hence structural change would be held up. Moreover, quota systems contradict the basic idea of a customs union: production cannot move to those regions and enterprises that are the most efficient (see Chapter 6). It has been agreed to end the milk quota system on 1 April 2015. The sugar market regime has also been changed: prices have been cut by 36 per cent, and the distinction between A and B quotas was abolished in 2006. The main forces pushing for the changes were international agreements. First, a WTO panel decided that the EU was no longer allowed to export the so-called C sugar. C sugar used to be those quantities produced above the EU quota and sold to the world market without export subsidies. The panel had argued that C sugar could be exported profitably only because there was internally a much higher price for A and B sugar. Economies of scale made the production of C sugar profitable even at world market prices. Second, the EBA agreement raised the fear that the least developed countries would have an incentive to increase their exports to the EU significantly at highly protected EU sugar prices.

CONSUMPTION SUBSIDIES EU policy-makers use different forms of subsidy. Payments for price reduction as described above are special subsidies. There are others, offered to reduce production costs, such as interest subsidies for investment or for stimulating demand. Let us examine the latter.

Consumption subsidies are most important in the milk market. Some 50–90 per cent of the total annual EU demand for skimmed milk powder has been supported in this way over the past twenty years. The figure for butter is 15–35 per cent. Hence, without these subsidies, the exportable surplus would be much higher.

The budget effects of the subsidy schemes are difficult to assess. If the alternative was to get rid of the surplus by exporting a higher volume, the answer would be straightforward. If domestic demand for the subsidized product is price inelastic and world market demand for the additional EU exports is completely elastic (small country assumption), budget outlays would be higher with subsidizing EU demand. The comparison is depicted in Figure 20.13. Total revenue for producers is financed by consumers, export revenue and budget outlays. The original situation for the domestic market price p_d is shown in the figure. If the government decided to subsidize domestic consumers, the demand curve would shift to the right, increasing

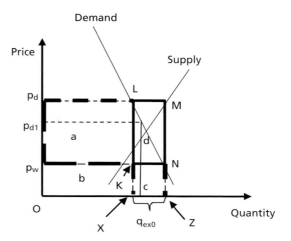

Producer revenue = $OP_dMZ = a + b + c + d$
Budget outlay at price p_d and exports of q_{ex0} = KLMN = d
Consumer expenditure at price $p_d = OP_dLX = a + b$
Export revenue = XKNZ = c

Figure 20.13 Budget effects of EU demand for domestic consumption as compared to export subsidization

the demand at price p_d. This would have the same effect as lowering domestic prices, say from p_d to p_{d1}. However, consumer expenditure at price p_{d1} would be lower than at price p_d if the price elasticity of demand were smaller than 1 (in absolute terms), a condition that definitely holds for EU butter demand. Moreover, if domestic consumers expanded their purchases on the domestic market, the exportable surplus would decline. Hence, revenue from sales to the world market declines. Thus the area $a + b + c$ would be smaller than in the initial situation. Consequently, budget outlays have to be larger to cover producer revenue.

The assessment of the subsidies on butter and skimmed milk powder would lead to a different result were welfare effects the focus. The marginal willingness to pay at price p_d is larger than the world market price. Reducing consumer prices through subsidies creates additional welfare. The analysis is presented in Figure 20.14.

Reducing domestic prices through subsidies increases demand; the increase in the willingness to pay is equal to the bold-bordered trapezoid, but the loss in revenue is only the rectangle given by the export quantity in the initial situation multiplied by the world market price. Hence there is an overall welfare gain. Actually the welfare gain would be even higher

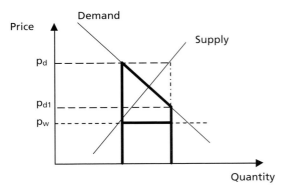

Figure 20.14 Welfare effects of consumer subsidies

if domestic consumers were confronted with world market prices by subsidizing the difference between producer and the world market price. This proves once more that budget effects are not related to welfare effects.

20.6 Rural development policy

Rural development policy was formally created under *Agenda 2000* (CEU 1997b) reforms and was termed the 'second pillar of CAP'. Some of the policy instruments have been in place as part of EU structural policy since the 1970s and 1980s, but most of them have been introduced in the 1990s.

There are some sound economic arguments for placing stronger emphasis on structural measures than on market and price policy. First, the EU has been enlarged significantly over time and this has widened the heterogeneity between MSs and between the regions (see Chapter 22). Therefore, the market and price policy became less effective over time, increasing the demand for specific structural measures. Nevertheless, one may wonder whether the second pillar instruments and, in particular, the method of financing, are a true rationalization for CAP.

The regulation quotes three objectives for rural development policy:

1. improving competitiveness of the agricultural sector;
2. protection of environment and landscape; and
3. improving living standards in rural areas and support of diversification.

There is a menu of more than forty measures from which the countries may select as many as they want. However, in implementing the measures the countries have to follow strict EU-enforced rules. The rules include the application of a specific evaluation and monitoring schemes. As the approach is bottom-up based, it could be supportive of a rationalization of CAP.

However, the list of instruments clearly shows that agriculture is considered the main sector that should be supported when aiming at rural development. Indeed the preamble of the regulation makes it clear that the focus should be on agriculture or activities closely related to agriculture. Moreover, it is clearly stated that payments to farmers in cases of environmental measures should be calculated on the basis of income foregone, and could surpass income foregone by as much as 20 per cent.

It may be surprising that rural policy focuses mainly on agriculture when the sector is not dominant in terms of rural GDP, and even less so with respect to regional employment. Data for England and for the UK as a whole reveal that the contribution of agricultural GDP to regional GDP was, respectively, only 1.2 per cent and 1.5 per cent in 1997.[12] The share of agricultural employment in rural areas was 4 per cent in the UK in 1996, the same as for construction, but much less than for distribution, hotels and restaurants, with 24 per cent, and services, with 20 per cent.[13] These figures are only averages for one country. Of course, there is a huge variance across countries and regions. However, there is a general trend indicating declining shares for agricultural GDP and employment. Moreover, conventional agriculture has become a highly capital-intensive sector, resulting in an even lower agricultural share in regional employment than in regional GDP. Hence agriculture is hardly the dominant sector in rural areas today in most EU regions, and is less likely to be so in the future.

The objective of 'enhancing the competitiveness of agriculture' raises major economic concerns. Policy-induced improved competitiveness of a specific sector in a region does not necessarily enhance the competitiveness of that region. The New Bundesländer in Germany proves the opposite: agriculture was highly subsidized, not only by high price support, but also by investment aid. The policy resulted in a highly capital-intensive agricultural sector, but with very high rural unemployment rates. Agriculture would have employed more L with less investment aid and the region would have been better off if support had not focused so much on agriculture. It is strange that advocating investment in farms is still considered a reasonable instrument for supporting agricultural competitiveness. There are some evaluations of investment aid which clearly show that the overall effect is not positive or cannot be identified when positive.

Second, the second pillar measures raise the suspicion that policy-makers aimed to compensate farmers for their loss in income due to the enforced reduction in support provided by first pillar measures. This suspicion is also supported by the created linkage between expenditure for first pillar measures and those for the second pillar. Direct payments, introduced to compensate the income losses due to price reductions, will be partly reduced over time and the savings will be incorporated into the second pillar measures. Again, this procedure could be a basis for rationalizing CAP, but only if it were accompanied by a change in the distribution of funds between countries and regions. Such a change would be necessary, since the need for rural development measures varies significantly between countries and regions. Such redistribution is not built into the new scheme. Of course, that would be understandable were the main purpose of the new approach only to stabilize support for agriculture, even if the term had to be changed.

A major problem of the second pillar measures is due to co-financing. The regions have to decide what measures they want to apply for selected projects. However, it has to be agreed by the national centre and thereafter by the EU. It is unlikely that the regions base their selection on an adequate cost-benefit analysis where they use shadow prices instead of market prices, and thus take into account the economic effects of the measures applied in the region or elsewhere. The selection is most likely highly distorted due to the system of co-financing applied between the EU and MSs, and within MSs between the national centre and the regions. The form of support differs across countries with respect to one-time grants, subsidized interest rates, loan guarantees and initial diminution of payback of loans.

Third, rules for co-financing differ significantly between MSs, concerning most of all the share of total investment costs that the regions, MSs and the EU contribute to public finance – for example, the EU contributes to public expenditure 23 per cent in Germany, 70 per cent in Greece and 55 per cent in Poland, whereas the local governments contribute 31 per cent in Germany and nothing in Greece and Poland.

Fourth, the share of investment costs to be financed by MSs and their regions varies largely across countries and regions. The EU contributes up to 75 per cent in Objective 1 Regions and up to 50 per cent in Non-Objective 1 Regions. As the national governments also contribute, but a non-uniform share among MSs, the remaining residual to be borne by regions varies greatly (Bergschmidt *et al.* 2006).

Fifth, the EU defines the programmes, but MSs have to implement them. They have to select the investment projects based on the application of individual potential investors, and have to ensure that the investors have followed the set EU rules. Also, MSs may select the evaluators who have to assess the performance of the programmes. Moreover, MSs have to report irregularities to the EU and may have to repay some of the finances donated by the EU. It is quite obvious that there are great differences in the implementation of the farm investment programmes across MSs, and hence the effects may vary significantly across countries. It is not possible to assess the programme in each individual country; we will generally focus on one specific country, namely Germany. However, based on the short survey of the application of the programme across MSs, some general conclusions concerning EU-wide effects can be drawn.

Policy-makers praise the introduction of the second pillar as a major step of rationalization of CAP. Indeed, as mentioned above, the move could be a real improvement;[14] however, the importance of the second pillar as indicated by the share of CAP expenditure is still fairly small (see Figure 20.15), and the impact is in many cases questionable, partly due to co-financing, but also to the specifics of the measures and the interplay among them.[15]

20.7 The future of CAP

As already described, there have been specific driving forces behind the evolution of CAP. Figure 20.16 clearly shows that support for agriculture has declined over time and the pattern of expenditure has changed significantly. Export subsidies and market support are not dominant any more, but have been replaced by direct

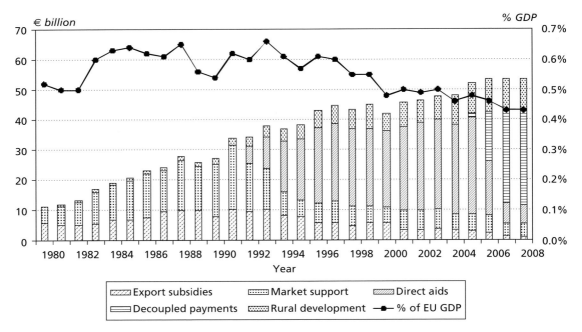

Figure 20.15 Breakdown of EU expenditure for agriculture

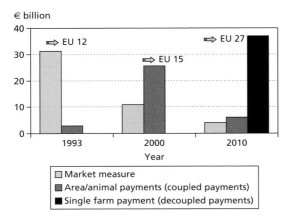

Figure 20.16 Market support and direct payments

payments. Moreover, expenditure for rural development has been growing over time, but is still relatively small.

The driving forces behind the reform were mainly changes on the political market for agricultural protection. Initiated by international agreements such as that of the Uruguay Round, and the preferential treatments extended to the least developing countries and the former ACP nations, the Council has lost power. The

European Council, as well as the EP, have gained influence. Thus the power of agricultural lobby groups has been eroded. The financial framework for the period 2007–13 signals that the time of ever-increasing CAP expenditure has come to an end. The total amount of money earmarked for CAP has not been programmed to increase annually as in former times. The constraining forces are likely to become stronger in the near future. First, it is questionable whether the present CAP is able to cope with the present constraints imposed by the WTO. It is likely that the price reduction for sugar beet will prove inadequate, and growing preferential imports may enforce further price cuts for sugar.

Second, the ongoing Doha Round will most likely require further adjustments to CAP. The EU has already agreed on abolishing export subsidies up to the year 2013. However, final agreement concerning the gradual timing of the downsizing of export subsidies and other changes has not yet been formally reached. Nevertheless, it can be expected that the Doha Round – if there is eventually a final agreement – will result in a complete abolition of export subsidies. This change will require further reform steps. Take the case of milk: if there are no export subsidies for milk products, yet domestic milk production still surpasses domestic consumption, dairy exporters can only pay world market prices on the domestic market. If intervention prices are above world market prices there would be no exports and the surplus would have to be bought in by intervention agencies. That would certainly not be a sustainable situation. Therefore, it can be predicted that prices of products presently in surplus would either fall to the level of world market prices, or to a higher level where domestic production equalled domestic consumption. However, the latter situation would probably prove unsustainable in the long run; it would imply price ratios on domestic markets that are not in line with world market prices. Export products would be implicitly taxed relative to products in self-sufficiency or imported. It would be rational from an economic point of view to move to world market prices for all products. Thus the new regulation, allowing no payments of any export subsidies, might open the door for pressure to liberalize agricultural markets completely.

Third, the 2003 CAP reform did not completely achieve its objective, namely the complete decoupling of payments. The final agreement allows MSs significant leeway in implementing the new system. There are only few countries that follow the basic idea of the proposal by the Commission. National derogations may be needed in order to allow for differences in national interests due to the homogeneity of the countries. However, the present variation in implementing direct payments conflicts with WTO objectives and also distorts the production pattern within the EU. For example, model calculations show that suckler cow production is declining in Germany due to complete decoupling, but increasing in France due to partial decoupling (Küpker *et al.* 2006). It is hardly credible that WTO members would allow a continuation of this policy, and some member countries may also ask for changes if they realize the distortive effects.

Fourth, further EU enlargements are likely (other Balkan countries and possibly even Turkey; see Chapters 1 and 2). It is questionable whether some NMSs, as well as the prospective ones, have the administrative capacity to apply CAP in its present form. These fears concern most of the second pillar measures. The ECA has stated many times that there are many irregularities and even frauds accompanying the implementation of these measures. Hence improvement in governance is strongly needed. Hopefully, a

new system will be created that does better than the present one in terms of subsidiarity, transparency and accountability.

20.8 Conclusion

Since the prospects for change have already been discussed, the conclusion should be in the nature of an assessment of CAP as it has developed over the five decades or so since its inception. Before doing so, however, it should be reiterated that the CAP support system has become rather complicated, since it retains the original system for certain products while applying new methods for others and/or building them on top of the old ones.

Judged in terms of the need at the time of EEC formation for a common policy, CAP is obviously a success. Also, judged in terms of its own objectives, the policy-makers agree that it seems to have had several successes. However, it is questionable whether CAP has contributed to its own objectives, let alone to its overall goal.

Any assessment of a policy cannot just focus on the development of specific variables, such as productivity or income. Instead, it has to be based on a comparison of 'with' and 'without' CAP. The situation 'with' is easy to observe; not so the situation 'without', since one has to specify what alternative policy would have been in place (one would need a reference situation or base line: the *anti-monde* discussed in Chapter 9). Second, the effects of this alternative policy would have to be analysed. The first point certainly contains a value judgement, as there is no consensus on how to specify the alternative policy; if analysts based their assessment on different reference systems, their results would necessarily differ. If, for example, agricultural policy-makers claim that there is no alternative to the given policy, they implicitly assess present costs as zero.

Here it is assumed that the alternative would have been a less protective CAP. What, then, would have been the effects of CAP according to the objectives mentioned in the treaties?

1. *Effect on agricultural productivity.* Assume that there is a production function, as mirrored in Figure 20.17. Given factor input F_0, production would be q_0,

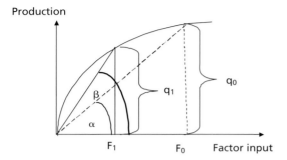

Figure 20.17 The effect of price support on productivity

hence the productivity tan α. Reducing prices, the marginal suppliers have to leave the sector, leading to productivity tan β. As tan β > tan α, productivity at lower prices would have been higher. As price support reduced migration out of the sector, resulting in the survival of marginal farms, it affected productivity negatively. It should be noted that this reasoning holds even if the productivity increase in EU agriculture had been greater than in other countries and in excess of that for the industrial sectors.

2. *Effect on agricultural income.* There is no doubt that the total income generated in farming is higher with support prices than without. However, the important question is whether *income per unit of L* is higher. Economists tend to argue that income per unit will be equal to the opportunity cost in the long run. Price support will increase income in the adjustment period, but after adjustment the income differential will be the same as at lower prices. Indeed there is some evidence for this argument. Take the German case. Agricultural prices had to be lowered in 1967/8, when the common prices were set. Out-migration increased, and after the adjustment agricultural income was again about 60 per cent of average income, reflecting preferences. Higher prices do not only increase the income of those who are in the sector; they also influence decisions to take up farming. Hence employment in the agricultural sector depends on the price level. Thus one has to take into consideration the transfer efficiency of price support. Part of the income lost by those in the non-agricultural sector results in dead-weight losses (negative welfare effects); another part is transferred through the market mechanism to others who were not targeted – in

particular, landlords, who are the main winners of price support.

3. *Effect on the stability of markets.* If CAP was supposed to stabilize prices, it has been a great success. Intervention prices helped to stabilize market prices. However, if CAP was supposed to stabilize revenue or income, it has probably failed. A shortfall in production due to a bad harvest might be compensated by higher prices in free markets. Actually, the revenue would be less volatile if the price elasticity of demand were larger than 0.5 in absolute terms. Taking into account the demand for storage and for inter-regional trade, it is likely that the elasticity is larger than 0.5.

4. *The effect on food security.* High support prices help to increase supply under normal conditions. However, food security only becomes a problem under abnormal conditions, such as natural catastrophes, wars or trade conflicts. Even if a country is able to feed its population under normal conditions, it is not at all sure that it will have the capacity to produce enough food under abnormal conditions. Take, for example, the case of milk production. It was stated above that EU farmers partly produce the milk on the basis of imported feed. Moreover, a lot of imported energy is needed in order to supply the market. Had trade ties fallen apart, these requirements would not have been met. Hence the present production level does not allow one to conclude that food would have been available in emergency situations.

5. *Effect on reasonable consumer prices.* It is quite clear that CAP was, from the very beginning, a burden for the EU consumer. Thus CAP has failed badly in trying to achieve the policy objectives set for it.

Has it done better in attempting to achieve general economic or overall policy objectives? Concerning the former, the answer is clearly in the negative, given the welfare effects identified in the analysis above. Nevertheless, one has to accept two positive political effects. The first is that CAP has mitigated the adjustment process, albeit not in the most efficient way. It has been argued that income transfers linked to the personal income situation of farmers would have been more efficient from the viewpoint of economics. Lack of endorsement of this alternative may be due to its political infeasibility: policy-makers can only select those alternatives that are acceptable to the electorate.

Of course, what the electorate would accept would depend, among others things, on information about the alternatives and their effects. Perhaps economists should have been more forceful in addressing both the population at large and politicians on this alternative, but could their academic performance match farmers' political clout?

It has been shown that there is a strong path dependency in agricultural policy, since the decisions taken at the outset have influenced ensuing development. It is arguable whether policy-makers had an alternative at that time. MSs had to be convinced to give up their national autonomy in agricultural policy and there was only a little political leeway left: it was necessary to incorporate agriculture into the European integration scheme. Policy-makers achieved this at the beginning, but the evolution of the policy has not much improved the situation. National markets are not well integrated because of quotas for milk, sugar and tobacco, and also because of EU expenditure constraints, such as limits on direct payments. Nevertheless, the Council decisions of June 2003 create hope for improvement, at least with regard to the main pillar of CAP.

Summary

- Before CAP inception practically all MSs had their own agricultural policies. This was due to several factors, the most important being:
  1. concern with food security;
  2. the low level of agricultural incomes;
  3. agricultural inefficiency; and
  4. instability of agricultural markets.
  To these are now added concerns with:
  5. food safety; and
  6. the environment.
- The institutions pertinent to CAP are:
  1. financial solidarity – that is, financing common agricultural activities out of a common budget; and
  2. preference for agricultural products – that is, domestic producers should exhaust domestically produced food before turning to imports.
- There are three constraints on CAP policy-makers:
  1. international trade agreements;
  2. the budget allocation; and
  3. the influence on non-agricultural pressure groups.
- CAP has an extremely complex set of instruments and regulations, which have changed greatly since the days of its inception, but the chapter deals only with the present ones:
  1. import regulations, which comprise variable levies and specific import tariffs, ad valorem tariffs, tariff rate quotas and preferential access;
  2. export regulations, especially since the conclusion of GATT's Uruguay Round in 1994; and
  3. domestic market regulations, which include intervention purchases, direct payments, production quotas and consumption subsidies.
- CAP has a rural development policy that was formally created under *Agenda 2000* reforms and was termed the second pillar of CAP. Some of the policy instruments have been in place as part of EU structural policy since the 1970s and 1980s, but most of them were introduced in the 1990s.

Questions and essay topics

1. Why was agriculture (ignore transport) singled out for special treatment by the EEC?
2. How can you demonstrate the changing role of agriculture in EU economies?
3. What are the six reasons for regulating agriculture as opposed to leaving it to the mercy of market forces?
4. What is the principle of financial solidarity?
5. What is the principle of preference for agricultural products?
6. What are the three constraints on CAP policy-makers?
7. What are the four instruments used by CAP for import regulations?
8. Which export regulations impinge on CAP?
9. What are the four CAP domestic market regulations stated in the chapter?
10. What is rural development policy?
11. Discuss the proposition that without CAP there would have been no EEC.
12. Discuss the allegation that CAP failures emanate mainly from its misconceived institutional structure.

13. Evaluate the proposition that EU farmers would have fared better without CAP.

FURTHER READING

Koester, U. and Senior, S. (2010) 'PILLAR II: a real improvement of the CAP?', in N. S. Senior and P. Pierani (eds.), *International Trade, Consumer Interests and Reform of the Common Agricultural Policy*, Routledge Studies in the European Economy, Oxford University Press.

NOTES

1 A rough indication of the average levels of income for farmers, relative to the incomes of those in other occupations, can be obtained by comparing the share of agriculture in total labour force and national output. Such a comparison indicates that at the time of EEC inception, average agricultural incomes in the three largest countries (France, Germany and Italy) were only about 50 per cent of those in other occupations (Ritson 1973, p. 96).

2 'Agricultural incomes have risen, but in France, Germany and Italy there is little evidence that the gap in incomes between agriculture and other occupations has diminished' (Ritson 1973, p. 97).

3 That is, a country that has no impact on world prices.

4 A policy failure indicates that policy decisions have reduced welfare for society at large.

5 See, for example, the divergence in national interest for implementing the set-aside programme (Koester 1989b, pp. 240–8).

6 It should be noted that Article 33 of the treaty neither mentions that policy-makers are supposed to achieve a specific income objective, nor states that prices should be set to contribute to the achievement of the income objective.

7 Expected external costs are defined as disadvantages to an individual due to constraints imposed on the individual by collective decisions.

8 This point is discussed in more detail and empirically supported in Koester and Tangermann (1990).

9 Indeed this observation should not be surprising for students of public choice. Western democracies have strong pressure groups, which strongly resist fundamental changes.

10 The invisible transfer, due to producer prices being higher than import or export parity prices, was considerably higher than the visible transfer before CAP reform; see Ballenger, Dunmore and Lederer 1987.

11 The producer support estimate is a measure used to indicate by how much farm income is increased by governmental interference.

12 DEFRA 2006.

13 Ibid.

14 See Koester and Senior 2010.

15 Ibid.

21 The Common Fisheries Policy

ALI EL-AGRAA

The tables referred to in this chapter can be found online at www.cambridge.org/el-agraa

21.1 Introduction

The Common Fisheries Policy (CFP) illustrates both the potential and the limitations of EU policy. Fisheries are an inherently difficult sector to manage. Issues such as competing views on property rights and tensions between scientists, fishers and conservationists are well known in fishing communities across the world. The crisis in most major fish stocks has heightened tensions in debates over the conservation and management of stocks. Key aspects of the sector, such as trade, processing and ownership, are becoming increasingly internationalized, but this has been a difficult process in a sector where individualism and a strong sense of community run deep. One of the challenges for fishery regimes is to compete effectively in the global market, but at the same time to cushion communities from social costs and economic decline.

It would seem logical for the EU to have a common fisheries policy, since much fishing activity is conducted across and beyond national territorial waters and fish take no notice of national boundaries. Fish such as mackerel, herring and cod often migrate hundreds of miles during their life cycles. They may spawn in one area, become juveniles in another and reach maturity in a third. About 90 per cent of North Sea cod, for example, spend their first year in waters off the coasts of Denmark, Germany and the Netherlands, but by the time they are three years old and ripe for catching most of them will have migrated to UK territorial waters. If successful, in the long run, the conservation of fish stocks could be a positive sum game for all the member states (MSs) in a situation of declining resources, and the conservation of fish resources lies at the very heart of heightening concern with the environment; hence anyone who thinks the CFP is not worth studying must have their mind examined.

However, an analysis of CFP shows how difficult it is to design a policy for the management and regulation of a common European pond, and the 'problem' of CFP is one that has bedevilled the EU since the inception of the policy in 1970. By the early 2000s, the policy had reached a crisis point, having failed to manage dwindling fish stocks, to respond to wider environmental concerns or to satisfy competing national interests. A number of fish stocks, including North Sea cod, were in a state of collapse, despite a significant decline in the fishing fleet. The policy lacked legitimacy because it imposed regulations in a highly diverse sector where there were no strong norms of obligation to a commonly accepted set of rules or institutions. There is a long chain of command from the politicians and scientists in Brussels to the fishers who are operating the policies on the high seas. One of the major problems facing the CFP is that many fishers do not comply with the detailed rules and regulations emanating from Brussels. Opinion is divided about whether the solution to this problem of non-compliance is greater uniformity and centralization or a move towards a more regionalized form of the CFP, which would bring the institutions closer to the stakeholders. The Commission has acknowledged that one reason for non-compliance may be that the stakeholders do not feel sufficiently involved in the policy-making process. At the same time it has made strenuous efforts to try to ensure more effective methods of compliance across the EU – for example, by establishing Commission inspectors.

This chapter will begin by setting out the background to the development of the CFP. It will go on to outline the main policy objectives and the nature of the policy-making process. It will then outline the recent CFP reforms. Finally, it assesses the institutional and governance issues associated with delivering a more effective CFP, which will be able to address the challenges of fish stock collapse and wider environmental concerns.

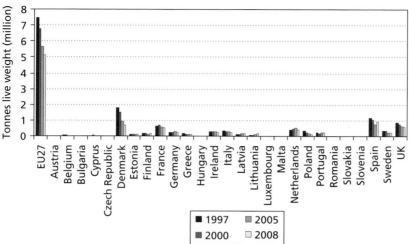

Figure 21.1 EU fish catches

21.2 Understanding the fisheries industry

The fisheries sector, comprising fishing, fish processing and aquaculture, is small in the EU. Measured in terms of output and employment, even when associated activities are taken into consideration, the sector accounted for 1 per cent of EU GDP in the early 1970s, but less than half a percentage point by 2009.[1] EU employment in the sector has been in steep decline: 1.2 million in 1970 in the EU15 (that is, the EU before the 2004/7 enlargements), coming down to about 400,000 in 2009 for the EU27, or about 0.4 per cent of total employment. Despite this, the EU fishing industry is the world's fourth largest, producing 6.4 tonnes (live weight) annually, or 4.6 per cent of the global total; China leads with 32.8 per cent, followed by India and Peru, with 5.2 per cent each. What is even more striking is that although fisheries are only a small sector of the EU economy, the activity tends to be concentrated in peripheral regions where there is often little alternative employment. The pain has been unevenly spread, depending on the type of catch, and the four largest producers – Spain (15.84 per cent of total catches and aquaculture), France (12.34 per cent), the UK (12.27 per cent) and Denmark (10.62 per cent) – account for over half the EU catch. See Figure 21.1 for a comparison of the catches for selected years and note how the four countries stand out. See also Tables 21.A1 and 21.A2 of the statistical appendix on the accompanying website for, respectively, the data for 1997–2008 and the percentages for 1993 and 2008.

In 2007 (latest) 1.3 million tonnes, valued at 3.2 billion euros, or about 20 per cent of the total volume of EU fisheries production, was by aquaculture. Aquaculture is a growing industry worldwide, and to some extent it compensates for the decline of sea fisheries. Even so, the EU as a whole imports more fish (5.7 million tonnes in 2008) than it exports (1.8 million tonnes), with only Denmark, Estonia, Ireland, Latvia, Lithuania, the Netherlands and Malta having positive trade balances in fishery products in 2008 (see Table 21.A3 of the statistical appendix). For a longer perspective on the trade balance, Figure 21.2 covers the period 1988–2007. Figure 21.3 shows that the major export items in 2008 were: bluefin tuna (82 per cent of which went to Japan, with 8, 7 and 3 per cent heading for Panama, the USA and South Korea respectively); flours, meals and pellets of fish; saltwater fish; and frozen mackerel. And Figure 21.4 reveals that the major import items were: fresh and chilled Pacific salmon (95 per cent of which was supplied by Norway and 5 per cent by the Faroe Isles), frozen shrimp and canned tuna.

The industry and its representatives tend to be highly fragmented. In any one country fishermen are divided among types of fishing (long distance or inshore) and structure of ownership (individual, family, conglomerate). Modernization has been asymmetric across the EU and there is a growing gulf between artisanal fishing and the highly technological deep-sea fleets.

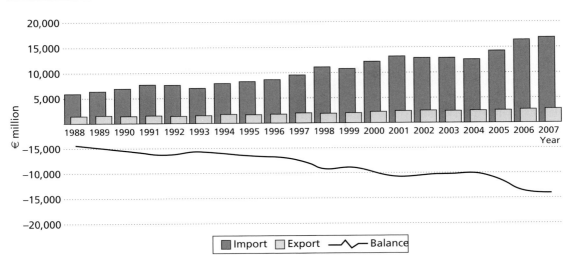

Figure 21.2 Extra-EU trade in fish and fishery products, 1988–2007 *Source:* Eurostat 2010g

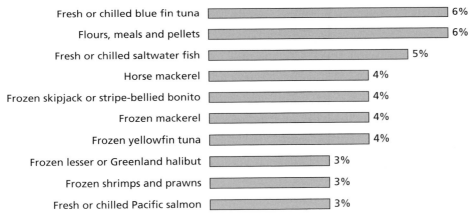

Fresh or chilled blue fin tuna	6%
Flours, meals and pellets	6%
Fresh or chilled saltwater fish	5%
Horse mackerel	4%
Frozen skipjack or stripe-bellied bonito	4%
Frozen mackerel	4%
Frozen yellowfin tuna	4%
Frozen lesser or Greenland halibut	3%
Frozen shrimps and prawns	3%
Fresh or chilled Pacific salmon	3%

Figure 21.3 EU fisheries: exports, 2008 *Source:* Eurostat 2010g

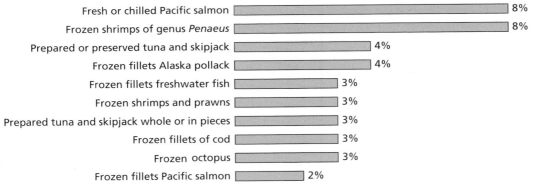

Fresh or chilled Pacific salmon	8%
Frozen shrimps of genus *Penaeus*	8%
Prepared or preserved tuna and skipjack	4%
Frozen fillets Alaska pollack	4%
Frozen fillets freshwater fish	3%
Frozen shrimps and prawns	3%
Prepared tuna and skipjack whole or in pieces	3%
Frozen fillets of cod	3%
Frozen octopus	3%
Frozen fillets Pacific salmon	2%

Figure 21.4 EU fisheries: imports, 2008 *Source:* Eurostat 2010g

As with agriculture (see Chapter 20), the diversity of the sector adds to the difficulty of constructing an effective common policy. This has been compounded by the political salience of the issue. The dangerous and to some extent romantic nature of the occupation, the strong sense of community and, in recent years, the linking of fishing not only to regional, but also, in some cases, to national identity, has meant that fishing interests often carry disproportionate weight within the EU.

Fisheries were included in the definition of agricultural products in the Treaty of Rome (see Chapter 20 and Article 38.1 of the Treaty on the Functioning of the European Union, TFEU), and the two industries do have much in common. Both are subject to price instability: in the case of fisheries, this is because of the highly specialized human and physical capital in the industry, making its short-term supply highly inelastic, and also because fish has a rather low price elasticity. Both have low income elasticities for their products and both are prone to random shocks from natural causes over which there is little control. During the 1950s both sectors were made up of large numbers of small, self-employed producers. Both policies are set within an international regulatory framework and face the challenges of internationalization, globalization, and increasing environmental and consumer pressure. There are, however, fundamental differences between the two sectors. Agriculture is about managing excess, while fisheries is about managing scarcity. Fisheries interests are much more diffuse and poorly organized at the EU level. Finally, and most importantly, the nature of ownership of resources is much more fiercely contested in fisheries than in agriculture.

The development of the CFP followed a pattern typical of many other policy areas: authority for the policy was vested in the Treaty of Rome; general principles were laid down some years later; and the detailed aspects of the policy were negotiated subsequently over many years, with successive enlargements and the changing international framework acting as catalysts for policy change. In the early 1960s fish stocks were relatively evenly spread among the six MSs and there was little international regulation of fishing. By the mid-1960s, the French and Italian governments became aware that their industries were becoming increasingly uncompetitive, especially compared to the German fishing fleet, and began to put pressure on the Community to devise structural aid for their fisheries. However, the real drivers for the establishment of the CFP were changes in the international situation and the impending enlargement to include Denmark, Ireland, Norway and the UK.

Historically, states had ownership over narrow territorial waters (typically 3–4 miles) and competed for stocks on the high seas that were deemed to be common property. This practice was workable because stocks were plentiful and 'belonged' to no one until they were caught. The increasing technical capacity of ships in the post-Second World War period, and the growing awareness of threats to stocks, meant that this regime began to be questioned. During the 1960s, there was an agreement that any vessel could fish anywhere outside a 12-mile coastal limit, which was reserved for the country whose coast bordered this zone or for states that had fished there historically. However, prompted by unilateral action by Iceland in 1970, claiming exclusive fishing rights within 50 miles of its coast, the United Nations (UN) decided in 1976 that any state could establish an exclusive economic zone (EEZ) in waters up to 200 nautical miles from its coastline.

This policy (eventually ratified in 1982 under the UN Convention on the Law of the Sea) had dramatic implications for EC MSs, most of which had traditionally fished far from their shores in deep-sea waters. The EC responded by setting up its own EEZ in January 1977. Once the decision had been taken by the EC to set up an EEZ, policy-makers had to evolve a system for distributing the stock among MSs (for further details, see Wise 1996).

The second factor precipitating the development of the CFP was the impending enlargement of the Community to include the fish-rich nations of Denmark, Ireland, Norway and the UK. These countries had large fishing stocks and the existing states were obviously keen to establish the principle of 'equal access' to fish-rich Community waters before enlargement took place. A policy was quickly hatched so that it became part of the *acquis communautaire* that the new states had to accept on joining. In 1970 an agreement established the right to equal conditions of access to fishing grounds and set the guidelines for a common structural policy. It also laid down some provisions for conservation measures and for financial aid for restructuring the industry. While the UK, Denmark and Ireland strenuously opposed the equal access principle, the issue was not high enough up the political agenda for it to jeopardize the long-awaited and much disputed EC membership. In the end, Norway declined to join the EC, partly because it feared the effects of the equal access principle on its fisheries (see Chapter 2). The CFP did not come into force fully until 1983, when it was successfully negotiated because of the impending accession of Spain and Portugal. These two countries had larger fleets than any of the existing MSs and had also lost much of their long-distance fishing opportunities in the 1970s. However, pressure from the UK, France and Ireland meant that Spain and Portugal were prevented from having equal access to EC waters until 2002.

The current CFP has evolved in response to a number of factors: biological (the condition of stocks), economic (the Single European Market, SEM (see Chapter 7), and trade liberalization) and political (the protection of national interests and enlargement) (see Wise 1996). The CFP and its interpretation by the European Court of Justice (ECJ) is guided by two key principles: equal access to fishing grounds within the common pond (with the exception of 6- and 12-mile coastal strips and special derogations such as the North Sea box around Shetland); and relative stability, which fixed the rights of MSs' access to waters. Relative stability, which is a highly contentious principle within the CFP, and which in fact distorts the principle of equal access, is based on historic fishing patterns and special interests. For example, in 1983 the UK received an additional cod quota to compensate for the losses from the Icelandic stocks that it had traditionally fished.

The ECJ has, over the years, maintained the principle of non-discrimination in fisheries by upholding the right of non-nationals to buy vessels (and hence a proportion of fishing quota) from other MSs. Typically, Spanish (and in some cases Dutch) owners have bought UK vessels, thus entitling them, for example, to fish hake in Irish waters and land their catches directly in ports in north-west Spain. This practice is highly controversial, and states such as the UK and France have retaliated by tightening up on licence regulations. The ECJ has now stipulated that there needs to be an economic link between coastal communities and vessels that have access (through flags of convenience) to national quotas by insisting that a certain percentage of fish caught is landed in the home port. In practice, policing such complex arrangements has proved

very difficult. The case of 'quota hoppers' is interesting because it is an example of a free market principle at work within fisheries, and shows the tension between supranational rules and national identities (Lequesne 2000b).

Until the 1990s the main objective of the CFP was to manage catches so as to ensure an equitable access to supplies across MSs, rather than to promote the welfare of the marine system, and fisheries were viewed more as an economic good than as a natural resource (McCormick 2001). Conservation of resources was not an issue until 1983, and it is only since the mid-1990s, under conditions of severe decline in stocks, that there has been any serious attempt to develop an ecosystem approach to stock management. This shift towards a more precautionary approach to fisheries was also influenced by the changing international agenda and the growing importance of environmental groups.

The search for equity and uniformity at the European level led to a highly complex system of rules and regulations. Superficially, the policy is marked by its centralization, with a reliance on regulations rather than directives (for definitions, see Section 3.4, page 43). In practice, however, there is a great deal of diversity and unevenness of implementation and enforcement across MSs.

21.3 Policy objectives

The CFP negotiated in 1983 gave the EU considerable leeway to prescribe detailed sets of rules for four main policy areas: marketing, structure, conservation and external relations.

Under the *marketing* policy, fisheries are subject to similar principles to agriculture, including common marketing standards, the institution of a price support system and the establishment of producers' organizations (POs). POs play a key role in many states – for example, in the UK, the twenty[2] POs decide the allocation of quotas and the granting of licences and permits. The marketing policy is commonly viewed as one of the few successful parts of the policy and has been little modified over the years. Until recently, consumer interests have not played a large part in the CFP, but since the mid-1990s there has been growing pressure on the industry to deliver fresh and wholesome fish. This is part of a changing culture within the

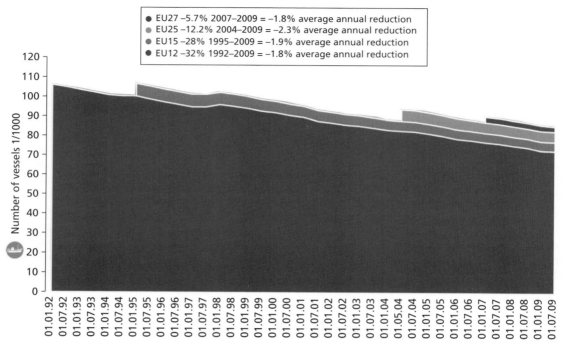

Figure 21.5 Evolution of the number of vessels in EU fishing fleet, 1992–2009 *Note*: The increse in the number of vessels in 1998 is due to the inclusion of vessels registred in the French outermost regions in the EU Fishing Fleet Register. *Source*: Eurostat 2006b

food industry in general, but also reflects the activities of pressure groups in the area. An example of a more environmentally oriented outlook is the initiative between the multinational Unilever and the World Wide Fund for Nature to set up the Marine Stewardship Council. This council supports more responsible fishing by giving certification to processors who restrict their purchases to fish that are being managed sustainably. Although this has been criticized by some as a marketing gimmick, the council has been quite successful in raising the public's awareness in campaigns such as 'dolphin-friendly' tuna.

Structural assistance for fishing was instituted in 1970 to 'promote harmonious and balanced development' of the industry and the 'rational use of marine resources' (Holden 1994). Until the mid-1980s, the key aim of the structural policy was to invest in the European fleet in order to catch more fish. However, over time the structural policy has become more flexible and more integrated with other aspects of the CFP. A growing awareness of the damage that overcapacity was having on Europe's fish stocks led in 1983 to the introduction of multi-annual guidance programmes (MAGPs), designed to link structural and conservation policy. Increasingly, MAGPs are used to achieve effort limitation and reduction rather than fleet renewal, although they seem to have somewhat limited effectiveness in this role (Suris-Regueiro *et al.* 2003) (see Figures 21.5 and 21.6). The targets put forward by the Commission under MAGPs are vigorously debated, and invariably moderated upwards, by fisheries ministers, who are keen to ensure that the burden of cutback is as small as possible and is fairly distributed among MSs. Financial assistance for communities dependent on fisheries was integrated into a single Financial Instrument for Fisheries Guidance, renamed the European Fisheries Fund (EFF) in 2007, which forms part of EU structural funds (see Chapters 19 and 21). EU aid for fishing (see Figure 21.7 and Table 21.A4 of the statistical appendix for the assistance, and Box 21.1 for explanation) now systematically requires some form of co-funding from MSs. Financial assistance cannot be given if states have failed to meet their decommissioning targets.

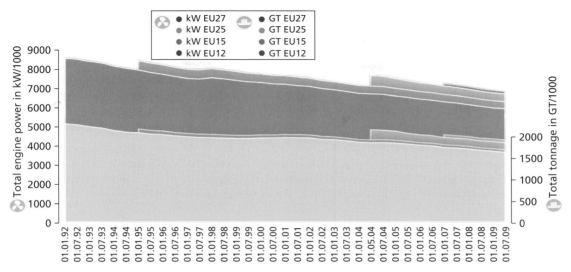

Figure 21.6 Evolution of EU fishing fleet capacity, 1992–2009 *Note*: The apparent tonnage increase registered between 1999 and 2001 is due to the transition from national tonnage systems to the EU system. On average, a vessel's tonnage on GT is greater than its tonnage measured in national units. The increase in engine power in 1998 is due to the inclusion of vessels registered in the French outermost regions in the EU Fishing Fleet Register. *Source*: Eurostat.

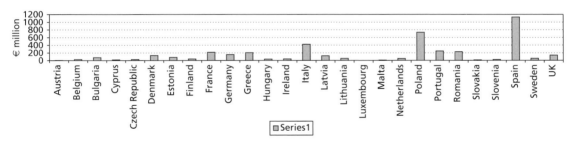

Figure 21.7 Financial assistance to the fisheries sector, 2007–2013

The aim of *conservation policy*, which now forms the core of the CFP, is the responsible exploitation of living marine resources on a sustainable basis (Council Regulation nos. 170/80 and 3760/92), taking into account its implications for the marine ecosystem and socio-economic implications for producers and consumers. There are two main conservation policies: quotas and total allowable catches (TACs); and technical instruments.

TACs are now used as a means of conserving stocks, although they were originally introduced as a means of allocating shares of available resources to MSs. The Commission bases its policy recommendations on information received from the International Council for the Exploration of the Seas (ICES). ICES scientists

monitor stocks and their relative health by setting a precautionary level of spawning stock biomass (SSB – total weight of a species capable of reproducing) for each fish type, below which stocks should not be allowed to fall, and a precautionary fishing rate above which the EU fleet should not go. Scientific evidence is often fiercely contested by fishermen on the grounds that it is out of date and is not sufficiently sensitive to changing conditions. Fisheries science does depend on highly complex biological and economic modelling. The inter-related life cycles of many fish (approximately 50 per cent of fish are eaten by other fish or marine predators), the multi-species nature of most stocks, and the complex nature of the ecosystem mean that predicting fish stocks, either through scientific

---

Box 21.1 EU financial assistance to the fisheries sector

EU financial assistance to the fisheries sector is now provided through the European Fisheries Fund (EFF), which began operations on 1 January 2007, having replaced the Financial Instrument for Fisheries Guidance. It has been allocated a budget of about 4.305 billion euros for 2007–13, including 75 per cent for regions whose development is lagging behind (see Chapter 22 for detailed information). The EFF helps to finance projects presented by companies, public authorities or representative bodies.

The strategic objectives of the EFF and priority 'axes' are defined by the Council:

- *Axis 1:*   Adaptation of the EU fishing fleet to the available resources, which provides aid for permanent or temporary cessation, small-scale coastal fishing, investments on board fishing boats, and the like.
- *Axis 2:*   Aquaculture, inland fishing, processing and marketing of fishery and aquaculture products, which advances productive investments in aquaculture, aqua-environmental measures, public health measures, and so on.
- *Axis 3:*   Measures of common interest, assisting the protection and development of aquatic fauna and flora, promotional campaigns, transformation of fishing vessels for a different use, and so on.
- *Axis 4:*   Sustainable development of fishing areas by assisting local projects for sustainable development, diversification of economic activities, and so on.
- *Axis 5:*   Technical assistance intended to facilitate the implementation of aid from the EFF to finance the work of public services, which manage the funds, and so on.

---

data or through experiential knowledge, remains fundamentally uncertain.

The advice provided by national teams reporting to ICES is assessed by ICES's Advisory Committee on Fisheries Management (ACFM) and the Commission's Scientific, Economic and Technical Fisheries Committee (STEFC). The Commission then tries to strike a balance between the ICES advice and what is likely to be politically acceptable when it draws up proposals on quotas and TACs for the December meeting of the Council of Fisheries Ministers. Once the ministers have agreed TACs, it is the responsibility of MSs to share out the quotas among their fishers and to enforce these quotas.

A second element of conservation policy is technical conservation. These measures include: minimum mesh sizes; minimum landing sizes; catch limits; selective gear, including square mesh panels and escape hatches for undersized fish; limits on the length of beam and size of drift nets (since 1 January 2003 a ban on drift nets for tuna and swordfish has been in place to remove the negative impact on dolphins and other non-target species); tonnage/power regulations; and the closure of fishing grounds for part of the year.

In *external relations* the Commission has the sole power to negotiate and conclude fisheries agreements with non-member states (NMSs; see Chapter 24). These include reciprocal arrangements over fishing rights, access to surplus stock, access to stock in return for financial compensation and, more recently, the development of joint enterprises. The EU currently has agreements in place with some thirty countries (for more details, see Lequesne 2005). The EU's external policy has become more important with the shrinking of the EU's own resources (see Chapter 19). It has come under heavy criticism from environmentalists and from the European Parliament (EP), because it has been seen as exporting the EU fisheries problem by exploiting the resources of developing countries. There is little coordination between the external aspect of the CFP and the EU's international development policy (see Chapter 25).

21.4 Policy process

Fisheries policy-making is characterized by a multi-level system of governance, ranging from the international arena, where a legal framework is set by the international fisheries regime, to the European, national, regional and local levels, which are responsible for the implementation and much of the monitoring of policy. At the core of this policy-making process lie the supranational institutions of the EU – the EP, the ECJ, the Commission and the Council (see Chapter 3). The EP only has a consultative role in the CFP, but its Fisheries Committee is becoming an increasingly important player in shaping policy and in liaising between fishers and the Commission. The ECJ has also been active in fisheries policy, with landmark decisions made upholding principles of non-discrimination in the fisheries sector. Historically, the key interests in the fisheries sector have been fishers and industry representatives, but increasingly environmental groups and consumers are entering the policy arena.

The policy-making process for fisheries is as follows. Policy initiatives come from the Commission's DG Fisheries, renamed Maritime Affairs and Fisheries (MAF) in 2009, which makes proposals against a background of scientific advice provided by international scientists. MAF will typically consult with its advisory committee, regional fisheries interests and other Commission directorates. This policy process is very complicated and can be inaccessible to many fishers, who are not part of an established policy community. Proposals from MAF are typically watered down in the Council, where MSs advocate on behalf of their fishermen. Policy within the Council is largely decided on the basis of qualified majority voting (QMV; see Chapter 3), leading to a series of trade-offs and bargains between MSs.

The final policy emerging from the Council seldom reflects the scientists' advice because of the way this is supplied (Daw and Gray 2005), bargained and traded through an intense political process (see Ritchie and Zito 1998; Payne 2000; Lequesne 2005). The example of the evolution of a policy to cope with the 2002 stock crisis illustrates this point.

When it came to advising on TACs for 2003, ICES and the STEFC recommended a moratorium on the cod fishery and the cod-related fisheries of whiting and haddock. In view of the likely detrimental social and economic impact, the Commission recommended to Council a substantial reduction in cod and related TACs. The Council, at the December 2002 meeting, set the 2003 TACs for the three stocks at substantially higher levels than the Commission had recommended. The eventual decision (Council regulation (EC) no. 2341/2002 of December 2002) saw a 45 per cent cut in the cod TAC. Haddock was cut by 50 per cent, whiting by 60 per cent and plaice by 5 per cent. CFP reform and the management of the stock crisis at the end of 2002 were marked by interventions from, among others, then British prime minister, Tony Blair, and French president, Jacques Chirac, on behalf of their fishermen.

Once the policy recommendations are made they are passed on to MSs, who then share out the nationally allocated quotas. MSs are also responsible for the implementation and monitoring of a large number of technical and conservation measures, such as the days-at-sea regulations, tonnage and gear size regulations, minimum landing sizes and vessel capacity. Responsibility for the implementation of policy falls to a variety of national, regional and local agencies across MSs. Thus, although the December 2009 Lisbon Treaty assigns the EU exclusive competence for the policy of fisheries conservation, to be decided by QMV in the Council, in reality MSs are fully involved. This complexity of institutional arrangements adds to the unevenness of policy implementation across the EU (Lequesne 2005, p. 368). One of the key CFP difficulties is ensuring that fishers comply with the rules. There are a number of reasons for non-compliance. First, some operators ignore the regulations because adherence may be too costly (especially when profit margins are small), they are too complex to work out, too bureaucratic to comply with or quite simply too difficult to implement in small craft. Second, many regulations have technical inconsistencies. Finally, many rules are simply ignored or flouted.

There are about as many ways of flouting CFP rules as there are rules to keep. Three key problems are the landing of illegal or 'black' fish, discarding fish back into the sea and the misreporting of information. 'Black' fish are landed illegally and are not reported as landings at the designated port, or are landed at other EU ports or outside the EU, where no record is taken. Landing illegal fish not only depletes stocks, but also undermines the accuracy of stock and TAC predictions, which is a particularly serious problem when stocks are in decline. A second problem is the discarding of fish that are not the right size or species. This is a major problem within the CFP, with estimates of 50 per cent for some catches. Discarded fish are a waste and also a major pollutant of the marine environment. Again, discarding is to some extent caused by the rigidity of some CFP rules, such as the requirement for single-species landings in some areas. The final key group of problems are misrecording or misreporting stock, or misdeclaring species in catches that are legally landed in other respects. All this creates havoc with the science on which the decisions on quota allocations are mainly based.

This discussion of the policy process has shown that effective collective solutions and radical policy change are inhibited by national and political interests, and that the policy structure leads to short-term political interests shaping policy. One of the main problems is that while the Commission is trying to effect a medium-term policy, TACs and quotas have historically been negotiated annually. Another problem is that representatives of the fishing industry have little direct role in the decision-making process (Symes 1995). Finally, procedures and guidelines are misunderstood, ignored, circumvented, falsified or merely flouted (Cann 1998). One of the Commission's responses to this problem has been to put forward more controls. This has served to further alienate the fishers.

21.5 Reform of the CFP?

The CFP has in many ways been in a process of reform since 1983, with the EU's Mediterranean enlargement, when a commitment was given to review the CFP and, in particular, the principle of relative stability in 2002. The promised reform and renegotiation of the CFP was to some extent deflected by the emergency measures that had to be put in place to deal with the crisis in stocks, and many commentators were disappointed by the limited changes proposed, particularly given the range of interests consulted during the drawing up of the reforms.

21.5.1 The 2002 reforms

Between 1998 and 2002 there was an unprecedented period of consultation of stakeholders and the industry by the Commission. The consultation began with 350 questionnaires being sent out to representatives and organizations involved in fishing in all EU MSs. This survey revealed a great deal of dissatisfaction with the CFP and emphasized problems with the conservation policy, enforcement difficulties and issues of equity. The Commission then organized a number of regional consultations (or roadshows) across all the

major EU fisheries regions, which led to more in-depth discussion of governance and institutional questions. In March 2001, on the basis of these two consultations, the Commission launched a consultative Green Paper (GP1) on CFP reform, with open invitations for evidence and comment. Over 300 submissions were made from stakeholders, ranging across inshore and deep-water fishermen, processors, anglers, environmentalists, the food industry and consumer organizations. Finally, the Commission held a public hearing in Brussels in June 2001, which was attended by 400 delegates from across the EU. This hearing gave particular emphasis to whether management of the CFP should be regionalized. The polarity of views expressed ranged from an anti-regionalist perspective adopted by the Spanish contingent, to a proposal for a full regionalization of decision-making powers put forward by the British, Dutch and Swedish delegates. Other key issues discussed, which elicited mixed and polarized responses, were the privatization of the CFP (through the introduction of a form of individual transferable quota) and issues of enforcement and compliance.

On the basis of the numerous consultation exercises and GP1, the Commission drew up a reform of the CFP. This was put to the Council in December 2002 and a Council Regulation followed on 20 December,[3] generally referred to as Basic Regulation (2371/2002). The reform, hence the Regulation, inevitably represented a compromise between the different views (above), especially on highly charged issues such as regional management. On the issue of the privatization of quotas, the Commission did seem to have taken note of the majority opinion during the consultation exercise by allowing flexibility at the level of MSs. Many of the traditional areas of the policy, such as relative stability and special derogations, remained, although after January 2003 Spanish, Portuguese and Finnish vessels were allowed to fish for unallocated quota in the North Sea.

To be specific, the Regulation contains a number of modest changes for the governance and management of the CFP, but no radical reform. Here is a summary, with the full details provided on the accompanying website:

1. Central to the reform is the adoption of a longer-term perspective to fisheries management by

setting multi-annual targets instead of the annual exercises of the past (Article 6.3).

2. There is a renewed and stricter commitment to capacity reduction and control, to bring the fleet in line with available resources (Article 13).

3. The reforms also stress the importance of ecosystem management and the precautionary principle.

4. In response to considerable discussion about increasing the role for industry and stakeholders, Article 31 calls for the setting up of regional advisory councils (RACs). These include mainly fishermen and representatives of interest in the CFP, such as the aquaculture sector, environmental and consumer groups, and scientists.

5. Conservation and sustainability remain the CFP cornerstone (Articles 4–10).

6. The objective of the structural policy remains the achievement of a 'stable and enduring balance between the capacity of fishing fleets and the fishing opportunities available to them in and outside of Community waters', hence adjustment of fishing capacity is the essence (Article 11).

7. Since 2004 fisheries agreements have been known as 'fisheries partnership agreements' (FPAs) to denote a new focus in external relations; sixteen FPAs are currently in force.

8. The Regulation outlines a whole series of measures designed to improve the control and enforcement of the CFP by both the Commission and MSs (Articles 21–28).

These reforms have failed to resolve the fundamental problem with the CFP: the inability to limit catches to a sustainable level (Daw and Gray 2005; Gray and Hatchard 2003). Thus, although catches have been reduced (see Figure 21.1 and Tables 21.A1 and 21.A2), this reduction has left catches in excess of safe biological limits. Overall fishing in EU waters exceeds these limits and the excess has been growing. The situation in relation to particular types of fish is even more serious.[4] EU situation can be contrasted with that of Iceland where national conservation measures have enabled the catch to be sustained.

21.5.2 The 2013 reforms

Article 35 of the Regulation asks the Commission to report to the EP and the Council on CFP operation regarding conservation and sustainability (Regulation, Chapter II) and the adjustment of fishing capacity (Chapter III) before the end of 2012. The Commission started this review in exactly the same manner as it did for the 2002 reforms: it published a Green Paper (GP2) in 2009,[5] followed it with a consultation period, with a closure of written responses on 31 December 2009, and issued a working paper synthesizing them in 2010.[6] Thus the process is all set for the 2013 deadline.

GP2 confirms what is in the last paragraph (p. 7):

the objectives agreed in 2002 to achieve sustainable fisheries have not been met overall . . . 88% of [EU] stocks are being fished beyond [maximum sustainable yield] . . . 30% of these stocks are outside safe biological limits, which means that they may not be able to replenish . . . 93% of cod in the North Sea are fished before they can breed . . . European fisheries are eroding their own ecological and economic basis

Also, few EU fleets are profitable without public support, due to chronic overcapacity. Moreover, there is high political pressure to increase short-term fishing opportunities at the expense of the future sustainability of the industry. Furthermore, not only is the industry provided with heavy EU support, but it also receives a number of indirect subsidies, the most important of which is overall exemption from fuel taxes.

These points are fully explained on the website and since the decisions are yet to come, there is no need to spend space on them here. It should be mentioned, however, that nothing dramatic has been suggested, hence the final outcome is not likely to be a call for radical change, only fine-tuning of the current policy situation.

21.6 Conclusion

CFP reform has not marked a radical shift in the way the EU organizes fisheries. However, there are signs of change. A new level of governance has been introduced. A more consultative approach is in evidence and there is more coherence in the technical aspects of the policy. The CFP is placing more emphasis on a medium-term strategic management of stocks, and the discourse of ecosystem management is becoming more common.

There are fundamental problems still confronting EU fisheries – declining stocks, overcapacity, cumbersome rules and regulations that are poorly implemented, and competing national interests. Solving these problems will require not only further technical reform and tough conservation methods, but an improved system of governance which has the support of its major stakeholders.

Summary

- It is logical for the EU to have a CFP, since much fishing activity is conducted across and beyond national territorial waters and fish take no notice of national boundaries.
- Although the EU's fisheries sector, comprising fishing, fish processing and aquaculture, is small in terms of both production and employment, the EU fishing industry is the world's fourth largest, and, vitally, fishing activity tends to be concentrated in peripheral regions where there is often little alternative employment and the industry and its representatives tend to be highly fragmented.
- The CFP has evolved since 1970, but was not formalized until 1982, operative from 1983. It has four aspects:
  1. *Marketing*, which includes common marketing standards, the institution of a price support system and the establishment of producers' organizations (POs).
  2. *Structural assistance*, with the aim of promoting 'harmonious and balanced development' of the industry, the 'rational use of marine resources' and multi-annual guidance programmes.
  3. *Conservation*, which is the responsible exploitation of living marine resources on a sustainable basis, taking into account its implications for the marine ecosystem and socio-economic implications for producers and consumers, the two main conservation policies being quotas/total allowable catches (TACs) and technical instruments.
  4. *External relations*, based on fisheries partnership agreements (FPAs) with NMSs, which include reciprocal arrangements over fishing rights, access to surplus stock, access to stock in return for financial compensation and, more recently, the development of joint enterprises.

- EU financial assistance for communities dependent on fisheries is provided by the European Fisheries Fund (EFF), which forms part of EU structural funds (see Chapters 19 and 22); EU aid for fishing now systematically requires some form of co-funding from MSs and is conditional on meeting fleet decommissioning targets.
- Fisheries policy-making is characterized by a multi-level system of governance, ranging from the international arena, where a legal framework is set by the international fisheries regime, to the European, national, regional and local levels, which are responsible for the implementation and much of the monitoring of policy.
- CFP has been in a process of reform since 1983, with the EU's Mediterranean enlargement, when a commitment was given to review the CFP and, in particular, the principle of relative stability in 2002. The 2002 reforms, which apply until 2013, include:
  1. the adoption of a longer-term perspective to fisheries management by setting multi-annual targets instead of the annual exercises of the past;
  2. renewed and stricter commitment to capacity reduction and control, to bring the fleet in line with available resources;
  3. the importance of ecosystem management and the precautionary principle to 'ensure exploitation of living aquatic resources and of aquaculture that provides sustainable economic, environmental and social conditions';
  4. increasing the role for industry and stakeholders by the setting up of regional advisory councils (RACs);
  5. simplified and streamlined regulations for easier and fairer application; and
  6. EU aid to support coastal communities as the industry restructures while fleet overcapacity is reduced.
- The reform process for 2013 is under way but is not expected to result in any radical changes.

Questions and essay topics

1. Why is it deemed necessary for the EU to have a CFP?

2. Why did the policy agreed in 1970 not become a CFP until 1983?

3. What are the four aspects of the CFP?

4. What are TACs?

5. What is sustainability?

6. What are the priority axes?

7. Who is involved in CFP policy process?

8. What financial assistance does the EU provide for fisheries communities?

9. What conditions does the EU set for its financial assistance?

10. What are FPAs?

11. 'It is not necessary to have a CFP since the most effective policy is one of national responsibility.' Discuss.

12. 'FPAs are the most effective way to protect the fisheries globally.' Discuss.

FURTHER READING

Churchill, R. and Owen, D. (2010) *The EC Common Fisheries Policy*, Oxford University Press.

Crean, K. and Symes, D. (1996) *Fisheries Management in Crisis*, Blackwell Science, Oxford.

NOTES

1 Unless otherwise stated, statistics are from Eurostat.

2 Overall, the EU has 169 POs for small-scale, coastal, off-shore and deep-sea fishing, and 35 for aquaculture and other types of fishing. Of the major six fishing nations, Italy has 30 and 7 respectively; Spain 28 and 12; France 23 and 7; the UK 20 and 1; Germany 17 and 1; and Portugal 14 and 2. In the other EU nations they are: the Netherlands 6 and 5; Poland and Sweden 5 and 1 each; Denmark 3 and 1; Ireland 5 and 0; Estonia and Greece 3 and 0 each; Latvia, Lithuania and Romania 2 and 0 each; and Belgium 1 and 0. Austria, Bulgaria, the Czech Republic, Cyprus, Finland, Hungary, Luxembourg, Malta, Slovenia and Slovakia have none.

3 Council Regulation (EC) No. 2371/2002 of 20 December 2002 on the conservation and sustainable exploitation of fisheries resources under the Common Fisheries Policy.

4 Demersal (species that live on shallow ocean beds), pelagic (species that swim together in shoals in the open ocean), benthic (species that live just above the sea bed) and industrial (other species caught for processing); see Eurostat for annual data.

5 Green Paper on the Reform of the Common Fisheries Policy (COM(2009) 163 final, 22 April 2009).

6 'Synthesis of the consultations of the reform on the Common Fisheries Policy', Commission Staff Working Document SEC(2010) 428 final.

Regional policy

HARVEY ARMSTRONG

22.1 Introduction

[Member states of the] European Economic Community are anxious to ensure their harmonious development by reducing the differences existing between the various regions and the backwardness of the less favoured regions (Preamble to the Treaty of Rome, 1958)

In order to promote its overall harmonious development, the Community shall develop and pursue its actions leading to the strengthening of its economic and social cohesion (Article 158, Consolidated Version of the Treaty Establishing a European Community, 2002)

[The EU] shall promote economic, social and territorial cohesion, and solidarity among the member states (Article 2, Treaty of Lisbon, 2009)

These three quotations, spanning the whole EU history, illustrate the strength and continuity of its commitment to regional policy (RP). Indeed, far from weakening over time, the quotations show a broadening of the policy, from an initial emphasis on *economic* disparities to incorporate both *social* and now *territorial* cohesion as well. The strength of the commitment is mirrored by the scale of financial resources devoted to EU RP, some 34.9 per cent of the EU budget in 2010 (€49.4 billion). The commitment to RP at first sight seems curious. The EU has aspirations to become something approaching a federal system. RP of the type we know in the EU, however, is rarely found in long-established federal countries such as the USA, Canada and Australia. Understanding EU RP requires an appreciation of the uniqueness of the EU situation, with its patchwork of sovereign member states (MSs).

This chapter examines EU RP at an important moment in the step-by-step process of EU integration. The accession of ten new member states (NMSs) in 2004, and a further two in 2007, significantly widened EU regional economic disparities, and in doing so forced the EU to bring in major changes in EU RP during its current 2007–13 'programming period'.

This chapter begins with an examination of the case for having EU RP running alongside the RPs operated by each MS's government. This is followed by an overview of the ways in which economic integration can affect regional disparities. Attention will subsequently be concentrated on EU RP as it is being practised during the current 2007–13 programming period. Finally, the key issues that confront EU RP in the immediate future will be examined.

22.2 The case for an EU regional policy

RP has always been controversial. It is undeniably interventionist. Those who distrust the competence of governments fear that RP penalizes successful businesses in prosperous regions, while simultaneously encouraging unsuitable economic activities in the depressed regions. To those who hold this opinion, regional disparities are the inevitable outcome of the market system – something to be tolerated until market forces such as labour migration, capital investment and expanding trade combine to automatically revitalize low-wage depressed regions. Supporters of RP are much more sceptical of the ability of market forces to solve long-standing regional problems.

Even if one accepts the view that there is a case for government intervention in the form of RP, this does not in itself constitute a case for EU RP. The crucial question from an EU point of view is why a separate EU RP is required *in addition to* those of the individual MSs, which have continued alongside EU RP since 1975 (when the European Regional Development Fund, ERDF, was established; see Section 22.4.1, page 356). There is no suggestion that they should be laid aside in favour of a single EU RP.

Several distinct arguments can be advanced in support of a RP operated at EU level. Each argument will be considered in turn.

22.2.1 The vested interest argument

EU MSs are becoming increasingly integrated economies. Rapidly expanding trade links (see Figure 5.8, page 76), together with much freer capital mobility and more slowly growing cross-border labour migration, have been and continue to be stimulated by EU initiatives such as the Single European Market (SEM; see Chapter 7) and European monetary union (EMU; see Chapters 10–12). Increasingly, the economic well-being of citizens of one MS depends on the prosperity of the economies of other MSs. The presence of disadvantaged regions experiencing low incomes and high unemployment is in the interests of no one. Put another way, the citizens of one MS have a *vested interest* in ensuring that the regional problems in *other* MSs are reduced. An EU RP can therefore be justified as a mechanism that allows one MS to become involved in policies which stimulate economic activity in the regions of other MSs.

22.2.2 The financial targeting argument

The second main argument in support of an EU RP is concerned with the effectiveness with which RP is operated in the EU. RPs are expensive to operate and resources must be found from public sector budgets. The disadvantaged EU regions are not evenly distributed among MSs. Some MSs carry such a burden of disadvantaged regions that they constitute depressed regions in their own right. This has traditionally been the case with some of the Mediterranean MSs in the south of the EU – for example, Greece. EU enlargement in 2004 to incorporate the significantly poorer NMS10 (Czech Republic, Cyprus, Estonia, Hungary, Latvia, Lithuania, Malta, Poland, Slovakia and Slovenia) and Bulgaria and Romania in 2007 (NMS12) greatly expanded the number of MSs of this type.

Given the inevitable pressure on public sector budgets, it is not surprising to find that it is precisely those MSs with the most severe burden of regional problems that have the greatest difficulty financing an RP. Leaving RP wholly to MSs is therefore not effective from an EU perspective. MSs such as the UK and Germany,

with fewer regional problems, have been best able to afford an active RP. Those with the most severe regional problems, such as Greece and Poland, face chronic budget difficulties and find it hard to fund their domestic RPs adequately. Only the EU, it can be argued, is capable of drawing resources from more prosperous parts of the EU and ensuring that they are allocated to the most heavily disadvantaged regions.

22.2.3 The coordination argument

The third argument that can be made in support of an EU RP concerns the advantages of a coordinated approach. The EU has immense potential to improve the effectiveness of RP by acting as a supranational coordinating body. Regional development initiatives within MSs are offered by a bewildering array of organizations. As well as MSs' governments, typically also involved are regional governments, local governments, non-elected development agencies and, increasingly, private sector organizations, community and voluntary organizations, as well as an array of joint venture schemes between private and governmental bodies.

Lack of coordination can be very wasteful. Firms seeking assistance in the disadvantaged regions may be bewildered and deterred by the complexity of the types of help on offer. Different regions may compete, using RP subsidies as a weapon, for one another's firms or for the inward investment projects of US and other foreign firms (a process known as competitive bidding). In addition, valuable development opportunities – for example, cross-border transport links (see Chapter 16) may not be properly implemented as a result of coordination failures. The coordination agenda for an EU RP is clearly a wide one.

22.2.4 The effects of integration argument

This is the most controversial of the arguments advanced in support of an EU RP. EU involvement in RP, it is argued, is necessary to overcome the adverse regional impacts of the integration process. This argument rests on two suppositions. The first is that economic integration, if left to its own devices, tends to cause a worsening ('divergence') of regional disparities. The second is that it is the EU, rather than MSs, that is best placed to tackle the regional problems that develop as integration proceeds. Both suppositions have been the subject of fierce debate. The effect of integration on regional disparities is an issue of immense importance and will be considered further in Section 22.3.

22.2.5 The effects of other EU policies argument

A further argument frequently advanced in support of EU RP is that it is needed to help mitigate the adverse regional effects of other EU policies. A number of EU policies are known to have particularly severe effects on the disadvantaged regions. VAT, for example, a major source of EU revenues, has long been known to be a regionally regressive tax (CEU 1979c; van den Noord 2000; and Chapter 15). Other EU policies have also long been known to have their own distinctive patterns of regional effects (CEU 1996d, 2001c, 2003g). The adverse regional effects of the Common Agricultural Policy (CAP), for example, have meant that, despite repeated CAP reforms, more prosperous northern regions continued to benefit most throughout the 1980s and 1990s (CEU 2000e). More recent evidence has shown that a succession of reforms since McSharry's of 1992 have slowly ameliorated the adverse CAP regional impacts (see Chapter 20), but its regional impacts remain far from favourable (CEU 1996d, 2003g).

The ideal solution to the problem of policies with adverse regional impacts, of course, would be to alter the nature of the policies themselves. Reforming an EU policy at source, however, is only possible to a limited degree, and there are usually dangers to the integrity of the policy itself if it is pushed too far in a 'pro-regional' direction. EU RP initiatives must therefore be designed, wherever sensible, to help to mitigate the adverse regional effects of other EU policies.

The list of arguments in favour of a separate EU RP is a long one. The case is a strong one too. It should be noted, however, that there is no logical case here for a *complete* transfer of RP powers from MSs to the EU. Indeed the EU's own commitment to 'subsidiarity' – the maximum devolution of powers – requires that MSs, regional and local governments and other partner organizations all have a role (see Chapters 2 and 3). The vast majority of modern types of RP initiatives – for example, advice to firms and training policies – also require an active local input to be effective. The remoteness of Brussels from many of the problem regions, the lack of specialist local knowledge and experience at the centre, and the virtue of allowing variety and experimentation in RP all suggest that partnership and not dominance is the appropriate EU role.

22.3 The effects of integration on EU regional disparities

The implications of economic integration for EU regional disparities are still imperfectly understood. The economic processes at work are complex and long-lasting. The regional effects even of the creation of the original customs union have not yet been fully experienced, and the regional implications of the SEM process are still really only in their relatively early stages (see Chapter 7), even though the legislation for it was largely completed by 1992. Add to these the regional ramifications of the 1996 enlargement (which saw the accession of Austria, Finland and Sweden), together with the geographic effects of EMU in 2002 and the accession of the NMS12 in 2004/7, and one can see just how complex the effects of economic integration are. Each of these steps in the process of economic integration has its own very distinctive 'regional footprint', and each has set in train effects that will take decades to emerge fully. Nor will the system have time to draw breath in the decade ahead. EMU remains an incomplete process (see Chapters 11 and 12) and any further future extensions of the Eurozone, combined with additional new accessions, perhaps Croatia and Turkey, would trigger yet more complex regional footprint effects right across the EU.

An examination of the existing pattern of EU regional disparities reveals an array of problems that are formidable by comparison with those in other parts of the world, such as the USA. Figure 22.1 shows EU regional GDP per capita, at purchasing power parities, for 2006. The EU already had wide regional disparities prior to the 2004 eastern enlargement. The GDP per capita disparities within the EU15 were already more than twice as great as those found in the USA. Prior to the eastern enlargement, for the EU15 countries which then comprised the EU, GDP per capita in the richest 10 per cent of regions was around 2.6 times greater than that in the poorest 10 per cent. Following the eastern

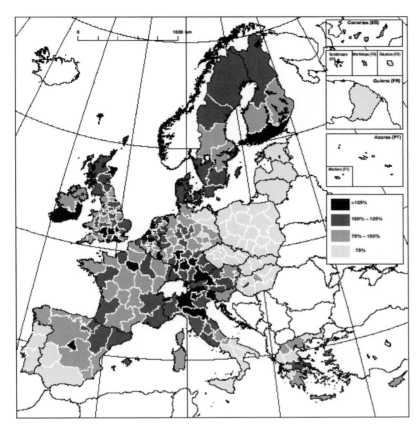

Figure 22.1 Regional gross domestic product per head, at purchasing power parties, 2006 *Source*: Eurostat 2006c (Map 1)
© EuroGeographics Association for the administrative boundaries

enlargement, for the EU27 this ratio has risen to around 5:1, revealing a dramatic widening of regional disparities. Just how stark are the additional challenges being posed for EU RP by the NMS12 accessions is clearly revealed in Figure 22.1. GDP per capita data for 2006 show that the region of the EU27 with the highest GDP per capita, Inner London, was more than thirteen times more prosperous than the poorest, north-east Romania (Eurostat 2009a).

Figure 22.2 shows the extent of EU regional disparities using another popular indicator, the regional unemployment rate. The picture here is much less clear than the broadly core–periphery pattern revealed in Figure 22.1 for GDP per capita. Nevertheless, the figure reveals just how severe the regional unemployment rate disparities are in the EU27. In 2007 regional unemployment rates ranged from a mere 2.1 per cent in Zeeland in the Netherlands (the region with the lowest

EU27 unemployment rate) to a massive 25.2 per cent in Réunion (a French Département d'Outre Mer and the region with the highest EU27 unemployment rate).

The regional problems confronting the EU are extremely diverse as well as being severe. EU RP in the past has variously recognized a whole array of different types of regions with distinctive problems. These have included lagging regions (regions whose GDP per capita is below 75 per cent of the EU average and whose regional problems are the most severe in the EU), declining manufacturing areas, certain rural regions, fishing communities, mining and steel regions, inner city areas, low population sub-Arctic regions in Sweden and Finland, island economies and the remote, outermost regions – that is, the Azores, the Canary Islands, French Guyana, Guadeloupe, Martinique and Réunion. In other words, EU RP has always clearly recognized just how diverse the *types*

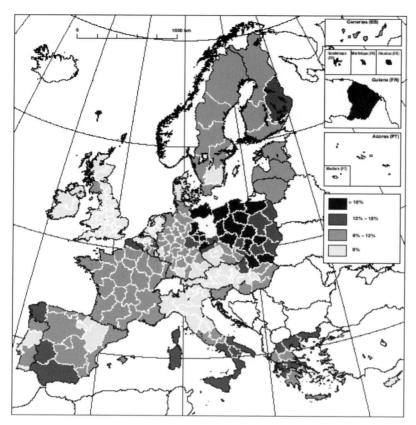

Figure 22.2 Regional unemployment rates (males plus female), 2007 *Source*: Eurostat 2007b (Map 1)
© EuroGraphics Association for the administrative boundaries

of regional problem faced are, as well as how *severe* a challenge they represent.

Despite the great variety of EU regional problems, the overwhelming impression that one obtains from statistics such as those presented in Figures 22.1 and 22.2 is that there appears to be something of a core–periphery pattern to EU regional disparities. A high proportion of the more prosperous regions lie at the geographical centre of the EU, whereas disadvantaged regions tend to be grouped around the periphery. Within the existing EU27, the most disadvantaged regions tend to be particularly (but by no means wholly) in the Mediterranean south and among NMSs of Central and Eastern Europe. Prior to 1995 the core–periphery pattern was even more pronounced than it appears now, because Ireland (both Northern Ireland and the Republic), as well as parts of northern and western Britain, were also highly disadvantaged. As Figure 22.1

shows, however, extremely rapid growth of both GDP and employment in Ireland (and to a lesser extent in western Britain) in the 1990s transformed these areas, so that the underdevelopment of the EU's 'western periphery' is much less pronounced than it once was. The traditionally prosperous core of the EU stretches from central England to northern Italy. There is evidence of the more recent emergence of a growth belt from northern Italy through the south of France and into northern Spain, and, as we have seen, across western Britain into eastern Ireland. This does not, however, alter the overall conclusion that a core–periphery situation prevails in the EU. All of these statistics, of course, predate the global recession triggered in 2008 (more on this later).

The core–periphery nature of EU regional problems has existed for many years. It is the outcome of economic processes predating the EU's existence, and others that have come into existence as a result of the EU. Economic integration is a process that is progressing continuously on a worldwide scale. Improvements in transport have gradually reduced freight cost barriers to trade. Moreover, in the post-war period there has been a consensus in favour of freer trade, which has led to successive international steps designed to reduce the barriers to trade – for example, WTO agreements and the policies of the IMF and the World Bank aimed at developing countries (see Chapters 24 and 25). EU MSs have participated in these worldwide processes of integration, and the pattern of *intra-EU* regional disparities that we observe today has been affected by them.

In addition to the broad integration processes common to all countries, the EU has acted to trigger its own distinctive, accelerated integration. The current maps of regional disparities (such as Figures 22.1 and 22.2) have been affected by these too. The regional effects of the SEM process have not yet been fully experienced, partly because the complete SEM has yet to be implemented, and partly because the effects are extremely long-term in nature. The effects of the convergence process *leading up* to full EMU in 2002 were felt in the 1990s – for example, via pressures on MSs' budgets – but the longer-term regional impacts of EMU itself have yet to be experienced. Moreover, existing regional disparities continue to be affected by the creation of the original customs union in 1958, and by its successive widening to include new MSs in 1973 (Denmark, Ireland and the UK), 1981 (Greece), 1986 (Spain and Portugal), 1991 (East Germany), 1996 (Austria, Finland and Sweden) and 2004/7 (NMS12).

No two rounds of economic integration ever have an identical effect on regional disparities. Each round in the integration process can be thought of as having two groups of effects: a unique regional imprint or pattern of effects, combined with a core–periphery effect in common with other rounds. The creation of the original customs union, for example, involved the removal of tariffs that had previously provided most protection to *manufacturing* industries. The most severe effects of this act of integration were therefore experienced in regions most heavily dependent on manufacturing industries. The creation of the SEM between 1989 and 1992 involved the removal of an array of non-tariff barriers. In this round of integration both manufacturing and service industries were affected. It is thought that a distinctive group of some forty manufacturing sectors were most affected by the SEM, along with certain types of services, such as banking and finance (CEU 1988a; Quévit 1995; Begg 1995). Some regions are clearly more at risk than others, giving rise to a distinctive regional imprint. EMU has plunged most EU15 regions into a larger single currency area than before, and has stripped Eurozone MSs of exchange rate and monetary policy powers frequently brought to bear in the past to help disadvantaged regions (see Chapters 10 and 12). Eventually, EMU too is therefore likely to impinge more on some regions than on others (Ardy *et al.* 2002).

While it is obvious that each round in the integration process has its own distinctive regional impact, why EU integration should exhibit systematic core–periphery effects as well is less clear. Evidence to date suggests that integration tends to trigger two sets of countervailing forces, one set tending to cause regional *convergence*, while the other tends to bring about regional *divergence*. The existing core–periphery pattern of regional disparities suggests that at least in some periods in the past the divergence forces must have predominated.

In more recent years there seems to have been something of a rough balance between divergence and convergence forces. Which set of forces will predominate in the years to come is an issue of major importance to the EU. Interestingly, the most recent evidence available suggests that while at the present time there seems to be a rough balance between the forces of regional convergence and divergence within the EU, the picture is actually rather more complex than this. The period since 1995 has witnessed a situation in which economic disparities – for example, in GDP per capita – *between countries* have narrowed. However, this has been accompanied by a widening of regional disparities *within some MSs*, leading to an overall situation of only a very slow decline in regional disparities (CEU 2005a; Cambridge Econometrics and Ecorys-NEI 2004; Monfort 2008; Dall'erba and LeGallo 2006). The widening of regional disparities within MSs is most dramatically seen in the NMS12, where the regions containing the capital cities – for example, Prague, Bratislava, Budapest – have gained rapidly compared with the more peripheral regions; but countries within the EU15, such as the UK, have also seen within-country disparities widen since 1995. Why this pattern of simultaneous convergence and divergence is happening within the EU is not well understood, but is clearly of profound importance for the task that EU RP must face.

The forces tending to bring about *convergence* of regional disparities within the EU are predominantly a series of automatic equilibrating processes that occur whenever a system of freely functioning markets is in operation. Free trade in goods and services will, it is argued, lead to regions specializing in the production and export of goods and services in which they have a comparative advantage. Under traditional trade theory, such as the Heckscher–Ohlin model, all regions benefit from this process, and regional differences in wage rates and capital rentals are also eliminated (Armstrong and Taylor 2000). The convergence effects of freer trade are reinforced by the effects of freer factor mobility (see Chapter 8). Where wage rates differ significantly between regions, there is an incentive for labour to migrate from low-wage to high-wage regions, a process that reduces regional wage inequalities. Capital investment, meanwhile, is attracted to the disadvantaged regions by the low wages and excellent labour supply available there. This too reduces regional inequalities. The combination of freer trade and large-scale factor mobility offers real hope for the convergence of regional disparities in the EU, and these processes lie at the heart of modern, neoclassical, conditional convergence theories of regional growth, which predict the convergence of regional disparities (Sala-i-Martin 1996). It is thought, however, that these processes operate only very slowly and that decades will be required before their full effects are felt. Moreover, there are forces leading to divergence of regional disparities. It is to these that we now turn.

At the heart of the economic integration process set in motion by the EU has been a desire to achieve free trade and the free movement of labour and capital. In order to enjoy the benefits of integration (Emerson *et al.* 1988; CEU 1988a), it is essential that a major restructuring of industry should occur. The various allocation and accumulation effects generating economic gains from integration require regions to switch production and concentrate on those goods and services for which there is a comparative advantage (Baldwin *et al.* 1997). The greater the integration envisaged, the greater the potential benefits, but the greater too are the restructuring implications. Painful though the restructuring process is for those involved, in principle it should be experienced by all regions. The crucial question,

therefore, is why EU integration seems to be associated with systematic core–periphery effects. A series of different divergence forces are thought to accompany the integration process:

1. *Economies of scale.* These represent a potent source of benefit from integration. The concentration of production at larger plants can lead to great efficiency gains. Firms seeking to exploit economies of scale are likely to be attracted to regions at the geographic core of the EU. Input assembly costs are lower, and access to the whole EU market is much easier from central locations. Moreover, the core regions are already the most prosperous regions and therefore represent the strongest markets.

2. *Localization and agglomeration economies.* Localization economies arise when firms in the same industry locate close to one another – for example, because of access to labour with appropriate skills, information flows, ability to subcontract work. Agglomeration economies occur when firms from many different industries locate close to one another – for example, because of transport facilities, financial facilities. These 'external economies' effects tend to strongly favour the core EU regions. Firms are drawn towards existing successful agglomerations of economic activity. The core EU regions contain almost all of the main financial, industrial and capital cities, and are a potent magnet for new activity. The traditional 'Marshallian' localization and agglomeration economies have been incorporated in a variety of new theories, which predict industrial clustering and hence a concentration of economic activity in those regions fortunate to have been able to develop successful industrial clusters. Theories such as post-Fordism have stressed the advantages of clustered small firms in new industrial districts such as those in the 'Third Italy', within the traditional geographic core of the EU (Dunford 2000; Bagella and Becchetti 2000). Porter's work has also highlighted the interacting sets of forces that can generate industrial clustering and the geographic concentration of economic activity (Porter 1990), as have social capital theories of regional growth (Putnam 1993). Within mainstream economics, new economic geography models of regional growth and some versions of endogenous growth theory also predict clustering,

and hence the possibility of divergent growth (Midelfart-Knarvik *et al.* 2000; Fujita *et al.* 2009).

3. *Intra-industry trade and dominant market positions.* Modern trade theory is increasingly sceptical of the ability of all regions to share equally in the growth associated with freer trade. There is evidence that intra-industry trade (IIT) in similar products has shown the most rapid growth among the more prosperous core regions and EU MSs (Neven 1990; and Chapters 6, 9 and 24). Regions in the Mediterranean south of the EU have fallen behind in participation in this important trade. IIT is important because of the fast pace of expansion of this type of trade, particularly the horizontal exchange of almost identical products. By contrast, NMSs in Central and Eastern Europe do appear to be engaging in an increasing amount of IIT, but of the less lucrative vertical IIT category, supplying Western Europe with semi-processed inputs. Similarly, much EU trade in manufactured goods is now dominated by large multinational enterprises. These firms are already concentrated in EU core regions and it is thought that they may exploit their ability to dominate markets in ways that disadvantage peripheral regions. Opening up peripheral regions to competition from large multinational firms could have serious effects for the smaller and less powerful firms more frequently found there.

4. *Lack of competitiveness in peripheral regions.* Research commissioned over the years by the EU (IFO 1990; CEU 1999c; Cambridge Econometrics and Ecorys-NEI 2004; CEU 2010d; Basile 2009) has provided powerful evidence that many firms in the EU's peripheral regions face severe problems in meeting the competitive challenges posed by integration. The lack of competitiveness is based on a combination of factors largely outside the control of the firms themselves. These include poor location, weak infrastructure facilities – for example, transport, telecommunications – low-skill labour forces, and local tax and financial sector problems.

5. *Selective labour migration.* The peripheral regions are also weakened, as integration proceeds, by the loss of migrants. The freeing of labour mobility stimulates migration from peripheral to core regions. Migration is highly selective. It is the young, the skilled and the economically active who migrate. Their loss is a severe blow to peripheral regions seeking to compete in an integrated EU. The surge in migrants from some of the main NMS12 countries towards those EU15 countries willing to accept them initially – for example, the UK – is a worrying example of this type of process at work.

6. *The loss of macro-policy powers in peripheral MSs.* This is a particular problem at the present time because of EMU. Those MSs that have joined the Eurozone have lost control of their exchange rates, as well as other aspects of their monetary policy such as interest rates. Full EMU has meant the complete loss of powers to try to protect a weak local economy by way of currency devaluation, and to use monetary policy to stimulate a weak local economy (see Chapters 10–12). Even fiscal policy has been to some degree constrained under EMU because of the Stability and Growth Pact (SGP; see Chapters 11 and 12) and constraints on MSs' public sector budgets within the Eurozone. Peripheral MSs face a future of very limited macro-policy powers. This will restrict their ability to protect their local economies.

The divergence forces set out above seem convincing and strong. There has been considerable discussion of the possibility that the divergence forces may interact and reinforce one another in such a way that *cumulative causation* occurs. This is where the loss of firms and a continuous outflow of migrants so weakens a peripheral economy that it can no longer attract new economic activities and hence goes into a downward spiral of decline. This is by no means a theoretical possibility. A number of EU rural regions – for example, the west of Ireland and parts of southern Italy – have historically experienced depopulation on a large scale.

Evidence from federal countries with a long history of being fully economically integrated, notably the USA, suggests that in the long term integration is associated with convergence of regional disparities rather than divergence (Sala-i-Martin 1996). This evidence implies that the convergence forces at work eventually come to predominate over the divergence forces. The ensuing balance of forces results in a process of convergence that is slow, but is also sustained over a long period.

The evidence for convergence among EU regions is much more contested, partly because good statistics do not exist for the long periods of time necessary to check whether or not convergence is occurring. The balance of the evidence that is available suggests that cumulative causation has not occurred in the EU. Most researchers have found that prior to the mid-1970s regional disparities in the EU had experienced quite a long period of narrowing. This was followed by a period of widening disparities in the late 1970s and early 1980s. As noted earlier, the EU's regional disparities, at least as far as GDP per capita figures are concerned, seem to have stabilized in the later 1990s and to have begun very slowly narrowing again (Armstrong 1995a, b; CEU 1999c, 2001d, 2003c, 2005a; Monfort 2008). However, this evidence remains rather controversial, since some analysts have also found evidence for *divergence* among EU regions, at least for certain periods of time (Dunford 1996; Magrini 1999; Barrios and Strobl 2009). Moreover, as also noted earlier, recent years have seen convergence between MSs being accompanied by divergence between regions within many MSs. What can be said, however, is that the spells of overall regional divergence that have been observed tend to have been apparently short-lived. Economic integration does appear, on the whole, to be associated with a narrowing of regional disparities, although currently at a painfully slow rate.

22.4 Current and future EU regional policy

22.4.1 The origins of modern EU regional policy: the reforms of 1989, 1994 and 1999

EU RP traces its origins to the decision in 1975 to create the ERDF. The policy subsequently underwent minor reform in 1979 and 1984 (Armstrong 1978, 1985), followed by a major reform in 1989 (CEU 1989a). The 1989 reform was specifically designed to accompany the introduction of the SEM and integrated a number of previously separate EU funding mechanisms, renaming them the 'structural funds'. The EU's structural funds comprise the ERDF, together with the European Social Fund (ESF), the Guidance Section of the European Agricultural Guidance and Guarantee Fund (EAGGF) and, from 1994, a Financial Instrument for Fisheries Guidance (FIFG; see Chapter 21), renamed

the European Fisheries Fund (EFF) in 2007. The Cohesion Fund (CF), also created in 1994, acts like one of the structural funds in many ways, although it is not strictly one of them.

EU RP continues to this day to be operated in its essential characteristics on the basis of the reform to the structural funds introduced in 1989. The reformed policy provided the basis for further reforms in 1994 (designed to accompany steps towards EMU; CEU 1996d) and 1999 (designed to prepare the way for enlargement, to include the Central and Eastern European Countries, CEECs; CEU 2000c). The 1994 and 1999 reforms both incorporated massive increases in funding for EU RP, resulting in its current status as the second largest EU policy. The 1999 reforms were for the programming period 2000–6. The current programming period is 2007–13 and this followed yet another major reform in 2007. While this most recent set of reforms again left the 1989 system largely intact, the need to try to cope with the challenges posed by eastern enlargement has meant that the 2007 reform had to be a far-reaching one (CEU 2006l, m, n).

22.4.2 EU regional policy 2007–2013: cohesion policy

As noted earlier, the current 2007–13 EU RP, now named cohesion policy, is being operated in all of its essential characteristics on the basis of the major reform to the structural funds of 1989. In order to ensure that funding is as precisely targeted as possible (the principle of *concentration*), since 1989 the structural funds have been given the task of attaining specific *priority objectives*. At one time there were no fewer than seven priority objectives. During 2007–13 these have been cut back to just three, as Table 22.1 shows.

Objective 1 (called the lagging regions objective between 1989 and 2006, and the convergence objective in 2007–13) is focused on the most disadvantaged EU regions – that is, those whose GDP per capita, at purchasing power parities, is less than 75 per cent of the EU average – and is designed to help them to catch up – that is, converge – with the rest of the EU. This objective is by far the most generously funded of the three, commanding some 81.4 per cent of total funding in 2007–13 (€282.9 billion at current prices), and with less stringent requirements than for the other objectives

Table 22.1 Priority objectives in the 2007–13 budget period

Priority objective	Funds
1. *Convergence* To speed up the real convergence of the least developed regions and member states	ERDF ESF CF
2. *Regional competitiveness and employment* Strengthening regions' competitiveness and attractiveness, as well as employment through innovation, the knowledge society and investment in human resources	ERDF ESF
3. *European territorial cooperation* To strengthen cross-border cooperation through joint local and regional initiatives – cross-border, transnational and inter-regional cooperation	ERDF

in terms of percentages of investment costs met and national matching funding targets.

Since the EU sets the criterion for eligibility for Objective 1 regions, the map of eligible regions is effectively set by Brussels, not by MSs. Figure 22.3 shows the eligible regions during 2007–13. As can be seen from the figure, within the EU15 the Objective 1 regions are concentrated in the southern Mediterranean and in parts of Ireland and the UK. The figure reveals that the accession of NMS12 in 2004/7 brought in a huge swathe of regions in CEECs that are automatically eligible. Indeed, apart from Malta and Cyprus, only small enclaves within the NMS12 – for example, Prague – are *not* automatically eligible for assistance.

Although the EU RP budget was increased for the current 2007–13 programming period, the sheer scale of regional problems in the NMS12 meant that a major shift eastwards had to be incorporated in funding arrangements for 2007–13. Many regions in Western Europe, particularly in Finland, Greece, Ireland, Italy, the UK and Sweden, which had formerly enjoyed Objective 1 funding, found that they lost this in 2007. These are shown in Figure 22.3 as 'phasing in' and 'phasing out' regions. Phasing in regions are those whose growth rates prior to 2007 had been sufficient to lift their GDP per capita values above the Objective 1 threshold and hence would have lost Objective 1 status after 2007 in any event. Phasing out regions, sometimes called statistical effect regions, are those unfortunate enough to have fallen foul of the fact that the accession of the twelve much poorer NMSs in 2004/7 led to a significant fall in overall average GDP per capita in the EU. These are therefore regions that would have

retained their status in 2007–13 had the EU remained at the EU15, but which found themselves exceeding the 75 per cent GDP per capita criterion for Objective 1, which by 2007 was based on the lower EU27 average. Some transitional assistance has continued in 2007–13 for the phasing in and phasing out regions in the EU15, but this is quite small (only €11.4 billion and €14 billion respectively).

Objective 2, as Table 22.1 shows, is called the regional competitiveness and employment objective. The name reflects the desire to use EU RP not only as a means of providing relief for very poor regions, but also to help the EU as a whole to maintain its competitiveness in an increasingly competitive global trading environment. During the 2007–13 period, EU RP is expected to throw its weight behind the so-called EU Lisbon Agenda objectives – growth, competitiveness and environmental sustainability (see Chapter 14). The name of Objective 2 closely reflects the Lisbon Agenda ideals, and the Commission's detailed guidelines for EU RP in 2007–13 are based very firmly on growth and competitiveness aims (CEU 2006l, m). The types of policies favoured by Objective 2 are also very much focused on competitiveness – policies to stimulate innovation, the knowledge society, entrepreneurship, the protection of the environment and the enhancement of workers' skills.

Figure 22.3 suggests that the areas eligible for Objective 2 comprise all regions other than Objective 1 regions – that is, effectively a non-regional objective. This is misleading, however, because MSs are allowed to establish their own priorities and eligible areas (within the budget limits set by the Commission).

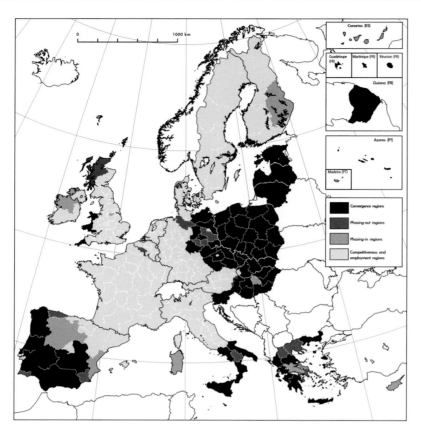

Figure 22.3 Cohesion policy eligible areas, 2007–13 *Source*: Drawn by Armstrongs' technical staff, using data from Eurostat, obtained from the DG Regions website (http://ec.europa.eu/regional_policy).

In practice, a diverse range of regions receive support, including regions suffering from industrial – that is, manufacturing – decline, certain disadvantaged rural areas, certain urban areas suffering severe economic, social and environmental problems, fishing communities in decline, and a series of regions suffering geographic handicaps, such as islands, mountainous regions and the very remote, outermost EU regions (the Azores, the Canary Islands, Madeira, Guadeloupe, Réunion, Martinique and French Guyana). Objective 2 is much less generously funded than Objective 1, being allocated only €55 billion for the 2007–13 period, only 15.8 per cent of the EU RP budget.

Finally, as Table 22.1 shows, there is Objective 3: European territorial cohesion. This has been allocated only a small pot of money (€8.7 billion or 2.5 per cent of the 2007–13 EU RP budget) to stimulate cross-border and transnational economic development initiatives.

It builds on previous small, yet successful cross-border schemes funded under a programme called Interreg, but is in fact rather more significant than either its name or small budget suggests. As noted in the introduction to this chapter, the EU has long been concerned with reducing economic and social disparities. However, in the 2007–13 period a commitment to territorial cohesion has been added to economic and social cohesion. Strengthening the drive for better territorial cohesion is currently being actively debated within the Commission for the post-2013 EU RP. The nature of spatial imbalances within the EU, notably core–periphery issues, disparities between the performances of the major cities of both the core and periphery, urban–rural system dysfunction and the challenges of regions with specific geographic handicaps have been highlighted (Monfort 2008). The precise meaning of territorial cohesion also continues to be debated

Table 22.2 Regional policy in 2007–13: indicative allocations (€ million, current prices)

Country	Convergence	Regional competitiveness and employment	Territorial cohesion objective	Total
Austria	177	1,027	257	1,461
Belgium	638	1,425	194	2,258
Bulgaria	6,674	0	179	6,853
Cyprus	213	399	28	640
Czech Rep.	26,423	419	389	26,692
Denmark	0	510	103	613
Estonia	3,404	0	52	3,456
Germany	16,079	9,409	851	26,340
Greece	19,575	635	210	20,420
Finland	0	1,596	120	1,716
France	3,191	10,257	872	14,319
Hungary	22,890	2,031	386	25,307
Ireland	0	751	151	901
Italy	21,641	6,325	846	28,812
Latvia	4,531	0	90	4,620
Lithuania	6,775	0	109	6,885
Luxembourg	0	50	15	65
Malta	840	0	15	855
Netherlands	0	1,660	247	1,907
Poland	66,553	0	731	67,284
Portugal	20,473	938	99	21,511
Romania	19,213	0	455	19,668
Slovakia	10,912	449	227	11,588
Slovenia	4,101	0	104	4,205
Spain	26,180	8,477	559	35,217
Sweden	0	1,626	265	1,891
UK	2,912	6,979	722	10,613
Inter-regional	0	0	455	455
Tech. assistance	0	0	0	868
Total	282,855	54,965	8,723	347,410

Notes:
1 Due to rounding, figures may not add up exactly to the totals shown.
2 'Convergence' objective column includes Cohesion Fund (€69,578 million) and phasing out funding (€13,955 million).
3 'Regional competitiveness and employment' column includes phasing in funding (€11,409 million).
Source: Commission DG Regional Policy website

(Armstrong *et al.* 2010), but it is clear that Objective 3 and its successor after 2013 will be about much more than simply cross-border and transnational schemes.

As noted earlier, Objective 1 dominates the structural funds. Table 22.2 sets out the indicative allocations for MSs for funding in 2007–13 ('indicative' since the actual expenditures will depend on how MSs and regions actually spend the money over the full budget period).

Table 22.2 illustrates both the dominance of Objective 1 funding (81.4 per cent of the total 2007–13 budget) and also just how much money is being targeted on the NMS12 (€178,503 million or 51.3 per cent of the total budget), despite the presence of transitional funding within EU15 countries. Transition funding is only a small amount of the total, comprising some €13,955 million (4.02 per cent of the budget) for the phasing out regions and €11,409 million (3.28 per cent of the budget) for the phasing in regions – the safety net for (mostly) EU15 regions losing eligibility as a result of eastern enlargement is therefore not a very large one.

22.4.3   Strategic planning, programming, partnership and additionality

As well as the commitment to concentration of assistance and much closer coordination of the activities of the EU's financial instruments, the EU RP that has emerged in the aftermath of the 1989 reforms places great emphasis on four further principles. They are the use of a system of multi-annual programmes of assistance; the need for a close partnership between all those involved in EU RP; a commitment to subsidiarity (the retention at EU level of the minimum necessary powers; see Chapter 2); and a desire that EU money should be a genuine supplement to EU RP spending by MSs (additionality). None of these principles was entirely new to the 1989 reform package, but the 1989 reforms represented the first comprehensive attempt to create an EU RP delivery system that would allow the principles to be achieved. These four great principles continue to underpin EU RP.

22.5 Some key issues for the future

EU RP has shown itself to be capable of evolution and change over the years since its introduction in 1975. Some of the key issues that EU RP must confront in the immediate future are legacies of the past – for example, additionality and the underfunding of the policy. Others, such as the response of EU RP to EMU and eastern enlargement, are much newer issues. Each will be considered in turn.

22.5.1   The challenge of eastern enlargement

The EU has always found it necessary to make changes to EU RP whenever new accessions have occurred.

In most cases this has taken the form of an increase in the EU RP budget and a re-designation of the map of the assisted areas, but without the fundamental principles of the policy itself being disturbed. At first sight, the current 2007–13 EU RP appears to be simply another new episode in this process of accommodating new MSs. Unfortunately, the eastern enlargements of 2004/7 have proved much more difficult to deal with, and the resulting decisions for the 2007–13 period leave a lot to be desired. As Figures 22.1 and 22.2 have shown, NMSs continue to have much lower GDP per capita levels than most of Western Europe and also, by and large, higher unemployment rates. The problems posed by eastern enlargement have clearly not been fully resolved thus far by the 2007–13 EU RP. On the contrary, a series of issues remain. Each will be considered in turn.

Institutional capacity and corruption

Many of the NMS12, despite rapid progress in some countries, remain within a painful period of adjustment and transition from their former communist economic, legal and political systems towards a more Western model. This fact alone is of major importance for EU RP because it means that the governance structures in some of the acceding states continue to make it difficult for them to effectively absorb cohesion policy money directed at them. Nor is it just a question of effectively absorbing the money going their way. Many of the NMSs lack strong regional tier governments and are frequently highly centralized, having limited administrative capacity in the more peripheral regions. Moreover, closely associated with institutional and legal capacity problems is the issue of corruption. Corruption, of course, is by no means confined to CEECs. The EU has struggled, however, to prevent fraud in EU15 RP programmes, and the challenge in some of the NMSs is an even greater one.

The underfunding of regional policy

The EU budget is dominated by two items: CAP and cohesion policy. Between them they command the majority of the full EU budget (see Chapter 19). The economic decline in many of the CEECs which followed the collapse of Communism in the early 1990s, together with the decision to encourage them to seek early accession, triggered an enormous debate on how the challenge to adequately fund EU RP in both the

NMSs and the EU15 could be met. This challenge was even more severe as several NMSs are major agricultural producers and hence became eligible for very large CAP assistance, as well as cohesion policy. The 2007–13 budget decisions taken by the EU were effectively a compromise. The NMS12 have indeed seen their eligibility for both CAP and cohesion policy funding honoured. However, to avoid a massive increase in the overall size of the EU budget, the NMS12 have had to accept a phasing in, year on year, between 2007 and 2013, of the funding allocated to them, while simultaneously many regions in EU15 countries, as we have seen, have lost cohesion policy eligibility and been given less generous EU RP help. EU RP is therefore even more underfunded than it was prior to NMS accession. It is therefore perhaps unsurprising that regional disparities remain so large in the EU. This problem would almost certainly have continued after 2013 even had the global recession of 2008/9 not occurred. The nature of the current recession is likely to exacerbate the underfunding issue for many years to come. The major public sector spending cuts triggered in countries facing sovereign debt problems, starting with Greece in 2010, mean that MSs' own RP budgets have come under severe pressure in the very EU countries with the most severe regional problems. If MSs' RP budgets are heavily cut, the burden will shift further to the already underfunded EU cohesion policy.

The regional impact of enlargement

Eastern enlargement has posed a further challenge to cohesion policy. As noted earlier, each act of economic integration tends to produce a set of broad core–periphery effects within the EU, and also a distinctive geographic pattern of losing and gaining regions. Eastern enlargement is also thought likely to be having its own distinctive set of regional impacts within the EU15 MSs. Estimates suggest that it has been the new entrants themselves that have gained most. However, within the EU15 it is likely that it will be the relatively prosperous regions of the north of the EU (especially in Germany, France and the UK) that will eventually gain the most from eastern enlargement, particularly Germany (Baldwin *et al.* 1997). The structural funds within the existing EU15 countries are therefore having to cope not only with budget cuts and restricted eligible areas, but also with a new set of strains on the existing regional disparities.

22.5.2 EU regional policy and EMU

The attainment of EMU for the majority of the EU15 MSs in 2002 has important implications for EU RP that have yet to be confronted. EMU is effectively a further step in the long process of economic integration. Like the customs union and the SEM, for example, EMU is certainly resulting in a distinctive regional footprint, combined with some general core–periphery effects. Moreover, all regions are experiencing structural change as the full implications of EMU work their way through the economic system. That this would occur has been known for many years (CEU 1990a; Emerson *et al.* 1991).

Precisely what the regional impacts of EMU will be remains a controversial issue, and one made more uncertain by the fact that some MSs, such as the UK, have not yet decided when (if ever) they will join the Eurozone. The SGP continues to bring pressure to bear on MSs' budgets, and hence on their ability to ameliorate regional problems by way of public spending in disadvantaged regions. In the longer term it remains very unclear whether EMU will lead to convergence or divergence in regional disparities. By accelerating the process of economic integration, EMU should enhance the convergence forces at the heart of the neoclassical growth model. However, 'the theoretical and empirical evidence suggests that convergence can occur, but it is not inevitable' (Ardy *et al.* 2002, p. 17). Those who take a less sanguine view of the regional impact of EMU point to the loss of exchange rate and monetary policy powers that have been used in the past by some MSs to protect their weaker regions.

The Eurozone is also some distance from being an optimum currency area (OCA; see Chapters 10 and 11). The inadequate nature of labour and capital mobility within the EU, together with the absence of the kinds of inter-state and interpersonal fiscal transfer mechanisms that exist in genuine federal states (and which cushion economic changes with adverse regional effects), remains a serious worry. Just how serious a concern this might be has been revealed by the sovereign debt crisis in the EU in 2010, beginning with enormous pressure on Greece to fund its large budget deficit, but also the pressure on other EU MSs, particularly in the south of the EU, and NMSs with similar problems. OCA theory suggests that the inability of countries such as Greece to devalue, together with the absence of US-type federal fiscal transfers, means that additional unemployment and real wage decline will occur in the MSs most affected. There is no other way for them to regain their competitiveness. EU regional problems may well worsen, therefore, in the immediate future.

22.5.3 Attaining the Lisbon Agenda objectives

The 2007–13 cohesion policy places great emphasis on refocusing EU RP on 'hard' economic objectives, particularly the enhancement of competitiveness in international markets. This is an enormous challenge. By definition, EU RP must spend its resources in some of the most deprived parts of the EU. Even within the relatively more prosperous parts of the EU15 it has not in the past proved easy to ensure that EU RP funds are well spent. This is, after all, one of the reasons why the regional disparities are proving so stubborn to eliminate. The 1990s saw what can best be described as 'mission creep' in structural funds programmes, with many types of projects having rather 'softer' environmental, social inclusion and anti-discriminatory objectives being funded. It continues to be very difficult for disadvantaged regions to find sufficient suitable projects that can meet the harsher requirements of the Lisbon Agenda.

22.5.4 Additionality and subsidiarity

Despite the successive reforms of the structural funds, it is clear that additionality remains a serious problem for EU RP. MSs faced with domestic public sector budget problems will always be tempted to cut their local regional policy efforts as EU RP is expanded. Similar comments apply to subsidiarity, where some MSs remain reluctant to release powers to regional and local partners.

22.6 Conclusion: regional policy after 2013

Attention has already shifted to the nature of EU RP that will follow the current 2007–13 programme. The debate on the nature and extent of policies aimed at territorial cohesion has been noted already in this chapter

and will figure prominently in any new reforms. More surprising has been the attack on the very basis of EU RP. The continued sluggish pace of convergence of economic disparities across the EU, together with rather disappointing (to some) evidence from the formal evaluations of EU RP for the 2000–6 period (CEU 2010e), have triggered some to question the very existence of EU RP. This was put most lucidly in the Sapir Report (Sapir *et al.* 2003a), which, while it did not call for a complete abolition, did criticize the effectiveness of EU RP and called for it to be redirected to become much more of a policy for the CEECs – that is, not really an RP policy at all – and for more focused priority objectives.

The Commission has mounted a vigorous defence of EU RP. The Barca Report (Barca 2009) has set out a detailed restatement of the economic, social and political governance case for a strong EU RP, drawing together arguments from new theories of regional development and empirical evidence of the processes at work. The Barca Report argues not only for the retention of a strong EU RP after 2013, but also for a more focused policy effort. The traditional twin *efficiency* and *equity* aims for EU RP are retained and restated, with the more modern and wider aim of 'social inclusion' replacing the rather narrower income redistribution aim embodied in 'equity'. However, the Report strongly urges a much tighter focus within these two broad aims on policies for innovation, climate change, migration, children, skills and ageing. The debate continues (CEU 2008d), but the two reports have been timely reminders that EU RP must continue to both reinvent itself and produce strong evidence of its success if it is to survive.

The 2008/9 global recession also poses new challenges that will almost certainly spill over into 2013 and beyond. All recessions have their own distinctive geographic footprints. Traditionally it was manufacturing regions that tended to suffer the most in recessions. This cannot now be taken for granted. The particular geographic footprint of the current recession is not yet known and it will be some time before it becomes clear. It is likely that regional disparities will worsen somewhat in the EU, since the less competitive regions, by definition, tend to struggle most when times are hard. Traditionally, recessions have also posed challenges for those seeking to justify an RP. When unemployment is high in all regions it is difficult to justify subsidies only to some. The evidence of past recessions suggests that EU RP needs to adapt to economic downturns by switching emphasis from 'softer' help to businesses towards infrastructure and training policies. These, it is argued, lay the foundations for a stronger and longer recovery in the disadvantaged regions. It will be interesting to track how well EU RP can adapt to the new situation.

Summary

- The EU has demonstrated a continuing commitment to RP since its inception in 1957. However, EU RP originated in 1975 with the creation of the first ERDF. It was greatly expanded in 1989, and then again in 1994, 2000 and 2007. Three funds currently combine to lead the attack on regional problems: the ERDF, the ESF and the CF.
- In 2010 EU RP (now called cohesion policy) commanded 34.9 per cent of the full EU budget, making it the second largest spending programme after CAP.
- The economic case for EU RP being complementary to those of the individual MSs is both complex and multi-faceted. The key justifications lie in the mutual self-interest of MSs in tackling regional problems; the EU ability to collect and target funds on the most disadvantaged regions; and in order to bring about better coordination of RP effort.
- EU regional disparities, particularly those depicted by the very important GDP per capita criterion, show a broadly core–periphery pattern, with most of the disadvantaged regions being in the east and south of the EU27.
- EU regional problems are not just severe, but are also very diverse in nature, ranging from lagging regions with very low GDP per capita, to regions suffering industrial decline, declining fishing and rural areas and very remote 'outermost territories'.
- The process by which lagging regions catch up with the more prosperous ones has proved to be a slow and intermittent one within the EU. In recent years progress has been painfully slow, with convergence between countries being accompanied by widening of disparities *within* many MSs. This suggests a rough balance between forces of convergence and divergence at the present time.

- Current EU RP has three priority objectives: convergence (81.5 per cent of the budget), regional competitiveness and employment (16 per cent) and territorial cohesion (2.5 per cent).
- In the years ahead EU RP faces a number of key challenges: how to cope with the continuing effects of eastern enlargement in 2004 and 2007, a process that brought many highly disadvantaged regions into the EU; continued underfunding; meeting the impact of the regional effects of EMU; and attacks on the very basis of the policy itself.

Questions and essay topics

1. What is the *economic* justification for an EU RP separate from that of individual MSs? Do you think that there are also *social* or *political* justifications too?
2. Since the beginning of the global recession in 2008, to what extent has EMU, in the form of the Growth and Stability Pact (see Chapters 11 and 12), helped or hindered MSs with many disadvantaged regions – for example, Greece, Spain – in their attempts to tackle their regional problems?
3. What economic processes can lead to regional disparities *narrowing* over time, and what processes can lead to their *widening*?
4. Can a case be made for strengthening RP in order to help the EU meet its wider Lisbon Agenda competitiveness and employment objectives?

FURTHER READING

Bachtler, J. and Gorzelak, G. (2009) 'Reforming EU regional policy: a reappraisal of the performance of the structural funds', in D. Bailey and L. de Propis (eds.), *Industrial and Regional Policies in an Enlarging EU*, Routledge, London.

CEU (2008d) *Regions 2020: An Assessment of Future Challenges for EU Regions*, Commission Staff Working Document SEC(2008), Brussels.

CEU (2008) *Turning Territorial Diversity into Strength: Green Paper on Territorial Cohesion*, Office for Official Publications of the European Communities, Brussels.

Moore, C. (2008) 'A Europe of the regions vs. the regions of Europe', *Regional and Federal Studies*, vol. 18.

23 Social policies: the employment dimension

BRIAN ARDY AND ALI EL-AGRAA

23.1 Introduction

Social policy is a broad term that could encompass government policies on education, health, employment, social security, social exclusion, and the like.[1] There are very wide divergences in these policies in the member states (MSs) of the European Union (EU), and because they are related to the nature of society and considered sensitive, they are issues of high political salience. This meant that a uniform policy was not possible, that decision-making powers had to remain with MSs and that policies would differ across MSs.

The next section looks at the development of social and employment policy, and the rest of this chapter examines EU employment policy, in particular the European Employment Strategy (EES). There is a consideration of the economic theory and evidence relating to employment performance on which the EES is based. Then the nature of open method of coordination is analysed and EU employment performance is discussed, particularly in relation to EES targets. The final assessment considers the relationship between the EES and EU employment performance.

23.2 The development of social and employment policy

In the 1957 EEC Treaty, social policy was restricted to the free movement of labour[2] and gender equality in payment terms, and political sensitivities in these areas were recognized by insisting on unanimous decision-making. These two policies were established in the 1960s, but further initiatives were limited until the Single European Market (SEM; see Chapter 7) in the 1980s. The SEM encouraged further social policy development for two reasons: first, there were fears that SEM competition would encourage a race to the bottom in social policy areas affecting companies' costs, such as working conditions; second, there was a desire to show that the SEM was not just about big business, but that it benefited working people too. Thus the 1987 Single European Act (SEA) included working conditions as part of EC policy, and began to extend qualified majority voting (QMV; see Chapter 3) to these 'traditional' areas of social policy.

This process was further developed by the 1989 Social Charter (which led to an extension of EU social policy in the Maastricht Treaty), a process that was carried through in the subsequent Amsterdam, Nice and Lisbon treaties. This means that today the free movement of labour, gender equality, working conditions, worker information/consultation, modernization of social protection, public health and coordination of social security are all areas of EU social policy, hence decided by QMV, with the European Court of Justice (ECJ; see Chapters 3 and 4) ruling on the application of legislation.[3] Other areas are potentially within the EU remit but require unanimous agreement by MSs; they include anti-discrimination, social security, protection of workers (employment termination) and employment of third country nationals. Some of these areas are subject to a separate mode of policy development: the open method of coordination (OMC). So although it is still true that welfare considerations remain national, with the EU not responsible for individual entitlements, national government's sovereignty in social policy is increasingly constrained within a Europeanized multi-tiered policy process.

Although social and employment policies remain very differentiated across the EU, there is a view that there is a distinctive European social model (ESM), which is differentiated from the US market-driven model. The ESM involves generous benefits and a high level of rights for workers, with the USA's being very limited in both respects. The ESM is justified not only on social grounds, but also in efficiency terms: it is argued that workers' greater attachment to the companies they work for results in higher productivity and a better trained workforce. The US model is supposed to protect workers by encouraging high levels of job creation as a result of the flexibility of the workforce and a more entrepreneurial culture. The challenge to the ESM is maintaining the benefits in the face of a recession, with rising unemployment and an ageing population. The challenge for the EU is generating jobs to replace those that have been lost in the recession. The ESM has influenced EU employment policy, which has to try to balance high benefits and workers' rights with sufficient flexibility to try to improve employment performance, but whether this has been successful is disputed (Raveaud 2007).

This chapter will concentrate on employment policy for four reasons. First, employment encompasses many of these areas of social policy. Second, the complex nature of EU decision-making is well illustrated in the employment arena. Third, employment policy is the most important aspect of social policy not only for economists, but also for specialists in other social disciplines. Fourth, we are not qualified to deal with its sociological and psychological considerations. Employment policy has also become increasingly important in the EU as the result of a generally deteriorating employment performance and the consequent EU desire to be seen as taking action on this important issue. The SEM has limited MSs' room for manoeuvre in employment policy and increased the importance of ensuring that competition is fair. EMU (see Chapters 10–12) has meant that Eurozone countries can no longer rely on changes in exchange rates to remain price competitive, so the ability to adjust depends on wage rates being flexible.

23.3 The development of the European Employment Strategy

The following areas of government policies affect employment and, because these policies are bound up with national traditions and institutions, they also differ substantially between MSs:

1. *Taxation*. Income taxes affect choices over whether to work, how much to work, where to work and what work to do. Other taxes can have similar effects. Income taxes have a negative substitution effect on work by making leisure cheaper, and a positive income effect by making workers poorer and so encouraging them to work more. Income tax and social security contributions combine to determine the overall tax on labour. Implicit tax rates[4] on labour in the EU27 in 2008 averaged 36.5 per cent, but there is a wide variation, between 20.2 per cent in Malta and 42.8 per cent in Italy[5] (Eurostat 2010c).

2. *Social security*. This affects choices over whether to work and how much to work, and interacts with the tax system, to give rise to unemployment traps (very high rates of tax on moving from unemployment to employment). It is not only the levels of benefit that are important, but their duration, the qualifications for receiving them and the way the system is administered.

3. *Education and training*. These are important in determining the quality of the workforce, its skills and adaptability, and thus its employability. With the increasing rate of structural change in the economy, the emphasis is on lifelong learning, so that workers are able to use new technology and to move into new occupations. The quality of education and training systems varies a great deal across the EU (OECD 2006b).

4. *Employment protection*. This refers to the legal rights of workers, particularly with regard to dismissal/redundancy and types of employment – fixed-term versus permanent, part-time versus full-time. The EU has a wide range of employment protection, from very limited protection in the UK, Ireland and the new member states (NMSs), to high levels of protection in Sweden, Germany and Italy.

5. *Employment services*. This covers the provision of advice, information and incentives to encourage unemployed workers to find new jobs. These services can be supplied by public or private employment agencies. They will be important in determining the efficiency with which the unemployed are matched with vacancies.

6. *Industrial relations*. This is the system by which workers and employers reach agreement over wages and other conditions of employment. Collective bargaining between trade unions and employers is the norm, but this can take place at the plant, company, industry or even, to a certain extent, the

national level (Ireland and the Netherlands have national agreements to determine overall wage increases). So there is a spectrum ranging from the very decentralized in the UK and NMSs, to centralized systems in many other EU countries.

7. *Minimum wages.* These are fixed by legislation. Some EU countries do not have minimum wages – for example, Italy[6] – and even where they do exist, their level in relation to average wages varies a great deal, from less than 29.1 per cent in Romania to 50.5 per cent in Luxembourg (Eurostat 2009b).

8. *Active labour market measures.* These are policies to try to influence employment directly – for example, employment subsidies, work experience, training. Active measures try to increase the possibility of employment, while passive measures just provide the unemployed with financial support. Sweden has invested heavily in such measures, while they are much less important in other countries such as Greece and Spain.

Given the sensitivity of the issue, it is not surprising that in the heady high-growth, low-unemployment era of the 1950s employment was not a central issue for the EEC Treaty. However, a high level of employment is now one of the major aims of the common economic policy in the treaties. Employment was referred to in Article 118 in connection with European collaboration in the field of social policy, but employment policy played only a subordinate role compared to the – mainly neoliberally inspired – economic integration of this period. Community activities were therefore limited to the coordination of national social policies, including measures concerning the free movement of workers (Articles 48–51), the European Social Fund (Articles 123–7) and vocational training measures (Article 128).

In the 1960s low unemployment was the norm, so employment was not a European issue, but this all came to an end with the oil crises of the 1970s. Growth slowed, employment fell and unemployment increased. In the early post-war period US unemployment had been higher than European unemployment, but after 1974 European unemployment rose faster, and while US unemployment fell from the early 1980s, Europe's remained high (see Figure 23.1).

The EU response to the oil shocks was MS-based: governments tried to solve their own problems with

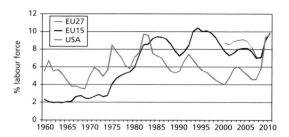

Figure 23.1 Unemployment in the EU and the USA, 1960–2010 *Source*: Eurostat 2010b

macroeconomic expansion and the new protectionism. There were some EU action programmes on social policy, but coordination of national employment policies remained limited. With EU unemployment high, and generally poor economic performance in the 1970s and early 1980s, the SEM was developed (see Chapter 7). It was hoped that this would raise EU economic performance, creating jobs and reducing unemployment (Emerson *et al.* 1988). These hopes were not fulfilled, and unemployment rose even higher in the early 1990s. Since then, however, the rise in EU employment and the fall in EU15 unemployment have been taken by some as indication of a fundamental shift of performance (Boeri and Garibaldi 2009). This seems rather premature given the rise in unemployment in the recent recession. Nevertheless, in 2009 EU and US unemployment levels were similar, although the better recessionary performance in Europe has meant that employment has fallen less than output, so productivity has been hit (OECD 2010a).

The continuation of weak employment performance in the 1980s meant that the fight against unemployment was becoming a major EC objective, and employment policy shifted from being a facet of social policy to an important aspect of economic policy. Given concerns over public support for the EC, the EC had to be seen to be tackling the major economic problem of the time. The aim of a high level of employment was – for the first time – integrated into the EC legal framework with Article 2 of the Maastricht Treaty in 1992. This development was supported by the 1993 Delors White Paper on growth, competitiveness and employment (CEU 1993b) and the 1994 European Council summit in Essen. The summit also introduced a multilateral monitoring mechanism for employment, and the emphasis of policy was shifted from employment protection towards employment promotion (Ferrera *et al.* 2000, pp. 77–8). Five priorities were identified, which later became central to the EES: improving employment opportunities; increasing the employment intensity of growth; developing active labour market policies; adopting measures to entice the long-term unemployed back to work; and reducing non-wage labour costs.

This 'Essen Strategy' was included in the 1997 Amsterdam Treaty, to promote broader convergence between MSs' employment policies by involving a wide range of political and social actors, while at the same time national labour market systems were to be respected. The integration of the title into the Treaty on European Union (TEU) was in order to foster the development of an EU employment strategy, particularly promoting 'skilled, trained and adaptable workforce and labour markets responsive to economic change with a view to achieving the objectives defined in Article 2 of TEU and in Article 2 of this Treaty' (Article 125). The same year, a special European Council on employment took place in Luxembourg to put into operation the new coordination mechanism. Hence the employment chapter became effective before the official ratification of the treaty by MSs; the Essen Strategy became the Luxembourg process; and the EES was launched. The Lisbon European Council added the non-binding target of an employment rate of 70 per cent by 2010 (European Council 2000c). The Stockholm European Council set additional targets of a 60 per cent female employment rate and a 50 per cent employment rate for older people (55–64 years; European Council 2001).

23.4 Employment performance: economic theory and evidence

The rising long-term trend in EU unemployment and its associated low level of employment have been subject to extensive economic research. Of particular interest has been the disparity in measured performance between the USA and the EU, and the very substantial differences between European countries. This section surveys this research in order to identify the way in which economic systems and institutions may be modified to promote higher employment.

The labour market in advanced economies is subject to constant change, with myriad factors altering demand and supply conditions. Some firms and sectors are shedding workers, while others are hiring new workers. This process determines the overall volume of job creation,[7] which will in turn depend on levels of and changes in wage rates, the structure of wages[8] and productivity. Given the complexity of this process, there will always be frictional, structural and regional unemployment. Beyond this, unemployment will be determined by real demand, and in the long term unemployment will tend towards a level consistent with stable inflation – the natural rate of unemployment (NAWRU; see page 378). Unless wages are flexible, wage rates may not adjust to ensure that supply and demand are reconciled at a reasonably high level of employment/low level of unemployment. The functioning of the labour market and its institutions will influence the extent of this unemployment by determining the efficiency with which the unemployed and vacancies are matched, and the flexibility of wages.

Economic theory suggests that unemployment can be viewed in two extreme ways. First, frictionless equilibrium: in this case, labour markets adjust rapidly to shocks (productivity, oil prices or interest rates) and the market is generally near to its long-term equilibrium with regard to unemployment (NRU; or rather the non-accelerating inflation rate of unemployment, NAIRU; see Chapter 10, page 152). Thus the actual employment rate approximates to the long-term equilibrium rate – the rate at which trade unions, employers and workers have no tendency to change their behaviour, provided the exogenous variables that they face do not change. Second, prolonged adjustment: in this case, the response of the labour market to external shocks is sluggish because of the costs and difficulty of adjustment. In such a labour market unemployment can differ substantially from the long-term equilibrium rate for prolonged periods because of this hysteresis. In this case, Keynesian remedies of expanding demand could have long-term effects on employment. With these as the polar cases, most economists believe that actual labour market behaviour contains elements of both extremes. The positioning on the spectrum between these extremes will have a strong effect on the explanations for unemployment and the policy prescriptions for its reduction.

Besides differences in the dynamics with which equilibrium is approached, the concept of equilibrium can be viewed in stock or flow terms. Stock approaches consider the relationship between the employment from firms (aggregate demand for labour) and the available work-force (aggregate supply of labour).[9] Flow approaches consider the relationships between people entering and leaving unemployment over a period of time. So the stock approaches emphasize the total number of unemployed, and the flow approaches the turnover of the unemployed and the length of unemployment.

23.4.1 Labour market flexibility

The EES can be regarded as building on the Organization for Economic Cooperation and Development (OECD) jobs strategy (OECD 1994, 1997) and is concerned with raising labour market efficiency, based on the frictionless equilibrium models of the market. Here the labour market, and in particular the real wage, will respond to shocks to establish the NRU. The actual unemployment rate lies close to the long-term equilibrium, and the upward trend in EU unemployment is therefore the result of exogenous changes that affect the efficiency of the market in creating employment and reducing unemployment (Layard *et al.* 1991; Morgan and Mourougane 2001). The dynamics of the process are seen to have little effect on the NRU (Nickell 1997; Blanchard and Wolfers 2000; Daveri and Tabellini 2000). Rising unemployment is in this view the result of changes in structural factors affecting the NRU.

The stock of workers and the flow into the market will largely be determined by demographics,[10] with younger workers and women returnees entering the labour market and older workers retiring or becoming inactive. An efficient labour market would find work for the available workforce, so an increase in younger people, with their higher employment rate, could lead to an increase in employment and a decrease in the unemployment rate. Shimer (1998) suggests that 70 per cent of the fall in US unemployment since 1979 could be attributed to demographics. But others believe that the workforce is endogenous to employment opportunities because of variations in the participation rate and immigration (Garibaldi and Mauro 2002, p. 84).

The prospects of finding jobs for those entering the workforce and for the unemployed depend on how well they match the requirements of employers' vacancies in terms of the geographic location of employment, education, skills and experience. They will also depend on the ability of labour market institutions to match the unemployed to the available vacancies.

The willingness of workers to accept jobs will vary with the generosity and availability of benefits compared with the real wage on offer. There are four aspects of the benefit system that could influence equilibrium unemployment: the level of benefits; the duration of benefits; the coverage of the system; and the strictness of its operation. These factors will affect the workers' reservation wage – the wage required to entice an unemployed worker back into employment. The level and duration of benefits do seem to be positively related to the NRU (OECD 2006c, pp. 58–61). Bassanini and Duval (2006) estimate that reducing the gross replacement rate[11] by 10 per cent would decrease the unemployment rate of men aged 25–54 years by 1.2 per cent and increase their employment rate by 1.7 per cent. Generosity of benefits seems to affect the employment rates of young, old and female workers particularly, and to increase the duration of unemployment. However, these disincentive effects can largely be offset by sanctions for failure to undertake job search or to accept reasonable offers of employment (de Koning *et al.* 2004). But changing the rules is not enough; enforcement is crucial (Grubb 2000). Given the large increase in numbers on non-employment benefits in the 1980s and 1990s, which has still to be reversed (OECD 2006c, p. 76), it is important that these activation approaches are extended to non-employment benefits. Otherwise the unemployed can easily end up on these other benefits, nullifying the reforms to unemployment benefit.

Social security contributions and indirect taxes drive a wedge between the wage cost to an employer and the real wage of the employee. The effect of this wedge on the supply and demand for labour depends on sensitivity to wages. The effect on labour supply is ambiguous, because the income effect of taxation encourages work effort, and the substitution effect discourages it. The actual effects are difficult to measure because of the differing circumstances of workers and potential workers, and the complexity of the tax and benefit systems. The effect is greatest where the increase in tax is combined with benefit withdrawal to create unemployment traps: increases in the financial returns of low-wage workers lead to higher levels of employment (OECD 2005d, Chapter 3). The effect seems to be greatest on entry to/exit from the market, rather than on the number of hours worked, and to affect partners in couples with only one worker and lone parents (Carone and Salomäki 2001).

OECD countries exhibit a large increase in the size of the wedge from the 1960s to the 1990s, so this is an obvious candidate to explain the secular rise in unemployment. The effect on unemployment, however, depends crucially on the extent to which employees can pass part of this increase on to employers (Pissarides 1990; Nickell and Layard 1999). Most empirical studies find that the tax wedge is positively related to unemployment and negatively related to employment, and thus accounts for a substantial proportion of the secular rise in unemployment (see, for example, Daveri and Tabellini 2000; Bassanini and Duval 2006).

The number of vacancies available could also be affected by employment protection legislation (EPL). The legal protection of workers will tend to make employers more reluctant to hire workers because it is more difficult to reduce employment. EPL, however, also discourages employers from making workers redundant during a recession. So its effects on unemployment are ambiguous, at least in the short term. Evidence of the effects of employment protection legislation on unemployment is inconclusive (Elmeskov *et al.* 1998; Nickell *et al.* 2002; Bassanini and Duval 2006). Part of the problem here may lie in the difficulty of accurately measuring changes in the severity of EPL, because the devil is in the detail of the legislation and its implementation (Bover *et al.* 2000). While EPL protects existing jobs, it concentrates labour turnover and job insecurity on groups such as young people, women and the long-term unemployed (Bertola *et al.* 2002); partial reform compounds these problems (Blanchard and Landier 2002). It also seems to undermine employment by reducing productivity (Bassanini *et al.* 2009).

Wage levels will also be affected by the strength of trade unions and their ability to bargain for higher wages. This strength cannot be measured directly, so proxies have to be used. Density measures the proportion of workers in trade unions. Coverage is the proportion of workers whose wages are determined as a result of collective bargaining agreements between trade unions and employers. Generally, studies have not found a significant relationship between union density and coverage and unemployment (OECD 2006c, p. 84). This may be, in part, because unions' effect on wages may be offset by coordination[12] of wage bargaining (Nickell *et al.* 2005; Nickell and Layard 1999; Booth *et al.* 2000), which is more likely to occur when unions are strong.

Labour market adjustment can take place via the physical movement of workers – migration. Migration seems to be an important method of adjustment in the USA, but not in the EU. Inter-regional migration is much more sensitive to changes in wage differentials in the USA than in the EU (Eichengreen 1993; Obstfeld and Peri 1998b). Migration from NMSs to the EU15 has been higher (CEU 2006g, pp. 79–84), and this may have been a factor moderating wage growth in Ireland and the UK, but its impact has been marginal for most EU15 countries. For NMSs it does moderate unemployment, but at the expense of the loss of young, enterprising and educated workers, although as the migration may be temporary this effect could ameliorate over time (Diez Guardia and Pichelmann 2006, p. 7). Extra-EU immigration is also significant for some countries, such as Spain, allowing faster employment growth.

Active labour market policies (ALMP) seek to increase the likelihood of the unemployed obtaining a job and encompass a wide range of policies, including training, work experience, employment subsidies and help with job applications. Macroeconometric studies find that increased spending on ALMP reduces unemployment (Scarpetta 1996; Nickell 1997; Elmeskov *et al.* 1998), but there are some statistical problems with these studies. A more sophisticated study indicates that only spending on labour market training reduces unemployment, and that this expenditure can be used to offset the effects of higher unemployment benefit levels (Bassanini and Duval 2006). Studies using micro data show that the efficiency of different types of measure varies: with job search, assistance is generally effective, but employment subsidies are not (Robinson 2000; Martin and Grubb 2001; Kluve 2006).

One important difference between the original OECD (1994) job strategy and the reassessment (OECD 2006d, pp. 18–19) is the recognition that market flexibility is not the only way to improve employment performance. Market flexibility, decentralized wage bargaining, low benefits, low taxation and weak employment protection do raise employment, but with widening income inequality. Flexi-security is an alternative, consisting of coordinated collective bargaining, generous welfare benefits, higher levels of employment protection, and activation of the unemployed through benefit administration and active labour market policies. This achieves high employment and low-income inequality, but with high levels of public expenditure. Successful policies are shaped by and have to respond to the institutional environment of each country. While the EES allows national variation, it is shaped around a common prescription, which may not always be appropriate for the heterogeneous group of countries to which it is applied (Seferiades 2003).

23.4.2 Persistence and unemployment

Alternative explanations stress the importance of lags and persistence mechanisms in the labour market's process of adjustment to shocks. One of the more developed examples is the chain reaction theory of unemployment, which views unemployment as part of a prolonged adjustment process (Henry *et al.* 2000; Karanassou *et al.* 2002; Hall 2009). Rising EU unemployment is the result of the interplay between labour market shocks and the slow process of adjustment to these shocks. Each shock has a chain reaction impact on unemployment, which extends over a considerable period of time. The long-run equilibrium is the NRU, but actual unemployment can differ substantially from this rate, because of its long adjustment. The fundamental difference between these models, therefore, is the speed of the adjustment process.

These differences are important for two reasons. First, the emphasis on policies designed to reduce unemployment will be different according to the view taken of its determination. If it is believed that the rise in EU unemployment is the result of an increase in long-run equilibrium unemployment, then the emphasis will be on factors that influence this equilibrium. Thus the measures taken to reduce it would concentrate, for example, on the amount and duration of unemployment benefits, the wedge, the power of trade unions, and so on. In contrast, if persistence is believed to be the problem, then concentration should be on reducing employment protection and on active labour market policies and training. The effects of policies may be different according to the theoretical perspective. Thus, from the point of view of the NRU, employment protection legislation has an ambiguous effect, discouraging hiring and firing. In terms of persistence, reducing firing costs lessens job inertia and contributes to the reduction in unemployment. Second, the German experience of the shock of unification will have had a much longer-lasting effect on unemployment according to the persistence hypothesis.

23.4.3 The macroeconomy and unemployment

The approach of the jobs strategy and the EES has been criticized as ignoring the other essential component of employment policy – that of macroeconomic management to achieve full employment. The macroeconomic policy mechanisms within the EU are geared towards economic stability, particularly price stability, not full employment. Thus the EES views employment and unemployment as strictly labour market problems (Schettkat 2001) and problems for the unemployed themselves (Serrano Pascual 2003). But employment levels depend crucially on the macroeconomic situation, as is shown by the decline in employment in the current recession. Prolonged periods of high unemployment and high long-term unemployment because of their effect on employability are likely to raise the NRU (Ball 2009). This provides an important reason for government macroeconomic policy to try to limit the rise in unemployment associated with the current recession (International Monetary Fund 2010a).

23.5 The European Employment Strategy

Given the range of policy areas it encompasses, it is not surprising that employment policy derives from several areas of the treaties, and thus different decision-making procedures apply to different aspects. However, the most sensitive areas of employment policy require the unanimous agreement of MSs before EU law can be introduced. There is, of course, some ambiguity over the delineation between these areas: the Work Time Directive was introduced as a health and safety measure, which the UK government contested, but the ECJ confirmed that this was the correct basis for this law.[13] The introduction of the employment title has made clear that the sensitive areas of employment policy will be coordinated under OMC, despite the existence of a treaty base for legislation under the traditional 'community methods'.

23.5.1 The open method of coordination

The OMC is a new method of policy coordination that is being applied to new areas of EU policy. To understand the OMC it is necessary to contrast it with the traditional or classical community method – the coordination of policy by harmonized legislation. The classical method has the following characteristics:

- *Supranational.* Laws are agreed on a Commission proposal by co-decision between the Council and the European Parliament (EP).
- *Uniform.* EC laws provide the basis of the policy, which is applied in the same way across the EU.
- *Enforcement by penalties and incentives.* MSs have to introduce and implement the legislation. Failure to do this could ultimately lead to fines. Where expenditure is involved, compliance with the rules is required to receive funding.
- *Oversight.* The Commission is responsible for the operation of the policy, typically delegated to MSs. Periodic review occurs on the basis of Commission reports, which are considered by the Council and the EP.

The OMC has somewhat different characteristics:

- *Intergovernmental.* Guidelines, not laws, are based on a joint report by the Commission and the Council, with the Council making the decision by qualified majority voting (QMV; see Chapter 3) after consulting the EP.
- *Subsidiarity.* The guidelines contain targets and suggest areas where action is needed, but policies are entirely at the discretion of each MS.
- *Enforcement by recommendation, peer pressure and benchmarking.* Recommendations can be addressed to MSs, but there are no penalties for non-compliance and no financial incentives. But there is peer pressure from other MSs, possible adverse publicity for failure to achieve benchmarks, and learning from the successes and failures of other countries.
- *Oversight.* This is provided by the Council and, to a limited extent, the EP, on the basis of reports by the Commission and the Council.

Thus OMC is a flexible, decentralized instrument of policy coordination, leaving the implementation of measures defined by the EU broadly to MSs. The OMC operates through persuasion, peer pressure ('naming, blaming and shaming'), mutual socialization, epistemic convergence, public accountability and experimental learning, and includes elements of flexibility, subsidiarity, multi-level and policy integration, inclusion and participation, deliberation and

knowledge-sharing (CEU 2002m). 'OMC represents a new form of regulation that is softer than the classical legalistic approach, but is more than a simple non-binding recommendation or a political declaration' (de la Porte and Pochet 2002, p. 12). It can be defined as a new form of soft coordination within the framework of EU decision-making and intergovernmental cooperation procedure, incorporating supranational elements. By issuing guidelines, the OMC develops a relatively clearly defined EU policy in areas that have traditionally been out of the EU remit. Thus, even if the OMC has no binding forces (one of its main weaknesses), it contributes to the development of common views and ideas when it comes to problem-solving in the EU.

23.5.2 The EES process

The EES is part of the annual general economic policy coordination process in the Broad Economic Policy Guidelines, which reviews and coordinates macroeconomic policy and economic reform (see Chapter 12). The Employment Guidelines (EGs) is the document that the EES contributes to this process. EGs specify the objectives and policies to be pursued by MSs to achieve the overall employment targets. EGs are accompanied by Employment Recommendations (ERs), which identify the particular employment problems of each MS and indicate what actions are necessary to tackle these problems. EGs and ERs are adopted by the Council on a Commission proposal, acting by QMV, after consulting the EP, the Economic and Social Committee, the Committee of the Regions and the Employment Committee (see Chapter 3).

EGs, and more particularly ERs, are derived from the Joint Employment Report (JER) prepared by the Commission and the Council. The JER provides an overview of the employment situation and an assessment of the progress made by MSs in the implementation of EGs in the previous year. The remaining challenges for MSs are also highlighted. The JER contains both an analysis of progress across the EU under the major agreed objectives and guidelines, and a brief country-by-country review. Key common indicators underpin the analysis and are summarized in the annexes. The analysis in the JER in turn draws on the reports on MSs, called the National Action Programmes (NAPs). NAPs describe national performance against EES targets and indicators under the various headings, the measures taken and proposals for further action. They are drawn up by national governments in conjunction with lower tiers of government and in consultation with the social partners. This annual cycle can be characterized as a permanent monitoring and review process through the JER, the recommendations to MSs and peer review of policies. This cycle is accompanied by a multi-annual (medium-term/five-year) evaluation of the EES, in which the national and overall progress of EU employment policy is assessed and reviewed.

Until 2003 EES objectives were grouped around four pillars: employability, entrepreneurship, adaptability and equal opportunities. The employability pillar contained both specific objectives, such as reducing youth unemployment and preventing long-term unemployment, and more general ones, such as developing skills. These followed quite closely conventional economic ideas on improving employment performance; hence a more employment-friendly tax and benefit system was an objective. The second pillar, entrepreneurship and job creation, aimed to create and support new businesses, new sources of employment and certain sectors of the economy, particularly services. These aims relate to the general improvement of the economic environment, and therefore the employment performance of the economy. Thus these two pillars are concerned with raising employment performance by improving the operation of the labour market and economic performance more generally.

The third and fourth pillars reflected the EU's wide social objectives for employment policy. Thus the third pillar, adaptability, is concerned with flexibility in work, which affects productivity and hence employment performance, but this had to be achieved with job security. Therefore, although there are minimum standards of employment protection, employment security is seen more in terms of functional flexibility, achieved through high-quality training and lifelong learning. Thus this pillar is concerned with improving employment performance and the quality of work. The fourth pillar, equal opportunities between men and women, was related directly to achieving a 60 per cent employment rate target for women.

EGs were revised for the period 2003–10.[14] The Commission identified four major issues for EES reform (CEU 2002p). First, is the need for clearer objectives. Second, is the need to simplify the policy guidelines. Third, is the need to improve governance. And fourth, is

the need for consistency and complementarity with the BEPG (CEU 2002p). As a result, the Commission now presents the implementation and evaluation of the BEPG, the EES and the IMS (internal market strategy) at the same time each year – in January and after the Spring European Council Summit in April – hence the different areas of economic policy are now synchronized and coordinated.

Instead of the rather ambiguous pillars of the old policy, there are now three clearer, overarching EES objectives (Council 2003c): full employment, improving productivity, and strengthening social cohesion and inclusion. The clearer EES should help the policy become more effective, but there are concerns that the concentration on employment is at the expense of the wider objectives of the policy in areas such as workers' rights and benefits.

23.5.3 The EES and employment policy

The EES is designed to improve EU employment performance by encouraging MSs to redesign their national employment policies, incorporating successful features from other countries. This process is supposed to occur as a result of policy learning, peer review, benchmarking and naming and shaming. While the EES could be criticized for its lack of sanctions, this was inevitable in such a sensitive policy area, and in any case, the effectiveness of such sanctions could be questioned in view of their failure in the coordination of economic policy (see Chapter 12). However, the effectiveness of the policy can be questioned: it is difficult to establish an impact on national policy, and there does not seem to be a clear institutional pathway through which national policy is influenced (Watt 2000). Naming and shaming is unlikely to be effective because of the low public profile of the policy, with very little debate in national parliaments or reporting in the press. Interviews with policy-makers in the UK and Germany suggested that the effect of the strategy on national policy-making was very limited (Ardy and Umbach 2004). The policies introduced were based on national preferences and priorities, although the EES may have had some impact on agenda setting. Similarly, the impact of the peer review process has been minor (Casey and Gold 2005). The involvement of the social partners in the process was also rather perfunctory, and the process was predominantly in the hands of an expert elite. One of the more significant attempts at reform, the Hartz reforms in Germany, do not seem to reflect the EES (Watt 2003), although Kemmerling and Bruttel (2006) find evidence of some policy diffusion. The effect of the EES is also reduced by the extent to which MSs can water down Commission proposals so that the restraints on national policy are substantially reduced (Watt 2004, pp. 131–3). It may be that the effect of the strategy is more subtle, influencing the views of this elite in the long term, and thus gradually influencing policy.

National employment policies have moved in the way that the EES intended. The duration of unemployment benefits has been reduced and conditions tightened, but their generosity has not been decreased. These changes are shared with the rest of the OECD, and some EU15 countries have not implemented changes (OECD 2006c, p. 58). Similar developments can be found for labour taxation, including social security contributions and ALMP, although the record is more patchy for the latter (OECD, 2006c, pp. 89, 70). There are, however, concerns over the extent to which declared intentions carry through to policy; spending on ALMP has not increased, despite falling 'passive' labour market expenditure (European Trade Union Institute 2003, p. 19). What all this seems to indicate is that governments have implemented EES policies where this fitted in with their own priorities (Zeitlin 2005), but whether it will be effective in shaping national employment policies in the long term is an open question, although some more recent evidence suggests that it is having an effect (Weishaupt 2009; Tholoniat 2010).

23.6 The EES and EU employment performance

The fundamental problem in assessing the effect of any policy is to identify what would have happened in its absence – that is, the *anti-monde* (see Chapter 9). In the case of the EES this problem is complicated still further, as argued above, by the weak link between the EES and national employment policy. However, there has been a general drift towards the employment policies contained in the EES. This section considers whether this shift has been accompanied by improved employment performance, without ascribing causation.

There is a very wide range of possible measures of employment performance and these different measures may rate countries' performance differently. The measures of performance considered here are employment and unemployment rates, the relationship between economic growth and employment and the NRU. The EU incorporates a wide range of performance on these and other employment indicators – one reason why it was thought that the policy learning process incorporated in the EES would be productive in this area.

23.6.1 Employment rates in the EU

The employment rate (ER) is the number of employed and self-employed divided by the total population of working age. This is probably the most reliable measure of employment performance; it avoids problems associated with the manipulation of unemployment figures – for example, the misuse of incapacity benefits in the UK (see Section 23.6.3, page 377). There are still some problems with ERs, which may be distorted by an increase in part-time work.[15] ERs also overemphasize the benefits of paid employment and undervalue the social activities of the economically inactive, such as childcare. The EU wants to increase the employment rate to improve the sustainability of welfare policy by reducing the dependency ratio – those not employed as a proportion of those employed. ERs are also sensitive to cyclical factors, rising in booms and falling in recessions, so in analysing trends it is important to identify the effect of these cyclical factors. This is complicated by the possibility that factors such as labour market reforms may also permit higher rates of economic growth.

In the early 1960s, the EU15 ER was higher than that of the USA, but the rate in the EU15 drifted lower while that in the USA rose, so that after 1977 the EU15 rate was lower (see Figure 23.2). From 1985 the EU15 ER rose until 2009, when the recession took its toll on employment. The US ER rate rose steeply until 1990, remained at a high level until 2000 and then fell, particularly steeply in 2008–9, with the recession. So although the EU15 ER began rising prior to the EES, most of the increase in ER has coincided with the EES, at a time when the US ER was falling. The individual EU15 countries show a very large variation in employment rates, but similar trends over time, with the ER drifting lower and then rising from 1985 (see Figure 23.3). As might be anticipated, the improvement in employment rates is generally greatest where they were lowest – for example, in Spain and Ireland. These countries also suffered the largest fall in employment rates associated with the recession.

The process of transition and structural change in the Central and Eastern European Countries (CEECs) led to substantial reduction in ERs followed by their rising, as economic growth created employment: average ERs rose from 58.9 per cent in 2000 to 63.8 per cent in 2008 (see Figure 23.4).[16] Employment performance is more variable across NMSs, related to different progress with transition and variations in its success. ERs are lower than in the EU15, with only

Cyprus having an employment rate of more than 70 per cent in 2008. Malta, Hungary and Romania have stagnant ERs, in the 50–60 per cent range. Bulgaria, Slovakia, Lithuania, Latvia and Estonia all experienced rapid employment growth until 2008, but employment has fallen significantly in the recession. Cyprus and Slovenia, with the highest ERs among NMSs, have experienced more moderate employment growth and a smaller fall in employment. Poland's employment growth started late in 2003 from a low base, but has been quite rapid since then and continued in 2009.

Total ERs hide large differences between different categories of workers, such as male, female and older workers.[17] Male workers have higher ER rates (74.2 per cent in 2008) than female workers (60.4 per cent), so it is understandable that the increase in the male ER during 1994–2008 was relatively small, at 3.8 per cent. The growth in male employment varies across countries, being negatively related to ERs and positively related to employment growth, so male ERs grew most in Spain, Finland, Ireland and the Netherlands. But countries with similar ERs in 1994 have very different improvements in their ERs. This indicates that in this area the possible impact of the EES has been variable.

Female ERs are increasing in all EU15 countries: the average rate increased from 49.3 per cent in 1994 to 60.4 per cent in 2008. They grew most in countries with the lowest female ERs and the greatest overall employment

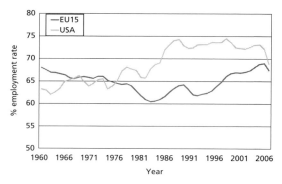

Figure 23.2 Employment rates in the EU15 and the USA 1961–2007 *Source*: Eurostat 2010b

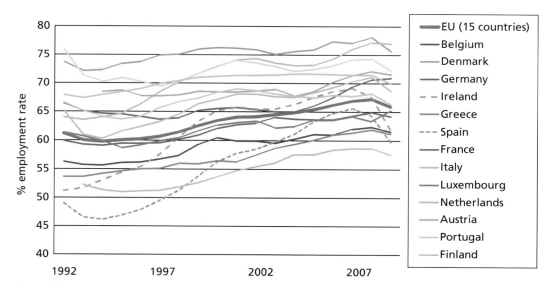

Figure 23.3 Employment rates in the EU15, 1992–2008 *Source*: Eurostat 2010b

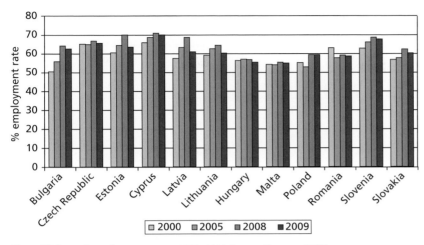

Figure 23.4 NMS employment rates, 2000–2009 *Source*: Eurostat 2010b

growth: Spain, Ireland and the Netherlands. However, they increased significantly in all countries, but there was a modest fall in 2009. The differences between countries remain substantial, with Danish, Dutch and Swedish female ERs exceeding 70 per cent in 2009; and Finland, Austria, Germany, the UK, Portugal and France between 60 and 70 per cent. Ireland, Luxembourg, Belgium and Spain have ERs between 50 and 60 per cent. Greece and Italy have much lower rates, at 48.9 per cent and 46.4 per cent respectively.

There are very wide differences in the employment rates of older workers[18] in the EU15, ranging in 2009 from 70 per cent in Sweden to 35.3 per cent in Italy; these differences are the result of a combination of factors, such as variation in statutory retirement age, generosity of pensions and the overall employment situation. Across the EU15, ERs of older workers improved substantially between 1994 and 2008, from 35.7 per cent to 48.0, but the improvement is very uneven: in the Netherlands older workers' ERs increased over this period by 23.9 per cent, whereas in Greece the increase was only 2.7 per cent. This indicates that the policies to raise the employment rate of this group are available, but the EES has not persuaded all countries to use them.

The picture that emerges from this analysis of employment is one of general improvement. There is considerable variation in performance, however, with the employment situation in NMSs being worse than in the EU15, although the pace of transition is

slowing, and with the benefit of relatively rapid economic growth the employment situation is improving. There has also been an improvement across the board in EU15 employment performance, which started before the EES was launched, but which has been sustained in the EES period.

23.6.2 Employment and economic growth in the EU

The improvement in EU employment since 1997 may be due to the EES or to other factors affecting employment, most notably higher economic growth. As can be seen from Table 23.1, the average GDP growth rate for the EU15 was the same over the period 1980–97 as it was during 1997–2008: 2.2 per cent per year. Every period has its idiosyncrasies, and 1980–97 includes German unification and very severe recessions in Sweden[19] and Finland,[20] which meant that employment fell in these countries. The elasticity of employment to GDP was very low, 0.2 for the EU15, which implies that a 1 per cent increase in the GDP growth rate leads to a 0.2 per cent increase in the employment growth rate. At 0.6, the elasticity is much higher for 1997–2008, when every EU15 country except Greece increased the employment intensity of growth. This is a very crude assessment because the relationship is probably not linear: there is likely to be a threshold level of GDP growth below which employment will contract, which may account for the very poor

Table 23.1 EU15 employment and GDP growth, 1980–2008

	1980–97			1998–2008		
	Employment	GDP	Elasticity	Employment	GDP	Elasticity
EU15	0.4	2.2	0.2	1.3	2.2	0.6
Belgium	0.2	2.1	0.1	1.2	2.2	0.6
Denmark	0.3	2.1	0.1	0.9	1.7	0.5
Germany	0.7	2.1	0.3	0.7	1.6	0.4
Ireland	0.9	4.6	0.2	3.7	5.8	0.6
Greece	0.8	1.1	0.7	1.3	3.9	0.3
Spain	0.7	2.5	0.3	3.3	3.5	0.9
France	0.2	1.9	0.1	1.1	2.2	0.5
Italy	0.3	2.1	0.1	1.3	1.2	1.0
Luxembourg	2.1	4.4	0.5	4.0	4.9	0.8
Netherlands	1.4	2.5	0.6	1.4	2.6	0.5
Austria	0.3	2.1	0.1	1.1	2.5	0.4
Portugal	0.2	3.3	0.1	0.8	1.8	0.4
Finland	−0.3	2.4	−0.1	1.5	3.5	0.4
Sweden	−0.2	1.7	−0.1	1.1	2.9	0.4
UK	0.3	2.2	0.1	1.0	2.7	0.4

Source: CEU 2010c; own calculations

performance during 1990–97. But it is apparent that the improved recent performance is not just the result of increased GDP growth. It looks as if the EU will be experiencing a period of very slow growth of GDP and employment, so a longer data period will be needed to confirm this improvement.

The improved employment intensity of growth is not all good news, however, because of its relationship with productivity. The growth of employment is equal to the increase in GDP minus the increase in productivity. For example, if GDP growth is 2 per cent and labour productivity growth is 2 per cent, then the existing employed workers can produce all of this increase in output, and employment growth will be zero. Employment can be increased by raising the growth rate or by decreasing productivity growth. The increased employment intensity of EU growth means that the growth of labour productivity in the EU has slowed, which implies more but not better jobs. Higher productivity growth is not incompatible with higher employment, because if it improves competitiveness output could expand faster than productivity. Lower labour productivity growth may reflect factors that are perhaps less damning than this implies – for

example, if it is the result of fewer hours worked (see Chapter 14). EU unemployment has fallen most heavily on workers with lower skills and lower productivity: employment of these lower-skilled workers, while obviously desirable, would tend to lower overall productivity growth.

23.6.3 Unemployment in the EU

The unemployment rate is the number of unemployed divided by the labour force (the number in employment and self-employment plus the unemployed). In the past, measurement of the unemployed was ambiguous, but now International Labour Organization (ILO) standardized unemployment is the generally accepted measure: the number of people not in employment who are looking for work, measured by surveys. The other side of the ratio, the labour force, remains problematic; the labour force equals the population of working age minus the inactive (those not in employment or looking for work). The inactive is not a stable group. It is affected by the proportion of women who work, which is increasing over time; the increasing numbers of full-time students; early retirement; and other factors. Despite falling unemployment in the UK, there were substantial numbers of economically inactive people who wanted jobs. Two significant groups of working age are inactive rather than unemployed as a result of government measures: on incapacity benefit or on government training and employment schemes. Thus, in 2007, UK unemployment was reported to be just over 0.9 million, but it was estimated that there were an additional 1.7 million hidden unemployed (Beatty *et al.* 2007). This problem of hidden unemployment distorting the figures is not confined to the UK. For example, Sweden recorded unemployment at a relatively low 6.3 per cent in 2004, but total unemployment, including hidden unemployment, was estimated to be much higher, at 15 per cent (Bengttson *et al.* 2006). Hence comparisons of unemployment need to be made carefully.

EU15 unemployment rates in 2009 ranged from 3.4 per cent in the Netherlands to 18 per cent in Spain. From 1998 to 2008 unemployment fell across the EU, with the exception of Luxembourg and Portugal. In 2009 unemployment started to rise with the recession, most notably in Spain and Ireland, countries that had experienced very large reductions. But the increase in unemployment was less severe in Finland and the Netherlands, which had also reduced unemployment substantially. The 1.9 per cent increase in the unemployment rate in 2008–9 in the EU15 was much less than the 3.5 per cent increase in the USA; rather than reducing workforces as output fell, EU firms were encouraged to engage in short-time working and to retain their workforce (CEU 2009b). This response mitigates the social effects of the recession and means that the skilled workforce is retained, but runs the risk of delaying necessary adjustment.

NMSs generally had higher unemployment rates in 2009: from 5.3 per cent in Cyprus to 17.1 per cent in Latvia. Unemployment in NMSs rose sharply with the recession, with particularly large increases in Estonia, Latvia and Lithuania. Hence some of the large reductions in unemployment that had been achieved were not sustainable.

Younger and older workers are particularly vulnerable, and the EES targets reductions in the unemployment rates of these groups. Youth unemployment is high because of the problematic transition from education to employment, and because of the group's lack of experience and employment record. In 2009 youth unemployment[21] in the EU15 averaged 19.2 per cent, compared to the overall rate of 9 per cent, with very large differences between the 15, from 37.8 per cent in Spain to 6.6 per cent in the Netherlands, largely reflecting the differences in overall employment rates. Average youth unemployment has been falling in the EU15, but this is because of large falls in France, Greece, Italy and Spain; the rate is rising in almost as many countries (seven) as it is falling (eight). Youth unemployment has also risen steeply during the recession.

The accuracy of the youth unemployment rate as a measure of the youth employment situation, however, is questionable. The central problem is that a substantial and increasing proportion of the 15–24 age group is in full-time education, and they may be employed, unemployed or inactive. The unemployment rate compares the total of 15- to 24-year-olds who are unemployed with the sum of the employed and the unemployed. Hence youth unemployment rates are sensitive to the number of young people in full-time education, and the proportion of this group that works. Thus comparisons of youth unemployment rates across countries will be distorted by variations in these proportions.[22]

Most unemployment is for relatively short periods, but some people remain unemployed for lengthy periods. Long-term unemployment (LTU) is not only dispiriting for the unemployed, it also affects the employability of those involved, who can drift into economic inactivity. LTU is sensitive to the overall level of unemployment because when unemployment rises, the period of job search lengthens. Also employers can be more selective. So for vulnerable groups, such as those without formal educational qualifications, LTU increases (Dickens *et al.* 2001). LTU is measured by the proportion of the labour force that has been looking for work for more than a year. In the EU15 such unemployment has fallen dramatically; the average has dropped from 5 per cent in 1994 to 2.6 per cent in 2008, with Portugal being the only country with rising LTU. The recession has led to a rise in LTU in most EU15 countries. LTU has fallen sharply in NMSs to levels similar to those in the EU15. Care is needed in interpreting these statistics because they are sensitive to government measures to cope with unemployment – the problem of hidden unemployment, already discussed.

23.6.4 The natural rate of unemployment

The measures of labour market performance considered so far are partial; one possible measure of overall performance is the non-accelerating wage rate of unemployment (NAWRU). This is the level of (structural) unemployment, reconcilable with a constant rate of inflation. This derives from the expectations-augmented Phillips curve (see Section 10.4.2, page 152) in monopolistic product and labour markets (Layard *et al.* 1991). According to this view, structural unemployment represents an equilibrium in the sense that, once established, workers and employers have no incentive to change real wages. The NAWRU equilibrium occurs when expectations are met with wages rising in line with prices, after taking into account the growth of productivity. Structural unemployment will not necessarily be constant. Over time, if structural factors in the economy change, then structural unemployment will change (McMorrow and Roeger 2000). It could be argued that NAWRU follows the actual employment rate because of persistence effects (Gordon 1998) or that there might be a multiplicity of NAWRU (Akerlof *et al.* 2000; de Vincenti 2001). If NAWRU is a little more than the existing unemployment rate, its utility in explaining differences in unemployment is clearly diminished. This is illustrated by the large negative effect of the recession on NAWRU in 2009. Obviously, care is need in interpreting the concept of NAWRU and in its estimation (Staiger *et al.* 1997).

Bearing in mind these qualifications, it can be seen (Table 23.2) that during 1991–2008 there was an improvement of 0.5 per cent in EU15 NAWRU, most of which was eliminated in 2009 by the recession. There are large variations in NAWRU, ranging from 3.5 per cent in the Netherlands to 14 per cent in Spain. There have been reductions in NAWRU in nine MSs, particularly spectacularly in Ireland; this reinforces the general impression of improving EU15 labour market performance. But there have been large increases in NAWRU in Sweden, Portugal and Luxembourg.

There is also variability in NMSs, with NAWRU ranging from 5.5 per cent in Cyprus to 13.1 per cent in Latvia. In eight of these countries, NAWRU is increasing, but in the others it is falling.

23.7 Conclusion

There is little doubt that employment policy in EU MSs has changed since the introduction of the EES, and this has been associated with an improvement in employment performance. What is less clear is the association between these changes. Similar change in employment policy (OECD 2006c) and employment performance has occurred across the whole of the OECD (OECD 2006d), so the independent influence of the EES is difficult to identify. The OMC used by the EES seems to work in a similar way to the OECD job strategy, by influencing the conventional wisdom on employment policy, so its added impact seems to stem from the more intensive nature of the interaction between the EU and national governments and administrations. The increasing acknowledgement of the importance of the interaction between different aspects of employment policy and the national institutional setting means that the national differentiation of the common policy has become more important. So the continued success of the EES depends not only on its ability to identify desirable employment policy reform, but also to appropriately differentiate between MSs – not an easy task.

It has also become clear that the EES operated until 2007 in an exceptionally benign economic situation. The extent to which the gains in employment can be maintained during the more difficult economic circumstances of today will be a demanding test of the success of the EES in raising EU employment performance.

Summary

- Social policy covers a very wide range of policy areas, and across the EU the policies vary a great deal.
- In most of these areas the EU has only limited powers, but while the policies remain national, they are increasingly constrained within a Europeanized policy process.
- The idea that there is a distinctive European social model, which places greater emphasis on equality and workers' rights relative to North America, remains an important influence on policy.
- This chapter concentrates on employment policy because it encompasses so many areas of social policy and is the most important economic area of social policy.

Table 23.2 Non-accelerating wage rate of unemployment, 1991–2009

	NAWRU (%)				Change
	1991	1997	2008	2009	1991–2008
Netherlands	6.0	4.3	3.3	3.5	−2.5
Denmark	6.2	5.5	4.3	4.7	−1.6
Austria	3.4	3.8	4.4	4.7	1.3
Luxembourg	2.1	2.4	5.1	5.3	3.2
UK	8.9	7.0	5.8	6.3	−2.6
Sweden	3.0	6.9	6.8	7.5	4.4
Finland	8.1	12.9	7.2	7.6	−0.5
Italy	8.8	9.3	7.9	7.9	−0.9
Belgium	7.6	8.7	7.8	8.0	0.4
Germany	7.0	8.1	8.3	8.1	1.0
Portugal	5.2	5.2	8.0	8.8	3.5
France	9.1	9.9	9.0	9.0	−0.1
Ireland	15.0	9.3	7.1	9.2	−5.8
Greece	7.4	9.3	9.6	10.1	2.7
Spain	15.0	14.4	11.9	14.0	−1.0
EU15	**8.4**	**8.6**	**7.9**	**8.3**	−0.1
					Change 1997–2008
Cyprus		2.9	5.0	5.5	2.6
Slovenia		6.9	5.7	5.9	−1.1
Czech Rep.		3.5	6.4	6.6	3.0
Malta		5.8	6.8	6.8	1.0
Romania		4.9	6.8	6.8	1.9
Bulgaria		14.4	7.3	6.9	−7.5
Hungary		8.4	8.3	9.0	0.6
Poland		11.8	10.4	9.2	−2.6
Estonia		6.9	8.4	9.8	2.9
Lithuania		3.3	8.5	10.1	6.8
Slovakia		11.4	12.3	12.1	0.7
Latvia		14.7	10.7	13.1	−1.6

Source: CEU 2010c

- EU low employment and high unemployment rates on average encouraged the development of the European Employment Strategy (EES).
- The EES was seen as necessary to facilitate adjustment to structural change and to enable wages to be a more effective adjustment mechanism in the European monetary union (EMU).
- Economic theory and evidence suggest that flexible labour markets can be developed by changing: benefits and the rules under which they are offered; taxation and the interaction between taxation and benefits; employment protection legislation; trade unions and collective bargaining; active labour market policies, such as training, work experience, and so on.
- There are differences of opinion and the evidence is not always clear-cut on whether it is important to maintain low unemployment, because periods of high unemployment will raise the natural rate of unemployment (NRU), the minimum rate that can be maintained in the long term.
- The EES tries to encourage the adoption by national governments of best practice in MSs' employment policy, by policy learning, setting targets and

publicizing failure to meet targets (naming and shaming): the open method of coordination (OMC).

- MSs' employment policies have moved in the desired direction, but it is not clear whether this is the result of the EES.
- EU employment performance has improved, employment rates have risen and unemployment rates have fallen. The improvement began before the EES, but it has been maintained until the recession.
- If this improvement is maintained in the less benign economic circumstances that follow the recession, the policy will have been a success.

Questions and essay topics

1. Why does social policy differ so much between EU MSs?
2. What is the European social model and why is it important?
3. What policies fall within the remit of employment policy?
4. Why is employment policy important?
5. What is the wedge, and why is it important that it should be reduced?
6. What is flexi-security, and why is it particularly attractive for the EU?
7. What is the NRU and why is it important?
8. What is the OMC and how does it differ from the traditional community method?
9. How does the EES operate?
10. Assess the effect of the EES on EU employment rates.
11. How have EU unemployment rates changed? Do you think the EES has reduced unemployment rates?
12. 'The employment intensity of growth in the EU has increased.' Explain what this means and consider whether it is a desirable development.

FURTHER READING

Boeri, T. and Garibaldi, P. (2009) 'Beyond Eurosclerosis', *Economic Policy*, 59.

CEU (2009) *Employment in Europe 2009*, OOPEU, Luxembourg, Chapters 1–2.

Raveaud, G. (2007) 'The European employment strategy: towards more and better jobs?', *Journal of Common Market Studies*, vol. 45.2.

NOTES

1 Social exclusion policies aim to reduce the extent to which certain groups are unable to participate fully in society.
2 Which includes discrimination on the grounds of nationality and social security coordination.
3 EU policy involvement in these areas, however, still varies substantially.
4 ITR is the total tax revenue as a proportion of the value of the activity being taxed; for labour it is total income tax and social security as a proportion of income.
5 The lowest rates in the EU15 are in Ireland (24.68 per cent) and the UK (26.1 per cent).
6 But there may be other institutional arrangements to set effective wage floors.
7 Or destruction.
8 Problems could arise, for example, if low wages were too high to generate sufficient employment for the low-skilled.
9 Or, more usually, the wage curve that reconciles the demands of trade unions with those of employers. Since both have market power, wages are determined by a bargaining process.
10 Since, according to these models, unemployment is near to its natural rate.
11 The level of unemployment benefits as a percentage of earnings.
12 Coordination can be achieved by centralized bargaining or by institutional features, as in Germany.
13 Thus the ECJ ruled that working time was a health and safety measure to which QMV applied.
14 The economic crisis meant that a further evaluation has not taken place.
15 Eurostat figures include everyone who has had at least one hour's paid work in the week of the survey.
16 Data are only available for a short period for NMSs, so the detailed discussion here is confined to the EU15.
17 There are also differences in employment for young people, but because of the large numbers in full-time education, the employment rate is not a reliable indicator for this group. They will be considered when unemployment is analysed.
18 Aged 55–64 years.
19 Due to a banking crisis.
20 Due to the end of the cold war division of Europe.
21 Under 25 years.
22 A further complication concerns differences in the amount of work undertaken in the informal economy.

Part VI EU external relations

Part VI of the book deals with the external relations of the EU. Chapter 24 covers EU trade relations with its major partners within the context of the Common Commercial Policy (CCP) run by the European Commission on behalf of all EU member nations. Chapter 25 tackles EU relations with the developing world in terms of trade, aid and preferential trading arrangements.

24 External trade policy

MIRIAM MANCHIN AND ALI EL-AGRAA

24.1 Introduction

The external trade policy of the European Union (EU) involves nearly one-fifth of world trade. Hence an understanding of the principles and practice of EU trade policy, the Common Commercial Policy (CCP), is of vital importance for understanding the EU's role and impact on the global economy.

With growing trade, falling transaction costs, better information and communication technologies, global economic integration is increasing; 'globalization' is on the rise (if one wanted to be trendy). Global production chains are common in most industries and are essential for maintaining competitiveness. Thus the EU's external trade policy has an increasing role to play in promoting the competitiveness of the European industries and ensuring EU economic growth.

While the CCP originally focused on tariffs and quantitative restrictions affecting trade in goods, its scope today is much more diverse. As tariffs were reduced in successive rounds of multilateral trade negotiations, other policy areas related to regulatory issues have become increasingly relevant to international trade. Thus the European Commission's (Commission) communication 'Global Europe: competing in the world' (CEU 2006p; see also Chapter 25) sets out some main policy objectives for the CCP that address the challenges of globalization. The communication's main objective is to define a trade policy that would both stimulate growth and create jobs in Europe. It also defines some of the links between the EU's external and internal policies, and emphasizes the importance of both the multilateral and bilateral liberalization

processes, as well as the CCP's role in achieving competitiveness. It calls for the CCP to address, among other issues, non-tariff barriers to trade (NTBs), liberalization of trade in services and securing/protecting intellectual property rights (IPR). Throughout, the importance of external liberalization is emphasized, which is well illustrated by the following statement: 'openness to others, and their openness to us, are critical and mutually reinforcing factors in European competitiveness'.

The CCP has also developed a highly complex set of trade relations with third countries, reflecting in part the way the granting of trade preferences was virtually the sole instrument of EU foreign policy in the past. The resulting hierarchy of preferential trading schemes has been determined by a mixture of trade and strategic and foreign policy concerns, in which the conflicting interests of member states (MSs), as well as hard bargaining between EU institutions and MSs, have played an important role.

The CCP is shaped by the EU's obligations (and reciprocal rights) under the World Trade Organization (WTO), which now administers the General Agreement on Tariffs and Trade (GATT), effective from 1995. The purpose of the WTO is to establish and monitor the rules for trade policy-making in its members, and to encourage the liberalization of trade through successive rounds of trade negotiations to reduce tariffs and other barriers to trade in goods and services. One of its core principles is that of most favoured nation (MFN) treatment, which means that members undertake not to discriminate in their treatment of imports originating from different members (see Chapter 1). The EU played a major role

This chapter was originally contributed by El-Agraa, who then persuaded Dermot McAleese to replace him. McAleese was joined in later editions by Marius Brülhart, and, when he retired, Alan Matthews co-authored it with Brülhart. We are greatly indebted to all three of them, but especially to Alan, who, despite heavy commitments, including membership of an elite group looking into ways to make savings in Ireland's national budget, has helped us greatly with this version.

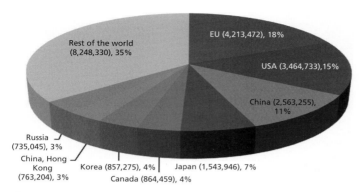

Figure 24.1 Main traders (value in US$ million) and share of trade (exports + imports) in goods of the eight most important trading nations, 2008 *Source:* UN Comtrade (http//comtrade.un.org); authors' own calculations

in the Uruguay Round Agreement conducted under the auspices of GATT. It was among the strongest proponents of the further comprehensive round of trade negotiations that was initiated in Doha, Qatar in November 2001. The difficulties in reaching an agreement within the Doha Round have revived the tension between the EU's commitment to multilateral trade liberalization through the WTO and its ongoing concern with regional and bilateral agreements outside that organization.

This chapter investigates these themes in four separate sections. The first describes the pattern of trade between the EU and the outside world. The second presents an overview of the EU's decision-making mechanism in the area of trade policy. The third reviews the main instruments used for the EU's CCP. The final section considers the EU's trade policy towards its main trading partners and the EU's engagement in multilateral trade negotiations.

24.2 EU trade patterns

The EU is the world's leading exporter and second largest importer of goods and the first trading power in services. Figure 24.1 shows the value of exports and imports in millions of US dollars for the biggest traders, together with their share of total goods trade in 2008. The EU's exports and imports amount to 18 per cent of world totals, but the USA and China are also significant, with 15 per cent and 11 per cent respectively. Hence it should be natural that the leading position of the EU as a global trader greatly influences its role in both multilateral and bilateral trade negotiations and

agreements. This section will provide an overview of the patterns of EU trade as well as trade in services, given their increasing importance.

24.2.1 EU trading partners

Most EU trade takes place between EU MSs – that is, it is intra-EU. As Figure 5.8 (page 76) shows, about two-thirds of both exports and imports are intra-EU; only one-third is conducted with the outside world – that is, extra-EU. Although intra-EU trade is obviously far more important for the EU as a unit, there are variations between MSs in this respect.

Figure 24.2 sheds light on the remaining one-third of EU trade by depicting the share of different countries in extra-EU exports and imports. The EU's biggest source of imports is China, with almost one-fifth of all extra-EU imports. The USA is the second most important partner, accounting for 13 per cent of all extra-EU imports. Russia, with 10 per cent, is the third main source of EU imports, which are dominated by natural resources. On the export side, the USA is the major destination for EU exports, absorbing 19 per cent of all extra-EU exports. Among the top trading partners are also some EU neighbours: Norway, Turkey and Switzerland; between them, they account for 17 and 15 per cent of total extra-EU exports and imports respectively.

Although trade in services is relatively less important than that in goods, it is increasingly gaining in significance. This is revealed in Figure 24.3, which depicts EU imports from and exports to its main partners and the rest of the world, for both goods and (commercial) services in 2008. The main EU partner country

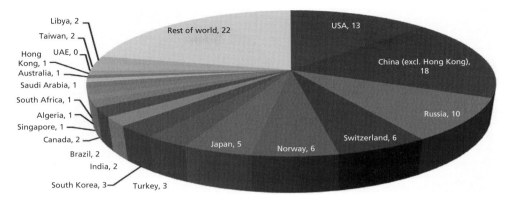

Share of imports by partner (%), 2009

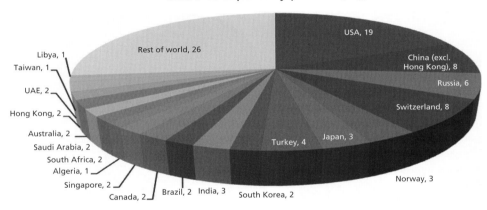

Share of exports by partner (%), 2009

Figure 24.2 Share of imports/exports by partner countries in total extra-EU imports/exports of goods, 2009 *Source:* Eurostat (http//epp.eurostat.ec.europa.eu)

in services trade is the USA, with the ratio of services to goods trade being remarkably high in comparison with the other main trading partners – for example, the share with China, one of the EU's main trading partners in goods, is minuscule. As with trade in goods, intra-EU services trade is more important than extra-EU trade: in 2009, 58 per cent of services trade took place within the EU, amounting to €641.4 billion (Eurostat).

For a direct comparison of EU trade in services and goods with its main partners, it is more revealing to use similar charts; hence consider Figures 24.3 and 24.4 together. Figure 24.4 shows a somewhat different pattern for the two trades, in particular the share of services trade with the USA dominates that of other

countries, unlike in the case of trade in goods. It can also be seen from the figure that EU services exports to all its main partners, except for India, is higher than its imports. Total EU for services exports is about 17 per cent larger than its imports.

24.2.2 Composition of EU trade

There is a difference in the structure of EU exports and imports. While machinery and transport equipment dominate EU exports, representing 42 per cent of total EU exports (see Figure 24.5), their share in imports is only 29 per cent. Another important difference is in the share of minerals: as Figure 24.5 shows, the EU is

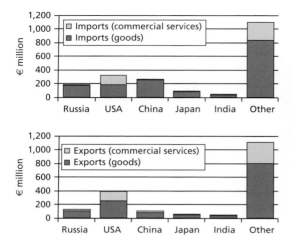

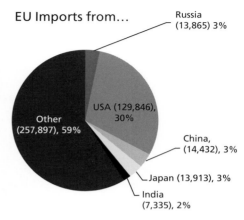

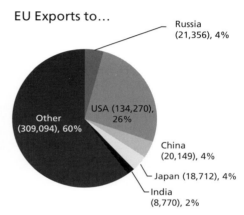

Figure 24.3 Trade in goods and commercial services, 2008 *Source*: EU, DG Trade (http//ec.europa.eu/trade/statistics)

basically an importer of mineral fuels and related materials, products representing 24 per cent of total imports.

Figure 24.6 depicts a breakdown of the composition of commercial services exports and imports relative to their respective total. The share of travel services is higher in EU imports (22 per cent) than in exports (14 per cent). Other commercial services, which also include financial services, has a somewhat higher share in EU exports (60 per cent) than in EU imports (52 per cent).

24.3 EU trade decision-making procedures

The key provisions of the common external trade policy, the CCP, are stated in Articles 188B (ex 131) and 188C (ex 133) of the Treaty of Lisbon, formally, the Treaty on the Functioning of the European Union (TFEU). Article 188B contains the well-known aspiration:

By establishing a customs union in accordance with Articles 24 to 27, the Union shall contribute, in the common interest, to the harmonious development of world trade, the progressive abolition of restrictions on international trade and on foreign direct investment, and the lowering of customs and other barriers.

The cornerstone of the CCP is Article 188C. It sets out the important rule that:

Figure 24.4 Trade in commercial services, 2008 *Source*: EU, DG Trade (http//ec.europa.eu/trade/statistics) *Note*: All figures are € million, apart from Russia, which is € billion.

The [CCP] shall be based on uniform principles, particularly with regard to changes in tariff rates, the conclusion of tariff and trade agreements relating to trade in goods and services, and the commercial aspects of intellectual property, foreign direct investment, the achievement of uniformity in measures of liberalization, export policy and measures to protect trade such as those to be taken in the event of dumping or subsidies. The [CCP] shall be conducted in the context of the principles and objectives of the Union's external action.

The Lisbon Treaty introduced important changes in the CCP area. One of the objectives of these is to reinforce the position of the EU as a global actor. Thus the treaty created the post of High Representative of the

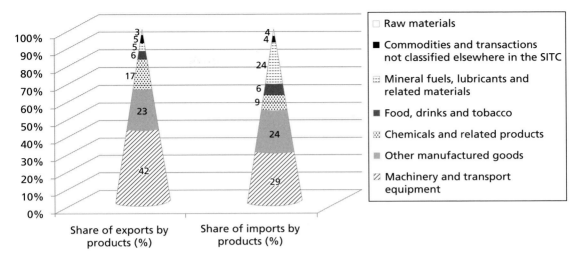

Figure 24.5 Main product categories in extra-EU exports and imports of goods, 2009 *Source*: Eurostat (http//epp.eurostat. ec.europa.eu)

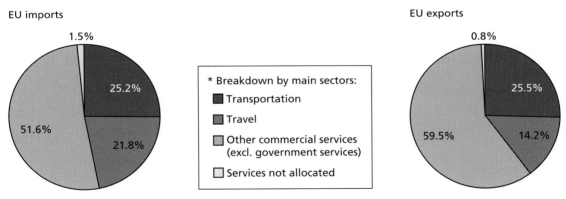

Figure 24.6 Composition of EU exports and imports in services, 2008 *Source*: EU, DG Trade (http//ec.europa.eu/trade/ statistics)

Union for Foreign Affairs and Security Policy, who is also a vice-president of the Commission (see Chapter 2), and whose role is to reinforce the coherence and visibility of EU external action. Recall from Chapter 2 that the High Representative is responsible for controlling general foreign policy (outside of trade, development and enlargement, which has to be made together with the Commission).

24.3.1 Decision-making in goods trade

Decision-making concerning trade in goods functions on the basis of qualified majority voting (QMV; see Chapter 3, page 38) in the Council. Subject to the Council's approval, the Commission is empowered to conduct negotiations in consultation with a special committee appointed by the Council for this purpose. For example, the Commission negotiates on behalf of MSs in the WTO. In the cut and thrust of negotiations, the Commission may sometimes interpret its mandate in a way with which some MSs may disagree, and this has been a source of tension in the past. Bilateral association agreements, such as the economic partnership agreements with the African, Caribbean and Pacific (ACP, see page 14 and Chapter 25) states, require unanimity in the Council, and the European Parliament (EP) also has to give its consent.

The Lisbon Treaty, which entered into force on 1 December 2009, added some improvements to the existing procedures. The aims of the introduced changes were to achieve better working methods, more efficient decision-making processes, and to reduce the perceived democratic deficit by allowing a greater role for the EP and national parliaments. With the Treaty of Lisbon the EP also obtained more legislative powers in some areas of trade policy.

24.3.2 Decision-making beyond trade in goods

As tariffs have been gradually decreased over time, the importance of NTBs has increased. As new protectionist measures gained significance and the magnitude of trade in services increased, the role of the different institutions and EU competence had to be defined accordingly. In 1994 the European Court of Justice (ECJ) was asked to rule on the division of competences with respect to services and intellectual property rights. The ECJ ruled that the EC had exclusive competence with respect to cross-border trade in services, but that MSs retained joint competence with the EC for trade issues involving commercial presence and factor movements. As a result, the WTO agreement was signed by representatives of both the Council and MSs. In 1997 the Amsterdam Treaty granted the EC powers to negotiate agreements on services and intellectual property, but only on the basis of unanimity. In 2001 the Nice Treaty further tilted the balance towards exclusive competence by extending majority voting to these areas (with certain exceptions). Unanimity continues to prevail in instances where it is required for internal decisions, such as taxation matters (see Chapters 3 and 15) – this is called the principle of parallelism. The absence of QMV in these areas could make the conclusion of future trade negotiations cumbersome where the outcome is presented as a 'single undertaking', because, de facto, unanimity is required for the entire agenda (OECD 2000b). The Lisbon Treaty extends the scope of the CCP to include foreign direct investment (FDI), which should facilitate trade negotiations covering FDI provisions as well.

24.4 Instruments of the external trade policy

24.4.1 Tariffs

MFN tariffs are applied on imports coming from countries whose products do not enjoy EU preferential treatment. There are only nine countries in the world with which the EU does not have a preferential trade agreement (PTA) and who are members of the WTO, hence the common external tariff (CET) applies only to imports from them. However, trade with these countries represents about one-third of EU external trade, so understanding the structure of the CET is necessary and may shed light on the benefits or otherwise of having preferential or tariff-free access to the EU.

Figure 24.7 reveals that, overall, 25 per cent of all product categories entering the EU face zero tariffs. Thus countries exporting products falling into this category would not benefit from having PTAs with the EU. Figure 24.7 also shows that in the sectors where average tariffs as well as tariff peaks are low, the share of products entering the EU market duty-free is high. The most protected sector by far is agriculture, where average tariffs are about 18 per cent (see Chapter 20) and the highest tariff in the sector has an equivalent to a 604 per cent *ad valorem* tariff rate. Two other sectors have rather higher protection: fish and fishery products, and textiles and clothing. In the textiles and clothing sector the share of products entering the EU duty-free is the lowest, amounting to only 2 per cent.

24.4.2 Non-tariff barriers

In addition to tariffs, the EU has made significant use of various NTBs to limit imports (see Chapters 6 and 7). These include quantitative restrictions, price controls and regulatory barriers. Specific examples include import quotas, voluntary export restraints, discretionary licensing, anti-dumping duties or prohibitions for health and safety reasons. As mentioned, NTBs have assumed importance due to the substantial reductions in tariffs that have been achieved over time; it

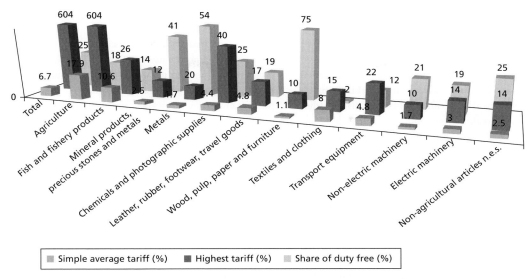

Figure 24.7 EU tariff structure, 2008 *Source*: Eurostat (http//epp.eurostat.ec.europa.eu)

is therefore useful to discuss those that have become especially prevalent, albeit briefly.

Quantitative restrictions

Quantitative restrictions on imports have similar effects to tariffs (see Chapter 6) in that they raise the price in the domestic market, but they will not provide revenue (rent) to the government unless the government collects the quota rents instead of the importer or exporter firms. Import quotas are generally not permitted under WTO rules, but were imposed on clothing and textiles under successive Multifibre Agreements (MFAs), and have been regulated by the WTO Agreement on Textiles and Clothing since 1995. Under this agreement, the EU eliminated these quotas by 2005 in a phased fashion. Quotas on banana imports designed to protect the market for ACP banana exporters were removed from 2006. Quotas remain in place for imports of steel from non-WTO countries – for example, Kazakhstan, Russia and Ukraine each have a yearly quota, specifying the maximum amount of steel that can be imported from each country.

Anti-dumping measures

Dumping is defined as selling in export markets below some 'normal' price. The 'normal' price of a good is commonly defined as the price prevailing in the exporter's home market. Such divergences could arise

if firms exported products at very low prices in order to capture markets abroad and eliminate competition. The imposition of anti-dumping measures is permitted under WTO rules, if dumping 'causes or threatens material injury to an established industry ... or materially retards the establishment of a domestic industry'. Complex pricing policies and adjustment for indirect cost factors leave a degree of arbitrariness in the calculation of dumping margins and 'material injury'. WTO rules also permit countries to take countervailing action against exports that have benefited from subsidies in the exporting country, provided such exports cause or threaten to cause material injury to a domestic industry. Safeguard clauses under WTO provisions allow signatories to take special measures against import surges or particularly low import prices that cause material injury to domestic industries.

The EU has had frequent resort to anti-dumping measures. Over the period 1995–2005 the EU had the third largest number of product categories with anti-dumping measures initiated, after India and the USA. Anti-dumping actions take one of two forms: (a) anti-dumping duties equivalent to the dumping margin, or (b) undertakings by exporting countries not to sell to the EU below an agreed price. The most affected product categories are iron and steel products, consumer electronics and chemicals. The EU rarely applies countervailing duties, and, in almost all cases, the investigations concern products that are also subject to an anti-dumping investigation.

Regulatory barriers

Regulatory barriers have also become important tools for restricting imports. Products imported into the EU must comply with relevant regulations, where they exist, to meet health, safety and environmental objectives. Technical regulations are mandatory rules laid down by the EU or MSs, while standards are non-mandatory rules approved by a recognized body such as a standards institute, which provides an assurance of quality to consumers. Compliance is established by means of conformity assessment procedures. Regulations may lay down product characteristics or their related process and production methods, or they may deal with the terminology, symbols, packaging and labelling requirements applying to a product or production method. Examples include noise and emission limits for machinery, or labelling requirements such as health warnings on tobacco products or the energy consumption levels of household appliances. Such regulations raise the cost of exporting where a manufacturer has to meet a different set of standards or pay for the cost of demonstrating compliance with the importing country's rules.

The EU's use of regulations and standards must comply with its obligations under the WTO Agreement on Technical Barriers to Trade (TBT Agreement) and, for food safety and animal and plant health measures, the WTO Agreement on the Application of Sanitary and Phytosanitary Measures (SPS Agreement). These obligations generally require the EU to use international standards where they exist (unless they can be shown to be inappropriate), in order to avoid discrimination against imported products and avoid creating unnecessary obstacles to international trade. Between 2000 and 2008 the EU or its MSs notified between 76 and 148 new regulations annually under the TBT Agreement (World Trade Organization 2009). Some of the more important trade disputes involving the EU have occurred around the use of regulatory import barriers, such as its ban on the import of hormone-treated beef, maximum aflatoxin levels in cereals, dried fruit and nuts, and its labelling requirements for genetically modified foods.

24.5 EU trade relations

Most EU external trade relations are governed by different regional and bilateral PTAs, which extend preferential treatment to partner countries. Almost all of these agreements are reciprocal; thus EU exports to partner countries receive the same preferential treatment. This section first discusses the EU's PTAs, then trade relations with the USA and China, since they are the most significant in terms of overall trade (see Figure 24.2), while the final part provides an overview of some important multilateral issues.

24.5.1 Preferential trade relations

The EU has a complex web of bilateral and regional PTAs. With the exception of only nine (Australia, Canada, Hong Kong , Japan, New Zealand, Singapore, South Korea, Separate Customs Territory of Taiwan, Penghu, Kinmen and Matsu, and the USA), all WTO members have PTAs with the EU (see Figure 24.8).

PTAs sometimes cover only manufacturing goods. But occasionally they involve deeper forms of economic integration, incorporating trade in services and harmonization of regulations, often with numerous annexes containing highly technical rules and exceptions, and thus can be rather complex. WTO rules (Article XXIV; see Chapter 1) allow the formation of PTAs only if trade barriers on average do not rise after integration; tariffs and NTBs are eliminated within the area on 'substantially all' intra-PTA trade (usually interpreted to mean 90 per cent of intra-PTA trade); they are established within a reasonable time; and the project is notified to the WTO in time for it to determine whether these conditions are satisfied.

The geographic coverage of the EU's PTAs exaggerates the relative importance of trade links with preferred partners in value terms. The share of extra-EU imports from non-preferential partner countries has been about one-third of total EU imports for a decade or so. In fact, the share of imports entering under non-preferential terms may be substantial given the importance of product categories where zero tariffs apply and of administrative rules that restrict the use of the preference schemes by the beneficiary countries. An example of the latter are rules of origin (RoO), which determine whether a product has undergone sufficient processing to qualify as originating from a preference-receiving

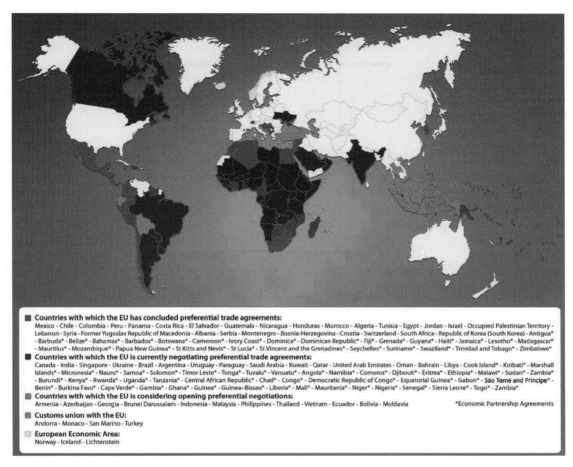

Figure 24.8 EU's PTAs *Source*: EU, DG Trade (http//trade.ec.europa.eu/doclib/docs/2006/december/tradoc_118238.pdf)

country. By making the rules more restrictive, the EU can disqualify many exports from receiving preferential treatment (see Cadot *et al.* 2005). The costs of these rules are estimated to be in the range of 2–8 per cent of the value of trade (see, for example, Carrère *et al.* 2006). Manchin (2006) found the costs of RoO for ACP countries to be around 4 per cent. The EU's Pan-Euro system, introduced in 1997, ensures that the same RoO applies to all preferential agreements signed by the EU, which might help to lessen the degree of complexity of preferential regimes under the CCP (Estevadeordal and Suominen 2005).

There are several issues that are likely to change the importance of the preference schemes in their current form. First, as global trade liberalization gathers steam and trade barriers crumble, the practical usefulness of trade preferences has diminished. Preference erosion is likely to accelerate markedly over the next decade. This will pose special problems for ACP countries that have enjoyed advantageous access to the EU market for many years, although taking into account the utilization rate of current preference schemes and the administrative costs of satisfying the requirements for obtaining the preferences reduces the magnitude of erosion costs significantly (Hoekman *et al.* 2006). Second, attention is likely to focus more on issues such as the right of establishment in services markets, attraction of foreign investment, rights to tender for public sector contracts in partner countries and competition law. Third, developing countries will have to provide reciprocity in future PTAs if they are to be acceptable under WTO rules. This means they will have to reduce their own import barriers as well. For some there will be a serious loss of government revenues as a result and some (small) danger of trade diversion. While some developing country governments tend to see the reduction in tariffs as a 'concession', trade theory suggests the opposite conclusion. Properly managed, the liberalization of imports can bring considerable benefits to their economies.

Generalized system of preferences

The generalized system of preferences (GSP) is a unilateral scheme providing preferential access for 176 developing countries in the form of reduced tariffs for their goods when entering the EU market. It is applicable for a period of three years at a time, and is then revised and renewed. The renewals provide some flexibility for the EU, but could also create some uncertainty for traders.

The GSP consists of three arrangements. The first is for all eligible countries. The second is a 'special incentive arrangement for sustainable development and good governance' (GSP+), which provides further preferences to those countries that implement international standards in sustainable development and good governance. The third is the Everything But Arms (EBA) initiative, the most generous arrangement, offering duty- and quota-free access to the EU market for least developed counties (LDCs) (for rice and sugar, tariff-free and quota-free access was introduced in 2009, for bananas in 2006) (for more on GSP, see Chapter 24).

Economic partnership agreements between the EU and African, Caribbean and Pacific countries

The first agreement between the EU (then the EEC) and ACP countries dates back to 1963, when the Yaoundé Agreements were signed. These were in effect during 1963–75. The objective was to foster economic cooperation between the EU and ACP countries, including through development assistance.

However, despite benefiting from one of the most generous trade preference schemes of the EU, providing free access (subject to RoO) for 95 per cent of their exports, it is a generally accepted view that ACP countries have been unsuccessful in taking advantage of their preferential status and, indeed, have performed poorly relative to other developing countries

(McQueen *et al.* 1997). Even the Commission acknowledges the failure of the agreement to deliver its objective: 'preferential access failed to boost local economies and stimulate growth in ACP countries'.[1]

The EU substantially revised the preference scheme, with the new EPAs dating back to the signing of the Cotonou Agreement in 2000. The new agreement gradually moves away from unilateral preferences towards reciprocal preferences between the EU and ACP countries (see Chapter 24).

Euro-Mediterranean trade agreements

The Euro-Mediterranean partnership was launched in 1995 (the 'Barcelona Process'). All the countries in the Mediterranean region (Algeria, Egypt, Israel, Jordan, the Palestinian Authority, Lebanon, Morocco, Syria, Tunisia and Turkey[2]), with the exception of Syria, signed association agreements with the EU. The agreements afford them duty-free access to the EU market for manufactured goods, and preferential treatment for exports of agricultural, processed agricultural and fisheries products. Tariffs will gradually be dismantled for EU exports to these countries.

Compared to some of the Europe agreements signed with the Eastern European countries in the mid-1990s, the Barcelona process is characterized by somewhat limited bilateral free trade areas (FTAs). This is due to lack of coverage: agriculture and services are rarely included; and also to lack of depth: substantial (and probably increasing) technical barriers to trade remain, due to differences in regulatory requirements and the need to duplicate testing and conformity assessment when selling in overseas markets. They are also limited by rules: restrictive RoO and lack of cumulation constrain the degree of effective market access (Brenton and Manchin 2003). (See more on the Barcelona process in Chapter 25.)

Euro-Mediterranean trade agreements are characterized by a hub-and-spoke structure, where the EU is in the centre of the web, with the sizes of the trading partners being very different. While trade with most of the partner countries represents only a small share of total EU trade, the EU is the most important trading partner for most of them. This hub-and-spoke structure is further reinforced by limited regional integration between the non-EU nations. Due to this asymmetry, the EU dominates the region's trade relationships.

European Free Trade Association

A series of bilateral FTAs were negotiated in the early 1970s between some of the European Free Trade Association (EFTA) nations (Austria, Finland, Iceland, Norway, Sweden and Switzerland) and the EU, most of which came into force in 1973, after Denmark and the UK left EFTA to join the EU (see Chapters 1 and 2). These applied to virtually all trade in industrial products, but excluded agricultural goods. While these EFTA producers did not have to pay tariffs (when RoO were satisfied), they faced important NTBs, which substantially increased costs when selling on the EU market. In order to achieve further integration, a new agreement, the European Economic Area (EEA), was concluded in 1992 and entered into force in 1994; all EFTA nations bar Switzerland (which rejected EEA membership in a referendum) signed the agreement (see Chapter 2). Liechtenstein joined the EEA in 1995. Due to the accession of Austria, Finland and Sweden to the EU in 1995, and the non-participation of Switzerland, the EFTA side of the EEA is now limited to two small European nations and a territory: Iceland, Liechtenstein and Norway. Today the EEA extends the Single European Market to these three, but they have no say in its legislation (see Chapters 2 and 6).

Commonwealth of Independent States

Although the EU does not have an FTA with the Commonwealth of Independent States (CIS; see Chapter 1), there are some agreements in place which touch on trade and possible future integration. One of the EU's most important trading partners is Russia: it is the third most important exporter to and importer from the EU, accounting for 10 per cent of total EU external imports and about 6 per cent of EU external exports. Other CIS countries play a lesser role, with about 2.5 per cent of total EU external exports and imports originating from them, but some of them are in the EU's GSP.

With the 2004 and 2007 EU enlargements, the physical border of the EU shifted towards the east, and several CIS countries (Russia, Ukraine, Belarus and Moldova) are now immediate neighbours of the EU. The Commission proposed a 'differentiated, progressive, and benchmarked approach' to the new neighbours, which was specified in the European Neighbourhood Policy (ENP) Strategy Paper.[3] On the basis of this strategy, bilateral action plans were agreed with each participating country. The ENP aims, among other things, to create grounds for possible further trade liberalization and for gradual participation in the SEM. Negotiations for a new Partnership and Cooperation Agreement are ongoing. Francois and Manchin (2009) estimated the effects of a potential FTA between CIS countries and the EU, and found that CIS countries would only benefit from it if it were to incorporate deeper forms of integration and not be limited to liberalization of tariffs on goods.

Western Balkans

In 2000 the EU granted autonomous trade preferences to all the Western Balkan countries, allowing nearly all their exports (except some agricultural products) to enter the EU duty-free. Also, the Western Balkans have been offered Stabilization and Association Agreements (SAAs): the two with Croatia and Macedonia are already in force, and one has been signed with Serbia. The trade part of the SAAs is effective with Albania, Bosnia and Herzegovina and Montenegro. The agreements aim to progressively establish an EU–Western Balkans FTA. These agreements are similar to the Europe Agreements that were signed between the Eastern European candidate countries and the EU in the mid-1990s, covering somewhat more than just goods trade liberalization (aligning rules on EU practice and protecting intellectual property).

Other non-regional preferential agreements

Numerous PTAs have either been signed or are under negotiation between the EU and other non-European countries or regions. The EU has FTAs with Chile, Mexico and South Africa, as well as with the Gulf Cooperation Council (GCC, comprising Bahrain, Kuwait, Oman, Qatar, Saudi Arabia and the United Arab Emirates; see Chapter 1). The EU and Mercosur (Brazil, Argentina, Uruguay and Paraguay; see Chapter 1) have been negotiating (on and off) an FTA since 1999. Negotiations are also ongoing with South Korea, ASEAN (Brunei, Cambodia, Indonesia, Laos, Malaysia, Myanmar, the Philippines, Thailand, Singapore and Vietnam), and with Canada, Central American countries, Colombia, Peru, India, Singapore and South Korea.[4]

24.5.2 Trade relations with some other important partners

As mentioned above, this section covers relations with the EU's two main partners, China and the USA.

China

China is the EU's fastest-growing goods exports market, worth €81.7 billion in 2009. EU goods imports from China amounted to €214.7 billion for the same year. China is the world's largest exporter and second largest importer. The EU, in turn, is China's biggest trading partner, ahead of the USA and Japan, and accounting for about 20 per cent of Chinese exports. EU–China trade has been increasing significantly in recent years and more than doubled during the period 2003–7 (see El-Agraa 2007 for a perspective during 1981–2003). Thus trade relations between the EU and China are increasingly important for both. The Commission states that 'China is the single most important challenge for EU trade policy'.[5]

The EU and China have a formal relationship, instigated by the EU in 1995 and endorsed by China in 2003 (El-Agraa 2007). Also, the 'EU–China High Level Economic and Trade Dialogue' was launched in 2008. It aims to deal with the most important issues related to EU–China trade and economic relations, including issues in the areas of investment, market access and protection of intellectual property rights. Furthermore, negotiations on a Partnership and Cooperation Agreement (PCA) started in 2007.

The EU–China trade relationship is not running smoothly, however, due to some EU concerns, mainly related to the EU's trade deficit with China. Some of these were raised by the EU during China's Trade Policy Review at the WTO in 2010.[6] They included problems related to China's NTBs, investment restrictions on foreign companies, protection of intellectual property rights and unjustified state interference in the economy. Note that although the EU's trade deficit with China is substantial, the overall EU trade deficit is negligible; while the trade deficit with China is increasing, that with the rest of the world has been decreasing. Also, many countries export to the EU via China, not from their home countries (Erixon and Messerlin 2009).

USA

The EU–USA bilateral trade relationship is the most important in the world in value terms. In 2009 EU goods exports to the USA amounted to €204.4 billion, with imports being €159.8 billion. For services trade the EU exported €119.4 billion and imported €127 billion in 2009. This is despite the fact that the two have no PTA, but are of course the power base of the WTO.

Although EU trade with industrial countries is in principle governed by WTO rules, this has not prevented controversy arising on many specific issues. EU economic relations with the USA have been based on strong political and cultural ties, as well as common economic interests. Yet at times it appears as if the two partners are locked in a state of perpetual crisis. In the past, trade wars have threatened to erupt because of disputes over issues as diverse as steel, hormone-treated beef, aircraft noise, subsidies to Airbus, genetically modified crops and bananas. Although full-scale trade wars have threatened to break out on many occasions, the strong mutuality of interests between the USA and the EU has, on each occasion thus far, brought them back from the brink. Trade relations are characterized by constant levels of minor friction rather than a deep divergence of interests.

On a regular basis, high-level EU–US summits take place to discuss relevant issues and possibilities for facilitating economic links between them. At the 2007 summit the two signed a Framework for Advancing Transatlantic Economic Integration between the USA and the EU. The framework included the establishment of the Transatlantic Economic Council (TEC), which aims to increase economic integration between them. The 2005 summit identified regulatory cooperation as the prime aim of transatlantic cooperation. Regulatory cooperation is directed towards reducing EU–USA NTBs, which are important barriers to trade in both goods and services. This is because bilateral tariffs between the two countries are less important, since those on goods traded between the two countries are low. Thus reducing NTBs is of the essence. Ecorys (2009) finds that abolishing the 'removable' EU–USA NTBs would result in considerable economic benefits for both: an increase in EU GDP by €122 billion per year, with exports rising by 2.1 per cent; and a €41 billion per year increase in US GDP, with a 6.1 per cent enhancement of US exports.

24.5.3 Multilateral trade policy

In 2001 the WTO concluded the Fourth Ministerial Conference with a decision to launch a new round, the Doha Development Agenda, comprising both further trade liberalization and new rule-making, underpinned by commitments to provide more effective special and differential treatment to developing countries. Although the negotiations were scheduled to end in three years, they are still ongoing, partly due to the emergence of the BRICs (Brazil, Russia, India and China) as a strong bargaining group on behalf of the developing world. The last set of formal negotiations in July 2008 collapsed due to lack of compromise on agricultural import rules. Since then, several countries have called for negotiations to restart, with the 2009 G20 summit declaring the intention to complete the round.

The EU had four stated objectives at the time of the launch of the Doha Round: (i) to further liberalize access to markets for goods and particularly services; (ii) to strengthen coverage in the areas of investment, competition, transparency in government procurement, intellectual property and trade facilitation; (iii) to ensure that more assistance is provided to developing countries to help with their integration into the global economy; (iv) to get the WTO to focus more on issues of public concern, such as the environment, animal welfare and food safety, ensuring that trade rules are compatible with the wider interests of society as a whole. A more implicit objective, but one which nonetheless carries much weight in the actual negotiating process, is the EU's desire to shape WTO rules on agricultural trade to enable it to maintain support for the European model of agriculture (see Chapter 20). This section examines some of the issues at stake in this comprehensive agenda.

Trade and intellectual property rights

Intellectual property is an increasingly important part of international trade. Most of the value of new medicines and other high-technology products lies in the research, innovation, design and testing involved. People who purchase CDs, videos, books or computer programmes are paying for the creativity and information they contain, not for the materials used to make them. Considerable value can be added even to low-technology goods, such as clothing or shoes, through design and the use of brand names. These 'knowledge goods', ranging from computer programmes to pop songs, and 'reputation goods', such as trademarks or appellations of origin, account for an unquantifiable but undeniably growing share of the value embodied in traded products. The nature of trade policy with respect to such knowledge and reputation goods differs radically from policy aimed at liberalizing merchandise trade, since the main concern is not to abolish obstacles to imports (as countries are generally keen to attract knowledge goods), but to safeguard owners' property rights. Negotiations on intellectual property rights therefore do not consist of bargaining on abolition of barriers, but on agreements to set up minimum standards of ownership protection.

From a theoretical viewpoint, the enforcement of intellectual property rights is a double-edged sword (see Primo Braga 1995). In the short run, protecting owners of knowledge goods – for example, through patents – violates the rule that public goods, whose marginal usage cost is zero, should be free. Static efficiency considerations therefore advocate a lax implementation of such property rights, to allow maximum dissemination. In the long run, however, the generation of additional knowledge goods is costly: resources have to be invested in research and development, and this will only occur if a future pecuniary return on such an investment can be safely anticipated. A zero price of knowledge goods is therefore socially sub-optimal in a dynamic sense, because it discourages innovation.

Property rights on reputation goods also have their advantages and drawbacks in equity terms. Trademark protection increases the monopoly power of owners, on the one hand, thereby restricting competition, but on the other hand it can increase consumer welfare, by allowing product differentiation and facilitating product information.

Both sides of the theoretical argument have been advanced in multilateral negotiations on intellectual property rights. Since developed countries, including the EU, tend to be the owners and exporters of intellectual property, while developing countries are net importers, the former generally argue in favour of stricter property rights enforcement than the latter. This was particularly evident during the Uruguay Round. These negotiations culminated in the Agreement on Trade-Related Aspects of Intellectual Property Rights (TRIPS), which, alongside GATT and GATS, forms one of the three pillars of the WTO. TRIPS negotiations were championed mainly by the USA and the EU, against much initial opposition from developing countries. Divisions surfaced again when it appeared that TRIPS protection would prevent developing countries from gaining access to generic drugs as part of their public health programmes. At Doha in November 2001 WTO ministers issued a declaration emphasizing that the TRIPS agreement should not prevent MSs from protecting public health. They confirmed the right of countries to grant compulsory licences (authorization, under certain conditions, to produce a drug or medicine without the consent of the patent holder) and to resort to parallel imports (where drugs produced by the patent holder in another country can be imported without their approval) where appropriate. A further waiver was agreed in 2003, to allow countries producing under a compulsory licence to export to eligible importing countries. This was particularly important for the least-developed countries, which do not have the indigenous pharmaceutical manufacturing capability to produce their own generic drugs.

Under the TRIPS agreement, signatories have to establish minimum standards of intellectual property rights protection, implement procedures to enforce these rights and extend the traditional GATT principles of national treatment and MFN practice to intellectual property. It was agreed that twenty-year patent protection should be available for all inventions, whether of products or processes, in almost all fields of technology. Copyright on literary works (including computer programmes), sound recordings and films is made available for at least fifty years. Under the agreed transition period, most countries had to take on full TRIPS obligations by 2000, while the least-developed countries were allowed to postpone application of most provisions until 2006, which is now extended to 2013 in general, and to 2016 for pharmaceutical patents and undisclosed information.

Trade and competition policy

The relationship between trade and competition policy was first raised by the USA, which, for many years, like the EU, claimed that Japanese corporate groups undermined market access for foreign suppliers by buying largely from each other and maintaining closed distribution chains. More recently, the EU has made the running, arguing that anti-competitive practices by businesses can have a significant impact on access to markets. It has sought rules that would require countries to introduce a national competition policy and to enforce it. It has also highlighted the need for more international cooperation to deal with questions such as international cartels and multi-jurisdictional mergers. This market access agenda is not necessarily shared by developing countries, who have been more concerned about possible anti-competitive behaviour by large multinational companies at their expense. They are also unhappy at the prospect of undertaking additional commitments in an area where they have limited capacity and foresee limited gains. Reaching agreement is also made more difficult, as in the case of intellectual property rights, by theoretical disagreements as to what appropriate competition policy should be.

The EU succeeded in establishing a WTO working group on the interaction between trade and competition policy at the WTO ministerial meeting in Singapore in December 1996. This group discusses the relevance of fundamental WTO principles of non-discrimination and transparency for competition policy. There is no question of trying to harmonize domestic competition laws, but even reaching agreement on a more general framework is proving difficult. The Doha Declaration had set the objective of establishing a multilateral framework on competition policies, but this topic was dropped from the remit of WTO negotiations in 2004. The question being of evident concern to the EU, it is certain to appear again sooner or later on the international policy agenda.

Trade and the environment

Environmental policy moved to a prominent position on the trade agenda during the 1990s (see Chapter 18). Until then, virtually the only environmental concern to affect trade policy was the protection of endangered species. With the rise of ecological awareness and trans-frontier pollution problems, such as ozone depletion, acid rain and global warming, trade policy came to be seen as a significant element in a country's overall environmental policy.

The main trade policy issue in this debate relates to the use of import restrictions on goods whose production creates negative trans-border environmental externalities. Economic theory suggests that in such circumstances the most efficient remedy is to apply direct environmental policy at the source of the externality – for example, through pollution taxes, eco-subsidies or regulation (see Chapter 18). However, environmental policies are often difficult to enforce, so this first-best option may not be feasible. In that case, import restrictions may be the only practicable policy tool. The main drawback of import restrictions against polluting countries is that they provide protection to domestic producers of the importable good, and ecological arguments are therefore vulnerable to abuse by domestic protectionist lobbies. For this reason, trade measures should be temporary and accompanied by efforts to implement environmental policies in the polluting countries.

Even if the externalities are dealt with by environmental policies adopted at the source, new problems can still emerge. Environmental policies affect the competitiveness of open economies. Thus countries with lax environmental legislation are blamed for 'ecological dumping', and import-competing industries in countries with stringent laws may lobby for protection to ensure a level playing field. As before, the first-best way of ensuring a level playing field is by achieving some degree of coordination in environmental policies across countries. This does not necessarily mean that all countries must adopt exactly the same environmental regime, but it provides a powerful rationale for seeking agreement on environmental policies on a multilateral basis. Even if an agreed way of eradicating ecological dumping could be found, it remains questionable if trade restrictions are the most appropriate remedy. Restricting imports can be counterproductive, as it promotes the domestic activities that the environmental policy is attempting to restrain.

On another tack, some environmentalists argue that the rising volume of international trade in itself is causing serious damage to the environment. Oil leakage from tankers and pollution from increased road haulage are classical examples. They recommend a reduction in trade, if necessary by protection, as a solution. The standard economic response would be that trade restrictions are inefficient and that policy should instead be aimed at the source of the problem – for example, taxation of oil shipments and on the use of polluting fuels by lorries. One could agree with this, while pointing out that such correct policy action may not be politically feasible. Witness, for example, the way in which the Commission's proposals for a carbon tax have been resisted by business interests (see Chapter 18).

We conclude that trade policy is certainly not the best, and can often be an inappropriate, instrument to protect the environment. International dialogue and agreed domestic policy measures are a more efficient alternative. The main platform for such negotiations is the WTO Committee on Trade and Environment, which was established in 1995. Discussions in this committee have so far been a mere stocktaking exercise, and its reports have rarely contained specific proposals. The EU, like everybody else, supports the case for multilateral environmental agreements, but the difficulty lies in getting countries to agree.

Trade and labour standards

The social dimension to increased international trade has received increasing attention, given the concern that trade and investment flows should benefit people at large and not just international business. This has led to calls for a social clause in WTO rules that would allow trade barriers to be invoked against imports from countries deemed to violate minimum labour standards. Human rights and moral advocates of a social clause see it as a way of promoting and enforcing core labour standards and helping to eradicate exploitative working practices. The difficulty is that trade sanctions will do little for the bulk of the labour force in developing countries, which is employed in the informal sector, and could even have the opposite effect to the one desired. A less well-founded argument is that lower labour standards, especially in developing countries, give them an 'unfair' competitive advantage, which will either lead to 'social dumping' (the ability to sell goods abroad more cheaply, analogous to 'ecological dumping'), or to the erosion of existing social standards in developed countries (the 'race to the bottom' argument), as footloose firms threaten to uproot to take advantage of laxer standards elsewhere. This version of the pauper labour argument is no less a fallacy for being restated in modern guise. Focusing only on labour costs ignores the substantially higher productivity of labour in developed countries. Developed countries are perfectly able to compete in the sectors where they have a comparative advantage.

The 1995 World Summit on Social Development in Copenhagen identified four core labour standards for the first time, and these were later confirmed by the 1998 International Labour Organization (ILO) Declaration on Fundamental Principles and Rights at Work. The four core standards are freedom of association and collective bargaining; the prevention of child labour; the elimination of forced labour; and the outlawing of discrimination. The EU is strongly committed to the protection of core labour rights, but the debate is about the appropriate role for the WTO in this task. The ILO enforcement mechanism, being limited to ratified conventions, is rather weak; hence the attraction of using the WTO, with its rules-based system and binding dispute settlement mechanism, as the means to ensure compliance.

In the first WTO ministerial conference in Singapore in December 1996, the EU was among those suggesting that a WTO working party be created to look into the links between international trade and working conditions. The proposal was fiercely resisted by the developing countries, which saw it as a guise for protectionism and a cover for more restrictive trade measures. The final declaration confirmed that the ILO was the competent body to 'set and deal' with labour standards. At the Seattle ministerial conference in 1999, the USA returned to the working party proposal, while making clear that its ultimate objective was to incorporate core labour standards into all trade agreements and make them subject to trade sanctions. This was a major reason for the failure of the Seattle conference (see Chapter 25). Labour standards therefore do not feature on the agenda of the Doha Round negotiations. In 2001 the Doha Ministerial Declaration reaffirmed the declaration made at the Singapore Ministerial Conference regarding internationally recognized core labour standards.

The EU has opposed sanctions as a way of enforcing core labour standards, but it continues to insist on the necessity of showing that trade liberalization does not lead to a deterioration in working conditions. It has proposed strengthened mechanisms within the ILO to promote respect for core labour standards, a review mechanism between the WTO and the ILO, as part of which a trade angle would be linked to the reviews conducted by the ILO, and support for private sector and voluntary schemes (such as codes of conduct and ethical labelling schemes) (CEU 2001a, CEU 2006o). It has also used social incentives, under its GSP scheme, to promote core labour standards by providing additional trade preferences for countries that comply with these standards, and allowing for the withdrawal of preferences where beneficiary countries practise any form of slavery or forced labour.

24.6 Conclusion

The EU is one of the world's most important traders. While initially EU trade policy mainly consisted of tariffs and import quota restrictions on goods, the importance of the former has gradually diminished and today is marginal, with the exception of tariffs on agricultural products. While tariff protection has waned, NTBs have assumed increased importance – hence the SEM of 1992. But the SEM is a family affair, so there is still scope for realizing further global integration through the removal of NTBs between the EU and its trading partners. Apart from tariff reductions, the EU has also facilitated access to its markets to numerous countries by establishing a complex system of preferential trade agreements, leading to the now familiar 'spaghetti bowl' depiction. Furthermore, the EU continues to be a very active leader in multilateral trade liberalization through the WTO. Agriculture still remains a sensitive area, both in multilateral liberalization negotiations and bilateral agreements, where the coverage in agricultural goods is often not the same as in manufacturing goods.

There are important challenges ahead for EU trade policy. The EU needs a secure system of rules of international trade, given that it relies heavily on trading with other nations. This implies the need for an efficiently functioning dispute settlement system at a multilateral level. Due to the increasing relative importance of non-tariff barriers, there is an increasing need to address the problem arising from divergence in regulatory systems between countries. The economic downturn, coupled with concerns about food and energy security, makes these issues even more challenging to tackle.

Some recent changes introduced in the Lisbon Treaty, such as the reinforcement of the EU's external actions by the new High Representative, and the extension of the scope of CCP to include FDI, might facilitate future negotiations in the area of trade. However, the precise form of the EU's future external policy will depend on several factors. Among these are that the increasing heterogeneity among EU MSs is likely to make it more difficult to reach consensus, and that the current economic crisis might lessen the enthusiasm for further integration.

Summary

- The EU is the world's largest trader and on average trades more within itself. Its main trading partners in goods are China, Russia, Switzerland and the USA. The EU's trade in services is of lower value relative to goods, and with many countries it is only a small share of total trade. The most important EU exporting sectors are machinery, transport goods and other manufactured goods. These sectors also represent an important share of imports, together with mineral fuels and related materials, which amount to one-quarter of total imports.
- The Commission has sole responsibility for EU external trade relations, and is in charge of negotiations with the outside world, in consultation with a special committee appointed by the Council. All trade agreements are subject to Council approval and, increasingly, jointly with the European Parliament, especially after the changes introduced by the Lisbon Treaty in December 2009.
- EU common external tariffs are rather low, with the exception of agricultural goods and textile and clothing products. With the reduction of tariffs on imports over time, some non-tariff barriers have gained more importance.
- Most EU external trade is governed by different regional and bilateral preferential trade agreements, which constitute a complex web of preferential trade links depicted as the 'spaghetti bowl'. Although only nine countries do not have preferential agreements with the EU, some of them are among the EU's most important trading partners, accounting for about one-third of EU external trade. Of these countries, the two most important partners, China and the USA, were reviewed.
- The EU is one of the most prominent actors in multilateral liberalization within WTO.
- In the context of the last round of multilateral liberalization negotiations, the EU aimed to achieve further liberalization of access to markets for goods and services, and to strengthen coverage in the areas of investment, competition and intellectual property. These last negotiations collapsed in 2008, due to lack of compromise on agricultural import rules.

Questions and essay topics

1. What does a common commercial policy mean?
2. What is the role of the Commission when it comes to EU external trade policy?
3. If an outside country, say, Japan, has a trade dispute with, say, France, can the two settle the matter between themselves?
4. Which countries are the EU's most important trading partners in goods and services trade?
5. Why does the EU have a 'special relationship' with China?
6. Which sectors are the most protected by the EU's common external tariffs?
7. What kinds of important non-tariff trade barriers does the EU have?
8. Which are the EU's most important regional preferential agreements?
9. Discuss the developments of different trade policy instruments over time.
10. 'Providing preferential access to the EU market which is limited to elimination of tariffs on imports from the partner country would not be worth much.' Discuss.
11. Discuss the possibilities of future directions of EU trade policy towards China.

FURTHER READING

Baldwin, R. E. (1994) *Towards an Integrated Europe*, CEPR, London.

Hoekman, B. (2007) 'Regionalism and development: the European neighbourhood policy and integration a la carte', *Journal of International Trade and Diplomacy*, vol. 1, no. 1.

Hoekman, B. and Kostecki, M. M. (2001) *The Political Economy of the World Trading System: The WTO and Beyond*, Oxford University Press.

Sapir, A. (2000) 'EC regionalism at the turn of the millennium: toward a new paradigm?', *World Economy*, vol. 23, no 9.

NOTES

1 http://ec.europa.eu/trade/wider-agenda/development/economic-partnerships

2 Turkey has a customs union with the EU on industrial goods excluding agriculture.

3 It was approved by the Council in June 2004 in the Council's Presidency Conclusions 10679/2/04.

4 Up-to-date information about ongoing negotiations can be found on the DG Trade's website: http://ec.europa.eu/trade/creating-opportunities/bilateral-relations

5 http://ec.europa.eu/trade/creating-opportunities/bilateral-relations/countries/china

6 Trade Policy Reviews (TPR) on China take place regularly. These reviews not only have a WTO transparency function, but also provide negotiation and dispute settlement functions. They allow WTO members to review openness to trade and raise questions and concerns over market barriers.

25 The EU and the developing world
ALI EL-AGRAA

25.1 Introduction

The EU's economic size and its role in world trade mean that it is a key player in structuring the global economic environment for developing countries (DCs) through its aid and trade policies. EU member states (MSs) are the largest trading partner of DCs, absorbing about one-fifth of their exports in 2009 and accounting for a similar portion of their imports. Also in 2009 the EU and its MSs provided 56 per cent of total official development assistance (ODA) worldwide. Moreover, the EU has a significant indirect influence through its active participation in international organizations that manage the world economic system – for example, the World Bank, the World Trade Organization (WTO) and, before it, the General Agreement on Tariffs and Trade (GATT, managed by the WTO since 1995). Furthermore, the EU development cooperation policy is comprehensive in its approach, including trade arrangements, ODA and political dialogue,[1] with important and even radical changes having been adopted by the EU in 2009 in its development policy. But more significant than all these considerations is that the EU's relationship with DCs goes back to the time of the creation of the European Economic Community (EEC), when the ex-colonies, especially those of the French, had to be accommodated before the 1957 Rome Treaties could become a reality, with the admission of the UK and the Iberian nations extending and enhancing the Community, to encompass African, Caribbean, Latin American and Asian nations.

This chapter explores the way the EU interacts with DCs through both its trade and its development cooperation policies. It then concentrates on the trade arrangements that are intended to benefit DCs, followed by discussion on the development cooperation or financial aid arrangements. Unfortunately, due to space limitations, other aspects of development aid, such as EU humanitarian or food aid, will not be covered except in passing. The conclusion highlights some of the main issues in the current debates on the EU's relations with DCs.

25.2 Essential background

Before getting down to the set task, it is necessary to provide some essential background information. First, the economic environment in which the EU's relations with DCs are played out is changing fast. The most striking feature of the global economy over the past three decades has been the growing differentiation in economic performance. Overall differences in gross national income (GNI) per capita between advanced nations and DCs remain large: in 2008 average income per capita was $39,687 in the high-income countries, but only $2,780 in the low- and middle-income DCs. However, for some DC regions the gap has been narrowing rapidly. This is particularly the case for the Asian 'tigers' (Hong Kong, Singapore, South Korea and Taiwan) and the East Asia and Pacific region, dominated by China. During the 1990s, GNI per head in these country groups had an annual growth rate of 4 per cent and 6.3 per cent respectively, compared to just 1.8 per

This area was only touched on in my external relations chapter in the first edition. It blossomed into a full chapter under Alan Marin, then Enzo Grilli, then Alan Mathews. Sadly, Alan has decided to make a clean break, with imminent retirement, so all I have done is to update and simplify his excellent contribution. Nevertheless, he has commented on various drafts of the chapter and made helpful suggestions; I am therefore greatly indebted to him in more ways than one. I am also grateful to Miriam Manchin for helpful comments and suggestions on various drafts of the chapter.

cent in the Organization for Economic Cooperation and Development (OECD) countries, and China has been growing by more than 10 per cent for about a decade.

The economic performance of Latin America and the Caribbean has been less strong. Following an average 3.3 per cent annual growth in the 1970s, the region was devastated by the debt crisis in the 1980s, which led to a 'lost decade' for development in which living standards declined. Recovery in the early 1990s started weakly, but overall performance has matched that of the 1970s, despite fears of the financial fragility of the region in the aftermath of Argentina's default on its foreign debt in 2001; the biggest default in history. Moreover, its performance has been stronger than that of either the Middle East and North Africa or Sub-Saharan Africa. In the latter, average living standards have contracted steadily for two decades, as a result of a combination of natural disasters, slumping commodity prices, economic mismanagement, civil strife and, most recently, the AIDS epidemic. World Bank forecasts for the period to 2015 project that these differences will persist, with yearly per capita growth rates of 5.3 per cent in east Asia and 4.2 per cent in south Asia, contrasting with 2.6 per cent in the Middle East and North African region and 1.6 per cent in sub-Saharan Africa. As we shall see below, the latter are the two regions on which EU development policies have a particular focus. Thus EU development policy is required to address an increasingly disparate group of DCs, where the appropriate mixture of policy instruments is going to vary, depending on the circumstances of the particular country or country grouping being considered.

Second, many of the old foundations of past EU relationships with DCs are being swept aside. These relationships were based on a mixture of trade preferences and development aid to promote trade and development in the weaker DCs, while restrictive trade measures (high protection against agricultural imports, quotas on the imports of textiles and clothing, and anti-dumping duties on the import of particularly competitive manufactured goods) and the absence of financial aid characterized EU relations with the more advanced DCs. Many DCs pursued inward-looking development strategies and were little interested in attracting private foreign investment. The liberalization of world trade and capital movements in recent years is gradually transforming these relationships.

Trade preference schemes are weakening for two separate reasons. The first is economic: trade liberalization under the auspices of the WTO/GATT is reducing the value of trade preferences and the EU has been searching for new models of cooperation. The second is legal: the EU's network of discriminatory preference schemes runs counter to GATT/WTO rules on regional trade arrangements (RTAs; see Chapter 1), but for years the EU was able to persuade other WTO members to condone them. In the mid-1990s the cost of obtaining these waivers became too high and the EU decided instead that it would enter into WTO-compatible trade arrangements with its DC partners. These are required to be free trade areas (FTAs), covering substantially all trade between the contracting parties (see Article XXIV in Chapter 1). Thus the EU has been actively pursuing with many DCs the conversion of its selective preferential agreements into FTAs.

Third, EU development cooperation policy is evolving rapidly. Private capital flows have come to dwarf the role of development aid as a source of investment capital in DCs. In the face of growing dissatisfaction with the outcome of aid programmes and growing 'aid fatigue', the search has been on to define new roles for aid and to see where it can be used most effectively. The EU has undertaken a comprehensive re-evaluation of its development cooperation policy objectives, which has placed poverty alleviation at the centre; indeed the 2009 Treaty on the Functioning of the European Union (TFEU, the Lisbon Treaty) clearly states that the EU's development cooperation policy 'shall have as its primary objective the reduction and, in the long-term, the eradication of poverty' (Article 280.1). Also, the EU has been an enthusiastic supporter of the Millennium Development Goals (MDGs) launched at the UN Millennium Development Summit in 2000, which include the goal of reducing global poverty by 50 per cent from its 1990 level by 2015. At the same time, development cooperation is also required to come to terms with the changed world after 11 September 2001. There is now a closer link between security and development policy, as emphasized in the 2003 EU Security Strategy, which defined security as the 'first condition for development'. The higher salience of South–North 'contagion effects' arising from issues such as terrorism, migration, disease and pollution may lead to aid being driven more by the security concerns of the donor rather than by the development interests of the recipient in the future.

Fourth, EU development cooperation policy has been characterized by a strong regional emphasis, with particular groups of partner countries, such as the African, Caribbean and Pacific (ACP) states, Asia and Latin American (ALA) countries, the Mediterranean nations, and, more recently, PHARE and TACIS countries (these are the Central and Eastern European countries, CEECs, and the former Soviet Union, respectively; see Section 25.3.2, page 405). The most long-lived and comprehensive of these regional arrangements has been the relationship with ACP countries, originally under successive Lomé Conventions and now under the Cotonou Agreement. The Lomé Convention, first signed in 1975, was hailed at the time as a model for a new type of development partnership between industrialized countries and DCs. Its innovations of partnership, deep trade preferences and long-term contractual aid commitments were certainly novel at the time. However, the EU's geographic priorities changed rapidly in the 1990s, following the end of the cold war and reflecting the changing importance of different DC regions in international trade. Priority is now given, under the European Neighbourhood Policy, to the stability and development of neighbouring countries, and to aid for countries in crisis in the regions nearest to the EU. The ACP countries are no longer as central to EU development cooperation policy as was once the case. On the other hand, in 2005 the EU launched its Africa Strategy, which reemphasized its commitment to support for African countries, which remain among the poorest and least-developed in the world (Council 2005b). Not surprisingly, these shifts and realignments have generated considerable controversy and debate. There is a continuing tension between those who stress the regional approach based on recognition of historical and strategic linkages with former European colonies and neighbouring countries, and those who argue for a more global approach concerned predominantly with poverty reduction.

25.3 Trade policy

Trade is a key mechanism for development. At the multilateral level, trade policy can contribute to ensuring a fair and equitable trading system, which facilitates the integration of DCs into the international trading regime at their own pace. At EU level, trade policy can facilitate access to EU markets by lowering trade barriers through multilateral liberalization, bilateral agreements and preferential schemes. EU trade policy

can also influence DCs' own trade policies, through economic and trade cooperation agreements and by encouraging regional arrangements between them.

The EU's trade policy towards DCs originally took the form of autonomous non-reciprocal preferential arrangements. These were of two kinds: the generalized system of preferences (GSP) available to all DCs, and special preferential schemes for particular groups of countries (see Chapter 24). The two most important special schemes were the trade preferences under the Lomé Convention (since 2000 the Cotonou Agreement) with ACP countries, and those with the EU's neighbours in the southern and eastern Mediterranean. Non-reciprocity meant that DCs were not required to offer similar preferential access to their markets in return for the access privileges they are granted to EU markets. The schemes differed according to the products covered, their contractual basis and the size of the concessions offered. Together, they formed a hierarchy of preferences, with the ACP signatories to the Lomé Convention in the most preferred category, the Mediterranean countries in an intermediate category and most ALA countries in the least preferred category, with GSP preferences only.

This trade policy has become even more diverse since the mid-1990s. In 2001 the EU decided to admit all products from countries on the UN's list of least-developed countries (LDCs) duty- and quota-free (though duty-free imports of bananas, rice and sugar remained subject to quotas for a further transition period). At the same time, the EU initiated moves to convert its special preferential schemes with the Mediterranean and ACP countries into reciprocal FTAs. It has also forged FTAs with some distant trading partners, notably South Africa, Chile and Mexico. In 2010, under the TFEU, it signed an FTA with South Korea and concluded negotiations with Columbia and Peru and countries of Central America. Negotiations with Mercosur were initiated in 1999, but remain ongoing. What explains these different strategies, and what does the future hold for the EU's trade relations with DCs? We seek to provide answers to these questions in this section.

25.3.1 The generalized system of preferences

Preferences contradict the WTO's most favoured nation (MFN) principle (see Chapter 1), but a provision known as the enabling clause which granted a waiver for autonomous tariff preferences to DCs was adopted in 1971 for a ten-year period, and renewed for an indefinite period as part of the final outcome of the Tokyo Round of GATT negotiations in 1979. This legitimizes the grant of general non-reciprocal preferences to DCs, and further allows deeper preferences in favour of LDCs. The EU introduced its GSP scheme in 1971. It covered all DC-manufactured exports, but only some agricultural and food products. GSP products are divided into sensitive and non-sensitive categories. Originally, non-sensitive products were offered duty-free access, while the preferences for sensitive products were characterized by quotas and ceilings, thus limiting the quantities involved.

In its 1995 revision of its GSP scheme, the EU did away with quotas and replaced them with tariff preferences that varied according to the sensitivity of the products. A further simplification took place in 2001. Under the general GSP scheme available to all DCs, including China, the EU granted duty-free access on non-sensitive products and partial tariff preferences on sensitive products. The usual tariff preference on sensitive products was a flat 3.5 percentage points (replaced for textiles and clothing by a 20 per cent preference margin, which, on a tariff of 15 per cent, for example, would yield a preference of 3 percentage points). For many exporters, these relatively small margins are not worth the extra paperwork involved in applying for GSP status.

Additional preferences were available under social, environmental and drug trafficking clauses (the 'super GSP'). For products receiving the flat rate preference of 3.5 percentage points under the general arrangements, the extra preference was 5 percentage points. In the case of textiles and clothing, an additional 20 per cent preference was available under these arrangements. The additional incentives under the social clause were available to countries complying with so-called 'core labour standards' (see Chapter 24), while those under the environmental clause were available to countries complying with international standards on forest management. The incentives to encourage countries to fight drug production and trafficking were initially introduced in the form of duty-free access for certain products originating in the Andean Community, but were subsequently extended to some other Latin and Central American countries, and later to Pakistan.

Partly in response to this ruling, the new EU GSP scheme introduced on 1 January 2006 reduces the number of GSP arrangements from five to three. Preferential margins under the general arrangement for all GSP beneficiary countries are maintained, although the product coverage is extended, mostly in the agricultural and fishery sectors. In addition, a GSP+ arrangement has been introduced for poorer and more vulnerable economies, conditioning them on human and labour rights (see page 411). This extends duty-free access to all sensitive products, provided that beneficiary countries can show that they comply with a range of conditions on human and labour rights, environmental protection, the fight against drugs and good governance. However, the arrangement is limited to lower-income economies, landlocked countries, small island nations and those countries that can demonstrate that their economies are poorly diversified. This open-ended list based on published criteria ensures that the new EU scheme complies with the WTO's ruling to give equal treatment to all similarly situated GSP beneficiaries. The third arrangement maintains the Everything But Arms (EBA; see Chapters 22 and 24) scheme of duty-free and quota-free access for all imports from LDCs. Apart from arms and ammunitions, which are permanently excluded products, the extension of the scheme to bananas was delayed until January 2006, for rice until July 2009 and for sugar until September 2009. The essential value of EBA is that it extends duty-free access to those agricultural products that are otherwise excluded from the GSP. While seen as the 'jewel in the crown' of EU trade relationships with DCs, its overall importance should not be exaggerated. The immediate impact of EBA has been negligible, largely because LDCs currently export so little in the product categories that were liberalized.

The EU's scheme has always provided for the 'graduation' of more competitive suppliers. This is defended by the EU on the grounds that it is intended to ensure that the preferences are targeted on those countries that genuinely need them, but it also reduces the competitive pressures on EU domestic firms. Based on certain criteria, a country may be excluded from the GSP altogether or graduated from certain products. Under the 1995 scheme, the criteria applied for exclusion were a complex combination of income level, a development index and an export specialization index. Under the 2006 scheme, these have been replaced with a single, simpler criterion: the country's share of the EU market expressed as a share of exports from all GSP countries. The threshold has initially been set at 15 per cent, with a 12.5 per cent limit for textiles and clothing.

The EU's GSP is intended to stimulate exports from DCs in three ways. First, trade is generated, as improved market access makes imported goods more attractive relative to domestically produced alternatives; this is trade creation (see Chapter 6). Second, to the extent that DCs and industrial countries are exporting similar products, preferential tariff reductions may help to switch trade to the DC supplier; this is trade diversion (see Chapter 6). From the point of view of DCs, both effects are additive and positive. Third, the GSP may have a longer-term effect to the extent that it enhances the attraction of the preference-receiving country as a location for inward foreign direct investment (FDI) seeking to export to the EU.

Generally, analysts have had difficulty in finding a positive effect of the GSP on DCs' exports, apart from the rent transfer accompanying the duty-free entry of goods (rents arise because DC exporters can benefit from the remaining tariff protection to the EU market against third countries). Critics point to a number of flaws with the GSP. Non-reciprocal GSP preferences lie outside the WTO's rule purview, and thus can be unilaterally modified or cancelled by donor countries at any time, which creates uncertainty, likely discouraging investment in beneficiary countries when enhanced investment is meant to be one of the GSP's primary rationales. The EU's scheme has offered minimal concessions on sensitive products (more than half of the total), which are often those in which DCs have a comparative advantage. Because there is a cost to firms in learning about and making use of preferences, it is often not worth their while to apply for preferential treatment. In the case of textile and clothing imports, quotas were maintained on all significant suppliers under the Multi-Fibre Arrangement until it was dismantled at the end of 2005 (see Chapter 24). Tariff preferences on agricultural products have been very limited, mainly because of the difficulty in reconciling preferential access with the protection provided by the Common Agricultural Policy (CAP; see Chapter 20), but also even in the case of tropical products, which the EU does not produce itself, in order to protect the margin of preference provided to more preferred ACP and Mediterranean suppliers. The value of preferences is also reduced by restrictive rules of origin (RoO; see Chapters 1 and 24).

25.3.2 Relations with the ACP states

The relationship with the ACP states began with the inception of the EEC in 1957, with the Yaoundé Conventions. This was followed by a series of five-year Lomé Conventions, starting in 1975, after the UK's accession in 1973. Since 2000 relations with the ACP countries have been governed by the Cotonou Agreement, which was signed in 2000 and came into force in 2003. This introduced significant changes in philosophy and instruments compared to Lomé Conventions. As noted earlier, Lomé Conventions were based on a partnership model, deep trade preferences and contractual financial commitments. This section concentrates on the trade preferences provided, while the aid element is examined in Section 25.4.3 (see page 416).

Under the conventions, the EU offered duty- and quota-free access to exports from the ACP countries, although, again, a major exception was exports covered by CAP. However, more preferential treatment than to other countries was extended for CAP products. In addition, four commodity protocols annexed to the Lomé Convention provided preferential access for a specified quantity of exports from a selected group of traditional ACP suppliers of bananas, rum, sugar and beef. This trade regime was extended under the Cotonou Agreement until the end of 2007.

Despite the fact that the ACP states were at the top of the EU's hierarchy of preferences, with the most favourable conditions of access to EU markets, they have become increasingly marginalized as EU trade partners over time; the share of ACP exports to the EU has fallen by more than a half. Furthermore, 50 per cent of total ACP exports came from only four products: oil (26 per cent), diamonds (11 per cent), cocoa (9 per cent) and wood (4 per cent). These data are often used to argue that trade preferences have not worked, and indeed there is some support for this, but it is not the whole story. The importance of the trade preferences granted is often overstated. On average, 50–60 per cent of ACP exports to the EU never received any preferences because they were non-dutiable, irrespective of source. Another 5–10 per cent fell under the special CAP import regulations (see Chapter 20). Ultimately, only about 35–45 per cent of ACP exports were eligible for preferences. These were mainly tropical beverages, for which demand is quite price inelastic and is reaching saturation in the EU. Further, the margin of preference enjoyed by the ACP states fell as the EU's MFN tariffs were cut under successive GATT negotiations for products such as coffee, cocoa and vegetable oils.

Trade preferences require a supply capacity to make them effective, and arguably economic mismanagement and supply-side difficulties also limited ACP exports. But even with good economic management, the ACP countries have been specialized in commodities with poor market prospects, and where the deterioration in export prices has had a devastating effect on development efforts. It can be argued that trade preferences failed to promote the necessary diversification. On the other hand, where progress in diversification was made, the products to benefit (such as textiles, fisheries and horticultural products), were those which had enjoyed a substantial margin of preference over the EU's MFN and GSP tariffs. On balance, however, ACP trade preferences have not been seen as a success, and this was one of the factors leading to their revision in the Cotonou Agreement in 2000.

In 1996 the Commission published a Green Paper to promote discussion on the post-Lomé relationship with the ACP states. Central to this discussion was the nature of future trade relationships in the context of the WTO rules. Because the EU's special preferences for ACP countries are clearly discriminatory in the context of the WTO enabling clause discussed in the previous section (see page 404), the EU had to seek a waiver from the WTO to permit it to offer this more favourable market access. This waiver came under sustained attack during the 'banana dispute' in the WTO, and the EU indicated right from the start of post-Lomé negotiations that it was not willing to seek further waivers to defend its trade regime with the ACP countries. It therefore sought new WTO-compatible trade arrangements in the form of reciprocal FTAs with the ACP states.

This shift was implemented in the Cotonou Agreement. In future, trade relations with the ACP countries will be based on reciprocal FTAs, which will take the form of economic partnership agreements (EPAs). EPAs will cover not only trade in goods and agricultural products, but also services, and, in addition, will address tariffs, NTBs and technical barriers, such as competition policy, protection of intellectual property rights, sanitary and phytosanitary measures, standardization and certification, trade and labour standards, trade and environment, food security, public procurement, and so on.

The Cotonou Agreement lays out the basic principles and objectives of the new economic and trade cooperation between the ACP countries and the EU, but does not itself encompass a fully-fledged trade regime. Negotiations started in 2002, with a view to bringing new reciprocal trade agreements into force by the expiry of the WTO's waiver on 1 January 2008. The Commission negotiated not with individual ACP countries, but with six regional groups. These were West Africa, Central Africa, Eastern/Southern Africa, the Southern African Development Community, the Caribbean and the Pacific. EPAs are thus intended to consolidate regional integration initiatives within the ACP countries. However, the task was complicated by the overlapping membership and fragmented nature of African regional groupings (see Chapter 1 and El-Agraa 2004). Many non-governmental organizations (NGOs) were critical of what they saw as undue pressure being put on weak economies to open their markets for both goods and services to EU exports, and to agree to rules on investment that they had previously rejected in the ongoing Doha Round of multilateral trade negotiations. They are concerned at the implications of the loss of tariff revenue for the ability of ACP economies to maintain minimum levels of government expenditure (Oxfam 2006). The Commission's view is that EPAs are a way to help the ACP countries to break out of their situation of economic dependency by helping them to build productive capacity and regional markets. It argues that the ACP countries will have a long transition period over which to lower their tariffs, and will continue to be able to protect their sensitive sectors even in a WTO-compatible FTA. It also points to its significant commitment to provide funding to help the ACP countries to meet the challenges of preparing for free trade with the EU.

By the deadline, only the CARIFORUM group of Caribbean countries was in a position to sign a fully-fledged EPA. Individual ACP countries in Africa and the Pacific made different decisions, depending on the importance of maintaining their preferences in EU markets. Some countries, such as Nigeria, opted out of EPAs and now export under GSP preferences. Other LDCs benefit from duty-free access under EBA, without the need to sign EPAs. Other ACP countries have signed interim EPAs, which introduced a simplified trade regime for goods only, while committing the signatories to continue negotiations on a fully-fledged EPA that would cover a much wider range of topics. Under the interim EPAs, the EU introduced with immediate effect duty- and quota-free access for ACP signatories (with a transition period for sugar). Effectively, this grants to some of the more developed ACP countries the same access conditions as the LDCs enjoy. In return, the ACP countries have committed to reducing tariffs on up to 80 per cent of EU imports over a lengthy transition period, sometimes up to twenty years.

One long-run consequence may be the fragmentation of the ACP countries, which are now divided into a number of different groups, each with different access conditions to EU markets. Whether the ACP states will be able to maintain a unified negotiating position under this new trade framework is an open question.

25.3.3 Relations with the Mediterranean and the Middle East

Formal relations with the countries of the south and east Mediterranean go back to the 1957 EEC Treaty, which enabled France, through a special protocol, to keep its special relationships with its former colonies, Morocco and Tunisia (Algeria was still an integral part of France at the time). The 1973 Israel/Arab war, followed by the oil embargo, led to renewed efforts for improved cooperation. The first common EU policy was the Global Mediterranean Policy (1973–92), which involved all non-EU Mediterranean countries except Libya and Albania. Bilateral cooperation agreements were signed, covering not just trade preferences but also aid through financial protocols. The southern EU enlargement to include Greece, Portugal and Spain in the 1980s reduced the benefits of trade preferences, particularly to the Maghreb countries (see Chapter 1 and page 392), given the similar export patterns of the two groups of countries. The new political climate in the early 1990s, following the 1991 Gulf War and the fall of the Berlin Wall, led to a renewed Mediterranean policy (1992–6). This increased the amount of development aid and extended trade preferences, as well as cooperation, to issues such as human rights, the environment and the promotion of democracy (see page 411).

In the mid-1990s, under pressure particularly from Spain, there was an attempt to breathe new life into the Euro-Mediterranean relationship through the Barcelona process or the Euro-Mediterranean Partnership. This was launched by the Barcelona Declaration, issued following a conference of the fifteen EU MSs and twelve Mediterranean countries in November 1995. The twelve Mediterranean partners are: Algeria, Morocco and Tunisia (Maghreb; see Chapter 1); Egypt, Israel, Jordan, the Palestinian Authority, Lebanon and Syria (Mashrek); Cyprus, Malta and Turkey. Cyprus and Malta became EU MSs in May 2004. Turkey has had a customs union agreement with the EU since 1996, and has been a candidate country since 1999. Libya has observer status at certain meetings. Thus currently the Euro-Mediterranean Partnership associates nine countries with the EU.

The Barcelona Declaration extends three partnerships on: politics and security; economy and finance; and society and culture. The first is for establishing peace and stability, based on fundamental principles including respect for human rights and democracy (see page 411). The second aims for the progressive establishment of free trade between the EU and its partners and among the partners themselves, to enable the creation of a Euro-Mediterranean FTA by 2010, with the EU providing financial support for partners' structural reforms and to help them cope with the socio-economic consequences that ensue.

The FTA is implemented through bilateral Association Agreements between the EU and the nine Mediterranean countries. These replaced the earlier cooperation agreements concluded in the 1970s, which provided for non-reciprocal preferences. By 2006 Association Agreements had been signed between all Mediterranean partners and the EU, with the exception of Syria. All Association Agreements provide for trade liberalization of manufactured goods, with free access for Mediterranean exports and gradual tariff dismantling over a transitional period for EU exports. For agriculture, asymmetric reciprocal preferences are granted by the parties. The agreements also include provisions relating to intellectual property, services, technical rules and standards, public procurement, competition rules, state aid and monopolies. In these areas, the partner countries are expected to approximate their laws to the EU's in order to facilitate trade.

As well as bilateral trade liberalization, the Mediterranean partners are committed to implementing regional free trade among themselves, but only limited progress has been made to date. In May 2001, four members of the Barcelona process (Egypt, Jordan, Morocco and Tunisia) signed the Agadir Declaration, under which they aim to establish an FTA among themselves. In practice, the partnership resembles more a hub-and-spoke arrangement, in which the EU has negotiated Association Agreements with the North African and Middle Eastern states. As a result, the EU–Mediterranean Partnership has not yet fulfilled the high hopes held out at the time of the Barcelona Declaration. In the political background is the Arab–Israeli conflict and the Middle East peace process. The Madrid Peace Conference and the breakthrough at Oslo were major factors in making the Barcelona process possible. Conversely, the cessation of the peace process has slowed down progress towards the objectives set out in the Barcelona Declaration.

25.3.4 Relations with Asia and Latin America

The remarkable growth of the east Asian economies in the 1980s and the first half of the 1990s was reflected in a significant expansion of trade and investment flows between the EU and developing Asia. The EU–ASEAN Cooperation Agreement, signed in 1980, was the cornerstone of EU Asia policy for many years. ASEAN initially emphasized economic and development cooperation and did not intend the creation of an FTA. The 1992 decision to create the ASEAN Free Trade Area by 2003 (see Chapter 1 on this and membership) reignited EU interest in the region. In 1994 the Commission produced its first overall Asia Strategy paper (CEU 1994c), which was updated in 2001 (CEU 2001b). In 1996, at the initiative of Singapore's prime minister, a series of Asia–Europe meetings (ASEM) were introduced which now provide the framework for political dialogue. The Asian partners include many ASEAN countries as well as China (see next paragraph), Japan and South Korea. Following pressure from EU exporters, a trans-regional EU–ASEAN trade initiative was launched in 2003, to promote regulatory cooperation between the EU and ASEAN on topics such as sanitary, phytosanitary and technical barriers to trade. The EU has expressed interest in building on this initiative to create a fully-fledged EU–ASEAN FTA.

China deserves special mention. As stated above and

in Chapter 24, China is now the EU's second largest trading partner, behind the USA, and the biggest source of extra-EU imports. Also, the EU has become China's biggest trading partner. In 2006 the Commission adopted a major policy strategy (Partnership and Competition) in relation to China, and in January 2007 negotiations started on a comprehensive Partnership and Cooperation Agreement (PCA) to upgrade the 1985 EC–China Trade and Economic Cooperation Agreement. In the background of all this is the EU–China Relationship, instigated by the EU in 1995 and endorsed by China in 2003 (El-Agraa 2007). The High Level Economic and Trade Dialogue (HED) has become a very important meeting between the EU and China; no fewer than fourteen commissioners participated in the meeting of May 2009, matched by twelve Chinese ministers and vice-ministers. China–EU cooperation also incorporates social security, increasingly recognized by China as an important component to stimulate domestic purchasing power and to create confidence for spending by Chinese consumers and release savings. Similar programmes on social security are piloted with Malaysia.

As was the case for Asia, EU Latin American policy was almost non-existent in the early EEC years. The EU's attention was focused on Africa and no MS had a particular interest in Latin America. In the early 1970s political contacts were maintained through meetings with the group of Latin American ambassadors in Brussels, and in 1971 Latin American countries became beneficiaries of the EU's GSP. Relations remained limited in the 1980s, partly because of the debt crisis, which meant that EU investors lost interest in the region, and partly because of differences over the Falklands War between the UK and Argentina, which led to the suspension of the Brussels dialogue.

Since the mid-1980s, however, cooperation has been intensifying. EU membership of Portugal and Spain in 1986, with their traditional links with Latin and Central America, provided the impetus for this. At the same time, however, Latin American countries were throwing off the old import substitution model of economic development and beginning to open up their markets under the influence of the Washington consensus. The EU's share of Latin American imports had been falling, which provided another reason for forging closer links. Formal institutional ties have been established since 1990 with the Rio Group, which now comprises all of Latin America, as well as representatives from the Caribbean. Ministerial meetings have been held annually between the EU and the Rio Group since 1987. Political dialogue with Central American countries began just a little earlier, in 1984, with the San José Dialogue. Political relations with Mercosur (see Chapter 1) were institutionalized by a cooperation agreement in 1995, while political dialogue with the Andean Pact countries was institutionalized in the Rome Declaration in 1996. Regular biannual summits are now held between EU, Latin American and Caribbean heads of state, to develop a strategic partnership between the two regions. Conflict resolution, democratization and human rights, social progress and the reduction of inequality and the environment are among the themes emphasized in these dialogues.

Political dialogue with ALA countries has been accompanied by attempts to forge closer trade relations and by increasing flows of EU development assistance. Trade relations have been based on the GSP since 1971. During the 1970s the Commission promoted trade agreements with a number of ALA countries, but their substantive significance was small. They generally confirmed MFN reciprocal recognition, while sometimes granting quotas under more favourable access terms for some ALA exports. As noted above, Andean Pact and some Central American countries received more favourable GSP preferences in order to help them in the fight against illegal drugs. On the other hand, ALA countries have been the most frequent targets of EU anti-dumping actions (see Chapter 24) – for instance, in the textiles and clothing sector, for which GSP preferences are already very restricted and where quantitative restrictions on imports applied until the end of the Multifibre Arrangement (MFA) in 2005.

The 1990s saw a new phase in trade relations with Latin America, beginning with discussions on association agreements with Mexico (which entered into force in 2000) and Chile (concluded in 2002). These initiatives were undertaken to minimize the consequences of trade diversion arising from similar US agreements with these countries. The negotiations on an FTA with Mercosur initiated in 1999 (see above and Chapter 24) were also in response to the USA's initiative to launch a free trade area for the Americas; the negotiations collapsed in 2004, with both sides unhappy with the extent of the market-opening offers from the other side, although discussions continue at a technical level.

Negotiations on political and cooperation agreements have now been concluded with Central America and Columbia and Peru, to create the conditions for future arrangements similar to those with Mexico and Chile.

25.3.5 Evaluation of EU trade policy towards developing countries

The major thrust of EU trade policy towards DCs is a move away from the autonomous preference-based and regionally discriminatory trade arrangements of the past, to a more horizontal but differentiated policy, emphasizing reciprocal free trade arrangements with low- and middle-income DCs, and duty- and quota-free access now offered to all LDCs under EBA. The EU argues that free trade agreements will have positive outcomes for the partner countries, through encouraging a more efficient allocation of resources and greater competition, and by creating a more attractive location for FDI. However, some potential drawbacks should be noted.

For ACP and Mediterranean partners, entering into an FTA is an asymmetric liberalization process. For manufacturing products, these countries already enjoyed duty-free access to EU markets (though in the case of Mediterranean countries ceilings operated for sensitive products such as textiles and clothing), so the main impact is the unilateral removal of trade barriers on EU exports entering partner country markets. While consumers and producers who will now have the possibility of importing cheaper intermediate products will benefit, many firms, particularly small and medium-sized enterprises, may be forced to close, with a consequent rise in unemployment. Also, the continued barriers to agricultural trade in the agreements, which is the sector where many of the partner countries have their comparative advantage, make adaptation to the required structural changes more difficult. Some fear that a consequence of this asymmetric liberalization may be trade diversion (see Chapter 6 and page 405) in favour of EU exports, which would add to the economic costs of these agreements for EU partners (for estimates of the impact on the Euro-Med partners, see the studies cited in McQueen 2002).

Proponents of these agreements therefore emphasize the likelihood of dynamic gains, particularly that the contractual nature of these agreements will lower uncertainty by locking in trade liberalization policies in the partner countries, thus helping to attract greater FDI flows. Also potentially important are the provisions to tackle NTBs, thus lowering the transaction cost of trade and reducing the impact of regulatory trade barriers. For the ACP countries, a further issue that needs to be addressed is the reduction in tariff revenues as duties on EU imports are eliminated. This could curtail government spending at the same time as increased support for industrial restructuring and assistance to cushion the costs of transitional unemployment is required, unless other means to broaden the tax base are found.

The EU announced a self-imposed moratorium on new FTA initiatives prior to the 1999 Seattle WTO Ministerial Council, in order to focus EU efforts on promoting the new WTO multilateral trade round. Following the suspension of Doha Round negotiations in July 2005, the EU indicated a revision of this position in its 'Global Europe' document the following year (CEU 2006t). This document noted that the EU's existing FTAs serve its neighbourhood and development interests well, but its trade interests less so. The content of existing agreements is too limited, in that they fail to address regulatory and 'behind the border' trade barriers (see Chapter 24). The EU does not have agreements with the world's most dynamic markets, particularly in Asia, while many of these priority markets are negotiating FTAs with its competitors (such as ASEAN members with China, Japan and Korea and each other, or Korea with the USA, concluded in June 2007), threatening the EU with a loss of market share. The document therefore announced the EU's interest in concluding a range of further FTAs, particularly with countries with significant market potential and where existing barriers to EU exports were high. Based on these criteria, the document highlights agreements with ASEAN, the Gulf Cooperation Council, India, Korea, Mercosur and Russia as of direct EU interest. While at the same time restating its commitment to a successful conclusion of the Doha Round, the document clearly signals that the EU is 'open for business' when it comes to concluding a range of FTAs with DCs in the future.

25.4 Development cooperation

This section examines the EU's development cooperation programme, referring to the provision of development aid. Development assistance is a shared

competence between the EU and its MSs. We will refer to EU aid as external assistance managed by the Commission unless it is otherwise clear from the context that aid provided by MSs is also included. But first it is important to note that ODA is defined by the OECD's Development Assistance Committee (DAC) as grants or loans to DCs provided by the official sector on concessional financial terms, with the promotion of economic development and welfare as the main objective. Box 25.1 provides information on the EU's ODA sources of finance and political responsibility

In 2009 the EU and MSs disbursed €48.2 billion in net ODA, which amounted to 9 per cent of the EU budget plus the European Development Fund (EDF) (see Chapter 19). Of this, €10 billion, or about 21 per cent, was by the Commission. According to the OECD, this represented 56 per cent of global ODA: $67 billion out of a total of $120 billion (see Figure 25.1). Figures 25.2 and 25.3 (see page 412) offer a longer-term perspective, covering 2001–9; note for later the differences between aid commitments and disbursements. Figure 25.4 displays the sectoral breakdown and Figure 25.5 the geographic distribution of the EU's aid (see page 413).

The EU development assistance policy evolved in a haphazard fashion, without clear objectives or justification for many years. Its modest start was when eighteen African countries, mainly ex-colonies of France and Belgium, were associated with the EU under the Yaoundé Convention (1965). UK accession to the EU raised the question of the treatment of its ex-colonies in Africa, the Caribbean and the Pacific. This led to the Lomé Convention in 1975, which over the next quarter of a century determined the use of the EDF for both groups of countries. In the following year aid resources were made available to other DCs for the first time, and in 1977 cooperation agreements were signed with neighbouring countries in the southern Mediterranean. Bilateral arrangements were subsequently made with countries in Asia and Latin America, and in the 1990s countries in Eastern Europe and central Asia gained their own regional programmes. The historical legacy of this evolution was a diffuse array of policies, budgets, administrative procedures and aid instruments. This section describes the EU ODA programme and some of the recent changes in its management, designed to make it a more efficient and effective instrument in contributing to the sustainable economic and social development of DCs.

Box 25.1 EU ODA: financing sources and political responsibility

Sources of financing:

The EU's external assistance programme has two distinct sources of funding: funds allocated through the EU budget and contributions by MSs outside the EU budget to the EDF. Decisions on budget funds are made with the involvement of the European Council, the European Parliament (EP) and the Commission (co-decision procedure; see Chapter 3). The final decision is made by the EP, but within the limits/ceilings agreed in the financial perspective. EDF funds are contributed by MSs on a voluntary basis, according to a specific distribution key, and decision-making power rests with the Council, without any legal basis for involvement of the EP and the Commission, although these funds are managed by the Commission on behalf of MSs. EDF funds are allocated solely to the ACP countries and overseas countries and territories (OCTs), while aid via the EU budget is provided mainly to non-ACP countries. Budgetized assistance is allocated according to either a geographic or thematic approach, under specific budget headings.

Political responsibility:

Responsibility for EU external assistance is divided among five departments (for a long time known as Directorates General, DGs; see Chapter 3): Development, which provides policy guidance on development policy and is responsible for aid to the ACP states; EuropeAid Development and Cooperation; Humanitarian Aid; Enlargement, which provides pre-accession assistance for potential future members in the western Balkans; and External Relations, which is responsible for remaining external assistance, mainly to Asian, Latin American and Mediterranean countries. Recently, however, all EU development aid is implemented by EuropeAid Development and Cooperation, with the External Relations Department having no responsibilities in this connection apart from programming policy. But with the entry into force of the TFEU on 1 December 2009, the European External Action Service (EEAS; see Chapters 2 and 3), which is in the process of being established, is expected to take full responsibility.

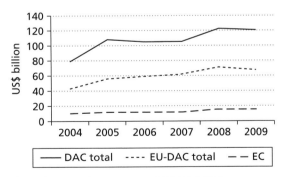

Figure 25.1 Total DAC ODA and EU-DAC ODA disbursements, 2004–9 *Source*: OECD QWIDS (http//stats.oecd.otg/qwids)

25.4.1 EU development cooperation principles

As noted above, before the Treaty on European Union (TEU) in 1992, EU development cooperation policies had evolved piecemeal and in a fragmented fashion.

The main innovation of the TEU was to establish policy objectives for EU development cooperation and to set out how it should relate to MSs' policies. Three policy objectives are stated in Article 177:

[EU] policy in the sphere of development cooperation, which shall be complementary to the policies pursued by [MSs], shall foster:

- the sustainable economic and social development of [DCs], and more particularly the most disadvantaged among them,
- the smooth and gradual integration of [DCs] into the world economy,
- the campaign against poverty in [DCs].

The Article further states that the EU's policy in this area shall contribute 'to the general objective of developing and consolidating democracy and the rule of law, and to that of respecting human rights and fundamental freedoms'. The emphasis on the complementary nature of the EU's policy implies that development aid is an area of shared competence where the EU operates

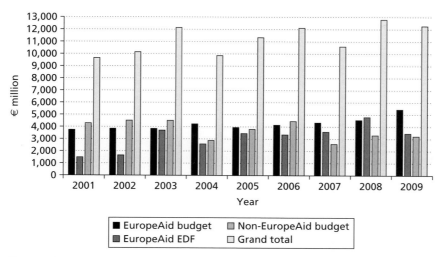

Figure 25.2 EU external assistance (commitments; €million) 2001–9 *Source*: CEU 2010o (p. 172)

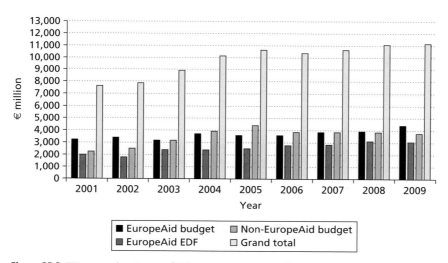

Figure 25.3 EU external assistance (disbursements; € million), 2001–9 *Source*: CEU 2010q (p. 172)

in parallel with MSs (in contrast to trade policy, which is broadly an EU prerogative alone; see Chapters 2, 3 and 24). This is reiterated in the TFEU:

> In the areas of development cooperation and humanitarian aid, [the EU] shall have competence to carry out activities and conduct a common policy; however, the exercise of that competence shall not result in [MSs] being prevented from exercising theirs (TFEU, Article 214)

Article 178 establishes the important principle of policy coherence, in that it requires that the EU 'shall take account of the objectives referred to in Article 177 in the policies that it implements which are likely to affect [DCs]'. Article 179 sets out that decision-making should be based on qualified majority voting (QMV), using the co-decision procedure (see Figure 3.1, page 46). However, decisions on EDF, an extra-budgetary arrangement designed to provide financial support to the ACP countries (see page 410), are explicitly

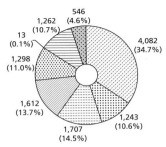

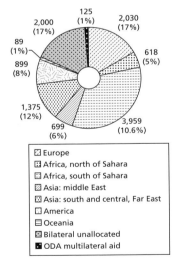

☑ Social infrastructures: education, health, water, government and civil society, other

⊞ Economic infrastructures and services: transport, communications, energy, other services

☒ Production: agriculture, forestry and fishing, industry, mining and construction, trade and tourism

☒ Multisector/Crosscutting: environment, other

☒ Budget support, food aid, food security

☐ Action relating to debt

☰ Emergency assistance, reconstruction relief

☒ Other/Unallocated: administration costs, support to NGOs, unspecified

Figure 25.4 EU ODA sectoral breakdown commitments (€ million; per cent), 2009 *Source*: CEU 2010o (p. 11)

☑ Europe
⊞ Africa, north of Sahara
☒ Africa, south of Sahara
☒ Asia: middle East
☒ Asia: south and central, Far East
☐ America
☰ Oceania
☒ Bilateral unallocated
◼ ODA multilateral aid

Figure 25.5 Regional distribution of EU ODA (€ million; per cent), 2009 *Source*: CEU 2010q (p. 174)

excluded from this provision and continue to be taken on the basis of unanimity.

The relationship between the EU aid programme and those of MSs is addressed in Article 180:

[The EU] and [MSs] shall coordinate their policies on development co-operation and shall consult each other on their aid programmes, including in international organisations and during international conferences. They may undertake joint action. [MSs] shall contribute if necessary to the implementation of [EU] aid programmes.

The significance of this Article is that it gives the EU the legal responsibility to coordinate its own development cooperation policy with MSs' policies. As noted by the OECD, this makes the EU 'a unique donor in that it plays a dual role in development, as a bilateral donor providing direct support to countries, and as a co-ordinating framework for EU [MSs]' (OECD 2002a, p. 21).

Development cooperation policy is thus based on four principles (the so-called four Cs):

- *complementarity* between the development policies of MSs and the Commission;
- *coordination* between MSs and the Commission in the operation of these policies;
- *coherence* of all EU policies so that they take development objectives into account;
- *consistency* of all external actions of the EU in the context of all external relations, including security, economic and development policies.

While the strategic focus on poverty reduction as the main development policy objective in the treaty was welcome, this needed to be refined and made more specific for operational purposes. The diversity of the different programmes and projects supported by the EU threatened to overwhelm the Commissions' institutional capacity to manage these programmes, both in Brussels and in the field. A more selective prioritization of what the EU should try to do was clearly desirable. The first attempt to set out these priorities was the Statement on the European Community's Development Policy in November 2000 (Council 2000). This statement identified six priority areas for EU action, based on where the EU could demonstrate value added and comparative advantage in contrast to other donors. These were: macroeconomic policies and the promotion of equitable access to social services; food security and sustainable rural development; transport; trade and development; regional integration and cooperation; and institutional capacity-building, particularly for good governance and the rule of law. In addition, four cross-cutting issues were identified, namely, human rights, gender equality, protection of the environment and conflict prevention. Humanitarian assistance was seen as an additional activity, but not as a priority area for long-term development assistance (OECD 2002a).

The 2000 statement has since been superseded by the European Consensus on Development, which was jointly adopted by the Commission, MSs meeting within the Council, and the EP in December 2005 (Council 2005c). Unlike the 2000 statement, the Consensus on Development sets out, for the first time, the common vision that guides the actions of both the Commission and MSs in development cooperation. It takes into account the commitments made by the EU at various international conferences in the preceding five years as part of its support for MDGs, as well as advances made in development best practice to ensure more effective aid. Unlike the earlier statement, the consensus document was preceded by a wide public consultation process, which gives it much greater legitimacy. The consensus is divided into two parts: the EU common vision on development is the subject of Part 1, whereas Part II, entitled *The European Community Development Policy*, sets out the policy guiding the implementation of this vision for the EU's aid programme under the Commission's responsibility. The key elements of the common vision are: the joint commitment to poverty eradication; ownership of development strategies by partner countries; delivering more and better aid; and promoting policy coherence for development. It identifies the particular role and comparative advantage of the EU's aid programme relative to those of MSs, and highlights eight areas for EU action: trade and regional integration; the environment and sustainable management of natural resources; infrastructure, communications and transport; rural development, agriculture and food security; governance, democracy, human rights and support for economic and institutional reforms; conflict prevention and fragile states; human development; and social cohesion and employment. While this may seem a comprehensive list of development activities, the commitment to complementarity and greater coordination between the Commission's programme and those of MSs is intended to ensure more effective aid delivery in the field.

As mentioned earlier, these developments have been fully incorporated in the TFEU, which also elevates the EP's role. Article 207.3 calls on the Commission to report regularly to the EP on progress

with negotiations. Article 218.10 provides that the EP must be 'immediately and fully informed at all stages of the procedure'. In terms of the information provided to it, the EP's International Trade Committee (INTA) is upgraded to a level similar to that of the Council Trade Policy Committee (previously called the Article 133 Committee). Article 218.6a stipulates that the European Council must obtain the EP's consent in order to adopt a decision to conclude an agreement; and the Commission has an interest in hearing the EP before the Commission proposes a Council decision for provisional application of an agreement under Article 218.5. In case of uncertainty regarding the conformity of the envisaged agreement with the treaties, the EP can request the opinion of the European Court of Justice (ECJ; TFEU Article 218.11). Trade negotiations, of course, are conducted by the Commission (see Chapters 3 and 24).

Also, the TFEU calls for the establishment of a European External Action Service (EEAS; see Chapter 2), which is now under construction. EEAS is envisaged as serving as the EU's 'foreign ministry' and diplomatic corps, headed by the newly established High Representative for Foreign Affairs and Security Policy (see Chapters 2 and 3). How EEAS will be involved in development cooperation is unclear, but its establishment is an opportunity to broaden the EU's relationship with DCs with politically and economically more sophisticated strategies. The TFEU specifies the values that underpin such strategies, which must be based on international human rights treaties. No matter what the exact scope of EEAS is, it is clear that this body will need to assess its promotion of EU interests abroad against the objective of eradicating poverty in all DCs. A question that will challenge policy-makers in TFEU implementation is how to find common ground between this objective and the stronger EU role in defending EU interests at the global level. For this, the EU is now involved in the first serious attempt to operationalize a policy coherence on development.

25.4.2 Aid volumes and trends

In the 1990s the volume of EU aid grew at an average annual rate of 5.3 per cent. The growth was largely in terms of budgetized aid (see Box 25.1, page 411), as disbursements through the EDF remained static in real terms and even dipped in the mid-1990s (OECD 2002a).

During this period the volume of aid provided by MSs declined, so that by 2000 the EU accounted for around 20 per cent of total EU ODA. This proportion was as high as 50 per cent for Italy, but only around 5–10 per cent for those countries, such as Denmark, the Netherlands and Sweden, that exceed the UN target contribution of 0.7 per cent of GNI. As mentioned above, since 2000 total EU ODA has increased sharply (including an exceptionally high figure for debt relief of $14.7 billion in 2005), in response to the commitments made at the UN Millennium Summit. Also, the Commission's contribution in 2009 rose slightly, to about 21 per cent of the EU's combined total (see page 410).

In response to the challenge of meeting Millennium Development Goals (MDGs), the Commission encouraged MSs to increase their ODA contributions at the European Council meeting in Barcelona in March 2002. In 2002 the combined EU MSs had a weighted average ratio of ODA to GNI of 0.32 per cent. The Commission target at the Barcelona Council meeting was to raise the average amount of ODA to 0.39 per cent of GNI by 2006, with a minimum country target of 0.33 per cent. More ambitious targets were set in 2005 and reconfirmed in the European Consensus, when the EU adopted a timetable for MSs to reach the 0.7 per cent of GNI target set by the UN by 2015, with an intermediate collective target of 0.56 per cent by 2010 (in 2009 it was only 0.41 per cent). These commitments were expected to double total EU aid (Commission plus MSs) to over €66 billion in 2010. Through this effort, based on DAC calculations, the EU will provide 78 per cent of the expected additional global ODA by 2010. The European Consensus states that at least half of this increase in aid will be allocated to Africa. In 2009 total EU aid (€48.2 billion) was equivalent to 0.41 per cent of EU GNI, which suggests that the EU as a whole is way off target, unless something miraculous happens in a year's time. But of course there has been a global economic and financial crisis since 2007.

A feature of EU development assistance cooperation is the importance of geographic programmes. During the 2000–6 Financial Perspective, these were: the pre-accession programme for East European countries (PHARE); the technical assistance programme for Eastern Europe and central Asia (TACIS); community assistance for reconstruction, development and stabilization in the Balkans (CARDS); external assistance to Asia and Latin America (ALA); support to the Mediterranean and Middle East countries (MEDA); and EDF for the ACP countries (EDF). Each of these programmes had its own management committee, made up of the Commission and MSs. There were a further fifteen thematic programmes, dealing with issues such as food security, poverty diseases, reproductive health, the environment and NGOs. Finally, the EU is the largest funding agency for emergency and distress assistance, much of which is channelled through ECHO, the EU's Humanitarian Aid Office.

Managing the EU's aid programme on the basis of such a mixed and complex set of instruments in an efficient and coordinated way was becoming an increasingly difficult task. A simpler framework has been agreed for the 2007–13 Financial Perspective. The new framework comprises six instruments only, four of them new (the instruments for humanitarian aid and macro financial assistance continue without modification). In addition, the number of thematic programmes has been rationalized from fifteen to seven. The relative importance of the various instruments in the new framework of EU external action is shown in Table 25.1 (page 416), which underlines the growing attention paid by the EU to its immediate neighbours and to security issues.

The EU has also responded to the criticism that its aid programme was not sufficiently poverty-focused. For example, an OECD (2002a) peer review of the EU aid programme highlighted the declining share of the poorest nations in EU aid disbursements, arising from the change in the geographic priorities for EU aid. Since the reform of external assistance in 2000, the share of low-income countries has grown from 32 per cent of disbursements in 2000 to 46 per cent in 2005, and the share of LDCs from 22 per cent to 33 per cent (CEU 2005l). Another indicator is the pattern of aid allocation by sector, where the EU programme was criticized for the low proportion spent on social sector spending. However, by 2005 the share of EU aid devoted to the social sector amounted to 45 per cent, compared to 16 per cent for economic infrastructure, 16 per cent for budget support, 10 per cent for emergency aid and just 6 per cent for production activities, with a further 6 per cent spent on multi-sectoral and cross-cutting issues. Not surprisingly, analysts have queried if the balance has not swung too much against support for the production sectors, and in particular agricultural and rural development, given the dependence of most

Table 25.1 Overview of expenditure within heading 'EU as a global partner', in the 2007–13 financial perspective (€ billions at 2004 prices)

	2006	2007	2008	2009	2010	2011	2012	2013	Total	Change 2006/13 (%)
Instrument for pre-accession	1,121	1,193	1,290	1,353	1,452	1,565	1,660	1,700	10,213	52
European neighbour-hood and partnership instrument	1,274	1,390	1,400	1,437	1,470	1,530	1,640	1,720	10,587	35
Development cooperation instrument	1,862	2,000	2,060	2,116	2,167	2,190	2,246	2,324	15,103	25
Instrument for stability	531	232	268	338	363	400	430	500	2,531	–6
Common foreign and security policy	99	150	185	220	250	285	310	340	1,740	245
Provi-sioning of loan guarantee fund	220	188	185	181	178	174	171	167	1,244	–24
Emergency aid reserve	221									–100
Other	894	1,046	1,081	1,094	1,129	1,196	1,222	1,278	8,046	43
Total for the EU as a global partner	6,222	6,199	6,469	6,739	7,009	7,339	7,679	8,029	49,463	29

Source: CEU 2006v

poor people on food production for their livelihoods. The query still stands: as Figure 25.4 shows, although the 45 per cent for social infrastructure has come down to 34.7 per cent, a decline of about 22.9 per cent, those for production and budget support have fallen about 33 and 31 per cent respectively (see page 412).

25.4.3 The Cotonou Agreement and the European Development Fund

As noted, the Cotonou Agreement succeeded the Lomé Conventions in 2000 and governs the EU's relationships with the ACP countries. The new agreement is distinguished from the old by its more comprehensive political dimension, its emphasis on the participation of civil society and the private sector, a strengthened focus on poverty reduction, a new framework for trade and economic cooperation, and a reform of financial cooperation. The Agreement lasts for twenty years, with financial protocols setting out the resources for EDF agreed at five-year intervals. However, the period for the ninth EDF, starting in 2000, was extended to 2007, based on the transfer of uncommitted balances from previous EDFs. It was subsequently agreed that the tenth EDF would run for six years, from 2008 to 2013, to coincide with the termination of the EU's

2007–13 financial perspective. The first revision of the Cotonou Agreement was concluded in early 2005. It strengthens the political dimension and cooperation in the area of security, as well as making minor adjustments in the management of EDF funds. Although it was intended to include the amount to be allocated to the tenth EDF as part of this revision, this was not settled until the end of 2005, as part of the overall negotiations on the EU's financial perspective for the 2007–13 period.

The aid component of the agreement is divided into programmable and non-programmable allocations. The programmable ones are extended to individual ACP countries and regions through National and Regional Indicative Programmes. They are given every five years on the basis of a formula reflecting objective criteria based on demographic, geographic and macroeconomic conditions (GNP per capita, external debt, and so on). One of the innovations in the Cotonou Agreement was a shift to including performance indicators as well as needs in the allocation of EU aid resources. The main instruments for programming grants are the country and regional strategy papers. These papers set out general guidelines for using the aid, as well as an indicative operational programme specifying how the money will be spent. A regular programme of review of these papers provides the means whereby performance measures are taken into account in future allocations of EDF funds.

Non-programmable funds are generally quick-disbursing instruments, and prior allocations by country are not defined. They are granted on a case-by-case basis to whichever countries meet the specified conditions. The main non-programmable resources of Lomé were support for structural adjustment, STABEX and SYSMIN, and humanitarian and rehabilitation assistance. STABEX was introduced in Lomé I to compensate the ACP countries for the shortfall in export earnings due to fluctuations in the prices or supply of non-mineral commodities, largely agricultural products. The idea was to encourage economic development by stabilizing the purchasing power of export earnings. STABEX was joined in Lomé II by SYSMIN, a scheme to help alleviate fluctuations in revenue arising from the production and sale of minerals. Funds could be requested by the ACP countries that were dependent on mineral exports for a substantial part of their export earnings, or if there were problems in the production of minerals, or development projects were threatened by a substantial fall in export earnings.

Under the Cotonou Agreement, STABEX and SYSMIN came to an end, although a new system was introduced to mitigate the losses caused by shortfalls in export earnings. The balance between programmable and non-programmable resources has shown a clear trend away from non-programmable resources towards programmable resources, and in particular towards budget support rather than project grants. This is in line with the EU's commitment to improve the effectiveness of aid by aligning it more closely with recipient countries' own priorities and procedures. Indeed, the EU believes that fiscal responsibility lies at the very heart of good governance, hence its emphasis on budgetary support (see CEU 2010o).

The volume of EDF resources was not increased significantly under the Cotonou Agreement. The Financial Protocol for the ninth EDF amounted to €15.2 billion, compared to €14.625 billion for the eighth EDF. In addition, the remaining funds from previous EDFs (amounting to €2.9 billion in 2003) have been transferred to EDF9 and are used in accordance with the new conditions. Although an increase in nominal terms, it represents a reduction in real terms, and even more so in per capita real terms. The amount allocated to the tenth EDF, beginning in 2008 and covering a period of six years, was eventually agreed at €22.68 billion in December 2005. EDF budgetization, as proposed by the Commission, was once again rejected by MSs, and the EDF will continue as an extra-budgetary fund. The agreed amount was intended to ensure that the funds available would be maintained at least at the same level as the ninth EDF, taking into account the effects of inflation, growth within the EU and the 2004 enlargement to include the ten new MSs. A further small adjustment was made due to Bulgaria and Romania joining the EU. However, many of the committed resources only reach the ACP countries many years after they have been allocated. The slow disbursement of EU aid was just one of the factors that led to a radical overhaul of the management of the EU aid programme at the end of the 1990s.

25.4.4 Management of EU development assistance

Despite the growth in the volume of EU ODA, its management and effectiveness were severely criticized in a number of reports at the end of the 1990s. Particular attention was drawn to the following weaknesses:

- The complexity of the development cooperation system, which before the 1999 reform of the Commission under Commission President Prodi (see Chapter 3), involved five commissioners and four DGs in addition to ECHO.
- The splintered framework of aid management, based around geographic programmes, meant that there was no coherent vision of aid priorities and little consistency in the weights given to the different aid elements in each geographic programme. There was a proliferation of ad hoc programmes, each with its own budget line, regulations and procedures, which made the overall programme very inflexible.
- Too much emphasis was placed on monitoring procedures and inputs, and too little on evaluating outputs and results. Projects and programmes rarely had performance indicators and almost no evaluations had been undertaken prior to the 1990s to document what had been achieved.
- The decision-making process was very centralized, with little authority delegated to field offices. Approval of policies, regional and country strategies, individual projects and contracting was centralized in Brussels.
- Staffing had not kept pace with the growth in disbursements, leading to a great reliance on external consultants for the design and implementation of projects and programmes.

A particular concern was the large and growing problem of disbursing funds that had been committed (compare Figures 25.3 and 25.4, pages 412–13). While in 1990 outstanding commitments stood at three times annual disbursements for the EU, by 2000 this had grown to a multiple of four for EU budget funds and to a multiple of six for EDF funds (OECD 2002a). The Court of Auditors' reports noted that as much as half of the annual budget would be committed in a rushed manner in the last month of the year. There may be good external reasons for the difficulties in drawing down funds, including the low absorption capacity of recipient country administrations, especially in the ACP countries, and restrictions arising from the abuse of human rights or the breakdown of the rule of law. However, internal problems, such as inadequate staff

numbers to administer the programme and the large number of different budget lines and instruments, created inefficiencies and inflexibilities. Reform of the EU's aid management system was desperately needed.

The reform process was initiated when a new Commission took charge in 1999, with a restructuring of the external relations (RELEX) services. The overall objective of the reform was to speed up implementation of external assistance and to improve the quality of aid delivery. The configuration of political responsibilities introduced then was broadly maintained when the first Barroso Commission took office in 2004 (see Box 25.1, page 411). The number of budget lines had been reduced from over thirty to just six when the 2007–13 financial perspective came into force. The idea of a single External Relations Council to ensure greater consistency in the EU's external actions was introduced in 2002, thus abolishing the Development Council, although some development NGOs regard this as a retrograde step, fearing that development will become subordinate to foreign policy within the RELEX family. But, as shown in Box 25.1, the newly created EEAS, now under construction, will take over and hopefully cater for this problem.

In January 2001 EuropeAid was created to strengthen the implementation of EU development programmes worldwide and to bring consistency to programme management. EuropeAid's mission is to implement the external aid instruments of the Commission, which are funded by the EU budget and the EDF. It does not deal with pre-accession aid programmes (PHARE, ISPA and SAPARD; see Chapter 22), humanitarian activities or macro-financial assistance. It has undertaken a series of reforms to improve the efficiency and effectiveness of EU aid, including strengthening the project evaluation process and devolving project and programme management to Commission delegations in the field (CEU 2005h). Since 2001 the Commission has published an annual report on EU development policy and the implementation of external assistance, which provides greater transparency on this area of activity. More recently, the focus has shifted to implementation of the international agenda to improve the coordination and harmonization of aid procedures. The EU signed the Rome Declaration on Aid Harmonization in 2003, and the Paris Declaration on Aid Effectiveness in 2005, which commit it to specific targets to improve aid delivery by 2010. As noted above and in Box 25.1, EuropeAid has recently assumed sole responsibility for EU development aid and will continue to do so until EEAS takes over.

25.5 Conclusion

From an aid relationship with its ex-colonies, the EU has evolved a complex set of relationships with DCs, embracing trade preferences, development assistance and political dialogue. This chapter has summarized the main features of these relationships and how they are changing over time. For reasons of space, not all aspects of these relationships could be covered. The chapter concentrated on trade arrangements and development assistance, and not much was said, for example, about EU humanitarian aid or food aid.

Both trade and development cooperation policies have been areas of dynamic policy development in recent years. Three themes in particular stand out as shaping the EU's relations with DCs over the next decade. First, the forging of FTA agreements with DCs brings the EU into uncharted territory. These agreements not only require reciprocal tariff concessions from the EU's partners, but are also much more comprehensive in their scope than anything the EU has negotiated with its DC partners until now.

Second, the changing status of the ACP countries in the EU's development policy priorities is clearly evident. The success of this grouping in maintaining a negotiating unity, when it is bound together more by historic links to the EU than by common interests, has been remarkable. But it does look like an increasingly fragile unity. The EU's insistence on negotiating regional EPAs will fragment the ACP countries into regional groupings, leaving EDF funding and political dialogue as the only unique parts of the EU–ACP relationship.

Third, despite the European Consensus on Development, there remains ambiguity about the role that the EU's aid programme should play relative to those of MSs.

Is cooperation between national, bilateral agencies in the context of the Paris Declaration sufficient, or should MSs channel a larger share of a growing aid budget through the EU? Apart from any general unwillingness among MSs to cede further authority to the EU,

there has been an often justified view that the quality of the EU's aid programme has not matched the standards of MSs' programmes. However, there has been a generally recognized improvement in EU aid policy since the substantial reforms in 2000. The effectiveness of EU aid has been enhanced since the creation of EuropeAid as a single implementing agency; the simplification of the legal basis for development assistance in the new financial perspective; the decentralization of management authority to delegations in the field; and the commitment to harmonization and alignment with the Paris Declaration. It is problematic, however, whether the EU's aid programme will be rewarded for this improved performance. The total budget for external action in the new financial perspective, as well as the size of the tenth EDF up to 2013, are now fixed. The increases agreed, in the context of the overall EU commitment to reach the UN target of 0.7 per cent of GNI by 2015, imply a sharp fall in the relative size of the EU's programme. In the absence of any revision of the financial perspective, or the creation of some special-purpose instrument that would channel more bilateral aid resources through the Commission, the weight of the EU's aid programme will gradually diminish over the next decade.

Summary

- Initially, the EU's relationship with DCs was in terms of association agreements, mainly with African nations. The relationship has widened with EU enlargements, however, especially with the accession of the UK and Iberian countries, each adding ex-colonial and cultural-link dimensions. The ACP–EU Cotonou Agreement is its latest manifestation.

- The TFEU dictates that the relationship should be firmly based on the principle of poverty eradication, and calls for all EU policies that impinge on DCs to do likewise.

- With the TFEU, the relationship comes under the EU External Action Service (EEAS), which supports the EU High Representative for Common Foreign and Security Policy (CFSP), now being founded, together with the Commissioners for Development and Humanitarian Assistance. The TFEU also dictates that the EP must approve international trade agreements.

- The relationship was built on cooperation in trade, regional arrangements and aid.
- The proliferation of the EU's special trade relationships with DCs and groups thereof has devalued the preferential trade cooperation schemes, and the WTO has criticized these as discriminatory. There is therefore a need for a new approach to:
  1. strengthen regional trade cooperation;
  2. avoid discrimination; and
  3. promote the overarching objective of poverty eradication.
- The EU's new trade cooperation models with DCs are resulting in a proliferation of bilateral agreements, in which the EU is advancing issues on which agreement in the WTO is lacking – for example, trade in services and government procurement policies.
- The EU is carefully watching how China is expanding its cooperation with DCs, and China's role in this regard will have a major impact on the future of the EU's relationships with DCs.
- The EU is aiming to make human rights a stronger factor in its preferential trade agreements with DCs.
- The Commission and MSs combine to provide 56 per cent of total global ODA in 2009. The Commission manages 10 per cent of all ODA, disbursing around €10 billion in 2009. MSs implement their own bilateral and multilateral programmes in addition to the EU's, managed by the Commission.
- The Commission is a strong protagonist of government-to-government aid, providing general budgetary support to further good governance. It allocates only a very small proportion of its programme to basic health and education.

Questions and essay topics

1. What is the Yaoundé Agreement?
2. What is the Lomé Convention?
3. What is the Cotonou Agreement?
4. Why does the EU have a special relationship with MSs' ex-colonies?

5. What are the Millennium Development Goals (MDGs)?
6. What sort of aid does the EU extend to DCs?
7. Who is responsible for the disbursement of EU development aid?
8. How does the EU help DCs export to the EU?
9. What are EPAs?
10. How many EPAs does the EU have with DCs?
11. What does the TFEU specify as the guiding principle of the EU's aid to DCs?
12. What are the four principles on which EU development cooperation aid is based?
13. Has the EU been able to meet the aid targets it set itself?
14. Explain and discuss the claim that the EU has failed miserably to promote exports by DCs to its markets.
15. What do you think of the EU's aid to DCs being conditional on the recipients' adherence to human rights?
16. Evaluate the effectiveness of EU aid to DCs in terms of the EU's set objectives.

FURTHER READING

CEU (2010) *Annual Report 2010: On the European Union's Development and External Assistance Policies and their Implementation in 2009* (available on the EU website).

Collier, P. (2007) *The Bottom Billion: Why the Poorest Countries are Failing and What Can Be Done About It*, Oxford University Press.

Mold A. (ed.) (2007) *EU Development Policy in a Changing World: Challenges for the 21st Century*, Amsterdam University Press.

NOTES

1 A number of studies have analysed the different elements of the EU's relations with DCs, which have provided a better understanding of the dynamics behind these relationships (Cosgrove-Sacks and Scapucci 1999; van Dijck and Faber 2000; Arts and Dickson 2004; Stokke and Hoebink 2005).

26 The future of the EU

Part VII of the book is naturally concerned with the future of the EU: where it is heading. It examines the views of all those who play influential roles in the drive behind European integration, and sets them against the vision of the founding fathers.

26 The future of the EU

ALI EL-AGRAA

26.1 Introduction

This final chapter is devoted to the question of where the European Union (EU) is heading in the future. By future we do not mean the intermediate term, which would be concerned with how the EU should deal with the aftermath of the financial crisis, the euro's problems, budget deficits, Turkish membership and the like; these are dealt with in the relevant chapters. Concentration here is on a longer perspective.

To offer a meaningful answer, one needs to take into consideration the views of all those who play influential roles in the drive behind European integration, and set them against the vision of the founding fathers. It is, however, neither feasible nor desirable to provide a full and detailed chronological account, due to the need for brevity and that only major episodes highlighting the visions are of the essence.

26.2 The vision of the founding fathers

As fully documented in Chapter 2, the founding fathers dreamed of the creation of a United States of Europe. This was because they believed that there was no other means of putting an end to the continent's woeful history of conflict, bloodshed and suffering – that is, they saw unity as the only way to achieve eternal peace in a continent with a long history of deep divisions and devastating wars.

The switch of emphasis to economic integration came later, but in a reinforcing manner. There were two facets to it. In the early 1950s, with war wounds fresh in people's minds, it was felt that although political integration remained the ultimate objective, it was out of the question then. That is why, when calling for the creation of the European Economic Community (EEC), the Benelux countries reasoned that experience gained

through working together in the economic field would pave the way for political unification later on: experience clearly borne out by the success of the European Coal and Steel Community (ECSC). Second, Europe then, and now, stood no chance of being on a par with the USA and Japan in terms of economic excellence and influence in world affairs, without being united on both fronts. Thus, with economic unity being only a means to an end, until a single European nation became the reality, the energies of those dedicated to the dream of the founding fathers were/are still devoted to finding ways of realizing it; political unity was to be introduced through the backdoor of economic integration.

However, there are those who question the wisdom, in the modern age, of creating one nation, either for the purpose of peace or for economic prosperity. With regard to peace, they argue that the ethnic-based struggles in Eastern Europe and the splitting of Czechoslovakia and Yugoslavia show that separation may be a more stable equilibrium, especially with Russia now being relatively weak and focusing on economic reform and industrial rebuilding.[1] They can appeal to reality to reinforce their argument by claiming that today there are not many of the founding fathers around, and vehemently asserting that their dream is not shared by the new generation of Europeans, who have not experienced war. Add to this the resurgence of national sovereignty, with even Germany, the central protagonist of integration, prepared to assert its national interest. However, European integration has ebbed in the past, especially in difficult economic times, only to re-emerge with renewed vigour. For example, the lost decade after the first oil crisis was followed by the Single European Market (SEM).

As to the benefit of size for economic excellence, some argue that the experience of smaller nations such as Switzerland, Singapore and New Zealand is ample proof that size does not matter. That may be so, but successful individual small nations' destiny is highly vulnerable to the activities of the larger nations, now including China. Hence, in this context, size is of the essence, as the rise of China's economy and political power clearly demonstrate.

There is therefore no need to dwell on this issue, because the political vision of the founding fathers relates to the long term, and the road is inevitably far from smooth. It is vital, however, to learn what EU leaders think the EU's future will entail, since one wants to know if their vision contradicts or lends support to that of the founding fathers.

26.3 The vision of contemporary politicians

Turning to the vision of contemporary political leaders, one needs to know their views regarding whether the SEM, economic and monetary union (EMU) and the implementation of the Treaty of Lisbon (the Treaty on the Functioning of the European Union, TFEU) are ends in themselves, or merely staging posts on the way to greater economic and political union. To concentrate attention and liven the debate, we shall consider interchanges between the leaders of the main driving forces behind EU integration: France, Germany and the European Commission (Commission), as well as the largest reluctant partner, Britain. Due to space limitations, we shall concentrate on two examples of interchange, one between them, before the adoption of the euro, the other relatively recent, but ongoing, since these should enlighten us about general trends, as well as show us if Britain is still out on a limb (see Young 1998 for excellent documentation and analysis).

26.3.1 The vision of political leaders: the 1980s and 1990s

The first example relates to the interchanges that took place between then British prime minister, Margaret Thatcher, the Commission president during the late 1980s, Jacques Delors, and Germany's chancellor, Helmut Kohl. During the summer of 1988 Delors predicted that 'in ten years time 80 per cent of economic, and perhaps social and tax legislation, would be of Community origin'. In early September of the same year, he followed this with a speech to the UK's Trade

Union Congress (TUC), in which he spoke strongly of the 'social dimension' of the SEM, and called for a 'platform of guaranteed social rights', including the proposal that every worker should be covered by a collective agreement with his or her employer: a proposal that is close to the hearts of most British trade unionists.

Later, during the same month, Thatcher responded in very strong terms: 'We have not rolled back the frontiers of the state in Britain only to see them re-imposed at a European level, with a European superstate exercising a new dominance from Brussels.' Subsequently, and on many occasions, Thatcher repeated similar phrases regarding the 'nightmare of an EC government'. Nor did she confine her attacks to broad policy issues. She also attacked every single practical measure by which her fellow EU leaders sought to achieve progress within the EU. She told the somewhat bemused Italian prime minister, Ciriaco De Mita, 'I neither want nor expect to see a European central bank or a European currency in my lifetime or . . . for a long time afterwards.' A few years later, she declared that she regretted having endorsed EMU during the 1989 Madrid Summit, and backed William Hague for the leadership of the Conservative Party to succeed her immediate replacement (John Major), simply because Hague had vehemently announced that qualification for membership in his shadow cabinet would require unwavering commitment to ensuring that the euro would have no place in Britain. Hague's choice of Michael Portillo as shadow chancellor soon after the latter's return to politics was consistent with that stance, since Portillo was, and continues to be, a vehement opponent of the UK adopting the euro, and actually believes in its imminent demise on the grounds that no single European currency has ever succeeded.

The first rebuttals of Thatcher's vehement utterances came not from the 'socialist' leaders of the other EC member nations,[2] but from the more right-wing.[3] The most outspoken was Chancellor Kohl, hitherto Thatcher's closest ally. He declared flatly in Brussels in November 1988 that:

1. All internal frontiers within the EC must disappear by 1992.
2. Tax harmonization is indispensable.
3. A European police force is the answer to crime and terrorism.

4. By pooling sovereignty, EC states will gain, not lose.

5. The EC must have (in alliance with the USA), a common defence policy, leading to a European army.

He did not mention Thatcher by name, but every point he emphasized was one on which she was on record as taking the opposite view.

It should be stressed that Thatcher's stance on these matters suggested that she believed that the EU was predominantly a zero-sum game: every increase in EU sovereignty was at the expense of that of the member nations, especially the UK. However, most of the other EU leaders had fewer illusions about what the medium-sized EU member countries could achieve by themselves: very little indeed. They reckoned that by 'pooling sovereignty' they would increase the range of possibilities for the EU as a whole, and thus for their own countries as well.

In short, it could be claimed that the other EC leaders saw Thatcher following the example of Charles de Gaulle, whose anti-EC policies in the 1960s held back the EC development, ironically including UK admission (see Chapter 2). The comparison may have been one which Thatcher herself found flattering; would she have realized, however, that de Gaulle's intransigence eventually did much to undermine French influence for a long time, both within the EC and outside it? Yet despite all this, one should not forget what de Gaulle stood for; in 1967 he said: 'if a united Europe is to be built by itself and for itself without being subjected to an economic, monetary or political system that is foreign to it, if Europe is to counterbalance the immense power of the United States, then the ties and rules that hold the community together must be strengthened, not weakened'.

So what is the message behind this interchange, in terms of the vision of EU leaders in the 1980s regarding the future of the EU? The answer is that, during that period, Germany and the Commission president, as well as the silent majority of EU nations, saw the EU as evolving beyond the commitments entered into then. In short, they envisaged the EU becoming more than an EMU with a common currency and coordinated policies on foreign affairs, defence and justice and home security. Britain took a different view and was supported by Denmark, her closest ally since well before the creation of EFTA in 1960, after it became clear that Britain could not go along with what the Original Six aspired to (see page 25 and Chapter 2). However, since Britain had always seen a different role for itself from that envisaged by the 'continent', one can claim that the countries most involved with EU integration acted in a manner that suggested that the future would bring about deeper integration. Although this was not expressed in the form of concrete political unity, what is pertinent is that their vision for the next steps to be taken for further EU integration was on the whole consistent with the dream of the founding fathers.

26.3.2 The vision of more recent political leaders

We now turn to the second example of interchange, by considering what more recent EU leaders think of how the future should be shaped for the EU.

The post-Maastricht leaders

Following the Thatcher–Kohl exchange, without a shadow of doubt the debate was opened by Joschka Fischer, the German foreign minister, on 12 May 2000, in a speech delivered at Humboldt University. He began by asking his audience to allow him to 'cast aside . . . the mantle of . . . minister', and to speak in a purely personal capacity. He said that

in the coming decade, we will have to enlarge . . . [the] EU to the east and south-east, and this will, in the end, mean a doubling in the number of members. And at the same time, if we are to be able to meet this historic challenge and integrate the new member states without substantially denting . . . [the] EU's capacity for action, we must put into place the last brick in the building of European integration, namely political integration[4]

He added that this 'finalité politique' would be preceded by the formation of a 'centre of gravity' within the EU: an 'avant garde', the driving force for the completion of political integration. With regard to the institutional arrangement, he asked for 'a constitutional treaty centred around basic human and civil rights; shared sovereignty and a clear definition of competences between European and nation-state levels of governance; a division of powers among the European institutions, including a European Parliament with two chambers, a European government and, possibly, a directly elected president, with broadly administrative powers'. With this 'division of sovereignty' between EU institutions and the nation states, he thus distanced himself from a European superstate transcending and replacing the national democracies.

The speech attracted a great deal of criticism and generated open hostility in some quarters, where the word 'federation' is not in the dictionary of European integration. Also, scholarly reactions have ranged from criticism of Fischer's logical inconsistency in wanting a federation where the member states remain sovereign, to the fact that he had not worked out the path to be taken to the ultimate objective. With regard to inconsistency, Leben[5] argues that classical constitutional theory recognizes only confederate and federal states, and hence wonders if there can be a third type: 'a federation but not a federal state, as . . . Fischer's speech seems to suggest?' However, our concern here is with what political leaders think.[6]

A year later, on 30 April 2001, the German chancellor, Gerhard Schröder, added to Fischer's framework in the publication for the November congress for his Social Democrat Party. He called for the restructuring of EU institutions, including the building of the Commission into a strong executive, the transformation of the Council of the European Union into a chamber of European states, and the drafting of a constitution for the EU. Singling out the weaknesses of the common agricultural and regional policies, he laid stress on greater transparency by insisting that the member states (MSs) should themselves assume responsibility for the tasks that they can carry out more effectively than through a central administration, which is consistent with the subsidiarity principle, incorporated in the Amsterdam Treaty.

On 27 June 2000 the French president, Jacques Chirac, in a speech delivered to the German Parliament in Berlin, called for the formation of an 'inner core of EU members', willing to push more rapidly towards further integration, thus echoing Fischer's appeal for a centre of gravity, which some would rather call a two-speed Europe (see Chapter 2). Also, he endorsed the idea of a future constitution for the EU. Some analysts saw this as support for Germany's call for EU federalism; others as politically calculated rhetoric lacking in substance. He stressed, however, that neither France nor Germany envisaged the creation of a 'European super-state which would take the place of our nation states' – that is, he was advocating 'not a United States of Europe, but a Europe of united states'.

On 28 May 2001 Lionel Jospin, while still French premier, spelled out his vision for the EU as a 'federation of nation states', but rejected the German views of federalism and distanced himself from President Jacques Chirac's idea of a 'pioneer group' to forge ahead with integration. Noting that 'federation' might appear to be a simple and coherent word, but that it was subject to several interpretations (see next page), he went on to reject any model based on the German federal system. He added that 'if federation means a gradual, controlled process of sharing competences, or transferring competences to the union level, then this refers to the federation of nation states coined by [ex-EU Commission president] Jacques Delors and is a concept which I fully support'. Being a dedicated socialist, he reinforced his previous suggestions that the EU should enhance its social legislation with the adoption of a social treaty, firming up tax harmonization, and a tighter legal framework to enshrine the role of public services in the EU.

Of the EU member nations considered here, this leaves the British government. Tony Blair, the leader of the reformed Labour Party (some argue it is the old Conservative Party in a pleasant disguise), had been at the British helm for a decade and is warm towards the EU, and hence out of step with Baroness Thatcher. After assuming office in 1997 he was sympathetic towards the EU. In a speech (in Ghent, near Bruges, where Thatcher delivered hers) on 23 February 2000, he said that he believed that, by winning the argument for economic reform in Europe, he could mould the EU agenda, and in doing so simultaneously defuse much of the resentment Britons felt towards the EU. In short, he wants the UK to act from within the EU to the betterment of the EU itself and to make it attractive to Britons, adding that British ties with the USA have been undermined by the failure of the UK to play an active role within the EU. Later, he committed his government to the adoption of the euro, provided that Britain passed his chancellor's economic tests (see Chapter 11), and providing that UK citizens endorsed adoption in a referendum. However, he remained adamant that he did not see the EU going beyond the economic, and that the alliance with the USA would be strengthened – the events leading to the 2003 US-British (and alliances) war with Iraq clearly demonstrated that.

On 6 October 2000, in his speech to the Polish Stock Exchange in Warsaw, Blair came up with his proposals for EU political reform, which, given its date, were obviously his response to Fischer and submission to the Convention of the Future of Europe (see Chapter 2). First, he wanted the European Council to set the agenda, which is more or less what it actually does (by offering blueprints that the Commission develops into concrete proposals; see Chapter 3), but with the Commission president playing a part in drawing up the agenda, the Commission continuing as the guardian of the treaties, and the Council having term presidencies with greater continuity. Second, he did not want to see a single document called the EU Constitution, opting for continuation of the present system of treaties, laws and precedents – that is, to retain the British style of an unwritten constitution, and to decide on what is to be done and not done at EU level: thus be more specific about subsidiarity. Third, he wanted to have a second chamber for the European Parliament, whose most important function would be to review the EU's work. Fourth, he wanted to streamline the Commission, since with enlargement it would have thirty members and would become unworkable, but he indicated that there was no need to discuss this then. In short, he wanted to see the EU as a 'superpower, but not a superstate . . . an economic powerhouse through the completion of the world's biggest single market, the extension of competition, an adaptable and well educated workforce, the support for businesses large and small'. All of this amounted to saying 'no thank you' to Fischer, and though he wanted to stress his positive commitment to the EU, this went only as far as a slightly strengthened EU.

It is interesting to note that in his speech to the European Parliament on 23 June 2005, Blair said that the EU 'is a union of values, of solidarity between nations and people . . . not just a common market in which we trade but a common political space in which we live as citizens'. He added that 'I believe in Europe as a political project. I believe in Europe with a strong and caring social dimension.' And he rejected the 'division between the Europe necessary to succeed economically and social Europe', and stressed that 'Political Europe and economic Europe do not live in separate rooms.'

To complete the picture, one must consider the position of the then Commission president, Romano Prodi, who was the Italian prime minister during 1996–8 and 2006–8. His opinions are clearly shown in a speech delivered to the French National Assembly on 12 March 2003. He asked: 'What Europe do we want? What common projects are we aiming for? Just a "supermarket" or a political area that allows us to defend convictions on the world stage?' He also called 'for a Union that can "exercise the responsibilities of a world power"', and claimed that current disagreements between EU leaders about the war in Iraq 'will eventually help defend the idea on which European integration was founded', and 'when a political Union emerges, it will reap the benefit' of this approach.

Thus practically all the major players were still envisaging the EU not only going beyond its commitments then, but also evolving into some sort of a closer political union. The debate on whether this should be a 'United States of Europe' or a 'Europe of united states' does not undermine this, since, to reiterate, a federation can take different forms. Hence the vision of most of the former major EU political leaders was consistent with the substance of the dream of the founding fathers.

Before turning to the current leaders, some further consideration of federation is warranted. According to constitutional theorists, federalism fulfils two major functions. The first is a vertical separation of powers by assigning separate responsibilities to two government levels; the components and the federation are usually geographically defined, 'although "societal federalism" considers non-territorial units as components of a federation' (Börzel and Risse 2000). The second is the integration of heterogeneous societies, but without destroying their cultural and/or political autonomy (Börzel and Risse 2000). Implicit in both functions is that the components and the federation have autonomous decision powers that they can exercise independently; thus sovereignty is shared or divided, rather than being exclusively located at one level. Even without the legitimate monopoly of coercive force, the EU has acquired some fundamental federal qualities. As witnessed by this book, it possesses sovereignty rights in a wide variety of policy sectors. These range from exclusive jurisdiction in the area of EMU, to far-reaching regulatory competences in sectors such as consumer protection, energy, the environment, health/social security and transport. Also, the EU is 'increasingly penetrating even the core of traditional state responsibilities such as internal security (Schengen, Europol)' (Börzel and Risse 2000). In most policy areas, EU law is not only superior to national law; it can also deploy direct effect, giving citizens the right to litigate against their states for violating EU laws conferred on them (see Chapter 4). This is part of a second development, which has been addressed more recently. The

EU is transforming itself into a political community within a defined territory and with its own citizens, who are granted (some) fundamental rights by the European Treaties and the jurisdiction of the European Court of Justice ... With the Treaties of Maastricht and Amsterdam, however, the single market has been embedded in a political union with emerging external boundaries [Article 11 of the Union treaty refers to the protection of the integrity of the Union and its external boundaries] and proper citizenship (Börzel and Risse 2000)

Not only has the EU developed into a political community with comprehensive regulatory powers and a proper mechanism of territorially defined exclusion and inclusion (EU citizenship), but it also shares most features of what defines a federation. First, the EU is a system of governance that has at least two orders of government, each existing in its own right and exercising direct influence on the people. Second, EU treaties allocate jurisdiction and resources to these two main orders of government. Third, there are provisions for 'shared government' in areas where the jurisdiction of the EU and MSs overlap. Fourth, EU law enjoys supremacy over national law: it is the law of the land (see Chapter 4). Fifth, the composition and procedures of EU institutions are based not solely on principles of majority representation, but guarantee the representation of 'minority' views. Sixth, the European Court of Justice serves as an arbitrator to adjudicate on conflicts between EU institutions and MSs. Finally, the EU has a directly elected parliament (Börzel and Risse 2000).

The EU only lacks two significant features of a federation. One is that the MSs remain the 'masters' of the treaties – that is, they have the exclusive power to amend or change the constitutive treaties of the EU. The other is that the EU has no real tax and spend capacity – that is, it has no fiscal federalism. 'Otherwise ... [the] EU today looks like a federal system [see Chapter 18], it works in a similar manner to a federal system, so why not call it an emerging federation?' (Börzel and Risse 2000). In short, one wonders why the word 'federalism' frightens some EU nations and citizens so much.

One obvious reaction to the position of these political

leaders would be that their statements summarized above should not be taken seriously, since they were meant merely to set the scene for the Convention for the Future of Europe (see Chapter 2). In other words, given past experience, these positions would have to be greatly watered down if consensus were to materialize, and consensus would be needed since a new treaty would require unanimity. This was especially so when it was being claimed that the Convention was to be a historic moment for the EU, just as the Philadelphia convention was for America, since it would give the EU a single legal personality and provide all its institutions with a constitutional basis for their powers, as well as transfer sovereignties over internal affairs (immigration, cross-border crime, drug trafficking) to EU institutions. One should add, however, that Peter Hain, British Prime Minister Tony Blair's representative on the Convention, insisted that it would be much less important than the Maastricht Treaty.

It is pertinent, therefore, to refer to the draft constitution, submitted on 6 February 2003, to find out what light it sheds on the matter, and to follow this by considering the Treaty of Lisbon, since doing so will help shed light on the above-mentioned 'watering down' during negotiations. There is no need, however, to examine the final draft, adopted in the Thessaloniki Greek summit on 20 June 2003, and signed in Brussels in the intergovernmental conference in June 2004 (see Section 2.3.6, page 33), because it is the adopted treaty that is of the essence.

Consider the first articles of the 2003 draft constitution, largely attributed to Valéry Giscard d'Estaing, chairman of the Convention and former French president, and his twelve-member 'inner praesidium'.[7] It envisaged a major role for the EU in the economy, foreign policy and even space exploration. Sixteen of its forty-six articles dealt with EU aims, values and powers. Article 1, on establishing an entity for the EU, stated that it should be: 'A Union of European States which, while retaining their national identities, closely coordinate their policies at the European level, and *administer certain common competences on a federal basis*' (italics added). Article 3, on EU objectives, calls for, inter alia, the 'development of a common foreign and security policy, and a common defence policy, to defend and promote the Union's values in the wider world'. Indeed, 'the tone of the document is more federalist than expected', and in particular the 'Commission was pleased with the clause to allow national governments and the European Parliament to give . . . [the] EU more powers' (*Financial Times*, 7 February 2003), if needed, for the attainment of the objectives set by the Constitution.

These were labelled surprising proposals, given that the Convention had been entrusted with proposing a framework and structures for the EU that were geared to changes in the world situation, the needs of EU citizens and the future development of the union. In other words, the Convention was largely meant to simplify and restructure EU basic treaties (Giuliano Amato, one of the two vice-chairmen of the Convention and ex-prime minister of Italy, *Project Syndicate/Institute for Human Science* 2002). No wonder that Britain immediately labelled the draft 'unacceptable', claiming it went further than expected towards creating a federal Europe (*Financial Times*, 7 February 2003). However, Amato responded in the same article by arguing that the 'institutional structure . . . should also reflect and help develop Europe's broader aspirations. Europe must be more than a vehicle of economic integration.' What was even more interesting was that Giscard d'Estaing, the Convention's chairman, proposed the streamlining of the EU foreign policy apparatus by the creation of a single post of EU foreign minister (to replace the two roles then held by Javier Solana, EU foreign policy chief, and Christopher Patten, commissioner in charge of external relations), as well as scrapping the rotating six-month presidency of the European Council (*Financial Times*, 16 April 2003).

That was the draft, but how does it compare with Lisbon Treaty? Since this is detailed in Chapter 2, there is no need to dwell on it here. A glance at relevant sections of Chapter 2 and the treaty should reveal that the changes have been minimal. That is why many have claimed that the Lisbon Treaty is the constitutional treaty in disguise (see Section 2.3.6, page 33). Thus it would seem that the pre-Convention utterances were not mere political gesturing, and hence should be taken seriously.

The current leaders

Turning to the current leaders, there have been changes in all the major actors considered in this chapter. Angela Merkel has been German chancellor since 2005. Nicolas Sarkozy assumed the French presidency in 2007. David Cameron became UK prime minister in 2010 in a Conservative/Liberal Democrat coalition. José Manuel Barroso, ex-prime minister of Portugal, assumed the presidency of the Commission in 2004 and again in 2009. Romano Prodi was replaced as Italy's prime minister by Silvio Berlusconi in 2008.

Following the rejection of the constitutional treaty by France and the Netherlands in 2005, Merkel asserted that the failed Constitution must be revived, stressing that clearing the EU institutional mess must be a priority over economic reform. Sarkozy went along with her, and so did Barroso. And although there were some differences between EU political leaders, the Lisbon Treaty became a reality in 2009. Since, as just mentioned, the Lisbon Treaty is more or less the same as the constitutional treaty, it follows that the current visions of three of our main actors (two new, one old) are consistent with those of their immediate predecessors. This leaves the UK.

Cameron has been UK prime minister since 11 May 2010, and Hague is his foreign minister. Although he stated that Britain will play 'a positive, active [and] engaged' role in Europe, he added that 'We're not a member of the euro, nor are we going to become a member of the euro'. He also stressed that he would 'stoutly defend British red lines', warning that he was 'only willing to back proposals that left UK powers untouched'. Moreover, he declared after the summit that 'of course there are those . . . who want to press for greater integration or still seek treaty changes to bring that about', so 'You've got to be on your guard'. Add to this that he was absent from the pre-summit meeting of EU leaders from the centre-right European People's Party (EEP; see Chapter 3), which included Merkel, Sarkozy and Berlusconi, but this is consistent with his controversial decision in 2009 to pull Tory MEPs out of the EPP to form a new Eurosceptic group, the European Conservatives and Reformist group (ECR; see Chapter 3). Furthermore, his foreign minister Hague is sticking to his guns (see page 424). Hence the UK's position has become more Eurosceptic. It is interesting that Cameron's position has not changed, even though the partner of his coalition government, the Liberal Democratic Party, and its leader and the deputy prime minister, Nick Clegg, are all committed to the EU. Thus the coalition agreement rules out the transfer of any further powers to Europe without a referendum.

26.4 Conclusion

Thus, excepting those of Britain, the majority of European political leaders who really matter envisage a long-term future for the EU that is not limited to what it has achieved to date. Those who share the dream of the founding fathers would stress that this is tantamount to being on the road leading to the creation of a United States of Europe. They would differ, however, with regard to how soon they will arrive there and what precise form they want it to take. On the other hand, both the Eurosceptics and those who have no memory of past wars, or have not experienced them at all, would argue that all that is likely to happen is simply concretizing and fine-tuning the economic achievements to date.

FURTHER READING

Tsoukalis, L. (2005) *What Kind of Europe?*, Oxford University Press.

NOTES

1   See, inter alios, Feldstein (1997), pp. 24–6.
2   Such as France's François Mitterrand, Spain's Felipe Gonzalez and Greece's Andreas Papandreou.
3   Such as Germany's Helmut Kohl, Italy's Ciriaco De Mita, Holland's Ruud Lubbers and Belgium's Wilfred Martens.
4   Translated into English in Joerges *et al.* 2000.
5   In Joerges *et al.* 2000, p. 101.
6   Those interested in purely academic discussion should turn to the excellent collection in Joerges *et al.* 2000.
7   Easily accessible from the EU website at http://european-convention.eu.int

Bibliography

Throughout this book, all references to publications by the Commission of the European Community or Union are recorded as being authored by the CEU, since there is no need to follow historical incidence; all that matters is date of publication.

Within CEU publications, frequent reference is made to Communications from the European Commission/Union to the Council. These are recorded as COM(??) ???, where (??) tells the year and ??? the number; hence COM(88) 491 means Communication number 491, issued in 1988. To save on space and avoid distraction, they are not stated in the main text, but are fully stated in the relevant CEU entry in the references.

Any references to the 'Council of whichever minister' are entered under Council. Those pertaining to the European Council of Heads of States and Governments come under European Council.

Reference is also frequently made to the Treaties of the European Union, which are now easily available on the Europa website (at http://ec.europa.eu). We use TEU for the Treaty on European Union – that is, the Maastricht Treaty – and TFEU for the Treaty on the Functioning of the European Union – that is, the Lisbon Treaty. Others are mentioned by name: EEC Treaty, Amsterdam Treaty, Nice Treaty, and so on. Throughout the book, *EU Bulletin* is used to refer to the *Bulletin of the European Communities*, now *Union* (various issues), and *OJ C*, *OJ L* or *OJ CL* (where *L* stands for legal) refer to the Commission's *Official Journal of the European Communities/Union*. Again, the EC/EU's own system of referencing is clear.

Abbott, K., Keohane, R., Moravcsik, M., Slaughter, A.-M. and Snidal, D. (2000) 'The concept of legalization', *International Organization*, vol. 53, issue 3.

ABS (2010) 'General government expenses by purpose 2008/9 5512.0', Australian Bureau of Statistics (www.abs.gov.au/ausstats/abs@.nsf/mf/5512.0).

Acs, Z., Audretsch, D. and Feldman, M. (1994) 'R&D spillovers and recipient firm size', *Review of Economics and Statistics*, vol. 100, no. 2.

Adedeji, A. (2002) 'History and prospects for regional integration in Africa', paper presented on 5 March at the African Development Forum III, held in Addis Ababa, Ethiopia.

Adelman, M. A. (1969) 'Comment on the "H" concentration measure as a numbers equivalent', *Review of Economics and Statistics*, vol. 51.

Agha, A. and Houghton, J. (1996) 'Designing VAT systems: some efficiency considerations', *Review of Economics and Statistics*, vol. 78.

Aiginger, K. and Pfaffermayr, M. (2000) 'The single market and geographic concentration in Europe', presented at the EARIE Conference, Lausanne, 11 December.

Aitken, N. D. (1973) 'The effects of the EEC and EFTA on European trade: a temporal cross-section analysis', *American Economic Review*, vol. 68.

Akerlof, G., Dickens, A., Perry, W. and George, L. (2000) 'Near rational wage price setting and long-run Phillips curve', *Brookings Papers on Economic Activity*, vol. 30, no. 1.

Alesina, A. and Spolaore, E. (2003) *The Size of Nations*, MIT Press, Cambridge, Mass.

Alesina, A. and Giavazzi, F. (eds.) (2009) *Europe and the Euro*, University of Chicago Press, Chicago and London.

Allen, C., Gasiorek, M. and Smith, A. (1998) 'The competition effects of the single market in Europe', *Economic Policy*, 27.

Allen, P. R. (1983) 'Cyclical imbalance in a monetary union', *Journal of Common Market Studies*, vol. 21, no. 2.

Allen, P. R. and Kenen, P. (1980) *Asset Markets, Exchange Rates and Economic Integration*, Cambridge University Press.

Alston, P. and Weiler, J. (1999) 'An "ever closer union" in need of a human rights policy: the EU and human rights', *European Journal of International Law*, vol. 9.

Alter, K. (1996) 'The European Court's political power', *West European Politics*, vol. 19.

(1998a) 'Who are the "Masters of the Treaty"? European governments and the European Court of Justice', *International Organization*, vol. 52, no. 1.

(1998b) 'Explaining national court acceptance of European Court jurisprudence: a critical evaluation of theories of legal integration', in A.-M. Slaughter, A. Stone Sweet and J. Weiler (eds.), *The European Courts and National Courts: Doctrine and Jurisprudence*, Hart, Oxford.

(2000) 'The European Union's legal system and domestic policy: spillover and backlash', *International Organization*, vol. 53.

(2001) *Establishing the Supremacy of European Law: The Making of an International Rule of Law in Europe*, Oxford University Press.

Alter, K. and Meunier-Aitsahalia, S. (1994) 'Judicial politics in the European Community: European integration and the pathbreaking Cassis de Dijon decision', *Comparative Political Studies*, vol. 26.

Alter, K. and Vargas, K. (2000) 'Explaining variation in the use of European litigation strategies: EC law and UK gender equality policy', *Comparative Political Studies*, vol. 36.

Alter, K., Dehousse, R. and Vanberg, G. (2002) 'Law, political science and EU legal studies: an interdisciplinary project', *European Union Politics*, vol. 3.

Amiti, M. (1998) 'New trade theories and industrial location in the EU: a survey of evidence', *Oxford Review of Economic Policy*, vol. 4, no. 2.

Anderson, M. and Liefferink, D. (eds.) (1997) *European Environmental Policy – The Pioneers*, Manchester University Press.

Ardy, B. (1988) 'The national incidence of the European Community budget', *Journal of Common Market Studies*, vol. 26, no. 4.

(2002a) 'The EU budget and EU citizens', in S. Hatt and F. Gardner (eds.), *Economics, Policies and People: A European Perspective*, Macmillan, Basingstoke.

(2002b) 'The UK, the EU budget and EMU', in Ali M. El-Agraa (ed.), *The Euro and Britain: Implications of Moving into the EMU*, Pearson Education, Harlow.

Ardy, B. and Umbach, G. (2004) 'Employment policies in Germany and the UK: the impact of Europeanisation', Anglo-German Foundation for the Study of Industrial Society, London and Berlin (www.agf.org.uk).

Ardy, B., Begg, I., Schelkle, W. and Torres, F. (2002) *EMU and its Impact on Cohesion: Policy Challenges*, European Institute, South Bank University, London.

Argyris, N. (1993) 'Regulatory reform in the electricity sector: an analysis of the Commission's internal market proposals', *Oxford Review of Economic Policy*, vol. 19, no. 1.

Armington, P. S. (1970) 'Adjustment of trade balances: some experiments with a model of trade among many countries', *IMF Staff Papers*, vol. 17.

Armstrong, H. W. (1978) 'European Economic Community regional policy: a survey and critique', *Regional Studies*, vol. 12, no. 5.

(1985) 'The reform of European Community regional policy', *Journal of Common Market Studies*, vol. 23.

(1995a) *Growth Disparities and Convergence Clubs in Regional GDP in Western Europe, USA and Australia*, Report for DG16, European Commission, Brussels.

(1995b) 'Convergence among regions of the European Union', *Papers in Regional Science*, vol. 40.

Armstrong, H. W. and Taylor, J. (2000) *Regional Economics and Policy*, 3rd edn, Blackwell, Oxford.

Armstrong, H. W., Camagni, R., Dabinett, G. and Davoudi, S. (2010) 'Territorial cohesion policy in the European Union', *Italian Journal of Regional Science*, vol. 9.

Armstrong, K. (1998) 'Legal integration: theorising the legal dimension of European integration', *Journal of Common Market Studies*, vol. 36.

Armstrong, K. and Bulmer, S. (1998) *The Governance of the Single European Market*, Manchester University Press.

Armstrong, K. and Kilpatrick, C. (2007) 'Law, governance, or new governance? The changing open method of coordination', *Columbia Journal of European Law*, vol. 13, no. 3.

Arndt, H. W. and Garnaut, R. (1979) 'ASEAN and the industrialisation of East Asia', *Journal of Common Market Studies*, vol. 17, no. 3.

Arndt, S. W. (1968) 'On discriminatory versus non-preferential tariff policies', *Economic Journal*, vol. 78.

(1969) 'Customs unions and the theory of tariffs', *American Economic Review*, vol. 59.

Arnold, F. (1994) *Economic Analysis of Environmental Policy and Regulation*, Wiley, New York.

Arnull, A. (1990) 'Does the ECJ have inherent jurisdiction?', *Common Market Law Review*, vol. 27.

(1991) 'What shall we do on Sunday?', *European Law Review*, vol. 16.

(1996) 'The European ECJ and judicial objectivity: A reply to Professor Hartley', *Law Quarterly Review*, vol. 112.

(2006) *The European Union and its Court of Justice*, 2nd edn, Oxford University Press.

Arts, K. and Dickson. A. (eds.) (2004) *EU Development Cooperation: From Model to Symbol*, Manchester University Press.

Asdrubali, P. and Kim, S. (2008) 'The economic effects of the EU budget: a VAR analysis', *Journal of Common Market Studies*, vol. 46, no. 5.

Asdrubali, P., Sorensen, B. and Yosha, O. (2002) 'Channels of interstate risk sharing: United States 1963–1990', *Quarterly Journal of Economics*, vol. 111.

Atkin, N. D. (1973) 'The effects of the EEC and EFTA on European trade: a temporal cross-section analysis', *American Economic Review*, vol. 63.

Audretsch, D. and Thurik, R. (2001) 'Linking entrepreneurship to growth', *STI Working Papers 2001/2*, OECD, Paris.

Audretsch, D., Baumol, W. and Burke, A. (2001) 'Competition policy in dynamic markets', *International Journal of Industrial Organization*, vol. 19, no. 5.

Australian Society of CPAs (1998) 'Tax reform in New Zealand – the shape of things to come in Australia', discussion paper, May (cited in Cnossen 2002).

Bachtler, J. and Gorzelak, G. (2009) 'Reforming EU regional policy: a reappraisal of the performance of the structural funds', in D. Bailey and L. de Propis (eds.), *Industrial and Regional Policies in an Enlarging EU*, Routledge, London.

Badinger, H. and Maydell, N. (2009) 'Legal and economic issues in completing the EU internal market for services: an interdisciplinary perspective', *Journal of Common Market Studies*, vol. 47, no. 4.

Badinger, H., Breuss, F., Schuster, P. and Sellner, R. (2008) 'Macroeconomic effects of the Services Directive', in F. Breuss, G. Fink and S. Griller (eds.), *Services Liberalization in the Internal Market*, Springer, Wien and New York.

BAE Systems (2000) 'Updating and development of economic and fares data regarding the European air travel industry', *2000 Annual Report*, BAE Systems, Chorley.

Bagella, M. and Becchetti, L. (2000) *The Comparative Advantage of Industrial Districts: Theoretical and Empirical Analysis*, Physica-Verlag, Heidelberg.

Bailey, S. J. (2002) *Public Sector Economics: Theory and Practice*, 2nd edn, Palgrave, Basingstoke.

Balassa, B. (1961) *The Theory of Economic Integration*, Allen and Unwin, London.

(1967) 'Trade creation and trade diversion in the European Common Market', *Economic Journal*, vol. 77.

(1974) 'Trade creation and trade diversion in the European Common Market: an appraisal of the evidence', *Manchester School*, vol. 42.

(1975) *European Economic Integration*, North-Holland, Amsterdam.

Baldwin, R. (1989) 'The growth effect of 1992', *Economic Policy*, no. 9.

(1994) *Towards an Integrated Europe*, Centre for Economic Policy Research, London.

Baldwin, R. and Krugman, P. A. (2004) 'Agglomeration, integration and tax harmonization', *European Economic Review*, vol. 48, no. 1.

Baldwin, R., Haaparanta, P. and Kiander, J. (1995) *Expanding Membership of the European Union*, Cambridge University Press.

Baldwin, R., François, J. F. and Portes, R. (1997) 'The costs and benefits of Eastern enlargement: the impact on the European Union and Central Europe', *Economic Policy: A European Forum*, vol. 24.

Baldwin, R. E. (1971) *Non-Tariff Distortions of International Trade*, Allen and Unwin, London.

Ball, L. M. (2009) 'Hysteresis in unemployment: old and new evidence', working paper, no. 14818, National Bureau of Economic Research, Cambridge, Mass.

Ballenger, N., Dunmore, J. and Lederer, T. (1987) 'Trade liberalization in world farm markets', *Agriculture Information Bulletin*, vol. 516, May.

Bangermann, M. (1994) 'Information technology in Europe: the EC Commission's view', in *European Information Technology Observatory*, EITO, Frankfurt am Main.

Banister, D., Stead, D., Steen, P., Akerman, J., Dreborg, K., Nijkamp, P. and Schleicher-Tappeser, R. (2000) *European Transport Policy and Sustainable Mobility*, Spon, London.

Barca, F. (2009) *An Agenda for a Reformed Cohesion Policy*, independent report prepared at the request of Danuta Hübner, Commissioner for Regional Policy, Brussels.

Barents, R. (1982) 'New developments in measures having equivalent effect: a reappraisal', *Common Market Law Review*, vol. 19.

Barham, C. (2002) 'Economic inactivity and the labour market', *Labour Market Trends*, February.

Barnard, C. (1995) 'A European litigation strategy: the case of the Equal Opportunities Commission', in J. Shaw and G. More (eds.), *New Legal Dynamics of European Union*, Oxford University Press.

Barnard, C. and Sharpston, E. (1997) 'The changing face of Article 177 references', *Common Market Law Review*, vol. 34.

Barnes, P. and Barnes, I. (1999) *Environmental Policy in the European Union*, Edward Elgar, Cheltenham.

Barrell, R. (2002) 'The UK and EMU: choosing the regime', *National Institute Economic Review*, no. 180, April.

Barrell, R. and Pain, N. (1993) 'Trade restraints and Japanese direct investment flows', National Institute of Economic and Social Research, London.

Barrios, S. and Strobl, E. (2009) 'The dynamics of regional inequalities', *Regional Science and Urban Economics*, vol. 39.

Barrios, S., Huizinga, H., Laeven, L. and Nicodème, G. (2009) 'International taxation and multinational firm location decisions', *Taxation Papers*, EU Publications Office, Luxembourg.

Barry, A. (1993) 'The European community and European

government: harmonization, mobility and space', *Economy and Society*, vol. 22.

Barten, A. P. (1970) 'Maximum likelihood estimation of a complete system of demand equations', *European Economic Review*, vol. 1.

Barten, A. P., d'Alcantra, G. and Cairn, G. J. (1976) 'COMET, a medium-term macroeconomic model for the European Economic Community', *European Economic Review*, vol. 7, no. 1.

Basile, R. (2009) 'Productivity polarization across Europe', *International Journal of Regional Science*, vol. 32.

Bassanini, A. and Duval, R. (2006) 'Employment patterns in OECD countries: reassessing the role of policies and institutions', OECD Economics Department working paper, no. 486, Paris.

Bassanini, A., Nunziata, L. and Venn, D. (2009) 'Job protection legislation and productivity growth in OECD countries', *Economic Policy*, vol. 58.

Baumol, W. J. and Oates, J. E. (1988) *The Theory of Environmental Policy*, 2nd edn, Cambridge University Press.

Bayoumi, T. and Eichengreen, B. (1995) 'Is regionalism simply a diversion? Evidence from the evolution of the EC and EFTA', discussion paper, no. 1294, Centre for Economic Policy Research, London.

(1996) 'Operationalising the theory of optimum currency areas', discussion paper, no. 1484, Centre for Economic Policy Research, London.

BEA (2010) 'GDP by state', Bureau of Economic Analysis, Washington D.C. (www.bea.gov).

Beatty, C., Fothergill, S., Gore, T. and Green, A. (2007) 'The real level of unemployment 2007', Centre for Regional Economic and Social Research, Sheffield Hallam University.

Begg, I. (1995) 'The impact on regions of competition of the EC single market in financial services', in S. Hardy, M. Hart, L. Albrechts and A. Katos (eds.), *An Enlarged Europe: Regions in Competition?*, Jessica Kingsley, London.

Begg, I. and Grimwade, N. (1998) *Paying for Europe*, Sheffield Academic Press.

Begg, I., Enderlein, H., Le Cacheux, J. and Mrak, M. (2008) 'Financing of the European budget', Final Report, Study for European Commission DG Budget (http://ec.europa.eu/budget/reform/conference/documents_en.htm).

Bellamy, R. and Warleigh, A. (1998) 'From an ethics of participation to an ethics of participation: citizenship and the future of the EU', *Millennium*, vol. 27.

Bengtsson, K., Ekström, C. and Farrell, D. (2006) 'Sweden's growth paradox', *The McKinsey Quarterly*, Economic Studies Country Reports (www.mckinseyquarterly.com/home.aspx).

Benvenisti, E. (1993) 'Judicial misgivings regarding the application of international law: an analysis of attitudes of international courts', *European Journal of International Law*, vol. 4.

Berglas, E. (1983) 'The case for unilateral tariff reactions: foreign tariffs reconsidered', *American Economic Review*, vol. 73.

Berglöf, E., Eichengreen, B., Roland, G., Tabellin, G. and Wyplosz, C. (2003) *Built to Last: A Political Architecture for Europe*, Centre for Economic Policy Research, London.

Bergman, D., Brunekreet, G., Doyle, C., von der Fehr, N.-H. M., Newbery, D. M., Pollitt, M. and Regilbeau, P. (1970) *A Future for European Agriculture*, Atlantic Institute, Paris.

Bergmann, L., Brunekreeft, G., Doyle, C., von der Fehr, N.-H. M., Newbery, D. M., Pollitt, M. and Regilbeau, P. (1999) *A European Market for Electricity?*, Centre for Economic Policy Research, London and SNS, Stockholm.

Bergschmidt, A., Dirksmeyer, W., Efken, J., Forstner, B. and Uetrecht, I. (eds.) *Proceedings of the European Workshop on the Evaluation of Farm Investment Support, Investment Support for Improvement of Processing and Marketing of Agricultural Products*, Johann Heinrich von Thünen Institut, series Arbeitsberichte aus derv TI-Agrarö konomie, no. 03/2006.

Bergstrand, J. D. (1985) 'The gravity equation in international trade: some microeconomic foundations and empirical evidence', *Review of Economics and Statistics*, vol. 67, no. 3.

Bertola, G., Blau, F. and Kahn, L. (2002) 'Labor market institutions and demographic employment patterns', working paper, no. 9043, National Bureau of Economic Research, Cambridge, Mass.

Betlem, G. (2002) 'The doctrine of consistent interpretation: managing legal uncertainty', *Oxford Journal of Legal Studies*, vol. 22, no. 3.

Beutler, B. (2009) 'State liability for breaches of Community law by national courts: is the requirement of a manifest infringement of the applicable law an insurmountable obstacle?', *Common Market Law Review*, vol. 46, no. 3.

Bhagwati, J. N. (1969) *Trade, Tariffs and Growth*, Weidenfeld and Nicolson, London.

(1971) 'Customs unions and welfare improvement', *Economic Journal*, vol. 81.

Bishop, S. and Walker, M. (2002) *The Economics of EC Competition Law*, Sweet and Maxwell, London.

Bishop, W. (1981) 'Price discrimination under Article 86: political economy in the European Court', *Modern Law Review*, vol. 44.

Björksten, N. (1999) 'How important are differences between euro area economies?', *Bulletin*, Bank of Finland, Helsinki.

Blanchard, O. and Wolfers, J. (2000) 'The role of shocks and institutions in the rise of European unemployment', *Economic Journal*, vol. 110, March.

Blanchard, O. and Landier, A. (2002) 'The perverse effect of partial labour market reform: fixed-term contracts in France', *Economic Journal*, vol. 112, no. 480.

Blandford, D. (2002) 'Multifunctional agriculture and domestic/international policy choice', *The Estey Centre Journal of International Law and Trade Policy*, vol. 3, no. 1.

Blaszczyk, B. (2005) 'Lisbon Strategy: a tool for economic and social reforms in the enlarged European Union', *Studies and Analysis*, no. 310, Centre for Social and Economic Research, Warsaw (www.case.com.pl/upload/publikacja_plik/8442581_sa310.pdf).

Blom-Hansen, J. and Christensen, J. G. (2004) *Den Europaeiske Forbindelse*, Magtudredningen, Aarhus.

Bluet, J. C. and Systermanns, Y. (1968) 'Modèle gravitational d'échanges internationaux de produits manufacturés', *Bulletin du CEPRE-MAP*, vol. 1.

Bode, E., Krieger-Boden, C. and Lammers, K. (1994) *Cross-Border Activities, Taxation and the European Single Market*, Institut für Weltwirtschaft, Kiel (cited in Cnossen 2002).

Boehmer-Christiansen, S. and Skea, J. (1990) *Acid Politics: Environmental and Energy Policies in Britain and Germany*, Pinter, Washington D.C.

Boeri, T. (2005) 'Lost in translation', *Intereconomics*, March/April.

Boeri, T. and Garibaldi, P. (2009) 'Beyond Eurosclerosis', *Economic Policy*, vol. 59, 409–61.

Bollard, A. E. and Mayes, D. G. (1991) 'Regionalism and the Pacific Rim', *Journal of Common Market Studies*, vol. 30.

Boone, J., Sadrieh, A. and van Ours, J. C. (2004) 'Experiments on unemployment benefit sanctions and job search behaviour', discussion paper, no. 4298, Centre for Economic Policy Research, London.

Booth, A., Burda, M., Calmfors, L., Checchi, D., Naylor, R. and Visser, J. (2000) 'What do unions do in Europe', a report for the Fondazione Rodolfo DeBendetti, Milan (www.frdb.org/upload/file/report1_17giugno00.pdf).

Börzel, T. A. and Risse, T. (2000) 'Who is afraid of European federation? How to constitutionalise a multi-level governance system', in Joerges *et al.* 2000.

Bottasso, A. and Sembenelli, A. (2001) 'Market power, productivity and the EU single market program: evidence from a panel of Italian firms', *European Economic Review*, vol. 45.

Bouët, A. (2002) 'Commentaire sur l'article "Niveau et coût du protectionnisme européen" de Patrick A. Messerlin', *Économie Internationale*, vols. 89–90.

Bovenberg, A. L. (1994) 'Designation and origin based taxation under international capital mobility', *International Tax and Public Finance*, vol. 1, no. 3.

Bovenberg, A. L. and Cnossen, S. (1997) *Public Economics and the Environment in an Imperfect World*, Kluwer, Dordrecht.

Bovens, M. A. P. and Yesilkagit, K. (2005) 'De invloed van Europese richtlijnen op de Nederlandse wetgever', *Nederlands Juristenblad*, issue 10, 11 March.

Bover, O., García-Perea, P. and Portugal, P. (2000) 'Iberian labour markets: why Spain and Portugal are OECD outliers', *Economic Policy*, vol. 31, October.

Boyd, G. (ed.) (1998) *The Struggle for World Markets: Competition and Cooperation Between NAFTA and the European Union*, Edward Elgar, Cheltenham.

BP (2010) *Statistical Review of World Energy* (www.bp.com/liveassets/bp_internet/globalbp/globalbp_uk_english/reports_and_publications/statistical_energy_review_2008/STAGING/local_assets/2010_downloads/statistical_review_of_world_energy_full_report_2010.pdf), June 2010.

Brander, J. and Spencer, B. (1983) 'International R&D rivalry and industrial strategy', *Review of Economic Studies*, vol. 50.

Braunerhjelm, P., Faini, R., Norman, R., Ruane, F. and Seabright, P. (2000) 'Integration and the regions of Europe: how the right policies can prevent polarization', *Monitoring Integration*, vol. 10, Centre for Economic Policy Research, London.

Brenton, P. (2003) 'Integrating the least developed countries into the world trading system: the current impact of EU preferences under Everything But Arms', policy research working paper, no. 3018, World Bank, Washington D.C.

Brenton, P. and Winters, L. A. (1992) 'Bilateral trade elasticities for exploring the effects of 1992', in L. A. Winters (ed.), *Trade Flows and Trade Policy After 1992*, Cambridge University Press.

Brenton, P. and Manchin, M. (2003) 'Trade policy issues for the Euro-Med partnership', Middle East & Euro-Med working paper, no. 7, May.

Bretschger, L. and Hettich, F. (2002) 'Globalization, capital mobility and tax competition: theory and evidence for OECD countries', *European Journal of Political Economy*, vol. 18, no. 4.

Bright, C. (1995) 'Deregulation of EC competition policy: rethinking Article 85(1)', *1994 Annual Proceedings of Fordham Corporate Law Institute*, vol. 21.

Brittan, L. (1992) *European Competition Policy: Keeping*

the Playing Field Level, Brassey's Inc., Washington D.C.

Britz, W., Heckelei, T. and Péres, I. (2006) 'Effects of decoupling of land use', *German Journal of Agricultural Economics*, vol. 55 (Agrawirtschaft, Jahrgang 55).

Brooks, M. R. and Button, K. J. (1992) 'Shipping within the framework of a single European market', *Transport Review*, vol. 12.

Brown, A. J. (1961) 'Economic separatism versus a common market in developing countries', *Yorkshire Bulletin of Economic and Social Research*, vol. 13.

Buchanan, J. M. (1965) 'An economic theory of clubs', *Economica*, vol. 32, February.

Buchanan, J. M. and Tullock, G. (1962) *The Calculus of Consent*, University of Michigan Press, Ann Arbor.

Buckley, P. J. and Casson, M. (1976) *The Future of the Multinational Enterprise*, Macmillan, Basingstoke.

Buettner, T. and Ruf, M. (2007) 'Tax incentives and the location of FDI: evidence from a panel of German multinationals', *International Tax and Public Finance*, vol. 14, no. 2.

Buigues, P.-A. and Sekkat, K. (2009) *Industrial Policy in Europe, Japan and the USA: Amounts, Mechanism and Effectiveness*, Palgrave Macmillan, Basingstoke.

Buigues, P.-A., Ilzkovitz, F. and Lebrun, J. F. (1990) 'The impact of the internal market by industrial sector: the challenge for the member states', *The European Economy/Social Europe*, Office of Official Publications of the European Commission, Luxembourg.

Buiter, W. H. (2000) 'Optimal currency areas: why does the exchange rate regime matter? With an application to UK membership in EMU', *Scottish Journal of Political Economy*, vol. 47. no. 3, August.

Buiter, W. H., Corsetti, G. and Roubini, N. (1993) 'Excessive deficits: sense and nonsense in the Treaty of Maastricht', *Economic Policy*, vol. 16.

Bureau of Economic Analysis (2006) *Gross State Product* (www.bea.gov/bea/regional/gsp.htm).

Bureau of Labor Statistics (BLS) (2003) 'Federal executive branch employment', Bureau of Labor Statistics, Washington D.C. (www.bls.gov/oes/2001/oesi3_901.htm#b00-0000).

(2006) 'Employees by major industry sector', US Department of Labour (www.bls.gov/ces/home.htm).

(2010) 'Bureau of Labor Statistics', Federal Government (www.bls.gov/oco/cg/cgs041.htm#emply).

Burley, A.-M. and Mattli, W. (1993) 'Europe before the court: a political theory of legal integration', *International Organization*, vol. 47.

Burrows, N. and Greaves, R. (2007) *The Advocate General and EC Law*, Oxford University Press.

Buti, M., Eijffinger, S. and Franco, D. (2002) 'Revisiting the Stability and Growth Pact: grand design or internal adjustment?', Centre for Economic Research, University of Tilburg, Netherlands, November.

Button, K. J. (1984) *Road Haulage Licensing and EC Transport Policy*, Gower, Aldershot.

(1990) 'Infrastructure plans for Europe', in J. Gillund and G. Tornqvist (eds.), *European Networks*, Centre for Regional Science (CERUM), UMEA University, Stockholm.

(1992) 'The liberalization of transport services', in D. Swann (ed.), *1992 and Beyond*, Routledge, London.

(1993) 'East–west European transport: an overview', in D. Banister and J. Berechman (eds.), *Transportation in a Unified Europe: Policies and Challenges*, Elsevier, Amsterdam.

(1998) 'The good, the bad and the forgettable – or lessons the US can learn from European transport policy', *Journal of Transport Geography*, vol. 6, no.4.

(2000) 'Transport in the European Union', in J. B. Polak and A. Heertje (eds.), *Analytical Transport Economics: An International Perspective*, Edward Elgar, Cheltenham.

(2005) 'The European market for airline transportation and multimodalism', in European Conference of Ministers of Transport, *Airports as Multinational Interchange Nodes*, ECMT, Paris.

(2007) 'The implications of the commercialization of air transport infrastructure', in D. Lee (eds.), *The Economics of Airline Institutions, Operations and Marketing 2*, Elsevier, Oxford.

(2009) 'The impact of the EU-US "Open Skies" agreement on airline market structures and airline networks', *Journal of Air Transport Management*, vol. 15, no. 2.

(2010a) 'Countervailing power to airport monopolies', in P. Forsyth, D. Gillen, J. Müller and H.-M. Niemeier (eds.), *Competition in European Airports: The German Experience*, Ashgate, Burlington.

(2010b) *Transport Economics*, 3rd edn, Edward Elgar, Cheltenham.

Button, K. J. and Gillingwater, D. (1986) *Future Transport Policy*, Croom Helm, London.

Button, K. J. and Swann, D. (1992) 'Transatlantic lessons in aviation deregulation: EEC and US experiences', *Antitrust Bulletin*, vol. 37.

Button, K. J. and Keeler, T. (1993) 'The regulation of transport markets', *Economic Journal*, vol. 103.

Button, K. J., Hayes, K. and Stough, R. (1998) *Flying into the Future: Air Transport Policy in the European Union*, Edward Elgar, Cheltenham.

Byé, M. (1950) 'Unions douanières et données nationales', *Économie Appliquée*, vol. 3. Reprinted (1953) in translation as 'Customs unions and national interests', *International Economic Papers*, no. 3.

Bygrä, S., Hansen, C. Y., Rystad, K. and Søltoft, S. (1987) *Danish-German Border Shopping and its Price Sensitivity*, Institut for Graenseregionfroskning, Aabenraa (cited in Cnossen 2002).

Bzdera, A. (1992) 'The ECJ of the European Community and the politics of institutional reform', *West European Politics*, vol. 15.

Cadot, O., Estevadeordal, A., Suwa-Eisenmann, A. and Verdier, T. (2005) *The Origin of Goods: Rules of Origin in Regional Trade Agreements*, Oxford University Press.

Callon, M. (1986) 'Some elements of a sociology of translation: domestication of the scallops and fishermen of St. Brieuc Bay', in J. Law (ed.), *Power, Action and Belief: A New Sociology of Knowledge?*, Routledge, London.

—— (1998) 'Introduction: the embeddedness of economic markets in economics', in M. Callon (ed.), *The Laws of the Markets*, Blackwell, Oxford.

Calmfors, L. *et al.* (1997) *EMU – A Swedish Perspective Report of the Calmfors Commission*, Kluwer, Dordrecht.

Calmfors, L. and Corsetti, G. (2002) 'A better plan for loosening the Pact', *Financial Times*, 26 November.

Cambridge Econometrics and Ecorys-NEI (2004) *A Study on the Factors of Regional Competitiveness*, Report for the European Commission, DG Regional Policy, Brussels.

Cann, C. (1998) 'Introduction to fisheries management viewpoint', in T. S. Gray (ed.), *The Policies of Fishing*, Macmillan, Basingstoke.

Cappelletti, M. (1987) 'Is the European ECJ "running wild"?', *European Law Review*, vol. 12.

Carmin, J. A. and Stacy, D. (2004) *EU Enlargement and the Environment: Institutional Change and Environmental Policy in Central and Eastern Europe*, Routledge, Abingdon.

Carone, G. and Salomäki, A. (2001) 'Reforms in tax benefit systems in order to increase employment incentives in the EU', economic paper, no. 160, European Commission DG for Economic and Financial Affairs.

Carrère, C., de Melo, J. and Tumurchudur, B. (2006) 'Product-specific rules of origin in EU and US preferential trading arrangements: an assessment', *World Trade Review*, vol. 5, issue 2.

Casey, B. (2004) 'The OECD jobs strategy and the European Employment Strategy: two views of the labour market and the welfare state', *European Journal of Industrial Relations*, vol. 10, no. 2.

Casey, B. and Gold, M. (2005) 'Peer review of labour market policies in the European Union: what can countries really learn from one another?', *Journal of European Public Policy*, vol. 12, no. 1.

Casey, P. (2005) *After the Financial Services Action Plan: A Repeat of the Post-1992 Blues?*, Centre for European Policy Studies: Commentaries, Brussels, 17 June (www.ceps.eu).

Cathie, J. (2001) *European Food Aid Policy*, Ashgate, Aldershot.

Cecchini, P. (1988) *The European Challenge 1992: The Benefits of a Single Market*, Gower, Aldershot.

CEPII/EU Commission (1997) 'Impact on trade and investment', vol. 2, *The Single Market Review*, Office of the Official Publications of the European Communities, Luxembourg and Kogan Page, London.

CEPR/EU Commission (1997) 'Impact on trade and investment', vol. 3, *The Single Market Review*, Office of the Official Publications of the European Communities, Luxembourg and Kogan Page, London.

CEU (Commission of the European Union) (1957) *First General Report on the Activity of the Communities*.

—— (1961) *Memorandum on the General Lines of a Common Transport Policy*.

—— (1963) *Report of the Fiscal and Financial Committee* (Neumark Report).

—— (1968a) 'Premières orientations pour une politique énergétique communautaire', in *Communication de la Commission présentée au Conseil le 18 Décembre 1968*.

—— (1968b) *First Guidelines Towards an EC Energy Policy*.

—— (1970a) 'Report to the Council and the Commission on the realisation by stages of economic and monetary union in the Community', *EU Bulletin*, Supplement no. 11 (Werner Report).

—— (1970b) *Corporation Tax and Income Tax in the European Communities* (van den Tempel Report).

—— (1970c) *Industrial Policy in the Community*.

—— (1972) *First Report on Competition Policy*.

—— (1975) *Social Harmonization – Inland Waterways*, COM(75) 465 final.

—— (1976) *Fifth Report on Competition – EEC*.

—— (1977a) *Report of the Study Group on the Role of Public Finance in European Integration*, 2 vols. (MacDougall Report).

—— (1977b) *Twenty-Five Years of the Common Market in Coal: 1953–1978*.

—— (1979a) *Eighth Report on Competition Policy*.

—— (1979b) *Social Harmonization – Inland Waterways*, COM(79) 363 final.

—— (1979c) *Report of Committee of Inquiry on Public Finance in the Community* (MacDougall Report).

—— (1983) *Thirteenth Report on Competition Policy*.

—— (1984a) *Civil Aviation Memorandum No. 2: Progress*

Towards the Development of a Community Air Transport Policy, COM(84) 72.

(1984b) *Review of Member States' Energy Policies*, COM(84) 88.

(1985a) *Completing the Internal Market*, White Paper from the EC Commission to the EC Council, COM(85) 310.

(1985b) *Fourteenth Report on Competition Policy*.

(1985c) *Progress Towards a Common Transport Policy, Maritime Transport*, COM(85) 90 final.

(1987a) *Sixteenth Report on Competition Policy*.

(1987b) *European Environmental Policy*, Economic and Social Committee and Consultative Assembly.

(1987c) 'The Single European Act', *OJ L* 169, 29 June.

(1988a) *Research on the Cost of Non-Europe: Basic Findings*, 16 vols. (Cecchini Report).

(1988b) *Disharmonies in US and EC Agricultural Policy Measures*.

(1988c) *Commission Review of Member States' Energy Policies*, COM(84) 88 final.

(1988d) *The Main Findings of the Commission's Review of Member States' Energy Policies: The 1995 Community Energy Objectives*, COM(88) 174 final.

(1988e) *The Internal Energy Market*, Commission Working Document.

(1989a) *Guide to the Reform of the Community's Structural Funds*.

(1989b) *Council Resolution on Trans-European Networks*, COM(89) 643 final.

(1989c) *Communication from the Commission to the Council on Energy and the Environment*, COM(89) 369 final.

(1990a) 'One market, one money: an evaluation of the potential benefits and costs of forming an economic and monetary union', *European Economy*, vol. 44.

(1990b) *Second Survey of State Aids*.

(1991a) *Twentieth Report on Competition Policy*.

(1991b) *Opening up the Internal Market*.

(1991c) *Amended Proposal for a Council Regulation (EEC) Establishing a Community Ship Register and Providing for the Flying of the Flag by Sea-Going Vessels* (presented by the Commission pursuant to article 149(3) of the EEC Treaty) COM(91) 54/I final.

(1991d) *Commission Proposal for a Council Directive Concerning Common Rules for the Internal Market in Electricity*, COM(91) 548 final.

(1992a) *Transport and the Environment – Towards Sustainable Mobility*, COM(92) 80.

(1992b) *The Future Development of the Common Transport Policy: A Global Approach to the Construction of a Community Framework for Sustainable Mobility*, COM(92) 494 final.

(1992c) *A Community Strategy to Limit Carbon Dioxide Emissions and to Improve Energy Efficiency*, COM(92) 246 final.

(1992d) 'Proposal for a Council Directive introducing a tax on carbon dioxide emissions and energy', COM(92) 226 final.

(1993a) 'Stable money: sound finances', *European Economy*, no. 53.

(1993b) 'Growth, competitiveness, employment: the challenges and ways forward into the 21st century', White Paper, COM(93) 700.

(1994a) *The European Report on Science and Technology Indicators*, DG XII.

(1994b) 'EC agricultural policy for the 21st century', *European Economy*, Reports and Studies, no. 4.

(1994c) *Towards a New Asia Strategy*, COM(94) 314 final.

(1995a) *Citizens Network*, COM(95) 601.

(1995b) *High Speed Europe*.

(1995c) *An Energy Policy for the European Union*, White Paper of the European Commission, COM(95) 682.

(1995d) *Teaching and Learning: Towards the Learning Society*, White Paper, COM(95) 590 final.

(1996a) *Energy for the Future. Renewable Sources of Energy*, Green Paper for a Community Strategy, COM(96) 576.

(1996b) *Report from the Commission on the Application of the Community Rules on Aid to the Coal Industry in 1994*, COM(96) 575.

(1996c) *Services of General Interest in Europe*, COM(96) 443.

(1996d) *First Report on Economic and Social Cohesion*.

(1996e) *First Cohesion Report*, COM(96) final (http://ec.europa.eu).

(1996f) 'The 1996 single market review', *Commission Staff Working Paper*, SEC(96) 2378.

(1996g) *Green Paper on Relations Between the European Union and the ACP Countries on the Eve of the 21st Century*, DG VIII.

(1996h) *XXVth Report on Competition Policy 1995*.

(1996i) *Impact of the Third Package of Air Transport Liberalization Measures*, COM(96) 514.

(1996j) *The First Action Plan for Innovation in Europe*, COM(96) 589.

(1996k) *European Environmental Legislation*, vols. 1–7, DG XI.

(1996l) 'Community framework for state aid for research and development', *OJ C* 405, pp. 5–14.

(1996m) *Proposal for a Council Decision Concerning the Organization of Cooperation around Agreed Community Energy Objectives*, COM(96) 431 final.

(1997a) *Fifth Survey on State Aid in the European Union*

in the Manufacturing and Certain Other Sectors, COM(97) 170.

(1997b) *Agenda 2000: For a Stronger and Wider Union.*

(1997c) *XXVIth Report on Competition Policy 1996.*

(1997d) *Green Paper on Sea-Ports and Maritime Infrastructure*, COM(97) 678 final.

(1997e) 'Notice on the definition of the relevant market for the purposes of Community competition law', *OJ C* 372.

(1997f) 'Notice on agreements of minor importance', *OJ C* 372.

(1997g) *The Single Market Review*, 39 vols., CEU, Luxembourg and Kogan Page, London.

(1997h) *Action Plan for the Single Market*, CSE(97) 1 final, 4 June.

(1998a) *Proposed Regulations and Explanatory Memorandum Covering the Reform of the Structural Funds 2000–2006*, DG XVI.

(1998b) *Communication from the Commission to the Council and the European Parliament on Implementation and Impact of Directive 91/440/EEC on the Development of Community Railways and Access Rights for Rail Freight*, COM(98) 202 final.

(1998c) *Financing the European Union: Commission Report on the Operation of the Own Resources System*, DG Budget (http://europa.eu/index_en.htm).

(1998d) *Risk Capital: A Key to Job Creation in the European Union*, SEC(1998) 552.

(1998e) 'Convergence report 1998', *European Economy*, no. 65.

(1999a) *Sixteenth Annual Report on the Application of Community Law 1998*, COM(99) 301 final.

(1999b) *Mutual Recognition in the Context of the Follow-Up to the Action Plan for the Single Market*, COM(99) 299 final.

(1999c) *Sixth Periodic Report on the Social and Economic Situation in the Regions in the Community*, Luxembourg.

(1999d) *The Amsterdam Treaty: A Comprehensive Guide.*

(1999e) 'Regulation 2790/1999 on the application of Article 81(3) of the Treaty to categories of vertical agreements and concerted practices', *OJ L* 336.

(1999f) 'White Paper on modernisation of the rules implementing Articles 85 and 86 of the EC Treaty', *OJ C* 132.

(1999g) *Institutional Implications of Enlargement.*

(1999h) *White Paper on Food Safety.*

(1999i) 'Community guidelines on state aid for rescuing and restructuring firms in difficulty', *OJ C* 288.

(1999j) 'Financial services: implementing the strategy for financial markets – action plan', COM(99) 232.

(1999k) 'Convergence report 1998', *European Economy*, no. 65.

(2000a) *Agenda 2000 – Setting the Scene for Reform*, 2 vols.

(2000b) *Working Party on the Future of the European Court System*, Luxembourg.

(2000c) *Structural Actions 2000–2006: Commentary and Regulations.*

(2000d) *The Community Budget: The Facts in Figures*, SEC(2000) 1200, Luxembourg.

(2000e) *Second Progress Report on Economic and Social Cohesion: Unity, Solidarity, Diversity for Europe, its People and its Territory.*

(2000f) 'Guidelines on vertical restraints', *OJ C* 291.

(2000g) 'The application of Article 81(3) of the Treaty to categories of specialisation agreements', Regulation no. 2658/2000 of 29 November 2000, *OJ L* 304, 5 December.

(2000h) 'The application of Article 81(3) of the Treaty to categories of research and development agreements', Regulation no. 2658/2000 of 29 November 2000, *OJ L* 304, 5 December.

(2000i) *The European Community's Development Policy*, COM(2000) 212, 26 April.

(2000j) 'The European Community's development policy', Statement by the Council and Commission, 10 November.

(2001a) 'Promoting core labour standards and improving social governance in the context of globalisation', COM(2001) 416.

(2001b) 'Europe and Asia: a strategic framework for enhanced partnerships', COM(2001) 496 final.

(2001c) *Spatial Impacts of Community Policies and Costs of Non-Coordination*, Study for DG-Regional Policy.

(2001d) *Electricity Liberalization Indicators in Europe.*

(2001e) *European Transport Policy for 2010: Time to Decide*, White Paper.

(2001f) *Reinforcing Quality Services in Seaports: A Key for European Transport Policy*, COM(2001) 35.

(2001g) *Company Taxation and the Internal Market*, COM(2001) 582 final.

(2001h) *Green Paper Towards a European Strategy for Security of Energy Supply* (two documents, one of which is technical).

(2001i) *XXXth Report on Competition Policy 2000.*

(2001j) *European Economy*, Supplement A, *Economic Trends*, no. 12.

(2001k) 'Commission notice on agreements of minor importance which do not appreciably restrict competition under Article 81(1) of the Treaty establishing the European Community (de minimis)', *OJ C* 368, 22 December.

(2001l) 'Commission notice on the applicability of Article 81 to horizontal co-operation agreements', *OJ C* 3, 6 January.

(2001m) 'On the sixth environment action programme of the European Community "Environment 2010: Our future, Our choice" – The Sixth Environment Action Programme', COM(2001) 0031 final.

(2002a) 'Communication from the Commission to the Council and European Parliament', ECFIN/581/02-EN rev. 3, 21 November.

(2002b) 'Evaluation of the 2002 pre-accession economic programmes of candidate countries', Enlargement Papers, no. 14, DG ECFIN.

(2002c) *First Progress Report on Economic and Social Cohesion*, COM(2002) 46 final.

(2002d) *31st Report on Competition Policy 2001*, Luxembourg.

(2002e) 'Tableau de bord des aides d'état', COM(2002) 242 final.

(2002f) *Towards a European Research Area, Science, Technology and Innovation: Key Figures 2002*, Luxembourg.

(2002g) 'The EU economy 2002 review', Statistical Annexe, *European Economy*, no. 6.

(2002h) *Financial Report 2001*, DG Budget.

(2002i) *Excise Duty Tables*, REF 1.015, August, DG Taxation and Customs Union.

(2002j) *VAT Rates Applied in the Member States of the EU*, DOC/2908/2002-EN, situation at 1 May, DG Taxation and Customs Union.

(2002k) *Activities of the EU in 2000 in the Tax Field*, DOC (2003) 2101, 27 January, DG Taxation and Customs Union.

(2002l) 'Commission notice on immunity from fines and reduction fines in cartel cases', *OJ C* 45, 19 February.

(2002m) 'Co-ordination of economic policies in the EU: a presentation of key features of the main procedures', DG Economic and Financial Affairs, Euro-Papers, no. 45, July.

(2002n) 'Communication from the Commission on streamlining the annual economic and employment policy co-ordination cycles', COM(2002) 487.

(2002o) 'Consolidated version of the treaty establishing the European Community', *OJ C* 325, 24 December.

(2002p) 'Taking stock of five years of the European Employment Strategy', COM(2002) 416.

(2002q) 'The internal market – 10 years without internal frontiers', Commission working document (http://ec.europa.eu/internal_market/10years/docs/workingdoc/workingdoc_en.pdf).

(2002r) *Annual Report 2002 on EC Development Policy and the Implementation of External Assistance in 2001.*

(2003a) 'Evolution of the performance of network industries providing services of general interest', working paper by F. Bolkestein, P. Solbes Mira and D. Byrne.

(2003b) 'Commission opinion on the ECB recommendation on and amendments to Article 10.2 of the statute of the ESCB'.

(2003c) *Second Progress Report on Economic and Social Cohesion*, COM(2003) 34 final.

(2003d) *Eurobarometer*, no. 5, Public Opinion Analysis.

(2003e) 'Proposal for a Council regulation on the control of concentrations between undertakings', *OJ L* 20, 28 January.

(2003f) 'Establishing common rules for direct support schemes under the common agricultural policy and establishing certain support schemes for farmers and amending Regulations (EEC) no. 2019/93, (EC) no. 1452/2001, (EC) no. 1453/2001, (EC) no. 1454/2001, (EC) 1868/94, (EC) no. 1251/1999, (EC) no. 1254/1999, (EC) no. 1673/2000, (EEC) no. 2358/71 and (EC) no. 2529/20' (http://eur-lex.europa.eu/LexUriServ/site/en/consleg/2003/R/02003R1782-20060101-en.pd).

(2003g) *Analysis of the Impact of Community Policies on Economic and Social Cohesion*, report by Labor Asociados to the European Commission DG Regional Policy.

(2003h) 'Programme for the promotion of short-sea shipping: proposal for a Directive of the European Parliament and the Council on Intermodal Units', COM(2003) 155 final.

(2003i) 'Internal market strategy: priorities for 2003–2006', COM(2003) 238.

(2003j) *Annual Report 2003 on EC Development Policy and the Implementation of External Assistance in 2002.*

(2003k) 'External costs: research results on socio-environmental damages due to electricity and transport', DG Research, EUR 20198.

(2004a) 'Commission Regulation 773/2004/EC of 7 April 2004 relating to the conduct of proceedings by the Commission pursuant to Articles 81 and 82 of the EC Treaty', *OJ L* 123.

(2004b) 'Guidelines on the assessment of horizontal mergers under the Council Regulation on the control of concentrations between undertakings', *OJ C* 31.

(2004c) 'Commission Notice on the co-operation between the Commission and the courts of the EU Member States in the application of Articles 81 and 82 EC', *OJ C* 101.

(2004d) *Financial Report 2004*, Luxembourg.

(2004e) 'Building our common future – policy challenges

and budgetary means of the enlarged Union 2007–2013', COM(2004) 101 final.

(2004f) 'Financial perspectives 2007–2013', COM(2004) 487 final.

(2004g) 'Financing the EU: Commission report on the operation of the own resources system', COM(2004) 505 final, vol. I, report.

(2004h) 'Financing the EU: Commission report on the operation of the own resources system', COM(2004) 505 final, vol. II, technical annexe.

(2004i) 'Proposal for a system of the EC's own resources', COM(2004) 501 final.

(2004j) 'Proposal for a Directive of the European Parliament and the Council on evaluating port security', COM(2004) 76 final.

(2004k) 'Proposal for a directive on services in the internal market', COM(2004) 2.

(2004l) 'Commission Notice on cooperation within the Network of Competition Authorities', *OJ C* 101, 27 April.

(2004m) 'Five-year assessment of the European Union Research Framework Programmes 1999–2003', OOPEC, Luxembourg.

(2005a) *Third Progress Report on Cohesion: Towards a New Partnership for Growth, Jobs and Cohesion*, COM(2005) 192 final.

(2005b) 'Second implementation report of the internal market strategy 2003–2006', COM(2005) 11.

(2005c) *White Paper on Financial Services 2005–10*.

(2005d) *Eurobarometer*, vol. 64, first results.

(2005e) *Eurobarometer*, vol. 63.

(2005f) 'Proposal for a decision concerning the seventh framework programme of the European Community for research, technological development and demonstration activities (2007 to 2013)', COM(2005) 119.

(2005g) 'Working together for growth and jobs: a new start for the Lisbon Strategy', COM(2005) 24.

(2005h) 'Qualitative assessment of the reform of external assistance', Commission staff working document, SEC(2005) 963.

(2005i) *Report on Progress in Creating the Internal Gas and Electricity Market*, COM(2005) 568 final.

(2005j) 'Mergers and acquisitions', DG ECOFIN, note no. 2, June.

(2005k) 'State aid action plan: less and better targeted state aid – a roadmap for state aid reform 2005–2009', SEC(2005) 795.

(2005l) *Annual Report 2004 on EC Development Policy and the Implementation of External Assistance in 2002*.

(2006a) 'Directive of the European Parliament and of the Council on services in the internal market', COM(2006) 160.

(2006b) 'Transposition of Financial Services Action Plan Directives' (http://ec.europa.eu/internal_market/finances/actionplan/index_en.htm#transposition).

(2006c) 'Single market in Financial Services Progress Report 2004–5', SEC(2006) 17.

(2006d) 'Annual macroeconomic database AMECO', DG Economic and Financial Affairs.

(2006f) 'VAT rates applied in the member states of the European Community', DOC/1803/2006, DG Taxation.

(2006g) 'Excise duty tables part III, manufactured tobacco', Ref 1.022, DG Taxation and Customs Union, January.

(2006h) 'Excise duty tables part I, alcoholic beverages', Ref 1.022, DG Taxation and Customs Union, January.

(2006i) 'Implementing the Community Lisbon Programme: progress to date and the next steps towards a Common Consolidated Corporate Tax Base (CCCTB)', COM(2006) 157.

(2006j) 'Excise duty tables part II, energy products and electricity', Ref 1.022, January.

(2006k) *Structures of the Taxation Systems in the European Union 1995–2004*, DG Taxation, Doc. TAXUD E4/2006/DOC/3201.

(2006l) *A Reformed Cohesion Policy for a Changing Europe: Regions, Cities and Border Areas for Growth and Jobs*, Inforegio Factsheet.

(2006m) *The Growth and Jobs Strategy and the Reform of European Cohesion Policy: Fourth Progress Report on Cohesion*, COM(2006) 281.

(2006n) *The Community Strategic Guidelines on Cohesion 2007–2013*, COM(2006) 386.

(2006o) *Promoting Decent Work for All*, COM(2006) 249.

(2006p) 'Global Europe: competing in the world', Commission Staff Working Document, Brussels, 4 October, SEC(2006) 1230.

(2006q) 'Enlargement, two years after: an economic evaluation', *European Economy*, Occasional Papers, no. 24.

(2006r) 'Keep Europe moving – sustainable mobility for our continent', mid-term review of the European Commission's 2001 Transport White Paper, COM(2006) 314 final.

(2006s) 'State aid scoreboard: statistical tables', DG Competition.

(2006t) 'Global Europe: competing in the world', DG Trade.

(2006u) *Green Paper: A European Strategy for Sustainable, Competitive and Secure Energy*, COM(2006) 105 final (http://ec.europa.eu/energy/green-paper-energy/doc/2006_03_08_gp_document_en.pdf).

(2006v) *Annual Report 2006 on EC Development Policy*

and the Implementation of External Assistance in 2005, Annex.

(2006w) *A Financial Perspective for Europe's Future.*

(2006x) *Annual Report of the Financial Management of the 6th–9th European Development Funds (SDFs) in 2005.*

(2006y) *Regions and Cities for Growth and Jobs: An Overview of Regulations 2007-13 on Cohesion and Regional Policy*, Inforegio Factsheet.

(2007a) *A Single Market for 21st Century Europe*, COM(2007) 724.

(2007b) FSAP Evaluation Part 1 Process and Implementation (http://ec.europa.eu/internal_market/finances/actionplan/index_en.htm).

(2007c) 'Implementing the Community Programme for improved growth and employment and the enhanced competitiveness of EU business: further progress during 2006 and next steps towards a proposal on the Common Consolidated Corporate Tax Base', COM(2007) 223.

(2007d) *FSAP Evaluation Part I: Process and Implementation* (http://ec.europa.eu/internal_market/finances/actionplan/index_en.htm).

(2007e) 'Mid-term review of the Sixth Community Environment Action Programme', COM(2007) 225 final.

(2007f) *An Energy Policy for Europe* (http://europa.eu/legislation_summaries/energy/european_energy_policy/l27067_en.htm).

(2007g) *An Energy Policy for Europe* (http://europa.eu/legislation_summaries/energy/european_energy_policy/l27067_en.htm).

(2008a) 'Consolidated versions of the Treaty on European Union and the Treaty on the Functioning of the European Union', *OJ C*, 115.

(2008b) 'Vademecum: Community law on state aid', DG Competition.

(2008c) 'Report from the Commission to the Council in accordance with Article 18 of Council Directive 2003/48/EC on taxation of savings income in the form of interest payments', COM(2008) 552.

(2008d) *Regions 2020: An Assessment of Future Challenges for EU Regions*, Commission Staff Working Document, SEC(2008), Brussels.

(2008e) 'Antitrust: guidance on Commission enforcement priorities in applying Article 82 to exclusionary conduct by dominant firms – frequently asked questions', Memo 08/761 (http://europa.eu/rapid/pressReleasesAction.do?reference=MEMO/08/761&format=HTML&aged=0&language=EN&guiLanguage=en).

(2008f) 'Reforming the EU Budget, Changing Europe Conference', 12 November (http://ec.europa.eu/budget/reform/conference/documents_en.htm).

(2008g) *EMU@10: Successes and Challenges after 10 Years of Economic and Monetary Union*, DG ECOFIN, Brussels.

(2008h) *Turning Territorial Diversity into Strength: Green Paper on Territorial Cohesion*, Office for Official Publications of the European Communities, Brussels.

(2009a) *Internal Market Scoreboard*, no. 20, December.

(2009b) *Employment in Europe 2009*, OOPEU, Luxembourg.

(2009c) *EU Budget 2008 Financial Report*, Luxembourg.

(2009d) *Eurobarometer* 70, Luxembourg.

(2009e) 'Third strategic review of Better Regulation in the European Union', 28 January, COM(2009) 15 final, Brussels.

(2009f) 'Decision amending the Interinstitutional Agreement of 16 May 2006', COM(2009) 662.

(2009g) 'Total state aid by member states as a percentage of GDP (1992–2008)', DG Competition.

(2009h) 'State aid scoreboard: autumn 2009 update', SEC(2009) 1638.

(2009i) 'Commission staff working document', SEC(2009) 589, to accompany the communication: On the progress made under the 7th European Framework Programme for Research, COM(2009) 209.

(2009j) 'Guidance on the Commission's enforcement priorities in applying Article 82 of the EC Treaty to abusive exclusionary conduct by dominant undertakings', *OJ C* 45.

(2010a) 'EU budget 2009: financial report', OOPEC, Luxembourg.

(2010b) 'Europe 2020: a strategy for smart, sustainable and inclusive growth', COM(2010) 2020.

(2010c) 'Annual Macroeconomic Database (AMECO)' (http://ec.europa.eu/economy_finance/db_indicators/ameco/index_en.htm).

(2010d) 'The Regional Lisbon Index', *Regional Focus*, no. 03/2010, Brussels.

(2010e) 'Ex-post evaluation of cohesion programmes 2000–2006 co-financed by the ERDF: synthesis report', DG Regional Policy.

(2010f) *The Internal Market Scoreboard*, no. 20, December (http://ec.europa.eu/internal_market/score/docs/score20_en.pdf).

(2010g) *Staff by Directorate Generals and categories* (http://ec.europa.eu/civil_service/about/figures/index_en.htm).

(2010h) 'Excise duty tables: Part I – alcoholic beverages, Part II – energy products and electricity, Part III – manufactured tobacco, DG Taxation and Customs Union', ref. 1031, July (http://ec.europa.eu/taxation_customs/taxation/excise_duties/tobacco_products/rates/index_en.htm).

(2010i) *Eurobarometer* 70, Office of EU Publications.

(2010j) *Staff figures* (http://ec.europa.eu/civil_service/about/figures/index_en.htm).

(2010k) 'Analysis of options to move beyond 20% greenhouse gas emission reductions and assessing the risk of carbon leakage', COM(2010) 265 final.

(2010l) Transposition of FSAP Directives (http://ec.europa.eu/internal_market/finances/docs/actionplan/index/100825-transposition_en.pdf).

(2010m) *Lamfalussy League Table* (http://ec.europa.eu/internal_market/securities/docs/transposition/table_en.pdf).

(2010n) *Regulating Financial Services for Growth*, COM(2010) 301.

(2010o) *Annual Report 2010: On the European Union's Development and External Assistance Policies and their Implementation in 2009*.

Chalmers, D. (1993) 'Free movement of goods within the European Community: an unhealthy addiction to Scotch whisky?', *International and Comparative Law Quarterly*, vol. 42.

(1997a) 'Judicial preferences and the community legal order', *Modern Law Review*, vol. 60.

(1997b) 'Community trade mark courts: the renaissance of an epistemic community?', in J. Lonbay and A. Biondi (eds.), *Remedies for Breach of EC Law*, John Wiley, Chichester.

(1998) 'Bureaucratic Europe: from regulating communities to securitising unions', Council of European Studies, Baltimore, Md.

(1999) 'Accounting for "Europe"', *Oxford Journal of Legal Studies*, vol. 19.

(2000a) 'Postnationalism and the quest for constitutional substitutes', *Journal of Law and Society*, vol. 27.

(2000b) 'The positioning of EU judicial politics within the United Kingdom', *Western European Politics*, vol. 23, no. 4.

Chalmers D., Davies G. and Monti, G. (2010) *European Union Law*, 2nd edn, Cambridge University Press.

Chandler, A. (1990) *Scale and Scope: The Dynamics of Industrial Capitalism*, Harvard University Press, Cambridge, Mass.

Chlomoudis, C. I. and Pallis, A. A. (2002) *European Union Port Policy: The Movement Towards a Long-Term Strategy*, Edward Elgar, Cheltenham.

Choi, J.-Y. and Yu, E. S. H. (1984) 'Customs unions under increasing returns to scale', *Economica*, vol. 51.

Christiansen, T. (1997) 'Reconstructing European space: from territorial politics to multilevel governance', in K. Jørgensen (ed.), *Reflective Approaches to European Governance*, Macmillan, Basingstoke.

Churchill, R. and Owen, D. (2010) *The EC Common Fisheries Policy*, Oxford University Press.

Cini, M. and McGowan, L. (2008) *The Competition Policy in the European Union*, Palgrave Macmillan, Basingstoke.

Clavaux, F. J. (1969) 'The effects of the EEC on trade in manufactures', in H. Brugmans (ed.), *Intégration Européenne et réalité économique*, de Temple, Bruges.

Cnossen, S. (1987) 'Tax structure developments', in S. Cnossen (ed.), *Tax Coordination in the European Community,* Kluwer, Deventer.

(1999) 'What rate structure of Australia's VAT?', *Tax Notes International*, 24 May.

(2001) 'Tax policy in the European Union', *FinanzArchiv*, vol. 58, no. 4.

(2002) *Tax Policy in the European Union: A Review of Issues and Options*, University of Maastricht, METEOR.

(2003) 'How much tax coordination in the European Union', *International Tax and Public Finance*, vol. 10.

Cnossen, S. and Bovenberg, L. (1997) 'Company tax harmonisation in the European Union: some further thoughts on the Ruding Committee Report', in M. Blejer and T. Ter-Minassian (eds.), *Macroeconomic Dimensions of Public Finance: Essays in Honour of Vito Tanzi*, Routledge, London.

Cnossen, S. and Smart, M. (2005) 'Taxation of tobacco', in S. Cnossen (ed.), *Theory and Practice of Excise Taxation*, Oxford University Press.

Coase, R. (1937) 'The nature of the firm', *Economica*, vol. 16.

(1960) 'The problem of social costs', *Journal of Law and Economics*, vol. 3, no. 1.

Cobham, D. (1996) 'Causes and effects of the European monetary crises of 1992–93', *Journal of Common Market Studies*, vol. 34.

Cockfield, Lord (1994) *The European Union: Creating the Single Market*, Wiley Chancery Law, London.

Codognet, M.-K., Glachant, J.-M., Lévêque, F. and Plagnet, M.-A. (2002) *Mergers and Acquisitions in the European Electricity Sector: Cases and Patterns*, CERNA, Centre d'économie industrielle, École Nationale Supérieure des Mines de Paris, Paris.

Cohen, E. (2006) 'Theoretical foundations of industrial policy', *EIB Papers*, vol. 11, no. 2.

Coleman, D. (1985) 'Imperfect transmission of policy prices', *European Review of Agricultural Economics*, vol. 12.

Collier, P. (2007) *The Bottom Billion: Why the Poorest Countries are Failing and What Can Be Done About It*, Oxford University Press.

Collignon, S. (2003) *The European Republic*, Kogan Page, London.

Comité intergouvernemental créé par la conférence de Messina (1956) *Rapport des chefs de délégation aux Ministres des Affaires Étrangères*, Brussels.

Commission of the European Union and European Environment Agency (2010) 'Quality of bathing water – 2009 bathing season', EEA Report 3/2010.

Conant, L. (2001) 'Europeanization and the courts: variable patterns of adaptation among national judiciaries', in J. Caparaso, M. Cowles and T. Risse (eds.), *Transforming Europe: Europeanization and Domestic Structural Change*, Cornell University Press, Ithaca, NY.

(2002) *Justice Contained: Law and Politics in the European Union*, Cornell University Press, Ithaca, NY.

Cooper, C. A. and Massell, B. F. (1965a) 'A new look at customs union theory', *Economic Journal*, vol. 75.

(1965b) 'Towards a general theory of customs unions in developing countries', *Journal of Political Economy*, vol. 73.

Copenhagen Economics (2005) 'Economic assessment of the barriers to an internal market for services', *Copenhagen Economics* (www.copenhageneconomics.com/publications/trade4.pdf).

Coppel, J. (1994) 'Rights, duties and the end of Marshall', *Modern Law Review*, vol. 57, no. 6.

Corden, W. M. (1972a) 'Economies of scale and customs union theory', *Journal of Political Economy*, vol. 80.

(1972b) 'Monetary integration', *Essays in International Finance*, no. 93, Princeton University.

(1977) *Inflation, Exchange Rates and the World Economy*, Oxford University Press.

Cosgrove-Sacks, C. and Scappuci, G. (1999) *The European Union and Developing Countries: The Challenges of Globalisation*, Macmillan, Basingstoke.

Coudenhove-Kalergi, Count Richard Graf Nicolas (1926) *Pan-Europa*, Putnam, New York.

(1938) *The Totalitarian State Against Man*, F. Fuller Ltd, London.

(1943) *Crusade for Pan-Europe*, Putnam, New York.

(1953) *An Idea Conquers the World*, Hutchinson, London.

Council (of the European Union) (1962) 'First regulation implementing Articles 85 and 86 of the Treaty', Regulation No. 17, *OJ L* 013, 21 February.

(1975) 'Council Directive 76/160/EEC of 8 December 1975 concerning the quality of bathing water'.

(1977) 'Sixth Council Directive 77/388/EEC of 17 May 1977, on the harmonization of the laws of the Member States relating to turnover taxes – Common system of value added tax: uniform basis assessment', *OJ L* 145.

(1988) 'Decision of 24 October 1988 establishing a Court of First Instance of the European Communities', *OJ L* 215, 25 November.

(1989) 'Regulation 4064/89 on the control of concentrations between undertakings', *OJ L* 395.

(1992a) 'Council Directive 92/77/EEC of 19 October 1992 supplementing the common system of value added tax and amending Directive 77/388/EEC (approximation of VAT rates)', *OJ L* 316, 31 October.

(1992b) 'Council Directive 92/79/EEC of 19 October 1992 on the approximation of taxes on cigarettes', *OJ L* 316, 31 October.

(1992c) 'Council Directive 92/84/EEC of 19 October 1992 on the approximation of the rates of excise duty on alcohol and alcoholic beverages', *OJ L* 316, 31 October.

(1994) 'European Parliament and Council Directive 94/62/EC of 20 December 1994 on packaging and packaging waste'.

(1995a) 'Council Directive 95/59/EC of 27 November 1995 on taxes other than turnover taxes which affect the consumption of manufactured tobacco', *OJ L* 291, 6 December.

(1995b) 'Council directive concerning indirect taxes on the raising of capital', consolidated text, *OJ L* 2, 1 January.

(1996) 'Council Directive 96/82/EC of 9 December 1996 on the control of major-accident hazards involving dangerous substances'.

(1997a) 'Regulation 1310/97 amending Regulation 4064/89 on the control of concentrations between undertakings', *OJ L* 40.

(1997b) 'Council resolution of 15 December 1997 on the 1998 Employment Guidelines', *OJ C* 30, 28 January 1998.

(1997c) 'Directive 96/71/EC of the European Parliament and of the Council of 16 December 1996 concerning the posting of workers in the framework of the provision of services', *OJ L* 18.

(1997d) 'Treaty of Amsterdam', *OJ C* 340.

(1998a) 'Directive 98/34 Laying Down a Procedure for the Provision of Information in the Field of Technical Standards and Regulations', *OJ L* 204.

(1998b) 'Regulation 994/98 on the application of Articles 92 and 93 of the Treaty to certain categories of horizontal state aid', *OJ L* 142.

(1999a) 'Regulation 659/1999 laying down detailed rules for the application of Article 93 of the EC Treaty', *OJ L* 83.

(1999b) 'Council resolution of 22 February 1999 on the 1999 Employment Guidelines', *OJ C* 69, 12 March.

(2000) *The European Community's Development Policy*

Statement by the Council and the Commission, 10 November.

(2001) 'Council decision of 19 January 2001 on the 2001 Employment Guidelines', *OJ L* 22, 24 January.

(2002a) 'Council Directive 2002/10/EC of 12 February 2002 amending Directives 92/79/EEC, 92/80/EEC and 95/59/EC as regards the structure and rates of excise duty applied on manufactured tobacco', *OJ L* 046, 16 February.

(2002b) 'Council decision of 18 February 2002 on the 2002 Employment Guidelines', *OJ L* 60, 1 March.

(2003a) 'Council Directive 2003/48/EC of 3 June 2003 on taxation of savings income in the form of interest payments', *OJ L* 157, 26 June.

(2003b) 'The implementation of the rules on competition laid down in Articles 81 and 82 of the Treaty', Regulation no. 1/2003 of 16 December 2002, *OJ L* 1, 4 January 2003.

(2003c) 'Council decision of 22 July 2003 on the guidelines for the employment policies of the member states', *OJ L* 197, 5 August.

(2003d) 'Council Directive 2003/96/EC of 27 October 2003 restructuring the Community framework for the taxation of energy products and electricity', *OJ L*, 283.

(2003e) 'Council Directive 2003/48/EC of 3rd June 2003 on taxation of savings income in the form of interest payments', *OJ L* 157.

(2003f) 'Council Directive 2003/87/EC establishing a scheme for greenhouse gas emission allowance trading within the Community and amending Council Directive 96/61/EC'.

(2004a) 'Council Regulation (EC) no. 139/2004 of 20 January 2004 on the control of concentrations between undertakings (the EC Merger Regulation)', *OJ L* 124.

(2004b) 'Council decision of 2 November 2004 establishing the European Union Civil Service Tribunal', *OJ L* 333, 9 November.

(2004c) 'Directive 2004/35/CE of the European Parliament and of the Council on environmental liability with regard to the prevention and remedying of environmental damage'.

(2005a) 'Council decision of 12 July 2005 on the guidelines for the employment policies of the member states', *OJ L* 205, 6 August.

(2005b) *The EU and Africa: Towards a Strategic Partnership.*

(2005c) 'Joint statement by the Council and the representatives of the Member States meeting within the Council, the European Parliament and the Commission', in *The European Consensus on Development*, 14820/05.

(2005d) 'Council Regulation (EC) no. 1777/2005 of 17 October 2005 laying down implementing measures for Directive 77/388/EEC on the common system of value added tax', *OJ L* 288.

(2006) 'Council Directive 2006/7/EC of 15 February 2006 concerning the management of bathing water quality and repealing Directive 76/160/EEC'.

(2009a) 'Presidency Conclusions: European Council 11–12 December 2008'.

(2009b) 'Council Directive 2009/29/EC of 23 April 2009 amending Directive 2003/87/EC so as to improve and extend the greenhouse gas emission allowance trading scheme of the Community'.

(2010a) 'Council Directive 2006/112/EC on the common system of value added tax, consolidated version', *OJ L* 347, 9 April.

(2010b) 'Council Directive 2010/12/EU on the structure and rates of excise duty applied to manufactured tobacco', *OJ L* 50.

(2010c) *The Internal Market Scoreboard No 20*, December 2009 (http://ec.europa.eu/internal_market/score/docs/score20_en.pdf).

Court of First Instance (2002) *Statistics of the Judicial Activity of the Court of First Instance*, Luxembourg.

Cox, A. and Chapman, J. (2000) *The European Community Extend Cooperation Programmes*, European Commission.

Cox, A., Healey, J. and Koning, A. (1997) *How European Aid Works*, Overseas Development Institute, London.

Cragg, C. (2009) 'Chernobyl legacy', *European Energy Review*, May/June.

Craig, P. (1992) 'Once upon a time in the west: direct effect and the federalization of EEC law', *Oxford Journal of Legal Studies*, vol. 12, no. 4.

(1997) 'Democracy and rule-making within the EC: an empirical and normative assessment', *European Law Journal*, vol. 3.

(2001a) 'The jurisprudence of the Community courts reconsidered', in G. de Búrca and J. Weiler (eds.), *The European Court of Justice*, Hart, Oxford.

(2001b) 'Constitutions, constitutionalism, and the European Union' *European Law Journal*, vol. 7, no. 2.

(2004) 'Competence: clarity, containment and consideration', *European Law Review*, vol. 29, no. 3.

(2006) *EU Administrative Law*, Oxford University Press.

Craig P. and de Búrca, G. (2008) *EU Law: Text, Cases and Materials*, 4th edn, Oxford University Press.

Craig P. and de Búrca, G. (eds.) (2011) *The Evolution of EU Law*, 2nd edn, Oxford University Press.

Crawford, J.-A. and Florentino, R. V. (2006) 'The changing landscape of regional trade agreements', discussion paper, no. 8, World Trade Organization, Geneva.

Crean, K. and Symes, D. (1996) *Fisheries Management in Crisis*, Blackwell Science, Oxford.

Crombez, C. (2003) 'The democratic deficit in the European Union: much ado about nothing?', *European Union Politics*, vol. 4, no. 1.

Crouch, C. and Marquand, D. (1992) *Towards Greater Europe: A Continent without an Iron Curtain*, Basil Blackwell, Oxford.

Cruickshank, A. and Walker, W. (1981) 'Energy research development and demonstration policy in the European Communities', *Journal of Common Market Studies*, vol. 20, no. 1.

Culem, C. G. (1988) 'The locational determinants of direct investment among industrialised countries', *European Economic Review*, vol. 32.

Curtin, D. (1990a) 'The effectiveness of judicial protection of individual rights', *Common Market Law Review*, vol. 27, no. 4.

(1990b) 'The province of government: delimiting the direct effect of directives in the common law context', *European Law Review*, vol. 15, no. 1.

(2006) 'Making a political constitution for the European Union', *European Journal of Law Reform*, vol. 8.

Curzon Price, V. (1974) *The Essentials of Economic Integration*, Macmillan, Basingstoke.

Cuthbertson, K., Hall, G. H. and Taylor, M. P. (1980) 'Modelling and forecasting the capital account of the balance of payments: a critique of the "Reduced Form Approach"', National Institute discussion paper, no. 37.

Daintith, T. (ed.) (1995) *Implementing EC Law in the United Kingdom: Structures for Indirect Rule*, Wiley, Chichester.

Daintith, T. and Hancher, K. (eds.) (1986) *Energy Strategy in Europe: The Legal Framework*, de Gruyter, New York.

Dall'erba, S. and LeGallo, J. (2006) 'Evaluating the temporal and spatial heterogeneity for the European convergence process', *Journal of Regional Science*, vol. 46.

(2009) 'Narrowing spread in regional gross domestic product', Statistics in Focus, no. 75, Luxembourg.

Dam, K. W. (1970) *The GATT: Law and International Economic Organization*, University of Chicago Press.

Dashwood, A. and Johnston, A. (eds.) (2001) *The Future of the European Judicial System*, Hart, Oxford.

Daveri, F. (2004) 'Why is there a productivity problem in the EU?', working document, no. 205, Centre for European Policy Studies, Brussels.

Daveri, F. and Tabellini, G. (2000) 'Unemployment, growth and taxation in industrial countries', *Economic Policy*, vol. 30.

Daw, T. and Gray, T. (2005) 'Fisheries science and sustainability in international policy: a study of failure in the European Union's Common Fisheries Policy', *Marine Policy*, vol. 29, no. 3.

de Bruijn, R., Kox, H. and Lejour, A. M. (2006) 'The trade-induced effects of the Services Directive and the country of origin principle', Centraal Planbureau (Netherlands Bureau for Economic Policy Analysis), The Hague, document no. 108, February.

(2008) 'Economic benefits of an integrated European market for Services', *Journal of Policy Modeling*, vol. 30, no. 2.

de Búrca, G. (1992) 'Giving effect to European Community directives', *Modern Law Review*, vol. 55.

de Grauwe, P. (1975) 'Conditions for monetary integration: a geometric interpretation', *Weltwirtschaftliches Archiv*, vol. 111.

(2009) *Economics of Monetary Union*, Oxford University Press.

de Koning, J., Layard, R., Nickell, S. and Westergaard-Nielsen, N. (2004) *Policies for Full Employment*, Department of Work and Pensions, London (http://webarchive.nationalarchives.gov.uk/+/http://www.dwp.gov.uk/publications/dwp/2004/pol_full_emp/layard_report.pdf).

de la Fuente, A. and Domenesh, R. (2001) 'The redistributive effects of the EU budget', *Journal of Common Market Studies*, vol. 39, no. 2.

de la Mare, T. (1999) 'Article 177 in social and political perspective', in P. Craig and R. Dehousse (eds.), *The European Court of Justice*, Macmillan, Basingstoke.

de la Porte, C. and Pochet, P. (2002) 'Introduction', in C. de la Porte and P. Pochet (eds.), *Building Social Europe through the Open Method of Co-ordination*, Peter Lang, Brussels.

de Mooij, R. A. (2005) 'Will corporate income taxation survive?, *De Economist*, vol. 153, no. 3.

de Vincenti, C. (2001) 'Customer markets, inflation and unemployment in a dynamic model with a range of equilibria', *Metroeconomica*, vol. 2, no. 1.

de Witte, B. (1999) 'Direct effect, supremacy and the nature of the legal order' in P. Craig and G. de Búrca (eds.), *The Evolution of EU Law*, Oxford University Press.

Deaton, A. S. and Muellbauer, J. (1980) 'An almost ideal demand system', *American Economic Review*, vol. 70.

Decressin, J. and Fatás, A. (1995) 'Regional labour market dynamics in Europe', *European Economic Review*, vol. 39.

Decreux, Y. and Fontagné, L. (2006) 'A quantitative assessment of the outcome of the Doha Development Agenda', CEPII working paper, no. 2006–10, Paris.

DEFRA (2006) 'Rural economy and employment', UK Department for Environment, Food and Rural Affairs, London.

Dehousse, R. (1998) *The European Court of Justice*, Macmillan, Basingstoke.

Dehousse, R. and Weiler, J. (1990) 'The legal dimension', in W. Wallace (ed.), *The Dynamics of European Integration*, RIIA, London.

Deloitte (2006) 'Country snapshots' (www.deloitte.com).

Denis, C., McMorrow, K. and Röger, W. (2004) 'An analysis of EU and US productivity developments (a total economy and industry level perspective)', *European Economy: Economic Papers*, no. 208.

Denis, C., McMorrow, K., Röger, W. and Veugelers, R. (2005) 'The Lisbon Strategy and the EU's structural productivity problem', *European Economy: Economic Papers*, no. 221.

Denison, E. F. (1967) *Why Growth Rates Differ: Post-War Experience in Nine Western Countries*, Brookings Institute, Washington D.C.

(1974) *Accounting for United States Economic Growth 1929–1969*, Brookings Institute, Washington D.C.

Devereux, M. P. and Griffith, R. (2001) 'Summary of the "Devereux and Griffith" economic model and measures of effective tax rates' (Annex A of CEU 2001g).

Devereux, M. P., Griffith, R. and Klemm, A. (2002) 'Corporate income tax reforms and international tax competition', *Economic Policy*, vol. 17, issue 35.

Devroe, W. (1997) 'Privatization and Community law: neutrality versus policy', *Common Market Law Review*, vol. 34.

Dewatripont, M. and Seabright, P. (2006) 'Wasteful public spending and state aid control', *Journal of the European Economic Association*, vol. 91, nos. 2–3.

Dezalay, Y. (1992) *Marchands de droit. La réstructuration de l'ordre juridique international par les multinationaux du droit*, Fayard, Paris.

Dickens, R., Wadsworth, J. and Gregg, P. (2001) 'What happens to the employment prospects of disadvantaged workers as the labour market tightens', in R. Dickens, J. Wadsworth and P. Gregg (eds.), *The State of Working Britain: Update 2001*, LSE Centre for Economic Performance, London.

Diez Guardia, N. and Pichelmann, K. (2006) 'Labour migration patterns in Europe: recent trends, future challenges', *Economic Papers*, no. 256, CEU, DG Economic and Financial Affairs, Brussels.

Domenesh, R., Maudes, A. and Varela, J. (2001) 'Fiscal flows in Europe: the redistributive effects of the EU budget', *Weltwirtschaftliches Archiv*, vol. 136, no. 4.

Dosser, D. (1973) *British Taxation and the Common Market*, Knight, London.

Downs, A. (1957) *An Economic Theory of Democracy*, Harper, New York.

Doyle, C. and Siner, M. (1999) 'Introduction: Europe's network industries – towards competition', in Bergmann *et al.* 1999.

Drake, S. (2005) 'Twenty years after von Colson: the impact of "indirect effect" on the protection of the individual's community rights', *European Law Review*, vol. 30, no. 3.

(2006) 'Scope of courage and the principle of "individual liability" for damages: further development of the principle of effective judicial protection by the Court of Justice', *European Law Review*, vol. 31, no. 6.

Dullien, S. and Schwarzer, D. (2009) 'Bringing macroeconomics into the EU budget debate: why and how?', *Journal of Common Market Studies*, vol. 47, no. 1.

Dunford, M. (1996) 'Disparities in employment, productivity and output in the EU: the roles of labour market governance and welfare regimes', *Regional Studies*, vol. 30.

(2000) 'Catching up or falling behind? Economic performance and regional trajectories in the new Europe', *Economic Geography*, vol. 76, no. 2.

Dunning, J. H. (1977) 'Trade, location of economic activity and the MNE: a search for an eclectic approach', in B. Ohlin, P.-O. Hesselborn and P. M. Wijkman (eds.), *The International Allocation of Economic Activity*, Macmillan, Basingstoke.

ECB (2003) 'Recommendation on an amendment to Article 10.2 of the Statute of the ECB', Frankfurt, 3 February.

(2004) *The Monetary Policy of the ECB*, Frankfurt, August.

(2006) *Convergence Report 2006*, Frankfurt, May.

The Economist (2006) 'VAT fraud and trade: costly carousel', 1 June.

(2010) 'United in the cause of undermining Russian pipeline monopolies', 4 March (www.economist.com/node/15622359?story_id=15622359).

ECORYS (2008) 'A study on EU spending', final report, Study for European Commission DG Budget (http://ec.europa.eu/budget/reform/conference/documents_en.htm).

(2009) 'Non-tariff measures in EU-US trade and investment – an economic analysis', study for Commission, DG Trade.

EEA (European Environment Agency) (2005) *Market Based Instruments for Environmental Policy in Europe*, technical report, no. 8/2005.

(2010) *The European Environment – State and Outlook 2010: Synthesis*, European Environment Agency, Copenhagen.

EFSF (2010) 'EFSF Framework Agreement' (www.efsf.europa.eu).

EFTA Secretariat (1969) *The Effects of the EFTA on the Economies of Member States*, Geneva.

(1972) *The Trade Effects of the EFTA and the EEC 1959–1967*, Geneva.

Ehlermann, C.-D. (1995) 'State aids under European Community competition law', *1994 Annual Proceedings of the Fordham Corporate Law Institute*, vol. 21.

—— (ed.) (2003) *European Competition Law Annual 2001: Effective Private Enforcement of EC Antitrust Law*, Hart, Oxford.

Eichengreen, B. (1993) 'Labor markets and European monetary unification', in P. Masson and M. Taylor (eds.), *Policy Issues in the Operation of Currency Unions*, Cambridge University Press.

El-Agraa, A. M. (1979a) 'Common markets in developing countries', in J. K. Bowers (ed.), *Inflation, Development and Integration: Essays in Honour of A. J. Brown*, Leeds University Press.

—— (1979b) 'On tariff bargaining', *Bulletin of Economic Research*, vol. 31.

—— (1979c) 'On optimum tariffs, retaliation and international cooperation', *Bulletin of Economic Research*, vol. 31.

—— (1981) 'Tariff bargaining: a correction', *Bulletin of Economic Research*, vol. 33.

—— (ed.) (1983a) *Britain within the European Community: The Way Forward*, Macmillan, Basingstoke.

—— (1983b) *The Theory of International Trade*, Croom Helm, Beckenham.

—— (1984a) 'Is membership of the EEC a disaster for the UK?', *Applied Economics*, vol. 17, no. 1.

—— (1984b) *Trade Theory and Policy: Some Topical Issues*, Macmillan, Basingstoke.

—— (1988a) *Japan's Trade Frictions: Realities or Misconceptions?*, Macmillan and St Martin's, New York.

—— (ed.) (1988b) *International Economic Integration*, 2nd edn, Macmillan and St Martin's, New York.

—— (1989a) *The Theory and Measurement of International Economic Integration*, Macmillan and St Martin's, New York.

—— (1989b) *International Trade*, Macmillan and St Martin's, New York.

—— (1997) *Economic Integration Worldwide*, Macmillan and St Martin's, New York.

—— (1999) *Regional Integration: Experience, Theory and Measurement*, Macmillan, London and Barnes and Noble, New York.

—— (2002a) 'The UTR versus CU formation analysis and Article XXIV', *Applied Economics Letters*, no. 9.

—— (ed.) (2002b) *The Euro and Britain: Implications of Moving into the EMU*, Pearson Education, Harlow.

—— (2004) 'The enigma of African integration', *Journal of Economic Integration*, vol. 19, no. 1. A simpler version can be found in 'La integración regional en África: un

intento de análisis', *Tiempo de Paz*, vol. 67, November 2002.

—— (2007) 'The EU/China relationship: not seeing eye to eye?', *The Asia Europe Journal*, vol. 5, no. 2.

—— (2008) 'EU "economic and human rights" examined within the context of regional integration worldwide', *The Asia Europe Journal*, vol. 6, nos. 3–4, November.

—— (2009) 'Economic rights and regional integration: considering the EU and ASEAN charters within the perspective of global regional integration', *Journal of Economic Integration*, December 2009, vol. 24, no. 4.

—— (2010a) 'On the east and northeast Asian communities', *Journal of Global Issues and Solutions*, vol. 10, no. 3, May–June.

—— (2010b) 'The east Asian community and the EU: a mismatch?', *Journal Global Issues and Solutions*, vol. 10, no. 3, July–August.

—— (2011) 'What can the east and northeast Asian communities learn from the EU?', in J. A. Batten and P. G. Szilagyi (eds.), *Contemporary Studies in Economics and Financial Analysis: The Impact of the Global Financial Crisis on Emerging Financial Markets*, Emerlad, Hong Kong.

El-Agraa, A. M. and Hu, Y.-S. (1984) 'National versus supranational interests and the problem of establishing an effective EU energy policy', *Journal of Common Market Studies*, vol. 22.

El-Agraa, A. M. and Jones, A. J. (1981) *The Theory of Customs Unions*, Philip Allan, Oxford.

—— (2000a) 'UTR vs CU formation: the missing CET', *Journal of Economic Integration*, vol. 15, no. 2.

—— (2000b) 'On "CU can dominate UTR"', *Applied Economics Letters*, no. 7.

—— (2007) 'Macroeconomics of regional integration: withdrawal from a customs union', *Journal of Economic Integration*, vol. 23, no. 1.

El-Agraa, A. M. and Liu, W. P. (2006a) 'The direction and composition of China's trade: an "unexpected" composition of exports for a developing nation?', *Journal of Far Eastern Business and Economy*, vol. 3, no. 4.

—— (2006b) 'Rationalising the dramatic change in the composition of China's exports', *The Asia Pacific Economic Journal*, vol. 4, no. 1.

Eleftheriadis, P. (1998) 'Begging the constitutional question', *Journal of Common Market Studies*, vol. 36.

Elhauge, E. and Geradin, D. (2007) *Global Competition Law and Economics*, Hart Publishing, Oxford.

Elmeskov, J., Martin, J. and Scarpetta, S. (1998) 'Key lessons for labour market reforms: evidence from OECD countries' experiences', *Swedish Economic Policy Review*, vol. 1.

Emerson, M. (1988) 'The economics of 1992', *European Economy*, no. 35.

Emerson, M., Anjean, M., Catinat, M., Goybet, P. and Jacquemin, A. (1988) *The Economics of 1992: The EC Commission's Assessment of the Economic Effects of Completing the Internal Market*, Oxford University Press.

Emerson, M., Gros, D., Italianer, A., Pisani-Ferry, J. and Reichenbach, H. (1991) *One Market, One Money: An Evaluation of the Potential Benefits and Costs of Forming an Economic and Monetary Union*, Oxford University Press.

EMI (1998) *Convergence Report*, Frankfurt, March.

Eno Transportation Foundation/European Commission (2002) *Intermodal Freight Transport in Europe and the United States*, Eno Foundation, Washington D.C.

EOPUS (2010) 'Budget of the United States Government: historical tables fiscal year 2011' (www.gpoaccess.gov/usbudget/fy11/hist.html).

Erdmenger, J. and Stasinopoulos, D. (1988) 'The shipping policy of the European Community', *Journal of Transport Economics and Policy*, vol. 22, no. 3.

Erixon, F. and Messerlin, P. (2009) 'Containing Sino-European protectionism', *Economic Affairs*, vol. 29, no. 1.

Estella, A. (2002) *The EU Principle of Subsidiarity and its Critique*, Oxford University Press.

Estevadeordal, A. and Suominen, K. (2005) 'Mapping and measuring rules of origin around the world', in O. Cadot, A. Estavadeoral, A. S. Eisenmann and T. Verdier (eds.), *The Origin of Goods*, Oxford University Press.

EurActiv (2007) 'The 6th Environmental Action Programme', 29 June (www.euractiv.com/en/climate-environment/6th-environment-action-programme/article-117438).

(2010) 'Europe 2020: green growth and jobs' (www.euractiv.com).

Eureka (2006) 'Eureka projects in figures' (www.eurekanetwork.org).

Eurobarometer (2008) 'Attitudes of European citizens towards the environment', Special Report, DG Environment.

EUROCONTROL Performance Review Commission (2010) 'ATM cost-effectiveness (ACE) 2008', Benchmarking Report EUROCONTROL, Brussels.

European Council (1988) 'Brussels European Council', *Bulletin of the European Communities*, no. 2.

(1992a) *Run-up to 2000: Declaration of the Council of 18 November*, Collection of Council Statements on Development Cooperation, vol. I, 05/92.

(1992b) 'Edinburgh European Council', *Bulletin of the European Union*, no. 7.

(1997) 'Special Luxembourg European Council on Employment', *Bulletin of the European Union*, no. 11.

(1998) 'Cardiff European Council', *Bulletin of the European Union*, no. 6.

(1999a) 'Special Berlin Council 24–25 March, Conclusions of the Presidency', *Bulletin of the European Union*, no. 3.

(1999b) 'Cologne European Council', *Bulletin of the European Union*, no. 6.

(2000a) 'Presidency conclusions: Lisbon European Council 23 and 24 March 2000', *Bulletin of the European Union*, no. 3.

(2000b) 'Council Decision of 29 September 2000 on the system of the European Communities Own Resources', *OJ L* 253, 7 October.

(2000c) 'Lisbon European Council', *Bulletin of the European Union*, no. 3, I.5–I.17.

(2001) 'Presidency conclusions: Stockholm European Council 23 and 24 March 2001', *Bulletin of the European Union*, no. 3.

(2002a) *Presidency Conclusions: Copenhagen European Council*, 12–13 December.

(2002b) 'Brussels European Council, 15–16 December', *Bulletin of the European Union*, no. 12.

(2003) 'Financial perspective 2000–2006 (tables) – EU 25 in 1999 and 2004 prices', *OJ L* 147, 14 June.

(2005a) 'Brussels European Council, 20–21 March', *Bulletin of the European Union*, no. 3.

(2005b) 'Financial Perspective, 2007–13, CADREFIN 238', 15915/05.

(2005c) 'Declaration of the guiding principles for sustainable development', Presidency conclusions, Brussels, 16 and 17 June.

(2010a) 'The Treaty of Lisbon', *OJ C*, 306.

(2010b) 'Conclusion of European Council 17 June', EUCO 13/10 (www.european-council.europa.eu/council-meetings/conclusions.aspx?lang=en).

European Court of Auditors (ECA) (1995) Annual Report Concerning 2004, *OJ C*, 293, 30 November.

(2009) Annual Report Concerning the Financial Year 2008, *OJ C*, 286.

European Court of Justice (1983) '*Commission of the European Communities* v. *United Kingdom of Great Britain and Northern Ireland*. Tax agreements applying to wine', *Case 170/78 European Court Reports*, p. 02265.

(1996) *Notes for Guidance on References by National Courts*, Proceedings of the Court 34/96, Luxembourg.

(1998) '*Commission of the European Communities* v. *Kingdom of Denmark*. Free movement of goods – containers for beer and soft drinks', Case 302/86, *European Court reports 1988*, judgment of the Court, 20 September.

(2002) *Statistics of the Judicial Activity of the Court of Justice*, Luxembourg.

(2005) *Annual Report of the Court of Justice*, OOPEC, Luxembourg.

(2009a) *Annual Report of the Court of Justice*, OOPEC, Luxembourg.

(2009b) 'Information notice on references from national courts for a preliminary ruling, *OJ C* 297, 5 December.

European Economy (1996) 'Economic evaluation of the internal market', *Reports and Studies*, no. 4.

European Financial Services round table (2003) 'Message to the European Council: the single market for financial services – breaking the gridlock', EFSRT, Brussels (www.efr.be).

European Parliament (2001a) 'Task force, statistical annex, November, enlargement'.

(2001b) 'Tax coordination in the EU – the latest position', working paper, ECON 128, DG Research.

(2010) 'Parliament gives green light to new financial supervision architecture', press release, 22 September (www.europarl.europa.eu/en/pressroom/content/20100921IPR83190).

European Parliament, Council and Commission (2006) 'Inter-institutional agreement between the European Parliament, the Council and the Commission on budgetary discipline and sound financial management', *OJ C* 139.

European Research Group (1997) *The Legal Agenda for a Free Europe*, The Group, London.

European Trade Union Institute (ETUI) (2003) 'Economic and employment outlook', report by the ETUI to the ETUC Executive Committee (unpublished, cited by Watt 2004).

Eurostat (annual) *Basic Statistics of the Community*, Luxembourg.

(annual) *Statistical Review*, Luxembourg.

(2001) *European Union Foreign Direct Investment Yearbook 2001*, Luxembourg.

(2005a) *Structures of the Taxation Systems in the European Union*, Luxembourg.

(2005b) 'Regional unemployment in the European Union and candidate countries', *Statistics in Focus: Economy and Finance*, no. 3/2005, Luxembourg.

(2006a) *Facts and Figures on the CFP: Basic Data on the Common Fisheries Policy*, Luxembourg.

(2006b) *Fisheries Statistics Online*, Luxembourg.

(2006c) 'New Cronos database', Economic and Social Data Services (www.esds.ac.uk).

(2006d) 'Economy and finance', in Government Statistics, online.

(2008) *Energy Yearly Statistics 2008*, Luxembourg.

(2009a) 'Narrowing spread in regional gross domestic product', *Statistics in Focus*, no. 75, Luxembourg.

(2009b) 'Minimum wages in January 2009', *Data in Focus*, 29/2009.

(2010a) *Taxation Trends in the European Union 2010*, EU Publications Office, Luxembourg (http://epp.eurostat.ec.europa.eu/cache/ITY_OFFPUB/KS-QA-09-029/EN/KS-QA-09-029-EN.PDF).

(2010b) 'Employment rate by gender' (http://epp.eurostat.ec.europa.eu/portal/page/portal/eurostat/home).

(2010c) 'Government finance statistics' (http://epp.eurostat.ec.europa.eu/portal/page/portal/eurostat/home).

(2010d) 'Government budget outlays on R&D' (http://epp.eurostat.ec.europa.eu/portal/page/portal/statistics/search_database).

(2010e) *Balance of Payments*, statistical tables (http://epp.eurostat.ec.europa.eu).

(2010f) *Energy Yearly Statistics 2008*, Luxembourg.

(2010g) *Fisheries: Statistics*, Luxemborg (http://ec.europa.ea/trade/creating-opportunities/economic-sectors/fisheries/statistics).

Falkner, G. and Treib, O. (2008) 'Three worlds of compliance or four? The EU 15 compared to new member states', *Journal of Common Market Studies*, vol. 46, no. 2.

Fassmann, H. J., Haller, M. and Lane, D. (2009) *Migration and Mobility in Europe: Trends, Patterns and Control*, Edward Elgar, Cheltenham.

Fatás, A. (1998) 'Does EMU need a fiscal federation?', *Economic Policy*, vol. 26, April.

Faull, J. and Nikpay, A. (eds.) (2007) *The EC Law on Competition*, 2nd edn, Oxford University Press.

Feldstein, M. B. (1997) 'The political economy of the European economic and monetary union: political sources of an economic liability', *Journal of Economic Perspectives*, vol. 11.

(2002) 'The role of discretionary policy in a low interest rate environment', working paper, no. 9203, National Bureau of Economic Research, Cambridge, Mass.

Ferrera, M., Hemerijck, A. and Rhodes, M. (2000) *The Future of Social Europe: Recasting Work and Welfare in the New Economy*, Celta Editora, Oeiras.

Fielder, N. (1997) *Western European Integration in the 1980s: The Origins of the Single Market*, Peter Lang, Bern.

Finon, D. and Surrey, J. (1996) 'Does energy policy have a future in the European Union?', in F. McGowan (ed.), *European Energy Policy in a Changing Environment*, Physica-Verlag, Heidelberg.

Fischer, P. A. (1999) *On the Economics of Immobility*, Verlag Paul Haupt, Bern.

Fitzgerald, J., Johnston, J. and Williams, J. (1988) 'An analysis of cross-border shopping', paper no. 137, Economic and Social Research Institute, Dublin.

Fitzpatrick, P. (1997) 'New Europe and old stories: mythology and legality in the EU', in P. Fitzpatrick and J. Bergeron (eds.), *Europe's Other: European Law between Modernity and Postmodernity*, Ashgate, Aldershot.

Flam, H. (1998) 'Discussion', *Economic Policy*, vol. 27.

Fleming, J. M. (1971) 'On exchange rate unification', *Economic Journal*, vol. 81.

Forrester, I. and Norall, C. (1984) 'The laicization of Community: self-help and the rule of reason – how competition law is and could be applied', *Common Market Law Review*, vol. 22.

Franchino, F. (2004) 'Delegating powers in the European Community', *British Journal of Political Science*, vol. 34.

Francois, J. and Manchin, M. (2009) 'Economic impact of a potential free trade agreement (FTA) between the European Union and the Commonwealth of the Independent States', Institute for International and Development Economics, discussion paper, no. 20090805.

Frankel, J. A. (1997) *Regional Trading Blocs in the World Trading System*, Institute for International Economics, Washington D.C.

Frankel, J. A. and Rose, A. K. (2002) 'An estimate of the effect of common currencies on trade and income', *Quarterly Journal of Economics*, vol. 117, no. 2.

Frey, B. S. and Stutzer, A. (2006) 'Environmental morale and motivation', working paper, no. 288, Institute for Empirical Research in Economics, University of Zurich.

Friedman, M. (1975) *Unemployment Versus Inflation? An Evaluation of the Philips Curve*, Institute of International Affairs, London.

Frohberg, K. and Weber, G. (2001) 'Ein Ausblick in die Zeit nach vollzogener Ost-Erweiterung', Institut für Agrarentwicklung in Mittel- und Osteuropa, Halle, July (cited in Swinnen 2002).

Fujita, M. and Thisse, J.-F. (1996) 'Economics of agglomeration', *Journal of the Japanese and International Economies*, vol. 10.

Fujita, M., Piacenza, P. and Vannoni, D. (2009) 'An appraisal on the occasion of Paul Krugman's 2008 Nobel Prize in economic sciences', *Regional Science and Urban Economics*, vol. 39.

Fuller, L. (1964) *The Morality of Law*, Yale University Press, New Haven.

Gardner, B. L. (1992) 'Changing economic perspectives on the farm problem', *Journal of Economic Literature*, vol. 30, no. 1.

Garibaldi, P. and Mauro, P. (2002) 'Anatomy of employment growth', *Economic Policy*, vol. 17, no. 34.

Garrett, G. (1992) 'International cooperation and institutional choice: the European Community's internal market', *International Organization*, vol. 46.

(1995a) 'The politics of legal integration', *International Organization*, vol. 49, no. 4.

(1995b) 'Capital mobility, trade and the domestic politics of economic policy', *International Organization*, vol. 49, no. 4.

Garrett, G. and Weingast, B. (1993) 'Ideas, interests and institutions: constructing the European internal market', in J. Goldstein and R. Keohane (eds.), *Ideas and Foreign Policy*, Cornell University Press, Ithaca, NY.

Garrett, G., Keleman, R. and Schulz, H. (1998) 'The European ECJ, national governments and legal integration in the EU', *International Organization*, vol. 52.

GATT (1986) *The Text of the General Agreement on Tariffs and Trade*, GATT, Geneva (www.wto.org/english/docs_e/legal_e/gatt47_e.pdf).

(1994) *Market Access for Goods and Services: Overview of the Results*, Geneva.

Gavin, B. (2001) *The European Union and Globalisation*, Edward Elgar, London.

Gay, S. H., Osterburg, B., Baldock, D. and Zdanowicz, A. (2005) 'Recent evolution of the EU Common Agricultural Policy (CAP): state of play and environmental potential', specific targeted research project, no. SSPE-CT-2004-503604, *Impact of Environmental Agreements on the CAP*, document no. MEACAP WP6.

Geddes, A. (1995) 'Immigrant and ethnic minorities and the EU's "democratic deficit"', *Journal of Common Market Studies*, vol. 33.

Gehrels, F. (1956–7) 'Customs unions from a single country viewpoint', *Review of Economic Studies*, vol. 24.

Geradin, D., Layne-Farrar, A. and Petit, N. (2010) *EC Competition Law and Economics*, Oxford University Press.

Gerber, D. J. (2001) *Law and Competition in Twentieth Century Europe: Protecting Prometheus*, Oxford University Press.

Geroski, P. and Jacquemin, A. (1989) 'Industrial change, barriers to mobility and European industrial policy', in A. Jacquemin and A. Sapir (eds.), *The European Internal Market: Trade and Competition*, Oxford University Press.

Gianella, C., Koske, I., Rusticelli, E. and Chatal, O. (2008) 'What drives the NAIRU? Evidence from a panel of

OECD countries', *OECD Economics Department Working Paper*, no. 649.

Giannetti, M., Guiso, L., Jappelli, T., Padula, M. and Pagano, M. (2002) 'Financial market integration, corporate financing and economic growth', European Commission economic paper, no. 179, Brussels.

Gibson, J. and Caldeira, G. (1995) 'The legitimacy of transnational legal institutions: compliance, support and the European Court of Justice', *American Journal of Political Science*, vol. 39, no. 2.

(1998) 'Changes in the legitimacy of the European ECJ: a post-Maastricht analysis', *British Journal of Political Science*, vol. 28.

Gill, S. and Law, D. (1988) *The Global Political Economy: Perspectives, Problems and Policies*, Johns Hopkins University Press, Baltimore, Md.

Gillingham, J. (2003) *European Integration, 1950–2003: Superstate or New Market Economy?*, Cambridge University Press.

Glachant, J.-M. (1998) 'England's wholesale electricity market: could this hybrid institutional arrangement be transposed to the European Union?', *Utilities Policy*, vol. 7.

Goldsmith, T. (2001) 'A Charter of Rights, Freedoms and Principles', *Common Market Law Review*, vol. 38, no. 5.

Golub, J. (1996a) 'The politics of judicial discretion: rethinking the interaction between national courts and the ECJ', *West European Politics*, vol. 19.

(1996b) 'Sovereignty and subsidiarity in EU environmental policy', European University Institute working paper, RSC no. 96/2.

(2007) *Global Competition and EU Environmental Policy*, Routledge, Abingdon.

Goolsbee, A. (1998) 'Does government R&D policy mainly benefit scientists and engineers?' *American Economic Review*, vol. 88, no. 2.

Gordon, R. (1998) 'Foundations of the Goldilocks economy: supply shocks and the time-varying NAIRU', *Brookings Papers on Economic Activity*, vol. 29, no. 2.

(2004) 'Why was Europe left at the station when America's productivity locomotive departed?', CEPR discussion paper, no. 4416, Centre for Economic Policy Research, London.

Gormley, L. (1994) 'Reasoning renounced? The remarkable judgment in Reck and Mithouard', *European Business Law Review*, vol. 63.

Gorter, J. and de Mooij, R. (2001) *Capital Income Taxation in Europe: Trends and Trade-Offs*, SDU Utigevers, The Hague.

Goyder, J. and Albors-Llorens, A. (2009) *Goyder's EC Competition Law*, Oxford University Press.

Granger, M.-P. (2003) 'Towards a liberalisation of standing conditions for individuals seeking judicial review of Community Acts', *Modern Law Review*, vol. 66, no.1.

Granovetter, M. (1985) 'Economic action and social structure: the problem of embeddedness', *American Journal of Sociology*, vol. 91.

Gray, T. and Hatchard, J. (2003) 'The reform of the Common Fisheries Policy's system of governance – rhetoric or reality?' *Marine Policy*, vol. 27, no. 6.

Green, R. J. (2001) 'Markets for electricity in Europe', *Oxford Review of Economic Policy*, vol. 17, no. 3.

(2006) 'Electricity liberalization in Europe – how competitive will it be?', *Energy Policy*, vol. 34, no. 16.

Green, R. J. and Newbery, D. M. (1992) 'Competition in the British electricity spot market', *Journal of Political Economy*, vol. 100, no. 5.

Greenaway, D. and Hine, R. (1991) 'Intra-industry specialisation, trade expansion and adjustment in the European economic space', *Journal of Common Market Studies*, vol. 29, no. 6.

Griffith, R., Hines, J. and Sørensen, P. B. (2008) *International Capital Taxation*, Institute for Fiscal Studies (www.ifs.org.uk/mirrleesreview/press_docs/international.pdf).

Grimm, D. (1995) 'Does Europe need a constitution', *European Law Journal*, vol. 1, no. 3.

Grinols, E. L. (1984) 'A thorn in the lion's paw: has Britain paid too much for Common Market membership?', *Journal of International Economics*, vol. 16.

Gros, D. (1996) *A Reconsideration of the Optimum Currency Approach: The Role of External Shocks and Labour Mobility*, Centre for Economic Policy Studies, Brussels.

(2005) 'Perspectives for the Lisbon Strategy: how to increase the competitiveness of the European economy?', working document, no. 224, Centre for European Policy Studies, Brussels.

(2006) 'EU services trade: where is the single market in services?', Centre for European Policy Studies, Brussels, Commentaries, 13 February.

Gros, D. and Steinherr, A. (2004) *Economic Transition in Central and Eastern Europe: Planting the Seeds*, Cambridge University Press.

Gross, L. (1984) 'States as organs of international law and the problem of autointerpretation', in L. Gross (ed.), *Essays on International Law and Organisation*, Martinus Nijhoff, Amsterdam.

Grossman, G. M. and Helpman, E. (1991) 'Trade, knowledge spillovers and growth', *European Economic Review*, vol. 35.

Grossman, G. M. and Hossi-Hansberg, E. (2006) 'Trading

tasks: a simple theory of offshoring', unpublished paper, Princeton University.

Grubb, D. (2000) 'Eligibility criteria for unemployment benefits', *OECD Economic Studies*, vol. 31, no. 4.

Grubel, H. G. and Lloyd, P. (1975) *Intra-Industry Trade: The Theory and Measurement of International Trade in Differentiated Products*, Macmillan, Basingstoke.

Grubert, H. (2001) 'Tax planning by companies and tax competition by governments: is there evidence of changes in behavior?', in J. R. Hines, Jr (ed.), *International Taxation and Multinational Activity*, University of Chicago Press.

Gullstrand, J. and Johansson, H. (2005) 'The disciplinary effect of the single market on Swedish firms', *Open Economies Review*, vol. 16, no. 4.

Guruswamy, I. D., Papps, I. and Storey, D. (1983) 'The development and impact of an EC directive: the control of discharges of mercury to the aquatic environment', *Journal of Common Market Studies*, vol. 22, no. 1.

Guzzetti, L. (1995) *A Brief History of European Union Research Policy*, Commission of the European Communities, DG XII (Science, Research, Development).

Gwartney, J., Holcombe, R. and Lawson, R. (2006) 'Institutions and the impact of investment on growth', *Kyklos*, vol. 59, no. 2.

Haas, E. B. (1958, 1968) *The Uniting of Europe*, Stevens, London.

Haberler, G. (1964) 'Integration and growth in the world economy in historical perspective', *American Economic Review*, vol. 54.

Habermas, J. (1996) *Between Facts and Norms*, Polity Press, Cambridge.

Haigh, N. (1989) *EEC Environmental Policy and Britain*, 2nd edn, Longman, Harlow.

Halberstam, D. and Möllers, C. (2009) 'The German Constitutional Courts says "Ja Zu Deutschland"', *German Law Journal*, vol. 10, no. 8.

Hall, L. (2009) 'Hysteresis in unemployment: new and old evidence', working paper, no. 14818, National Bureau of Economic Research, Cambridge, Mass.

Han, S. S. and Leisner, H. H. (1971) 'Britain and the common market: the effects of entry on the pattern of manufacturing production', University of Cambridge, Department of Applied Economics, occasional paper, no. 27, Cambridge University Press.

Hancher, L. (1997) 'Slow and not so sure: Europe's long march to electricity market liberalization,' *Electricity Journal*, vol. 10, no. 9.

Hancher, L., Ottervanger, T. and Slot, P.-J. (1999) *EC State Aids*, Sweet and Maxwell, London.

Harding, C. (1992) 'Who goes to court in Europe? An analysis of litigation against the European Community', *European Law Review*, vol. 17.

Harlow, C. (1996) 'Francovich and the disobedient state', *European Law Journal*, vol. 2.

Hartley, T. (1996) 'The European Court, judicial objectivity and the constitution of the EU', *Law Quarterly Review*, vol. 112.

(1999) *Constitutional Problems of the EU*, Hart, Oxford.

Hayek, F. A. (1945) 'The use of knowledge in society', *American Economic Review*, vol. 35, no. 4.

Hazlewood, A. (1967) *African Integration and Disintegration*, Oxford University Press.

(1975) *Economic Integration: The East African Experience*, Heinemann, London.

Hedemann-Robinson, M. (1996) 'Third country nationals, EU citizenship, and free movement of persons: a time for bridges rather than divisions', *Yearbook of European Law*, vol. 16.

Heitger, B. and Stehn, J. (1990) 'Japanese direct investment in the EC: response to the internal market 1993?', *Journal of Common Market Studies*, vol. 29.

Helm, D. and Hepburn, C. (eds.) (2009) *The Economics and Politics of Climate Change*, Oxford University Press.

Helm, D. R. (ed.) (2005) *Climate Change Policy*, Oxford University Press.

Helm, D. R. and McGowan, F. (1989) 'Electricity supply in Europe: lessons for the UK', in D. R. Helm, J. A. Kay and D. J. Thompson (eds.), *The Market for Energy*, Oxford University Press.

Helm, D. R., Kay, J. A. and Thompson, D. J. (eds.) (1989) *The Market for Energy*, Oxford University Press.

Hemmelgarn, T. and Nicodème, G. (2009) 'Tax coordination in Europe: assessing the first years of the EU-Savings Taxation Directive', CESifo working paper, no. 2675.

Hemming, R. and Kay, J. A. (1981) 'The United Kingdom', in H. Aaron (ed.), *The Value Added Tax: Lessons from Europe*, Brookings Institute, Washington D.C.

Henrekson, M., Torstensson, J. and Torstensson, R. (1996) 'Growth effects of European integration', discussion paper, no 1465, Centre for Economic Policy Research, London.

Henrichsmeyer, W. and Witzke, H.-P. (1994) *Agrarpolitik*, Band 2, Bewertung Willensbildung, UTB für Wissenschaft, Eugen Ulmer Verlag, Stuttgart.

Henry, S., Karanassou, M. and Snower, D. J. (2000) 'Adjustment dynamics and the natural rate', *Oxford Economic Papers*, vol. 52.

Hervey, T. (1995) 'Migrant workers and their families in the EU: the pervasive market ideology of Community law', in J. Shaw and G. More (eds.), *New Legal Dynamics of European Union*, Oxford University Press.

Hildebrand, D. (2002) *The Role of Economic Analysis in the EC Competition Rules*, Kluwer Law International, The Hague.

Hill, C. (1997) *Convergence, Divergence and Dialectics: National Foreign Policies and the CFSP*, RSC 97/66, EUI, Florence.

Hodson, D. and Maher, I. (2001) 'The open method as a new mode of governance: the cases of soft economics policy co-ordination', *Journal of Common Market Studies*, vol. 39, no. 4.

(2004) 'Soft law and sanctions: economic policy coordination and the reform of the Stability and Growth Pact', *Journal of European Economic Policy*, vol. 11, no. 5.

Hoekman, B. (2007) 'Regionalism and development: the European neighbourhood policy and integration a la carte', *Journal of International Trade and Diplomacy*, vol. 1, no.1.

Hoekman, B. and Konan, D. (1999) *Deep Integration, Non-Discrimination and Euro–Mediterranean Free Trade*, Development Research Group, World Bank, Washington D.C.

Hoekman, B. and Kostecki, M. M. (2001) *The Political Economy of the World Trading System: The WTO and Beyond*, Oxford University Press.

Hoekman, B., Francois, J. and Manchin, M. (2006) 'Preference erosion and multilateral trade liberalization', *The World Bank Economic Review*, vol. 20, no. 2.

Hoffmann, H. (2009) 'Legislation, delegation and implementation under the Treaty of Lisbon: typology meets reality', *European Law Journal*, vol. 15, no. 4.

Hoffman, L. (2009) 'Don't let the sun go down on me: the German Constitutional Court and its Lisbon judgment', *Journal of Contemporary European Research*, vol. 5, no. 3.

Hofheinz, P. and Mitchener, B. (2002) 'EU states agree to open energy markets by 2004', *Wall Street Journal Europe*, 18 March.

Holden, M. (1994) *The Common Fisheries Policy*, Fishing Book News, Oxford.

House of Commons, UK (2007) 'Emissions trading: government response to the Committee's Second Report of Session 2006–07 on the EU ETS', Environmental Audit Committee Eighth Report of Session 2006–07, HC 1072, Stationery Office, London.

House of Lords, UK (1992) *Enlargement of the Community*, Select Committee on the European Communities, Session 1991–92, 10th Report, HL55, HMSO, London.

(2003) 'Revision of the EC Bathing Water Directive 46th Report', House of Lords Session 2002–03, Select Committee of the European Union, HL Paper 193, HMSO, London.

Huizinga, H. (1994) 'International interest withholding taxation: prospects for a common European policy', *International Tax and Public Finance*, vol. 1, no. 3.

Huizinga, H. and Laeven, L. (2008) 'International profit shifting within multinationals: a multi-country perspective', *Journal of Public Economics*, vol. 92.

Huizinga, H., Laeven, L. and Nicodème, G. (2008) 'Capital structure and international debt shifting', *Journal of Financial Economics*, vol. 88.

IFO (1990) *An Empirical Assessment of the Factors Shaping Regional Competitiveness in Problem Regions*, study carried out for the EC Commission.

Ilkovitz, F., Dierx, A., Kovacs, V. and Sous, N. (2007) 'Steps towards a deeper economic integration: the internal market in the 21st century', *European Economy. Economic Papers*, vol. 271.

Inklaar, R. M., O'Mahony, M. and Timmer, M. (2003) 'ICT and Europe's productivity performance: industry level growth accounting comparisons with the United States', Groningen Growth and Development Centre, research memorandum GD-68.

(2005) 'ICT and Europe's productivity performance: industry-level growth account comparisons with the United States', *Review of Income and Wealth*, issue 4.

Institute for European Environmental Policies (2003) 'Environmental integration and the CAP', a report to the European Commission (http://europa.eu/index_en.htm).

International Energy Agency (2001) *Oil Supply Security: The Emergency Response Potential of IEA Countries in 2002*, IEA, Paris.

(2008) *Energy Balances of OECD Countries 2008*, IEA, Paris.

International Monetary Fund (2001) *Government Financial Statistical Yearbook 2001*, Washington D.C.

(2004) *Government Finance Statistics Yearbook, 2004*, IMF, Washington D.C.

(2010a) 'The challenge of growth, employment and social cohesion, discussion document, IMF-ILO (www.osloconference2010.org/discussionpaper.pdf).

(2010b) *Direction of Trade Statistics*, ESDS International (www.esds.ac.uk/international).

(2010c) 'Government financial statistics', ESDS International (www.esds.ac.uk/international).

Issing, O. (2008) *The Birth of the Euro*, Cambridge University Press.

Jacqué, J.-P. and Weiler, J. (1990) 'On the road to EU – a new judicial architecture: an agenda for the intergovernmental conference', *Common Market Law Review*, vol. 27.

Jamasb, T. and Pollitt, M. (2005) 'Electricity market reform in the European Union: review of progress toward liberalization and integration', *Energy Journal*, vol. 26, no. 3.

Janssen, L. H. (1961) *Free Trade, Protection and Customs Union*, Economisch Sociologisch Instituut, Leiden.

Jeppesen, T. (2002) *Environmental Regulation in a Federal System: Framing Environmental Policy in the EU*, Edward Elgar, Cheltenham.

Joerges, C. (1996) 'Taking the law seriously: on political science and the role of law in the integration process', *European Law Journal*, vol. 2.

Joerges, C., Mény, Y. and Weiler, J. (eds.) (2000) *What Kind of Constitution for What Kind of Polity? Responses to Joschka Fischer*, Robert Schuman Centre for Advanced Studies, European University Institute and Harvard Law School.

Johansson, B. K. Å. *et al.* (2002) *Stabilisation Policy in the Monetary Union – A Summary of the Report*, Commission on Stabilisation Policy for Full Employment in the Event of Sweden Joining the Monetary Union, Stockholm.

Johnson, H. G. (1965a) 'Optimal trade intervention in the presence of domestic distortions', in R. E. Baldwin (ed.), *Trade, Growth and the Balance of Payments*, Rand McNally, Chicago.

— (1965b) 'An economic theory of protectionism, tariff bargaining and the formation of customs unions', *Journal of Political Economy*, vol. 73.

— (1973) 'Problems of European monetary union', in M. B. Krauss (ed.), *The Economics of Integration*, Allen and Unwin, London.

— (1974) 'Trade diverting customs unions: a comment', *Economic Journal*, vol. 81.

Johnston, A. (1999) 'The EC Energy Law 1999: reciprocity and the gas and electricity directives', *CEPMLP Internet Journal*, vol. 4, no. 9.

— (2001) 'Judicial reform and the Treaty of Nice', Common *Market Law Review*, vol. 38.

Jones, A. J. (1979) 'The theory of economic integration', in J. K. Bowers (ed.), *Inflation Development and Integration: Essays in Honour of A. J. Brown*, Leeds University Press.

— (1980) 'Domestic distortions and customs union theory', *Bulletin of Economic Research*, vol. 32.

— (1983) 'Withdrawal from a customs union: a macroeconomic analysis', in El-Agraa 1983a, Chapter 5.

Jones, C. and Gonzalez-Diaz, F. E. (1992) *The EEC Merger Control Regulation*, Sweet and Maxwell, London.

Jordan, A. (1999) 'European water standards: locked in or watered down?', *Journal of Common Market Studies*, vol. 37.

— (2005) *Environmental Policy in the EU: Actors, Institutions and Processes*, 2nd edn, Earthscan, London.

Jordan, A., Huitema, D. and van Asselt, H. (2010) *Climate Change Policy in the European Union: Confronting the Dilemmas of Mitigation and Adaptation?* Cambridge University Press.

Kaldor, N. (1971) 'The dynamics of European integration', in D. Evans (ed.), *Destiny or Delusion?*, Gollancz, London.

Karanassou, M., Sala, H. and Snower, D. J. (2002) 'Unemployment in the European Union: a dynamic reappraisal', discussion paper, no. 531, IZA, Bonn (www.iza.org).

Keen, M. and de Mooij, R. (2008) 'Tax policy and subsidiarity in the European Union', in G. Gelauff, I. Grilo and A. Lejour (eds.) with M. Keen (2008) *Subsidiarity and Economic Reform in Europe*, Springer, Berlin.

Keller, W. (2002) 'Geographic localization of international technology diffusion', *American Economic Review*, vol. 92, no. 1.

Kemmerling, A. and Bruttel, O. (2006) '"New politics" in German labour market policy? The implications of the recent Hartz reforms for the German welfare state', *West European Politics*, vol. 29, no. 1.

Kenen, P. (1969) 'The theory of optimum currency areas: an eclectic view', in R. A. Mundell and A. K. Swoboda, *Monetary Problems of the International Economy*, MIT Press, Cambridge, Mass.

Kenny, S. (1998) 'The members of the ECJ of the European Communities', *Columbia Journal of European Law*, vol. 5.

Klamert, M. (2010) 'Conflicts of legal basis: no legality and no basis but a bright future under the Lisbon Treaty?', *European Law Review*, vol. 35, no. 3.

Klemperer, P. D. and Meyer, M. A. (1989) 'Supply function equilibria in oligopoly under uncertainty', *Econometrica*, vol. 57, no. 6.

Kluve, J. (2006) 'The effectiveness of European active labour market policy', IZA discussion paper, no. 2018, Bonn (www.iza.org).

Knight, F. H. (1921) *Risk, Uncertainty and Profit*, Houghton Mifflin, New York.

Koester, U. (1977) 'The redistributional effects of the EC Common Agricultural Policy', *European Review of Agricultural Economics*, vol. 4, no. 4.

— (1989a) *International Agricultural Trade Consortium*, Washington D.C.

— (1989b) 'Financial implications of the EC set-aside programme', *Journal of Agricultural Economics*, vol. 40, no. 2.

— (1991) 'Economy-wide costs of farm support policies in major industrialized countries', in K. Burger, M. N. de Groot, J. Post and V. Zachariasse (eds.), *Agricultural Economics and Policy: International Challenges for the Nineties*, Elsevier, Amsterdam.

(2010) *Grundzüge der landwirtschaftlichen Marktlehre*, 4th edn, Vahlen Verlag, Munich.

Koester, U. and Kirschke, D. (1985) 'Die hausgemachte Krise in der Agrarpolitik', *Wirtschaftsdienst*, vol. 65, no. 7.

Koester, U. and Tangermann, S. (1990) 'The European Community', in F. Sanderson (ed.), *Agricultural Protectionism in the Industrialized World, Resources for the Future*, Washington D.C.

Koester, U. and Senior, S. (2010) 'PILLAR II: a real improvement of the CAP?', in N. S. Senior and P. Pierani (eds.), *International Trade, Consumer Interests and Reform of the Common Agricultural Policy*, Routledge Studies in the European Economy, Oxford University Press.

Kok, W. (2004) *Facing the Challenge: The Lisbon Strategy for Growth and Employment*, report of the high level Group chaired by Wim Kok, OOPEC, Luxembourg.

Komninos, M. (2002) 'New prospects for private enforcement of EC competition law: *Courage* v. *Crehan* and the Community right to damages', *Common Market Law Review*, vol. 39.

Korah, V. (1998) 'The future of vertical agreements under EC competition law', *European Competition Law Review*, vol. 19.

(2004) *An Introduction to EC Competition Law*, 8th edn, Hart, Oxford.

Korah, V. and Sullivan, D. (2002) *Distribution Agreements under the EC Competition Rules*, Hart, Oxford.

Kouevi, A. F. (1964) 'Essai d'application prospective de la method RAS au commerce international', *Bulletin du CEPREL*, vol. 5.

Kouvaritakis, N., Stroblos, N., Paroussos, L., Revesz, T., Zalai, E. and van Regemorter, D. (2005) 'Impacts of energy taxation in the enlarged European Union, evaluation with GEM-E3 Europe', study for DG Taxation and Customs Union (http://ec.europa.eu/taxation_customs/taxation/excise_duties/energy_products/studies_reports/index_en.htm).

Kox, H., Lejour, A. and Montizaan, R. (2004a) 'The free movement of services within the EU', Centraal Planbureau (Netherlands Bureau for Economic Analysis), The Hague, document 69.

(2004b) 'Intra-EU trade and investment in service sectors and regulatory patterns'. CPB memorandum, no. 102, Centraal Planbureau (Netherlands Bureau for Economic Policy Analysis), The Hague, November.

Kramer, A. E. (2009) 'Falling gas prices deny Russia a lever of power', *New York Times*, 16 May.

Kramer, L. (2003) *EC Environmental Law*, 5th edn, Sweet and Maxwell, London.

Krause, L. B. (1962) 'US imports, 1947–58', *Econometrica*, April.

(1968) *European Economic Integration and the United States*, Brookings Institute, Washington D.C.

Krause, L. B. and Salant, W. S. (1973) *European Monetary Unification and its Meaning for the United States*, Brookings Institute, Washington D.C.

Krauss, M. B. (1972) 'Recent developments in customs union theory: an interpretative survey', *Journal of Economic Literature*, vol. 10.

Kreinin, M. E. (1961) 'The effects of tariff changes on the prices and volumes of imports', *American Economic Review*, vol. 51.

(1967) 'Trade arrangements among industrial countries: effects on the US', in B. Balassa (ed.), *Studies in Trade Liberalization*, Johns Hopkins University Press, Baltimore, Md.

(1969) 'Trade creation and trade diversions by the EEC and EFTA', *Economia Internazionale*, vol. 22.

(1972) 'Effects of the EEC on imports of manufactures', *Economic Journal*, vol. 82.

(1973) 'The static effects of EEC enlargement on trade flows', *Southern Economic Journal*, vol. 39.

(1979a) *International Economics: A Policy Approach*, Harcourt Brace Jovanovich, Orlando, Fla. (also subsequent editions).

(1979b) 'Effects of European integration on trade flows in manufactures', seminar paper no. 125, Institute for International Economic Studies, University of Stockholm.

Krueger, A. O. (1974) 'The political economy of the rent-seeking society', *American Economic Review*, vol. 64.

Krugman, P. A. (1979) 'Increasing returns, monopolistic competition and international trade', *Journal of International Economics*, vol. 9.

(1990) 'Policy problems of a monetary union', in P. de Grauwe and L. Papademos (eds.), *The European Monetary System in the 1990s*, Longman, Harlow.

(1991) *Geography and Trade*, MIT Press, Cambridge, Mass.

(1994) *Re-Thinking International Trade*, MIT Press, Cambridge, Mass.

Krugman, P. A. and Venables, A. J. (1990) 'Integration and competitiveness of peripheral industry', in C. Bliss and J. Braga de Macedo (eds.), *Unity with Diversity in the European Community*, Cambridge University Press.

(1996) 'Integration, specialization, adjustment', *European Economic Review*, vol. 40.

Kumm, M. (1999) 'Who is the final arbiter of constitutionality in Europe?: three conceptions of the relationship between the German Federal Constitutional Court and the European ECJ', *Common Market Law Review*, vol. 36.

Küpker, B., Hüttel, S., Kleinhans, W. and Offermann, F. (2006) 'Assessing impacts of CAP reform in France and Germany', *German Journal of Agriculture Economics*, vol. 55 (Agrarwirtschaft, Jahrgang 55).

Kyla, L., Tilden, M. and Wilsdon, T. (2009) *Evaluation of the Economic Impacts of the Financial Services Action Programme*, CRA International, Report for DG Internal Market (http://ec.europa.eu/internal_market/finances/docs/actionplan/index/090707_economic_impact_en.pdf).

Ladeur, K.-H. (1997) 'Towards a legal theory of supranationality – the viability of the network concept', *European Law Journal*, vol. 3.

Laffan, B. (1997) *The Finances of the European Union*, Macmillan, Basingstoke.

Laffont, J.-J. (1996) 'Industrial policy and politics', *International Journal of Industrial Organisation*, vol. 14, no.1.

Lamfalussy, A. (1963) 'Intra-European trade and the competitive position of the EEC', *Manchester Statistical Society Transactions*, March.

(2001) *Final Report of the Committee of Wise Men on the Regulation of European Securities Markets*, CEU, Brussels.

Landler, M. (2006) 'Europe's image clashes with reliance on coal', *New York Times* 20 June (www.nytimes.com/2006/06/20/business/worldbusiness/20eurocoal.html).

Langer, J. (2007) *Tying and Bundling as a Leveraging Concern under EC Competition Law*, Kluwer, Deventer.

Latour, B. (1993) *We Have Never Been Modern*, Harvester Wheatsheaf, London.

Layard, R., Nickell, S. and Jackman, R. (1991) *Unemployment: Macroeconomic Performance and the Labour Market*, Oxford University Press.

Lee, J.-W. and Swagel, P. (1997) 'Trade barriers and trade flows across countries and industries', *Review of Economics and Statistics*, vol. 79, no. 2.

Lehtinen, T. (2003) 'The coordination of European development cooperation in the field: myth and reality', discussion paper, no. 43, ECDPM, Maastricht.

Leinbach, T. R. and Capineri, C. (eds.) (2007) *Globalized Freight Transport: Intermodality, E-Commerce, Logistics, and Sustainability*, Edward Elgar, Cheltenham.

Lepori, C. (2010) *Sustainable Intermodal Freight Transport in Europe: Motorways of the Sea Services and Innovative Railway*, AP Lambert Academic Publishing, Saarbrücken.

Lequesne, C. (2000a) 'The Common Fisheries Policy', in H. Wallace and W. Wallace (eds.), *Policy Making in the EU*, Oxford University Press.

(2000b) 'Quota hopping: the Common Fisheries Policy between states and markets', *Journal of Common Market Studies*, vol. 38, no. 5.

(2005) 'Fisheries Policy', in H. Wallace, W. Wallace and M. Pollack, *Policy Making in the European Union*, Oxford University Press.

Liebscher, K., Christl, J., Mooslechner, P. and Ritzberger-Grunwald, D. (2007) *Foreign Direct Investment in Europe: A Changing Landscape*, Edward Elgar, Cheltenham.

Lin, J. and Monga, C. (2010) 'Growth identification and facilitation: the role of the state in the dynamics of structural change', policy research working paper, no. 5313, World Bank, Washington D.C.

Lindberg, L. N. and Scheingold, S. A. (1970) *Europe's Would-Be Policy Patterns of Change in the European Community*, Prentice Hall, London.

Lindner, J. (2006) *Conflict and Change in EU Budgetary Politics*, Routledge, London.

Linnemann, H. (1966) *An Econometric Study of International Trade Flows*, North-Holland, Amsterdam.

Lipgens, W. (1982) *A History of European Integration*, vol. I: *1945–47: The Formation of the European Unity Movement*, Clarendon Press, Oxford.

Lipsey, R. G. (1960) 'The theory of customs unions: a general survey', *Economic Journal*, vol. 70.

Lockwood, B., de Meza, B. and Myles, G. (1994) 'When are destination and origin regimes equivalent?', *International Tax and Public Finance*, vol. 1.

London Economics (2002) *Quantification of the Macroeconomic Impact of Integration of EU Financial Market*, London Economics for DG Internal Market (http://ec.europa.eu/internal_market/securities/docs/studies/report-londonecon_en.zip).

(2010) 'Study analysing possible changes in the minimum rates and structures of excise duties on alcoholic beverages', study for DG Taxation and Customs Union (http://ec.europa.eu/taxation_customs/taxation/excise_duties/alcoholic_beverages/studies_reports/index_en.htm).

Loveman, G. and Sengenberger, W. (1991) 'The re-emergence of small-scale production: an international comparison', *Small Business Economics*, vol. 3, no. 1.

Lucarelli, B. (1999) *The Origins and Evolution of the Single Market in Europe*, Aldershot, Ashgate.

Lucas, N. J. D. (1977) *Energy and the European Communities*, Europa Publications for the David Davies Memorial Institute of International Studies, London.

Lucas, R. E. (1988) 'On the mechanics of economic development', *Journal of Monetary Economics*, vol. 22.

Ludlow, P. (1982) *The Making of the European Monetary System: A Case Study of the Politics of the European Community*, Butterworths, London.

MacCormick, N. (1993) 'Beyond the sovereign state', *Modern Law Review*, vol. 56.

— (1996) 'Liberalism, nationalism and the post-sovereign state', in R. Bellamy and D. Castiglione (eds.), *Constitutionalism in Transformation: European and Theoretical Perspectives*, Blackwell, Oxford.

— (1999) *Questioning Sovereignty*, Oxford University Press.

Machlup, F. (1977) *A History of Thought on Economic Integration*, Macmillan, Basingstoke.

Magrini, S. (1999) 'The evolution of income disparities among the regions of the European Union', *Regional Science and Urban Economics*, vol. 29.

Maher, I. (1994) 'National courts as European Community Courts', *Legal Studies*, vol. 14, no. 2.

— (1995) 'Legislative review by the EC Commission: revision without radicalism', in J. Shaw and G. More (eds.), *New Legal Dynamics of European Union*, Oxford University Press.

— (1996a) 'Limitations on Community regulation in the UK: legal culture and multi-level governance', *Journal of European Public Policy*, vol. 3, no. 4.

— (1996b) 'A traders' charter? Free movement of goods and the Sunday dilemma', in G. Wilson and R. Rogowski (eds.), *Challenges to European Legal Scholarship*, Edward Elgar, Cheltenham.

— (2009) 'Functional and normative delegation to non-majoritarian institutions: the case of the European competition network', *Comparative European Politics*, vol. 7, no. 4.

Majone, G. (1994) 'The rise of regulatory policy making in Europe and the United States', *Journal of Public Policy*, vol. 11, no. 1.

— (1998) 'Europe's democracy deficit: the question of standards', *European Law Journal*, vol. 4.

— (2008) 'Unity in diversity: European Integration and the Enlargement Process', *European Law Review*, vol. 33, no. 4.

Major, R. L. and Hayes, S. (1970) 'Another look at the common market', *National Institute Economic Review*, no. 78.

Manchin, M. (2006) 'Preference utilisation and tariff reduction in EU imports from ACP countries', *World Economy*, vol. 29, no. 9.

Mancini, G. (1998) 'Europe: the case for statehood', *European Law Journal*, vol. 4.

Marer, P. and Montias, J. M. (1988) 'The Council for Mutual Economic Assistance', in El-Agraa 1988b.

Marin, A. (1979) 'Pollution control: economists' views', *Three Banks Review*, no. 121.

Marjolin, R. (1986) *Architect of European Unity: Memoirs 1911–1986*, trans. William Hall (1989), Weidenfeld and Nicolson, London.

Marques-Mendes, A. J. (1986) 'The contribution of the European Community to economic growth', *Journal of Common Market Studies*, vol. 24, no. 4.

Marshall, A. (1920) *Principles of Economics*, Macmillan, Basingstoke.

Martin, J. and Grubb, D. (2001) 'What works and for whom? A review of OECD countries' experiences with active labour market policies', *Swedish Economic Policy Review*, vol. 8, no. 2.

Martin, S. (2001) *Industrial Organization: A European Perspective*, Oxford University Press.

Martin, S. and Scott, J. T. (2000) 'The nature of innovation market failure and the design of public support for private innovation', *Research Policy*, vol. 29, nos. 4–5.

Mathä, T. (2006) 'The euro and price differences in a cross-border area', *Journal of Common Market Studies*, vol. 44, no. 3.

Mattli, W. and Slaughter, A.-M. (1998) 'Revisiting the European ECJ', *International Organization*, vol. 52.

Mayes, D. G. (1971) 'The effects of alternative trade groupings on the United Kingdom', PhD thesis, University of Bristol.

— (1974) 'RASAT: a model for the estimation of commodity trade flows in EFTA', *European Economic Review*, vol. 5.

— (1978) 'The effects of economic integration on trade', *Journal of Common Market Studies*, vol. 17, no. 1.

— (1983) 'EC trade effects and factor mobility', in El-Agraa 1983a, Chapter 6.

— (1988) Chapter 3, in A. Bollard and M. A. Thompson (eds.), *Trans-Tasman Trade and Investment*, Institute for Policy Studies, Wellington, New Zealand.

— (1993) *The External Implications of European Integration*, Harvester Wheatsheaf, London.

— (1996) 'The role of foreign direct investment in structural change: the lessons from the New Zealand experience', in G. Csaki, G. Foti and D. G. Mayes (eds.), *Foreign Direct Investment and Transition: The Case of the Visegrad Countries*, Trends in World Economy, no. 78, Institute for World Economics, Budapest.

— (1997a) 'Competition and cohesion: lessons from New Zealand', in M. Fritsch and H. Hansen (eds.), *Rules of Competition and East–West Integration*, Kluwer, Dordrecht.

— (1997b) *The Evolution of the Single European Market*, Edward Elgar, Cheltenham.

— (1997c) 'The New Zealand experiment: using economic theory to drive policy', *Policy Options*, vol. 18, no. 7.

— (1997d) 'The problems of the quantitative estimation of integration effects', in El-Agraa 1997.

— (2004) 'Finland the Nordic insider', *Cooperation and Conflict*, vol. 39, no. 2.

Mayes, D. G. and Begg, I. with Levitt, M. and Shipman, A.

(1992) *A New Strategy for Economic and Social Cohesion after 1992*, European Parliament, Luxembourg.

Mayes, D. G. and Virén, M. (2000) 'The exchange rate and monetary conditions in the euro area', *Weltwirtschaftliches Archiv*, vol. 136, no. 2.

(2002a) 'Macroeconomic factors, policies and the development of social exclusion', in R. Muffels, P. Tsakloglou and D. G. Mayes (eds.), *Social Exclusion in European Welfare States*, Edward Elgar, Cheltenham.

(2002b) 'Policy coordination and economic adjustment in EMU: will it work?', in El-Agraa 2002b.

(2002c) 'Asymmetry and the problem of aggregation in the euro area', *Empirica*, vol. 29.

(2002d) 'The exchange rate and monetary conditions in the euro area', *Empirica*, vol. 29.

Mayes, D. G. and Suvanto, A. (2002) 'Beyond the fringe: Finland and the choice of currency', *Journal of Public Policy*, vol. 22, no. 2.

Mayes, D. G., Hager, W., Knight, A. and Streeck, W. (1993) *Public Interest and Market Pressures: Problems Posed by Europe 1992*, Macmillan, London.

Mayes, D. G., Bergman, J. and Salais, R. (2001) *Social Exclusion and European Policy*, Edward Elgar, Cheltenham.

McCormick, J. (2001) *Environmental Politics in the EU*, Palgrave, Basingstoke.

McKinnon, R. I. (1963) 'Optimum currency areas', *American Economic Review*, vol. 53.

McMahon, J. (1998) *The Development Cooperation Policy of the EC*, Kluwer Law International, Dordrecht.

McManus, J. G. (1972) 'The theory of the international firm', in G. Paquet (ed.), *The Multinational Firm and the National State*, Collier Macmillan, New York.

McMorrow, K. and Roeger, W. (2000) 'Time-varying Nairu/Nawru estimates for the EU's member states', economic papers, no. 145, European Commission, DG ECFIN.

McQueen, M. (2002) 'The EU's free trade agreements with developing countries: a case of wishful thinking?', *The World Economy*, vol. 25, no. 9.

McQueen, M., Phillips, C., Hallam, D. and Swinbank, A. (1997) 'ACP-EU trade and aid cooperation post-Lomé IV', Brussels, ACP Secretariat, document ACP/28/065/97.

Meade, J. E. (1980) *The Theory of International Trade Policy*, Oxford University Press.

Meade, J. E., Liesner, H. H. and Wells, S. J. (1962) *Case Studies in European Economic Union: The Mechanics of Integration*, Oxford University Press.

Meij, J. (2000) 'Architects or judges? Some comments in relation to the current debate', *Common Market Law Review*, vol. 37.

Mélitz, J. (2001) 'Geography, trade and currency union',

discussion paper, no. 2987, Centre for Economic Policy Research, London.

Mélitz, J. and Zumer, F. (1998) 'Regional redistribution and stabilization by the center in Canada, France, the United Kingdom and the United States: new estimates based on panel data econometrics', discussion paper, no. 1892, Centre for Economic Policy Research, London.

Memedovic, O., Kuyvenhoven, A. and Molle, W. (eds.) (1999) *Multilateralism and Regionalism in the Post-Uruguay Round Era: What Role for the EU?*, Kluwer, Boston, Mass.

Merrills, J. (1998) *International Dispute Settlement*, Cambridge University Press.

Messerlin, P. A. (2001) *Measuring the Costs of Protection in Europe*, Institute for International Economics, Washington D.C.

Meunier, S. (2005) *Trading Voices: The European Union in International Commercial Negotiations*. Princeton University Press.

Midelfart-Knarvik, K. H., Overman, H. G., Redding, S. J. and Venables, A. J. (2000) 'The location of European industry', economic paper, no. 14, CEU, DG for Economic and Financial Affairs.

Mintz, J. M. (2002) 'European company tax reform: prospects for the future', *CESifo Forum*, 3/1 (www.cesifo.de).

Molle, W. and Morsink, R. (1991) 'Direct investment and European integration', *European Economy*, special issue.

Monfort, P. (2003) *An Agenda for a Growing Europe: Making the EU Economic System Deliver*, report of an independent high-level study group established on the initiative of the President of the European Commission, Brussels.

(2008) 'Convergence of EU regions: measures and evolution', DG Regional Policy working paper, no. 01/2008.

Monti, M. (1996) *The Single Market and Tomorrow's Europe: A Progress Report from the European Commission*, Office for Official Publications of the European Communities, Luxembourg and Kogan Page, London.

(2001) *The Future of Competition Policy*, Merchant Taylor's Hall, 9 July, Speech/01/340 (http://europa.eu/rapid/pressReleasesAction.do?reference=SPEECH/01/340&format=HTML&aged=0&language=EN&guiLanguage=en).

(2007) *EC Competition Law*, Cambridge University Press.

(2010) *A New Strategy for the Single Market: At the Service of Europe's Economy and Society*, Report to the President of the Commission, J. M. Barroso (http://ec.europa.eu/bepa/pdf/monti_report_final_10_05_2010_en.pdf).

Moore, C. (2008) 'A Europe of the regions vs. the regions of Europe', *Regional and Federal Studies*, vol. 18.

Moravcsik, A. (1998) *The Choice for Europe*, UCL Press, London.

(2006) 'What we can learn from the collapse of the European constitutional project', *Politische Vierteljahresschrift*, vol. 47, no. 2.

Morgan, J. and Mourougane, A. (2001) 'What can changes in structural factors tell us about unemployment in Europe?', ECB working paper, no. 81, October (www.ecb.int).

Motta, M. (2004) *Competition Policy: Theory and Practice*, Cambridge University Press.

Moser, S. and Pesaresi, N. (2002) 'State guarantees to German public banks: a new step in the enforcement of state aid discipline to financial services in the Community', *Competition Policy Newsletter*, no. 2, June.

Munby, D. L. (1962) 'Fallacies of the Community's transport policy', *Journal of Transport Economics and Policy*, vol. 1, no. 1.

Mundell, R. A. (1961) 'A theory of optimum currency areas', *American Economic Review*, vol. 51.

(1964) 'Tariff preferences and the terms of trade', *Manchester School*, vol. 32.

(1973a) 'A plan for a European currency', in H. G. Johnson and A. K. Swoboda (eds.), *The Economics of Common Currencies*, Allen and Unwin, London.

(1973b) 'Uncommon arguments for common currencies', in H. G. Johnson and A. K. Swoboda (eds.), *The Economics of Common Currencies*, Allen and Unwin, London.

Musgrave, R. A. (1959) *The Theory of Public Finance*, McGraw-Hill, New York.

Nam, C. and Reuter, J. (1992) *The Effect of 1992 and Associated Legislation on the Less Favoured Regions of the Community*, Office for Official Publications of the European Communities, Luxembourg.

Neill, Sir P. (1996) *The European ECJ: A Case Study in Judicial Activism*, European Policy Forum, London and Frankfurter Institut, Frankfurt.

Neumayer, E. (2001) 'Improvement without convergence: pressure on the environment in EU countries', *Journal of Common Market Studies*, vol. 39, no. 5.

Neven, D. J. (1990) 'Gains and losses from 1992', *Economic Policy*, April.

Neven, D. J. and Wyplosz, C. (1999) 'Relative prices, trade and restructuring in European industry', in M. Dewatripont, A. Sapir and K. Sekkat (eds.), *Trade and Jobs in Europe: Much Ado About Nothing?*, Oxford University Press.

Neven, D. J., Nuttall, R. and Seabright, P. (1993a) *Competition and Merger Policy in the EC*, Centre for Economic Policy Research, London.

(1993b) *Merger in Daylight*, Centre for Economic Policy Research, London.

Neven, D. J., Papandropoulos, P. and Seabright, P. (1998) *Trawling for Minnows: European Competition Policy and Agreements Between Firms*, Centre for Economic Policy Research, London.

Newbery, D. M. (1999a) *Privatization, Restructuring, and Regulation of Network Industries*, MIT Press, Cambridge, Mass.

(1999b) 'The UK experience: privatization with market power', in Bergmann *et al.* 1999.

(2001) 'Economic reform in Europe: integrating and liberalizing the market for services', *Utilities Policy*, vol. 10.

Nicholl, W. (1994) 'The battles of the European budget', *Policy Studies*, vol. 7, July.

Nickell, S. (1997) 'Unemployment and labor market rigidities: Europe versus North America, *Journal of Economic Perspectives*, vol. 11, no. 3.

Nickell, S. and Layard, R. (1999) 'Labour market institutions and economic performance', in O. Ahsenfelter and D. Card (eds.), *Handbook of Labour Economics*, vol. III, North-Holland, Amsterdam.

Nickell, S., Nunziata, L., Ochel, W. and Quintini, G. (2002) 'The Beveridge curve, unemployment and wages in the OECD from the 1960s to the 1990s', LSE Centre for Economic Performance (http://cep.lse.ac.uk/pubs/download/dp0502.pdf).

Nickell, S., Nunziata, L. and Ochel, W. (2005) 'Unemployment in the OECD since the 1960s: what do we know?', *Economic Journal*, vol. 115, no. 500.

Nicodème, G. (2001) 'Comparing effective corporation tax rates: comparisons and results', economic paper, no. 153, EU Commission, DG Economic and Financial Affairs.

Nicoletti, G., Scarpetta, S. and Boylaud, O. (2000) 'Summary indicators of product market regulation with an extension of employment protection legislation', working paper, no. 226, OECD, Paris.

North, D. C. (1990) *Institutions, Institutional Change and Economic Performance*, Cambridge University Press.

Notaro, G. (2002) 'European integration and productivity: exploring the gains of the single market', London Economics, London.

Oates, W. E. (ed.) (1977) *The Political Economy of Fiscal Federalism*, Lexington Books, Toronto.

(1999) 'An essay in fiscal federalism', *Journal of Economic Literature*, vol. 37, no. 3.

Obstfeld, M. and Peri, G. (1998a) 'Regional non-adjustment and fiscal policy', *Economic Policy*, vol. 26, April.

(1998b) 'Asymmetric shocks: regional non-adjustment and fiscal policy', *Economic Policy*, vol. 28.

Odudu, O. (2006) *The Boundaries of EC Competition Law – The Scope of Article 81*, Oxford University Press.

OECD (various years) *Economic Survey of Europe*, OECD, Paris.

(various issues) *Geographical Distribution of Financial Flows to Aid Recipients*, OECD, Paris.

(1988a) *The Newly Industrialising Countries: Challenges and Opportunity for OECD Industries*, OECD, Paris.

(1988b) *Taxing Consumption*, OECD, Paris.

(1994) *The OECD Jobs Study*, OECD, Paris.

(1997) *Implementing the OECD Jobs Strategy*, OECD, Paris.

(1999a) *SOPEMI: Trends in International Migration: Annual Report 1999. Continuous Reporting System on Migration*, OECD, Paris.

(1999b) *Implementing the OECD Jobs Strategy: Assessing Performance and Policy*, OECD, Paris.

(2000) *The European Union's Trade Policies and their Economic Effects*, OECD, Paris.

(2001) *Multifunctionality: Towards an Analytical Framework*, OECD, Paris.

(2002a) *European Community Development Cooperation Review Series*, OECD, Paris.

(2002b) *Revenue Statistics 1965–2001*, OECD, Paris.

(2002c) *Main Science and Technology Indicators*, OECD, Paris.

(2003) *Agricultural Policies in OECD Countries: Monitoring and Evaluation*, OECD, Paris.

(2005a) *OECD/EEA Database on Instruments Used for Environmental Policy and Natural Resources Management*, OECD, Paris (www2.oecd.org/ecoinst/queries/index.htm).

(2005b) 'The benefits of liberalising product markets and reducing barriers to international trade and investment in the OECD', Economics Department working paper, no. 463, OECD, Paris.

(2005c) 'The EU's single market: at your service?', Economics Department working paper, no. 449, OECD, Paris.

(2005d) *Employment Outlook*, OECD, Paris.

(2005e) *Main Science and Technology Indicators*, database, Economic and Social Data Services (www.esds.ac.uk).

(2006a) *Main Economic Indicators*, annual database, Economic and Social Data Services (www.esds.ac.uk).

(2006b) *Education at a Glance: 2006 Indicators*, OECD, Paris.

(2006c) *Employment Outlook: Boosting Jobs and Income*, OECD, Paris.

(2006d) *Boosting Jobs and Income: Policy Lessons from Reassessing the OECD Jobs Strategy*, OECD, Paris.

(2006e) *Labour Productivity Database* (www.oecd.org/topicsstatsportal/0,2647,en_2825_30453906_1_1_1_1_1,00.html).

(2006f) *OECD Economic Outlook*, 79, OECD, Paris.

(2009a) 'Deepening the single market', *OECD Economic Surveys: European Union 2009*, OECD, Paris.

(2009b) *PSE/CSE Database*, OECD, Paris.

(2010a) 'Moving beyond the economic crisis', *Employment Outlook* 2010, OECD, Paris.

(2010b) 'Productivity statistics, OECD Statistics Portal' (www.oecd.org/topicsstatsportal/0,3398,en_2825_30453906_1_1_1_1_1,00.html).

OECD QWIDS (http://stats.oecd.org/qwids).

O'Keeffe, D. (1998) 'Is the spirit of Article 177 under attack? Preliminary references and admissibility', *European Law Review*, vol. 23.

Olson, M. (1982) *The Rise and Decline of Nations: Economic Growth, Stagnation and Social Rigidities*, Yale University Press, New Haven, Conn.

Oort, C. J. and Maaskant, R. H. (1976) *Study of Possible Solutions for Allocating the Deficit which may Occur in a System of Charging for the Use of Infrastructure Aiming at Budgetary Equilibrium*, EU Commission.

OPEC (2009) *Annual Statistical Bulletin 2008*, Geneva.

Owen, N. (1983) *Economies of Scale, Competitiveness and Trade Patterns within the European Community*, Oxford University Press.

Owens, S. and Hope, C. (1989) 'Energy and the environment – the challenge of integrating European policies', *Energy Policy*, vol. 17.

Oxfam (2006) *Unequal Partners: How EU-ACP Economic Partnership Agreements Could Harm the Development Prospects of Many of the World's Poorest Countries*, Oxfam International, London.

Padoa-Schioppa, T. and Emerson, M. (1987) *Efficiency, Stability and Equity: A Strategy for the Evolution of the Economic System of the European Community*, Oxford University Press.

Page, E. (1998) 'The impact of European legislation on British public policy making: a research note', *Public Administration*, vol. 76.

Palazuelos, E. and Fernandez, R. (2010) 'Labour productivity: a comparative analysis of the European Union and United States, 1994–2007', *New Political Economy*, vol.15, no. 3.

Palmer, M. and Lambert, J. (1968) *European Unity*, Allen and Unwin, London.

Panagariya, A. (2002) 'EU preferential trade arrangements and developing countries', *The World Economy*, vol. 25, no. 10.

Paxton, J. (1976) *The Developing Common Market*, Macmillan, Basingstoke.

Payne, D. C. (2000) 'Policy making in nested institutions: explaining the conservation failures of the EU's Common Fisheries Policy', *Journal of Common Market Studies*, vol. 38, no. 2.

Pearce, D. and Barbier, E. (2002) *Blueprint for a Sustainable Economy*, Earthscan, London.

Pearson, M. and Smith, S. (1991) *The European Carbon Tax*, Institute for Fiscal Studies, London.

Peeperkorn, L. (1998) 'The economics of verticals', *EC Competition Policy Newsletter*, vol. 2.

Peeperkorn, L. and Verouden, V. (2007) 'The economics of competition', in Faull and Nikpay 2007.

Pelkmans, J. (2001) 'Making network markets competitive', *Oxford Review of Economic Policy*, vol. 17.

Pelkmans, J. and Winters, L. A. (1988) *Europe's Domestic Market*, Routledge, London.

Perju, V. (2009) 'Reason and authority in the European Court of Justice', *Virginia Journal of International Law*, vol. 49, no. 2.

Perman, R., Ma, Y., McGilvray, J. and Common, M. (2003) *Natural Resource and Environmental Economics*, 3rd edn, Pearson Education, Harlow.

Pescatore, P. (1983) 'The doctrine of 'direct effect': an infant disease of Community law', *European Law Review*, vol. 8.

Peterson, J. and Sharp, M. (1998) *Technology Policy in the European Union*, St Martin's Press, New York.

Petit, M. (1985) 'Determinants of agricultural policies in the United States and the European Community', International Food Policy Research Report 51, Washington D.C.

Phelps, E. S. (1968) 'Money–wage dynamics and labour market equilibrium', *Journal of Political Economy*, vol. 76.

Phillips, A. W. (1958) 'The relation between unemployment and the rate of change of money wages in the United Kingdom', *Economica*, vol. 25.

Phinnemore, D. (1999) *Association: Stepping Stone or Alternative to EU Membership?*, Sheffield Academic Press.

Phlips, L. (1993) 'Basing point pricing, competition, and market integration', in H. Ohta and J.-F. Thisse (eds.), *Does Economic Space Matter? Essays in Honour of Melvin L. Greenhut*, Macmillan, Basingstoke.

(1995) *Competition Policy: A Game Theoretical Perspective*, Cambridge University Press.

Pisani-Ferry, J. (2002) 'Fiscal discipline and policy coordination in the eurozone: assessment and proposals', CEU, Brussels.

Pissarides, C. (1990) *Equilibrium Unemployment Theory*, Basil Blackwell, Oxford.

Plötner, J. (1998) 'Report on France', in A.-M. Slaughter, A. Stone Sweet and J. Weiler (eds.), *The European Courts and National Courts: Doctrine and Jurisprudence*, Hart, Oxford.

Political and Economic Planning (PEP) (1962) *Atlantic Tariffs and Trade*, Allen and Unwin, London.

(1963) 'An energy policy for the EEC', *Planning*, vol. 29.

Pollack, M. (1997) 'Delegation, agency, and agenda-setting in the European Community', *International Organization*, vol. 51.

Pollard, P. (2003) 'A look inside two central banks: the European Central Bank and the Federal Reserve', *Federal Reserve Bank of St Louis Review*, January/February.

Polyhonen, P. (1963) 'A tentative model for the volume of trade between countries', *Weltwirtschaftliches Archiv*, vol. 90.

Porter, M. (1990) *The Competitive Advantage of Nations*, Macmillan, Basingstoke.

Posner, R. (1976) *Antitrust Law: An Economic Perspective*, University of Chicago Press.

Prechal, S. (2005) *Directives in EC Law*, 2nd edn, Oxford University Press.

Press, A. and Taylor, C. (1990) *Europe and the Environment*, The Industrial Society, London.

Prest, A. R. (1979) 'Fiscal policy', in P. Coffey (ed.), *Economic Policies of the Common Market*, Macmillan, Basingstoke.

Prewo, W. E. (1974a) 'A multinational interindustry gravity model for the European Common Market', PhD dissertation, Johns Hopkins University, Baltimore, Md.

(1974b) 'Integration effects in the EEC', *European Economic Review*, vol. 5.

Primo Braga, C. A. (1995) 'Trade-related intellectual property issues: the Uruguay Round agreement and its economic implications', in W. Martin and L. A. Winters (eds.), *The Uruguay Round and the Developing Economies*, discussion paper, no. 307, World Bank, Washington D.C.

Public Accounts Committee (2002) *Tobacco Smuggling*, 3rd report, session 2002–2003, HC 143, HMSO, London.

Pulliainen, K. (1963) 'A world trade study: an econometric model of the pattern of commodity flows in international trade 1948–1960', *Ekonomiska Samfundels Tidskrift*, no. 2.

Putnam, R. D. (1993) *Making Democracy Work: Civic Traditions in Modern Italy*, Princeton University Press.

Quigley, C. and Collins, A. M. (2004) *EC State Aid Law and Policy*, Hart, Oxford.

Quévit, M. (1995) 'The regional impact of the internal

market: a comparative analysis of traditional industrial regions and lagging regions', in S. Hardy, M. Hart, L. Albrechts and A. Katos (eds.), *An Enlarged Europe: Regions in Competition?*, Jessica Kingsley, London.

Quinlan, S. (2009) 'The Lisbon Treaty Referendum 2008', *Irish Political Studies*, vol. 24, no. 1.

Raisman Committee (1961) *East Africa: Report of the Economic and Fiscal Commission*, Cmnd 1279, Colonial Office.

Rameu, F. (2002) 'Judicial cooperation in the European courts: testing three models of judicial behaviour', *Global Jurist Frontiers*, vol. 2, issue 1.

Rasmussen, H. (1986) *On Law and Policy in the European ECJ*, Martinus Nijhoff, Dordrecht.

(1998) *European ECJ*, GadJura, Copenhagen.

(2000) 'Remedying the crumbling EC judicial system', *Common Market Law Review*, vol. 37.

Raveaud, G. (2007) 'The European Employment Strategy: towards more and better jobs?', *Journal of Common Market Studies*, vol. 45.2.

Rawlings, R. (1993) 'The Eurolaw game: some deductions from a saga', *Journal of Law and Society*, vol. 20, no. 3.

Rehg, W. (1996) 'Translator's introduction', in J. Habermas, *Between Facts and Norms*, Polity Press, Cambridge.

Reich, N. (1997) 'A European constitution for citizens: reflections on the rethinking of union and community law', *European Law Journal*, vol. 3.

Resnick, S. A. and Truman, E. M. (1974) 'An empirical examination of bilateral trade in Western Europe', *Journal of International Economics*, vol. 3.

Rietschel, E. Th. (2009) 'Evaluation of the Sixth Framework Programme for Research and Technological Development 2002–2006', report of the expert group (http://ec.europa.eu/research/reports/2009/pdf/fp6_evaluation_final_report_en.pdf).

Ritchie, E. and Zito, A. R. (1998) 'The CFP: a policy disaster', in P. Gray and P. Hart (eds.), *Public Policy Disasters in Western Europe*, Routledge, London.

Ritson, C. (1973) 'The Common Agricultural Policy', in *The European Economic Community: Economics and Agriculture*, Open University Press, Milton Keynes.

Rittberger, B. (2005) *Building Europe's Parliament: Democratic Representation Beyond the Nation-State*, Oxford University Press.

Robinson, P. (2000) 'Active labour-market policies: a case of evidence-based policy-making?', *Oxford Review of Economic Policy*, vol. 16, no. 1.

Robson, P. (1980, 1985) *The Economics of International Integration*, Allen and Unwin, London.

(1983) *Integration, Development and Equity: Economic Integration in West Africa*, Allen and Unwin, London.

(1997) 'Integration in Sub-Saharan Africa', in El-Agraa 1997.

Roca Zamora, A. (2009) 'How is the internal market performing?', Commission, DG Internal Market (http://ec.europa.eu/internal_market/score/relateddocs/index_en.htm).

Rodger, B. (1999) 'The Commission's white paper on modernisation of the rules implementing articles 81 and 82 of the EC Treaty', *European Law Review*, vol. 24.

Romer, P. M. (1986) 'Increasing returns and longrun growth', *Journal of Political Economy*, vol. 94.

(1990) 'Endogenous technological change', *Journal of Political Economy*, vol. 98, no. 5.2.

(1994) 'New goods, old theory and the welfare of trade restrictions', *Journal of Development Economics*, vol. 43.

Rosamond, B. (2005) 'The uniting of Europe and the foundations of EU studies: revisiting the neofunctionalism of Ernst B. Haas', *Journal of European Public Policy*, vol. 12, no. 2.

Rose, A. K. (1999) 'One money, one market: estimating the effect of common currencies on trade', working paper, no. 7432, National Bureau of Economic Research, Cambridge, Mass.

Rose, J. (2004) 'The rule of law in the western world: an overview', *Journal of Social Philosophy*, vol. 35, no. 4.

Ross, J. (1998) *Linking Europe: Transport Policies and Politics in the European Union*, Praeger, Westport, Conn.

Russell, C. S. (2001) *Applying Economics to the Environment*, Oxford University Press.

Ruttan, V. W. (1998) 'The new growth theory and development economics: a survey', *Journal of Development Studies*, vol. 35.

Sachs, J. D. and Shatz, H. J. (1994) 'Trade and jobs in U.S. manufacturing', *Brookings Papers on Economic Activity*, vol. 1.

Sala-i-Martin, X. (1996) 'Regional cohesion: evidence and theories of regional growth and convergence', *European Economic Review*, vol. 40.

Sala-i-Martin, X. and Sachs, J. D. (1992) 'Fiscal federalism and optimum currency areas: evidence from Europe and the United States', in M. Canzoneri, V. Grilli and P. Masson, *Establishing a Central Bank: Issues in Europe and Lessons from the US*, Cambridge University Press.

Salz, P., Buisman, E., Smit, J. and de Vos, B. (2006) 'Employment in the fisheries sector: current situation', final report (FISH/2004/4), LEI BV, Framian BV.

Sand, I.-J. (1998) 'Understanding new forms of governance: mutually interdependent, reflexive, destabilised and competing institutions', *European Law Journal*, vol. 4.

Sandford, C. T., Godwin, M. T. and Hardwick, P. J. (1989) *Administrative and Compliance Costs*, Fiscal Publications, Bath.

Sapir, A. (1995) 'Europe's single market: the long march to 1992', discussion paper, no. 1245, Centre for Economic Policy Research, London.

(1996) 'The effects of Europe's internal market programme on production and trade: a first assessment', *Weltwirtschaftliches Archiv*, vol. 132.

(1998) 'The political economy of EC regionalism', *European Economic Review*, vol. 42.

(2000) 'EC regionalism at the turn of the millennium: toward a new paradigm?', *World Economy*, vol. 23, no 9.

Sapir, A., Aghion, P., Bertola, G. *et al.* (2003a) *An Agenda for a Growing Europe: Making the EU Economic System Deliver*, report of an independent high-level study group established on the initiative of the President of the European Commission, Brussels.

(2003b) *An Agenda for a Growing Europe: The Sapir Report*, Oxford University Press.

(2003c) *An Agenda for a Growing Europe: Making the EU Economic System Deliver*, report of an independent high-level study group established on the initiative of the President of the European Commission, Brussels.

Sauter, W. (2008) 'Services of general economic interest and universal service in EU law', *European Law Review*, vol. 33

Scaperlanda, A. and Balough, R. S. (1983) 'Determinants of US direct investment in the EEC revisited', *European Economic Review*, vol. 21.

Scarpetta, S. (1996) 'Assessing the role of labour market policies and institutional settings on unemployment: a cross-country study', *OECD Economic Studies*, vol. 26.

Schepel, H. (1997) 'Legal pluralism in Europe', in P. Fitzpatrick and J. Bergeron (eds.), *Europe's Other: European Law between Modernity and Postmodernity*, Ashgate, Aldershot.

Schepel, H. and Wesseling, R. (1997) 'The legal community: judges, lawyers, officials and clerks in the writing of Europe', *European Law Journal*, vol. 3.

Scherer, F. M. and Ross, D. (1990) *Industrial Market Structure and Economic Performance*, Houghton Mifflin, New York.

Schettkat, R. (2001) 'Structural revolution: the interaction of product and labor markets', *Intereconomics*, vol. 36, January/February.

Schiff, M. and Winters, L. A. (1998) 'Regional integration as diplomacy', *World Bank Economic Review*, vol. 12, no. 2.

(2003) *Regional Integration and Development*, Oxford University Press.

Schilling, T. (1996) 'The autonomy of the community legal order – through the looking glass', *Harvard Journal of International Law*, vol. 37.

Schmalensee, R., Joskow, P. L., Ellerman, A. D., Montero, J. P. and Bailey, E. M. (1998) 'An interim evaluation of sulphur dioxide emissions trading', *Journal of Economic Perspectives*, vol. 12, no. 3.

Schreiber, K. (1991) 'The new approach to technical harmonization and standards', in L. Hurwitz and C. Lequesne, *The State of the European Community: Politics, Institutions, and Debates in the Transition Years*, Lynne Rienner, Boulder, Colo.

Schüler, M. and Heinemann, F. (2002) 'How integrated are the European retail financial markets? A cointegration analysis', Zentrum für Europäische Wirtschaftsforschung GmbH, ZEW discussion paper, no. 02-22 (ftp://ftp.zew.de/pub/zew-docs/dp/dp0222.pdf).

Schumpeter, J. (1934) *The Theory of Economic Development: An Inquiry into Profits, Capital, Interest, and the Business Cycle*, Harvard University Press, Cambridge, Mass.

Scitovsky, T. (1954) 'Two concepts of external economies', *Journal of Political Economy*, vol. 62.

(1958) *Economic Theory and Western European Integration*, Allen and Unwin, London.

Scott, J. (1992) 'European law', in I. Grigg-Spall and P. Ireland (eds.), *The Critical Lawyers' Handbook*, Pluto Press, London.

(1998) 'Law, legitimacy and EC governance: prospects for "partnership"', *Journal of Common Market Studies*, vol. 36.

Scully, R. (1997) 'The European Parliament and the co-decision procedure: a reassessment', *Journal of Legislative Studies*, vol. 3.

Seferiades, S. (2003) 'The European Employment Strategy against a Greek benchmark: a critique', *European Journal of Industrial Relations*, vol. 9, no. 2.

Sellekaerts, W. (1973) 'How meaningful are empirical studies on trade creation and trade diversion?', *Weltwirtschaftliches Archiv*, vol. 109.

Senden, L. (2004) *Soft Law in European Community Law*, Hart, Oxford.

Serrano Pascual, A. (2003) 'A contribution to evaluation of the European Employment Strategy: what lessons from the first five years of implementation of the EES?', in E. Gabaglio and R. Hoffmann (eds.), *European Trade Union Yearbook 2002*, European Trade Union Institute, Brussels.

Servan-Schreiber, J.-J. (1967) *Le défi américain*, Denoöl, Paris.

Shackleton, M. (1983) 'Fishing for a policy? The CFP of the

Community', in H. Wallace and W. Wallace, *Policy Making in the European Community*, Wiley, Chichester.

Shapiro, M. (1996) 'Codification of administrative law: the US and the EU', *European Law Journal*, vol. 2.

Shaw, J. (1996) 'EU legal studies in crisis? Towards a new dynamic', *Oxford Journal of Legal Studies*, vol. 16.

(1999) 'Postnational constitutionalism in the EU', *Journal of European Public Policy*, vol. 7.

Shaw, J. and Wiener, A. (1999) 'The paradox of the "European polity"', Harvard Jean Monnet working paper, no. 10/99.

Shibata, H. (1967) 'The theory of economic unions', in C. S. Shoup (ed.), *Fiscal Harmonisation in Common Markets*, vols. I–II, Columbia University Press, New York.

Shimer, R. (1998) 'Why is the US unemployment rate so much lower?', in B. Bernanke and J. Rotemberg (eds.), *NBER Macroeconomics Annual 1998*, National Bureau of Economic Research, Washington D.C.

Silvis, H., van Rijswijck, C. and de Kleijn, A. (2001) 'EU agricultural expenditure for various accession scenarios', report 6.01.04, Agricultural Research Institute, The Hague (cited in Swinnen 2002).

Sinn, H.-W. (1991) 'Taxation and the cost of capital: the "old" view, the "new" and another "view" ', in D. F. Bradford, *Tax Policy in the Economy*, vol. V, MIT Press, Cambridge, Mass.

Siotis, G. (2003) 'Competitive pressure and economic integration: an illustration from Spain, 1983–1996', *International Journal of Industrial Organization*, vol. 21.

Skully, D. W. (1999) 'The economics of TRQ administration', IATRC working paper, no. 99–6.

Slaughter, A. J. (1999) 'Globalisation and wages', Centre for Research on Globalisation and Labour Markets, research paper 99/5, Leverhulme Trust, London.

Slaughter, A.-M. (1995) 'International law in a world of liberal states', *European Journal of International Law*, vol. 6.

Slaughter, A.-M., Stone Sweet, A. and Weiler, J. (1998) 'Prologue', in A.-M. Slaughter, A. Stone Sweet and J. Weiler (eds.), *The European Courts and National Courts: Doctrine and Jurisprudence*, Hart, Oxford.

Smith, A. J. (1977) 'The Council of Mutual Economic Assistance in 1977: new economic power, new political perspectives and some old and new problems', in US Congress Joint Economic Committee, *East European Economics Post-Helsinki*.

Snell, J. (2008) '"European constitutional settlement", an ever closer union, and the Treaty of Lisbon: democracy or relevance?', *European Law Review*, vol. 33, no. 5.

Snyder, F. (1995) 'The effectiveness of European Community law: institutions, processes, tools and techniques', in T. Daintith (ed.), *Implementing EC Law in the United Kingdom: Structures for Indirect Rule*, Wiley, Chichester.

(1999a) *Global Economic Networks and Global Legal Pluralism*, EUI working paper, Law, vol. VI, Badia Fiesolana, San Domenico.

(1999b) 'Governing economic globalisation: global legal pluralism and European Law', *European Law Journal*, vol. 5.

Solow, R. M. (1957) 'Technical change and the aggregate production function', *Review of Economics and Statistics*, vol. 39.

(1987) 'We'd better watch out', *New York Times*, 12 July, Book Review 36.

Sørensen, P. (1998) 'Discussion', *Economic Policy*, vol. 27.

Staiger, D., Stock, J. and Watson, M. (1997) 'The NAIRU, unemployment and monetary policy', *Journal of Economic Perspectives*, vol. 11, no. 1.

Statistics Canada (2010) 'Federal general government expenditure' (www40.statcan.gc.ca/l01/cst01/govt02b-eng.htm).

Stavins, R. N. (1998) 'What can we learn from the Grand Policy Experiment?' *Journal of Economic Perspectives*, vol. 12, no. 3.

Stein, E. (1981) 'Lawyers, judges and the making of a transnational constitution', *American Journal of International Law*, vol. 75, no. 1.

Stefan, O. (2008) 'European competition soft law in European courts: a matter of hard principles?' *European Law Journal*, vol. 14, no. 6.

Stern, N. (2007) *The Economics of Climate Change: The Stern Review*, Cabinet Office, HM Treasury.

Stewart, K. and Web, M. (2006) 'International competition in corporate taxation: evidence from OECD time series', *Economic Policy*, January.

Stiglitz, J. (1997) 'Reflections on the natural rate hypothesis', *Journal of Economic Perspectives*, vol. 11, no. 1.

Stokke, O. and Hoebink, P. (2005) *Perspectives on European Development Cooperation*, Routledge, London.

Stone, J. R. N. and Brown, J. A. C. (1963) 'Input–output relationships', *A Programme for Growth*, no. 3, Chapman & Hall, London.

Stone Sweet, A. and Brunell, T. (1997) 'The European Court and national courts: a statistical analysis of preliminary references 1961–1995', *Journal of European Public Policy*, vol. 5.

(1998) 'Constructing a supranational constitution: dispute resolution and governance in the European Community', *American Political Science Review*, vol. 92.

Stone Sweet, A. and Caporaso, J. (1998) 'From free trade to supranational polity: the European Court and integration', in W. Sandholtz and A. Stone Sweet (eds.), *European Integration and Supranational Governance*, Oxford University Press.

Straathof, B., Linders, G.-J., Lejour, A. and Möhlmann, J. (2008) 'The internal market and the Dutch economy: implications for trade and economic growth', Centraal Planbureau (Netherlands Bureau for Economic Analysis), The Hague, document 168.

Strasser, S. (1995) 'The development of a strategy of docket control for the European ECJ and the question of preliminary references', Harvard Jean Monnet working paper, vol. III.

Streit, M. (1991) *Theorie der Wirtschaftspolitik, WiSo-Texte*, 4th edn, Werner-Verlag, Dusseldorf.

Striewe, L., Loy, J.-P. and Koester, U. (1996) 'Analyse und Beurteilung der einzelbetrieblichen Investitionsförderung in Schleswig-Holstein', *Agrarwirtschaft*, vol. 45, no. 12.

Stroux, S. (2004) *US and EC Oligopoly Control*, Kluwer Law International, The Hague.

Suchorzewski, W. (2003) 'Main transport policy issues in transitional economics in central and eastern Europe', in European Conference of Ministers of Transport, *Fifty Years of Transport Policy*, ECMT, Paris.

Sundelius, B. and Wiklund, C. (1979) 'The Nordic Community: the ugly duckling of regional cooperation', *Journal of Common Market Studies*, vol. 18, no. 1.

Suris-Regueiro, J. C., Varela-Lafuente, M. M. and Iglesias-Malvido, C. (2003) 'Effectiveness of the structural fisheries policy in the European Union', *Marine Policy*, vol. 27, no. 6.

Swank, D. (1998) 'Funding the welfare state: globalization and the taxation of business in advanced capitalist economies', *Political Studies*, vol. 46, no. 4.

Swann, D. (1973) *The Economics of the Common Market*, Penguin, London.

  (1988) *The Economics of the Common Market*, 4th edn, Penguin, London.

Sweet and Maxwell (regularly updated) *European Community Treaties*.

Swinnen, J. F. M., (2002) *Budgetary Implication of Enlargement: Agriculture*, policy brief, Center for European Policy Studies, Brussels.

Symes, D. (1995) 'The European pond: who actually manages fisheries?', *Ocean and Coastal Management*, vol. 27, no. 1.

Szyszczak, E. (1996) 'Making Europe more relevant to its citizens: effective judicial process', *European Law Review*, vol. 21.

Tamanaha, B. Z. (2004) *On the Rule of Law: History, Politics, Theory*, Cambridge University Press.

Tangermann, S. (1991) 'Agriculture in "international trade

negotiations"', in K. Burger, M. de Groat, J. Post and V. Zacharriasse (eds.), *Agricultural Economics and Policy: International Challenges for the Nineties*, Elsevier, Amsterdam.

Tani, M. (2002) 'Have Europeans become more mobile? A note on regional evolutions in the EU: 1988–1997', School of Economics and Management, University of New South Wales at the Australian Defence Force Academy.

Temple, J. (1999) 'The new growth evidence', *Journal of Economic Literature*, vol. 37, no. 1.

Temple Lang, J. (1998) 'Community antitrust law and national regulatory procedures', *1997 Annual Proceedings of Fordham Corporate Law Institute*, vol. 24.

  (2004) 'National measures restricting competition, and national authorities under Article 10 EC', *European Law Review*, vol. 29.

Teubner, G. (1997) 'Breaking frames: the global interplay of legal and social systems', *American Journal of Comparative Law*, vol. 45.

  (1998) 'Legal irritants: good faith in British law or how unifying law ends up in new divergences', *Modern Law Review*, vol. 61.

Thirlwall, A. P. (1979) 'The balance of payments constraint as an explanation of international growth rate differences', *Banca Nazionale del Lavoro Quarterly Review*, March.

  (1982) 'The Harrod trade multiplier and the importance of export-led growth', *Pakistan Journal of Applied Economics*, vol. 1, summer.

Tilford, S. and Whyte, P. (2010) *The Lisbon Scorecard X: The Road to 2020*, Centre for European Reform, London.

Tholoniat, L. (2010) 'The career of the open method of coordination: lessons from a "soft" EU instrument', *West European Politics*, vol. 33.

Thornton, D. L. (2002) 'Monetary policy transparency: transparent about what?', Federal Reserve Bank of St Louis, working paper, no. 2002-028A, November.

Tinbergen, J. (1952) *On the Theory of Economic Policy*, North-Holland, Amsterdam.

  (1953) *Report on Problems Raised by the Different Turnover Tax Systems Applied within the Common Market* (Tinbergen Report), High Authority of European Coal and Steel Community.

  (1954) *International Economic Integration*, Elsevier, Amsterdam.

  (1962) *Shaping the World Economy: Suggestions for an International Economic Policy*, Twentieth Century Fund, New York.

Tracy, M. (1989) *Government and Agriculture in Western Europe 1880–1988*, Harvester Wheatsheaf, New York.

Treutlein, D. (2009) 'Zooming in on transposition: national

execution measures for EU Directives 1986–2002', *CESifo Economic Studies*, 55(1).

Tridimas, T. (1994) 'Horizontal effect of Directives: a missed opportunity?', *European Law Review*, vol. 19.

(1996) 'The ECJ and judicial activism', *European Law Review*, vol. 19.

(2006) *The General Principles of EU Law*, Oxford University Press.

Tridimas, T. and Gari, G. (2010) 'Winners and losers in Luxembourg: a statistical analysis of judicial review before the European Court of Justice and the Court of First Instance (2001–2005)', *European Law Review*, vol. 35, no. 2.

Trubek, D. and Trubek, L. (2007) 'New governance and legal regulation: complementarity, rivalry and transformation', *Columbia Journal of European Law*, vol. 13, no. 3.

Trubek, D., Dezalay, Y., Buchanan, R. and Davis, J. R. (1994) 'Global restructuring and the law: studies of the internationalization of legal fields and the creation of transnational arenas', *Case Western Reserve Law Review*, vol. 44.

Truman, E. M. (1969) 'The European Economic Community: trade creation and trade diversion', *Yale Economic Essays*, spring.

(1975) 'The effects of European economic integration on the production and trade of manufactured products', in B. Balassa (ed.), *European Economic Integration*, North-Holland, Amsterdam.

Tsebelis, G. (1994) 'The power of the EP as a conditional agenda-setter', *American Political Science Review*, vol. 88.

Tsebelis, G. and Garrett, G. (1997) 'Agenda setting, vetoes and the EU's co-decision procedure', *Journal of Legislative Studies*, vol. 3.

(2000) 'Legislative politics in the European Union', *European Union Politics*, vol. 1.

(2001) 'The institutional foundations of intergovernmentalism and supranationalism in the European Union', *International Organization*, vol. 55, no. 2.

Tsebelis, G. and Kreppel, A. (1998) 'The history of conditional agenda-setting in European institutions', *European Journal of Political Research*, vol. 33.

Tsoukalis, L. (2005) *What Kind of Europe?*, Oxford University Press.

Tullock, G. (1967) 'The welfare costs of tariffs, monopolies and theft', *Western Economic Journal*, vol. 5.

UK Civil Aviation Authority (1993) *Airline Competition in the Single European Market*, CAP 623, CAA.

UK Government (1996) *Memorandum by the British Government to the 1996 Intergovernmental Conference on the European ECJ*, Foreign and Commonwealth Office, London.

UK Treasury (2003) *UK Membership of the Single Currency: An Assessment of the Five Economic Tests*, UK Treasury, London.

UNCTAD (2002) *Participation of the African, Caribbean and Pacific Group of States in International Trade*, UNCTAD/DITC/TNCD/Misc., 22 August, Geneva.

(2004) *Handbook of International Trade Statistics 2003*, New York.

(2006) *TRAINS Database*, Geneva.

Ungerer, H., Evans, D. and Nyberg, P. (1986) 'The European monetary system – recent developments', occasional paper, no. 48, IMF, Washington D.C.

Urrutia, B. (2006) 'The EU regulatory activities in the shipping sector: a historical perspective', *Maritime Economics and Policy*, vol. 8.

US Bureau of Economic Analysis (2003) *Regional Accounts Data* (www.census.gov).

US Census Bureau (2003) *State Population Estimates* (www.bea.gov/bea/regional/data.htm).

(2006) *Annual Population Estimates* (www.census.gov).

US Department of Energy, Energy Office Administration (1997) *Electricity Reform Abroad and US Investment*, September.

Valbonesi, P. (1998) 'Privatization and EU competition policy: the case of the Italian energy sector', in S. Martin (ed.), *Competition Policies in Europe*, Elsevier Science, Amsterdam.

Van Bael & Bellis (2009) *Competition Law of the European Community*, 5th edn, Kluwer Law International, Deventer.

van den Berg, R. J. and Camesasca, P. D. (2001) *European Competition Law and Economics: A Comparative Perspective*, Intersententia Publishing, Mortsel, Belgium.

van den Noord, P. (2000) *The Size and Role of Automatic Stabilisers in the 1990s and Beyond*, Economics Department, report no. 230, OECD, Paris.

van der Linde, J. G. and Lefeber, R. (1988) 'IEA captures the development of European Community energy law', *Journal of World Trade*, vol. 22.

van Dijck, P. and Faber, G. (eds.) (2000) *The External Economic Dimension of the European Union*, Kluwer Law International, Dordrecht.

Vanek, J. (1965) *General Equilibrium of International Discrimination: The Case of Customs Unions*, Harvard University Press, Cambridge, Mass.

Vanhalewyn, E. (1999) 'Trends and patterns in state aids', *European Economy Report and Studies: State Aid and the Single Market*, no. 3.

Vaubel, R. (2009) *The European Institutions as an Interest Group*, Institute of Economic Affairs, London.

Venables, A. J. (2003) 'Winners and losers from regional integration arrangements', *Economic Journal*, vol. 113.

Verdoorn, P. J. (1954) 'A customs union for Western Europe – advantages and feasibility', *World Politics*, July.

Verdoorn, P. J. and Meyer zu Schlochtern, F. J. M. (1964) 'Trade creation and trade diversion in the common market', in H. Brugmans (ed.), *Intégration Européenne et réalité économique*, de Temple, Bruges.

Verdoorn, P. J. and Schwartz, A. N. R. (1972) 'Two alternative estimates of the effects of EEC and EFTA on the pattern of trade', *European Economic Review*, vol. 3.

Vernon, R. (1966) 'International investment and international trade in the product cycle', *Quarterly Journal of Economics*, vol. 80.

Verwaal, E. and Cnossen, S. (2002) 'Europe's new border taxes', *Journal of Common Market Studies*, vol. 40, no. 2.

Vickerman, R. (1997) 'High-speed rail in Europe: experience and issues for future development', *The Annals of Regional Science*, vol. 31, no. 1.

Viegas, J. M. and Blum, U. (1993) 'High speed railways in Europe', in D. Banister and J. Berechman (eds.), *Transport in a Unified Europe*, Elsevier, Oxford.

Viner, J. (1950) *The Customs Union Issue*, Carnegie Endowment for International Peace, New York.

Vinois, J.-A. (2010) 'Energy Infrastructure Package', presentation at the US-EU Dialogue on Sustainable Energy Security, Prague, 16 June.

Volcansek, M. (1986) *Judicial Politics in Europe*, Peter Lang, Frankfurt.

von Bogdandy, A., Arndt, F. and Bast, J. (2004) 'Legal instruments in European Union law and their reform: a systemic approach on an empirical basis', *Yearbook European Law*, Oxford University Press.

von Geusau, F. A. (1975) 'In search of a policy', in F. A. von Geusau (ed.), *Energy Strategy in the European Communities*, Sijthoff, Leiden.

von Hagen, J. and Mundschenk, S. (2002) 'Fiscal and monetary policy co-ordination in EMU', Oesterreichische National Bank Working Paper 70, August.

von Thünen, J. H. (1826) *Der isolierte Staat in Beziehung auf Landwirtschaft und Nationalökonomie*, Perthes.

Vos, E. (1998) *Institutional Frameworks of Community Health and Safety Regulation: Committees, Agencies and Private Bodies*, Hart, Oxford.

Waddams Price, C. (1997) 'Competition and regulation in the UK gas industry', *Oxford Review of Economic Policy*, vol. 13, no. 1.

Waelbroeck, J. (1964) 'Le commerce de la Communauté Européenne avec les pays tiers', in H. Brugmans (ed.), *Intégration Européenne et réalité économique*, de Temple, Bruges.

Wallace, L. (2006) 'Ahead of his time: Laura Wallace interviews economist Robert Mundell', *Finance and Development*, September, International Monetary Fund, Washington D.C.

Wallace, W. (ed.) (1990) *The Dynamics of European Integration*, Pinter, London.

Walter, I. (1967) *The European Common Market: Growth and Patterns of Trade and Production*, Praeger, New York.

Walters, A. A. (1963) 'A note on economies of scale', *Review of Economics and Statistics*, November.

Wang, Z. and Winters, L. A. (1991) 'The trading potential of Eastern Europe', discussion paper, no. 610, Centre for Economic Policy Research, London.

Wanlin, A. (2006) *The Lisbon Scorecard VI: Will Europe's Economy Rise Again?*, Centre for European Reform, London.

Ward, I. (1996) *A Critical Introduction to European Law*, Butterworths, London.

Watt, A. (2000) 'What has become of employment policy? Explaining the ineffectiveness of employment policy in the European Union', *Basler Schriften zur europäischen Integration*, vols. 47–48.

——— (2003) 'The report of the Hartz Commission in the context of the European Employment Strategy', unpublished manuscript (cited by Watt 2004).

——— (2004) 'Reform of the European Employment Strategy after five years: a change of course or merely of presentation?', *European Journal of Industrial Relations*, vol. 10, no. 2.

WB-BML (Wissenschaftlicher Beirat beim Bundesministerium für Ernährung, Landwirtschaft und Forsten) (1998) *Integration der Landwirtschaft der Europäischen Union in die Weltagrarwirtschaft*, Angewandte Wissensschaft, Heft 476, Bonn.

WCED (1987) *Our Common Future*, Report of the World Commission on Environment and Development, World Commission on Environment and Development (Brundtland Report), Oxford University Press.

Weale, A., Pridham, G., Cini, M. *et al.* (2000) *Environmental Governance in Europe: An Ever Closer Union?*, Oxford University Press.

Weatherill, S. (2001) 'Breach of Directives and Breach of Contract', *European Law Review*, vol. 26, no. 2.

Weatherill, S. and Beaumont, P. (1999) *EU Law*, 3rd edn, Penguin, Harmondsworth.

Weck-Hannemann, H. and Frey, B. S. (1997) 'Are economic instruments as good as economists believe? Some new considerations', in Bovenberg and Cnossen 1997.

Weiler, J. (1993) 'Journey to an unknown destination: a retrospective and prospective of the European ECJ in the arena of political integration', *Journal of Common Market Studies*, vol. 31.

—— (1994) 'A quiet revolution: the European ECJ and its interlocutors', *Comparative Political Studies*, vol. 26.

—— (1997a) 'To be a European citizen: Eros and civilisation', *Journal of European Public Policy*, vol. 4.

—— (1997b) 'The EU belongs to its citizens: three immodest proposals', *European Law Review*, vol. 22.

—— (2001) 'Epilogue: the judicial Après Nice', in G. de Búrca and J. Weiler, *The European Court of Justice*, Hart, Oxford.

Weiler, J. and Haltern, U. (1998) 'Constitutional or international? The foundations of the community legal order and the question of judicial KompetenzKompetenz', in A.-M. Slaughter, A. Stone Sweet and J. Weiler (eds.), *The European Courts and National Courts: Doctrine and Jurisprudence*, Hart, Oxford.

Weise, C. (2002) 'How to finance Eastern enlargement of the EU: the need to reform EU policies and the consequences for the net contributor balance', working paper, no. 14, October, European Network of Economic Policy Research Institutes (www.enepri. org).

Weishaupt, J. (2009) 'Money, votes or "good" ideas? Partisan politics and the effectiveness of the European Employment Strategy in Austria and Ireland', *European Integration Online Papers-EIOP*, vol. 13, no.14.

Weiss, L. W. (1971) *Case Studies in American Industry*, 2nd edn, Wiley, New York.

Wemelsfelder, J. (1960) 'The short-term effects of lowering import duties in Germany', *Economic Journal*, vol. 70.

Wenneras, P. (2006) 'A new dawn for Commission enforcement under Arts. 226 and 228 EC: General and Persistent (GAP) Infringements, Lump Sums, and Penalty Payments', *Common Market Law Review*, 43(1).

Wesseling, R. (2000) *The Modernisation of EC Antitrust Policy*, Hart, Oxford.

—— (2005) 'The rule of reason and competition law: various rules, various reasons', in A. A. A. Schrauwen (ed.), *Rule of Reason – Rethinking Another Classic of European Legal Doctrine*, Europa Law Publishing, Groningen.

Wessels, W. (1997) 'An ever closer fusion? A dynamic macropolitical view on integration processes', *Journal of Common Market Studies*, vol. 37.

Whitwill, M. (2000) 'European deregulation: one year on', The Uranium Institute, 25th Annual Symposium, London, 30 August–1 September.

Wilhelmsson, T. (1995) 'Integration as disintegration of national law', in H. Zahle and H. Petersen (eds.), *Legal Polycentricity: Consequences of Pluralism in Law*, Dartmouth, Aldershot.

Wilkinson, D. (1997) 'Towards sustainability in the EU? Steps within the European Commission towards integrating the environment into other EU policy sectors', *Environmental Politics*, vol. 6.

Williamson, J. and Bottrill, A. (1971) 'The impact of customs unions on trade in manufactures', *Oxford Economic Papers*, vol. 25, no. 3.

Wils, W. (1999) 'Notification, clearance and exemption in EC competition law: an economic analysis', *European Law Review*, vol. 24.

—— (2000) 'The undertaking as subject of EC competition law and the imputation of infringements to natural and legal persons', *European Law Review*, vol. 25.

—— (2003) *Optimal Enforcement of EC Competition Laws: A Study in Law and Economics*, Kluwer Law International, The Hague.

Winters, L. A. (1984) 'British imports of manufactures and the common market', *Oxford Economic Papers*, vol. 36.

—— (1985) 'Separability and the specification of foreign trade functions', *European Economic Review*, vol. 27.

—— (2000) 'EU's preferential trade agreements: objectives and outcomes', in P. van Dijck and G. Faber (eds.), *The External Economic Dimension of the European Union*, Kluwer Law International, Dordrecht.

Wise, M. (1984) *The Common Fisheries Policy of the European Community*, Methuen, London.

—— (1996) 'Regional concepts in the development of the CFP', in K. Crean and D. Symes (eds.), *Fisheries Management in Crisis*, Blackwell Science, Oxford.

Wolf, M. (1983) 'The European Community's trade policy', in R. Jenkins (ed.), *Britain in the EEC*, Macmillan, Basingstoke.

Wolfram, C. D. (1999) 'Measuring market power in the British electricity spot market', *American Economic Review*, vol. 89, no. 4.

Wonnacott, G. P. and Wonnacott, R. J. (1981) 'Is unilateral tariff reduction preferable to a customs union? The curious case of the missing foreign tariffs', *American Economic Review*, vol. 71.

Wood, A. (1994) *North–South Trade, Employment, and Inequality*, Oxford University Press.

—— (1995) 'How trade hurt unskilled workers', *Journal of Economic Perspectives*, vol. 9.

Wooders, M., Zissimos, B. and Dhillon, A. (2001) 'Tax competition reconsidered', Warwick Economics Research Paper, no. 622, University of Warwick.

World Bank (1992) *Governance and Development*, World Bank, Washington D.C.

(2003) *Global Economic Prospects of Developing Countries*, World Bank, Washington D.C.

(2006a) *World Development Indicators Database*, Economic and Social Data Services International (www.esds.ac.uk/international).

(2006b) *Global Economic Prospects of Developing Countries*, World Bank, Washington D.C.

(2006c) *World Development Indicators Database* (http://siteresources.worldbank.org/DATASTATISTICS/Resources/GNIPC.pdf).

World Trade Organization (WTO) (2002) *Trade Policy Review: European Union 2001*, vols. I and II, Geneva.

(2004a) *Trade Policy Review: European Union 2004*, vols. I and II, Geneva.

(2004b) *Agreement Establishing the World Trade Organisation*, Annex 1A, WTO, Geneva (www.wto.org/english/docs_e/legal_e/10-24.pdf).

(2006) *International Trade Statistics Database* (www.wto.org/english/res_e/statis_e/statis_e.htm).

(2009) *Trade Policy Review, European Communities*, WTO, Geneva.

Yarrow, G. (1991) 'Vertical supply arrangements: issues and applications in the energy industries', *Oxford Review of Economic Policy*, vol. 7, no. 2.

Young, H. (1998) *This Blessed Plot: Britain and Europe from Churchill to Blair*, Macmillan, Basingstoke.

Zeitlin, J. (2005) 'The open method of co-ordination in action: theoretical promise, empirical realities, reform strategy', in Zeitlin and Pochet 2005.

Zeitlin, J. and Pochet, P. (2005) *The Open Method of Coordination in Action: The European Employment and Social Inclusion Strategies*, Peter Lang, Brussels.

Ziltener, P. (2004) 'The economic effects of the European single market project: projections, simulations – and the reality', *Review of International Political Economy*, vol. 11, no. 5.

Zürn, M. and Wolf, D. (1999) 'European law and international regimes: the features of law beyond the nation state', *European Law Journal*, vol. 5.

Author index

Subject index

Page numbers in *italics* indicate tables or figures.